HISTORY OF

THE GERMAN GENERAL STAFF

A Westview Encore Edition

Walter Goerlitz

History of
THE GERMAN
GENERAL STAFF

1657-1945

Translated by
BRIAN BATTERSHAW

Introduction by WALTER MILLIS

Westview Press / Boulder and London

Published in 1985 in the United States of America by Westview Press, Frederick A. Praeger, Publisher, 5500 Central Avenue, Boulder, Colorado 80301

Translation of *Der Deutsche Generalstab,* Verlag der Frankfurter Hefte, Frankfurt am Main. First U.S. publication in 1953 by Praeger Publishers.

Library of Congress Catalog Card Number: 85-50932
ISBN: 0-8133-0195-5

Printed and bound in the United States of America

6   5   4   3   2   1

PREFACE

By Walter Millis

TO two generations of Americans the German General Staff has stood as an object of hatred, fear and revulsion. In the two greatest of our wars Germany was our principal opponent; twice in a lifetime we have seen our normal world, if not our national existence itself, imperilled by her formidable and ruthless armies. Through the whole thirty years from 1914 to 1945 we were to live more or less under the shadow of the grimly expert, professional militarism by which those armies were led — a tradition nurtured, and in the world's eyes personified, by the German Great General Staff.

This remarkable organization seemed so much a thing of evil in itself that its extirpation became a chief object of the Treaty of Versailles. Duly it was abolished, and Germany forbidden ever to recreate such an instrument of military power; apparently, the only result was that twenty years later it was functioning as it always had, managing still greater armies, launching them with still greater precision and more deadly effect upon a shattered world society. The General Staff, which traced its origins to the armies of Frederick the Great, did not finally cease to exist until that apocalyptic moment in the ruins of the Reichskanzlei, when Germany was at last left without an army of any kind through which it might operate.

That it had left an indelible impress upon our national life, our history and our future was obvious enough. Less obvious — and certainly far less clearly understood — was the earlier influence which it had exerted upon our own institutions, in common with those of Western society as a whole. In the late Nineteenth Century it was far from seeming the evil power which it was later regarded as being; in the days of the elder Moltke it was, rather, a model, earnestly imitated by all the greater nations as they sought to bring their military systems and policies into line with the revolutionary changes which sociology and technology were working in the ancient art of war.

The Napoleonic era had posed, or clearly foreshadowed, certain fundamental military problems of great complexity. It had combined the invention of the democratic, popular mass army with the beginnings of a technological revolution which was to make possible the mobilization, supply, deployment and maneuver of such masses on an unparalleled scale. Both the ideological foundations and the technical apparatus had been provided for a "total" outpouring of the national energies in war to an extent which would have seemed incredible even as late as the mid-Eighteenth Century. How were such tremendous potential forces to be controlled; how were they to be commanded; how, in particular, were they to be related to the political and social ends of the state, which they were supposed to serve?

It was still just possible in Napoleon's time for individual genius (aided by such improvisations as the divisional system of command and the embryonic staff officer) to direct the new forms of military action which were coming into existence; but even with genius available, the results were not too happy. And a generation later it was already apparent to the thoughtful that something else would have to be developed to meet the growing problem of generalship in the modern technological state. The inevitable answer—in war as in commerce, industry or civil public administration — was system, organization and specialized training. And, rather curiously, it fell to the Prussian general staff, itself already an anachronism in more ways than one, to provide that answer in what for nearly a century was to seem its most efficient practical form.

The Prussian staff, as the opening sentences of this book observe, was "a product of a specific phase of European development. It grew out of that combination of absolute monarchy with standing armies which became so typical a phenomenon after the Thirty Years' War." But perhaps it was just because the roots of the institution ran so deep in an ordered past, that it survived into the tempestuous future of the Nineteenth Century as an example on which nearly every great military power —not only in Western Europe but in Japan and the United States as well—tended to model its military policies and systems.

Not a few of the basic precepts and traditions worked out by the Prussian and later the German Great General Staff were to enter into the military thought of every major military power.

The traditions of an almost monkish divorcement of military policy from political affairs, of thorough preparatory planning for every possible military eventuality (without regard for the influence which the military plan might have on the political crisis), of corporate anonymity in planning and command but of the highest level of individual competence and responsibility within the corporate leadership, of the strictest moral and intellectual and also caste standards maintained within the framework of selfless devotion to the sovereign and the state — these were the traditions and the principles developed by the German General Staff through the Nineteenth Century as answers to the basic problems of military command in the democratic-capitalist-technological society of the times.

That the answers did not work too well is painfully obvious in the light of later knowledge. But that they were widely admired and imitated is indisputable. The anonymous but overriding authority of the Staff, the secret preparation of war plans, the division of Staff responsibilities and labors, the incorporation of technological advance into military practice through Staff study, channelling and guidance, all became standard practice in the world that came up to catastrophe in 1914, and much of it is standard practice still. While the United States had during most of the Nineteenth Century remained outside the main lines of European military development, it was to the German General Staff that we turned for example when, after 1898, we realized that we would have to modernize our military system. And the staff method of organization, largely based on the German model, which Elihu Root instituted in our own Army in the Theodore Roosevelt era, remains to this day the basis of American military command and military policy formation.

The history of the German Great General Staff has been a great and pregnant influence in the affairs of Western Europe and America over at least a century and a half. Yet it is a history which few Americans understand or are even aware of. It is believed that this translation and condensation of Walter Goerlitz's massive account is the first book to appear in English which deals at all adequately with the subject. Actually, it is at once rather more and perhaps somewhat less than its title suggests. The author's approach is not through the technics of organization or even of plan, but through the succession of great and near-great or sometimes inferior personalities who, together with the social and economic backgrounds which produced them, made up the story. This is not an analysis of how the Oberquartiermeister *functioned in 1699 or of just how the* Truppenamt *(the name assumed by the General Staff after Versailles) was organized in the period before Hitler. It is the story of Scharnhorst, Boyen, Gneisenau, Clausewitz, the elder Moltke, Waldersee, Schlieffen, the younger Moltke, Hindenburg and Ludendorff, Seeckt, Schleicher, Beck, Blomberg, Halder, Rundstedt, Keitel, Guderian, Jodl and many more, by no means omitting the brilliant von Stauffenberg who organized and gave his life to the conspiracy of July, 1944, which sought to erase the madman, Hitler, and so tragically failed.*

As such it is less a history of the General Staff, perhaps, than a history of German generalship, formed and disciplined in the brick building in Berlin's Bendlerstrasse, *formed also out of a long tradition of military service going back to Frederick's feudal armies yet carrying forward into the appalling moral dilemmas of Hitler's demonic state. About half of the whole book is devoted to the Second World War and its immediate prelude. And it is a section of absorbing interest and, I suspect, of many surprises for American readers.*

The virtue of the earlier part of the book is that it puts facts which are generally well known, such as the recreation of the Prussian army after Jena, and the work of Scharnhorst and Gneisenau, in their proper social and economic setting. As one passes on into the Nineteenth Century one can see the triumphs of the elder Moltke and the subsequent schemes of Waldersee (who shares with the tragic Schleicher the dubious honor of being one of the two really "political" generals which the General Staff produced) leading inevitably to the Schlieffen Plan, which prepared the catastrophe into which the younger Moltke (and with him the whole of Western society) was to fall. But with the second part of the book, one sees the facts, hitherto obscure, behind the social and economic setting of the Hitler era, with which all are familiar.

It is an amazing story, and one certainly not well known in the West. Actually, the General Staff was not destroyed by the Treaty of Versailles (it merely changed its name and carried on as the Truppenamt *under the office of the* Heeresleitung) *but it was destroyed by Hitler. Hitler set up the* Oberkommando

Wehrmacht, (OKW) *under Keitel with its own staff under Jodl. The differences of opinion and purpose between the OKW and the General Staff became extreme; for a long period, for every war plan which the Staff produced in response to Hitler's demands, a counter-plan was also developed to render the plan ineffectual. The counter-plans were never actually put into effect until the abortive revolt of July, 1944, but the number and extent of the conspiracies into which the old-line officers, trained in the General Staff tradition, entered is astonishing.*

Dr. Goerlitz here is of course trying to make the best case possible for the traditional, monocled officer aristocracy which went down in the universal crash. It is not impossible that the case has been somewhat embroidered. But the underlying facts are there. The author does not conceal Schleicher's manipulations in the pre-war period, or defend the general attitude of an official and officer class which produced its own destruction along with that of a world society. He draws a picture of men like Beck or Halder or von Model or even Rommel in the end, tortured by their consciences and their fears, caught up upon the terrible wheel of Hitlerian Satanism, unable either to acquiesce or to oppose, bound by oaths which others had betrayed and dedicated to a national end which others had turned into a thing of loathing and putrefaction.

Such was the bitter end of the German Great General Staff, once the most precise and powerful director of military policy known to the Western world. Its ultimate failure, like its early successes, is a subject peculiarly worthy of study, now that we stand in an even more perilously militarized age, making even more imperious demands upon us to find answers for the basic problems of military command and military policy in a free society. The United States has undertaken military commitments and is maintaining standing armed forces on a scale vastly larger than anything we ever contemplated in peace time. We have engaged ourselves to the remarkable experiment of NATO — a military coalition involving command relations of an altogether novel delicacy and difficulty — and are trying to bring a new German army into it. Much of this latter problem turns upon the character and traditions of the German officer class — or what is left of it — and so gives this book an appositeness of another kind. Finally, our development of nuclear weapons has again raised the terrible potentialities of war to more dreadful levels, making it still more desperately urgent that we should learn better how to control and command such forces and bring them into a sounder integration with the rational aims of the civilian state.

The Great General Staff is dead, and no one can say that its answers for the central problems of military organization and command in a democratic-capitalistic society were the sound ones. But we can certainly profit by its example.

New York, 8 Dec. 1952

TRANSLATOR'S NOTE

THERE are in Herr Görlitz's story certain allusions which in this country would be unintelligible to all but the expert and certain passages which needed amplifying, clarifying and to some extent amending for the English reader. I therefore sought the Author's permission to edit and very slightly rewrite certain parts of this book. That permission was granted—a piece of magnanimity which must surely be rare in the annals of writing.

In carrying out my task I have in no way modified the general argument or implications of the book, nor did I feel any desire to do so. The picture Herr Görlitz draws of the General Staff and the German Military Caste as a whole is, I believe, accurate, and he is as much alive to certain of that caste's shortcomings as to what we must in fairness admit to have been its virtues. I have, however, met certain criticisms in regard to matters of fact which were made concerning the original German edition, and I have considerably shortened the book.

In the matter of terminology and in particular in the English rendering of military terms, I have followed an altogether admirable principle which is to follow no principle at all, but have dealt with each case as it occurred. In some instances where there was no close English equivalent I have left the German original version; in others I have rendered the term into English. I have in this connection received much kind and valuable assistance from Mr J. Y. Morfey, Senior Information Officer of the War Office, which I hereby most gratefully acknowledge.

Despite Mr Morfey's help, there may possibly have been occasions when I have fallen into a trap, and if that is so I ask the reader's indulgence. I do not think, however, that even the most captious will contend that this has seriously affected the value of the book. For here is pre-eminently a case where "the play's the thing", and I am sure that the reader will find the play as excellent as I have done myself.

BRIAN BATTERSHAW

CONTENTS

XIV. THE BEGINNING OF THE CAPTIVITY   378

Army *versus* S.S. in France—Russian troop concentration (I)—
Operation "Sea Lion"—The Blitz (II)—Hitler and Franco (III)—
The project of an attack on Russia—Underestimation of Russian
strength—Paulus made Halder's Deputy (IV)—Halder's mis-
givings about Russian campaign (V)—"Operation Marita"—
General Staff's status declines as its responsibilities grow—
Weakness of Tank arm (VI)—Preludes to Russian campaign—
"Operation Sunflower"—Rommel (VII)—A new resistance
group—Hitler's dominance increased by his success—Date of
Hitler's final decision to attack—The *Wolfsschanze* (VIII)—
Russian resistance believed broken—The Generals and the
"Commissar Order" (IX)—Hitler further curtails General Staff's
authority—Hitler dissipates his forces—Nazi "Colonial" policy
in Russia (X)—Despite his advisers, Hitler refuses to press home
attack on Moscow—Hitler's plans foiled by weather (XI)—
Further vacillation—The tide turns: Germans lose Rostov (XII)—
Brauchitsch resigns—Hitler takes over command of Army—
Guderian removed from post—Life at Hitler's Headquarters
(XIII)—The turning point of the war—Elastic *v.* inelastic De-
fence—Resignation of von Leeb (XIV).

XV. THE REVOLT   410

Manpower shortages—Todt succeeded by Speer (I)—Beck's
secret influence—Witzleben's plan for a coup (II)—The attack
on Stalingrad (III)—Dismissal of Halder (IV)—Zeitzler, Chief of
the General Staff (V)—Rivalries and cross purposes in high
policy (VI)—Paulus ordered to stand—Manstein vainly en-
deavours to relieve Paulus (VII)—Beck's new plan for a Field-
Marshals' revolt—Zeitzler seeks to reform structure of Command
—Approach of Stalingrad disaster—The opposition and "Unconditional Surrender" (VIII)—The Disaster of Stalingrad and its
effects—Stauffenberg—The first attempts by the military to
assassinate Hitler (IX)—Olbricht gives Stauffenberg an appointment—The caste of the great conspiracy—The conspirators'
political aims (X)—Second phase of the war begins (XI)—Further
conflicts between Hitler and General Staff—New types of
Generals (XII)—Russian counter-offensive (XIII)—Allied landing in Italy—The enigma of Himmler (XIV)—Final Russian
counter-offensive (XV-XVI)—The last act of tragedy—Heusinger
as military commander (XVII).

XVI GÖTTERDÄMMERUNG   454

Preparation to defend the west—Rommel on static defence (I)—
Rommel's doubts of Hitler (II)—Canaris in the shadows (III)—
The Allied invasion—Scepticism of Rundstedt (IV)—The enigma
of Kluge—Rommel a casualty (V)—The conspirators face a crisis—
The planning of the conspiracy—The 20th of July—The con-
spiracy in Paris (VI-XI)—Himmler commands *ersatz* Army—
Guderian Chief of Staff—Guderian's efforts to influence Hitler—
The end of the General Staff—Model (XII)—The Ardennes
offensive—The "Revolutionary Generals"—Russians break into
East Prussia (XIII-XIV)—Germany's death agony begins—
Wenck (XV)—Krebs succeeds Guderian (XVI)—The Battle
of Berlin—Hitler's death—The Great General Staff and the
Nuremberg Tribunal (XVII-XIX).

INDEX   501

ACKNOWLEDGEMENTS

THE publishers are grateful to the following for permission to reproduce photographs: to Ullstein Verlag for the portraits of von Clausewitz, von Waldersee, von Moltke (the Younger), von Schlieffen, von Falkenhayn, von Seeckt, Groener, Heye, von Schleicher, von Fritsch, von Stülpnagel, Beck, von Kluge, von Rundstedt, Zeitzler, Guderian, Olbricht, Canaris and Goerdeler, and the photographs of Hitler with his generals, and of Hindenburg with Ludendorff; to Archiv für Kunst und Geschichte for the portraits of Scharnhorst, von Gneisenau, von Moltke (the Elder), Hindenburg as a young man, and von Blomberg; to the Associated Press for the portraits of Blumentritt, Speidel and von Hassell; and to the *Picture Post* Library for the portraits of von Roon and von Hammerstein-Equord.

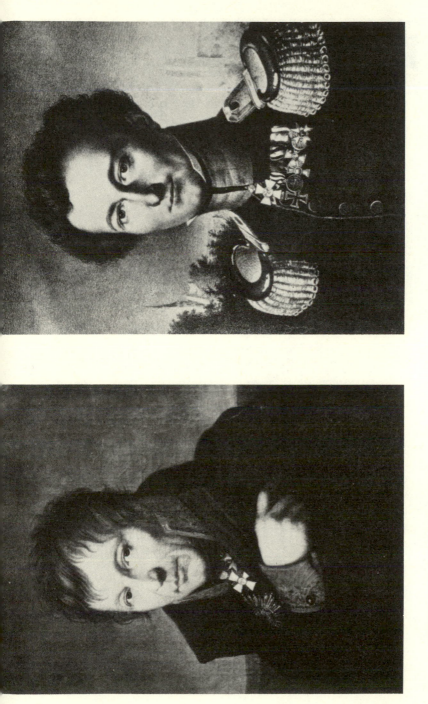

GERHARD SCHARNHORST

VON CLAUSEWITZ

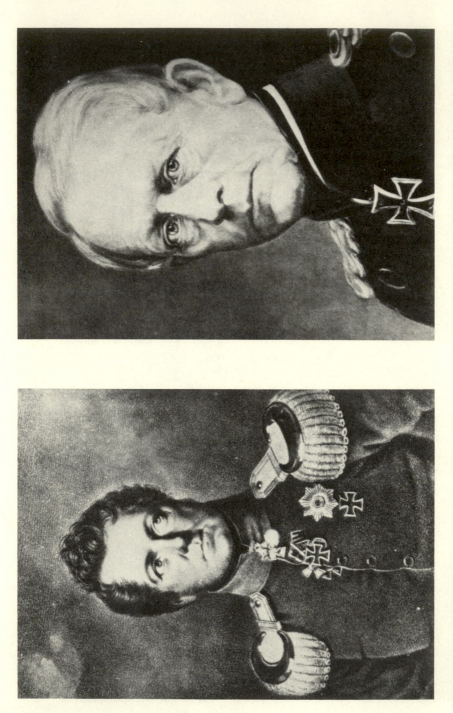

GRAF VON MOLTKE (The Elder)

GRAF VON GNEISENAU

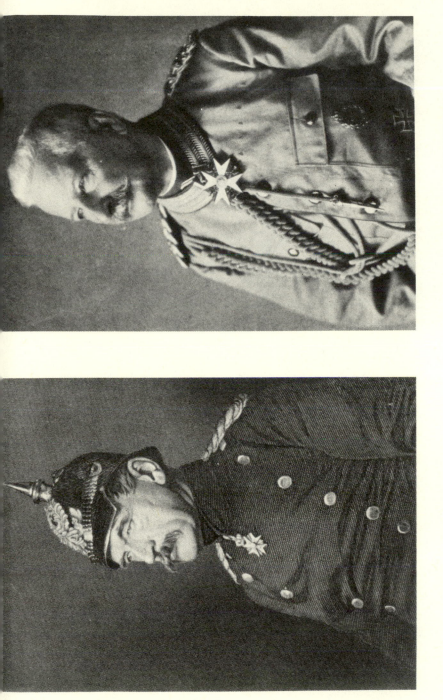

GRAF VON WALDERSEE

GRAF VON ROON

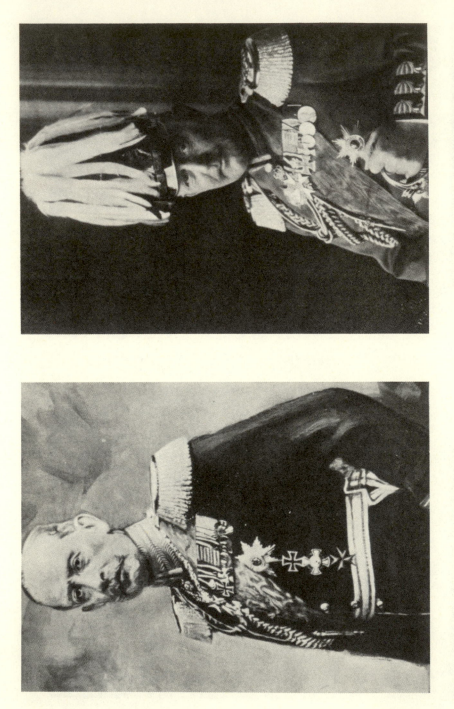

GRAF VON SCHLIEFFEN

GRAF VON MOLTKE (The Younger)

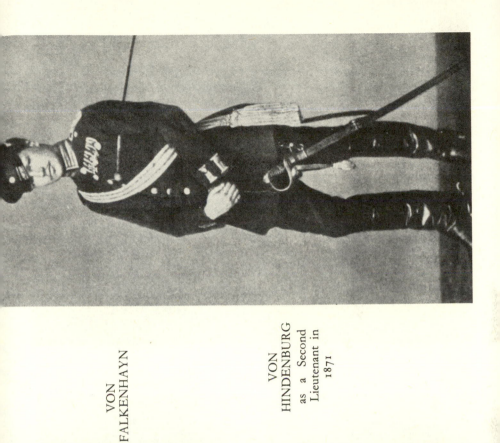

VON FALKENHAYN

VON
HINDENBURG
as a Second
Lieutenant in
1871

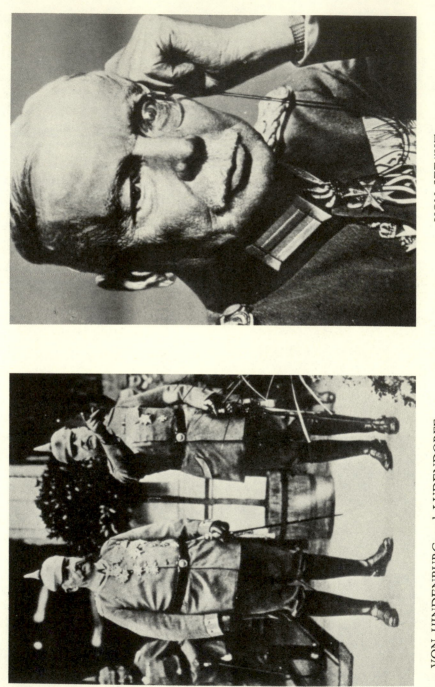

VON HINDENBURG and LUDENDORFF

VON SEECKT

GENERAL
WILHELM HEYE
aged 75

GENERAL
GROENER

Successor to
Ludendorff
after the
abdication of
the Kaiser

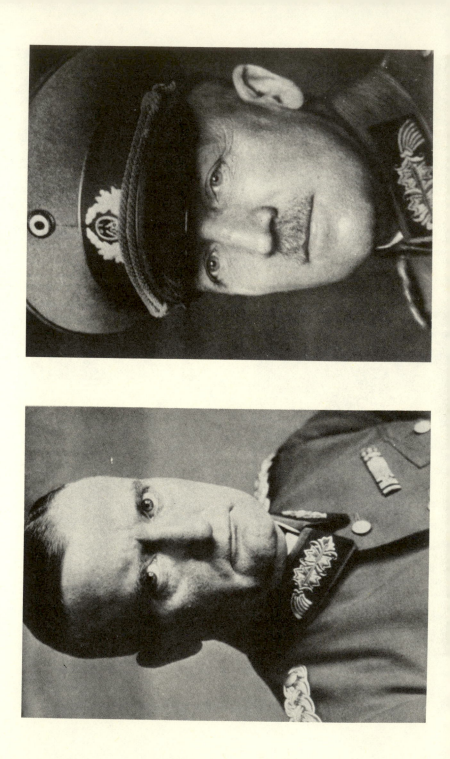

HITLER with (left to right) FIELD MARSHAL KEITEL, GENERAL HALDER and
FIELD MARSHAL VON BRAUCHITSCH

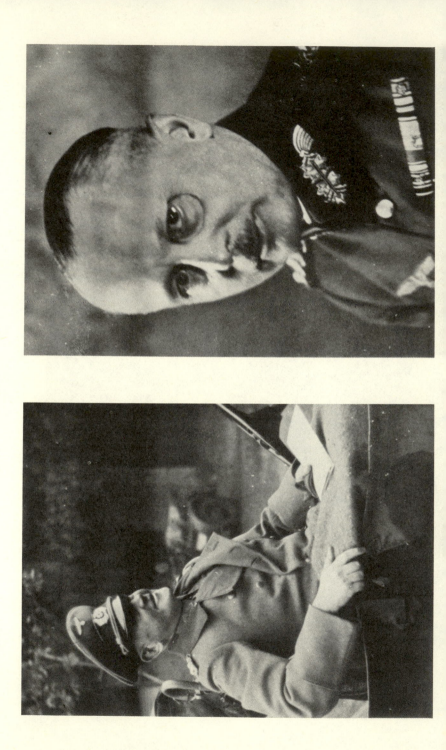

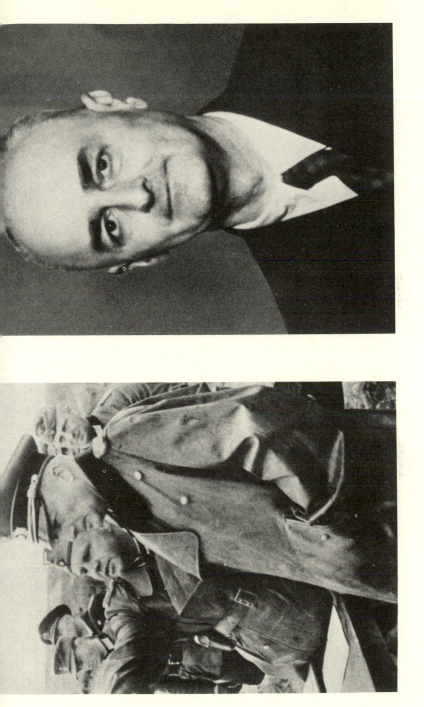

GÜNTHER BLUMENTRITT

VON KLUGE

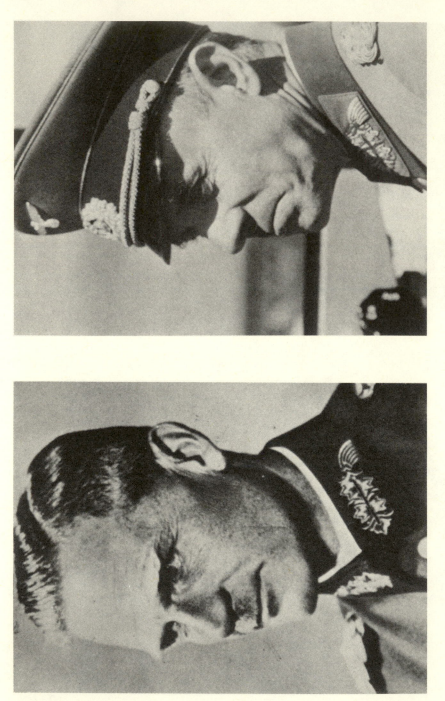

GENERAL LUDWIG BECK

VON STÜLPNAGEL

HANS
SPEIDEL
At one time
Rommel's
Chief of
Staff

VON
RUNDSTEDT

VON
HASSEL

GENERAL
OLBRICHT

ADMIRAL
CANARIS

DR GOERDELER
Oberbürgermeister
of Leipzig

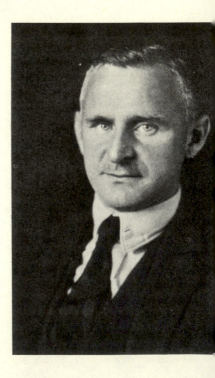

CHAPTER I

THE BEGINNINGS

I

THE Prussian General Staff is a product of a specific phase of European development. It grew out of that combination of absolute monarchy with standing armies which became so typical a phenomenon after the Thirty Years' War. In more than one instance, where that combination occurred, the military element was integral to the whole structure of the State. In the Spanish Empire it was the paid professional Army that held that scattered and heterogeneous thing together. In the Habsburg dominions with their diversified mixture of peoples the Army played a similar part.

Nowhere did this hold more true than in that composite state formed by the union of the Electorate of Brandenburg with the secularized inheritance of an East Prussian religious order. Writing towards the end of the eighteenth century, the military historian von Behrenhorst declared that the Prussian monarchy was not a country that had an army, but an Army that had a country which it used as a billeting area, and Mirabeau once made a somewhat similar remark. There is more than a little truth in these observations; the history of Prussia is essentially the history of the Prussian Army.

During the Thirty Years' War the speculative traffic in mercenaries had developed into something like a major industry. It was by bringing its bigger practitioners under his control, and also by forcing the recalcitrant nobility to do service to their sovereign, that the Great Elector laid the foundations of a standing Prussian force—and, with it, of Prussia. The chequered hotchpotch of the Hohenzollern possessions had come together through purchase, through conquest and through inheritance. It was the Army that formed the iron ring that held them together; one may even go so far as to say that in the strict sense there has never been a Prussian nation at all, though there has most certainly been a Prussian Army and a Prussian State.

Aside from the Army, the absolute monarchy of the Hohenzollerns had two other props, a Protestant orthodoxy with a peculiar Prussian colouring of its own, and a patriarchal system of land ownership. All matters of Church government were, of course, dependent upon the King, the Church's activating doctrinal principle being the subject's duty of obedience—which last was often inculcated to the neglect of more cardinal Christian virtues. As to the landlords, they were compensated for the sovereign's encroachment on certain privileges of their order by the retention of private jurisdiction and the continued dominion over their serfs.

Without the Junkers of East Elbia, without this Prussian aristocracy of sword and service which for two centuries supplied it with most of its officers, the Prussian Army is inconceivable, and this applies with even greater force to the Prussian General Staff. Indeed, the history of the General Staff is indissolubly linked with that of a comparatively small number of noble families. This Junker nobility differed markedly both in spirit and circumstance from what was often the much wealthier nobility of other parts of Germany. Its manorial estates were often far from profitable. As against this, they were free from taxes, save only for the *Lehnpferdegeld*, or Horse-money, an ancient feudal due, quite negligible in terms of actual cash. Military or administrative service was the normal career for the sons of such families—to this rule there was hardly ever an exception —though prior to 1806 few of the young men concerned enjoyed a university education.

Genetically, these people were a mixture. Families of Wendish, Cassubian or "Pruzzian" origin, like the Zietens, Quitzows, Mansteins and Yorcks, may be said to have constituted a sort of basic norm, but there were accretions to this. Huguenot settlement had brought in a sizeable French element, while the incorporation of Silesian and Polish territories introduced a strong Polish influx which was swollen by the tendency of the impoverished Polish noblesse to take service under the Prussian crown. Prior to 1806, about one-fifth of the higher and one-quarter of the lower ranks of the nobility were of Polish origin. Though these families became thoroughly Germanized in habit and outlook, the censorious might claim to see the marks of a distinctive origin in a haughtiness that was crude beyond the average and in their occasional tendency to wild extravagance.

II

The period round 1640, in which the Prusso-Brandenburgian Army was born, saw the beginnings of what was later to be referred to by the comprehensive term *Generalstabsdienst*, or "General Staff

Service". The Swedish Army stood at this time in high repute in Northern Europe, and it was on that model that the Great Elector may be presumed to have based himself in creating a so-called Quartermaster-General's Staff. The latter's function comprised all engineering services, the supervision of routes of march and the choice of camping sites and fortified positions. The first mention in the records of a Brandenburgian Quartermaster-General (a certain Lieutenant-Colonel and Engineer Gerhard von Bellicum, or Belkum) appears in 1657. He seems to have been assisted by one Lieutenant-Colonel and Engineer Jacob Holsten, who bore the title of Second Quartermaster-General.

The pay sheets show that the following belonged at this time to this so-called General Staff. There was, first, a Commissary-General, responsible for all matters of replacement, uniform, armament, food and shelter. This officer was assisted by a *Generalwachtmeister*; Sergeant-Major-General is the literal rendering: the rank was known to Cromwell's New Model Army. Further there were two Adjutants-General, one Provendermaster-General, a *General-auditeur*, who dealt with matters of military law, a Wagonmaster-General and an "Enforcer-General" (*Generalgewaltiger*) who with his constables was responsible for police matters. Actually, neither the Quartermaster-General nor the Commissary-General ranked as senior officer of the General Staff. That honour fell to the Master of Ordnance (*Feldzeugmeister*), in this instance Freiherr von Sparr, one of the Great Elector's truly great generals.

Among Bellicum's successors we find in the years 1670-73 a certain Philippe de Chiese, or Chiesa, less well known as a soldier than as the architect of the main building of Potsdam Castle and of the Berlin Mint, and also famous as the constructor of a post-chaise hung in slings, known as the "Berline". Chiesa was succeeded in the years up to 1699 by a number of officers of French origin, de Maistre, du Puy, Margace and de Brion. As regards the staff of the Quartermaster-General proper, this consisted of the following in order of seniority: the *Oberquartiermeister* or Senior Quartermaster (the rank is unknown in English), the General Staff Quartermaster and the Staff Quartermaster. These various functionaries constituted a technical and administrative body which, however, was never really organized on a permanent basis. What happened was that when war broke out, the General War Commissariat, as the General Staff began to be called, would on each occasion be assembled afresh.

In Austria, whose rulers tended to lack military experience and were not in the habit of taking the field themselves, a somewhat different institution had developed. This was the Court War Council, which surrounded the ruler with a body of persons with active service experience. In so far as this body drew up operation plans, it came closer to what we understand today by a General Staff.

In Prussia, however, the Great Elector was his own Generalissimo and his own Chief of Staff. His grandson, King Frederick William I, founded the tradition that the King was *ipso facto* the Supreme War Lord, leading his own army in the field. Under him, the uniform became the ruler's official livery, and so the most distinguished attire of social life. Service as an officer became the privilege of the nobility. The officer began to look upon himself as the servant of the monarch in whom the State was held to be personified, and the military oath in which the Junker swore loyalty to his sovereign gained a new and profound significance. Indeed, this conception of personal loyalty was the real moral foundation of the Army and was the thing that shaped the highly distinctive mental attitudes of the Prussian and later of the German officer corps as a whole.

Like that of Austria and Russia, the character of the new State was essentially military. Even the civil administration tended to borrow military forms, and the title of *Kriegsrat*, or War Councillor, for ordinary senior government officials is eloquent in this respect. With the exception of the Academy of Sciences, all educational institutions served purely military purposes, as, for instance, did the *Ritterakademie*, the Cadet Schools designed for the education of the nobility, and the *Militärakademie*. The *Ingenieurakademie* duly delivered military engineers, while the Medical School known as the *Pépinière* ensured the supply of regimental doctors.

It was under Frederick William I that the conception of so-called "Prussian Obedience" became a fundamental principle of this Prussian military nobility, and yet in those days, at any rate, it was not an obedience that was merely blind. A story is told of von Seydlitz, the cavalry leader, that when at the battle of Zorndorf, in 1758, Frederick the Great ordered him to attack the still unbroken Russian infantry, he replied, "Tell His Majesty that my head will be at his disposal after the battle, but that as long as the battle lasts I intend to use it in his service."

III

The Great Elector bequeathed an army of 30,000 men to his successor. Frederick I raised the number to 40,000, and Frederick William I increased it further to 80,000. When Frederick the Great died in 1786, the number had risen to 200,000. These rising figures mirror Prussia's ascent during the eighteenth century to the level of a great power. The three victorious Silesian wars and the proceeds of the partition of Poland in 1772 added West Prussia and Silesia to Frederick's possessions, while his victories at Rossbach and Leuthen in the Seven Years' War established the Prussian Army's reputation all over Europe, though it was Russia's change of sides, and not Frederick's military performance, that saved him from annihilation by his more powerful neighbours.

Like his predecessors, Frederick the Great was his own Chief of Staff, and the Quartermaster-General's staff remained much the kind of thing that has already been described, the number of officers serving on it totalling about twenty-five. We find, however, that this staff has now a corps of orderlies at its disposal to serve as messengers and despatch carriers, and also that the institution of the Brigade Major has come into being. Brigade Majors were officers who moved about from one place to another and assisted generals by means of reports and the compilation of useful data. It was in the nature of things that this Quartermaster-General's corps should work in close personal contact with the King. Indeed, in later times the latter made the training of these officers his own personal concern, the twelve best pupils of the *Academie des Nobles* in every year being taken for these posts. Even so, there is as yet no question of a genuine General Staff in our sense of the term. The King has as yet no responsible body of military advisers.

We must, however, note the growth of another institution with which the Quartermaster-General's department has a tendency to overlap, and with which in the course of time it develops a very sharp rivalry. This is the office of the Adjutant-General, the germinal cell of that most characteristic Prussian thing, the Military Cabinet of the Prussian kings. Under the first Prussian kings, this office was chiefly concerned with officers' records. Frederick the Great, however, somewhat extended its province in connection with the new system of "directives" which the exigencies of this particular time called into being.

The fact that during the Seven Years' War theatres of operation were scattered and often remote frequently necessitated the employment of large bodies of troops under what were really independent commanders. Within the framework of instructions of a general kind, such officers had to be given a certain freedom of decision. In such cases, apart from Brigade Majors and other more subordinate personnel from the staff, the King liked to attach to the field commander an Adjutant-General or an aide-de-camp, whose rôle was in the nature of that of a royal Commissar. There were during the Seven Years' War five such Adjutants-General attached to the infantry and two to the cavalry, and the best known among them, Hans von Winterfeld, one of the King's closest friends, actually had a number of units under his independent command.

From the year 1758 onwards, there was a single Adjutant-General who had a secretary attached to him. The most important of these was Heinrich Wilhelm von Anhalt. He was an illegitimate son of Prince Wilhelm von Anhalt-Dessau, his mother, a noted beauty, being a clergyman's daughter. This man joined the Prussian Army under the name of "Gustavsohn", served on the Quartermaster-General's staff and was raised by Frederick to the nobility in 1761, and from 1765 to 1781 held, with the rank of colonel, the posts of First Adjutant-General and Quartermaster-General. The interest of this figure lies in the fact that, during the partition of Poland and in the war of the Bavarian succession of 1778, he played so large a part in deciding on the commitments of various bodies of troops that one might almost speak of him as Frederick's Chief of Staff. He seems hardly to have been a very agreeable person, for he enjoyed the reputation of a surly and obstinate martinet, but he shared one characteristic with later chiefs of the General Staff: his work was largely done in secret and he remained almost wholly unknown to the public.

IV

War in the eighteenth century had its own governing principles. The economic and even the political power of the absolutist states was limited, and this, of course, in its turn set a limit to their military means. Moreover, the professional armies of the Hohenzollerns, the Habsburgs and the Bourbons were expensive instruments which were hard to replace, for they were instruments of high mechanical perfection. Infantry marched right into the battle line in firm, mathematically circumscribed formations. It fought in thin lines three deep, several sets of triple alignments being drawn up one behind the other. All evolutions were carried out according to rule, with the soldiers during all their ingenious wheeling and manoeuvring keeping strictly in step. The aim was the welding together of the men so that they moved and fired with the synchrony of a single machine. The individual as such was at a discount. Frederick the Great is said to have remarked that the soldier needed to fear the sergeant's stick more than he feared the bullets of the enemy; even of his own officers, the great Potsdam sceptic was in the habit of saying that if they ever started to think, not one of them would remain with the colours. There were really only two considerations—speed of march and speed of fire, of which the latter was greatly enhanced by the use of the iron ramrod (introduced into the Prussian Army by Duke Leopold of Anhalt-Dessau) since wooden ramrods were liable to break under rapid manipulation.

The short range of firearms restricted the size of the battlefield, so that it was easy in those days for commanders to supervise their dispositions with their own eyes from any rising piece of ground. The provisioning of the well-nigh irreplaceable troops was done by means of a cumbersome system of storehouses, and this also narrowed down the field of operations. If military operations were on a modest scale, the aims of wars were equally restricted. Wars were waged for the possession of a fortress or a province. The merciless life and death struggle between whole peoples, let alone the war of ideologies, had not yet been born.

The strategy of the time was that of the chess board which concentrated on felicitous manoeuvring and avoided, wherever possible, the more painful decisions of a direct encounter. Count Wilhelm von Schaumberg Lippe, one of the most important military historians of the time, says in his *Mémoires sur la Guerre Défensive* that the art of war should be directed to the avoidance of war, or at any rate towards the mitigation of its evils. One of the most typical wars of the century was that of the Bavarian Succession, which was fought by Frederick the Great in 1778 to prevent the union of Austria and Bavaria. In this instance the King and his brother, Prince Heinrich, each with an army of 80,000 men, marched from Silesia and the Lausitz into Bohemia, while the Austrians took up an entrenched position on the Upper Elbe; yet a battle was risked by neither belligerent, and the issue was settled by diplomacy. Till then the notion of a war of extermination had only made its appearance in the Turkish wars which were waged against the House of Habsburg in the Balkans, and in this case the Osmanli Empire really does seem to have maintained the traditions of Timur the Tartar and Genghis Khan; but these wars took place in an area that lay somewhat outside the consciousness of eighteenth-century Europe.

Change, however, was already at work. In the middle of the century two events had erupted into that polished world of Rococo—the Industrial Revolution and the Enlightenment. The former had been most in evidence in England, but in France, too, it was a sign of the times that land speculators were buying up old ancestral homes. Middle-class business efficiency and the middle-class ability to make money began palpably to breach the charmed feudal circle, and the change finds expression in the military sphere. Technical proficiency begins to threaten the traditional precedence of a titled soldier caste— particularly in the artillery, which now becomes essentially the weapon of the third estate. Scharnhorst, the son of a tenant farmer, begins his career as an artillery officer in the Hanoverian forces. Even Prussia is not wholly immune against this hidden class war, which brings with it a steady dribble of middle-class officers into the artillery and the engineers.

Meanwhile, eighteenth-century military thought was effecting its own *reductio ad absurdum*. Moving, as it did, in a world of artifice and geometrical forms, it induced in a number of minds the conviction that the art of war was a matter of mathematical calculation. Von Templehof, a Prussian artillery colonel, from whose family came Ludendorff's mother, inclined to this persuasion, as did also a certain Dietrich Heinrich von Bülow, a Prussian officer who was dismissed the Army because of the irregularities of his life, but aspired to a post on the Quartermaster-General's staff on the merits of his theories. One of von Bülow's main concerns was the angle formed between the base of operations and the operational objective. An angle of ninety degrees was considered the most desirable. In the Prussian Quarter-master-General's staff itself, Colonel Christian von Massenbach was the best-known exponent of this general school of thought, and it was no doubt this kind of speculation, in which all feeling for effective forms of combat had disappeared, that led von Saldern, one of Frederick the Great's latter-day generals, to declare that the essence of all military training lay in the formal evolutions of the parade ground.

V

The petrifaction of Frederick's military system led to the bureaucratization of the Army command. Under Frederick's successor, Frederick William II, it became plain that the monarchy had grown much too large for a single individual to deal with the whole business of government, especially when that individual was as devoted to the pleasures of life as the potentate concerned. That was why in 1787 there was formed an *Ober-Kriegs-Kollegium* or Supreme War Council which under the direction of two Field-Marshals, the Duke of Brunswick and von Möllendorf, was to act as the highest military authority. This body had three departments, one for mobilization, provisionment and Army affairs in general, one for uniforms and equipment, and one to deal with the disabled. Also, theoretically at least, it had the departments of the Adjutant-General and that of the Quartermaster-General under its control. The department of the Adjutant-General was in the charge of the Adjutant-General of the infantry, whoever he might be, and concerned itself with officers' records, with garrison and armament matters and with all questions relating to regulations. The Quartermaster-General's staff, the strength of which at this time was from twenty to twenty-four officers, was now for the first time given its own uniform. In the case of infantry officers on this staff, this uniform consisted of a light-blue coat with red facings and dark-yellow waistcoat and trousers, the coat of cavalry officers being white. In addition to the duties already allotted to it in regard to fortresses and camps, this department was in 1796 asked to concern itself with a typical General Staff activity, namely the preparation of serviceable military maps. With this purpose in view, thirteen *Ingénieur-Géographes* were posted to the Quartermaster-General's staff, their office being in the royal castle at Potsdam. These "Engineer Geographers" were mostly people of middle-class origin, for it was looked upon as beneath the Junker's dignity to busy himself with coloured pencils and dividers.

There was further, from time to time, an exchange of personnel between the Adjutant-General's and the Quartermaster-General's departments. The First Adjutant-General of the infantry, Colonel von Geusau, himself later became head of the Quartermaster-General's staff. Even so the departments were rivals, and in the end the Adjutant-General's department not only secured ascendancy over that of the Quartermaster-General, which never rose beyond the level of a purely technical body, but also over the *Ober-Kriegs-Kollegium*, which suffered considerably under the disadvantage of divided control and had never more than a most nebulous conception of the nature of its functions. Thus the way was opened for the development which we have already noted, whereby the Adjutant-General's department was ultimately to blossom into the all-powerful military cabinet of the Prussian kings, a consummation that had its disquieting side, for the military cabinet's irresponsible *imperium in imperio*, and its ability to influence the sovereign by secret advice, was to provide at least one of the reasons for Stein's dramatic appeal for a reform of head and members. Whatever its shortcomings in this respect, however, the Adjutant-General's department can still claim the distinction of providing the nearest equivalent that the age could show to a modern General Staff.

VI

Strangely enough, the Prussian Army continued, while these changes were in progress, to be the accepted model for Europe, so much so that immediately before the Revolution the French Minister of War was considering the introduction of Prussian drill regulations and the Prussian military organization into France. Yet while life everywhere was congealing into ever stiffer forms, that same France rediscovered a new vitality of her own, and in the military sphere as in others the French Revolution proved a turning point.

Nothing could have offered a sharper contrast at this time than the mood of Germany and that of France. After the long struggle of the Seven Years' War, Germany was hungry for peace. That longing found its spiritual embodiment in Kant's tract, *Towards Everlasting Peace*, which condemns war as the destroyer of all that is good and the origin of all that is evil; it also found it in Schiller's glorification of World citizenship, and in much of the writing of Herder. French aspirations were very different. Moreover, the French Revolution not only propagated the ideas of the freedom and equality of man, it brought into being the Nation State, which in its turn produced the phenomenon of the nation in arms, and with it an altogether new potential of power. The Prussian elaboration of this conception was one of the Revolution's unforeseen consequences—a consequence which, thanks to the German example, was in due course passed on to the Slavs of the East.

French admiration for existing military arrangements only waned slowly, and Moderate leaders of the National Assembly who honestly sought, as many of them did, to reconcile the officers of the *ancien régime* with the Revolution, encountered little opposition on technical grounds. A proposal was even considered to offer the command of the armies of the Revolution either to the Duke of Brunswick or to the Hessian general and minister Count Ernst Heinrich von Schlieffen, both of whom had been trained in the school of Frederick the Great, and many a general of King Louis's army loyally served the Tricolor. The French Drill and Training Regulations of 1791 differed very little from those of the royal army.

A struggle against the old army began, however, when the more radical elements of the Revolution, the Jacobins, rose to power. Many officers were either murdered or executed simply because they were of noble descent, while the very barracks and parade grounds, and all else that recalled the ancient rigid discipline, became detested symbols of the old order. "Soldiers' Committees", prototypes of the "Soldiers' Councils" of 1918, were formed in many regiments, a congress of regimental delegates took place in Strasbourg, and 20,000 naval ratings mutinied at Brest. The National Guard, which the Marquis of Lafayette had originally formed to protect the propertied middle class, was gradually changed into the germinal cell of a new People's Army. When in 1792 Prussia, Austria, England and Spain formed a coalition against Revolutionary France, the leaders of the Revolution deliberately appealed to the patriotism of the broad masses, and the Deputy Dubois-Crancé introduced a bill for universal service into the National Assembly. That bill immediately became law, and with Barrès leading the panegyric, the glorification of the nation in arms began.

VII

The campaign of 1792, that crusade of the Princes which was so singularly short of crusaders, petered out in pitiable failure. The French popular army broke completely with tradition and developed wholly new forms of combat. Something very like open order fighting appeared, as did the tactic of packing huge numbers of men together for an offensive punch. There was little art in this manoeuvre, but it was exceedingly effective.   Moreover, the new French armies did not look upon war as the exclusive concern of a distant and detached authority with whom the rank and file had little in common, and this may explain their quite unprecedented powers of resilience. Certainly they contrived to recover from defeats which would have finished troops of the conventional type for good.

Another new element was economic. With the introduction of the mass army, cannon fodder was not only more plentiful but cheaper; no costly apparatus had now to be employed to recruit or press men to the colours. The new mass army had come to stay, the old feudal order disintegrated. Peace had to be made with France, for, as the Duke of Hohenlohe, one of the coalition's commanders, remarked, you cannot get the better of madmen.

The lessons went home. Men like Kant, Schiller, Hölderlin and Herder were by no means the only ones who greeted the Revolution with enthusiasm. A number of young officers of the more intellectual type, like Major von der Knesebeck of the Quartermaster-General's staff, and Lieutenant von Boyen (then a simple infantry officer in distant East Prussia), showed marked sympathy for the new spirit coming from the West. Military writers such as Georg Heinrich von Behrenhorst, like the von Anhalt previously mentioned, an illegitimate child of one of the Dukes of Anhalt-Dessau, now abandoned the conception of a mathematic science of war and set about explaining the relationship of military tactics to political upheaval. Behrenhorst's conclusions led him to propose the replacement of the professional army by a cadre army based on a militia. His brother-devotee, von Bülow, followed him in this and insisted in particular on the value of the new skirmishing tactics.

The new "Gospel of Belly-crawling", however, found no response in the *Ober-Kriegs-Kollegium* or in the Adjutant-General's department, and its apostles were treated with ridicule or contempt. Bülow in particular remained an outcast, who as manager of a troop of actors, glass manufacturer, speculator and author, led a precarious existence in England and America. Only a handful of generals, headed by Lieutenant-General von Rüchel and Lieutenant-General de Courbière, of whom the latter had commanded the Prussian Guard in the late campaign, made the cause of universal service their own and obtained occasional support from enlightened staff officers like Knesebeck. Unfortunately, such ideas clashed with the basic principles on which the East-Elbian landowners ran their estates, for they touched on their rights over their serfs and their private jurisdiction— and those rights were already none too secure. The effects of the French Revolution had reached far into the heart of Prussia. In Silesia, where conditions were particularly oppressive, a series of disturbances among the peasants necessitated the calling in of troops.

Whole villages were compelled by the military commanders to run the gauntlet, and so to undergo one of the worst punishments known to the old professional army, in which the prevailing absolutism still found its most typical expression.

Yet the French revolutionary wars had shattered the old scheme of things and brought about world-wide changes which not even the Prussian Army could indefinitely deny. They led to an unprecedented extension both of the area and the objectives of warfare. They also brutalized the whole business of fighting. Strangely enough, the birth of mass armies synchronized not only with the French Revolution and with the English Industrial Revolution but also with that very remarkable biological phase which multiplied human beings in every country in Europe.

The revolutionary masses, which now became militarized, broke with the limitations of what in the eighteenth century had become the aristocratic pastime of war. France now carried on war on the Rhine, in Southern Germany, in Belgium, in Northern Italy, in Egypt, in Syria, in Southern and Western France. She fought against the armies of Prussia, Austria, Spain, Sardinia, England, Russia and Turkey, and against her own counter-revolutionaries. In 1794 France had over a million men under arms.

The direction of so vast a host by a single commander was as impossible as was the simultaneous personal supervision of a number of campaigns carried on in widely separated theatres. Quite obviously the new situation demanded radical changes in technique. First, to be of tactical use, the mobilized masses needed a precise articulation into armies, corps and divisions. The practice of breaking fighting forces up into groups had not been unknown under Frederick the Great, but such groups had not been entities organized into a specific functional pattern. They had in each case been built up out of the different arms as necessity might require. All this now is changed, and the division comes into its own as the new tactical unit.

VIII

But this in its turn calls forth a new necessity, that of linking the division with the command, and so staff officers are attached to it to ensure the correct transmission, interpretation and even the correct execution of orders sent from above. Such officers must obviously be men of highly specialized training. Here the office of Carnot, the War Minister, played its part as a sort of staff officers' breeding ground, for although it was little more than an organization for reinforcements and supply and had no further authority, it did tend to train the kind of specialist whom the situation required. One feature of this office is especially notable in this connection, for its work was marked by that tendency to anonymity which today is almost the essence of staff work —a circumstance which once led General von Seeckt to remark that staff officers had no names.

The process, therefore, by which the conduct of war comes more and more into the hands of specialists, a process which accelerated with the technical developments of the nineteenth century, has its origins in the French revolutionary wars. It is a depersonalizing process on which the spirit of the mass age has clearly set its mark, and none is more palpably affected by it than the officer of the General Staff. Two sharply opposed influences have thus assisted in forming the character of the German General Staff, the stratified feudal society of old Prussia, and the new nationalism of the French Revolution. It was left to the great reformer Scharnhorst to make a synthesis of these two contradictory elements and so to reconcile the old with the new.

CHAPTER II

THE FATHERS

I

IN 1801 Gerhard Johann Scharnhorst applied to the King of Prussia for employment in the Prussian Army. He did this because the Prussian Army at that time was accounted the most important in Germany and held out greater prospects of advancement than either the Hanoverian or Danish Army, the latter of which had offered him an appointment. Scharnhorst added three curious requests to his application. He asked to be posted as a lieutenant-colonel. He also asked to be raised to the nobility and to be allowed to carry out a reform of the Prussian Army. Three essays on various aspects of military science were attached to the application, presumably as a proof of the applicant's qualifications.

Certainly this application argued an unusual character, and in Scharnhorst's case some unusual capacity was certainly required, since neither his circumstances nor any other visible trait recommended him for his chosen career. He had been born in 1755 in Bodenau as the son of a tenant farmer and sometime sergeant-major in the Hanoverian artillery. The father's brother delivered fish for the Hanoverian Elector's table, his brother-in-law was a miller, while Scharnhorst's mother was the niece of one of the suppliers of the Court kitchen. Further, the son's bearing quite singularly lacked that peculiar semi-military stiffness that the Prussians designate by the word *stramm*, while his face, with its fleshy nose and its slight trace of sarcasm about the mouth, was somehow not the right kind of face for an officer at all. He cut a bad figure on parade, his word of command was poor, and he lacked that special kind of eloquence that can at times both delight and inspire the rank and file.

It is to the credit of the Prussian Army that despite these departures from the customary norm, the major's application was approved, but the fact is that there were other reasons for this than his work in military science, and indeed the suggestion to draw him into the

Prussian forces had been made as far back as 1797. Scharnhorst had been brought up in the famous military school of Count Wilhelm von Schaumburg-Lippe, the reorganizer of the Portuguese Army and a champion of the revolutionary idea of universal service. He had earned high distinction in the revolutionary wars in Belgium. As Chief of Staff to General von Hammerstein, the Commandant of the fortress of Ménin, Scharnhorst directed the sortie when that place was besieged. This led to his being appointed Chief of Staff to Count Wallmoden, Commander in Chief of the Hanoverian forces and father-in-law to Reichsfreiherr von Stein, who was at that time congenially employed in administering the Westphalian possessions of the Hohenzollerns. Scharnhorst was thus already accounted a very knowledgeable officer. Moreover, he had an excellent pen and had already acted as editor of a respected military periodical.

II

When Scharnhorst entered the Prussian Army, the second coalition against Napoleon between England, Austria and Russia had come to an end on the battlefield of Marengo, while Napoleon himself had seized unlimited power by the *coup d'état* of the 18th Brumaire. Prussia was at the time passing through one of the less illustrious phases of her variegated history. True, she was no longer the Prussia of Frederick William II who had luxuriated in the deceptive but delightful twilight of the *ancien régime*. The swarm of colourful mistresses were there no longer, and there had been other salutary changes, but though the outrageous had disappeared from Prussian life, it was merely to make room for the futile, and in the fields of diplomacy, defence, administration and social life the State machine worked with a complacent incompetence which even by eighteenth-century standards was remarkable. Few denied the need for reform, but fewer ventured on action, and so Prussian policy was at this time marked by a timid conservatism which in the long run nearly ended by conserving nothing at all. Napoleon was at this time extending his power over Southern and Western Germany and over Belgium, Switzerland and Italy. From Egypt he was threatening Britain's possessions in India. Yet Prussia, gorged with her acquisitions from the second partition of Poland, sought diligently to retain her neutrality. This was not so much a policy as the result of having no policy at all.

Internally the picture was scarcely more heartening. The nobility, closely bound together by blood and marriage, poor, unyielding, ambitious and ravenous of emolument, held all the key posts in its hands. This applied particularly to the Army. All the generals and regimental commanders were titled, only the Artillery could produce an occasional colonel who was actually a commoner, the Fortress Artillery being distinguished by the possession of no less than three. Actually, this Junkerdom, which to a man like Stein seemed a caricature of genuine nobility, had, as a matter of fact, forfeited much of its old stubborn self-assurance, though this merely increased the obstinacy with which it clung to what it still possessed.

Meanwhile, under this uninspired leadership, the Army, the backbone of this State of warriors and colonizers, had gone from bad to worse. Its outmoded tricks of drill, its rough and brutal methods of discipline, its scourgings and runnings of the gauntlet, made it seem like a single huge antediluvian penal institution. Only too often in the little garrison towns of East Elbia the peaceful burghers were startled out of their sleep when the dull thunder of the alarm gun proclaimed through the darkness that a soldier, or perhaps a number of soldiers, had deserted.

It needed a stronger personality than the reigning monarch, Frederick William III, to set this ramshackle house in order, but if Frederick William singularly failed to do anything, he was not utterly blind to reality. For some time, though the notion came to nothing, he toyed with the idea of liberating the serfs, and he was certainly aware of the fact that something had to be done about the Army. In a memorandum of 1795 he refers to that institution as a diseased body which must be helped back to health. It was a striking but not an exaggerated description.

III

Whatever her defects, however, Prussia was in Scharnhorst's case as good as her word, and his somewhat novel request to be raised to the nobility was complied with shortly after his entry into the Prussian service. He was, moreover, posted to the Quartermaster-General's staff, where he undertook the supervision of military schools, but he found yet another at least equally important activity, for in July, 1801, Scharnhorst founded in Berlin the *Militärische Gesellschaft*, which had the reform of the Army as its aim.

The president of this society was Lieutenant-General von Rüchel, Inspector of the Guards and Governor of Potsdam. Rüchel's adjutant, Major von dem Knesebeck, was, as already related, an enthusiast for the ideas of 1789, and had at the time drawn up a memorandum on the strengthening of the Army through a territorial militia, and it was about this time that the idea came to Scharnhorst of using just such a national and universal militia as a stepping stone to a People's Army.

A number of young officers of lieutenant's and captain's rank joined the society, including Boyen, Grolman, Clausewitz and Rühle von Lilienstern, all of them wholehearted supporters of Scharnhorst. The ardour of these enthusiasts was, however, subject to the chastening influence of a number of adherents of the old school who had a certain scientific interest in the new but tended to bring what was perhaps a more critical spirit to bear. Such were Colonel von Phull, of the Quartermaster-General's staff, and Colonel Hans von Yorck, at that time commander of a regiment of the *chasseurs à pied*. The last named, who was probably the more captious of the two, had served under the Dutch in a foreign legion at the Cape and in Java, and had during this service made acquaintance with the new open order fighting. As a dour old Prussian traditionalist he naturally refused to recognize that the new tactics were based on the assumption of changes in the social structure. He also declared that there was too much learned talk in the society, more of it, in fact, than an "honest Prussian's" brains could cope with.

Actually, most of the generals doubted whether the success of the French "mob-heaps" offered ground for subjecting the system of Frederick the Great to re-examination. Even Rüchel was in the habit of saying that the Prussian Army possessed several generals of the quality of "Herr von Bonaparte". Such things, however, did not affect the clarity of Scharnhorst's insight, for the study of the Napoleonic wars had left him in no kind of doubt as to the epoch-making changes which the French Revolution had set in motion. He saw their military implications—the exploitation of all the resources of popular strength by means of universal service, the new type of infantry combat which was followed by the attack of huge massed columns, the subdivision of the Army into divisions composed of all types of weapons, and last, but by no means least, the creation of a proper Army General Staff—and Scharnhorst's convictions were sufficiently intense and the weight of his authority sufficiently great to make the ascendancy of the new ideas assured.

Two things however must be noted about this man. First, he was no revolutionary. He wished to see the new growing organically out of the old. He wished a retention of the valuable traditions of the past. In this respect he was a sort of double to Stein who, in the civilian sector, wanted reform to come as an orderly development in the process of history. Further, Scharnhorst was also perfectly clear in his mind that the creation of a militia, the introduction of universal service, necessitated the granting of political rights to the serfs on the great estates. This freeing of the peasants and the recognition of a universal duty of bearing arms were two things that went hand in hand. Hegel, who was to become the philosopher of the almighty State, had already indulged in reflections on an ideal German constitution. In these the correlation between universal service and popular representation, both of which the author demanded, had been clearly apparent.

As Director of the *Militärakademie*, Scharnhorst now became the educator of a new generation of officers whose representatives were to play a great part in the decades to come. It was a generation inspired by a high sense of moral responsibility and by glowing idealism. Among Scharnhorst's pupils were a number of young men who were later to earn distinction—Lieutenant Carl von Clausewitz, the son of an impoverished family of Protestant theologians, Staff-Captain Carl Wilhelm von Grolman, the son of a high Prussian judicial functionary descended from an ennobled merchant family in Bochum, Lieutenant August Rühle von Lilienstern, son of an ennobled Prussian officer from Frankfort with an estate on the Priegnitz, and Staff-Captain Hermann von Boyen. It is significant that all these men came, as did Stein and Hardenberg, not from the ranks of the rooted Pommeranian Junkers but from other regions and other sections of society. Scharnhorst's pupils, who were later to form the kernel of the Prussian General Staff, underwent a training which was both moral and intellectual. It was not for nothing that the curriculum of the old *école militaire* of 1790 had included the philosophy of Kant. Kant had brought the moral conduct of the individual into relationship with universal law, and something of Kant's categorical imperative continued to animate these men.

Scharnhorst himself was a man of high moral sensibility and a believing Christian, who was fully conscious of all the terrible aspects of the trade of war. He knew the fearful responsibility which the waging of a war entailed. He brought up a generation of men from whom one cannot withhold respect, and he brought them up in the conviction that war as a political expedient is only permissible in circumstances of desperate necessity, that it is only permissible when resorted to unwillingly as the last remaining expedient. Time and again he warned against a *Kabinettspolitik*, a policy conducted secretly and with unworthy motives in which the purely military point of view was allowed to prevail.

Without willing it, Napoleon had in the military field become the great instructor of the German states, but in one respect his imitators went beyond the original, for since Napoleon tended in the main to be his own Chief of Staff and to draw up his own operational plans, the French General Staff was limited to the Army General Staff pure and simple. There was nothing like a Great General Staff such as was ultimately developed in Germany. The French Emperor's Chief of Staff, Marshal Berthier, who had served as a French colonel in the American War of Independence, was, strictly speaking, nothing but the director of a military bureau, whose function it was to issue and transmit orders but who had no responsibility for advising his Commander in Chief.

That Prussia now struck out on a line of her own in this particular field is due to the educational work of Scharnhorst, but also to the imagination and organizing ability of that somewhat controversial figure, Colonel von Massenbach, of the Quartermaster-General's staff, who was another member, and a most active one, of the *Militärische Gesellschaft*. Von Massenbach was in many ways a remarkable individual. The scion of a noble Württemberg family, he was a small, squat, bald-headed man, with large, lively eyes. He was a man of restless mind, consumed by a devouring ambition, and incidentally a warm admirer of Napoleon. He was certainly a more brilliant man than Scharnhorst, though temperamental, unstable and cursed with an unfortunate manner. That is why, despite his considerable achievements, he disappears comparatively early from the stage and does so under something of a cloud.

Now, von Massenbach had in 1801 drawn up instructions relating to service on the Quartermaster-General's staff, and two important memoranda, dated January and November, 1802, respectively, justify his being called, at any rate as far as Prussia is concerned, the father of a unitary General Staff organization. In these memoranda, Massenbach pointed out the necessity of a permanent General Staff which was to function even in peace-time as a planning centre. He proposed, and this proposal is the essence of the whole concept, that even in time of peace operational plans for every conceivable military eventuality should be prepared, the work being divided into three fields, relating to three possible theatres of war, Austria, Russia and France.

Thus his projected General Staff consisted of three brigades, though it was in the east alone, with Russia or Austria, that is to say, that he foresaw the possibility of war. The thought of a war with the France that he so much admired does not seem to have entered his mind.

Further, he insisted, and this too was a proposal of the utmost importance, that as an integral part of the training programme, journeys should regularly be undertaken in peacetime for the purpose of reconnoitring the terrain of possible scenes of operations. Such reconnaissance journeys were also to be undertaken abroad. Other proposals related to the regular alternation of service with the General Staff and with the troops, and to what was to be the most important right of any future Chief of Staff—the *Immediatvortrag* to the sovereign, the right, that is to say, to have unhindered and uncontrolled access to the Supreme War Lord; so that no limits would be set to the Chief of Staff's influence on the latter's decisions; this last proposal was to be frequently repeated, but was only translated into reality comparatively late.

Frederick William III held Massenbach's memoranda to be so important that he referred them to the highest generals for their opinions. Only Rüchel expressed unreserved agreement; most of the others were doubtful. Field-Marshal von Möllendorf feared the danger of possible indiscretions if plans of operation were prepared in advance and then stored away. General von Zastrow was uneasy about the advisability of treating a General Staff as a training school. All generals, he felt, would now become endowed with field-marshal's talents and none of them would be willing to take orders from the other.

For all that, the King in 1803 acted on Massenbach's suggestions and ordered the reorganization of the Quartermaster-General's staff, Major-General von Gravert being entrusted with the task. Lieutenant-General von Geusau was appointed Chief of Staff, and was at the same time entrusted with the direction of the War Department of the *Ober-Kriegs-Kollegium* and with that of the Engineer Corps—a considerable extension of the Quartermaster-General's province.

The Quartermaster-General's staff now consisted of twenty-one officers, and all save Scharnhorst came from titled families. The special military ranks which these men carried being, it is believed, without any British counterparts, it will be best to give them in the original German. The twenty-one officers consisted of three *General-quartiermeisterleutnants*, equivalent in seniority to colonels, or in certain cases, apparently, to major-generals, six *Quartiermeisters*, equivalent to majors, six *Quartiermeisterleutnants*, equivalent to captains, and six adjutants. The number was supplemented by six "Officer-Geographers", together with a small staff of engravers, clerks, and orderlies. The whole corps was divided in accordance with Massenbach's plan into three brigades, each under one of the *Generalquartiermeisterleutnants* and each corresponding to one of the three "theatres of war". The three *Generalquartiermeisterleutnants* were Major-General von Phull, himself the son of a Württembergian general, Massenbach and Scharnhorst, the respective areas of the three brigades being as follows. The 1st or Eastern Brigade took over the territory on the right bank of the Vistula, the 2nd or Southern Brigade, Central and Southern Germany including Silesia, while the 3rd or Western Brigade took over Western Germany.

In some ways the auspices under which the new institution began were not too propitious, for the Chief of Staff and his three Brigade commanders were a somewhat diversified group. Lieutenant-General von Geusau was old; his wits had grown somewhat dull and he had lost such aptitude as he ever possessed for keeping his head above water in a sea of red tape. Phull was essentially a peevish pedant, though he had an occasional gleam of insight and could at least see that reforms were necessary. Massenbach was a *bel esprit* but unfortunately quite incapable of resisting the siren quality of his own eloquence. Further, Massenbach, as has already been told, was, among other things, a disciple of the mathematical school and could never permanently shake off the recurrent obsession that the peacetime registration of all the positions that would prove most favourable in any military eventuality was an adequate prescription for victory. Above all, his nervous instability, which once at a shooting party nearly cost a relative his life, set limits to his usefulness. Scharnhorst alone, whom Phull and Massenbach called a pedantic schoolmaster for his pains, had that combination of intellectual power and emotional balance to grasp exactly what was required to give a real meaning to Massenbach's creation.

Yet whatever the quirks of its principals, Prussia now had a proper General Staff and had never had such a thing before. The only trouble was that nobody knew the true use of this piece of apparatus and that among the organized disorder of the various military hierarchies the exact limits of its functions and authority remained extremely nebulous. Alongside of the Quartermaster-General's staff—

theoretically, indeed, above it—there was the *Ober-Kriegs-Kollegium* under Field-Marshal von Mollendorf and the Duke of Brunswick, of whom the former was nearing eighty while the latter was getting on for seventy. It was not these, however, but the Adjutant-General's department which possessed the greatest influence on the conduct of military affairs. The Adjutant-General's department was functioning, as we have seen, as a secret military cabinet and a kind of personal staff to the sovereign, and its head at this time was the Adjutant-General of Infantry, a certain Major-General von Köckritz, according to Stein, a typical product of the "Monk's obedience" of the Potsdam garrison, whose entire world consisted of cards, port and tobacco. Nobody had yet made up his mind how in an emergency the competencies of these various authorities were to be arranged.

Both the reputation and the work of the Quartermaster-General's staff rested for the time being entirely on Scharnhorst's personality, but Scharnhorst was not the advocate of any hard and fast system. He merely preached the realization of certain basically new ideas, the validity of which had lately been recognized—ideas such as the strengthening and completion of the Army by means of a militia, the creation of mixed divisions composed of all arms under their own staffs (staffs for which Scharnhorst was training the necessary staff officers) and the adjustment of combat methods to the needs of the time.

Napoleon's strategy aimed at a merciless annihilation of his enemy. Scharnhorst was still capable of visualizing a different type of war, but he saw one of the consequences of the increasing size of armies, he saw that as a result of this increasing size it was necessary to divide forces during the approach march. His principle, "Never stand in concentration, always do battle in concentration," was already formulated in anticipation of Moltke's thought, and this in its turn necessitated the presence of that 'operational' staff to which allusion has already been made.

IV

In 1805, the third Russo-Austrian-British coalition was formed against Napoleon. Sweden joined the alliance, and it was plain that as far as Prussia was concerned the crisis had come. The agreeable notion of Count Haugwitz, Prussia's Foreign Minister, that Prussia could stand aside and, as *tertius gaudens*, make profits out of the strife of the Great Powers, had proved illusory, as had the fear that the

Czar's request for right of way through Prussia concealed a sinister scheme to annex that kingdom. Moreover, the Czar had at least asked permission to enter Prussian territory, while France, without observing that tedious formality, had quietly violated it.

The result was the defeat of Haugwitz and his party. Prussia signed an alliance with France's enemies, though enough of her old caution remained for her to prefer armed mediation to the hazards (if these could be honourably avoided) of actual belligerency.

Such hesitancy on the part of her king was understandable and even praiseworthy, for Frederick William distrusted both his own abilities and those of his army. Scharnhorst, however, believed that there was no escape from conflict with Napoleonic France and used the opportunity to take a step of some importance. He sent a memorandum on the operational possibilities to Hardenberg, who had now superseded Haugwitz as Foreign Minister. The event is of some slight interest, for it marked the first occasion on which a senior officer of the Quartermaster-General's staff sought to play the part of a responsible adviser in a political decision.

Meanwhile, the Prussian Army was put on a war footing and in that stifling summer of 1805 that seemed so pregnant with disaster, Scharnhorst, with a view to reconnoitring certain areas of ground, arranged for the officers of his brigade to go on the first staff training journeys which formed so important a part of Massenbach's proposals. In later times these so-called General Staff journeys were to constitute one of the most important parts of the Prussian General Staff's training.

In October the Austrian armies under Mack were surrounded at Ulm. Napoleon's main army advanced into Moravia, where in December the Austro-Russian coalition suffered its annihilating defeat at Austerlitz. This reduced the idea of Prussian armed neutrality to absurdity before it had ever been properly born. Austria made peace with France, Napoleon united the South German States in the Confederation of the Rhine and very skilfully offered Hanover as a bait to Prussia in order to split her off from England.

Prussia was now nearly isolated, and her isolation was in due course rendered complete by her own diplomatic ineptitude. Apart from the Duke of Saxony Weimar, only the Electors of Saxony and Hesse-Cassel remained at her side. Russian help in case of war was distant and uncertain, the great opportunity for Prusso-Austro-Russian collaboration had been allowed to slip by, while Prussian finances had been prematurely exhausted by mobilization.

Stein, who since 1804 had been Prussian Minister of Finance, felt the urgency of the hour. He strove desperately for some kind of thoroughgoing reform and for the abolition of the irresponsible government of the King's cabinet. He was quite prepared to force the King to action by some kind of Palace revolution, provided only that all generals and ministers would act in concert with him. Unfortunately among the high-ranking generals only Rüchel, Blücher and Phull would give him support. Scharnhorst himself believed that the time for such a plan had gone by, war being, so to speak, at Prussia's door. Perhaps he was wise, though it is difficult to see how an over-precipitate reform could have produced worse results than those which actually eventuated.

V

In August, 1806, Prussia mobilized once more. The organization into divisions which had so long been advocated was now hurriedly carried into effect; but the Quartermaster-General's staff had no real authority and the Army and divisional staffs lacked the skill born of experience. Scharnhorst drew up a plan for a massing of forces, so placed that they could take the offensive against any French concentration either on the Rhine or the Main, and considering Prussia's inferior numbers, such a spoiling attack was probably the only possible strategy, for it might just conceivably have gained time, and time might have brought allies. But other counsels prevailed, and Scharnhorst's plan was abandoned in favour of the old-fashioned conception of a main and two auxiliary armies whose task would be to cover the territories of the allied Princes in Thuringia and Hessen. Thus Prussia's slender forces were quite needlessly extended and in fact largely dissipated in advance. When it became clear that Napoleon was deploying his forces on a long line between the Sieg and the Upper Palatinate, Scharnhorst again proposed a great offensive to effect a quick, bold breaching of this line. Again, thanks largely to the glibness of Massenbach, he failed to carry his point. "I know what we ought to do," he wrote to his daughter on October 7th, 1806. "What we *will* do is known to the Gods alone."

Thus a war accepted under the worst possible conditions was fought in the worst possible way, and what was ultimately to become the Great Prussian General Staff made its début on the stage of history with a fiasco. For this it can hardly be blamed, since it was crippled from the start, its highest officers being simply distributed among the various armies, so that the greater part of their usefulness was completely destroyed. Von Geusau and von Phull were posted to Royal Headquarters, where the Adjutant-General's department was playing the part of a sort of secret general staff on its own. Von Massenbach became Chief of Staff to Duke Hohenlohe, who was commanding one of the two Prussian armies in Thuringia. Scharnhorst was made Chief of Staff to the Duke of Brunswick, who commanded the second of the Prussian armies. There were thus in reality three general staffs, one headquarters, two army commanders, to say nothing of the activities of the Adjutant-General's department, which was a law unto itself.

The one quality that was not lacking in most of the commanders was a sublime self-confidence: "We two aren't half bad," wrote Rüchel to his superior, Blücher, who commanded the third Prussian army, while a Prussian colonel expressed his regret that his men had to drag muskets and sabres around with them. There would, he maintained, be no difficulty in driving the French curs out of the country with cudgels. Only Blücher seemed to be uneasy, for he saw the lack of unity and the confusion of counsel in the Command.

In the battles of Jena and Auerstadt, the Prussians were admittedly outnumbered. Even so, however, the determining element was precisely that faulty sense of timing which is the essence of poor generalship. The Prussians lay in what we have seen to be an over-extended line some distance west of the Elbe, and the strategy of Napoleon, pursued with immense energy, was to work round their left flank and so cut them off from their retreat across that river. As the development of this manoeuvre became apparent to his enemies, it was met by the dashing riposte of Prince Louis, whose heroic death upon the field earned a tribute even from Napoleon himself, but Prince Louis's effort failed, for as he sought to drive into the flank of the superior French forces, the French redeployed to meet the thrust with wholly unexpected speed.

This, however, was not decisive and the real cause of the catastrophe was threefold. First, Hohenlohe, who faced Napoleon's main forces on the great plateau above Jena, did not press home his attack at a time when there was some chance of success. There was some excuse for this since Brunswick, who lay to his rear near Auerstadt with the main Prussian force, had ordered him to keep to the defensive, and this brings us to the second cause, namely that Brunswick himself vacillated too long in making his decision whether to stand or withdraw across the Elbe. The result was that Hohenlohe's defence, which was acting as a screen to the main body behind, was worn down before that same main body had an opportunity to escape.

The third cause of the defeat lay in the tardy arrival of Rüchel, who was to have reinforced Hohenlohe. This delay was due to that over-extension of the Prussian forces which Scharnhorst had so ardently striven to avoid. We may add yet a fourth cause, and that a wholly irrational one. Napoleon, quite unaware of the fact that the great bulk of the Prussian forces were not with Hohenlohe but lay to the rear at Auerstadt, had sent Davout to work round the other Prussian flank, i.e. the right one. Davout thus encountered the superior main Prussian force and won an independent victory on his own, though at the end the twin Prussian disasters merged into one. Scharnhorst himself was wounded, having himself picked up a musket, as the whole Prussian force was beginning to go reeling to defeat, and taken his place in the line.

The melancholy light of an autumn evening saw the Prussian Army in flight. Some looting broke out among soldiers from the South Prussian and new East Prussian provinces, from the territories, that is to say, that had recently been Polish, while here and there officers who were especially hated were subjected to violence. Scharnhorst made his way from the field and at first joined the King's *entourage*. On this evening, however, he was riding a particularly unmanageable horse, with the result that he fell behind and got separated from royal headquarters in the dark. Chance determined that he should fall in with Blücher, who, with the remains of his cavalry, was trying to save the heavy artillery. Blücher, that rough, thoroughly ill-educated man, who was nevertheless endowed with an excellent natural intelligence, was the first Prussian officer to see the value of a scientifically trained and highly qualified Chief of Staff. He was retreating over the Harz mountains towards Mecklenburg—Yorck and his *chasseurs* joined him on the way— and thanks to that retreat, marked as it was by a number of stubborn engagements, considerable French forces were diverted from their main task, which was the occupation of the eastern provinces of Prussia, but the retreat was memorable for yet another reason, for during the course of it Scharnhorst became Blücher's indispensable adviser. The military marriage which was begun on this march was the first example of something that was to recur time and again in the history of the Prussian and German armies. It was the first example of the co-operation between a naturally gifted commander and a scientifically trained Chief of Staff.

Hindenburg and Ludendorff, Mackensen and Seeckt represent the final stages of that line of development.

Lack of ammunition and supplies at length forced Blücher and Scharnhorst to surrender at Rakau near Lubeck. They were almost the only ones who in the hour of defeat contrived to safeguard the honour of Prussian arms.

The rest of the story is as pitiful as it is ignominious. Lieutenant-General von Kleist capitulated in Magdeburg with 24,000 men, while General von Lecocq, himself a sometime reformer, surrendered in Hamlin. The strong fortresses of Küstrin and Stettin capitulated without a shot. Von Hohenlohe, with 12,000 men, the remains of his force, laid down his arms at Prenzlau. It was von Massenbach, who now had completely lost his head, that persuaded him to take that step.

In Berlin, the senior minister, General Count von der Schulenburg, heard the news of the defeat. At a loss for more felicitous expedients, he issued a proclamation which declared that His Majesty had lost a battle and that the citizen's first duty was to remain calm. Amongst others, the news of the double defeat moved Dietrich von Bülow to utterance. This, he said, was the result of locking up the generals and allowing incompetents to command. He was not far wrong, but in Prussia it was still dangerous to be right on such matters, though Bülow came to his inevitable end for his criticisms, not of the Prussian monarchy but of the Czar, whose generalship at Austerlitz had, he averred, not been all that might have been expected. Bülow was imprisoned and was shortly afterwards extradited at the Czar's request. He died on the journey to Siberia as the result of ill-usage by a Cossack.

VI

The old order had revealed itself bankrupt. It had proved incapable of either decision or leadership and had now lost any respect or affection on the part of ordinary citizens that it had ever possessed. Indeed, things had now reached the stage where the ordinary Prussian often derived actual pleasure from the downfall of the overbearing officer caste. In Silesia the established nobility had less fear of a French invasion than of the resentment of their miserable ill-used serfs, for the breakdown of the old dispensation was plain enough to see, and serfs were in many instances refusing their services.

It was in this dark hour of Prussia's history, when the court had fled to Eastern Prussia and French armies were flooding all the monarchy's dominions, that Stein drew up his plan for the setting up of responsible ministerial government on the English model, and many must surely have thought the moment had come for the reconciliation of the absolute monarchy of the Hohenzollerns, which had risen up as a warrior power nourished on the rough barren soil of the eastern plains, with the forces of the age and with those of the German spirit. Yet even now the unhappy vacillating monarch could not summon up the determination to give Stein a free hand in internal affairs. Indeed, when Stein persisted in his demands, he was dismissed.

Externally the situation seemed equally hopeless. The support provided by the Czar was insufficient, the Polish provinces were in full revolt and, despite the winter, which usually brought all operations to a standstill, French troops were preparing to advance on Königsberg.

In the military sphere, chaos was complete. Thanks to the fact that nobody really understood the function or purpose of the Quartermaster-General's staff, that staff had virtually been out of commission. Geusau had been suspended, Massenbach was in French captivity, while Phull had taken service with the Russians. The staff's chief, General von Laurens, was sitting impotently in Königsberg. The only man to whose advice the King was prepared to listen was the Adjutant-General, the old, dull-witted von Köckritz.

There was an exchange of prisoners of war. Scharnhorst returned and was sent to serve with General Lestocq, who commanded the special corps serving in East Prussia with the Russian armies; he was, however, not sent as Chief of Staff but as *Assistent*, though the post of such a military "Assistant" was without precedent or clearly defined duties. For all that, the quality of Scharnhorst's personality made its mark. When Bennigsen attempted to check the French advance at Eylau, Scharnhorst, under the sinister light of a winter sky, marched out with the Prussian Corps from Hussehnen. Leading his troops through a snowstorm, he took the enemy in the flank, a manoeuvre that decided the day. Despite heavy losses, Prussians and Russians maintained their ground, but the Russian commander failed to turn this indecisive battle to his advantage, and the defeat of Friedland in the summer of the following year sealed the fate of the Hohenzollern state. The Czar deserted his Prussian ally, and the King was forced to sign the Peace of Tilsit. The greater part of the Prussian monarchy remained under the occupation of French troops, large territories were lost, and the period of occupation was made dependent on the payment of an indemnity of indetermined amount.

It was the ultimate humiliation, but it was also the turning point, and the beginnings of a new climate in public affairs were marked by a novel and interesting manifestation, namely the appearance of parties, a thing so far unprecedented in Prussian history. In characteristic Prussian fashion, however, these had a military and bureaucratic rather than a political background, the reform party being very largely formed by soldiers. Massenbach, who had returned from captivity, attained, together with a certain *Kriegsrat* Frederick von Cölln, a kind of leadership as a critic of the system, while other supporters of the cause included Scharnhorst, Boyen, Grolman, Clausewitz and, above all, Lieutenant-Colonel von Gneisenau, who had made a name for himself by the successful defence of the fortress of Kolberg.

It was not given to Massenbach to see the triumph of a cause with which he had been largely, even if not always too felicitously identified. He resigned at an early stage from the commission and his military employment was in due course terminated. The fact is that his unstable temperament had been the undoing of him, and even when leading the party of reform he had largely damaged his own cause by slanderous exaggeration. Elsewhere, too, his insufferable dogmatism had made him unequivocally detested. Moreover, his conduct during the late campaign had been distinctly questionable. He passes into the shadows of history, a pathetic figure, to whom posterity may have given less than his deserts, for some slight share in the planning of the great edifice that is here described cannot be denied him.

Meanwhile, though Napoleon had insisted on the dismissal of Hardenberg, the reforming element in the higher bureaucracy was able to force the King into the recall of Stein. This happened in July 1807 and in that same month a committee for military reorganization was formed on which Scharnhorst, Gneisenau, Massenbach, Lieutenant-General von Bronikowsky and the newly-appointed Adjutant-General, Count von Lottum, were called upon to serve.

The object of this body's deliberations was the elimination from the Army of what were considered "unworthy elements", and the creation of a fighting force which was equal to the requirements of modern war. That this object was in course of time largely attained was due to an act of self-purification on the part of the officer corps that was wholly without historical precedent. All the higher officers submitted their conduct during the war to examination. Some 800 were disciplined, some being dismissed the Army or condemned to serve sentences in a fortress.

Scharnhorst now developed his comprehensive programme of reform. It contemplated the abolition of the long-service professional Army, which was to be replaced by a standing Army based on universal service. It also proposed the abolition of the privileges of nobility and of the cadet schools and the elimination of dishonouring punishments. Scharnhorst's Army was no longer to be the servant of the King but first and foremost the servant of the nation, whose power and capacities universal service was to liberate as it turned the subject into the citizen.

In his design for the instrument that was to lead this new national force, Scharnhorst approximated more closely to the picture that ultimately emerged than any rival draughtsman. Scharnhorst's plan here was for the formation of a "General Staff of the Army" with four sections (somewhat confusingly called Divisions). One was for strategy and tactics, one for matters of internal administration, one for reinforcements, and one for artillery and munitions. The Divisional staffs should similarly be composed of four sections. This was to some extent the model according to which the Great General Staff with its different sections, or *Abteilungen*, was formed. Further, the "Royal Mapping Office" which had charge of war maps was to be subordinated to the General Staff. Actually the highest military authority was to be a War Ministry to which both the Quartermaster-General's staff (as we must still call it) and the Adjutant-General's department (the department of the unhappy military cabinet) were to be subordinated.

Needless to say, the King did not take this invasion of his rights in good part, but lack of royal enthusiasm was but one of a number of obstacles which hindered the realization of the new proposals. The insecurity of the country, the precarious state of its finances, the impoverished condition of its agriculture, which was the backbone of Prussia's economy, and, above all, the uncertain future of the Prussian rump state, for that state could at any time be brought to an end by a stroke of Napoleon's pen—all these tended to relegate the programme of reform to the sphere of pious aspiration. In addition, there was the opposition of the old Prussian Junkers, who found an advocate in General von Yorck, but more especially in a nobleman from Brandenburg, Friedrich August Ludwig von der Marwitz auf Friedersdorf. These diehards held to the idea that the Army's prime

function must remain that of furnishing a livelihood for the sons of
the impoverished Prussian nobility, whom the King should continue
to provide in the cadet schools with the opportunity of a military
education. The officer corps was, as before, to remain a closed knightly
corporation, whose exclusiveness was not to be endangered by the
intrusion of a bourgeois-liberal system of education. The battle in the
Army between the *Federbüschen* and the *Federfuchsern* ("Plumes" and
"Quilldrivers") filled the whole nineteenth century.

Since they saw matters from this point of view, the reactionaries
showed particular hostility to Scharnhorst's proposed General Staff.
For these people Scharnhorst's plan reflected a partiality for a particular kind of education and culture which made the Prussian officer
of the old school feel ill at ease. Further, the Pommeranian nobility
protested against the introduction of universal service, which it
designated as "Revolutionary equality-mongering". In the eyes of
the reactionaries, the arming of subjects constituted revolution, and
by and large this point of view was shared by the King. Scharnhorst
and Gneisenau were stamped as "Jacobins".

All this was but part of a larger failure to achieve a general liberal-
izing of Prussia or the creation of a true constitutional monarchy
which might have served as a model for other German states to
follow, nor was it long before much of the reformers' idealism had
been completely dispersed. A few breaches were made. Stein succeeded in securing the abolition of serfdom, but representative
government remained a dream and that bulwark of old Prussian feud-
alism, the landlords' judicial powers and their rights to maintain their
own police, remained untouched. In the military sphere, Scharnhorst
contrived to get approval for the remodelling of the officer corps.
Something of the deep chasm disappeared which before Jena had
existed between the ordinary civilian and the officer. It was said that in
the old days the "Harmonie", a society to which wealthy and cultured
commercial circles in Magdeburg belonged, had a rule reading, "Dogs
and Officers Not Admitted". Now that the sons of commoners could
become officers, and that not only in the despised technical and light
troops, the artillery, engineers, Hussars and Chasseurs, the barrier
of distrust broke down. Since commissioned rank no longer depended
upon birth but upon the abilities of the individual concerned, it
might well have been thought that the old caste feeling would have
given place to a more egalitarian spirit. That this was not the case
was due less to the old officer corps than to the new elements that
began to be absorbed into it. The fact is that to generations of

middle-class Germans a commission in the reserve became a symbol of social elevation, and they prized the social status thus conferred more highly than any equality of political rights or political power. Indeed, in so far as this new bourgeois element introduced new values into the Army, they were not always of the most desirable kind, for the rising bourgeoisie produced its own myth and its own type of self-assertion. Expansionist ideas, such as those of the latter-day Pan Germans, affected the officer corps far less than many foreigners suppose, but in so far as they did so, it was from bourgeois origins that they derived.

The traditionalists were not the only people with whom Scharnhorst had to contend. Reformer as he was, he was also the saviour of the old officer corps. He firmly opposed all plans for the radical democratization of the Army which the example of the French National Guard tended from time to time to inspire. There was a time when he had not been too opposed to the notion of having officers elected by the rank and file. Yet when Hardenberg developed the idea that the troops should elect non-commissioned officers, and these in their turn the subalterns, Scharnhorst saw in it a danger to certain fundamental military values, and persuaded the reorganization commission to reject it. Scharnhorst had passionately defended the idea that the bearing of arms was for every citizen a duty of honour, and it was this conviction that had moved him to bring about the abolition of dishonouring corporal punishments in the Army. Yet he also held that discipline must have a firm moral foundation which, so he thought, a system of elected superiors would not secure.

The essence of Scharnhorst's scheme was, as we have seen, the combination of a standing Army and universal service. The Army, founded on the principle of strict submission to lawful authority, was to be the school of the entire nation, but although Scharnhorst's conception ultimately prevailed, the notion of a less authoritarian organization never wholly disappeared. A militia conceived along less strictly integrated lines, an institution into which a system of elective officers was easier to fit, still remained the idea of all liberal and socialist parties of later years. At the time of the wars of liberation there were several attempts to introduce an elective system in the Prussian *Landwehr*, while the transformation of the standing Army into a "People's Defence Force" later formed an essential point in the German Social Democratic party's Erfurt Programme. During all this time, needless to say, the General Staff threw the whole weight of its influence on the side of a disciplined standing Army.

On the organizational side Scharnhorst's most important measure was the articulation of the peacetime Army into Divisions composed of all arms. Since Prussia's financial position did not permit the up-keep of a numerically large Army, the Divisions were created in skeleton form under the name of Brigades. Every province had one of these Brigades allotted to it, and officers of the General Staff were posted to the Brigade staffs. In this way the foundations of the *Truppengeneralstab* (or Operational General Staff*) were laid. Con-siderations both of foreign and domestic policy moved the King to continue his objection to universal service, and this posed for Scharn-horst the problem of a reserve. He attempted to build up the number of reservists by having a certain percentage of short service volunteers trained in certain regiments. These so-called *Krümper*, who were the forerunners of the *Zeitfreiwillige* of the *Reichswehr* period, formed the foundation of a Territorial Army which, in its turn, acted as a drafting body for the standing Army. The latter was, of course, composed of men who engaged themselves for much longer periods.

We have already alluded to Stein's struggle against the irrespons-ible *imperium in imperio* of the royal cabinet counsellors and the Adjutant-General's department. We have seen how he sought to re-place this by responsible ministerial government on the English model, and had drawn up a plan for three departments which were to function within the framework of such a system. Stein was dismissed by Napoleon's orders, but Scharnhorst was able to continue with his task of transforming the clumsy *Ober-Kriegs-Kollegium* into a Min-istry of War which would have supreme authority in military affairs. It was a matter of some consequence that he should have bestowed on this matter the attention which he did. Napoleon, who had at first omitted to limit Prussia's forces, thinking that the country's bankrupt condition would keep her innocuous, now had his suspicions aroused and insisted on the reduction of the Army to 42,000 men. This meant that the new Ministry was called on to play a decisive part, for it was only among officers of high rank, such as Grolman, Gneisenau, Boyen and Scharnhorst himself, all of whom were now in close de-partmental association, that the cause of radical reform was still kept alive.

The new Ministry was divided into two sections, the General War

---

* The peculiar organization of the German General Staff into a "Great General Staff" and a *Truppengeneralstab* which worked with the actual armies, corps and divisions, has no exact parallel elsewhere. The term Operational General Staff will be used for *Truppengeneralstab* throughout this book.

Department, which exercised a general direction over the Army, and the Department of Military Economy, which dealt with administrative matters. The War Department consisted of three "Divisions". The first Division, under Grolman, had taken over the functions of the old military cabinet and the Adjutant-General's department, and in particular all business connected with officers' records. The second Division formed the General Staff, its direction being put in Boyen's hands. The old Quartermaster-General's staff was abolished. Scharnhorst, however, characteristically accorded this second Division a somewhat special place, for he considered it the intellectual centre of the Army and the school for higher officers. The third Division, that of weapon inspection, was placed under Gneisenau, who was also head of the Engineer Corps. It is an indication of the precarious nature of the reform party's position that Scharnhorst was not made Minister for War, though that might reasonably have been expected and was, no doubt, what Scharnhorst expected himself. That post, however, went to Count Lottum, a confidant of the King. Scharnhorst only obtained the General War Department, a heavy disappointment for him, in so far as the War Minister was *ipso facto* head of the General Staff.

Choosing Captain von Clausewitz as manager of his office, Scharnhorst threw himself into his task. His aim remained unchanged and it must be noted that throughout this time military and political reform were merely two aspects of the same problem and were inseparable from one another. The fusion of Army and nation, the transformation of the subject into the citizen who must not only defend his country but may, as of right, through his elected representatives, decide its fortunes—these were the great ends to be pursued. Gneisenau and Boyen urged the creation of a representative assembly and did so with all the passion of which they were capable, and they did this not from internal political considerations alone, for they saw in such *Reichstände* the moral basis of an uprising against Napoleon's tyranny. It is significant that Grolman himself became an active member of the *Tugendbund*, a secret organization which combined the object of just such a national uprising with the aspiration towards more liberal institutions at home.

Different men had different views as to the pattern of future events. Some thought there should be a *levée en masse* of the kind the French had successfully used against the coalition in 1792. Others looked back on the Vendee's bitter fight against the Revolution. A third party, which was also the most numerous, fixed its eyes on the fight of the Spanish people in 1808 against Napoleon's occupation, the war which the "Junta", the Spanish National Assembly, had waged by means of national levies and volunteers.

While Gneisenau stressed the political line of attack, Scharnhorst devoted himself quietly to the work of education. Three military schools were now to ensure a supply of officers who had been scientifically trained. A military academy for officers was created in Berlin. A Central Office for Military Education took charge of all such institutions. It was again not the "Jacobin" Scharnhorst, but a martinet of the old school, Major-General von Diercke, who was entrusted with the ultimate supervision of this work and was made responsible for military education as a whole. Curiously enough, the top class of the new Military Academy which was founded in 1810 was given the designation of "General Staff", despite the fact that all such matters really pertained to the second Division of the War Department. This merely show how imperfectly this concept had been defined. As against this, it was an indication of what Scharnhorst understood by this same term of General Staff, that he should have kept this top class or "Selecta" under his personal charge.

VII

It was precisely because honest Liberals like Boyen and Gneisenau were keenly conscious of the social and ethical implications of their reforms, and strove so vigorously to realize them, that they came at a very early stage into conflict with the King. The King was a sober minded, unemotional and somewhat unimaginative man who viewed the reformers' ideas regarding a sort of People's War against Napoleon with profound distrust. Like Stein, Boyen and Gneisenau tended to think in German rather than in Prussian terms. The King, however, had only one aim in view—the preservation of his dynasty.

When Austria, having found the terms of the Peace of Pressburg unendurable, again took up arms against Napoleon in 1809, Scharnhorst and Gneisenau believed that the hour for action had come, and when the King very definitely refused to share this view Grolman resigned and went to Austria, and later to Spain, where he fought against Napoleon in the *Tercio Estranjero* or Foreign Legion. Gneisenau similarly resigned, but remained in Prussian service as a secret agent and went to London and St. Petersburg to gather information about the possibilities of resisting Napoleon. The King thought —and the fair-minded critic will hardly blame him—that an attempt by Prussia to give Austria armed support while French forces were still occupying Prussian territory would amount to political and military suicide.

Most certainly the precipitate Prussian patriots were wrong. The time was not yet ripe for what they wanted. Yet though the reformers often came near to losing their patience, the reports that began to circulate of an intended insurrection in which even Scharnhorst was said to be implicated, were groundless. It is true that a certain Major von Schill, commanding a regiment of Brandenburg Hussars, took up arms on his own initiative, a venture that ended pitiably within the walls of Stralsund, but the case was an isolated one. Nor need we attach too much weight to Gneisenau's repeated declaration that if the King persisted in refusing the reformers' demands he would have to be replaced by his younger brother, Prince Wilhelm. Such outbursts singularly failed to issue in any action, and indeed, any thought of a military *coup d'état* was not Utopian but inconceivable. Prussian officers felt themselves bound by their military oath to the sovereign, whatever might be their personal opinion of his acts. Even Schill, who had hoped by his action to force the King to fall in with him, found no imitators, but paid the penalty of his courage by suffering expulsion from the Army. Prussia was not Spain.

One result of the chatter about a Jacobin revolution, however, was that Scharnhorst really did lose a great deal of his influence, a process that was accelerated by the fact that he had become suspect to Napoleon. He was removed from his post as Chief of the General War Department and relegated to the direction of the General Staff in the second Division. Even so, Count Hake, his successor, one of those submissive and dutiful officials that found special favour with the King, received instructions to keep Scharnhorst informed on all important decisions. Actually, Hake thought the whole business of reform was already over and done with.

The following year, 1811, was critical. The Czar had refused to take part in the blockade of the Continent against British goods, and Napoleon decided to bring Russia under his power. The deployment of the Napoleonic armies against the huge Russian domain was at the time the greatest military undertaking known to the history of Europe. Italians, Portuguese, Dutchmen, Germans of all kinds were now united under the French flag in a crusade against the East. Hardenberg had become Chancellor again in 1810 and was now confronted by Napoleon's demand for an alliance and an army corps.

For a time neither was forthcoming. Instead, Scharnhorst went to St. Petersburg to negotiate an alliance with Russia, and Prussia made secret preparations. Now for the first time the King declared that if the international situation permitted it he was prepared to agree to universal service. Meanwhile, however, Austria, now after her defeats at Wagram and Aspern once more Napoleon's ally, had also been asked for an army corps, and, what is more, had undertaken to provide it, and this meant that in the event of resistance, Prussia would simply be delivered up to a vast superiority of force. The King and Hardenberg therefore decided to accede provisionally to the French demands, and so when Scharnhorst returned to Prussia after excellent progress at St. Petersburg, he was confronted with a *fait accompli* and a disavowal of his acts, a development which led Boyen, who, since 1810, had been directing the first Division of the War Department, to protest and resign. Clausewitz and a considerable number of other Prussian officers refused to fight under the French flag and took service with the Russians. Scharnhorst was virtually deprived of all function and was ultimately sent to Silesia as Inspector of Fortresses. Here, incidentally, Blücher was living in unobtrusive exile. Napoleon had had him dismissed from his post as commander in Pommerania on the alleged ground of secret rearmament activity. Colonel von Rauch now became Chief of Staff.

General Yorck, that dour representative of the old Prussian tradition, had been put in charge of the army corps Prussia was supplying to France. After Napoleon's failure in Russia, when in the last days of 1812 his once proud regiments were streaming back in disorder through the icy storms of a Russian winter, Yorck made his historic decision. He entered into a convention with the enemy commander, von Diebitsch (von Diebitsch's adjutant was none other than Clausewitz), whereby he undertook to break off his connection with the French and place his troops at the Czar's disposal. Thus began that close Prusso-Russian co-operation which determined the shape of European politics for three generations and laid down the essential pattern of the *Reichswehr's* policy after the First World War.

Yorck's action opened the way for an uprising of Prussia. Nor was the King any longer obdurate now that Yorck had built the bridge and co-operation with the Russians was assured. He had himself gone to Breslau where the patriots and reformers had their abode, and he was now prepared to yield to their demands. The proclamation of universal service in March and the organization of a *Landwehr* were the measure of Scharnhorst's triumphs.

Meanwhile, the General Staff had been very quietly created. In 1813, the wars of liberation were to put it to the proof. Commanders of Prussian armies in Brandenburg and Silesia now for the first time receive authoritative advice from a Chief of Staff. It is characteristic for this new service that so long as a strong self-reliant personality has the command of an army in hand, staff officers remain in the background. Scharnhorst himself obeyed this unwritten law of anonymity, though since he himself ardently desired the supreme command in the field, he did so with an aching heart. Despite his own feelings on the subject, however, he suggested Blücher as commander in Silesia. Blücher's speech and manner were very much "of the people", and this made him a more popular man than Scharnhorst, and since he was also a commander of considerable natural gifts, it was Blücher that Scharnhorst chose. Scharnhorst himself was content to serve as Chief of Staff, while Gneisenau, who had returned from London, took over the post of so-called "Ia" or first General Staff officer. Beside Blücher's racy and somewhat elemental personality, with its impetuous will to attack, the figure of Scharnhorst, the quiet man of learning, made a strange contrast, for Scharnhorst was in a way the perfect exemplar for all Chiefs of Staff, he was *par excellence* the man who stands in the background, advises, warns and guides.

In close co-operation with Gneisenau, Scharnhorst drew up the plan of operations for the Prusso-Russian armies for the spring of 1813. The deployment plan provided for a main army and two flanking armies. The first of these flanking armies, under the command of the Russian General, Count Peter Witgenstein, was to advance from Pommerania over Berlin towards Magdeburg. The second was to move forward from Silesia over the Lausitz toward Saxony, and was to occupy Dresden. The main army in the centre was to remain about three days' march behind the two flanking armies. Should matters appear to be working towards a decisive engagement, it would then be able to give its support either to the one or to the other, as necessity might dictate. The principle of having separated elements advance concentrically for combined action was also to mark Gneisenau's plan for the autumn campaign. The application of this principle in the circumstances prevailing at that time was particularly daring. Bad roads and inadequate transport made any division of forces a dangerous expedient. It was only the advent of the railway age (by which this danger was considerably diminished) that made possible the full development in Moltke's plans of the principle of "marching separated, fighting united".

The great indecisive battles of the spring campaign in Saxony, in the Lausitz area, at Gross-Görschen and Bautzen, showed that as yet not even the combined power of the Prussian and Russian armies sufficed to defeat the great master of the art of war. Scharnhorst saw that the essential problem was that of getting Austria to take part in the war. Neglecting a foot wound which he had received at Gross-Görschen, he travelled, in May 1813, to Vienna for military negotiations. In Prague, he was stopped by Metternich's orders. Metternich, who strongly favoured the principle of a European balance of power, saw as much danger to the Habsburg monarchy in a strengthening of the powers of Prussia and Russia as in the existence of the Napoleonic Empire. He was thus constantly seeking to develop a policy of armed mediation, and with such a policy Napoleon was at this juncture not unwilling to co-operate. He needed a pause to recover and re-arm. That was why after Bautzen he had asked for an armistice.

Scharnhorst's wound grew worse; blood poisoning set in. He died in Prague on June 28th, lonely and deserted. A shadow of melancholy, possibly an inheritance of the Lower-Saxon temperament, had always overhung his life. It was not his to see the accomplishment of his purpose. He did but point the way. There is also this that is noteworthy about him, namely that his freedom from any kind of prejudice, his true human feeling, his Christian humility and his loathing of those horrors of war (though it was in the midst of war that he died) make him a man of very different kind from many that came after him.

VIII

In August, the armistice with Napoleon came to an end, and Austria took her stand by the side of Prussia, Russia, England and Sweden. A very different man from Scharnhorst now stepped into the post of Chief of the General Staff. August Wilhelm von Gneisenau was no quiet contemplative man of learning. He was, on the contrary, of passionate, one might almost say tempestuous, disposition. As a strategist, however, he had high gifts, his mind was clear and penetrating, and his will unshakable. Frankish and Austrian ancestors had given him the round, firmly-held head, the fleshy cheeks, the energetic mouth and alert-looking eyes. He once wrote that he was Scharnhorst's St. Peter (much as Clausewitz had claimed to be Scharnhorst's John the Baptist) and though he declared that compared with Scharnhorst he felt himself like a pygmy measuring himself with a giant, he was nevertheless a man who knew the value of his own great gifts and one who chafed under a General Staff officer's anonymity.

A new generation of General Staff officers was now changing the face of the Prussian Army. Gneisenau was Chief of the Prussian General Staff and adviser to Blücher; Boyen was Chief of Staff to General von Bülow (brother of the unfortunate Dietrich Heinrich von Bülow) who under the Crown Prince of Sweden commanded the troops of the Northern army. Grolman was Chief of Staff to General von Kleist, who commanded the main army in Bohemia. It was in such men as these that the new generation of Staff officers was finding its embodiment. It was Gneisenau who quite deliberately developed the conception of the joint responsibility of the various Chiefs of Staff for any decisions which the army commanders might take. The object—it was of prime importance—was to ensure the spiritual unity of the General Staff and to enable it to assert its will as a unitary organism against army commanders who were refractory and difficult. In the event of a difference of opinion between a Chief of Staff and an army commander, the former had special avenues open to him. He could communicate any complaints or doubts directly to the Chief of the General Staff himself.

Gneisenau also created the typically Prussian technique of command with its insistence on clarity, perfection of form, and speed and certainty of communication. He further developed the system of general directives which left the subordinate commander scope for individual initiative and independent action. Mental elasticity and flexibility of thought, speedy adaptability to changing circumstances, all these were to be combined with inflexible determination and persistence in pursuing the main objective. All this was really an extension of Frederick the Great's system of Directives into the age of the mass armies of the nation states, for the mass army had, as we have seen, necessitated articulation into the permanent tactical entities of the corps and the division.

The Gneisenau school of thought exercised great influence on the development of the allied Russian Army. Already, under Catherine the Great, the Russian "Main Staff", as the General Staff was called, had attained growing importance. It consisted largely of officers of German origin and German education, and the increasing weight it began to carry was due to the circumstance that a woman could not take the field. In the year 1813, a whole number of Prussian-trained General Staff officers rendered excellent service to the Russian Army. These included such men as Colonel Hofmann, who was Chief of

Staff to the Duke of Württemberg, Colonel von Lützow, who was Chief of Staff to the Cavalry Corps of Count von der Pahlen, and Clausewitz, who acted as liaison officer for the Russian command at Blücher's headquarters.

Gneisenau's strategic thinking, which has strong political implications, may be roughly summarized as follows: ruthless exploitation of the national potential—Gneisenau sought to carry this into effect in his organization of the *Landwehr* during the armistice; search for a decision with the object of annihilating the enemy force, all available means being used to this end; application of the strategy of encirclement to all operational plans. A survey of these conceptions makes it clear that we should think of Gneisenau not only as the man who found the answer to Napoleon's strategy of the mass and of the offensive, but as the spiritual father of the battle of encirclement, an idea which comes out ever more strongly in the General Staff's strategic thought till it results in the Cannae conception of Schlieffen.

Neither Gneisenau nor Boyen nor Grolman nor Rauch, however, were mere one-sided military specialists. That human type had not yet been born. They were highly individual personalities who were closely bound up with the spiritual life of their time. In their eyes war in its new form of a people's war could only be justified if it led to the moral and political freedom of the peoples who waged it. Gneisenau quite deliberately distinguished between the *Kabinettskrieg*, waged by the absolute rulers of the eighteenth century, and the modern war of nation states. It was not for nothing that he numbered Stein among his friends. In his eyes it was essential that the present war should become a war of liberation for all the nations of Europe, and from it the spirit of European progress must proceed. As to the parliamentarizing of the Hohenzollern monarchy, his ideas were much more radical than Stein's (for Stein was still to some extent mentally a prisoner of the old order); he was even more radical than Scharnhorst, who had never had a really burning interest in domestic politics. Indeed, Frederick William III must have found Gneisenau something of a trial.

Gneisenau's history was curious enough. He came from a noble but impoverished family in Upper Austria, which had taken its name from the fortified castle of Gneisenau, near Efferding. Gneisenau's father served as a lieutenant in the Saxon artillery. His mother, the daughter of an artillery officer (a commoner), accompanied her husband during the Seven Years' War and died during the retreat from Torgau immediately after giving birth to her son. Gneisenau's father subsequently engaged in a variety of schemes and professions, including those of surveyor and architect. At length, he entered on a new marriage and passed his declining years as a building inspector in Erfurt. The orphaned boy, who was entirely without means, grew up in abject poverty among some humble folk until some wealthy Würzburg relatives took him under their wing. After serving for a short while in an Austrian regiment of Hussars, he went in 1782 to Canada, as a lieutenant of Chasseurs in an Ansbach contingent. The Peace of Versailles, however, put an end to the American war before he had an opportunity of serving in the field.

Gneisenau now obtained employment in the Prussian service, hoping for a post on the Quartermaster-General's staff. In this last, however, he was disappointed, for he was kept for twenty years in wretched Silesian garrisons as an ordinary company officer, and it was as a company commander that he took the field in 1806. It was only in 1807 that the successful defence of Kolberg against the French laid the foundations for his advance. Some time after this we find him on the military reorganization commission and in the War Department, tilting at the windmills of Prussian reaction. Then came his mission to England from which he returned a firm believer in English liberalism and in the principle of constitutional monarchy, having added the advantages of military experience to the unusual combination, which we have already observed, of high military gifts with political insight.

IX

The general strategic plan of the autumn campaign of 1813 and the winter campaign of 1814 are largely Gneisenau's work. His strategic abilities are clearly apparent in the operations plan for the autumn campaign. The problem which the Allies had to face was this. Napoleon had taken up a position along almost the whole line of the River Elbe with his right wing resting on the fortress of Königstein and the mountains of Northern Bohemia, while his left extended past Torgau, through the fortresses of Magdeburg and Wittenburg to Hamburg itself. In the middle lay the entrenched camp of Dresden. This immense interior line was in the nature of a shield from the cover of which mortal blows might be directed against either Vienna or Berlin, and Napoleon had the best part of half a million men to accomplish this task.

Theoretically, his communications were over-extended, and his marshals sought to persuade him to choose not the Elbe but the line of the Saale or the Rhine, but Napoleon's judgment in this matter was probably good. He said, 400,000 men resting on a system of strongholds, on a river like the Elbe, cannot be turned. This was true. His line was, for those days, at any rate, so immensely long (and strong) that his enemies could not outflank him (even though they could have passed in between his fortresses) without incurring far greater risks from over-extended communications than he was running himself. At least they could not do this while Napoleon was compact and strong.

Napoleon knew well enough how difficult was the problem he was posing for the Allies. These were of necessity extended over a long arc, and it was not unreasonable on his part to suppose that sooner or later he would catch them in a false move and destroy them piecemeal.

The Allies had organized their forces in three armies: a northern army, commanded by the Crown Prince of Sweden, consisting of Prussian and Swedish troops, was based on Brandenburg and Pommerania; the Silesian army, consisting of Prussians and Russians, was under the command of old Blücher; while the main army—Prussians, Russians and Austrians—was in Bohemia and commanded by the Austrian von Schwarzenberg.

As so often happens in the forces of a coalition, there were wide divergencies of view between the different commanders. The Crown Prince of Sweden was inclined for political reasons to hang back, and the Austrian commander was a stickler for the strategic proprieties of the old school. This made it most desirable for Gneisenau to ensure for his own army, the Silesian one, a considerable measure of operational freedom. In this he succeeded, despite marked resistance at headquarters on the part of the allied monarchs, and despite the fact that both the Czar and von Schwarzenberg claimed the right to an overriding control of operations. It was a fortunate move, for it ensured to Gneisenau and Blücher an elasticity which they would not otherwise have enjoyed.

There was only one strategy for the Allies to pursue, and it is a tribute to Gneisenau's genius that his grasp of that strategy is evident in every move he made. Clearly their only hope was to make Napoleon uncover himself at some point so that they could strike home concentrically for the kill, but before this could be done there would necessarily be a period of feint and manoeuvre, a period in which they had to dodge their enemy's blows and at the same time if possible turn and make those blows as costly to him as possible.

This was the strategy pursued by Blücher. When Napoleon struck at him at Löwenberg, Blücher withdrew towards Silesia, and then riposted brilliantly on the Katzbach, where his enemy was extended and far from his base. As August drew on to September, the Allies had in several cases followed these tactics successfully, so much so that on the periphery Napoleon had suffered a number of defeats. At the core, however, he held firm and returned better than he received, and when Schwarzenberg struck at Dresden, Napoleon defeated him by a miracle of speedy concentration.

Then two things happened. A feat of great tactical brilliance at Kulm by a Prussian force commanded by Kleist saved the beaten Schwarzenberg from what might have been an overwhelming defeat, and so blunted Napoleon's strategy. The other was an excellently-timed movement carried out at Gneisenau's suggestion whereby a southern force moved through Napoleon's right flank to Leipzig, while a strong northern force, led by Blücher, crossed the Elbe at Wittenberg. With his own forces now increasingly committed, with time working for his enemy, whom he had failed to destroy and who was now daily gathering strength, Napoleon immediately reacted to the menace which was now inherent in that move. He fell back on Leipzig where the Allies, reinforced now by Bavaria, which had deserted the Emperor (the Saxons were to follow suit in a matter of days), closed in on him in what was very nearly (though not quite) the perfect battle of encirclement.

X

Frederick William wished to limit his demands to the liberation of Germany from French power as far as the Rhine. Metternich again developed his idea of a European balance of power, a conception to which a France of moderate strength was integral. The war threatened to peter out. Gneisenau now came forward (despite passionate opposition from old Blücher) as the advocate of military annihilation of Napoleon, a policy for which the occupation of France was essential. Schwarzenberg, still thinking in terms of strict military orthodoxy, held that France could and should be forced to surrender through the occupation of strategic points such as the plateau of Langres. Gneisenau, however, demanded a march on Paris, and the root and branch abolition of the Napoleonic régime. Gneisenau won his point, thanks to support by the Czar—Stein was acting as the latter's adviser—nor did he allow some quite definite reverses in

France, occasioned by a too hasty advance, to deter him from his purpose. For the first time in that century Prussian troops marched into Paris in March 1814, and Napoleon abdicated. This last was a triumph for Prussian inflexibility. It was also without any doubt an unavoidable necessity. How very much alive in Gneisenau's mind was the notion that this war had been a crusade for European freedom is shown by his idea that Napoleon should be brought before a world court and shot for crimes against law and justice. He further demanded that the peace should be dictated in Paris, a notion that was profoundly at variance with the late tradition in such matters and with the principle of solidarity between crowned heads.

A congress was called in Vienna to consider the reordering of Europe and the re-erection of a German Federal State. Meanwhile, Napoleon was exiled to Elba. From that place, however, he made one more attempt to seize power. That this attempt was defeated within one hundred days is again largely Gneisenau's doing. Gneisenau had once more become Chief of Staff under Blücher—and had complained bitterly because he had been denied the supreme command. On the evening after Ligny, Blücher had disappeared. His horse had been hit, and the old man severely bruised. It was Gneisenau who made the epoch-making decision ordering his horribly mangled Prussians to retreat towards Wavre. This meant that Napoleon had failed—despite the slaughter inflicted. He had failed in his strategic objective of driving a wedge between Blücher and Wellington. A defeated army would have taken the road due east. It was Gneisenau who determined that they were not defeated, that they could maintain their touch with the British according to the original plan. It was by carrying out that plan and making their magnificent counter thrust on to the French flank at Waterloo that Gneisenau enabled Blücher to turn the scale, made victory possible and encompassed Napoleon's ruin.

Again the Prussian Army marched into Paris. Yet the second Peace of Paris brought Gneisenau the heaviest disappointment of his life. His political programme envisaged, as did Stein's, a German Federal State with a strong centralized authority to govern it. That programme had already been rendered futile by the Vienna Congress, which in June 1815 had proclaimed a loose confederation of separate states. In external matters Gneisenau wanted a decisive weakening of France through the cutting-off of Alsace Lorraine (which would be made over to the South German states) and through the creation of a strong Belgium as a buffer state in the north. Both demands arose from the anxiety which the peculiar geographical position of Prussia, with a ring of stronger powers around her, tended to arouse in a soldier's mind. Such views, however, did not correspond with the policies of Austria and Russia, both of which saw in the latent Prusso-French antagonism a means of weakening both those powers.

At home, Gneisenau had hoped that victory would bring recognition of the forces of freedom and of the growing feeling of nationhood, forces which the defeat of 1806 had so unmistakably released. Prussia had received large accessions of territory through the decisions of the Vienna Congress. She had had Westphalia and Posen returned to her, also Eupen and the western part of the kingdom of Saxony. In Gneisenau's eyes this made the proclamation of a proper constitution by which all these territories would be united, absolutely indispensable. The enthusiasm with which youth from every section of society had, at the King's call, rushed to the colours in 1813, had not been nourished by patriotic fervour alone. It was fired by certain political hopes. In particular, young university students cherished the expectation that, as a result of the war, peace would bring them a voice in public affairs and powers of political decision. It was, of course, the educated middle class that tended to look upon the wars of liberation in this way. In Pommerania, East Prussia and Brandenburg, the rural population, who had only just received their freedom, were moved by a habit of traditional solidarity with their superiors, and, when universal service was proclaimed, simply followed the example of their landlords. As against this, in the most indigent parts of Silesia the indescribably poor weavers and other poor working folk had often to be brought to the colours in chains by the police. They simply could not understand what all this fighting was about. The King was not altogether without comprehension of the meaning of these aspirations for freedom, and in May 1815 he solemnly promised the proclamation of a constitution and the creation of a popular assembly.

XI

After the second Peace of Paris, Gneisenau held that the hour had come for these promises to be honoured, but the hour passed and not liberalism but reaction gained ground. After the war, Grolman was made Chief of the General Staff: Gneisenau was considered by the court too liberal—and too obstinate. He was sent as commanding general to the newly-created province of the Rhine, whose seat was at Coblenz. From the neighbouring Nassau Stein would sometimes make a visit and talk over the old wonderful plans of reform. Stein had also fallen out of favour, and people in Berlin would speak, half anxiously and half amused, of Gneisenau's circle of friends as "Wallenstein's camp". Nothing could be more childish than the secret fear behind this attitude. To think of Gneisenau marching on Berlin was ludicrous. What Stein and Gneisenau most probably discussed— for at this time the matter moved Gneisenau very strongly—was a reform of the nobility. He wanted to see the old, impoverished, place-hungry Junkerdom replaced by a nobility of property and achievement on the English model. At that time a somewhat different ideal of nobility was being proposed. Friedrich von der Marwitz, spokesman for old Prussia, was advocating the transformation of the nobility into a warrior caste. All those who were physically unfit, or had scientific or cultural inclinations, were to lose their patent of nobility.

In 1816, the embittered Gneisenau resigned. True, he had, like Yorck, Bülow and Kleist, been made a Count and had been rewarded with the estate of Sommerschenburg. In 1825, on the anniversary of Waterloo, he was raised to Field-Marshal's rank, but no employment could any longer be found for him in the public service. Only in 1831, when the outbreak of the Polish revolution against Russia endangered Prussia's Polish possessions, was Gneisenau again remembered and made Commander in Chief of the army which protected the eastern frontiers. He chose Clausewitz as his Chief of Staff and set up his headquarters in Posen. There, on August 21st, he died of the cholera which was sweeping over Europe from the east. Like Scharnhorst, he died in something like ill repute because he was a liberal at heart, and the Prussia of the era that succeeded the wars of liberation was anti-liberal and hostile to progress. Stein's generation had acted on the old Prussian substance, that strange mixture of warlike efficiency and servility, like a cataclyst. That was why it had been eliminated.

Because of Gneisenau's great military gifts, the Prussian General Staff had survived its first great test. It is well to remember that what safeguarded its infancy and gave it its first vigour was Gneisenau's self-reliance and independence of thought. The General Staff had become a superb instrument of potential leadership, yet even now its constitutional and functional position, and in particular its relation to the War Minister, the Adjutant-General's department and the reviving military cabinet of the King, was controversial and ill-defined. For all that, the General Staff now remained in being within the War Ministry even in peacetime.

It is in the nature of every human institution to strive for expansion and for the extension of its power. The peacetime function of the new instrument of leadership consisted fundamentally in the preparation for the next war. For this it busied itself with the education and scientific training of future higher officers, mapped the entire realm in order to produce serviceable military maps and studied the armies of its neighbours. For this also, irrespective of the international situation prevailing at the time, it prepared plans both for attack and defence for use in any conceivable military eventuality. Such activities are not peculiar to the Prussian General Staff. They became the function of every general staff everywhere in the world. There seemed nothing sinister in this at the time. It was only when a certain tension between the great nation states which the age of the revolution produced that this work of the General Staff appeared to become charged with a peculiar significance and a peculiar danger.

That time, however, had not yet arrived, and though its main function was established, its precise place in the official edifice was not. That naturally was bound up with other constitutional questions dealing with the position of the monarchy and of the relation of the Army, still in theory a purely royal affair, to a constitutional State.

These matters were now to be thrashed out before the Prussian General Staff, a thing born largely out of a political crisis, was to some extent to deny the circumstances of its origin and settle into its stride as that technically efficient and wholly unpolitical instrument which it ultimately became.

CHAPTER III

THE PHILOSOPHER OF WAR

I

AFTER Napoleon's downfall in 1814, the last hope of Prussian reform no longer centred in Stein and Gneisenau but in another personality, a man who was to lead a strange, shadowy sort of existence in the later pages of Prussian history. This was Major-General von Boyen. Boyen was made War Minister at this time. He was the son of a Prussian lieutenant and an enthusiast for Kant, and he was to prove himself the most revolutionary War Minister either Prussia or Germany was ever to have; for Boyen was far more radical than Noske, the only Social Democratic War Minister who has ever held office.

Boyen envisaged a broad scheme of social and political reform, the general spirit of which was to communicate itself to the Army. The anachronisms of the Royal Guards and the Military Cabinet were to be done away with, such things being held to be in contradiction with the rôle which Boyen felt the Army should play as champion and defender of the people. Since industry was expanding and seemed likely to play an increasing part in the life of the nation, Boyen also pressed for measures to protect the industrial worker. He further developed an extensive programme of rural resettlement. All these were relatively pardonable heresies. What was really serious was his view that the War Minister of the new age was not primarily re-sponsible to the King but to the nation.

Then there was the question of universal service. More recent generations have tended to look on universal military service as a symbol of Prussianism in the more invidious sense of that term, but that was not how it impressed contemporaries when it first appeared. Both King and Junkerdom objected strongly to it, for to such minds, as we have seen, it held the threat of a revolution. The great mass of rural serfs, though now made technically free by decree, still lived in a concealed unfreedom, but since duties in social life can never be wholly divorced from rights, universal service was bound sooner or later to imply a voice in the affairs of the State on whose behalf that service was undertaken. Since, therefore, the *Wehrgesetz* or universal service law of September 3rd, 1814, was a thoroughgoing affair, and provided with its *Landwehr* and *Landsturm* nothing less than military organization on a nation-wide scale, it is not surprising that Boyen should have had some difficulty in securing its passage. The *Landwehr*, which was Boyen's especial darling, was a particular stumbling block, for the *Landwehr* was a kind of militia made up of the older age-groups who had served their time. It was held that discipline would be poor in such a body, which was in any case much too exposed to the vagaries of popular sentiment. Also, the officers were largely middle class and often informed by distressingly liberal opinions. It must be admitted that these apprehensions were to prove not wholly groundless. The only units that ignored the mobilization orders during the disturbances of '48 were *Landwehr* units.

If the *Landwehr* was a subject of controversy, so was the problem of integrating the different departments of the War Ministry, the General Staff and the Adjutant-General's department being particularly troublesome; the whole matter was further complicated by the King's continuing habit of regarding the Army as a personal instrument of the royal house. Boyen suffered his first defeat when the King decreed the setting up of a Brigade of Guards (which soon attained the dimensions of an army corps), and claimed the right to appoint an Adjutant-General of his own. Against such dynastic self-assertion, Boyen's struggle was both lone and desultory. Prince Hardenberg, the Chancellor, was a liberal, but had long learned to accommodate his aspirations to circumstance. Also he was old and far too fond of his ease to take on a fight with the court camarilla and the King. Soon War Ministry Department III, which, it will be remembered, had taken over the business of the old Military Cabinet, showed distinct symptoms of becoming a law unto itself and of reviving that same Military Cabinet as a personal staff of the King, while Department II, that of the General Staff, caught the prevailing infection and showed a similar appetite for administrative self-determination.

This whole drift was intensified by the circumstance that it had behind it the tacit approval of the great body of regimental officers, who manifested a dislike as spontaneous as it was vehement against the broader processes of constitutional control. Despite the reforms, it was still the Junkers from whom those officers were chiefly drawn.

Just before the wars of liberation, the proportion of untitled as opposed to titled officers had attained forty per cent, but such untitled officers all too often got eliminated as "poor officer material". Indeed, the more the traditional officer class was threatened by the intrusion of what it considered to be an alien element, the more it drew together into a closed corporation; educational segregation in the cadet schools had in any case made that process instinctive so far as the sons of the older officer families were concerned, and so officer corps and reaction tended increasingly to be interchangeable terms.

Many of the Prussian phenomena found their Russian counterpart, nor is it surprising that a spiritual kinship should have its organizational consequence, for that kinship was very close indeed. Since the alliance of 1813, military plenipotentiaries had been exchanged between the King of Prussia and the Czar, these officials being the visible signs of a military secret diplomacy which often followed paths of its own. Whatever the cause, the parallelisms are noteworthy. Like his Prussian counterpart, the Czar had his private Military Cabinet. His brother and successor, Nicholas I, was in due course to copy the whole plan of Prussian General Staff organization and to found the Nikolai General Staff Academy entirely on the Prussian model. Meanwhile, relations between the two armies were so close that General von Rauch, who was inspector of fortresses and later War Minister in Prussia, combined the inspection of the Russian fortress system with his corresponding activity at home. Again like its opposite number in Prussia, the "Main Staff" in Russia enjoyed for a period a position of privileged independence until the War Minister, Prince Tchernschew, established the overriding authority of the War Ministry. In the following decades no appointment of a Chief of Staff was made in peacetime. Other European countries tended to show a somewhat different line of development. In France, though a General Staff Academy was created by Marshal Gouvion St. Cyr in 1818, the priority of the War Ministry was never called in question.

II

The Adjutant-General's department and the General Staff had rather different objects in view, but both were straining at their administrative shackles. Indeed, the General Staff quite as much as its rival was seeking not merely decisive influence over the Army but over the policy of the King, and the towering personality of Grolman, the head of Department II in Boyen's War Ministry, tended to make

it a most formidable force, for Grolman was a man of very pronounced views. Karl Wilhelm von Grolman, the new Chief of the
General Staff, the son of a high judicial functionary, was made a
major on the General Staff in 1813, and Quartermaster-General in
Blücher's headquarters in Belgium in 1815. He came from the Westphalian nobility, and his tall, strong body and lion-like face made him
a man whom no one could fail to notice. His character was marked
by pride, firmness and a strong sense of independence. He was at one
with Boyen in demanding a reform of head and members. Under his
leadership, the intellectual and scientific eminence of the General
Staff made it a discernibly anti-feudal element in feudal Prussia. His
educational work was fundamentally at variance with the old Prussian
officer's tradition, and indeed the bourgeois ideal of education encountered strong opposition from the officer corps right up to the fall
of the monarchy. Where, the defenders asked angrily, were the largely
impoverished nobility to find the means to give their sons the
necessary education if the officer's calling was to become a science and
the meagre knowledge imparted in the cadet schools was accounted
insufficient? General culture of the mind, technical knowledge and
science, these were the distinguishing marks of the coming bourgeois
industrial age, but the soldier still worshipped other gods.

To Grolman, the task of the General Staff was the provision of
military leaders with a scientific training, men who combined
thorough specialist knowledge with independence of mind and
character. To forestall the emergence of a spirit of caste, he introduced periodic exchanges between service on the General Staff and
regimental duty. This ensured a considerable degree of bodily training and elasticity but also fitted the General Staff more completely
for its rôle as a school of army leadership.

We have spoken, for the sake of convenience, of a "General Staff",
but it was only in 1817 that Department II actually received this
designation, and before that occurred certain organizational changes
had been introduced by which its character and function were more
precisely defined. In 1816, Grolman split Department II into three
"Theatres of War" and a Military History Section, for military history now began to play an important part in the work of the General
Staff and was treated as a medium of professional training, a conception that was always in danger of distorting the purpose of genuine historical study and research. In Grolman's view, however, the final and
supreme function of the General Staff still remained the acquisition
of data concerning the armies of neighbouring states and the close

examination of every possible military situation, together with the preparation of mobilization and deployment plans for every eventuality.

Grolman also attached great importance to the development of the road system. Prussia's disadvantageous geographical position and the absence of any natural frontier made it essential to offset these obstacles by good internal communications and the exploitation, wherever possible, of "internal lines" against an attack coming from several directions at once. All operations and deployment plans were based on that assumption. In such circumstances, good roads were indispensable.

Grolman's work, which was so closely associated with that of Boyen, went forward under an adverse star. When, in 1819, the King opposed a further extension of the *Landwehr*, Boyen resigned and Grolman followed his example. It was the year of the Carlsbad decrees, in which the German states, under pressure from Metternich, undertook measures against the growing spirit of liberalism and put schools, universities and the press under strict censorship.

III

With the retirement of Boyen and Grolman, liberalism abandoned its last hold on the Prussian Army. The Army was in future to remain a relic of the absolutist era. It was to remain a thing which lay beyond the influence of public opinion and was untouched by any spiritual force or inspiration coming from the people themselves. It is significant that in later times the chief object of all liberal striving in Prussia was the control of the Army and its expenditure. Yet a civilian parliamentary War Minister after the English model would in Prussian eyes have been a piece of sacrilege. The King's Army could only be administered by soldiers—that was an article of faith which was obstinately defended right up to the revolution of 1918. As far as their attitude to the Army's place and function was concerned, Boyen and Grolman were the last exponents of the idealism of the wars of liberation. Gradually, educated Prussians split into two groups, one vaguely liberal the other conservative in sentiment. Liberalism in due course came to connote a preponderantly German and anti-Prussian way of looking at things. The fact, however, that the thin stratum of rising bourgeois capitalists tended to hold liberal views caused the economic aspect of liberalism to be somewhat overstressed. The National Liberals of Bismarck's era set more store by an expansionist foreign policy than by the liberal ideas of the fathers of '48.

The "Jacobins" disappeared from the Prussian officer corps. Only a few isolated individuals at the time of the '48 revolution found themselves in sympathy with the great ideas of the time. The young heretical Prussian lieutenants who subscribed to the cause of the malcontents were eliminated as alien elements from the Army. When the revolution failed, they mostly went into exile. A few of them joined the Federal forces and fought in the American Civil War for the freedom of the slaves. The most original and also the most muddleheaded among them, August von Willich, who had exchanged the sword of the Prussian Artillery officer for the carpenter's saw, went to London, where he attached himself to or joined Socialist and Communist circles or groups and developed the idea of a military dictatorship on a socialist basis. This conception of Willich's of a fusion of factory and barracks was one day under other auspices to have a great and disastrous realization.

The Prussian officer corps was something in the nature of a small aristocratic republic, for though officers were technically appointed by the King, selection by the regiment was a precedent condition. A very definite tone and outlook thus tended to prevail, which remained quite unaffected by the influx of officers from the middle strata of society. At the time here under review, the officer corps once more became what it had been under Frederick the Great, a closed caste that lived unto itself. The change in the attitude of civil servants from that of personal servants to an absolute monarch to that of servants of a constitutional state found no parallel in the ranks of Prussian officers. The oath was sworn to the King, never to the constitution or the nation, even in those days when a constitution had actually been granted.

One of the most powerful influences shaping the general outlook of the officer caste was economic. The agrarian crisis which followed the wars of liberation together with encroachments of capitalism on to nearly all forms of economic enterprise led to extensive impoverishment among the landed Junkers, who in any case had never enjoyed great economic strength. If it is to remain the genuine article, a noble class must always have its roots in landed property, which ensures over generations the continuance of a specific tradition. Yet throughout the nineteenth century the Prussian nobility continued literally to lose ground. In Berlin of the early 'forties, the Wilhelmstrasse and the Wilhelmsplatz were still symbols of the dominion of great families like the Arnims, the Voss's, the Blüchers, the Radzi-wills, and the Schlippenbachs, all of whom had their palaces there. A generation later, the bureaucracy of the various ministries had moved in. In 1857, a number of the best-known families still possessed very extensive property. The Kleists had fifty-three estates, the Wedels forty-four, the Winterfelds twenty. In the same year, the Winterfelds had twenty-four officers serving in the Prussian Army.

Most of these estates were, of course, far from being latifundia. In his memoirs, Field-Marshal von der Goltz, who was still able to recollect this period, writes of Fabiansfelde, the East Prussian estate on which he was born, and describes the typical seat of an impover-ished Junker family. He shows us a square farmyard, around which are white-painted office and workshop buildings with thatched roofs. There is a pond, and the chief pride of the family home (also thatched) was the possession of stone fireplaces. Add to this the steward's house and a wretched little garden with a few oaks and wild pear trees, and you have the picture. Von der Goltz's mother could not even keep this poor habitation together, and it had to be sold. There was so little money that she considered having her son trained as a cooper.

It was just this kind of unprofitable little estate that suffered most in the crisis, and this was significant. In the century between 1820 and 1920 the leading personalities in the Prussian Army and General Staff, Moltke, Waldersee, Hindenburg, Goltz and Seeckt, come from just such impoverished, uprooted, landless families of the nobility. The exception, Schlieffen, whose parents still owned property in a relatively big way, proves the rule. This impoverished nobility found a calling in the Army that was not incompatible with that status concerning which it was so sensitive. It also found in the Army a few of the other things that it wanted from life; but though it avoided the wilder forms of ideological extravagance, it was much more narrowly nationalist than, say, the great and very rich families of the Silesian *haute noblesse*, or some of the great South German houses with their tranquil but dying lustre and their many internat:onal connections.

Perhaps the best picture of the point of view and the hard and enforcedly Spartan ideals of the old Prussian officers' families is pro-vided by Hindenburg's youthful recollections. The true wealth of the Prussian officer corps, he proudly wrote, consisted in its wantlessness. Such Spartan habits have been the mark of every warrior caste in history. The education of the sons of the nobility in the cadet schools, and outside the run of ordinary schools, contributed very greatly to this tendency towards a bare and simple style of life. The ideal was not happiness; rather was it obedience, self-denial and service—but this service was service of the ruling house, not of the people.

Thus in the days before the revolution of '48, the Army had become the symbol of reaction. At the Wartburg festival of 1817, the first great revolutionary demonstration of German students, the latter had burned a military pigtail and also a specimen of the detested *Korporalstock*, the non-commissioned officer's stick which was often put to other than ceremonial uses; but these symbolic acts had few permanent consequences and service in the Army suffered greatly under the dull formalism of the parade ground. Indeed, it was concentration on soulless routine which drove fiery spirits like Otto von Corvin to rebellion. However, such examples of revolt were very much the exception.

IV

After the resignation of Grolman, there was a sort of interim period during which the affairs of the General Staff were taken over by Major-General August Rühle von Lilienstern, once a favourite of Scharnhorst's, and in 1814 adviser to Stein in *Landwehr* matters. Then a staunch conservative was appointed. This was Lieutenant-General von Müffling.

Friedrich Karl Freiherr von Müffling had been Blücher's Quartermaster-General in 1813 and had afterwards commanded the Prussian occupation troops which were left behind in France. He was very much a martinet and very much the confidant of the King. Another such confidant was Count Hake, Boyen's successor as War Minister, another enemy of reform. Müffling adapted himself to the reactionary camarilla which set the tone at court, and soon after his appointment on January 11th, 1821, secured a considerable extension of the General Staff's authority. The Chief of the Great General Staff of the Army, as it was now called, was from 1821 onwards no longer subordinated to the War Minister but treated as his adviser. He could not act against the will of the War Minister, but the new regulation, which laid down that he must act in consultation with him, offered possibilities of further emancipation. Gneisenau was conspicuous among the supporters of this measure, which was very much in line with Massenbach's *Immediatvortrag* proposals.

In 1825, Department II was formally disbanded, that being the end of the subordination of the General Staff to a Minister. Small causes often have great results. The occasion for Müffling's step was really a question of rank. Müffling, when Chief of the Great General Staff, was the senior of Rühle von Lilienstern, who had remained on as head of Department II, and Müffling could not permanently take orders from a junior.

Thenceforward the General Staff was linked to the War Ministry as a parallel organization. Its head was not yet the authoritative adviser of the Supreme War Lord, as Massenbach, Scharnhorst and Gneisenau had desired, but only adviser to the War Minister. Moreover, in the long years of peace his advice was not often sought and he remained at bottom nothing more than the director of a planning office. A similar emancipation took place in Department III, which was that of the Adjutant-General, though it would be more accurate simply to say that the Military Cabinet was revived. The latter was recreated in 1824 under the designation of "Department for Personal Affairs", and was placed under the direction of the Adjutant-General, Major-General Job von Witzleben, a clever and industrious man of strong conservative sentiments who was counted among the King's closest friends. Being concerned with all matters relating to personal records, this department soon attained very great power. Witzleben, who became War Minister in 1833, acted as adviser to the sovereign even in such matters as mobilization which were really matters for the General Staff. Thus was created the triangle of forces which influenced the military policy of the Hohenzollern monarchy right up to 1918, the Military Cabinet, the War Ministry and the General Staff.

The personal pressure which could be brought to bear by the Military Cabinet and the General Staff caused the influence of the Ministry as a constitutional organization continually to decline. For a time it seemed as though Witzleben's son-in-law, the all-powerful and very ambitious Adjutant-General, Edwin von Manteuffel, would be the victor in this struggle of the two extra-constitutional Palace powers and secure the dominant influence for the Military Cabinet. After that, in the era of Moltke, thanks to the victories in the Danish, Austrian and Franco-German wars, the palm seemed to pass to the General Staff.

Müffling again reorganized the General Staff, which was now composed of three "Main Divisions". The first of these concerned itself with personnel matters—as such it anticipated the later Central Office—the second dealt with organization, training, manoeuvres, deployment and mobilization plans, while the third handled all technical and artillery matters.

The uniform became particularly handsome. It consisted of a blue frock coat with carmine red collar and facings (which were embroidered with silver), white trousers, silver epaulettes and a "Two-Master" hat with white plumes. The carmine red facings continued even in the age of field grey as the distinguishing mark of the General Staff. According to the records of 1821, the General Staff of the time consisted of eighteen officers stationed in Berlin, of whom two were major-generals, nine were majors, three were captains and four were *premier-leutnants*. Of these officers, thirteen were titled and five were commoners. Working in conjunction with the General Staff was a Trigonometrical Bureau with three officers and a Topographical Bureau with thirty-five officers on its establishment. Of the latter, over half were commoners, a sign that it was the technical services which formed the entry port into the Army for the middle class. Twenty-seven General Staff officers served at the headquarters of the army corps and twenty with the divisional commands, six others being employed abroad as military attachés.

Müffling revived Scharnhorst's practice of General Staff journeys for reconnaissance purposes. Further, by way of novelty, he introduced the practice of the *"Kriegsspiel"*, or war game, in which operational situations were followed through in the sandbox or on a map.

The story is told that on one occasion the Prussian military attaché, Prince Kraft von Hohenlohe, was describing these methods to a group of socially exalted Austrian officers. They listened in incredulous astonishment. Finally, one of them, Prince Thun, asked how they worked out the points in scoring. The Prussian replied that there were no points, since after all, the game was not played for money. Prince Thun: "Then what's the object of playing at all?" In 1866, the cold, exact and deadly thinking of the Prussian General Staff soon disposed of people with that kind of mentality.

In devising the nature of his Staff journeys, Müffling was very much under the influence of the defeat of 1806 and the thought that centrally-located Prussia might again be attacked by a coalition coming, as in the Seven Years' War, from west, south and east. Müffling suffered from the same feeling of encirclement that had caused Frederick the Great to determine on a preventive war with Saxony and by that "Flight in a forward direction" to unleash a war of world-wide dimensions. Müffling's imaginary situations dealt with invasions of Westphalia and the Ruhr by an enemy from the west, a war against an Austro-Saxon alliance (a quite realistic idea in view of the large acquisitions of territory by Prussia in 1815), and defence against an attack from the east in the Posen-West Prussia area. His thinking was strictly limited to wars of defence. The idea of a preventive war was alien to him both on moral and practical grounds.

The chief mark of the Müffling era is concentration on military education, and it was in these years that the connection began between the General Staff and the well-known Berlin publishing house of Ernst Siegfried Mittler & Son. For a hundred and twenty-five years these remained the General Staff's regular publishers, and most military writers had their works published here. These were the years in which Rühle von Lilienstern, as director of military education, and Clausewitz, as director of the *Militärakademie*, earned the right to be called the intellectual fathers of the Prussian officers' corps. Müffling himself sought to promote the establishment of war schools and compiled the first manual for officers of the Army General Staff. He also left behind a very detailed account of the campaign of 1813/15.

V

It was also under Müffling that Clausewitz wrote his classic treatise, *On War,* a work that was to direct the thought of the intellectuals on the General Staff for the next hundred years. The writer had only served on the General Staff in 1808, and then again from 1813 to 1815 and in 1831, but the book entitles him to be classed with the General Staff's most distinguished minds.

Carl von Clausewitz was born on June 1st, 1770. He came from one of those depressed and impoverished families of the petty nobility that are so characteristic of Prussia. Clausewitz's great-grandfather was a Protestant pastor in Leipzig, his grandfather Professor of Theology at Halle. His father, Friedrich Gabriel Clausewitz, was a lieutenant in a Prussian garrison regiment during the Seven Years' War; he was severely wounded and, as a disabled officer, was granted the poorly paid post of an excise collector in Brieg, where he married the daughter of a commoner, a town official from Merseburg.

The son, a slender, pleasant-looking lad, with a Goethe-like brow and a Goethe-like way of wearing his hair, entered a Prussian infantry regiment as a sub-lieutenant at the age of twelve, and later became one of Scharnhorst's favourite pupils. As the latter's collaborator, he was looked upon by the King as a "Jacobin". It was only Boyen who contrived to get him reappointed to the General Staff. During the campaign in Belgium he was Chief of Staff to the Second Army Corps. In 1818 he became director of the *Kriegsakademie* in Berlin, with the rank of major-general. In 1831 Gneisenau called him as Chief of Staff to Posen, where, like his commander, in that stifling late summer he died of the cholera.

"My life is an existence that leaves no traces," wrote Clausewitz after the catastrophe of 1806. This fear was to prove groundless, though this became apparent only after his death. With his curious mixture of devouring ambition and external diffidence, he was unwilling that his works should be published during his lifetime. It was only after his death that his widow allowed the book on war to appear. It was an examination of the five wars in which he had served (the war of 1792-5 against the Revolution, the campaigns of 1806, 1812, 1813/14 and that of 1815) and also of a hundred and thirty earlier campaigns. The purpose of the book was to lay the foundation of a philosophy of war and to evaluate war morally.

Clausewitz had inherited something from the Protestant preachers who had been his forebears. Like them, he was rooted in Christian thought. Fundamentally, however, he was a child of the age of idealism. He was a man of sentiment as well as of intellect, though suffering sometimes from a fanaticism which accorded ill with his Kantian training. Clausewitz's thought took its character from the transitional phase between the disintegrating institution of absolutism and the age of rising nationalism. War, so taught Clausewitz, once the instrument of despots, had been given back to the People. By its refusal to limit means, by its use of an ever-extending area (as in the Russian campaign of 1812), by its exploitation of the factor of numbers and its will to harness the entire power of a people by means of universal service, this essential human act of war was drawing nearer to its true nature and absolute perfection. Strategy and tactics were always determined by the character of the age.

In the era of the balance of power, "Chessboard wars" and "wars of observation" were the means of settling international differences. The new age demanded a new form of war. Now it was not a question of gaining possession of a fortress or a province or a strategic point, as it had been in the days of the dynastic wars. It was not even a question of defeating and putting out of action your enemy's army. Today, whole peoples fought for the right to live. Therefore, argued Clausewitz, the essence of modern leadership in war must be to achieve decision by the speediest and most ruthless means and it must achieve this aim by breaking into the actual structure of the enemy state. This was the Prussian "Revolution in War". Nineteenth-century war was no war of observation, but a war of decision and annihilation. "The more sublime and the stronger are the motives of a war," so wrote Clausewitz in his first volume, "the more it embraces the whole existence of Peoples, the greater the tension that precedes a war, the more will war approximate to its essential abstract power, the more will be its purpose to hurl the enemy to the ground, the more purely warlike, the less political will war appear to become."

On this law of tension depended the nature of the perpetual war preparations in which the General Staff was engaged and also the relative importance of that activity. Thanks to Prussia's (and later Germany's) unfavourable situation, Clausewitz's conception of the war of decision and annihilation influenced all strategic thinkers from Moltke to Schlieffen, and from Schlieffen to Ludendorff and Hitler.

Clausewitz's reasoning differed in one fundamental respect from that of the Ludendorff school of thought. Terror for Clausewitz could never be an end in itself. He was a contemporary of Hegel. There is, it is true, no proof that Hegel's philosophy had influenced him or that he had read his works, but very often the thought of a particular period seems to lie, so to speak, in the air. According to Hegel, the State was God's manifestation of Himself in the world. Its foundation was the power of reason manifesting itself as will. The essential stuff of history was the development of States. Coming as he did out of the world of the Prussian officer corps, Clausewitz too thought of the State as the great super-individuality which revealed itself in the unfolding of history. To the Prussian officer, not the people but the State was the essential reality. Politics was the personified intelligence of States and through their interaction the pattern of Divine thought revealed itself.

From this train of reasoning, Clausewitz arrives, in the first chapter of his first volume, at his famous conclusion: "War is a continuation of policy by other means." The mysterious base element of both was struggle as a creative principle of life, but since war was the continuation of a rational process this implied the demand that man must remain master of war. War and its conduct was not an affair for the military alone. It concerned the policy makers, the statesmen. Clausewitz, moreover, did not glorify the warlike character but the soldierly virtues. The German people in particular, he wrote, was not a warlike but a soldierly people. Only something in the nature of the Osmanli Empire could see the purpose of life only in war.

War, he emphasized, was the statesman's last expedient. How dangerous it was if a false policy hoped, by the use of warlike means, to attain ends that were contrary to nature. True, he demanded that in time of war the military commander should be given a seat in the Cabinet. He should not, however, have unlimited power. His judgment and counsel should merely ensure that statesmen reached the correct decisions. As against this, he held that the principle of moderation distorted the character of war. An essential condition for the war of annihilation was "a state system penetrated by the very highest consistency".

Implicit, however, in the conception of war as an instrument of policy was the idea that such an instrument might one day become superfluous. For a time, Clausewitz looked upon this idea as Utopian, but he recognized its justification. When the path had been prepared for Justice in the life of peoples, then with the help of firmly-founded Nation States, a common order might be created for the community of European peoples. So long as this was not the case, the dream of everlasting peace would remain a sin against the divine ordering of human affairs, and war would continue to be for the peoples the *ultima ratio*.

In these reflections it is noticeable that the only factors that appear to play any kind of part are the State and the Army. Right, freedom and the individual disappear completely into the background, although Clausewitz had originally been among the radical reformers. Yet the idea that the Army constituted the true content of the State had during the years of Prussia's defeat thrust the old ideals into the background. In a desperate situation, so Clausewitz now taught, the existence of the Army had priority over that of the State itself, a typically Prussian thought, in so far as the Army was the unifying factor of the Hohenzollern monarchy. It was also the principle which consciously or unconsciously guided the *Reichswehr* in the years from 1918 to 1933. The chasm between the Army and liberalism which opened up after 1815 turned Clausewitz into a conservative. Parties were for him merely an element of disunity in the State. The most he would admit, as a means of enabling the nation to voice its views, was a purely advisory Council of State, made up of men distinguished in public life. Democracy was to him the equivalent of disaster. His ideal was the "strong State" which guaranteed the soldierly education of its people. The State created the people, an idea that was later to influence the philosophers of Italian Fascism.

His foreign policy programme was in accord with such thinking. France was the great originator of unrest. The unity of Germany which Stein had wished to see brought about by the organic processes of history could, in Clausewitz's eyes, only be realized by the sword. One State would have to bring all the others into subjection. That State could only be Prussia with its strong Army. The time for this had not yet come, but he never doubted its coming. It was because of this that in 1815 he had demanded the aggrandizement of Prussia through the elimination of the Saxon, Thuringian and Hessian principalities. It was Bismarck's policy that was here anticipated.

Clausewitz's doctrine received its confirmation only after his death. It was only the development of science and industry that could actually give space and weapons their unbounded potential. It was still in Clausewitz's lifetime, however, that Alfred Krupp founded his great Prussian gun factory in Essen and transformed the smithy and steel factory which he had inherited from his father into one of the leading arsenals of Europe. In 1846 he developed the first rifled guns with a range far greater than that of the old smooth bores. In the 'sixties there followed breech loaders, with all the advantages they offered of speedier fire. Prussia, Austria, Italy and Russia all equipped their artillery with guns from Krupp. By 1870, Krupp was employing ten thousand workmen.

Other innovations played their part. In 1838 the first railway in Prussia was built between Potsdam and Berlin. While the steam engine was revolutionizing transport, the electric telegraph was having a similar effect on communications and on the technique of command. In 1840 Prussia equipped its fusilier battalions with Dreyse's breech-loading needle-gun, which raised the fire power of infantry to a degree that had been wholly unanticipated. The industrial revolution thus created the new type of Clausewitzian war, the scientific war of masses and machines. Marx, the first great interpreter of the idea that economic factors shaped mass destiny, was a pupil of Hegel. The Prussian view which isolated State and History as the essential realities had its counterpart in the Marxian view which saw in the class war the sole determinant of social form, and in the economic process the sole efficient historical cause. It was no mere chance that Marx, the scion of a Jewish Rabbi who had married a Prussian aristocrat, had Prussia as his place of origin. The growth of the mass in size and power, and the development of applied science, however, had yet another consequence, namely the disappearance of the German humanist ideal. Science created the specialist. In the military field, this meant the triumph of the anonymous General Staff officer, the embodiment of military specialism at its highest potential.

VI

In 1829, Müffling resigned from the General Staff in order to act as Prussia's special envoy, as a mediator, in the Russo-Turkish war. His successor was General Wilhelm von Krauseneck, the son of an untitled judicial official in Bayreuth. Krauseneck had begun his career in the Prussian Army in the ranks, as an *Ingenieurgeograph*. He was later made an officer in a fusilier battalion and raised to the nobility. Under Scharnhorst, he had taken part in drawing up the new Prussian Training Regulations. Later he had been made commanding general of the Sixth Army Corps.

While Krauseneck was Chief of the General Staff, the July revolution of 1830 occurred in France, and also the Polish insurrection. Troops had thus to be mobilized both in the west and in the east. For a time, an armed collision with France seemed imminent—this period saw the birth of the *Wacht am Rhein*. It was this crisis that caused Krauseneck to draw up a plan for protecting Germany's western frontier by a belt of fortresses, a sort of "West Wall".

It was under Krauseneck that the leaders of the great wars of the 'sixties and 'seventies first began to make their appearance on the General Staff. In 1833, Helmuth von Moltke first joined it as a *premier-leutnant*, and in 1836 Captain Albrecht von Roon, the iron War Minister of Bismarck's time. We also begin to encounter such names as Goeben, von Alversleben and Fransecky. Another notable development is the establishment of relations with the Turkish Army. Moltke, at the Sultan's request, went, together with other staff officers, as instructor to that body.

These were the first chords of the great symphony that was to come—and yet the era of Krauseneck was still subject to the paralysing influence of reaction. Even the recall of Boyen by Frederick William III changed very little. Krauseneck, being of bourgeois origin, might still have some liberal and progressive views, but even if he had not been hostile to the thought of his time he was helpless in trying to influence it. In 1848 he heard the news of the revolution in France with pleasure, but when the revolution spread to Berlin, he grew frightened and prayed for a return of the old order.

When the people of Berlin rose in revolt in March of 1848, the Army, after some hard street fighting, contrived to hold its own.

When victory seemed assured, the King vacillated and gave orders for the troops to evacuate the capital. To the officer corps this was a humiliation that for decades it was to remember. To those among the workers and middle classes who were struggling for equality of rights, the Army became a bulwark of reaction. Not a single unit mutinied, all stood by the old order, unshaken. Only the *Landwehr* showed a certain tendency to sympathize with the mood of the masses.

The Army treated the abuse with which it was assailed with contempt and even with pride. "Democrat", wrote Waldersee, who was Chief of Staff at a later time, was among officers simply a term denoting a bad lot. Bismarck, as the spokesman of Junkerdom, coined the phrase that troops are the only answer to democracy. In a typically Prussian regimental history of a famous regiment of Hussars, we read that the regiment had treated with contempt that "miserable clique that harboured the ideas of insurrection", and when a certain Rustow, a lieutenant of engineers, dared to step out of line and publish an essay attacking the Army as a State within a State, he was imprisoned by the War Ministry and subsequently fled to Switzerland, where he became one of the best-known military writers of his day.

The Frankfurt Parliament and the idea of a new German Federation left the Army cold. When the War Minister of that same Parliament, himself a sometime officer of the Prussian General Staff, demanded that the troops of the various German contingents should take the oath to the proposed Federal Constitution and urged the appointment of a Vicar Imperial to act as the Federation's head, the officer corps protested vehemently, for loyalty to the State meant loyalty to the King—and to nothing and nobody else but the King. In 1849, the Prussian Army suppressed the last remnants of the revolution in Saxony and South Germany. From this time dates the revival of the alliance between King, officer corps and Protestant orthodoxy, and the birth of that peculiar atmosphere which we associate with Waldersee.

Such was the background against which Lieutenant-General von Reyher took over the post of Chief of the General Staff. Reyher had been War Minister in the days of the March disturbances in '48, and was a man whose career, one would have thought, might make him more sympathetic to the democratic cause than he actually was. He was the son of a cantor and organist in a small Brandenburg village. In youth he had herded sheep, he had then entered a Prussian infantry regiment as a clerk, and was finally made an officer in a

Uhlan regiment by reason of his outstanding ability. In 1815, he was transferred to the General Staff, and later, as Chief of Staff of the Corps of Guards, had won the confidence of the King's brother, Prince William of Prussia, the heir to the throne—the man who fled to England in March of '48.

Reyher was a simple, straightforward man, but he was an officer, and having been raised to the nobility, had made the Prussian officer's point of view his own. He looked on the revolution with abhorrence, because it endangered order. He had the simple conviction of those Minden-Ravensburg peasants who in 1848 refused to take part in the elections to the National Assembly because, as they said, their good King had governed the country so long that he might as well go on doing it without their help. All Reyher's efforts were directed towards maintaining the special position of the General Staff in circumstances that made this particularly difficult. As War Minister, he had tried to dam up the power of the Military Cabinet, yet in the period of reaction which followed '48, the King tried his hardest, despite Parliament and constitution, to turn the Military Cabinet into a private Chancellery for Army affairs and to maintain his prerogative in all matters military. No less than six War Ministers came to grief between April '48 and December '51, owing to this embittered backstage conflict. Quite suddenly, under Manteuffel the Military Cabinet secured ascendancy, and for a time the idea gained ground to let the Military Cabinet actually absorb the General Staff. Reyher had the greatest difficulty in forestalling this plan.

The revolution of 1848 had, in the main, been a bourgeois revolution, but while the liberalism of the Stein-Gneisenau period had been chiefly concerned with spiritual and political freedom and had confined itself mainly to the educated classes, the revolution of 1848 had about it a touch of class war. The development of industry had brought into being a new powerful bourgeois element which in 1800 had not existed at all. It was avid of economic advancement and eager to claim the fullest equality, not only politically but socially as well. In the Habsburg monarchy, the upper strata of the middle class in the various nationalities now similarly took to an aggressive nationalism under the effects of which the old conceptions of loyalty to the dynasty tended to disappear. This tendency asserted itself also in Russia, the third great reactionary power. Here it was Pan-Slavism that provided the newly-risen higher bourgeoisie with the desired outlet for self-assertion, while the Germano-Baltic strata of potential leaders with their strong dynastic loyalties tended to lose ground. It was the conjunction of economic expansion and aggressive national-ism that finally produced militarism.

Now, in the conduct of war, science was becoming of greater moment than those romantic and colourful factors that had hitherto determined the more popular and pleasing conceptions of armed con-flict, a fact which finds its confirmation in the rising number of middle-class officers on the General Staff, since these predominantly entered through some technical appointment. Chivalric tradition and the clatter of cavalry were charming things in their way, but now of doubtful value as prescriptions for victory. The day had come for the specialist, and the specialist, precisely because he was a narrower man, was often more accessible to exaggerated nationalist ideas than the earlier generation of officers. For these had lived in close association with the great ideas of their time. They had lived in the age of Goethe and German humanism had given them a clear and comprehensive picture of what life was about. Before this dissolving scene there now appeared the figure of Moltke, on whom that humanism still shed the rays of its declining sun.

CHAPTER IV

THE MAN OF SILENCE

HELMUTH VON MOLTKE

I

I T is a curious coincidence that it was von Manteuffel of all people who should have suggested Moltke as Reyher's successor to the post of Chief of the General Staff. We have seen that it was von Manteuffel who had secured for what had originally been the Military Cabinet (and was now known as the Department for Personal Affairs) a dominant influence over its rival, the General Staff, yet it was none other than Moltke, his own nominee, who reversed the position and so decided this hidden conflict against him.

Von Manteuffel was very much a man of Rüchel's stamp, and Clausewitz might well have said of him, as he did say of Rüchel, that he was like an acid concentrate of pure Prussianism. He had had a rough military upbringing, possessed little culture and had that horror of "quill drivers" (what in Thackeray's novels is designated by the term "literary man") that was a mark of the school of Frederick the Great.

Manteuffel was personally inspired by two things, a devouring ambition and certain rather old-fashioned conceptions of chivalry. The mainspring of nearly all his action was his fury at the humiliation of '48 when at the bidding of its Supreme War Lord the Army had had to give way to the Canaille. There was no task that would attract him more, he once pointedly remarked, than the crushing of a revolution. Prussia for Manteuffel was simply the Army, and anything that in Prussia was not the Army incurred on Manteuffel's part not merely a lack of understanding but something like positive hatred. During his years of power, the industrial revolution was changing the face of Prussia, but for the immense potentials and the immense new problems thus brought into being, Manteuffel cared nothing whatever.

Beside the all-powerful Adjutant-General, the fifty-seven-year-old Major-General von Moltke presented the strangest of contrasts. He was at that time quite unknown to the Army. For the past two years he had been adjutant to Prince Frederick of Prussia, who was later to have so brief and tragic a reign as German Emperor. He had, however, never commanded a regiment, let alone a division. Physically, the contrast with Manteuffel was equally striking. Moltke's thin, refined and almost delicate features, high forehead, thin lips and curving nose suggested a lack of robustness, while his quiet, measured and controlled manner had too much of the classical about it to be really Prussian. It has been said that a man's taste in music and tobacco are good indications of his character, and for what that somewhat jejune observation is worth, Moltke loved Mozart, and was fond of smoking a good cigar in solitude. He was exceptionally well read and was definitely an officer of that learned type of which the final representatives were Seeckt and Beck.

Helmuth Karl von Moltke was born on October 26th, 1800, in Parchim in Mecklenburg. The family belonged to the old nobility, but their properties, which were in Mecklenburg, were in decay. Moltke's father, a curiously restless and unstable person, managed to run through an estate he had inherited, and became first a Prussian and then a Danish officer. His mother, however, the daughter of an old Lübeck family, was a much more significant personality. It was undoubtedly from that quarter that Moltke inherited his delicacy of feeling and his poise.

Moltke was educated in the Royal Cadet Corps in Copenhagen, and then became a lieutenant in a Danish infantry regiment. His youth was darkened by poverty, hopelessness and all the shadows that the decay of an ancient family is liable to cast, and the wounds which the brutality of that Danish cadet corps had inflicted on his sensitive spirit only healed slowly. On top of all else, his health was bad.

In 1821, after a visit to Berlin, Moltke exchanged the Danish uniform for the dark-blue frock-coat of a Prussian officer; the Prussian Army offered greater opportunities, though his brothers remained for the most part in the Danish service. Thus it was that Moltke became a lieutenant in the *Leibgrenadier* Regiment and began his ascent of the professional ladder in the placid provincialism of Frankfurt on the Oder.

Unfortunately, during these first years as a lieutenant the poverty of his family caused Moltke to be wellnigh penniless, and in order to earn a little money the young officer tried his luck as an author. His work was for the most part published anonymously. One piece of fiction seems to have come into being at this time, while the Polish revolution of 1830 produced a study of the internal conditions o

Poland. He did not, however, disdain the more remunerative obscurity of a translator, and when an enterprising publisher commissioned him to translate Gibbon's *Decline and Fall of the Roman Empire* (all twelve volumes of it) into German, he was ready enough to accept the offer.

Unquestionably Moltke had an artistic vein and also an unmistakable intellectuality, and it speaks much for the way the officer corps kept itself shut off from things that, despite the receptiveness of his mind, he was completely untouched by the political ideas of his time. Yet so it was. He was a soldier and a servant of the State. That State, the Prussia of pre-'48, appeared to him to be in process of steady and fruitful evolutionary development, the Stein-Hardenberg reforms having done all that was necessary to set that process in motion; the process would complete its work in its own good time. Prussia, he was still with commendable ingenuousness to write in the 'forties, was in the forefront of reform and a pioneer of "reasoned liberty".

After spending a number of years in the Topographical Bureau, where his undoubted talent for drawing proved useful, he was in 1833 transferred to the General Staff with the rank of *premier-leutnant*. In 1835 he was sent for study purposes to Turkey, where Sultan Mahmud II was anxiously seeking to apply the specific of Westernization to a State already in the more interesting stages of decay. It was a very great experience for Moltke, and one that was to have a determining effect on his whole future.

The journey was undertaken at a distinctly critical juncture in Turkish affairs. Greece, after a fierce struggle, had won her freedom, the Viceroy of Egypt had made himself a virtually independent ruler, while defeat by the Russian armies was now coming to be regarded less as a catastrophe than as a habit. The days when the Janissaries and the semi-feudal Siphai cavalry had been a terror to their enemies were over. The Sultan was now concerned to replace them by an army trained on Western lines, and since Frederick the Great, Prussian officers had been accounted the best in the world. These were the considerations which led Mahmud to approach the King of Prussia with a request for military instructors, and so to begin that connection between Prussia and Turkey that was to be of such importance in later times.

Moltke's original instructions had been to send his chief, von Krauseneck, a report about conditions and organization in the Turkish Army, but now, together with a number of other Prussian

officers, he formally entered Turkish service. In 1839, he accompanied, in the capacity of adviser, the Turkish commander, Hafiz
Pasha, to Syria on an expedition against insurgent Kurdish tribes, but
there was more serious business on hand, namely the ejection of the
Egyptian Army, under Ibrahim, from Syria. In this Moltke was less
fortunate, for since the Turkish commander preferred the advice of
his astrologers to that of his military experts, a characteristic he
shared with a more recent and less amiable autocrat, the decisive
battle at Nisib was most regrettably won by the Egyptians. Even so,
this Prusso-Turkish military marriage was not wholly barren, for it
did produce a literary progeny—Moltke's Turkish letters of travel,
which, thanks to their sensitive descriptions of land and people,
and their quiet humour, have a high place in German epistolary
literature.

In 1842 Moltke married. The bride was the stepdaughter of his
sister, who had married an Englishman, a landowner named John
Burt. The marriage, which, though there were no children, was
serenely happy, was followed after three years by his appointment in
Rome as adjutant to Prince Henry of Prussia. It was a curious employment, for that strange offspring of the Hohenzollerns had for
twenty years virtually cut himself off from the world, but it provided
occasion for the *Wanderings in Rome*, a continuation of the Turkish
letters and, like the latter, a literary achievement by no means devoid
of merit.

However, there was about this time another side to Moltke's
literary activity. It is one that chiefly interests us not so much for any
great originality of thought displayed but because it is a reflection of
the problem which cast its shadow over modern Germany from before its inception and has remained with it till our own day. It is the
problem of a people that has developed a vigorous culture and shown
considerable aptitude in the material arts, but nevertheless finds itself
so placed that it is almost wholly lacking in natural defences.

It was Germany's and perhaps the world's misfortune that she
should have become conscious of this problem at a time when
nationalism was still in its aggressive stage, when considerations of
prestige weighed slightly more than they do today, when wars were
just a little less terrible than they are now and in consequence tended
to be accepted with rather less protest as part of the normal business
of mankind. The result has been a preoccupation with the problem
of security which has always weighed somewhat heavily on the German mind.

Moltke's concern with these matters, though by no means morbid, is naturally marked. Like many others, he could never forget the fact that Prussia was surrounded by powerful neighbours who might view her rise with mixed feelings or even, as in the case of Austria (who had never forgotten Frederick the Great), with resentment. This is the basic idea in the article published in 1841, in Cotta's *Deutsche Vierteljahresschrift* on the problem of Germany's western frontier. In this from purely military considerations Moltke championed a union of all German races, and took the line that even in peacetime Prussia must look upon herself as an army encamped facing a mighty enemy; and this brings us to Moltke's quarrel with the revolution of 1848.

Moltke was at that time a Staff officer on the Rhine—and the revolution was for him first and foremost a danger to Prussia's preparedness; but it also clashed with his belief as a conservative aristocrat that progress could only take place within the framework of law. For better or worse Moltke's political *credo* was order. The democratic illusion was spreading like a "moral cholera" through Europe, he once wrote, and a letter to his wife pleads for "some kind of authority, *any* kind of authority, anything is better than being governed by lawyers, literary men and officers kicked out of their jobs".

There was, however, yet another ground for his hostility. Moltke, as we have seen, believed in the unification of Germany, but he also believed, let us freely admit it, that this unification of Germany could only be achieved by the sword, for, needless to say, Moltke had read his Clausewitz. For other modes of achieving the German nationalist ideal, he had neither sympathy nor confidence, and the lucubrations of the Frankfurt Diet filled him with the most unutterable contempt. The moralist must make what he pleases of these shortcomings, if shortcomings they be. The historian is bound to record them.

II

In October 1848 reaction won its victory. Windischgräts and Jelacic captured Vienna. In Prussia, Count Brandenburg's ministry took the "strong measures" Moltke had so ardently desired. On November 10th, Field-Marshal Wrangel entered Berlin with 15,000 troops, disarmed the *Bürgerwehr* and sent the Prussian National Assembly about its business.

True, there were concessions. The King proclaimed a constitution providing for a hereditary monarchy, a two-chamber system of government and a national Diet elected on a graded franchise which gave the propertied and educated classes a preponderance of votes, an arrangement which, with a deplorable disregard of the proprieties of history and the nuances of sociological fashion, persisted right through the Weimar Republic. But though, for the next decade and a half, the fear of some kind of fresh revolutionary impulse dominated not only Moltke's mind but that of all Prussian officers, the essential victory had been won. The insurrections in Southern Germany on behalf of a free German Empire were finally quelled by Prussian troops in 1849, and in 1850 Moltke wrote to his brother that the curtain had come down on Prussia's worst enemy, democracy.

For all that, it began to appear that reaction, yes, even Prussian reaction, was not immune from blemishes. Moltke took especial comfort in the thought that the Prussian police state had remained fundamentally unshaken by the revolution. Yet events had already shown how little that police state was able to hold its own against other powers, when, in 1849, Prussia so singularly failed to assert the leadership of Germany against Austria. What concerned Moltke even more intimately was that the ensuing mobilization of 1850 had been little better than a fiasco. Fortunately the time when that could be crucial was not yet at hand.

After some years of responsible routine work at General Staff Headquarters, Moltke received the appointment already referred to, as adjutant to Prince Frederick. In that capacity he learned something of the great world of Europe, visiting Windsor and Balmoral—Frederick was shortly to become Queen Victoria's son-in-law—and also becoming acquainted with the Tuileries, the Kremlin and the Winter Palace. The Empress Eugenie, with that implication of profundity which sometimes marks royal perceptions of the obvious, remarked that he was a gentleman of few words, but anything rather than a dreamer. Her observation that he seemed like a man under continuous inner tension argues a slightly higher degree of perspicacity.

Such was the man who, in 1857, was provisionally appointed Chief of the General Staff, and on September 18th, 1858, was formally confirmed in that office. Nor did the moment at which he took it over seem auspicious, for unlike the Department for Personal Affairs, whose director, von Manteuffel, was quite deliberately aiming at the control of the entire Army, the influence and prestige of the post of

Chief of the General Staff had under Krauseneck and Reyher been steadily declining. The special position it attained under Müffling was merely the result of the latter's very positive personality.

Actually appearances were deceptive, nor could a man of Moltke's qualities have taken over at a more promising time, for the technical revolution had reached the stage where the whole business of soldiering was bound to be affected. So far the military significance of that revolution had only been imperfectly grasped. The rearmament of all infantry units with the breech-loading needle-gun had been proceeding since 1848, but the inertia of military conservatism was to delay the introduction of breech-loaders into the artillery till 1861.

What chiefly distinguishes Moltke in this connection is his exploitation of the new factor of railways, which militarily and so also politically had a profound effect on the whole future of Prussia. Moltke was not slow to grasp both the tactical and strategic implications of this new element which may be roughly summarized as follows.

Insufficient roads and poor facilities for Intelligence had caused Napoleon to rely on the expedient of packing great masses of men together for a concentrated punch. The use of a more scattered deployment for the attaining of a common tactical objective would, in such circumstances, be a matter of great difficulty and could only be employed in a very limited way. Circumstances had now changed, however; new means of transport and communication, together with the vast increase of effectives, led Moltke to develop a new form of scattered deployment at the decisive point.

This method implied a great widening of the area of operations. It also had other consequences. Jomini, the military writer of Napoleon's time, favoured movement along internal lines, indeed, held this to be the only correct procedure. Moltke is the author of the method of deployment on external lines.

However, this method in its turn made demands of its own, for it necessitates high mental qualities and a greatly enhanced capacity for independent decision on the part of subordinate commanders. Napoleon's marshals were the instruments of a despot who demanded blind obedience and had neither use nor respect for individuality or for peculiar capacities possessed by any particular people. Wherever, as in Spain, they acted alone, Napoleon's subordinates failed. Moltke's subordinates were trained to think and act on their own. Some writers have seen a profound moral and philosophical implication in this fact, and have connected this "moral freedom of the individual" with the less luminous reaches of German metaphysics. We need not follow them here, but this tradition of the subordinate's responsibility became a very real factor in the Prussian Army, particularly in the General Staff. Prince Karl of Prussia once pregnantly summed up this Prussian conception of obedience to an over-servile Staff officer. The King, he said, had put him on the Staff, because he had expected him to know when to disobey.

It was in the light of this general idea that Moltke now developed the method of General Directives into a guiding principle. "The advantage," he wrote later, "which a commander thinks he can attain through continued personal intervention is largely illusory. By engaging in it he assumes a task which really belongs to others, whose effectiveness he thus destroys. He also multiplies his own tasks to a point where he can no longer fulfil the whole of them." Moltke did not fall into this error. Because he had confidence in himself, he had confidence in others, and because his own strong sense of responsibility communicated itself to his subordinates, there thus came into being under him a generation of General Staff officers distinguished by a very high standard of morals and great simplicity of life. These men held a common body of military doctrine, and represented a military community of a very unusual kind; it was moreover one which had great influence on the Army, since nearly all the higher commanders passed through the school of the General Staff. The defects of this school did not lie in the military sphere, in which its quality was outstanding, but in its undoubted tendency to wall itself off from the intellectual and political developments of the time, a characteristic which tended to bedevil the German General Staff and the officer corps right to the end.

Another important result of the advent of railways was that it contributed at least something towards making Prussia's disadvantageous strategic position slightly less acute, and this too was grasped by Moltke, for, thanks to railways, Prussia could now for the first time rapidly throw troops from one side of the kingdom to the other. It was this fact that caused Moltke to declare that the development of the railway system was more important than frontier fortification. This new element of potential mobility also led Moltke to introduce field telegraph units, and to equip the infantry with portable camping equipment.

Certain organizational changes were made under Moltke. The old divisions of the Great General Staff were replaced by three departments which recalled the "Theatres of War" of an earlier day and now formed the basic framework of the whole institution. The first of these departments concerned itself with Sweden, Russia, Turkey and Austria, the second, subsequently known as the "German Department", with Germany, Denmark, Italy and Switzerland, while the third, which later tended to be designated quite simply as the "French Department", dealt with France, England, Holland, Belgium, Spain and the United States.

As a result of Moltke's systematic utilization of railways for purposes of mobilization and for moving troops up the line, a railway department was created. Since Moltke was convinced that in any future war a rapid deployment by rail was an essential condition of operational success, military time-tables were worked out, this work being done in co-operation with the Ministry of Commerce, which at that time was responsible for the railway system. The first great rail-transport exercises were held in 1862 and were planned to take place in the Hamburg-Lübeck area with a special view to a possible conflict with Denmark.

III

All these plans touched the general question of Army reform, as did certain proposals for a considerable strengthening of the field artillery (on which Moltke also had pronounced views), and Army reform had since 1858 become an exceedingly live subject. Indeed, the conflict it aroused between the Diet, the Army, and the King threw a shadow over Moltke's first year of office. The introduction of a three-year service period, the regrouping of the Army into thirty-nine infantry and ten cavalry divisions, the increase of reserves and the various other reforms meant that the Army would now absorb twenty-five per cent of the total State revenues. So large an expenditure was bound to be opposed by the somewhat leftist and so-called progressive majority of the Diet, for the Progressives continued to see in the Army an instrument of the old régime, and so to look upon it as a reactionary force, hostile to Parliament in sentiment.

There was some excuse for such an attitude. The control of the Diet over the Army was limited. Indeed, it had little more than the doubtful honour of voting it funds. The War Minister was not a member of the Diet but a general who considered his prime responsibility to lie to the King. Bodies like the Military Cabinet were wholly withdrawn from Parliamentary influence.

Thus the quarrel about Army estimates became Prussia's leading constitutional issue, and here the three-class franchise proved a two-edged sword. As already explained, it secured a preponderance of votes to the propertied classes, but it was just the propertied classes that were beginning to have very definite ideas of their own importance and were fighting for an effective voice in affairs.

Moltke kept his General Staff out of this conflict, but the General Staff could no more remain wholly untouched by it than could the Department for Personal Affairs, which the Progressives attacked with quite peculiar vigour. Indeed, Moltke himself had very definite views. Popular representation was in harmony with the spirit of the times, but it must never be allowed to touch the very foundation of the State, which was the Army.

Now, there were unfortunately many who shared Moltke's ideas without possessing his coolness of temper, and in the officer corps something of the old fury revived which had been engendered by the humiliation of March '48. Moreover, since nothing would have suited many people better than to have matters settled with a little blood-shed, the prospect of a popular uprising became the occasion not so much of apprehension as of hope. Thus when in 1861 the Prince Regent ascended the throne as King William I, the atmosphere was somewhat charged.

At first that monarch showed signs of an honest desire to co-operate with the Diet, so long as the royal power over the Army was left intact, while Prince Karl von Hohenzollern-Sigmaringen's ministry contained a number of men like Moltke's friend, von Patow, the Finance Minister, who were not averse to a compromise. There were also other signs of an accommodating spirit in high quarters. Princess Frederick, in a manner admirably suited to a daughter of the Prince Consort, had in the previous year composed a paper on the parliamentarizing of Prussia, and her husband was quite definitely a progressive at heart. All this, however, was something of a false dawn, and in the matter of the Army William not only refused to yield but was quite ready to pay the price of his intransigeance. In darker moments he visualized the possibility of deposition, and even the more distressing fate of England's Charles I, but even these did not deter him. The Army was the backbone of the monarchy. Compromise was thus unthinkable.

Three years previously an event had occurred which was to have some slight influence on the future, in so far as it precipitated into politics the somewhat formidable personality of General von Roon.

Von Roon, who was at that time commanding the 14th Infantry Division at Düsseldorf, was a great mountain of a man, whose dark blue eyes, bushy brows and aggressively upturned moustache suggested the stereotype of the Prussian sergeant. Indeed, "the King's sergeant" was what he liked to call himself. Others, however, had a different terminology, and in a considerate desire to distinguish him from other members of his family spoke of him as "Ruffian Roon".

Now, in 1858 Roon had handed in a paper on what he more or less untranslatably called "a Fatherlandish Constitution". This interesting document provided for a three-year service period, an increase in the strength of the Army and a fusion of the younger year groups of the *Landwehr* with the first-line troops.

The paths of political ascent were in those days more smooth than those of a later generation, and this document, which had attracted William's attention while he was still Prince Regent, brought about Roon's elevation to the post of War Minister in 1859. Now, Roon's views were nothing if not decided. The Army, he held, was the aristocrat's professional school, and its natural head was the King. Roon's main concern was to preserve the constitutional theory of Frederick the Great inviolate against the seductions of the "Mock Monarchy of England", and to maintain the integrity of the monarch's position as supreme war lord in the midst of what he was pleased to call "confusions of constitutional thought". It is not altogether surprising that where Waldeck, the leader of the Progressives, was concerned, there was a marked divergence of views.

Apart from William's accession, the year 1861 had been marked by a number of interesting events. In July, a student of mixed Russian and Germanic origin made an unsuccessful attempt at regicide, the ruler of Prussia being the intended victim and the locale Baden Baden. Manteuffel challenged a member of the Diet, named Twesten, to a duel; the misguided man had compared Manteuffel to the all-powerful Austrian adjutant, General Count Grunne, who was held to be largely responsible for Austria's recent disasters. Twesten had also put the somewhat unkind question whether it was really necessary to have a Prussian Solferino before removing a disastrous individual from an equally disastrous post. Amid these varying happenings, two elements remained constant. The Diet continued to refuse passage to the Army estimates, and Roon continued as Minister of War.

Yet beneath this relatively placid surface there was a stirring of larger happenings, for both Manteuffel and Roon believed that their opponents in the Diet might one day send out a call to the streets. Roon quite honestly hoped for this, and spoke with characteristic delicacy of the "cleansing mud bath" that an attempted revolution would bring about. Manteuffel went one better and decided that the hour had come to take military measures to forestall this not wholly unwelcome eventuality, and what was really a plan for a military *coup d'état* against the Diet was the result.

The idea of reacting to any distasteful political development with a *coup d'état* from above was subsequently to occur time and again in the Prussian officer corps, it being always understood that the thing was legal so long as the sovereign raised no objections. On this occasion General Hiller von Gaertringen received orders to work out details of a march on Berlin, only troops from the reliable military areas being used. Incidentally, it is noteworthy that the General Staff was short-circuited when the plans for this march were drawn up, a thing that even as little as ten years later would have been quite impossible.

The plan in question provided for the occupation of Berlin by a force of some thirty-five thousand men with a hundred guns. This force was to occupy a fortified position around the castle in the centre of the city until such time as troops from other parts of the country could reach it, and telegraphic communication was established between the castle and the barracks. In the event of possible resistance by the masses, the occupation was to be preceded by a bombardment. The generals commanding in Stettin, Breslau and Königsberg received sealed orders containing this plan, with instructions to break the seals on receipt of a telegraphic code-word.

Manteuffel and Roon picked old Field-Marshal Wrangel to lead the enterprise, and the whole plan was made known to the King, who himself signed the secret orders before they were despatched under seal. When thereafter the King lost his nerve and again started to talk of abdication, there was a dramatic scene with Wrangel. The old Field-Marshal declared that there could be no question of abdication. The secret orders threatened any officer with a court-martial who came to any kind of terms with the people. The King could, it is true, not be court-martialled, but even the King was subject to the judgment of God.

For the moment, however, His Majesty was given no occasion to fear that awful tribunal, the situation which the excellent Wrangel had envisaged being much more hypothetical than he supposed. The plan to get rid of the Diet by the forcible impositions of a ministry of generals assumed that the Diet would really call the masses on to the streets. Unfortunately, this was exactly what the Diet failed to do. Lasalle, who in the spring of 1862 made the first attempts to form a social-democratic Labour party, advised the Progressive leaders to resort to passive resistance and to refuse any kind of co-operation with the State, but even that was too extravagant a demand. The Progressives, guessing, no doubt, that the Army was only waiting for the moment when they would let themselves be pushed into an actual breach of the law, most inconsiderately determined to cling to legality. The battle thus resolved itself into the constitutional proprieties of a parliamentary motion when on March 6th, 1862, Adolf Hagen demanded the itemization of all heads of expenditure and in this demand, of course, the Army estimates were included.

The Diet was dissolved and the liberal ministers dismissed, but the new elections again returned a Progressive majority, and Moltke went to watch Diet sessions from the gallery in order, as he wrote, to have a look at the men whom the people thought could run things better than His Majesty. On September 25th, the Diet resolved to disallow all expenditure relating to Army reform. Yet once again the King was moved to thoughts of abdication, while Manteuffel and Roon again toyed with the idea of a *coup d'état*. At this moment, however, a much more subtle mind appeared as saviour of the situation in the person of a middle-aged man who was at that time Prussian Ambassador to France. His name was Otto von Bismarck.

Bismarck had diagnosed the Progressives' weakness with exquisite discernment. Secure in that knowledge, he affirmed that he would secure passage of the Army reforms without Parliament but also without resort to force. He honoured that promise by roundly declaring that circumstances compelled him to sanction the estimates, dispensing, if necessary, with the tedious formality of constitutional approval.

It was on September 30th that he delivered that famous speech in which he declared that the burning questions of the day were not settled, as men had thought in '48 and '49, by speeches and parliamentary resolutions, but by blood and iron. It was among the least felicitous of his remarks, and he was afterwards at some pains to explain what he meant—probably because he so largely meant what he said.

The sealed orders remained in force till 1864 and were not with-drawn till the end of the Danish war. But the tide had turned. The great triumvirate of Bismarck, Moltke and Roon was now at least potentially in being.

IV

Moltke, till 1862, had experienced all the discomforts of sitting in a power vacuum, and it is natural enough that the new Army laws should have brought him a sense of relief. Even had Prussia been before that date the victim of aggression, as well she might have been, Moltke would have had to submit to all the inconveniences and the irritation of letting the strategic initiative pass to his enemy. The routine plans of 1857-8 for the event of hostilities with France show that very clearly. They provide for little more than the taking of a defensive position on the Rhine.

When in 1859 the Franco-Austrian war in Italy produced the very real possibility of a conflict with France, Von Bonin, the War Min-ister, one of the first to recognize Moltke's importance, asked him for his views, and incidentally gave orders that the Chief of Staff was in future to report to him direct and not through the channels of the General War Department. Moltke was for fighting at Austria's side on this occasion because that was where German interests seemed to lie. In the end Prussia actually mobilized and there were staff talks with Saxony and Hanover, but one may doubt whether Moltke accepted the risk with any enthusiasm.

The crisis led Moltke to re-examine his deployment plans in the west, and the results of these reflections are particularly interesting, for he now begins to assume that Holland and Belgium would take part in any future war with France, either on one side or the other. Should that occur, it was, for a time at least, Moltke's plan to thrust through Belgium towards the Seine basin and strike at Paris. This was the first anticipation of the plan which was to be developed by Schlieffen with such momentous effects on human history, though Moltke himself did not intend to put it into execution unless Belgium joined in the war of her own independent volition.

One thing seems clear however. It is that Moltke was perpetually haunted by the eternal German dilemma and that the prospect of war with a France that would both seek and find allies, oppressed him like a nightmare. Moltke foresaw that France would not passively accept the sudden appearance in Central Europe of a Germanic power centre. Moreover, the Italian war had sharpened the peril. The extension of French power into the "Romance area" might well whet France's appetite for possessions on the Rhine. What would happen if France could strike a bargain with another power? After all, Napoleon did have something of an aptitude for making capital out of third party grievances.

The more Moltke thought of these things, the more gloomy he became. In a memorandum written at the turn of the year 1859/60, he falls into an idiom which was soon to become distressingly familiar. He paints the picture of a possible union of the Romance and Slavic peoples, i.e. France and Russia, against Germanic Central Europe; though he did not believe the time for such a "Battle of the Titans" was yet at hand. In 1862, his confidence in Prussian power has definitely increased, and when in that same year Prussia intervenes in Hesse-Cassel to restore law and order, and is threatened with an Austro-Bavarian/French coalition, he is for drastic action, and even for preventive action in the style of Frederick the Great. Happily the sagacity of Bismarck was for a time at least to remove the occasion for such desperate measures.

It was in the main fortunate that Moltke was a disciple of Clausewitz. Military men are rarely militarists, but they sometimes tend to underestimate the difficulty of adapting military means to secure political ends. Clausewitz makes it clear, or at least it is implicit in his doctrine that the choice of ends, and also to some extent the choice of the limits within which any set of means is to be employed, lies outside the soldier's sphere, and in this Moltke followed his master, for in the main he submitted himself to Bismarck's direction, though his personal relations with him were cool. It was Germany's tragedy that this twin star constellation of the great soldier and the great statesman was to remain unique and was never to be repeated in her history.

V

In 1864, the old problem of the Schleswig-Holstein Duchies flared into open war, Denmark, Prussia, Austria and the German Federation all being involved. The position of the General Staff on this occasion proved not unlike that of the Quartermaster-General's staff in 1806. Nobody knew exactly what use to make of it. Old Wrangel, who was given the supreme command, declared that a General Staff was wholly unnecessary and that it was a shame and a disgrace for a

Royal Prussian Field-Marshal to have a lot of "damned clerking" put on to him.

From this status of an impotent, not to say incomprehensible, nuisance, the General Staff was now to be gradually emancipated. At the outbreak of hostilities Moltke's function was still limited to making suggestions through the War Minister, while directives for the conduct of the campaign went from the King, again via the War Ministry, direct to the Supreme Command. Moltke was not even given the official reports on the progress of the campaign, but was confined during the early stages of the war to private reports sent to him by General von Blumenthal, who was Prince Karl Friedrich's Chief of Staff. It was only when operations were well advanced that he was even able to visit General Headquarters.

Moltke's promotion to a position of greater responsibility has for the story-teller that charm of the fortuitous which is the essence of all good nursery tales. It is true that after the Danes had withdrawn to their fortified position on the Düppel, and the question of an attack on it began to be discussed, Roon had asked the King to draw Moltke into active consultation. Even so, when the King himself took the field, Moltke remained in Berlin. His ultimate advancement was due less to the sober recognition of his merits than to the fact that Wrangel's Chief of Staff, General Vogel von Falckenstein, a difficult man of quite peculiar obstinacy, had to be removed. This necessitated the appointment of a successor, and Moltke was provisionally given the post.

The storming of the Düppel fortifications was the first of the great Prussian victories, and when the mediation of England and Sweden resulted in an armistice, and Wrangel was replaced as Commander in Chief by Prince Friedrich Karl, the latter asked for Moltke to remain. On the resumption of hostilities, Prussian troops entered the island of Alsen and occupied the whole of Jutland. Peace followed in the autumn.

These successes first brought Moltke's personality to the notice of the general public. They also attracted the attention of the King. Moltke had patiently awaited the hour in which his work would be confirmed by success, and now thought it time to retire on grounds of age, but the King had recognized his importance, as also had Roon. Roon now took an important step. He secured the dismissal of Manteuffel and had him replaced as director of the Department for Personal Affairs by Major-General von Tresckow, a quiet, objective man, who in many important respects had a certain spiritual kinship with Moltke. This appointment had a far-reaching consequence, since it was Tresckow who persuaded the King to let Moltke attend all discussions of the Ministerial Council whenever General Staff matters were on the agenda. It was a beginning of momentous things, but not by any means the end of the story.

Habsburg and Hohenzollern had acted as allies in the matter of the duchies, and the question which of the two was to have the hegemony of Germany would no longer wait for an answer. Sound legitimist that he was, Moltke heartily disliked the idea of war against Austria, and there were others who shared his uneasiness. The Catholics of Silesia and the Rhine were loud in their objection, while even an enthusiast would have been sobered by the unrelieved pessimism of Moltke's royal master, who already saw Austrians before Berlin.

Yet there could be no question of the direction of Bismarck's policy, and in the winter of 1865-6 Moltke reviewed the situation with a strictly military eye. He foresaw that France and Russia would be neutral, while Saxony and the South German states were Austria's natural allies. He was not sure of the attitude of Kurhessen and Hanover, but had no doubt that a community of interests made Italy a potential Prussian ally. Moltke believed that the Austrians would take the offensive and strike at Berlin through Saxony, and proposed to counter this by a concentric march into Bohemia from Saxony and Silesia.

Now, despite Tresckow's good offices, Moltke's position as the King's adviser and as intermediary between the King and the War Minister was still very insecure, the more so since in military matters the King liked to draw the second Adjutant-General, von Alvensleben, into consultation. It was thus not easy for Moltke to carry his point. Yet in spite of these difficulties and the protests of conservative theorists like Alvensleben and Colonel Döring of the General Staff, he planned for the concentric convergence of four separated Army groups upon the main Austrian force in Bohemia. In this he was favoured by the fact that Prussia had the better railway and mobilization system. Prussia had no less than five railway lines at her disposal, while Austria had only one.

Moltke now drew the bow of that deployment over a distance of nearly 300 kilometres—from Saxony to Lower Silesia—the intention being that the armies closing in on this great curve should not unite till they were in the actual presence of the enemy, one might almost say on the actual battlefield itself. Six-sevenths of all Prussian forces were to be used in this operation, no regard being had to the fate of those provinces like the Rhineland and Silesia that were left without protection. In Central Germany, a weak army under General Vogel von Falckenstein was to mask Hanover, should the latter decide to join the belligerents. At a later stage this army was to move in the direction of the Main against contingents from South German states that had espoused the Austrian cause.

Moltke's strategy was undoubtedly sound. Either, however, the principles of strategy (which are essentially simple) were less generally understood than they seem to be today, or the personalities who had necessarily to be consulted were almost reprehensibly cautious. Whatever the explanation, Moltke, having successfully overcome his Dörings and his Alvenslebens, came up against a more august and formidable obstacle in the person of the Crown Prince. The latter insisted, and insisted successfully, on some forces being left to protect Silesia, despite Moltke's vigorous protest that Silesia would be protected—and saved—in Bohemia.

The attacking armies were now reduced to three. It is, however, refreshing to record that when Bismarck (of all people), with the help of Roon but otherwise on his own authority, decreed that the 8th Army Corps should remain in Coblenz to protect the Rhine Province, Moltke secured the King's aid in getting the decision reversed.

The King also now formally outlined Moltke's position and powers. On June 2nd, 1866, a Cabinet order was issued by which, subject to his keeping the War Minister informed, the Chief of the General Staff was declared competent to issue orders on his own authority. Hitherto the latter had merely been concerned with the drafting of operational plans, not with their execution. The Cabinet order marked the first step on the road to the emancipation of the Great General Staff.

VI

Royal blood unfortunately carries no guarantee of exceptional tactical endowment, and the fact that two of the three Prussian armies were led by royal princes should, by the working of the law of averages, have militated against rather than in favour of the enterprise's success. It did not do so, however, at least not to any decisive extent, nor does Moltke seem to have had any apprehensions on the matter, having too much confidence in the perfection of his planning and in himself.

He would have been even more sanguine, however, had he realized how admirably his enemies were co-operating to ensure his victory.

It was part of Moltke's plan that the rôle of the Italian Army should be limited to what was virtually a holding action south of the Alps, a more ambitious scheme which involved their attacking Vienna having, perhaps prudently, been abandoned. In view of the limited part the Italians were to play, it was unfortunate for the Austrians that they should have wasted their best soldier on them. Yet that was what they did. The Imperial House did not wish to expose itself to the danger of having one of its members defeated by a mere Prussian, and so the Archduke Albert, by far the ablest of the Austrian generals, was relegated to the Italian command.

Here the worst that could happen to him would be that he would be prevented from doing anything in particular, while the best he could hope for was an indecisive victory, which in point of fact he gained. As against this, the Emperor gave the command over the Bohemian forces to the Commanding General of the Ordnance Department, von Benedek, though the latter, who had a thorough knowledge of the Italian terrain and knew absolutely nothing of Bohemia, implored to be employed where he could be of some use. Francis Joseph brushed such considerations aside. It was, he said, a question of the honour of his house. After the war, Benedek, having duly lost his battle, had to listen in respectful acquiescence when his Emperor complained of military law's knowing no punishment for deficiency in the higher intellectual gifts. The way of an Austrian general was hard indeed.

Prussia mobilized on May 12th. Despite a few blunders by subordinate commanders and a display of misplaced originality by Vogel von Falckenstein, the deployment went on the whole according to plan. The Prussian columns broke into Bohemia from three sides. The white-coated Austrian infantry, still equipped with muzzle-loaders, attacked with the bayonet. It was quite like old times. In the preliminary engagements at Soor, Skalitz, Münchengrätz, Trautenau and Schweinschädel, except at one point the murderous fire of the needle gun carried the day. On July 3rd the three Prussian armies united on the battlefield, exactly as planned by Moltke, and fought what was at that time the greatest battle of encirclement in history.

Yet while the guns were thundering at Königgrätz, Moltke was still a man unknown to most of the generals. "This seems all ship-shape and proper," a divisional commander remarked on receiving orders from the Chief of Staff, "but who on earth is this General von

Moltke?" Yet Königgrätz was Moltke's battle—and Moltke's triumph. Rainsoaked roads delayed the arrival of the Crown Prince's force, and during the morning things had seemed critical as Moltke sat his horse, together with the King and Bismarck, on the Rokosberg near the village of Sadowa. One of the corps commanders fighting near Bistritz called again and again for help; but Moltke would not allow supports to be thrown in prematurely and at the wrong place. He sat waiting patiently for his plan to work itself out. Bismarck offered him his cigar case. Moltke quietly picked the best of the cigars and, while lighting it with slow deliberation, remarked to the King, "Your Majesty is not merely winning the battle today. You are winning the campaign."

And so indeed he was. The Crown Prince's thrust at the Austrian centre settled the matter precisely as Moltke had foretold. Vienna lay open to the Prussian troops. Reactions in Europe were somewhat varied, and in Rome, the Cardinal Secretary of State cried out that the world was going under.

Meanwhile, at the castle of Nikolsburg, not far from the scene of the action, a conflict was in progress almost as significant as Königgrätz itself. In that conflict were the first signs that the General Staff's very devotion to its task carried its own dangers. No man would have been more horrified than Moltke if anybody had regarded war otherwise than as a finite means to a finite end—he was too good a pupil of Clausewitz to do otherwise—but the very one-sidedness of the soldier's training had tended to narrow his vision and to blind him to the limits within which the instrument of war must be applied.

At Nikolsburg the General Staff declared for a ruthless exploitation of their military success, many officers dreaming of a march into Vienna. The King sided with his generals and was for annexing Saxony (which had fought on the side of Austria), Austrian Silesia and the Sudeten territory. Bismarck was more far-sighted and more moderate. In his eyes a settlement with France was bound to come sooner or later, for France would never acquiesce in a Prussian hegemony in German affairs.

It was a bitter fight. The generals savagely reproached Bismarck and accused him of carelessly revealing military secrets to his wife who in an equally light-hearted manner was stated to have passed them on to foreign diplomats in her drawing-room. Yet Bismarck won his victory against both King and generals. The Peace of Nikolsburg which he made with Austria was a rational peace without annexations.

Prussia left the Habsburgs their living space, and in return secured indemnity against counteraction for the annexation of Hanover, Hesse-Cassel, Frankfurt and Nassau. The Northern and Central German states joined a North German Confederation under Prussian leadership.

Yet, despite his calculated moderation towards Austria, there was never any question of the driving motive in Bismarck's mind. Stein had once dreamed of a union of Germans which went hand in hand with the internal reform of all states, with Prussia providing the model for the rest. Bismarck now subordinated the will for unity to the Prussian will for power. It was significant that the North German Federation was denied a Federal War Minister, though a concession to democracy was made by granting it a Federal Assembly based on universal suffrage. In the Federal Assembly the Prussian War Minister acted as spokesman not only for the Prussian Army but, *faute de mieux*, for the contingents of other members of the Federation who were bound to the Prussian Army by military conventions, a constitutional anomaly for which a parallel would be difficult to find.

As to Moltke himself, victory brought him tangible honours. The Kings of Prussia had never been miserly in rewarding military success with gifts of money and land. Moltke received a handsome gift of money which enabled him to buy the estate of Kreisau. Also he entered the Federal Assembly as member for Memel-Heydekrug—another sign of the changing times.

Moltke was now a personality. Königgrätz had made his name known throughout Europe, and even the General Staffs of South German states like Baden and Württemberg put out feelers to Prussia. The Prussian General Staff had suddenly become a new potential in international politics.

VII

Prussia had made history without French permission, and France was not likely to forgive the impertinence, nor was she likely to acquiesce in the birth of a new Central European power centre. Bismarck had no illusions on the matter and knew that the issue had inevitably to be settled by the force of arms, but he was too cool a calculator to seek such a settlement otherwise than at his own convenience.

France sought an approach to Austria and Archduke Albert travelled to Paris for discussions with the French generals and the

French Minister of War. A plan was talked of according to which the French armies were to press forward along the line of the Main and unite with the Austrians for a decisive battle on the historic plain of Leipzig. It might have been a profitable arrangement, for France at that time already possessed the first magazine rifle and the *mitrailleuse*, the first quick-firing gun. Its only defect was that it never progressed beyond the discussion stage.

Moltke had wanted to march as early as 1867, when Napoleon put forward his claim to Luxemburg, but Bismarck was waiting for a chance to put France in the wrong, and with an ineptitude that has few parallels in diplomatic history, France fell into the trap. When the Hohenzollerns put up a candidate for the vacant throne of Spain, she reacted with a gusto appropriate to the best melodrama but scarcely calculated, where so subtle and so undaunted a practitioner as Bismarck was involved, to achieve the larger ends of policy. Though Napoleon, already sick unto death, had on the whole little appetite for battle, and though Bismarck's royal master rather flunked his lines, a slight but ingenious abridgement in re-editing the historic Ems despatch put the last-named matter to rights, and Bismarck had his war.

In the night of July 16th, Prussia mobilized for the third time within a decade. Moltke declared that he had never had less to do, and indeed he had made his preparations well. The General Staff had now full power of command and was working with the precision of clockwork. It moved into the field in three mobile groups. Apart from the Chief, his two adjutants and three lieutenant-colonels who had charge of the three groups, it consisted of only nine General Staff officers, three majors, six captains and one *premier-leutnant*, a very small number when the General Staff's newly-won importance and its responsibility are taken into account.

In making his plans, Moltke had relied on two things, the backwardness of the French railway system and the general rustiness of the French Army. The kernel of the latter consisted of long-service professional soldiers. These had, it is true, been equipped with the quick-firing weapons; yet despite such an asset, the French Army suffered from the fact that its leaders had neither great intellectual qualities nor flexibility of mind. Even so, it might be possible for the Prussians to be placed at a disadvantage. The French plan was, broadly speaking, to take the offensive with two armies in the general direction of the Black Forest in order to sever the northern and southern states from one another. The most unfavourable eventuality that Moltke had to reckon with was that in carrying out this plan the French might have crossed the Rhine by July 25th, for in such a case they would have cut through the Prussian deployment. On the other hand, if the French held up their offensive till August 1st, Moltke thought it possible to seek a decision on the left bank of the Rhine. If they went so far as to delay till August 4th, it was his intention to seek a decision on French soil.

Moltke's original conception was to have three armies which would set out from a fairly constricted area between Mainz, Speyer and Trier. These armies would move around the enemy on either flank and force him to a battle of annihilation on the Saar. Despite the fact that the French took all the time over their deployment that Moltke could have wished, this plan had to be modified owing to the fact that General von Steinmetz, one of the army commanders, hurried forward too fast and so upset Moltke's calculations. Moltke now gave the order for the Prussian armies to wheel right from the line Wittich—Landau and cross the Moselle with the object of detaching the French armies from Paris and pressing them against the frontier of neutral Belgium. This plan, too, only half succeeded owing to the mistakes of certain army commanders like Steinmetz, the downright failure of others such as Prince Friedrich Karl, the untimely interference of the King and his Minister of War. The battles of August at Metz, Colombey, Nouilly, Vionville and Mars-la-Tour, Gravelotte and St. Privat led to certain partial successes which had not been anticipated. One of the French armies under Marshal Bazaine was shut up in Metz (where it capitulated after a long siege) while the other, which was accompanied by the Emperor, was encircled at Sedan and forced to surrender. This last was the Prussian General Staff's greatest triumph, and what is more it was recognized as such, and Moltke and his collaborators became known in the Army as the demigods. Two men, both unknown at the time, who were to be leaders of the German Army on another occasion, were witnesses of the drama of Sedan. One of these was August Mackensen, at that time a sergeant in the 2nd *Leibhusaren*, the other was a young officer then serving as Battalion adjutant in the 3rd Regiment of Foot Guards. His name was Paul von Hindenburg.

Yet as success crowned his arms, Moltke encountered two forces both of which set limits to the field within which his principles could be applied. The first of these forces was—again—Bismarck. As on a previous occasion, Bismarck acted as the exponent of limited war, a conception which, however much it formed a part of his formal doctrine, Moltke's training prevented him from making fully his own. There is a record of a conversation with the Crown Prince in which this shortcoming is vividly illuminated. The Crown Prince had asked what would happen after Paris had been taken. Moltke replied: "Then we shall push forward into the South of France in order finally to break the enemy's power."

The Crown Prince: But what will happen when our own strength is exhausted—when we can no longer win battles?

Moltke: We must always win battles. We must throw France completely to the ground.

The Crown Prince: And what then?

Moltke: Then we can dictate the kind of peace we want.

The Crown Prince: And if we ourselves bleed to death in the process?

Moltke: We shall not bleed to death, and if we do, we shall have got peace in return.

The Crown Prince then asked whether Moltke was informed about the current political situation, which might perhaps make such a course seem unwise. Moltke replied: "No, I have only to concern myself with military matters." Fortunately the course of events relieved Moltke of the necessity of having to translate his intentions into fact.

It is unfortunate that the real differences in the outlook of Bismarck and Moltke, though very apparent when it came to discussing terms of peace, were obscured by their respective attitudes regarding the bombardment of Paris. As the war dragged on, Bismarck, who feared Austrian or British intervention, wanted at all costs to bring it to an end. For that, the capture of Paris was essential, and it seemed impossible to effect this save by merciless bombardment. Moltke objected that he was short of heavy guns and munitions, and that this deficiency would first have to be made good from Germany. Bismarck followed a practice of which he was guilty on a number of other occasions, and professed to see personal motives where only technical considerations were at work. The fact is that the Crown Princess, Queen Victoria's daughter, had voiced strong moral objections to the bombardment, and it so happened that Moltke had married an English wife.

Bismarck now accused Moltke of being under English influence. Moltke defended himself, insisting that his reasons were purely military, but matters went so far that he decided to compel the King to choose between himself and Bismarck. He set down his grounds for this step in a memorandum, yet it was characteristic both of the man and of the tradition he left behind, that this memorandum was never delivered: it was merely filed. It was as though Moltke had simply wanted to purge his soul of resentment by committing his thoughts to paper.

When it came to discussing peace terms, each of the two men once more stood fully revealed. Moltke's proposals reflected the feelings of the all-out victor. He pressed for the union of the old Imperial territories of Alsace-Lorraine with the new German Empire, the creation of a strategic glacis in the west, comprising Western Lorraine, parts of Burgundy and such important points as Nancy, Lunéville, Briey, Belfort and Montbéliard, all of which were later to form part of France's eastern defensive system. He wished to make victory secure, and was already determined that in another Franco-German war France should from the beginning be at a disadvantage. Bismarck asked for the return of Alsace-Lorraine, and seems even to have done this reluctantly and on political rather than military grounds. It was to be the common possession which would give unity to the Empire. Of a strategic glacis he would hear nothing whatever. All that Moltke could obtain was the fortress of Metz.

The second of the new forces which Moltke encountered was personified in Léon Gambetta. This young Jewish lawyer had sat on the extreme left in the French Chamber, and it was in him that Moltke first encountered modern mass democracy. In the Government of National Defence which took office after Sedan, he combined the functions of War and Finance Minister and of Minister of Internal Affairs; with a fanaticism that must for Moltke have been a wholly novel experience, he stamped new armies out of the ground in Northern and Western France, and deliberately unleashed a people's war against the Prussian invaders.

The siege of Paris, accompanied as it was by the activities of the Garde Mobile and the Francs Tireurs, shattered Moltke's conceptions of war. Moltke had always conceived of war as essentially a conflict between regular armies. This in itself was bad enough, he wrote to his brother Adolf at this time, but now war was taking on an ever more hate-inspired character. "It is all wrong to lead whole peoples against each other. That is not progress, but a return to barbarism." The fact is that Moltke was experiencing the first faint indications of what war is like when it escapes from the control of the statesman's guiding hand. The seventy-year-old man, who said that his favourite reading was the Bible, and who with St. Paul held charity to be the highest of the virtues, was already looking into the Gorgon visage of a wholly new kind of war. And yet for that kind of war, though he did not know it, he had himself prepared the way. A generation later, a man like Ludendorff was to see the only true form of war precisely in a war of this character, and to declare that the campaign of 1870, with its battles of the classical type, was no true war at all.

VIII

The new German Empire was a strange compound containing elements of a constitutional State and survivals from the era of monarchical absolutism. It had a Reichstag, or Imperial Diet, based on universal suffrage, and an Imperial Chancellor, but the latter had nothing in the nature of an Imperial Cabinet to work along with him, merely a handful of subordinated Secretaries of State. It is noteworthy that among the latter there was no Secretary of State for War, who might to some extent have substituted for a genuine Imperial War Minister—the absence of any such functionary has already been noted—but Bismarck wished, as we have seen, to leave the final responsibility in such matters to the Prussian Army. As a result, the Prussian General Staff was the highest military planning authority; the Bavarian General Staff still continued to live on, but became a mere shadow and an authority of second rank. The other states of the Empire frequently sent their officers to serve with the Prussian General Staff. A plan to create a Federal Command Office did not go further than the discussion stage, since the position of the King of Prussia and German Emperor as Supreme War Lord would thereby have been called in question. By and large, the constitution of the Empire was tailored to fit Bismark's personal policy.

The German Empire now possessed the best Army in the world, and a General Staff that was a model to all the rest. Also, for the conduct of its foreign policy it could turn to one of the greatest statesmen of the time. Yet all was not well. One had to be grateful for Bismarck, wrote the Crown Princess to her mother, Queen Victoria, at this time, but figs could not be gathered from thistles, and so one could not expect to obtain from him that for which Germany hungered and thirsted, namely peace between the different classes of society and between the different races, religions and parties, friendly relations with one's neighbours, freedom and respect for the Right.

The Princess may have been a biased witness, yet her words cannot be dismissed as meaningless.

Princess Frederick's father, the Prince Consort, had once dreamed of a German Empire that was truly free, and perhaps a larger dose of constitutional freedom would have helped. The generation that had witnessed the great years of social conflict was not yet dead. It still found inspiration in the liberal attitudes of the handsome Crown Prince, and its hopes seemed to be further strengthened by the vast economic upswing that followed the war. Yet the new stream of money brought new problems of its own. Germany as a nation had arrived late on the European scene, and so was handicapped in the African and Asian power race. The result was a haunting fear that she might be left behind everywhere, and a consequent curious *malaise*, which tended to express itself in a somewhat crude self-assertion. The arrogant, snarling, half-slovenly tone of the typical German officer, which Nietzsche so detested, was the sign of a new, false, overbearing pride in German material efficiency. It was in line with the crude display of wealth by the new captains of business and industry. The palace of the railway king Strousberg in Berlin now outshone the old town mansions of the landed nobility. Moltke's world was slowly dying.

In 1874 Heinrich von Treitschke obtained the chair for History at the University of Berlin. Treitschke was the son of a Saxon general of Czech extraction. He had begun his career as a liberal, but had later become the typical exponent of the new "National Liberalism" which set its national above its liberal sentiments, and finally forgot the latter altogether. He preached the evangel of a "Greater Prussia", and was the pioneer of that school of noisy militarist *littérateurs* which caused the name of Prussia to be a symbol to so many Europeans not so much of brutality as of intellectual shoddiness and bad manners. Only tired, uninspired and devitalized ages, declared Treitschke in his *Politics*, dreamed of everlasting peace; war was "the terrible medicine of the human race" from which it ultimately derived great benefits.

In this spiritual atmosphere the General Staff acquired an almost mystical power over men's minds. It was already surrounded, thanks to the victories of 1866 and 1870, by the nimbus of invincibility, and the extreme reserve which it practised in regard to all current questions increased the awe in which it was held. Thus there grew up the legend that here was a dark force, something more than human, weaving the threads of national destiny according to a terrible pattern of its own.

Meanwhile, the General Staff concerned itself with the more pedestrian tasks of its actual, as distinguished from its fictional, business. It was at this time that there came into being opposite the Reichstag the red brick building that was from now on to serve as the General Staff's headquarters. Its personnel was being continually increased. In 1857 Moltke had found sixty-four General Staff officers at his disposal. In 1871 there were a hundred and thirty-five. When he resigned in 1888, the number had risen to two hundred and thirty-nine, of which one hundred and ninety-seven belonged to the Prussian Army, twenty-five to the Bavarian General Staff, ten to that of Saxony, and seven to that of Württemberg. The General Staff mirrored the extent to which the officer corps was being invaded by bourgeois elements. In 1872, roughly one-third of all General Staff officers were untitled. One was even a Jew.

The period was also marked by further organizational changes. The *Kriegsakademie*, the chief training centre for the officer corps, was placed under the General Staff as far as scientific work was concerned, a considerable extension of the General Staff's range of influence. Areas of command over the railway system were multiplied in connection with the working out of time-tables for the mobilization plan, the railway section itself being placed under Department II, the "German" Department, which was responsible for all deployment and operational plans. For all personal questions, a central department was formed which came directly under the Chief of Staff.

Admission to the General Staff entailed attendance at the *Kriegsakademie* and the successful passage of its final examination, after which there followed a two-year probationary period on the Staff itself, with an examination at the end. Candidates were selected strictly on the recommendation of superiors. The climax of the General Staff officer's training was the annual practice journey carried out under Moltke's personal supervision.

In 1871 appeared Moltke's essay on strategy, which was a kind of legacy to the German people. Fundamentally, the secret of his school was that it had no secret. In war, he said, nothing is certain except the commander's capital in will and energy. Situations often cannot be fully foreseen in advance, and strategy is nothing but a system of *ad hoc* expedients, the value of which must be judged by their capacity to achieve their object, whatever that object may be.

Moltke thought highly of historical research as a strategical training medium, but while insisting in the main on strict truthfulness he also held it a "duty of piety and patriotism" not to destroy certain traditional accounts if these involved an issue of prestige and ascribed historical victories to specific personalities. If this was a fault, however, it was an amiable one, and Moltke's system of training had a somewhat more serious defect to show. His well-known maxim, "Be more than you seem", expressed his high moral conception of the Staff officer's task; yet it was perhaps unfortunate that this ideal of quiet detached fulfilment of duty within a specialist sphere should have been so firmly inculcated in an age already somewhat marked by over-specialization, or that Schlieffen, with his "Achieve much but keep in the background," should have followed so closely in his master's footsteps; for the result was a type of military specialist who, despite his moral principles, was helpless and uncertain of himself outside his own domain.

Meanwhile, the reputation of the General Staff continued to spread. Greek, Rumanian and Turkish officers came to Berlin to study its methods. In 1871, General Miribel organized his *État-Major Général de l'Armée* on the Prussian model, dividing it into four *Bureaux*, of which the *Deuxième Bureau*, which was concerned chiefly with the study of the German Army, was in due course to achieve almost legendary fame. In 1882, a military mission went to Turkey under General von Kaehler, and in the following year Colmar von der Goltz was called to Constantinople by Abdul Hamid II as Inspector of Military Schools, and was shortly thereafter placed at the head of the Turkish Military Reorganization Commission. Italy created a General Staff on the Prussian pattern, as did Japan, which in 1884 obtained General Clemens Meckel as instructor for the Army.

Other appointments were to follow. Lieutenant-Colonel von Falkenhayn went as Military Adviser to China in the 'nineties, while Captain Körner was called to Chile, where he later became a general and Chief of the Chilean General Staff. Von der Goltz's son, also a General Staff officer, later served as an instructor in the Higher Military School in Buenos Aires. Of these various appointments, however, only that of von der Goltz in Turkey had political significance, for it helped determine the line of Germany's Eastern policy.

In 1883 a special Cabinet order secured the Chief of the General Staff the right on the *Immediatvortrag*, that is, of direct access to the Supreme War Lord, even in peacetime. This step, which had been urged for half a century, was now enforced by the logic of events, for the pace was growing hotter and Germany's neighbours and rivals were actively keeping abreast of her in military development. Under the influence of General Miribel, France introduced universal service in 1872, and Miribel became the creator of the French Army Reserve. Russia also adopted universal service. General Dragomirow, one of the most important military theorists of his day, had accompanied the campaign of 1866 as the Czar's military plenipotentiary, and the Russian "Main Staff" was now equipped with a railway department on the Prussian model.

Meanwhile, Germany was faced by her ancient danger. A possible war of revenge launched by France was a risk which Bismarck could face with relative equanimity. The peril lay elsewhere. Bismarck owed his recent victory largely to the somewhat precarious neutrality of other powers, and the likelihood was small, unless he did something about it, that they would all be equally considerate on another occasion. It was unfortunate, to say the least, that the two powers principally concerned, Russia and Austria, were almost continually on bad terms—and likely to continue so while the Turkish question remained unsolved. It was not easy to cultivate the friendship of the one without incurring the suspicion of the other. Yet Germany most desperately needed the goodwill of both. It was the triumph of Bismarck's diplomacy that this is exactly what he contrived to obtain, though it was not till the reinsurance treaty of 1887 that the whole system was really secure.

There were anxious moments for Moltke while Bismarck's diplomacy was getting to work, though a memorandum dated April 1871 shows him confident enough at the beginning of this period. France had been weakened by defeat, and Russia's garrisons in the western part of her huge empire were widely scattered. This led Moltke to believe that in the event of a Franco-Russian combination, the German Army would be strong enough to take the offensive in both directions. Relations between Berlin and St. Petersburg were, it is true, at that time undisturbed; Colonel Kutusow, the military plenipotentiary at the Prussian court, had witnessed the victory at Sedan with sincere pleasure. But one never knew with Russia. As the Berlin Congress was to show, a lack of sufficient warmth by a neighbour in the espousal of Russian causes was liable to be interpreted as downright hostility.

In 1872 the meeting of the Emperors of Germany, Austria and Russia, and the conclusion of a Russo-German military convention in the following year, laid to rest for a moment the spectre of a Franco-Russian alliance. Now, however, France was once more recovering, and was seeking to make the uttermost use of her manpower by means of universal service. This meant that in order to gain the advantage of Germany's superior numbers, Moltke was compelled to put her human potential to more effective use. This in its turn led him to ask for an increase in the reserve formations, a strengthening of the field artillery, the turning of the telegraph troops into completely self-contained units, and an increase in railway troops. Unfortunately it was Bismarck's practice to draw up the estimates first for a period of five years, and then of seven; the object was to make them immune against the changing currents in the Reichstag. The practice, however, made it very difficult to adapt German armaments to changes in the armies of her neighbours. It is possible that a more flexible and democratic system would have produced greater confidence between legislature and executive, and thus, so far from hurting the Army, might actually have advanced its interests.

Between 1872 and 1876 Moltke planned, in the eventuality of war, to take the offensive against France from Lorraine. He took Swiss neutrality for granted, and believed that the fear of British intervention would prevent France from attacking through Belgium. This reasoning also made him consider it absurd for Germany to violate Belgian neutrality herself, and in this he was fully at one with Bismarck. As the French Army grew steadily stronger, he weighed from time to time the theoretical advantages of a preventive war, but on that issue Bismarck's attitude was quite unequivocal, and so theories such notions remained.

The Berlin Congress left Russia resentful and dissatisfied, and in the years which followed Russia pushed her armies forward to her western frontier. At the same time, France created the great frontier fortresses of Verdun, Toul, Epinal and Belfort, which were connected by further outer forts, the whole making a formidable military barrier. The final alignments now began to crystallize. In 1879 a memorandum of Moltke's on the new Russian military dispositions helped to undermine the resistance of the old Emperor to Bismarck's proposed alliance with Austria. Hitherto the Emperor had objected to such a treaty as an affront to the good faith which till then had united Romanoffs and Hohenzollerns. Thus began the dual alliance with Austria which, when deprived of the counterbalance of the reinsurance treaty, was to bring Bismarck's work to ruin and wreck the German ship of state.

IX

It was in the year 1879 that a villager from Liebstadt approached Moltke and asked him to intervene with the Emperor so as to obtain some lessening of the burden of military expenditure. Moltke replied that any war, even a victorious one, was a misfortune for the nation concerned, but that it did not lie even within the Emperor's power to make everybody realize this. That would only become possible when all nations had had better moral and religious training than they at present enjoyed. It was a fruit that would not have ripened within the lifetime of either of them. In a somewhat similar vein he replied to Professor Bluntschli, the great Heidelberg teacher of constitutional law, when the latter was championing the cause of international law and of an international peace organization. "Everlasting peace," he wrote when Bluntschli sent him one of his books, "is a dream and not even a beautiful dream, and war a link in God's ordering of the world." International agreements would never have the force of law, and the best that war could do was to settle disputes as quickly as possible by all legitimate means. When a Russian pacifist writer, named Goubarew, once approached him, he expressed the hope that war, "this ultimate expedient", would become ever more infrequent as civilization progressed, but that no State could wholly renounce it. Finally he quoted Schiller's words from *Wallenstein*:

> Oh, war is terrible as any trial
> The Heavens do send us, yet is it a good,
> A thing fate wills ...

According to Stresemann, Hindenburg once said that as an old soldier he did not believe in any rational substitute for war. The same could have been said by Moltke. The General Staff knew only one principle: *Si vis pacem, para bellum*—which is arguing in a circle with the deadly certainty of getting nowhere at all.

From the year 1879 onwards, two deployment plans were worked out every year, one against France, one against Russia. The strength of the new French fortifications caused the chances of a quick success in the west to grow steadily smaller. Nevertheless, quick decisions and short wars represented the ideal at which Moltke always aimed, if only because he knew the horrors of war only too well. The deployment plan for 1879 therefore provided for defensive action in the west—if necessary, for a retirement to the right bank of the Rhine into the area Mainz-Frankfurt—while, in the east, Austria and Germany were to act together and make an attack with half a million men. In the event of France marching through Belgium, it was intended to receive the French blow on the lower Rhine and to press the French Army back against the Dutch frontier. Belgium was now also resorting to universal service and was building a large chain of fortifications. Thus the attack in the east remained the essential solution during Moltke's lifetime and for some time after it. For the defence of the west, he relied on some Italian help. Six Italian army corps were to be thrown across the Alps on to the Upper Rhine.

In 1882 came the first great strengthening of the Army. Thirty-four new battalions were formed, together with 40 batteries of field and two battalions of heavy artillery. Six years later, these additions were supplemented by 30 more infantry battalions and 23 further batteries. Two new army corps were created, the 16th and 17th, while in 1884, following the French example, the first balloon troops were created and placed directly under the General Staff.

In 1887, Moltke drew up a memorandum recommending offensive action against Russia in conjunction with Austria, a proposal which Bismarck described as "premature". In his *Thoughts and Memories* Bismarck wrote that the General Staff's desire for a preventive war had its origin in the spirit which such an institution was bound to foster, and which he for his part did not wish to see it lack. The only question was what would happen when you got an aggressive Chief of the General Staff in combination with a weak and incompetent monarch and a Chancellor without political perspective and without authority. The foundations for such an unhealthy development were already laid when Bismarck wrote those lines.

From 1882 onwards the ageing Moltke, who had repeatedly asked for his release, had had to accept the services of General Count Waldersee as Quartermaster-General and Deputy. Yet the old man with the finely cut, wrinkled and venerable face—he was nearly ninety—was still the master in the red house on the Königsplatz. Anyone who met him walking in the Tiergarten in his long general's cloak and simple service cap might almost have taken him for some philosopher of antiquity. In actual fact, however, he had long been a lonely man. In 1868, his wife, whom he loved above everything in the world, had departed from him. Twenty years later he saw two Emperors die, his old master and the poor, doomed Frederick, the champion of German liberalism.

On August 10th, 1888, his new master, the Emperor William II, granted his request for permission to resign. He went to Kreisau, the entailed estate which his nephew, Count Wilhelm von Moltke, was to inherit. One day, in Germany's darkest hour, Count Wilhelm's grandson was to show forth that spirit which had marked Helmut von Moltke's declining years, the spirit of wisdom, goodness and reason.

The erratic, vain and nervous bearing of the new Emperor aroused a foreboding in Moltke that Germany had a difficult time ahead. In one of his last speeches in the Reichstag—he delivered it in 1890—he again dealt with the great war which he held to be inevitable. If that war should break out which hung like a sword of Damocles over the head of the German nation, then no end to it could be foreseen; for the strongest and best equipped powers of the world would be taking part in it. None of these powers could be completely crushed in a single campaign. The war might thus last for seven, perhaps for twenty, years. "And woe to him that sets fire to Europe." The picture of a short war was fading. The old man saw more sharply than his contemporaries, although his eyes that once had been so bright had begun to dim.

In the spring of the following year he was in Berlin on a visit. On the morning of April 24th he attended a session of the Prussian Upper House, and in the evening listened to music in the company of his hosts. He grew tired and went into an adjoining room. Since he did not come back, one of his nephews, who was in the house at the time, went to see where he was. He found him sitting bent forward on a chair. He was still breathing, but could not speak. He was carried to his room and laid on the bed. For a few minutes his gaze remained fixed on a picture of his wife that hung upon the wall. Then he breathed his last.

CHAPTER V

PREVENTIVE WAR OR *COUP D'ÉTAT*

WALDERSEE

I

BOUT the turn of the century there appeared a novel by a
young unknown author named Franz Adam Beyerlein, entitled
Jena or Sedan. This book, though lacking much literary merit,
aroused considerable interest, for it touched on a matter of some
topical importance.

Scharnhorst, Gneisenau and Boyen had insisted that the Army
should be the school of the nation, but now large sections of the
nation had begun to turn away from many of the assumptions on
which the Army was built, and this, as Beyerlein's book showed, was
not without its effect on morale. In the story of the fictitious Osterland
80th Field Artillery Regiment, the officers have for the most part
become a body of place hunters and careerists who give little thought
to the real nature of their duties but fulfil them merely as a matter of
routine. There are wasters, fops and libertines among them, and those
of middle-class origin seem only too ready to make the traditional
snobbish social code their own. The commander of the regiment, a
man with some of Moltke's traits of humanity, moderation and goodness, produces almost an antiquated effect. The one real idealist ends
by putting a bullet through his head, and the man who has military
reform at heart and holds the view that the old system of military
education led nowhere, ends by resigning and taking a post in the
armament industry, which at least knows how to put competence to
use. Last, but not least, the typical, simple, dutiful soldier, Lance-
Corporal Vogt, is driven into the ranks of the socialists by the arro-
gance of one of the young officers.

No doubt the picture is somewhat overdrawn—as happens in all
novels that are written with a specific purpose—but for all that the
author was inspired by an honest and well-founded anxiety, for the
faults he described were genuine faults. The fact is that the essentials
of military organization had remained unchanged for a hundred years

but life and circumstances had not. The training of the barrack square, which in the long years of peace had lost more and more of its vitality in eternal parades, and the tacit assumption that the rank and file were imbued with a simple-hearted patriotism, of which many were entirely innocent—these things left something to be desired when regarded as the main expedients for maintaining the discipline and efficiency of a modern army. The serene assurance that the troops would always accept a semi-patriarchal system of human relationships, and the rigid and even penal measures taken against all who were in any way suspected of socialist sympathies were cognate pieces of folly.

The truth is that vast changes had taken place in the social and economic structure, and there had been no corresponding changes in the Army. Nor did the majority of the older generals want any. When one of the few truly great reformers of the time, General von Schlichting, remarked in his training regulations of 1888 that the old regulations had helped to win three wars, von Pape, the commander of the Guards, engagingly asked why they wanted new ones, and von Pape was unfortunately an all too dominant type.

A personality of genius taking hold of the Army at this juncture and given a free hand, might conceivably have worked changes that would have affected the whole future, not of the German Army alone but of Germany itself. Moltke's successor, Waldersee was not a man of genius, though he had energy and intelligence of a very high order. Also, and most unquestionably, he was possessed of charm.

That elusive quality no doubt contributed to the eminence he achieved—though there was also his background. The princely house of Anhalt-Dessau had been as distinguished for its misalliances as for its military achievements, and we have already seen that one of Frederick the Great's adjutant-generals was the offspring of one of these princely liaisons. The military historian von Behrenhorst was another. The von Waldersees were also a left-handed offshoot of this great family and had over more than a century distinguished themselves both in the civilian and in the military branches of the Prussian service.

Alfred Count von Waldersee was born in 1832 as the son of a Prussian general, his mother also being a general's daughter. He grew up in the Berlin of the 'forties, which was dominated by the old narrowly demarcated aristocracy, whose mansions still lined the Wilhelmstrasse. He passed through the inevitable schooling of the cadet corps, and in 1830 joined the Artillery of the Guard as a lieutenant. In the campaign of 1866 he was adjutant to Prince Karl of Prussia, who at that time occupied the somewhat decorative post of Master General of Ordnance and chief of the Artillery Corps. In the summer of the following year he was transferred to the General Staff. Service on the General Staff, a number of appointments as adjutant and finally the post of military attaché in Paris just before the outbreak of the Franco-German war were the experiences which determined his career. They turned him from a somewhat shy and sickly young man to an officer who was at home both in court and diplomatic circles. Nature had given him an agreeable exterior, a certain suppleness of character, powers of quick and accurate mental perception which sometimes carried a danger of superficiality. His acquaintance with a world which most Prussian officers had little opportunity of entering strengthened his self-assurance and gave him the pleasing certainty that, with his quick wits and the prestige he enjoyed as an officer of the General Staff, there was no situation in which he could not find his bearings and no task he could not master. Unfortunately he wholly lacked the ability to assess his own limitations or to see himself from the outside. This was a pity, for despite his charm, his very naïveté sometimes made him mildly ridiculous. When the King once said to him that he was really a sort of maid of all work, the joke filled him with immense pride. His brother Staff officers, however, had a different name for him.

His despatches from Paris contained remarkably accurate estimates of both the strength and weakness of the French Army of the Second Empire, for in a matter of that kind there was never any question of his talent, and these despatches attracted the attention of Bismarck, Moltke and the Kaiser. Thus he went to the front as the Kaiser's aide-de-camp. Immediately after the conclusion of hostilities he became Prussian chargé d'affaires in Paris as Bismarck's confidential man, and thereafter returned to the Army.

It seemed to be Waldersee's good fortune to obtain military appointments which held out the possibility of political influence, for after commanding for a short time the 13th Uhlans, a crack regiment, he became Chief of Staff to the 10th Army Corps, which again put him under a princely superior, namely Prince Albert of Prussia. To crown everything, he married about this time a rich American lady, originally a Miss Mary Lee, who had previously been married to a Schleswig Prince. This had important consequences. His own family had lost their fortune in the crisis following the wars of liberation, and the marriage enabled him to keep house and entertain in a big way.

It was a good career by any standard, but what makes the whole figure of Waldersee of interest to the historian is his diary. The habit of keeping a diary is often the solace of the sententious, whom a sound instinct guides to keep their less stimulating observations to themselves, or at any rate to confine them to the privacy of an unheard monologue, and certainly if Waldersee's conversation had partaken of the complacent ineptitude which marks most of the observations that fill these long-suffering volumes, it seems unlikely that anyone would have listened to him—let alone have tolerated him. The fact is, however, that he was popular, and that in a high degree, so that we cannot but suppose that despite the technical identity of the two, Waldersee the diarist was a rather different figure from Waldersee the officer, charmer and man of the world.

II

And yet Waldersee had enemies. In the correspondence between the Crown Princess and Queen Victoria, the former on one occasion remarked to her mother that Waldersee had not half Moltke's military talent and that he was unreliable and false. Since the exalted lady's capacity for judgment on the first of these complaints can hardly have been considerable, not too much weight need be attached to it. The second is more easy to understand, particularly since Waldersee waged relentless war against the liberalism of the Prince Consort's daughter and of his son-in-law, both of whom he designated as "English democrats". Moreover, Waldersee really was a man with a natural appetite for intrigue, while certain innovations which he introduced, in themselves innocuous enough by modern standards, must have struck those educated in an older and simpler tradition as the very hallmark of the disingenuous. A Chief of Staff who organized press attacks on his opponents, and incidentally laid himself open to similar attacks in return, must have appeared to such excellent people as a very paragon of impropriety.

Yet the strange thing is that Waldersee's was fundamentally not a subtle mind but a very simple one. There were for him no nuances in either politics or morals. Revolution was to be combated, preferably by force. The Churches were simultaneously to be sustained and kept in their place, and threats from any quarter were to be countered by preventive war. He could see no merit in Bismarck's diplomatic artistry, which he designated as the policy of the see-saw. That estimate is typical of his disastrous imperviousness to the finer political shades. Confronted by an international situation which was either threatening or precarious, it was Waldersee's invariable tendency to "panic forward". It is a common military failing. Waldersee had it to a degree that was astonishing.

Also, he misread men abominably. He pinned his hopes to young Prince William, thinking to discern in him a kindred spirit to his own. Never was man more deceived, and the mistake was to cast the shadow of futility and disappointment over his declining years.

Yet a certain magnetism about the man is undeniable. Even Bismarck in those days had an excellent opinion of him, and Moltke considered him a man of outstanding gifts. So did most other people, for Waldersee made conquests everywhere. He seemed to release a wave of confidence in a jaded and doubting world, and that confidence, as his diary shows, infected himself.

In 1878 he was mentioned as a possible candidate for the post of Ambassador in Vienna. Then, when attempts were made on the life of the old Emperor, he coveted that of president of the Berlin police; he believed he was particularly fitted to finish once and for all with the subversives. "How I despise the liberal gang that has captured the Chamber," he writes, apropos of one of these attempts at regicide. "They are prisoners of their own verbose unrealism, and are setting the country back further from year to year." Blessed indeed are they who see the world in such clean and simple colours—but they rarely succeed in shaping the destinies of nations.

III

One day, General Albedyll, who had replaced Tresckow as Chief of the Military Cabinet, remarked that Waldersee should watch his health for his hour would one day come. Waldersee seems to have seen nothing extraordinary in the remark. Perhaps the most astonishing thing about it—at least to those who view the man in retrospect— is that it happened to be largely true. We have seen how, in 1881, Moltke was finding the burden of office increasingly unbearable and asked for a deputy to take some of the work off his shoulders, and how he expressed the wish to use Waldersee in this capacity. He clearly regarded Waldersee's freshness, courage and readiness to take decisions as a welcome vitalizing element. High military circles widely approved the choice. So it came about that in 1882 Waldersee was appointed Quartermaster-General to the Great General Staff, and thus, since Moltke left him the most complete freedom, became for all practical purposes the director of its affairs.

Politics was something which Moltke almost nervously avoided. Waldersee was temperamentally incapable of keeping out of them, and he seized the opportunity, which his new post almost lavishly provided, with an uninhibited, one might almost say guileless, spontaneity which is not devoid of charm. He was, of course, helped by Moltke's prestige, but he also found an ally in General Albedyll, who shared with him a desire to disencumber himself of the influence of the War Ministry, for the War Ministry most inconsiderately continued not merely to exist but actually to exercise a not inconsiderable degree of authority.

This was particularly galling in the delicate matter of approaches to the Emperor, and it was at this point that he made his first major assault. By 1883 Waldersee had established his right to approach the Emperor without informing the War Ministry at all. Moltke had never felt the need for any such extension of his personal power. It had been his habit to say that if the Emperor had need of him, he would send for him, but Waldersee had plans which were very much his own.

This was a good beginning, yet it was to lead to even better things. One of Waldersee's first steps was to secure, again in conjunction with Albedyll, the replacement of Kameke by a more acceptable War Minister, namely General Paul Bronsart von Schellendorf, sometime head of the Operations section of the General Staff. The new incumbent had no objection whatever to the fullest use of the rights of the *Immediatvortrag*, and had indeed been one of those who had pressed for the General Staff's emancipation from the War Ministry. Waldersee, however, actually aimed higher. He wished to see the War Ministry reduced to a purely administrative central office, while all powers of command that derived from the ruler's rights and authority passed on to the General Staff. He never reached his goal, though in the years that followed (and this was Waldersee's doing) the General Staff became responsible for the working out of combat principles and the conduct of manoeuvres. But Waldersee was not the man to think that his energies should properly expend themselves in a pedantically circumscribed departmental sphere. Again short-circuiting the War Ministry, he also maintained contact with the Foreign Office, where he had confidential relations with Holstein. In addition to this, he created, with the help of the military attachés, an unofficial, half military, half diplomatic, intelligence service. Soon the

Ambassador in St. Petersburg, General von Schweinitz, was writing that the Waldersee-Albedyll régime had constructed a "very respectable secondary tyranny" inside of Bismarck's own.

From the vantage point he had attained, the intrepid officer dived into the yet uncharted seas of public relations. A press office was opened under Major Zahn, the head of the intelligence service, and a number of retired officers who had been active with their pens were employed as so-called "Press Hussars"—these included Major Scheibert, sometime military observer with the army of Robert E. Lee. For the most part these gentlemen wrote for the ultra-conservative *Kreuzzeitung*, whose publisher, the distinctly pleasure-loving and eternally indebted Freiherr von Hammerstein, was under obligation to Waldersee in yet other respects. With the help of his rich American wife, Waldersee had secured him a sum of 100,000 marks for his paper. Nor did Waldersee hesitate to tread even more devious paths. He established contact with Ernst Schumann, for some time correspondent of the *New York Herald*, a doubtful character who played a highly questionable part in the Xanten ritual murder case. It was strange company for one of Gneisenau's spiritual progeny.

In matters of high policy, in which a man of Waldersee's restless temperament could hardly refrain from endeavouring to take a hand, his ideas had an *ad hoc* directness which must have been—and in point of fact often was—a nightmare to those trained in the more hesitant traditions of mere diplomacy. The Empire, he declared, with touching ingenuousness, had too many enemies. Frenchmen, Slavs and Catholics—all these were hostile. Only a great war could offer an escape from this difficulty. He would have liked to try conclusions with France in 1873, but, sharing as he did with Moltke the conviction that the east was the decisive theatre, he viewed Russia as the most suitable object for his attention. In 1878, he wanted, for no immediately apparent reason, to fight Russia with English help, and cheerfully spoke of mobilizing Austria, Italy and Turkey against her.

In 1882—it was the year he met young Prince William, the Crown Prince's son, who, so the diary says, "made an agreeable impression" —Waldersee again had thoughts of an attack on Russia and had deliberately worked for a close association with von Beck, the Austrian Chief of General Staff. At the same time he also initiated a newspaper campaign against Russian rearmament with the double purpose of influencing the Reichstag in favour of rearming Germany and of depressing Russian shares on the stock exchange. Meanwhile, he intensified mobilization plans and pressed for heavier armaments.

Closer relations were established with the armaments industry, and it was during this period that General Budde, the head of the General Staff's railway section, became manager of the Löwe gun factory.

The great problem, if Waldersee was ever to stand forth as the man he hoped to be, was the attitude of the Reichstag. The victory of the Franco-German war had inspired the population as a whole with a feeling of security which was in marked contrast to the very genuine anxiety of the General Staff. New armaments seemed to most people a needless expense. By and large, that simple villager's letter to Moltke was an index of a widespread feeling that military expenditure was a burden on men's backs, and people had little time for the man by whom that burden threatened to be imposed.

There was also opposition at court and in the Army. One such centre of intransigeance was the Crown Prince, which caused Waldersee to organize with a quite peculiar determination a campaign of intrigue against General Mischke and Count Marshal von Normann, two active members of the Crown Prince's *entourage*. Opposition also came from a group of generals of the Guards Corps, in particular from General von Winterfeld, the commander of the Guards Cavalry division. But generals did not make policy, nor, for that matter, was it very important that these essentially moderate-minded people held Schlichting to be Moltke's obvious successor, Schlichting having expressed Moltke's ideas in a number of first-rate books. Waldersee merely committed the characteristic observation to his diary that compared with Schlichting he was the better man, and that opinion seems to have prevailed widely enough to be effective.

Waldersee's great hope was the Emperor's grandson, young Prince William, whom he accompanied in 1884 on a visit to the Czar. In 1885 his diary speaks of an intimate friendship with this vain and disquietingly neurotic young man. Waldersee speaks of him as having an open mind, and describes him as fresh, a real lover of work, agreeably mannered, markedly Prussian and as a man of unshakably conservative views. Certainly he had not much heart, but since the future would be hard, this might actually be an advantage. In these years Prince William was the man under whom he felt that he could realize his plans. He hopes, so the diary reads, still to give him excellent service. But the courtier was in a hurry. He was playing for a bigger prize than a young Prince with a still uncertain future could at that time have secured. Waldersee raised his sights.

IV

In 1886 he began secretly to attack the "see-saw" policy of Bismarck and to hint that the old Chancellor's energy was declining. It was the first sign of that ambition the frustration of which filled his declining years with the strange poignant melancholy of the unappreciated, for Waldersee was at last aiming at the chancellorship. His tragedy was that despite his superficial brilliance he was at heart too simple to know how completely he was unfitted for that post, nor could he understand that even the Byzantine Germany of William II, which he rightly came to distrust, had at least enough sanity left to refuse it him.

However, Waldersee's energy carried him sufficiently far along this path to make him definitely Bismarck's rival. Bismarck relied in the Reichstag on a coalition of the middle parties, which included the National Liberals, while Waldersee found support on the right wing of the Conservatives, since these had quarrelled with Bismarck. It was a more mixed company than its name might suggest, and a not untypical representative of this inwardly disintegrating world of old Prussian Junkerdom was a man to whom allusion has already been made. The publisher of the *Kreuzzeitung*, Freiherr von Hammerstein, was a man of not inconsiderable abilities, but he was somewhat unbalanced by his rooted conviction that conventional standards of right and wrong did not apply to persons of exalted birth.

Then suddenly, in 1887, the rivalry reached a critical phase, for in that year the Crown Prince was found to be suffering from cancer. He was within a year to succumb to that malady, and Waldersee knew well enough that something of this kind might happen. The possibility that the way might be opening for young Prince William, whose favourite he was, gave interesting food for thought. The sparring intensified, the first round of the new phase being fought largely around the person of the court chaplain, Stoecker. Stoecker was a man of humble origin who had worked as a tutor in the houses of a number of great landowners and been impressed—perhaps over-impressed—by the kind of life he found there. He had also worked as a pastor in some industrial slum areas, and had there learned something of the depth of the social problem. He was now directing the Berlin City Mission and seeking to win the masses back from Socialism to Christianity. With this man Waldersee struck up an alliance, though how far he shared Stoecker's quite genuine zeal for souls and how far he was merely actuated by the ingenuous conviction that a small dose of spiritual sedative would banish what was often a justifiable discontent, is difficult to say.

As a matter of fact, Stoecker's activities did not have the happiest kind of issue. He became the founder of the Christian Social Workers Party, which in the course of time gave birth to the Christian Social movement. This last soon ceased to be noticeably Christian or to have very much to do with the workers, for it became a nucleus of the discontented petty bourgeois and palpably anti-Semitic. For the moment, however, Stoecker appeared to serve Waldersee's purpose tolerably well.

Bismarck watched Stoecker's career with mistrust, for he feared that the Catholic Centre Party might now have an evangelical counterpart. Actually it was the Stoecker affair which brought matters to a head. Towards the end of 1887 there was a gathering in Waldersee's house of ultra-conservative aristocrats. A number of Ministers were present, so was the President of the Reichstag and so was Prince William of Prussia, who came accompanied by his pious young wife. Now Prince William made a speech—the object of the meeting was the financing of the Berlin City Mission—and dwelt upon the need for reawakening Christian feeling among the labouring poor. Bismarck pricked up his ears. The heir to the throne must be above party, he commented to Waldersee. The thrust was at Waldersee, and Waldersee knew it. He professed to agree—and secretly carried on his war against the Chancellor with greater zeal than ever. On points it was Bismarck's round—but by a narrow margin.

At the end of that year Waldersee knew beyond any doubt whatever that the detested Crown Prince was marked for death. When the aged Emperor closed his eyes, it would not be long before the sceptre passed to Prince William, and then the real tussle would begin.

With Albedyll in the Military Cabinet and von Schellendorf at the War Ministry, Waldersee was excellently placed for a fight. Against him were ranged the Bismarcks, father and son, the Crown Princess, the "Army of Liberals" and Caprivi, then State Secretary of the Imperial Navy Office. Before the year was out, Waldersee at last had a collision with Bismarck which was serious. He had on his own authority let it be known in Vienna that there was no need for Austria to fear a Russian attack. Bismarck, whose policy it was to keep all parties in a state of mutual distrust, complained—and that not unreasonably—of this interference of the General Staff in diplomatic affairs.

So far from being deterred by this rebuff, Waldersee developed a new energy in pushing his own brand of policy, for which he could always get a certain backing from the military party in Vienna and which cut right across that of his rival. In 1888 he was again pressing for attack in the east. There had already been staff talks with representatives of Italy and Austria, and Waldersee was counting on Rumanian help once the shooting had started.

Actually, Waldersee did not by any means lack support. There was, for instance, General von Loe, of the Cavalry. Von Loe had already written to Waldersee in 1886 that Bismarck's "Appeasement Policy" had failed and that the chances for a "double war" were excellent. The thing was to activate England, Turkey and Italy against Russia, and to get British officers to train the Turkish Army, though so far the British War Office had shown no appetite for this interesting activity and the Turks no wish to benefit by it.

Yet to Waldersee and his friends, it all seemed plain sailing. Russia, it is true, was getting steadily stronger, but Germany had herself completed much of her rearmament. She had carried out the equipment of her infantry with the magazine rifle, a new howitzer had been introduced into the foot artillery. Also there was a new type of high explosive shell and new shrapnel ammunition. In the eyes of Loe, as of Waldersee, all this made the moment extremely favourable for a "double war", and had Prince William been the man whom Waldersee took him to be, the war might well have eventuated. What saved Europe from Waldersee was not the genius of Bismarck but the fortunate circumstance that William was largely a fraud.

V

The old Emperor died in March of '88, his heir receiving the news in San Remo with his own death staring him in the face. Had the new Emperor's health been sound, Waldersee would inevitably have had to reckon with resignation. As it was, he had little to fear, and the conflict between himself and the Chancellor intensified.

Meanwhile, in contrast to his dying father, William was positively bursting with vitality. He drilled the Guards on the Templehofer Feld and sometimes invited Waldersee to these exercises. Then Crown Prince and Quartermaster-General would ride back into Berlin at the head of the troops with bands playing, fifes shrilling and drums beating, and with the crowds along the Linden roaring their cheers as they went by. It was at times almost as though they were anticipating the triumphal return from that great war of Waldersee's dreams.

Waldersee was watching intently for what he called his "moment". Hammerstein adjured him to save the Empire from the Bismarck Dynasty, since Bismarck was unmistakably working to secure his son Herbert's succession to the Chancellorship. In the *Kreuzzeitung* Major Scheibert was advocating a preventive war in the east. Bismarck in return arranged for the "War Party" to be assailed in his own tame press. Waldersee's diary grew indignant about these "disgraceful attacks" and abused "the House of Bismarck and its Mamelukes".

So far there was no sign of a setback and Moltke was still behind him. When Bismarck asked Moltke whether Waldersee was really the right man in the right place, Moltke replied with an unqualified affirmative. Perhaps Moltke was no longer capable of recognizing the background of intrigue behind Waldersee's activities, or it may have been that the obstinacy and inflexibility of age made him averse to change. One cannot tell.

Meanwhile, all things seemed, as far as Waldersee was concerned, to be working together for good. In the Reichstag, in the spring of 1888, the middle parties held war to be a certainty if Prince William came to the throne, and Waldersee was allowed to be his Chief of Staff. Even Bismarck was under the impression that William wanted war. Neither Bismarck nor Waldersee was alive to the fact that William was acting a part, that of Supreme War Lord, and that more than to anybody else he was acting it to himself. His various warlike ancestors had collaborated in writing the play—its acts were Fehrbellin, Rossbach, Leuthen, Königgrätz and Sedan—and what with the powder-smoke, the cries of the wounded and the dying, the thunder of cavalry charges and the roar of cannon, it was good, rough, virile but somewhat sanguinary stuff. The part for which his ancestors had cast him was traditional, but it was too difficult for a man congenitally averse to the whole business of bloodshed, so he made up for more essential qualities by the sheer noise of his speeches and his sabre rattling; but it was not a good performance.

In his diary Waldersee found comfort in the thought that his own position was secure, since the new ruler lay dying. Then shortly after that unhappy man was actually dead we find Waldersee writing: "Few mortals are as fortunate as I. Perhaps I am at the zenith of my life." He was not so very far wrong.

A new wind was blowing. Many old generals were removed. On

August 10th, Moltke retired. Waldersee became Chief of the Great General Staff. The diarist could hardly have remained dumb on such an occasion. "The appointment did not surprise me," he writes. "One of the most brilliant careers is behind me, and the whole world is looking towards me. The merit for my getting as far as this is not my own. It is the goodness of God. ... Sometimes the thought comes to me that this cannot go on and that there must be reverses."

The immediate effect of the appointment, however, was that reverses were suffered by others. Waldersee's first deed as Chief of the General Staff was to stab his own camarilla in the back. When the new Emperor expressed the wish to have General von Hahnke, who commanded the 1st Guards Infantry Brigade, as Chief of the Military Cabinet, Waldersee, without even an attempt at an excuse, sent his old friend Albedyll into the wilderness. Similarly, he was responsible for a change of War Ministers. It seemed likely that General von Verdy du Vernois would be even more accommodating than von Schellendorf as War Minister, and so Verdy du Vernois obtained the post through Waldersee's backing.

In many quarters Waldersee was urged to unite the General Staff and the War Ministry in his own hands. He declined the suggestion, to which Bismarck would in any case never have agreed, but the fact that it was made is to some extent an index of the change in position of the General Staff, which had once been little better than an adjunct to the War Ministry. That change, too, had largely been Waldersee's work.

VI

The new Chief of Staff had an extensive programme. He was all for Army reform, but this for him was not a matter of internal reorganization but simply of numbers. He was curiously lacking in any sense for the great technical innovations of his time, though the armies of other countries had begun to concern themselves with these matters. As a convinced anti-modernist, it was natural in a way that he should have little interest in such things. It was not machines that had brought Prussia her victories, but courage and discipline—and yet Waldersee did not wholly scorn the material factor. He did believe that God was on the side of the big battalions.

In co-operation with the War Minister, Verdy du Vernois, he drew up a programme for the most ruthless application of the principle of universal service. Every man who could possibly be made liable was to be trained and that for the full three-year period. Both Infantry and Artillery were to have substantial increases. Waldersee also re-organized the General Staff. The different departments were placed under three *Oberquartiermeisters*, corresponding to the Brigades of the old Quartermaster-General's staff. *Oberquartiermeister I* got the rail-ways and the old Department II (the "German Department") which dealt with matters of organization, mobilization and armaments. This was the so-called Deployment Department. *Oberquartiermeister II* dealt with training, fortresses and maps, while *Oberquartiermeister III* had the old Departments I and III which looked after those parts of Europe that fell outside the "German Department". Directly under the Chief was the Central Department, the Military History Depart-ment and the Survey section.

Change of a more fundamental kind, however, was in the air. The new industrial development had brought imperialist aspirations, and each of these things reacted on the other. The colonial question was born, and with it dreams of vast new conquests in Africa, Asia, and Goltz's activity in Turkey laid the foundations of an Oriental policy. German undertakings were included among those which made their way to Mesopotamia and the Middle East.

This caused some people to view the General Staff in a new light, namely as the technical and organizational apparatus by which Ger-many would maintain her hold in a world that was steadily expand-ing. It was not for nothing—and perhaps it was no accident—that fifty per cent of the officers of the General Staff were now of bour-geois origin. The hold of Pan-Germanism on the General Staff was never strong, but its Pan-German champions, such as they were, came from just these bourgeois strata. In the General Staff it was untitled officers such as Captain Keim and Major Liebert who established the first links with the *Flottenverein* (the naval propaganda organization) and similar bodies. The old Prussian Junkers had never really understood what purpose a strong navy was supposed to serve. It was the new wealthy commercial class that was clamouring for the protection of German commerce and German overseas possessions, though it was the Emperor, with the picture of his grandmother's navy ever before his eyes, who vowed that he would one day have as big a fleet of his own and so made these aspirations effective.

The Navy was now the new lodestar, an agent of growing lustre for the German name, to the more pedestrian patriot a stumbling block but to the true visionary a mystical, almost holy aspiration. It was in 1889 that the first naval plans passed through the Reichstag and the

Navy obtained its own chief command which was independent of the Imperial Navy Office. The Emperor also created his own Naval Cabinet which, even as a peacetime arrangement, was thrown together with the Military Cabinet and formed into an Imperial Headquarters under General von Wittich. For a time there was talk of a plan for a Supreme Command Staff, a sort of Super Staff or Imperial General Staff, and even though this came to nothing, Waldersee realized that he was confronted by an entirely new development and one which went counter to his own plans, for with all his faults, Waldersee in more senses than one had his feet upon the ground. Germany in his view was essentially a continental power, and naval rearmament was liable to interfere with the development of a land army, which had been Prussia's traditional source of strength.

As early as August 1888, immediately, that is to say, upon his assumption of office, this question had begun to cause him serious concern and it marked the first scarcely perceptible divergence between the Emperor and himself. He was far too intelligent not to realize that the Empire could not afford the luxury of a powerful fleet on top of its land armaments, and the fact that such a fleet could play no decisive part in a war with either France or Russia added weight to his consideration. It was the first glimmer of Waldersee's disillusionment regarding the Emperor, who he now began slowly to realize seemed to think he understood everything and interfered in matters of which he understood nothing whatever.

VII

Hammerstein had been strengthening Waldersee's conviction that he was the coming Chancellor whose drastic surgery was destined to lead the Empire to a new phase of healthful development—it was about this time that the *Kreuzzeitung* got its hundred thousand marks —but when the opposition press made open allusions to his ambitions in this matter Waldersee excelled himself in righteous indignation. In secret he asked himself whether he had not so deeply enmeshed himself in his own intrigues that his instinct was failing him so that he could no longer seize the psychological moment for an open bid for power. His doubts were increased by the fact that Bismarck still enjoyed enormous prestige both at home and abroad. Officially Waldersee and Bismarck would exchange mutual assurances that they were in no sense rivals, but this did not stop Waldersee burrowing, though he was careful to let others do his less reputable work in public, the attack on Bismarck being left in the willing hands of Stoecker and Hammerstein.

Yet things were by no means easy. New men were threatening to supersede him in the Emperor's favour. There was in particular Count Philip Eulenburg, Prussian Ambassador in Munich, a soft, dreamy sort of man who played the piano, composed and sang and was also something of a poet. Waldersee had enough sense to cultivate Philip Eulenburg's favour. The Eulenburgs, however, were not so much a family as a pullulation. There was another member of this great East Prussian clan, Count Augustus Eulenburg, who was Deputy Master of Ceremonies, while Count Botho Eulenburg, sometime Prussian Minister of the Interior, was playing quite a part as a conservative politician. It was this family that was now edging into the foreground; the Emperor was a frequent guest of a collateral branch, the Dohna-Schlobittens, with whom he liked to shoot. The going was getting harder. It was a trying experience for a favourite.

On April 15th, 1889, Waldersee confided the thought to his diary that Bismarck's reputation and skill should be used to the full until such time as German armaments were completed. Once that had been achieved, the decisive war with France and Russia should be deliberately brought about. "Till then with the Chancellor, but when things get serious, without him—or even against him." When Russia wanted to take up an armaments loan in Berlin, the Emperor was inspired by Waldersee to prevent this. Bismarck was more cautious. He got his press to attack Waldersee, which really meant that the Emperor was himself the object of the attack. Waldersee was openly accused of wanting war for war's sake. He replied by angrily complaining of all this talk about a "War Party". The Prussian Army, he declared, knew no parties, but somehow it did not sound convincing.

Waldersee now thought it politic to make approaches to other parties—the "free-conservative *Reichspartei*" and the National Liberals—but at this stage there was a new development. It became evident that the Emperor was inclined to be conciliatory on the social question, and it looked as though as a result the antagonism between Chancellor and Sovereign might now break out into an open quarrel. Waldersee was himself disappointed by the Emperor's attitude. A fight with labour was what he had always wanted; he wanted it now, and the consequence was a somewhat paradoxical parallelism between Bismarck's ideas and his own.

Towards the end of 1889 and in the early part of 1890, there was reason to believe that Bismarck was playing with the thought of a *coup d'état*. The Reichstag had been his own creation, but parents are often disappointed with their children. The essence of the contemplated coup lay in determining the Federal Treaty with the Princes and drawing up a new one. Universal suffrage would then be replaced by a thoroughly reactionary electoral system. Now it was hardly to be expected that the socialist masses would passively acquiesce in such proceedings, and that would be the moment for troops to settle the issue by force. Such a policy of reactionary violence would, Bismarck believed, pay dividends not only at home but abroad. The Czar, whom the Nihilists and their bombs had contrived to put into a state of chronic terror, would, he felt, be delighted with it. The whole thing was very much in tune with Bismarck's prevailing mood, which caused him at this time to admonish the Emperor that a Hohenzollern should know how to die fighting upon the steps of his throne.

Waldersee only got to know indirectly of what was supposed to be in Bismarck's mind, but *coups d'état* were something to which he was by no means unsympathetic, and he thoroughly subscribed to Bismarck's diagnosis of universal suffrage as a cancerous growth. Nevertheless if there was to be a *coup d'état*, he was determined that he himself was to carry it out and not Bismarck.

Yet none of these schemes materialized. In March of 1890 came the crisis which ended in Bismarck's fall. "The great row has come" is the comment of Waldersee's diary on the 15th of that month. Waldersee attacked the Chancellor furiously before the Emperor and charged that his whole foreign policy had been a failure. It should have been the great schemer's hour of triumph, and yet the triumph was denied, and its denial was probably a heavier blow than the diarist's wistful resignation suggests: "*Die Eitelkeit, Kanzler zu sein, plagt mich wirklich nicht,*" he writes, which may be very loosely rendered, "I really do not hanker after such slight satisfaction of my vanity as the Chancellorship would afford." He adds that if the Emperor were to summon him, then, as a soldier, he would obey. When, smooth courtier that he remained to the end, Waldersee told the Emperor that he prayed that God would let him choose the right successor, the Emperor, standing half way through the doorway of the audience chamber, replied: "Oh, I think we'll manage. Good hunting!" And that for the moment was that.

VIII

Both Waldersee and Eulenburg had talked the Emperor into the idea that only a general could be a possible successor to Bismarck at such a moment, though the motives of the two men were very different. The result was Caprivi, a general of Infantry who had served on the General Staff in the 'sixties under Moltke and was certainly an able officer. Indeed, Bismarck himself remarked that it was a pity so good an officer should go into politics. Caprivi, however, abandoned the keystone of Bismarck's policy, which was the reinsurance treaty, because, as he said, he was not equal to such masterpieces of juggling—a transparent piece of nonsense, for there was no more juggling in the business than normal diplomacy can show a dozen times in a decade.

The effects of the blunder were visible immediately. In 1890 the French Deputy Chief of General Staff, General Boisdeffre, for the first time attended Russian manoeuvres. In 1891 a Franco-Russian military convention came into being. In part this was directed against England, whose colonial acquisitions in Africa and the Far East France was viewing with uneasiness, but it was also very definitely directed against Germany. Waldersee had for some time advocated the mobilization of England against Russia, but that genius in mis-calculation, Holstein, was now conducting the secret policy of the Foreign Office and wanted no firm ties with that country. The obsession that England might use Germany as a continental sword against Russia haunted him to the end. It resulted in Russia being England's ally, thus invalidating another of Holstein's axiomatic ineptitudes—namely that the Lion and the Bear were irreconcilable enemies and so would always be on opposite sides. So no Anglo-German understanding ever came into being, though this was the obvious answer to the Franco-Russian convention.

Waldersee had yet other cares. At first he had welcomed Caprivi's appointment. Soon it became apparent to him that *Der Biedermann* (the solid citizen), as he called him in his diary, was pursuing an original policy, which was as a matter of fact an eminently sensible one, though Waldersee could hardly be expected to like it, for among other things Caprivi arranged for the military attachés to be subord-inated for the future to their respective civilian diplomatic chiefs, so that a kind of private intelligence service which Waldersee had built up was virtually destroyed. In the matter of Army reform,

Waldersee's conceptions of which were in any case unrealizable, Caprivi actually held that a reduction of the period of service was unavoidable.

In the autumn, Verdy du Vernois resigned and was replaced as War Minister by General von Kaltenborn, and now Waldersee became uneasy. The Emperor was becoming completely absorbed by his master passion for the Navy, and to make matters worse Waldersee, at a critique on manoeuvres, had propounded a solution different to the Emperor's own. Waldersee's solution happened to be the correct one, but His Majesty could never be wrong. It was a strange error for so supple a courtier to make—and a disastrous one.

He began to wonder whether he had not been completely mistaken in the Emperor. Vanity and the fevered pursuit of popularity were failings of Waldersee's own. He found them unbearable in others. In the autumn of 1890, the Emperor, under pressure from Caprivi, made an effort to get rid of his obstinate and inconvenient Chief of Staff. He offered him the command of the 13th Army Corps in Stuttgart, and in doing so developed the startling theory that a commanding general in what was after all a federated state was a kind of Prussian Viceroy. Waldersee knew instinctively that what was intended was his relegation to obscurity, and declined. Old Moltke, who still had glowing opinions of him, sought to warn the Emperor and declared openly to him that one could not change one's Chief of Staff whenever one happened to please. But who now listened to Moltke?

At last Waldersee saw that the Emperor had come too early to the throne. His days were a whirl of journeys, parades, manoeuvres, inspections and shooting parties, punctuated at intervals by the trumpet-like blare of his speeches. The actor was becoming intoxicated with his part. Already he had used the words, "*I* will lead you towards glorious times." What horrified Waldersee most of all was a speech of the Emperor at a swearing-in of recruits for the Guards Corps. On that occasion, having revolution temporarily on the brain, he said that if *he* ordered it they would have to fire on their own fathers and brothers. That would be regrettable but might be unavoidable. To Waldersee's ears it was a horrifying remark. According to his code, the possibility of the soldier's refusing obedience should never even be discussed. The thing touched him on the raw, for with a persistence that had something of the pathetic about it he still pursued the idea of a *coup d'état* which he held to be the final means of solving the social question, and the success or failure of any such plan depended on military obedience being unconditional. Small wonder that William's words should have distressed him.

IX

There were further setbacks. Towards the end of 1890 the Emperor developed the idea of fortifying the harbour of Memel and of using it as an eastern naval base. Waldersee was against fortifications in principle. The war he was planning was a war of lightning offensives. It was in attack that lay the chief strength of the Prussian infantry. About this time the old boy was again propounding plans for an attack on Russia under the pretext that she was seeking to dismember Turkey; but William wanted no war, war games were all he cared for—war games and magnificent manoeuvres (which were also magnificent anachronisms) with charges by Cuirassiers in white tunics, gleaming breastplates and the rest of it.

On January 15th of the following year, a darkly apprehensive Waldersee recorded that he was no longer invited to Imperial dinners. On the Emperor's birthday, the latter presented Waldersee with the Cross of the Grand Commander of the Order of the House of Hohenzollern and took this occasion to tell him that he wished to entrust him with an army corps.

This was his death sentence. After the Emperor's birthday dinner with the Great General Staff, Waldersee had a discussion with Schlieffen and another officer, General Oberhoffer. Then he went to the Emperor and asked for permission to retire. The Emperor was in excellent humour. "I only want my Chief of Staff to be a sort of amanuensis," he said, "and for that I need a younger man." He proposed, he added, to give Waldersee the 9th Army Corps in Altona. That was a very important post. From Altona he could keep an eye on Bismarck, who since his retirement was living at Friedrichsruh. It was also close to Hamburg with its tens of thousands of Proletarians. Then there were the Mecklenburg Princes who could do with some watching. Waldersee persisted in his request for retirement. He was now badly shaken. "He wants to be his own Chief of Staff. God help our country." That is one of the diary's few genuine *cris de coeur*.

The Emperor, however, continued to reject both written and oral requests for retirement. On the 31st he received Waldersee again. Waldersee told him on this occasion that the Army had deteriorated. "That's the first time anyone has said that to me," was the astonished rejoinder. This time Waldersee yielded and took the Altona command. Schlieffen succeeded him as Chief of the General Staff.

On the whole Waldersee's departure produced a happier atmosphere both in the General Staff and in the Army. Political intrigue was alien to the average officer. Soldiers did their duty and obeyed orders. Waldersee had largely lost the affection of the Army through his restless political ambition, in the same way that Schleicher was to lose it somewhat later. Only the ultra-conservatives and the warmongers among generals and politicians still looked to him as to a man who yet had greatness before him.

The remainder of his career, which was spent in Altona, was not happy. There were rumours of scandals and some striking at his creatures. Two officers of the General Staff, Majors Zahn and Liebert, who had been his "Press Hussars", were reprimanded and removed from their posts on the ground of improper association with journalists and parliamentarians. Stoecker had fallen from Imperial grace a year before.

X

The ageing man still itched with the nostalgia for power. He refused to despair. He still awaited the signal and from time to time it seemed that men were beckoning to him. In the years 1892 to 1894, a number of anarchist outrages occurred in France, Spain and Italy, culminating in the murder of the French President Carnot. These things had their effect in Germany, where the coal magnate, Freiherr von Stumm, started a campaign for energetic counter-measures. Again Waldersee believed that his hour had come. Again reactionaries cast their eyes toward the "strong man", now an exile in Altona. That other great exile in Friedrichsruh had now acquired the wisdom to warn his countrymen against the more fatuous kind of political escapade, but the eternal boys of politics remained; there were still the romanticists, the crusaders and all the other incorrigibles, and everlastingly of course there were the disgruntled.

At home, storm signals were out. Caprivi was having a stiff fight over the Army estimates which caused the Emperor to declare that if the "half-crazy Reichstag" baulked him further, he would send it to the Devil, and of course in certain quarters that meant more whispered advice, more promptings, more discreet and knowledgeable prods. The younger Moltke advised Waldersee to keep in the background, as His Majesty would be sending for him, while

Hammerstein insisted there was only one course—to provoke the workers and then start shooting.

Again, there was talk of a military dictatorship. Waldersee seems to have taken this nonsense seriously enough to cause a certain amount of discreet alarm. Holstein sweated, and there was a flutter among the Eulenburgs. Philip Eulenburg in particular seemed to be afraid that France and Russia might use the occasion of Germany's internal difficulties for a preventive war of their own, and things did actually go far enough for the French press to speculate on the Empire's possible disintegration, and for a certain Captain Molard, of the French General Staff, to publish a book in which he claimed for France the left bank of the Rhine.

On October 26th, 1894, the Emperor, under pressure from the East Prussian agrarians, dismissed Caprivi. In Stoecker's eyes the moment had now come for a "Greater action". Waldersee must become Chancellor, finish with the Reichstag and the subversives, and replace universal suffrage by some adequate system of professional and class representation. The Emperor, however, did not want Waldersee, because having Waldersee would have meant a fight, and William, neither now nor later, had much appetite for fighting. What William wanted was to be friends with everybody.

Meanwhile, Caprivi's fiscal policy had led to a crisis among the East Elbian landowners, as a result of the importation of cheap Russian grain. A number of the less efficient estates of the old landed nobility came under the hammer. A number of sinister scandals provided evidence that the class which had once supplied the nation with its leaders was disintegrating. At court, a titled Master of Ceremonies was falsely imprisoned for writing obscene anonymous letters, the real culprit being another Master of Ceremonies, also titled. Waldersee nearly became involved when two Berlin journalists and an official of the political Police were prosecuted for spreading false reports. The man Schumann, whom Waldersee had used as a source of information, was mixed up in the affair, and Waldersee had to help him escape secretly to Italy. All these things helped to create a kind of cloak and dagger atmosphere congenial to thoughts of dictatorship, and indeed to some it seemed the only salvation. Waldersee was ready. One could still have shooting, he somewhat pathetically declared. The Army would still obey its officers against the Social Democrats. Yet no one seemed to have much taste for fratricide, and there was no shooting.

XI

Things began to get quiet around Waldersee. In 1895 the indiscretion of an actress, who had been Hammerstein's mistress, revealed that the publisher of the *Kreuzzeitung*, the slogan of which was "With God for King and Country", had committed forgeries to the extent of 200,000 marks and used the money to finance his personal extravagance. Hammerstein had been Waldersee's political mentor and his warmest personal admirer. Now he fled to Tirol, thence to Greece, where he was arrested. He was brought home and sentenced to three years' imprisonment.

Oddly enough, Waldersee still counted as a great potential war leader and the irony of it is that in actual war he might have justified himself, for if war came, he was to command in the east. However, he rejected the new theories of Schlieffen that the first offensive was to be directed against France, and in other respects his convictions remained equally rigid. In a memorandum of 1897 he again appealed to the Emperor to solve the social question by force while reliance could still be placed on the Army, which caused the Emperor to remark smilingly to him during an inspection that if ever it came to shooting he was sure Waldersee would make a good job of it. Waldersee in reply hoped that His Majesty would not wait till he was too old, to which the Emperor rejoined, still smiling, "Well, we'll have to look into that"—and that, again, was that.

But Waldersee gradually lost hope. After attending the solemn procession at the New Year's Day reception at the Berlin Castle in 1900, he asks himself in that ineffable, that incredible, that interminable diary whether such a procession would be taking place in the Castle in a hundred years' time. His conclusion is negative. In 1900 the Boxer rebellion broke out, and the German Ambassador was murdered in Pekin. Waldersee was appointed Commander in Chief of the German Expeditionary Force, and the Emperor secured the agreement of the other powers sending forces to China to put their contingents under him and made him a Field-Marshal for the occasion. However, when he arrived there, Pekin was already occupied by forces from the combined European navies, so that warlike fame was denied him. This provided all the more fun for the liberals at the expense of the *Weltmarschall*.

Up to the time of his death in 1904, he held the post of inspector of the 3rd Army inspection area in Hanover, a post which was accounted as a preliminary to command at one of the fronts in the event of war. One of his last remarks before he died was: "I pray God that I may not live to witness what I see coming."

These words, spoken almost in the presence of death, may betoken Waldersee's realization that he had been travelling the wrong road— or again they may indicate that Waldersee died convinced that his country's end was near because she had rejected his advice.

So ended Waldersee. There is about the figure of this undoubtedly able man a kind of nimbus of futility. Of all the major personalities of the Great General Staff he alone approximates, though very distantly and imperfectly, to the popular stereotype. He did not plan world conquests on the crude Pan-German formula, yet he did display an embarrassing proclivity for fighting pretty well anybody—for no better reason in most cases than the simple principle that it is better not to put off till tomorrow what you can do today. That seems to be the general idea behind his theory of preventive war. He was not quite the brutal and repressive type of anti-democrat who was one day to hag-ride Wilson's imagination, though some of his utterances tend to suggest that he would rather have relished the part. Nevertheless, there are certain overtones in his romantic authoritarianism which the modern ear has become apprehensively ready to catch.

If Waldersee had attained his ambition, the results for Germany might well have been disastrous—but was there really ever any danger of that? He was never a man in tune with more than a fraction of his contemporaries. He was both too naïf to be taken seriously as a statesman and too forthright for the time-servers, and so fell between two stools. The great tides of history were pulling in other directions than those of his choosing, and the significant thing about Waldersee is that he failed.

CHAPTER VI

THE MASTER PLAN

SCHLIEFFEN

I

THE creator of the *Reichswehr*, General von Seeckt, frequently remarked that the task of the Great General Staff was not to produce geniuses, but to concentrate on the training of ordinary men who could display efficiency and common sense. His ideal was a state of affairs in which one General Staff officer could at any time take over the work of another and apply to it the same body of basic ideas and the same principles of operational thought. He wished to see identity of training result in uniformity of type. This ideal tended rather to enforce on men the characteristic limitations of the expert and to produce a certain one-sidedness of mind, and this tendency may be said to have asserted itself with the appointment of Count Schlieffen as Chief of the General Staff.

Schlieffen was a very different man from his brilliant predecessor. The family did not trace back its descent into the misty regions of the princely elect. They were descended from a line of Kolberg burgesses who had been mayors and aldermen, and their great successor had the habit of attributing his own industry to the traditions of these simple, dutiful folk. It was only under the Prussian kings that the family acquired land and attained nobility.

Count Alfred von Schlieffen was born in 1833, his father being a major in the 2nd Foot Guards. His physical type was that of the highly-bred but somewhat effete aristocrat. There was a quality both of pride and aloofness about his face, though a certain veiled look about the eyes may have been due to shortsightedness. Indeed, the latter defect made it questionable whether he would be able to enter military service. After attending school with the *Herrenhüter* in Niesky and at the Joachimsthal *Gymnasium* in Berlin, he spent a short time studying law, but the school was probably the major influence, for something of the piety of the *Herrenhüter* remained with him all his life. He was a profoundly religious man. He had especial need of the comfort and support derived from that, for he was a man who shut his heart up and so did not greatly savour life or derive much joy from it.

In 1854, he joined the 2nd Guard Uhlans as a second lieutenant. For a few years he plunged into the gaieties of a young officer's life, in a way that contrasts strangely with his serious nature, earning the nickname "Crazy Schlieffen". Probably this frenzied, one might almost say desperate, pursuit of pleasure should be ascribed less to some quality of his personal make-up than to the fashion of the time. He was posted to the General Staff in 1865. In due course he married a cousin, a Countess Anna Schlieffen, whom death took from him after four years of exceedingly happy married life. Anna Schlieffen seems to have been a woman with great gifts of heart, and the husband never sought to make good his loss.

His first experience of war was Königgrätz. He was present on that occasion in the capacity of a staff officer with Prince Albrecht of Prussia's Cavalry Corps, and the impression seems to have been indelible in his mind; it is significant that Königgrätz was a battle of encirclement. In the Franco-German war he was a staff officer with the corps of the Grand Duke of Mecklenburg-Schwerin, who was fighting Gambetta's levies on the Loire. In 1884 he became head of the military history section of the Great General Staff—Hindenburg was at that time serving on the General Staff as a captain—and in 1889 was made General, *Oberquartiermeister* and Deputy to Waldersee.

The contrast between the Chief of Staff and his multiplicity of interests and his *Oberquartiermeister I* must indeed have been remarkable, for the latter seemed entirely absorbed in the technicalities of his work and had no interest whatever for anything outside it. There was also this difference between the two men, that whereas Waldersee deliberately sought to bring about a war, Schlieffen looked upon that coming war as an ineluctable decree of fate. The only problem to which the human will was free to apply itself, successfully or otherwise, was that of discovering how a power with inferior numbers could beat a superior combination of enemies. This fatalism, by the way, was soon to find eloquent expression in the pages of another General Staff officer who was also a historical and political writer of some distinction, Count Yorck von Wartenburg. Von Wartenburg saw clearly that the weakness and incompetence of German policy could only have one issue. The realization drove him to a full-blown advocacy of preventive war, a notion which Schlieffen only entertained at one period, and then only very tentatively.

Schlieffen's complete imperviousness to anything that lay outside the sphere of his professional interest could at times be astonishing. Once on a Staff journey, after a tiring night of travel between Königsberg and Insterburg, the adjutant who was accompanying him drew his attention to the magic of the Pregel Valley that lay before them in the morning sun. Schlieffen looked at the scene, remarked, "An unimportant obstacle", and relapsed into silence. In human relationships he was equally insensible. One of his closest colleagues, General von Kuhl, relates how on every Christmas Eve he received a military problem the solution of which had to be returned by Christmas Day.

This side of his character was apparent in nearly all that he did. Moltke in dealing with his Staff had been kindness and consideration itself. They had all been like one great family. Schlieffen was proud, distant, and often wounded people with his sarcasm. If he succeeded in getting a subordinate to entangle himself in a self-contradictory solution of some particularly difficult problem in a war game, he often seemed positively pleased at his discomfiture. General von Schlichting, of whom more will be said in a moment, wrote of Schlieffen that he had great strategic talent but was not a great character. His worst fault was that he would brook no rivals and would suffer no one near him with real originality of mind. Officers with real integrity and firmness of purpose were either relieved of their posts or consigned to ineffectiveness. Their places were filled by men who were ready simply to take orders.

Even when he knew a thing was right, Schliffen would never put up a fight for it, a truth which applies both to the question of the needed completion of Army reform and to the planning of the great autumn manoeuvres. In the latter he gave a free hand to the Emperor, who liked to take the lead personally on these occasions; Schlieffen would them magnanimously overlook the brilliant cavalry charges and other magnificent impossibilities by which William's theatrical battles were decided. There was an element of Byzantinism in this that accorded strangely with Schlieffen's coldness and reserve. Those who got to know him intimately, like Captain Mackensen, his adjutant during the 'nineties, could not do enough in their reminiscences to try and explain the peculiar fascination he exercised over them. The fact is, however, that our values are conditioned by the age in which we happen to live, and the ideal of that particular time was the inspired but impersonal expert, absorbed in his work and wholly disinterested in anything else, and for that part Schlieffen was, as we have seen, most admirably cast. What men admired was the incorruptible clarity of Schlieffen's mind, of whose deadly one-sidedness they wholly ceased to be conscious.

II

It had now become axiomatic for the General Staff that Germany would have to fight a two-front war, yet once this assumption was given the character of a decree of destiny, it meant that all future planning had to be carried on in the atmosphere of a nightmare. In this desperate position, it was natural that the military planners should search for some encouraging precedent, and their gaze again fell on Frederick the Great.

By operating on interior lines, Frederick the Great had once successfully fought a war on several fronts. He had beaten the French and Imperial armies at Rossbach in November 1757 and had then hurried to Silesia with 32,000 men, and, by means of a brilliant out-flanking operation, beaten 82,000 Austrians at Leuthen. True enough, these victories had not brought about the end of the war; that had come six years later as a result of a change in the composition of the enemy coalition. For all that, the thing dominated Schlieffen's mind, and the geographical separation of France and Russia, the two great powers who were his probable opponents, suggested a parallelism with Frederick's situation which was both seductive and illusory.

The fundamental problem was simple; it was a question of beating one opponent by concentrating against him the greatest possible superiority of force and then falling as rapidly and as violently as possible on the other. Moltke had ensured the speed of such a blow, for he had made railway transport into something like a master weapon. It fell to Schlieffen to try and add the element of weight to that of speed, and so he pressed for a further strengthening of the Army. He gave way on this when he encountered opposition, for he held the view—and held it strongly—that he was not called upon to do more than warn and advise.

Nevertheless, between 1893 and 1905 three new army corps were created and there was considerable strengthening of the technical arms. Even so, hundreds of thousands liable for military service failed to receive training because the Reichstag was unfriendly on the subject of military expenditure. Schlieffen followed with interest the development of military means of communication by the telegraph, the telephone and the heliograph. He seems rather to have overlooked the military potentialities of the internal combustion engine, and the most important innovation which he succeeded in introducing was the equipment of the field army with mobile heavy artillery of 15 to 21 centimetre calibre.

Schlieffen's main concern was the development of existing means. In 1896, the General Staff organization was improved. It now had a Quartermaster-General as Deputy to the Chief of General Staff, and four *Oberquartiermeisters*. Yet though he was at pains to perfect this important apparatus, his thought was vitiated by one grave fallacy. He believed that because mass armies were so expensive, no power could finance a protracted war. He did not realize that such mass armies would involve the mobilization of industry and so release forces which had hitherto been hidden.

The great question was on which front the first annihilating blow could be delivered with the greatest prospect of success. Schlieffen at first adhered to the plans of Moltke and Waldersee which provided for the main deployment to be in the east. Then the prospects of a quick decision, either east or west, began to fade. France completed General Rivière's plans for a fortress belt on her eastern frontier, while Russia massed ever-increasing numbers of troops in Poland and began a system of fortresses in the area Ivangorod, Brest-Litovsk, Kovno and Warsaw. This barred the terrain of the Naref, against which Moltke wished to deliver his main attack.

In the end, Schlieffen's gaze moved towards the west; Moltke and Waldersee had wished to await the French offensive in Lorraine. It was their intention not to go over to the attack themselves until the decision had fallen in the east and the French offensive had been held. The idea now came to Schlieffen of marching round the flank and into the rear of the French fortress system and of forcing the enemy to battle with his front reversed.

Now, on one flank of this fortress system lay Switzerland, while Belgium lay on the other. Switzerland was easily defensible and offered no passage for troops. The opposite was true of Belgium, and here he already had to reckon with the possibility that French forces might themselves pass through it, outflank the line of the Rhine and threaten the Ruhr. Round about 1892, Schlieffen conceived the thought of sending a powerful flanking army through Luxemburg, while remaining on the defensive in Lorraine. However, this territory was too small to serve as a deployment area and had too few roads. It is true that the Ardennes were the weakest point in the French defensive system. The "Luxemburg Gap" was only covered by two antiquated fortresses which had not been improved because the French relied on the difficulties of the terrain. The Ardennes were thickly wooded and had only a few inferior hill roads.

In so far as these considerations proved decisive for Schlieffen, the French calculations may be said to have been justified, but with the Ardennes ruled out, there remained only Belgium. Prussia, like all other leading European powers, had guaranteed Belgian neutrality when Belgium achieved her independence. An orderly political leadership, such as existed under Bismarck, would probably have refused to go back on that pledge—assuming that such a leadership would ever have allowed the political situation to deteriorate to a point where so dangerous a venture could have had attraction—but Schlieffen's relations with Hohenlohe, the Chancellor, and with Bülow, his successor, were quite superficial. Neither of these men, in the eyes of the General Staff, commanded Bismarck's prestige, and so within their own province the military planned entirely on their own. When he heard of the plan to violate Belgian neutrality, Holstein, the secret manager of the Foreign Office (from whom Schlieffen derived such knowledge of international affairs as he possessed), preferred to let sleeping dogs lie, and no doubt vaguely hoped that the occasion for applying it would not arise.

Schlieffen knew enough history to realize that a violation of Belgian soil carried the danger of British intervention. He set no great store by the possibility of an English landing in Denmark, or of an attack on the Kiel canal, believing, as he did, that he could defend himself in that quarter with negligible forces. If, on the other hand, British forces appeared in Belgium or Northern France, they would simply be drawn into the general catastrophe of the French Army and reduced to impotence.

III

Every year the plans were worked over afresh, but it was only slowly that, under the influence of events as a whole, the great master plan began gradually to take shape. Through the greater part of the 'nineties, the bogey of encirclement gave it actuality; then, in 1898, 1899 and 1901, England sent out feelers to see if an understanding could not be arranged between the greatest sea power and the greatest land power. But the opportunity was thrown away; neither Bülow nor Holstein approved of firm commitments for Germany, who would thus lose her bargaining power and so fall between two stools.

Finally, England gave up her search for an Anglo-German *rapproche-ment*. In 1904, she settled outstanding differences with France and brought her policy into line with that of her neighbour. Meanwhile, Belgium, growing alarmed at continual rumours that found their way into the press concerning German intentions to march through her territory, began to fortify Liège and Namur, whereas hitherto Antwerp had played the principal part in her defences, which up till then had been mainly directed against France.

Round about the turn of the century, Schlieffen's plan in the west provided for the assembly of six armies on the line St. Vith-Strassbourg, and a flanking army which was to move in echelon out of the area Aix-la-Chapelle-Düren. As late as 1902 it was still assumed on the Staff journey that the neutrality of Belgium and Luxemburg must not be violated by Germany unless it had already been violated by France. Even so, the conclusion drawn from this particular exercise was that a French army attacking out of the Vosges might suffer a frontal defeat but would by no means necessarily be annihilated. Yet just such speedy annihilation of the French force was the assumption underlying the delaying tactics employed against Russia.

Here indeed was the essential dilemma; the Russians must be contained east of the Vistula, but this was impossible unless a knock-out blow could be delivered against their allies, and that blow could only be struck through Belgium. It is not true that Schlieffen came lightheartedly to his decision. He wrestled with the Belgian problem long and arduously, but the more he examined it, the clearer it became that the problem admitted of only one solution.

At length, in 1905, there came into being the Schlieffen plan that is known to history. According to its provisions, the main mass of the western army, on paper usually made up of nine army corps, five cavalry divisions and seven reserve corps, was to be assembled in the area Cologne-Düsseldorf-Aix-la-Chapelle for attack in the direction of Belgium; seven weaker armies drawn up in echelon southwards as far as Saarbourg were also to advance. In a word, a vast force was to execute a gigantic wheeling movement through Belgium on the pivot Diedenhofen-Metz, and bring the enemy to battle in the Seine basin so as to force him back till he was facing inwards with his own frontier fortresses in his rear or was driven into Switzerland. Meanwhile, the Upper Rhine was to be held by the Italian force of ten infantry and two cavalry divisions with which Schlieffen was still reckoning at this time, though a French advance across the Upper Rhine into Baden would actually not have been unwelcome to

Schlieffen, in so far as it would have drawn away forces from the French defence.

In the east, a weak force of three army corps, four reserve divisions, two to four cavalry divisions and some *Landwehr* troops was to cover East Prussia, while a diversionary action was prescribed for the Austrian Army in Galicia. A thorough discussion of these plans with the Austrian General Staff never took place, nor were any binding assurances of the Italian co-operation on which Schlieffen relied ever actually received. Even the German naval command remained without any information on the General Staff's plans.

Schlieffen's plan—he insisted that every army leader should have a complete grasp of it—demanded a certain depersonalizing of subordinate commanders. A single Vogel von Falckenstein taking some action on his own initiative could have cut right across it and rendered it worthless. In implicit, though reluctant, agreement with this provision, a corps commander once said to a young staff officer who sought to develop his own strategic ideas, "His Majesty only keeps one strategist, and neither you nor I is that man." Schlieffen expected armies to move with the precision of a battalion on parade, and it was no accident that it was just at this time that large manoeuvre areas were created where great numbers of troops could carry out their exercises without damage to agriculture or industrial activity. The plan also seemed to exclude that element which Clausewitz had designated as "Frictions", that is to say, the unexpected incidents and unforeseen developments which he held to be characteristics of every war.

Grolman had once warned against the "Great Plan" that was designed years in advance in the study as a certain prescription for victory. Now "The Plan" had been the ultimate expression of military wisdom. In the case of the Commander in Chief himself, the demand was for iron nerves and a fanatical will—a will which must not weaken—even if British troops should carry out a successful operation from Denmark, or the Russians launch an offensive on the Vistula. Nominally the Emperor would be Commander in Chief in war time in the west, and if war broke out, it would be against the Emperor that the Chief of Staff would first have to assert himself, but since the very fact of having Schlieffen as Chief of Staff had actually fortified William's well-nigh pathological self-confidence, this would be no easy task.

IV

It was not granted to Schlieffen to see his plan carried into effect. Yet when the excellence of the Imperial Army of 1914 is taken into account, and the cold efficiency of the General Staff, there can be no doubt that if it had been carried out in its original form by a man of, say, Ludendorff's brutal energy, it would have achieved an overwhelming initial success. France would have been hurled into the dust. The question would then have arisen whether either England or Russia would have given up the struggle, and we can now almost certainly say that they would not.

Unfortunately, this truth was insufficiently appreciated. The militarist notion that a single purely military victory can effect a permanent political settlement was among the most dangerous but most persistent delusions of the age. It was still not seen that modern war releases all the powers of a people, and, thanks to modern technical and economic development and the growth of population, those powers are so enormous as to give even a nation that has suffered severe reverses almost unlimited capacities for resilience. Yet there were those who had begun to grasp something of all this. Colmar von der Goltz had commenced as far back as 1877 to lay the foundations of his reputation as a military writer with his *Léon Gambetta and his Armies*. Later, in his *People in Arms*, he showed an insight that was often remarkable. Von der Goltz saw clearly (and Schlieffen, one cannot help thinking, did not) that the war of the future, Ludendorff's genuine war, was not a mere matter of armies but of entire nations dedicating themselves to the task of survival. Not lightning victories in the field but the physical and moral exhaustion of one of the combatants would ultimately decide the conflict. Goltz also prophesied that a war of mass armies increasingly exploiting the triumphs of technology would necessarily lead to a loss of mobility, and that extensive fortifications would in the future play a determining part. In the short run, one must admit, that prophecy proved to be true.

V

The praises of the Schlieffen plan became for a time so loud that people have forgotten the volume of criticism to which Schlieffen had to submit until the publication of his military studies cast a new lustre on his name. On General Staff journeys it was made plain to him that neither the General Staff itself nor the great body of his brother generals fully accepted his fundamental ideas. General von Bülow, who was Quartermaster-General to the General Staff in 1902/3, favoured the frontal breakthrough, as did General von Bernhardi, the head of the military history section at the time and one of the leading military writers of the day. Von der Goltz, who some time after his return from Turkey became Commander in Chief in East Prussia, was unreservedly, and perhaps not unnaturally, hostile in principle to the conception of an offensive at all costs, and advocated the erection of a huge frontier fortification system. It was quite in keeping with his idea that he should not visualize the coming war primarily as a land war at all. He saw England as the principal opponent of the extension of Germany's influence in the world, and wanted Turkey to be activated for undertakings against India and Egypt. He further advocated the occupation of Holland as a sally port against England and close co-operation with the Navy. Such notions were the wildest fantasy for Schlieffen.

Actually, the essential anti-Schlieffen in the Army was not Goltz but General Sigismund von Schlichting, for some time Chief of Staff to the Corps of Guards, who in the 'eighties had earned a considerable reputation as a military writer. Schlichting was retired without adequate explanation in 1896, a sacrifice, as he put it, to the mechanical brains of the Army, but came out five years later with a remarkably outspoken book, *Moltke's Legacy*. Schlichting, a vehement opponent of blind dependence on the set piece battle, went counter not only to Schlieffen's ideas but to the whole spirit of the man. Like Field-Marshal von Haeseler, who after a short service as *Oberquartiermeister* on the General Staff was removed as "inconvenient", like General von Bernhardi who in his book, *On Modern War*, had added his own warning against entering a war under the impression that victory was a matter of recipes, so Schlichting put up a fight for more flexible principles and, above all, for the preservation in the Army of the subordinate's right and ability to think for himself and take responsibility on his own shoulders. The enormous extension of the areas of manoeuvre and the increase in the size of armies led Schlichting to believe that they should be broken up into smaller bodies. These smaller bodies needed not only first-class Staff officers, which the General Staff was already training, but army commanders capable of thinking out problems on their own and of making their own decisions. Unfortunately these last were not being produced by the era of William II, and Schlieffen had done nothing to remedy this defect.

VI

Schlieffen himself, to do him justice, attached great weight to his assertion that his plan was not an infallible formula for victory by a weaker power over a number of more powerful ones; but a simple faith in planning was in the spirit of the age, and Schlieffen's adherents elevated the Great Plan to a dogma almost in spite of themselves. There is also other evidence that Schlieffen did not by any means underestimate the toughness of his problem. In a discussion on the military situation in 1905, he was already assuming the possibility that France and Russia would not be Germany's only enemies, but that they would be joined by England, Belgium, Italy, Serbia and Rumania. That presumably is why, when Russia suffered defeat in the Japanese war and the first Russian revolution broke out, he thought, at least for a moment, of a preventive war against France. The Emperor and Bülow were not tempted, though a number of commanding generals, including Hindenburg, then commanding the 4th Army Corps, were not unfriendly to the idea.

As it is easy to exaggerate Schlieffen's confidence in his own brainchild, it is also possible to over-simplify his somewhat complex attitude to the past, and actually his plan was not based on historic precedent at all. Rather did it derive from a novel realization that modern methods of transport and communication could force the factors of space and, in a sense, time into his service, thus enabling him to deploy over an enormous area and endanger his enemy in flank and rear. Correspondingly, he saw that in the age of mass warfare the frontal punch carried out in depth had become impossible; that was how Napoleon had met disaster at Waterloo, and Benedek at Königgrätz.

For all that the study of past battles was for Schlieffen a profound psychological necessity, he did not share Schlichting's view that modern armies might become too large to be manageable by the will of a single man; he was too deeply imbued with the Prussian officer corps' tradition of obedience for that. Yet a torturing uncertainty on the soundness of his design never deserted him. It drove him to search through the whole of military history for reassuring examples because there was nowhere else where that reassurance could be found, and thus to lay the basis for a number of studies, remarkable for their purity of style and the perfection of their literary form.

For a time, all his enthusiasm was for Leuthen, though there was also a period when he gave pride of place to Napoleon's defeat of Mack at Ulm, as the perfect example of a battle of encirclement, yet he does not seem to have reflected that Leuthen no more decided that particular war than Ludendorff's victory at Tannenberg, another classic battle of encirclement, decided World War I. But instead of heeding these things, Schlieffen merely delved deeper into history. At last, Hannibal's victory at Cannae, in which he had completely surrounded his enemy despite his inferior forces, became for Schlieffen the perfect pattern of a battle.

He published a study on Cannae in a military periodical, yet there is no evidence of his realizing that this very battle was the perfect object lesson of the necessity for exploiting a victory of this kind by adequate political leadership. The Suffetes of Carthage had had no idea of what to do with Hannibal's success. The war dragged on for fourteen years and ended in Hannibal's defeat at Zama. Cannae was the perfect illustration of the truth that a battle does not win a war.

VII

In August 1905 Schlieffen was kicked by a companion's horse during his morning ride. He was badly hurt in the leg and was unable to attend to his duties at the very time when the world was holding its breath because of the Moroccan crisis. Schlieffen was getting old, and for some years now the question of a successor to the master-strategist had been under discussion. There was no doubt about von der Goltz being the ablest man in the Army—even if his head was somewhat full of Utopian political notions. Unfortunately, von der Goltz was a man of just that inflexible and determined type whom the Emperor found intolerable. The next likely candidate was von Bülow, the Quartermaster-General, but in the autumn of 1903 this officer had been displaced by a favourite of the Emperor's, Helmuth von Moltke the younger, the nephew of the creator of the Great General Staff and for many years his adjutant, who was appointed Deputy to Schlieffen and Quartermaster-General in 1904. It was the name that fascinated the Emperor, in addition to which the younger Moltke had an impressive military appearance; he was tall and broad, a regular cuirassier's figure, and the Emperor, in the simplicity of his heart, really seems to have believed that a nice big man at the head of the General Staff would strike terror into other nations' hearts.

While riding in the Tiergarten one morning in 1905, Prince Bülow, the Chancellor (not to be confused with his military namesake), asked him whether he would care to become Schlieffen's successor. Moltke was by no means certain of himself, in fact he had grave doubts, for he knew his Imperial master well, and when sent for by the latter he was at pains to ensure for himself complete freedom of action. He told the Emperor openly that the great manoeuvres at which the Emperor took the lead were meaningless, if regarded as training for actual war, since etiquette demanded that he should never lose. At this the Emperor grew thoughtful, and Moltke further disclosed to him that he had no high opinion of his own abilities. Much that was said in that hour echoed a similar interview between Benedek and Francis Joseph. Moltke also very significantly warned on that occasion that the coming war, which would be a people's war, could not be ended by a single battle. The Emperor's strategic war games always ended, with Schlieffen's concurrence, with the capture of the entire enemy army, a kind of super-Sedan.

Schlieffen returned to duty towards the end of October to be present at the dedication of the Moltke memorial. During his absence, however, and without his knowledge, Moltke the younger had already circulated an order recommending commanding generals to practise frontal attacks involving large numbers of troops, a distinct reaction against Schlieffen's somewhat one-sided conceptions. In a memorandum dated December 20th, Schlieffen again stressed that in the event of war France could only be beaten by means of a flank attack through Belgium. The relation of strength between the right and left wings should be approximately seven to one. At the end of the year he retired.

When Schlieffen left it, the General Staff consisted of one Quartermaster-General, four *Oberquartiermeisters*, one of whom—another Moltke, as it happens—was seconded for duty with the Emperor, and a hundred and two officers. Forty-four of these officers were of bourgeois extraction, and among the latter we already find names which were to become famous during the First World War. Major Ludendorff worked in the deployment section, Captain Groener in the railway section. It is noteworthy that at this time more than half of the officers of the General Staff had passed through the *Gymnasium*, only thirty per cent having been educated at one of the old cadet schools. One hundred and eighteen officers had been seconded from their regiments for service with the General Staff, among whom was Captain Düsterberg, who at a later date was to become leader of the *Stahlhelm*. A number of princely personages were at this time also being seconded to the General Staff; these included, among others, the Empress's brother, Prince Ernst Günther of Schleswig-Holstein and Prince Frederick William of Prussia. The more orthodox members of the General Staff still frowned upon this practice. They did not wish their organization to become a forcing house for Byzantinism.

VIII

Before retiring, Schlieffen had already spoken of himself as an unprofitable servant from whose shoulders a burden was being lifted which his decaying body could no longer bear. This was resignation in more senses than one, and one might almost use the same term of his attitude to the whole problem of a war on several fronts. As a military technician, he accepted this task without ever questioning its necessity or propriety, nor did he feel called upon to point out to the civil authorities the dangers inherent in such a conflict. The fact is that, though from time to time he formed views on such matters as the need for a preventive war, he held to the principle that as a soldier the discussion of political issues lay outside his province. In this he differed markedly from Schlichting. For instance, he never ceased to represent Germany's encirclement as an accomplished fact to be accepted with such stoicism as one could muster, while Schlichting suggested that instead of talking everlastingly about encirclement, Germany might set diplomacy to work to do something about it. As to Germany's geographical position, which kept the Schlieffenites in a constant pathological obsession of impending strangulation, he maintained that this might actually be a source of strength; all that was necessary was a sensible policy in Central Europe. He also held that England might become the most powerful of Germany's enemies, and asked what point there was in gratuitously provoking her. But if such ideas ever occurred to Schlieffen, he did not think it was within his competence to utter them.

This was of course the attitude of the military technician pure and simple. The fearful thing was that there was no longer any leadership in external policy by which the military technician could be directed. Schlieffen was the first and perhaps the greatest of the military technicians in that declining Prussia, and his most characteristic setting is that great map room of the General Staff where in the early hours of almost any morning, even before his customary ride in the Tiergarten, he could be found at work. Later, when nobody would any longer listen to him, an air of tragedy began to surround this ageing figure. We have seen how he searched the pages of history in the desperate hope of persuading himself and the world that he might after all have discovered the saving formula, the formula that would ensure victory over all opponents. He ended by pursuing that search with terror in his heart for the sinking fortunes of his country and for the dynasty which he and his ancestors had so faithfully served.

In 1909, the year in which Schlichting died forgotten and at variance with the world he could no longer understand, Schlieffen attempted in the *Deutsche Revue*, which at that time had a wide circle of readers, to draw a picture of modern war as he saw it. He wrote of a Germany ringed by a Chinese wall. The French fortresses barred the line from the Ardennes to the Jura, while the Belgian fortress triangle Antwerp-Liège-Namur barred the ancient passage through the Sambre and Meuse country. In the east was the threat of the Russian fortress system surrounded by rivers and marshes. England was a fortress in itself, surrounded by water. Denmark had built Copenhagen into a huge *place d'armes*. Italy had strengthened against Austria her fortifications on the borders of Istria and Southern Tirol. If ever the drawbridges of all these fortresses were to be let down, then armies of millions would stream into the heart of Central Europe—a nightmare! The only hope of peace lay in the closer economic integration of the powers in question and in the fact that the various dynasties all feared revolution. The essential thought, however, was that the enemy coalition was prepared—though, as a matter of fact, it was nothing of the kind.

There was, according to the author, only one thing that could produce a favourable decision for Germany; that was a correct deployment of her forces. Schlieffen rightly foresaw that the increased effectiveness of weapons and the consequent importance of cover would empty the surface of the battlefield. He drew a correct picture of the modern commander sitting in his office far behind the front and pouring over his maps while telegraph and telephone, supplemented by Staff officers in cars and on motor bicycles, kept him in touch with the battling masses. He foresaw the potentialities of aerial observation by plane and captive balloon. In all these matters he proved himself an accurate prophet, yet his thought continued to be vitiated by the persistent conviction that sheer economic necessity would cause the war to be short, and that a single giant battle would decide its issue.

Even as late as 1912 he was still busy with his theoretical planning, and in that year—he had come to recognize the growth of the offensive spirit in France—he began to develop the idea of attacking along the whole front all the way from Belgium to Switzerland. But even in the hour of death, the great plan continued in his thoughts. His last words were: "See you make the right wing strong."

CHAPTER VII

WAR WITHOUT GENERALS

I

THE face of Europe was darkening—Franco-German relations had been strained by the Moroccan crisis and the first Russian revolution was already history—when, on January 1st, 1906, the younger Moltke somewhat diffidently assumed the office in which his uncle had served with such distinction. Moltke, who was born in 1848, had served as his uncle's adjutant from 1882, and had received under the new Emperor the command of various Guards regiments. It was a time in which a dashing military appearance still counted for something, and Moltke, in addition to that, had charming manners. It was not long before he was in high favour with the Emperor, who sent him as his personal representative to the coronation of Nicholas II of Russia and to that of Alfonso XIII of Spain.

To some extent Moltke's social graces caused him to have preferment thrust upon him. The Crown Prince once compared him to Benedek, and, as we have seen, there was point in the remark. Schlieffen had taught that generals are born and not made, and Moltke did not feel that he was a general born. Moreover, as so often happens with those who inherit a great name, Moltke found this distinction something of a burden. This is not very surprising, for he was by temperament diffident. He was exceptionally well read and had a wide range of literary interests, Goethe's *Faust* being his inseparable companion on all Staff journeys. His intellectual interests were further enlivened by his marriage to a distant relative, a woman of considerable mental attainments but possessed of an appetite for somewhat exotic types of religion. The couple displayed a curious interest in mesmerism, and at one time took up Christian Science. Rather significantly, Moltke was a ludicrously bad rider. On Staff rides and at steeplechases he took too many tosses for the matter not to arouse comment.

For so intellectual a type his views were marked by an astonishing simplicity. He was hag-ridden by the fear of revolution, but this made him cling all the more firmly to the belief that in Germany the Prussian Army and the Prussian officer corps were a kind of spiritual citadel and the guardian of an order that was sacrosanct. He accepted the hostility of France and Russia as an unalterable fact, and his judgments on England seem to have got no further than artless *clichés* about perfidious Albion, shopkeepers' hypocrisy and the alleged backstairs intrigues of Edward VII.

His political philosophy was equally ingenuous. He held that the diplomat's function was not to avoid wars but to ensure that the country which he served was placed as advantageously as possible when the inevitable war broke out. For all that, he looked upon that coming war with horror, and in his darker moments began to despair of any possibility of victory. Believing, as he did, that his own abilities were sufficient for peacetime requirements but incapable of doing justice to more arduous demands, he actually drew some comfort from the Emperor's frequent declarations that in the event of war he would himself assume command in the west.

Nevertheless, he absorbed himself in his work—largely to escape from a world that seemed with every year to grow more tawdry. His main concern was the yearly manoeuvres, and here he proved as good as his word and tried honestly to make conditions approximate to those of actual war. The pretty pictures, with their charges of brightly uniformed cavalry, to which the Emperor had such loving addiction, should, he urged, disappear—and disappear they did.

Meanwhile an air of even greater reserve than that of Schlieffen's day began to surround the Red House on the Königsplatz. An attempt was made—unsuccessfully, it is true—to impose a censorship by the General Staff on all publications of a military nature, even on the memoirs of leading military men—surely not a sign of strength. Increasingly careful note was also now taken of developments in the armies of Germany's neighbours, and in the main the picture so obtained was accurate. Thanks to the reforms of General Suchomlinoff, the Russian Army was recovering with surprising speed from the defeat and revolution of 1905 and was becoming once more a respectable military instrument. The same, since Haldane's reforms, applied to the British Army, which was now equipped with a properly organized expeditionary force consisting of six infantry and one cavalry division. All this was, of course, taken into account, but the warlike potential of the British Empire as a whole and the military capacities of Canada, Australia and New Zealand were underestimated. A particularly bad mistake was the assumption that the danger of unrest in India would exclude the possibility of employing Indian troops.

The first decade of the twentieth century saw considerable strides made in the perfection of mechanical weapons. The French introduced their celebrated 75 mm. recoiling field gun, equipped with an armoured shield. The German artillery developed more or less along French lines, but the ballistic superiority of the French seventy-five remained undisputed right up to 1914. All armies now began to establish cyclist and motor transport units, to develop further the potentialities of telephone, telegraph and helio, and to experiment with airships and aeroplanes. German military aviation had been endeavouring to turn Count Zeppelin's airship to military use, but once Bleriot had flown the Channel in 1909, Moltke realized that planes had far greater possibilities than airships.

Actually the Chief of the General Staff had very little to say in these matters, since questions of armament were decided by the War Ministry, which was a stronghold of conservatism. That conservatism produced the effects that might have been expected. Whereas the French General Staff did all it could to exploit new inventions for military purposes—France was the first to establish military aviation units, and the French motor industry the first to produce an armoured car—Berlin delayed and hesitated. When three experimental types of armoured cars equipped with machine guns appeared at the manoeuvres of 1908, nobody had the least idea of what to do with them. No better fortune attended Lieutenant-Colonel Burstyn of the Austrian railway troops, who in 1911 offered the Prussian War Ministry the plans of an armoured machine-gun-carrying vehicle equipped with caterpillar treads, a genuine prototype of the tank. The idea was not even found worth carrying to the experimental stage.

What part this lack of vision played in determining events must remain a matter of speculation, but there is another department where the relation of cause and effect is much more palpable. The increase in Franco-Russian offensive power caused Moltke to subject his predecessor's plans to special re-examination, and it was typical of his methods that on this occasion he only drew into consultation von Stein, who was *Oberquartiermeister I*—the other *Oberquartiermeisters* were not consulted, the reason apparently being Moltke's fear of leaks.

It was in this atmosphere of almost conspiratorial secrecy that Moltke reached his vital decision. Conrad von Hötzendorf, the head of the Austrian General Staff, was in those days trying desperately to get approval for a big attack in the east, but Moltke had Napoleon's fate before his eyes and still remained bedevilled by the notion of a quick victory in the west. Unlike Schlieffen, however, he did not wish to stake everything on a single card, and therefore took the view that Alsace and the Upper Rhine should not remain without adequate cover. There were, of course, certain reasons for this. There was an undeniable danger of a powerful French army striking into Southern Germany, and so operating against the flank that was invading Belgium. There was also the Saar coal, about which specialists on the Staff, like Groener in the railway section, were distinctly nervous. These considerations brought it about that the Schlieffen plan was drastically modified, the weight of the German right wing being cut down to a point where it was insufficient for its purpose. It was a fateful step, but having taken it, Moltke held fast to his modified "western" solution, and plans for an attack on the east ceased to be given further consideration.

II

International tension continued to increase. In 1908 Austria occupied Bosnia and Herzegovina. Internally there were two crises— that of the Eulenburg scandals, which revealed the presence of homosexuality in high court circles (these revelations badly shook the Emperor's inflated self-esteem) and that of the *Daily Telegraph* letter. From the effects of this last the Emperor was never to recover, for the uproar it caused in press and parliament showed him that he no longer possessed the confidence of the broad mass of the people. From that year must be dated his decision that in the event of war the real responsibility for its conduct would not be vested in himself but in his so-called amanuensis, the Chief of the General Staff. It was another step in a centrifugal process that was once more reasserting itself, for, just as before the catastrophe of 1806, the different authorities that would be responsible for the conduct of war were beginning to fall apart. Hülsen-Haeseler, the head of the Military Cabinet, had died of a stroke while dancing before the Emperor in the costume of a ballerina. Under his successor, von Lyncker, this Cabinet sank to the level of a mere adjunct of the court, while the Ministry had long been concerned with little more than administrative questions, and with the problem of getting the Army estimates through the Reichstag. The Army's supreme planning centre, the

General Staff, continued to be surrounded with an aura of legend and to count for the public as the symbol of all the virtues of the old Army. In reality it was becoming dangerously isolated, while its Chief was being plagued by ever darker misgivings.

In 1911 came the Agadir affair. In Moltke's eyes the despatch of the "Panther" had most refreshingly served to clarify the situation, and he was all for the continuance of a bold forward policy, failing which he threatened to resign. Thus tempers shortened as the picture of coming events grew clearer.

As late as 1910 the General Staff had made the landing of an expeditionary force of 100,000 men by Britain at the Jutish port of Esbjerg the subject of a war game. It was now realized that the idea of a possible British invasion through Denmark had been abandoned, and that the British Expeditionary Force, if it turned up at all, would do so in Belgium or Northern France. Meanwhile, France was straining every nerve to increase her military efforts. The three-year service period was introduced, the 1912 and 1913 classes being called up together. Military expenditure per head of the population in France was more than three to two, compared with that of Germany. In the years that followed leading military personalities in France and Russia regularly visited each other's manoeuvres. In France there were some noteworthy military publications. In his *Nos Frontières de l'Est et du Nord* General Maitrot warned his countrymen of the impending thrust through Belgium, while General Malleterre pointed anxiously to the Ardennes gap. In Germany the atmosphere was further charged by the arrest of large numbers of spies, while in Austria Colonel Redl, Chief of Staff of the Prague army corps, was found to have betrayed the Austrian deployment plans to the Russian secret service.

The Balkan wars of 1912 and 1913 were another stage on the road, and raised anew the apparently insoluble question of the 100 per cent application of the universal service laws. Between 1905 and 1911 only the machine-gun detachments, the engineers, the heavy artillery and the transport and airship formations had had actual increases. In 1906 the infantry had had new training regulations which took account of experiences gained in the Boer and Russo-Japanese wars, experience which led in 1910 to the introduction of the field grey uniform. All these measures, however, did not touch the heart of the military problem, which was that every year the insufficiency of training facilities prevented tens of thousands of useful recruits from joining the colours, while France was calling up the last man.

III

In that same year of Agadir, 1911, Moltke's health gave way through a chronic infection of the tonsils. He was compelled to take sick leave, and there was considerable talk of his retirement. It was at this stage that a man began to make himself noticed who had hitherto done his work in comparative obscurity. This was Lieutenant-Colonel Ludendorff, head of No. 2 Department (the "German Department"), which contained the deployment section. As has already been said, Ludendorff was the great advocate of war in its so-called "true form". Professing to complete Clausewitz, but in reality contradicting him, he evolved the theory according to which war was not an instrument of policy. On the contrary, politics were, according to this theory, a part of warfare. The life of nations being thus viewed as essentially a biological struggle, it was logical enough in a way that Ludendorff should follow the French example and concentrate, almost to the point of idolatry, on the factor of numbers. Schlieffen had sought to offset Germany's numerical inferiority by increased mobility and elasticity. Ludendorff was for more direct and even brutal measures. His aim was to throw into the scales the whole physical potential of the German nation; and, as we have already seen, there was certainly a case for making that physical potential more effective. As things were, Germany's figure of annual births far exceeded that of France, yet whereas France called 82% of all those fit for service to the colours, the German figure was a mere 52%. In 1912, no less than 540,000 of those nominally liable for service never underwent training at all. It was here that Ludendorff believed himself able definitely to change the face of things—despite the fact that in such a matter the General Staff could only make its influence felt indirectly.

To achieve his ends Ludendorff put his demands through the mouth of Moltke, for in this matter Moltke gave him his most complete confidence. Indeed the somewhat unusual situation may be said to have arisen in which Ludendorff was operating as a sort of secret Chief of Staff himself, the remainder of the hierarchy of *Oberquartiermeisters* being short-circuited. Even so, these matters were, strictly speaking, concerns not of the General Staff but of the War Ministry, for they were primarily a matter of money. Ludendorff therefore decided to follow in Waldersee's footsteps and work on public opinion.

For this purpose he made use of Keim, now a retired general, who had relations with Class and his Pan-Germans, and who had already proved his usefulness in this connection under the Waldersee régime. The nature of this link between the General Staff and the Pan-German movement is worth careful notice. It did not come into being because the General Staff shared all the expansionist notions of the Pan-German League, but because Ludendorff took his tools wherever he happened to find them. We shall return to this subject later.

In 1912, Keim succeeded in calling into life the *Wehrverein*, or Union of Defence, to which Class and various personalities from heavy industry who had sponsored the Pan-German movement acted as godfathers. A number of personages prominent in the business and intellectual life of Germany also signed the initial appeal, and in this same year of 1912 the establishment of two new army corps was actually authorized, as well as increases in heavy and field artillery and aviation troops. The total increase in the Army amounted to 117,000 men, the costs being covered by the *Wehrbeitrag*, a special contribution which raised a thousand million marks. Ludendorff was not satisfied. He pressed for three new corps for 1913/14—an importunity which elicited from General Wandel, the director of the General War Department of the War Ministry, the observation that Ludendorff would end by driving Germany to revolution.

This was really a very illuminating remark. It shows that the legendary omnipotence of the General Staff, which has been so much talked about, existed chiefly in the imagination of its enemies. Actually, the War Minister, General von Heeringen, was opposed to an overhasty increase in the establishment, since he feared a lowering of the standard of training, and there was heavy opposition in the Reichstag. Even on the General Staff itself there was some opposition—on the part of those who would have the unpalatable task of presenting Ludendorff's financial demands to the authorities concerned. This general hostility had very concrete results. It was the custom in the General Staff that the head of the deployment section should in wartime become Chief of Operations, and so principal adviser to the Chief of Staff. This had been Ludendorff's great dream, but in January, 1913, he was removed from his post as "inconvenient", and sent to command a regiment in Düsseldorf. The increase in Army establishments was slowed down. There was an increase of 65,000 in 1913, but the setting up of the three new corps was not scheduled to take effect till between 1916 and 1921.

One is struck in this whole episode by a most curious division of counsel, which to some extent had its counterpart in that strange lack of co-ordination, which we have described, between authorities whom the prospect of an impending war should certainly have united. Army and Admiralty worked in the strictest separation from one another when formulating their requirements—and in other matters, too, for the Navy would not even accede to the General Staff's request for an exchange of intelligence reports. It may be presumed that by now the Chancellor had been apprised of the general intention to march through Belgium, but he appears to have sought no further exchange of ideas with Moltke on this vital matter. There was a corresponding lack of co-ordination between the staffs of the Dual and Triple Alliance, and here relations were definitely clouded by mistrust. Since the Bosnian crisis of 1908, the Austrian Chief of Staff had been in possession of a general assurance that after the decision in the west, say, about the thirty-fifth or fortieth day after mobilization, it would be possible to send German reinforcements to the east. Moltke however, refused to commit himself to any definite date. In Rome, the Chief of Staff, General Pollio, was accounted a firm supporter of the alliance with Germany. The King, however, was a vigorous opponent of the Habsburgs, and in any case the notion of taking part in a war in which England took sides with the French was for Italy a military absurdity. In March, 1914, a military mission spent some time in Berlin to discuss details of the transport of Italian troops over the Alps. It was, however, already clearly understood that these arrangements would only come into force if France was the only enemy in the west and the German Empire palpably the victim of aggression.

IV

On June 28th, 1914, Serbian fanatics murdered the heir to the Austrian throne, together with his wife. The Foreign Office seems to have recognized the dangerous potentialities of the situation, and at first both in Berlin and Vienna joined a warning against precipitate action to its expressions of sympathy. Unfortunately it was possible for Berchtold, the Austrian Foreign 'Minister, to get his Imperial master to send a special envoy to the Emperor in Berlin and to secure from the latter a promise of more or less unqualified support for anything Austria saw fit to do. Whether the Emperor realized the perilous nature of this undertaking, or whether, realizing it with one part of his mind, he sought to suppress that knowledge with the other, is a psychological mystery which will never be solved. All we know is that outwardly he acted as though there were no serious danger of a general war, and that it was in that tone that he spoke to the heads of his fighting services. He had an extremely hurried interview with Falkenhayn, his War Minister, who in reporting it to Moltke observed that he had not gained the impression of any warlike developments being imminent, but merely of energetic political action, and that he saw no reason for Moltke to curtail his vacation. Thereupon he himself went off to the seaside, while the Emperor went to continue his cruise in the North Sea.

Meanwhile there began in Vienna the preparation of the disastrous ultimatum to Serbia, an ultimatum which involved demands wholly incompatible with her existence as a sovereign State. The whole business was carried on in an atmosphere of intense secrecy, though the German Foreign Office was apprised in a general way of what was afoot, for the President of the French Republic, Poincaré, was paying an official visit to St. Petersburg and it was considered inadvisable to present the ultimatum while he was still in Russia.

Despite all precautions, however, some news leaked out to all the capitals of Europe. Thus, on July 16th, the English Ambassador in Vienna telegraphed to Sir Edward Grey that "A kind of indictment is being prepared against the Serbian Government for alleged complicity in the conspiracy which led to assassination of the Archduke," that the "Austro-Hungarian government will insist on immediate unconditional compliance, failing which force will be used," while Bunsen, the British Ambassador in Berlin, was confidentially informed by Count Lützow, German ex-Ambassador to Rome, that "Austria was determined to have her way this time and refused to be put off by anybody." Needless to say, these reports reached Poincaré in St. Petersburg, and the latter took occasion, somewhat improperly, at a reception to give a sharp warning to the Austrian Ambassador that France would stand by her friends, a sentiment which he also uttered with considerable emphasis at a banquet at the Peterhof.

On the morning of July 24th, just after Poincaré had begun his return journey to France, the Austrian ambassadors in all capitals informed the various governments of the ultimatum which had been delivered at Belgrade on the previous evening. The effect in St. Petersburg was immediate. Sentiment for giving support to Serbia was extremely strong, and the general feeling was that Russia could not stand aside and passively witness her destruction. The first plan of Sazonov, the Russian Foreign Minister, was a partial mobilization directed against Austria which, it was hoped, would deter Austria from taking irrevocable action. This plan was shelved on account of the technical difficulties involved, but on the following day an Imperial Council, at which the Czar presided, decided to proclaim what was known as a "period preparatory to war". This involved the calling up of reservists, the making of frontier posts ready for mobilization, the cancellation of leave, etc. This was not so drastic a measure even as partial mobilization, but it had the disadvantage of being directed against Germany quite as much as against Austria, and though an attack on Austria would have brought Germany into the war, the new Russian measure at least involved the theoretical possibility that hostilities might open with an attack on Germany herself.

Germany, placed as she was in the unenviable position of a man between two stools, had for some time begun to grow conscious of her peril. After its initial caution, the mood of the Foreign Office had changed somewhat, largely, no doubt, thanks to the Emperor's attitude, and sympathy had been growing for the Austrian point of view. This was natural enough. Austria was now Germany's only dependable ally, and a loss of prestige which might result if Austria remained passive to the Sarajevo conspiracy (in which there is strong reason to believe that certain members of the Serbian government were involved) might well have brought about the disintegration of the Austrian Empire. At the same time the German Foreign Office had no interest whatever in producing an international conflagration, and naturally wished to be kept informed of every step that the Austrian government took.

During the first part of July this wish was loyally complied with. Then, from mid-July onward, Berchtold became increasingly secretive. Even the text of the ultimatum to Serbia was not shown to Germany till two days before the handing over of the note, and then only at the insistence of the German Foreign Minister, von Jagow, backed, it may be added, by that of the Austrian Ambassador himself. The reason for this change of front was, of course, that on July 14th Count Tisza, the Hungarian Prime Minister, who had hitherto been opposed to war with Serbia, allowed himself to be brought into line. From then onwards Berchtold took the bit between his teeth.

When the ultimatum had been delivered, and answered on the part of Russia by the military measures described above, Germany's position became critical, and it was at this point that the determining technical factor came into play. Germany's great military asset against Russia was the relative speed of her mobilization. If, under cover of her "period preparatory to war", Russia was secretly mobilizing, her one great military advantage would be lost to Germany.

Realizing the growing peril to his country, the Emperor threw himself with almost desperate energy into the rôle of mediator, sending urgent appeals to the Czar to help in avoiding a calamity. By this time, however, despite Serbian compliance to a quite astonishing degree with the Austrian demands, Austria had already declared war, and though the Czar replied in a friendly and conciliatory spirit, his words held out little hope. "An ignoble war," he wrote, "has been declared on a weak country. The indignation in Russia, shared fully by me, is enormous. I foresee that very soon I shall be overwhelmed by the pressure to which I am exposed and compelled to take measures which will lead to war."

Such was the attitude of the rulers. Moltke, however, made increasingly anxious by the preparations inside Russia, felt that the time for parleying was past, and that the problem by which Germany was faced was no longer political but military. He feared in particular that Austria's delay in mobilizing would mean that the task of countering a Russian attack would fall wholly on Germany. On the afternoon of the 30th, when reports of a Russian mobilization were already trickling through, he spoke with the Austrian military attaché, Bienerth, urging that the mediation attempts by Sir Edward Grey (which Moltke was convinced would be unsuccessful) be ignored and that Austria should mobilize against Russia immediately. Moltke, whose attitude up to this date seems to have been scrupulously correct, has been criticized for this action, and technically such interference by the military in the sphere of policy was improper, but it cannot be said to have had any influence on events.

Actually Austria, which so far had only mobilized eight army corps, ordered general mobilization on the 31st, but by that time the die had already been cast, for on the 29th, as a result partly of a declaration by the German Ambassador that Germany would take counter-measures if Russia did not put a stop to her own preparations, and partly of the bombardment of Belgrade, the Czar had already signed the order for Russian general mobilization. There was, it is true, a slight delay in making that order effective, for while the instructions were actually going out from the central telegraph office, the Czar, as a result of a further conciliatory telegram from the German Emperor, commanded their cancellation; but persistent pressure brought to bear on the following day by Sazonov and the military, who now were all convinced that diplomacy had done its work and failed, caused the orders for general mobilization to go out again.

Meanwhile in Berlin the German Chancellor continued with an almost frenzied energy to work for peace, resisting with all his power the pressure of Moltke, who regarded war as inevitable and wanted military preparations to begin immediately, though even he seems to have been anxious to get yet further confirmation of the Russian mobilization. Telegram after telegram was sent to the German Ambassador in Vienna to try and put a restraining influence on Berchtold, though, as we have seen, reports of the impending Russian mobilization were already trickling through. Bethmann, however, refused to give up hope until he had certainty that the catastrophe could no longer be forestalled.

Early in the morning of the 31st Moltke was advised by telephone that the East Prussian frontier had been completely closed by the Russians and that notices of mobilization had been posted up. Moltke told his informant to procure one of these, as he could do nothing without positive evidence. Later in the morning, however, a telegram from Pourtales, the German Ambassador in St. Petersburg, gave the required confirmation. Hereupon "Threatening danger of war", which was the necessary preliminary to general mobilization, was proclaimed.

The question now arose whether Germany should send a formal declaration of war. Moltke and Falkenhayn were both opposed to this, believing as they did that Germany would thus brand herself as the aggressor, but Bethmann was anxious to adhere strictly to the Hague convention, and therefore instructed Pourtales to inform Sazonov of the German measures, and told him that mobilization must follow if Russia did not suspend every one of her own war measures, the time limit expiring at noon on August 1st.

At 5 o'clock on August 1st, Germany, having received no satisfactory reply from Russia, ordered general mobilization—a quarter of an hour after a similar step had been taken by France. Actually Germany was the last of the great Continental powers to mobilize. An hour later Pourtales called on Sazonov. Three times he asked the Russian Foreign Minister whether he could not give a favourable answer to the request the day before. Three times Sazonov answered in the negative. Thereupon Pourtales drew from his pocket a declaration of war which he handed to the Russian, and having done so went to the window, where he burst into tears. The First World War had begun.

The great plan had now to move forward. On the 31st Sir Edward Grey had addressed a note to the French and German governments asking for an undertaking to respect Belgian neutrality, but such an undertaking could obviously now no longer be given by Germany, and this failure swiftly ranged England on the side of Germany's enemies, a development which the General Staff had, of course, taken into account.

Before this occurred, however, there was a significant incident. As we have seen, the Emperor, on August 1st, ordered the mobilization of the Army and the Navy, and on this same afternoon Moltke attended a Crown Council at the Castle. When the meeting was over, he went to the General Staff building to issue the necessary orders. He was, however, recalled by the Emperor to learn that a despatch had come from Lichnowsky in London to the effect that England would be prepared to guarantee French neutrality against a German assurance that no hostile acts would be undertaken against France. In the presence of the Prussian War Minister, General von Falkenhayn, and of Bethmann-Hollweg, the Emperor blandly declared, "Well, now we'll simply march our whole army against Russia."

Moltke was horrified. The deployment of an army of millions was not a thing that could be improvised, such things took years to prepare. The Emperor remarked: "Your uncle would have given me a different answer." Moltke remarks aggrievedly in his memoirs that he had never claimed to be on the same level as the Field Marshal. At length he succeeded in persuading the Emperor that deployment would have to proceed as planned, though an assurance could be given to France about the absence of hostile intentions. Later troops could be diverted to the east. So a telegram was sent to London, declaring that for technical reasons the deployment could not be stopped and giving the requisite undertakings.

Late that night it transpired that Lichnowsky had been in error. There had never been any question of a British guarantee. "Now," said the Emperor, "you can do whatever you please." In his memoirs, Moltke, who, according to his own statement, had been in tears after the interview of the afternoon, states that he was never able to get over the effects of this experience. Something broke within him

which could never again be set right. It was while still under
the impact of that shattering experience that Moltke took the
field.

V

The German Field Army consisted in 1914 of two million men,
distributed among eight army commands. Behind these stood trained
and immediately available reserves which raised the figure to 3.8 million. There were available 18 airships, 33 aviation units and about
4,000 lorries and cars. Men actually liable for military service
totalled 12 million, of which 8.4 million could in extreme emergency
be called to the colours.

Of this Field Army, seven armies, comprising 1.6 million men, now
deployed between Krefeld and Basle. Five of these seven, under von
Kluck, von Bülow, von Hausen, the Duke of Württemberg and the
Crown Prince, prepared for the invasion of Belgium and Luxemburg.
Considerable cavalry forces were attached to them. On their southern
flank they joined on to the 6th and 7th Army commands under
Crown Prince Ruprecht of Bavaria and Colonel General von
Heeringen, the ex-Minister of War. The task of this latter force was
to pin down the enemy in Lorraine and hold the line of the Upper
Rhine, and for this purpose it was supplemented by some *Landwehr*
elements. One reserve corp remained in Schleswig-Holstein, as a safeguard against the bare possibility of a British landing and for the
protection of the Kiel Canal. Over against these armies were eche-
loned five French armies, stretching from the Ardennes to the Swiss
frontier, and numbering from north to south, 5, 3, 2 and 1. The
4th Army was drawn up in the rear of the 3rd, prepared for a thrust
into Belgium if necessary. In addition there were four territorial
divisions grouped round Lille, and the troops of the fortified area of
Greater Paris. There were further the five infantry divisions and one
cavalry division of the Belgian Army to be reckoned with, and the
six infantry divisions and one cavalry division of the British Expeditionary Force.

In the east the command of the 8th Army was taken over by
General von Prittwitz und Gaffron, while the main mass of the
Austrian Army took the offensive in Galicia, thus giving protection
both to the Silesian area and the Danube basin. The Russian deployment proceeded very much as the General Staff had foreseen. Two
very powerful armies, the 1st, or Niemen, Army under General

Rennenkampff, and the 2nd, or Naref, Army under General Samsonov, turned concentrically on East Prussia from east and south. Another army under General Ewerth was concentrating on the right bank of the Vistula in the Warsaw area, while three others under Generals Plehve, Russki and Ivanov faced Galicia. General Shilinski was supreme commander on the northern front, while the Grand Duke Nicholas Nicholaievitch, a master in the ruthless exploitation of his teeming human material, commanded in Poland.

Now, in the west, Schlieffen's *Bataillon carré*, whose task it was to wheel round on the pivot Metz-Diedenhofen in the direction of Brussels-Namur, was to have been seven times as strong as the covering flank in Alsace-Lorraine, but Moltke had reduced the relation between the offensive and defensive wings to one of three to one. The front of the operational wing was strong enough, but there were insufficient reserves for diversion to the siege of fortresses or for any special duty on the lines of communication, though the reserve corps in Schleswig-Holstein was to be thrown in on the western front as soon as it became plain that the British were definitely not going to land in Denmark. Meanwhile, Italy declared her neutrality, so that the Italian help on the Upper Rhine, on which Schlieffen had counted, did not materialize. France did not now even have to protect her frontier on the Alps.

Most serious of all was the fact that these seven armies, spread along a front of hundreds of miles, were such a large and unwieldy instrument that they needed a much more complex devolution in the hierarchy of command. The interpolation of army group commands between the supreme command and the armies themselves would have produced leadership that was both more flexible and more capable of quick and energetic adjustment to a given situation, and yet would have maintained sufficient detachment from the actual confusion of battle to concentrate uncompromisingly on the broad strategic idea. Instead of this, control of all operations was vested wholly in Headquarters, which followed the armies far too slowly and at far too great a distance.

This was not the only source of weakness. Officially the Chief of the General Staff was only the adviser of the Supreme War Lord, but now the sovereign himself felt that he was not equal to the task of commanding in the field. Unfortunately, his Chief of Staff felt himself even less qualified for this task than his master, though unlike the latter he could not evade its performance. Even physically he was no longer a sound man. The superbly trained German Army, which was now moving strictly according to plan against the Belgian frontier, thus resembled a huge and wonderful machine that was equipped with a defective mechanism of control. The battles by which the enemy forces in North-Western Europe were to be destroyed, were to be made up of a number of engagements, spreading over weeks, a circumstance which made it possible to engage in complex manoeuvring with large bodies of men, throwing them in at the exact place and time when their arrival would be most effective. It was a situation that the elder Moltke might well have dreamed about; but full advantage could only be drawn from it so long as the mind conducting operations continued to have a clear view of the picture as a whole, and the commanders of the various constituent forces kept the outline of the master plan clearly before their eyes. Neither of these conditions obtained.

In this matter Moltke measured up to requirements as little as did the successor of Ludendorff in the post of Chief of Operations. This last was Lieutenant-Colonel Tappen, an obstinate, slow-thinking man, singularly deficient in finesse. Further, of the various Army Chiefs of Staff only von Kluck's Chief of Staff, von Kuhl, was really imbued with the Schlieffen plan. In 1912 Schlieffen had already expressed the fear that owing to lack of operational experience among the higher commanders the whole operation might degenerate into a *wilde Jagd nach dem Pour le Mérite* (a wild hunt after decorations), and, with certain reservations, this may to some extent be said to have occurred. Finally, the General Staff does not seem to have recognized the necessity of giving the enveloping arm an adequate supply of cyclists, lorries and armoured cars so as to give it the maximum mobility. Much too great a strain was placed on horseflesh. The horses both of the French and the German cavalry were often exhausted before it ever came to any regular engagement.

VI

As Chief of the deployment section, Ludendorff had been working, as far back as 1908, on plans for a *coup de main* on the fortress of Liège. The whole invasion of Belgium depended on the assumption that this would succeed. After his removal from the General Staff, the intention had been that in the event of war he should go to Bülow as Chief of Staff of the 2nd Army. Chance had it that his immediate employment was as liaison officer with the commander of the six infantry brigades which were to carry out his own plans. The essence of these was that a body of troops was to worm its way in between the outer forts and penetrate to the heart of the city, and Ludendorff himself personally led this venture. The enemy was taken completely by surprise. There was no resistance, and eventually Ludendorff drove with his adjutant into the heart of Liège in a commandeered Belgian car and presented himself at the citadel, where some hundreds of very frightened Belgian troops surrendered to him in a body. The outer forts all fell within the next two days under the murderous fire of the German siege guns.

The speedy capture of Liège tore a huge hole in the Belgian defence system, and the field-grey flood spread all over Belgium. Some were surprised that at this stage General Headquarters did not move forward, but, out of consideration for the Emperor's person, remained in Coblenz, and there was some question whether Moltke's powers would stay the course. In the main, however, the war continued to progress successfully, and by August 20th had developed more or less according to Schlieffen's schedule. The German right wing had reached Brussels, and reports of victories followed one upon the other. Moreover, the Belgians had not succeeded in doing any noteworthy damage to their railway system, so that there was no difficulty in sending troops and supplies up the line.

On August 20th, Joffre, the French Commander, decided on what Schlieffen had always designated as "a most kindly act". He went over to the offensive with strong forces, though these did not represent all he had in hand, and he did so in the very area where his own encirclement was being attempted. Actually, he seemed, however, at the time to be running right into Germany's arms.

Between August 21st and 24th, the issue of the war lay with Army Commands 1, 2 and 3, which together had a superiority over the forces facing them of 100 battalions and 1,044 guns. The 1st and 2nd Armies under von Kluck and von Bülow were in point of fact both under the command of the latter, and on the 24th Bülow was able to report further success. Amongst other things, the British Expeditionary Force had been drawn into the general disaster. On the 25th, Tappen was declaring that "the whole affair" would be over in six weeks, and by the 27th it was obvious that the gate to the Seine basin and to Paris had been torn right open. With these in German hands, the armoured forts on France's eastern frontier would be worthless.

Unfortunately, Moltke had by this time wholly lost his grasp of the situation, which was made more complicated by the fact that the 6th and 7th Armies were now also engaged, and for a while nursed the belief that the campaign was really over. He decided to send six corps to the east, where East Prussia stood in danger of being swamped by the Russians.

Soon, however, he had occasion to grow more pessimistic, so much so that he decided to reduce the despatch of troops to the east from six corps to two, for, owing to the uncontrolled rush forward of individual bodies of troops and the lack of any adequate co-ordination of their efforts, the German offensive began to lose its cohesion. Tappen declared that all that was necessary for victory was to "go on hammering", but the advice was neither practicable nor effective. As we have seen, the right wing was already too weak, and Moltke had weakened it still more by withdrawing two corps to the eastern front; a further two and a half corps were used in masking the fortresses of Maubeuge and Antwerp. Moreover, the uninterrupted battles and marches of the past few days had made fearful demands on the troops, and eventually, towards the end of August, Bülow thought it advisable to stop extending his line. For this reason he ordered Kluck to change direction somewhat earlier than the plan had foreseen. Thus a common front would be formed which could drive down on the French and press them back in a south-easterly direction, away from Paris. Moltke got to know of certain differences of opinion between Bülow and Kluck, but, although already apprehensive, did not interfere. On the contrary, he approved Bülow's directives. Yet with that the whole idea of crossing the Seine west of Paris was simply abandoned, and the great fortress of Paris with all the troops that it contained was left to threaten the flank of Bülow's armies.

Moltke moved his headquarters to Luxemburg, but still refrained from intervening, his mind now being full of a kind of new Sedan. The 1st and 2nd Armies were to press forward to the Seine and the Oise, while the 4th, 5th, 6th and 7th Armies were to break through the French defences between Toul and Epinal, and so to grip the French right with a pair of pincers. The *"Extratour"*, a term which Groener somewhat deprecatingly applied in particular to the operations of the 6th Army, thus became the main operation and one fraught with enormous difficulties, since it meant breaking through the French lines at their strongest point. Something of Tappen's simple crudity seems to lie in this idea, for Tappen's confidence in the driving power of German infantry, after its well nigh superhuman achievement, was virtually unlimited.

Meanwhile, Joffre determined on a strategic retreat in the west in order to regroup his forces for a new attack, while General Galliéni, the military governor, put Paris in a state of defence. The French 6th Army was formed, and, under General Manoury, placed at his disposal. On September 3rd, when German outposts were within 18 kilometres of Paris, Galliéni saw the chance of striking at the flank of the 1st Germany Army, which was crossing the Marne facing south. After a stiff tussle, Joffre agreed. The critical hour had come.

Already, on August 29th, Moltke had written to his wife that nobody at Headquarters appreciated the seriousness of the position, and that the Emperor was going around in a sort of "Hip hip hooray" mood that was an abomination to him. On September 4th, Helfferich, the State Secretary for the Interior, heard him say: "Don't let's deceive ourselves. We've had a few successes, but we haven't won the war. Winning the war means destroying the enemy's power of resistance. When armies of millions stand facing one another, the victor has prisoners. Where are our prisoners?"

On the 5th, Gronau, with the 4th Reserve Corps, struck right into Manoury's flank attack, and in a series of heavy engagements slowed down the development of that manoeuvre. On that same day, Moltke sent Lieutenant-Colonel Hentsch, head of the General Staff's Intelligence section, as his confidential representative to the 1st and 2nd Armies to report on the position. Some regrouping was palpably necessary, since Kluck had had to draw heavily on the forces on his left in order to meet the French thrust and a gap had thus opened up between the two armies, the 2nd Army having moved too far over to the left, and this gap was only covered by a thin screen of cavalry.

Something drastic had obviously to be done, but Moltke was suffering from nervous exhaustion. Bülow was also in bad shape and showing signs of strain. On the 7th, Moltke had a message from Hentsch telling him that both armies were being heavily pressed and had for the time being been driven on to the defensive. Joffre's counter-stroke was developing and might, in conjunction with a boldly conceived operation of Galliéni's from Paris, develop into a pincers movement. Meanwhile, the German attack on France's fortified line in the east had come to a standstill and, despite desperate efforts, could make no further progress.

On the 8th, Tappen declared at Headquarters that the Army would simply have to fight the thing out, thus abandoning all his strategic responsibility. Moltke did much the same. He sent out Hentsch a second time, but without clear instructions, while British forces slowly thrust their way into the gap between the two armies. If absolutely necessary, Hentsch was to cause the 1st Army to retreat to the line Soissons-Fismes, in order to regain contact with the 2nd Army.

Hentsch drove to see Kluck. In the main, the battle was progressing favourably, and the French were themselves being threatened with an encircling movement. Kluck declined to take a serious view of the gap between himself and Bülow, since the British progress there was extremely slow. The 2nd Army, however, was in a much more pessimistic mood, and Hentsch, who was no optimist, gave Bülow (who was himself afraid that he could not hold out) a very discouraging picture of the 1st Army's position. On the 9th, Bülow decided to order a general retreat and sent appropriate instructions to Kluck. Hentsch's part in this business is obscure. He certainly was not an encouraging influence. Though Kluck and his Chief of Staff, von Kuhl, took a very different view to that of Bülow, Hentsch undoubtedly declared himself in favour of retreat.

This was, or should have been, Kluck's great moment. Galliéni had on that day, as we now know, thrown in his last reserve, an Algerian division which he rushed off in commandeered taxicabs and 'buses. One asks what would have happened if Kluck had ignored the authority which Hentsch seems to have assumed, carried Bülow along with him and continued the fight. It was what Seydlitz did at Zorndorf, but this kind of thing was not in the mode of the era of William II. So far from acting in the Seydlitz tradition, Kluck seems to have allowed von Kuhl simply to accept Hentsch's orders—and verbal ones, at that. Kluck on this occasion does not seem even to have seen Hentsch personally at all. However that may be (the facts, let us remember, are uncertain), Kluck, against his better judgment, retreated at the very moment when the French generals were themselves considering when their own retreat would become imperative, and nobody was more astounded at the German withdrawal than Joffre, Galliéni and Manoury.

Moltke, without troubling to obtain Imperial consent, now ordered the retreat of the 3rd, 4th and 5th Armies. In Varennes, the Crown Prince saw a broken man who told him with tears in his eyes that the whole Army had been beaten and was flooding back, and that no one knew where the business would end. Yet at this moment the Army, though under severe strain, was still full of fight and was completely unable to understand why it had been ordered to abandon the offensive.

VII

The time was now approaching for Moltke to be cast into that outer darkness which was the portion of all the Emperor's favourites from Waldersee to Eulenburg. On September 14th, General von Lyncker conveyed to him that His Majesty believed him to be too ill to go on directing operations and that provision had been made to appoint the Minister of War, von Falkenhayn, as his successor. Strangely enough, Moltke clung to the post which he had been so unwilling to accept. Together with Falkenhayn, he went to the Emperor and pointed out that a bad impression would be created if the Chief of the General Staff was dismissed immediately after a retreat. The Emperor replied that if that were so, Falkenhayn had better be Quartermaster-General but take the actual business of Chief of Staff into his hands. Falkenhayn protested that he could only conduct operations if he had absolute freedom of action. This was agreed to by Moltke, who later declared the ensuing weeks to have been a martyrdom. Having lost all influence, he at last succeeded in persuading the Emperor to let him go and assist General von Beseler at the siege of Antwerp. In October his health broke down again, and he asked to be relieved. By the end of the year, however, he had recovered and was given the post of Deputy Chief of Staff at home. So ended the career of yet another in the long list of imperial favourites.

Erich von Falkenhayn was fifty-three years old when he took over Moltke's post. He came from an old officer family, had been educated at the cadet school, served as a military instructor in China, as a Staff officer on the Far Eastern Expeditionary Corps, and on the General Staff. Finally, in 1913, he was made Minister of War. He now continued to hold that position; this was the first occasion on which the offices of Chief of Staff and Minister of War were united in the same person. Falkenhayn was a palpably different man from Moltke, less highly educated, perhaps, but a man endowed with great clarity and energy of mind. His defence of the Army against the press in the Zabern affair had brought his name before the public; for many people he represented the "strong man" they were hoping for.

For Falkenhayn, as for so many others, the Great Plan had been the last word in military thinking, and his first idea on taking office as Quartermaster-General had been to put something like the Schlieffen Plan once more into effect between Cambrai and Verdun, but this might have involved temporarily yielding some ground else-where, and Tappen would not agree to the yielding of an inch. Also, the attacking armies were running short of munitions and reserves. Falkenhayn was thus forced to abandon his proposed offensive, and for the time being to take up an entrenched position on the line Noyon-Rheims-Verdun. Positional warfare, which Schlieffen had so dreaded and which Bernhardi and other military writers had pre-dicted, now made its appearance. Germany was a beleagured fortress.

The lightning-like decision which was to bring a victorious end to the whole war was, according to Schlieffen, to have fallen in the west, and German professional soldiers still kept their eyes fixed on the mighty struggle between the Scheldt and the Vosges. Nevertheless, Fate had ordained that it was to be in the east that that perfect Cannae of which Schlieffen had dreamed was to be realized.

Prittwitz's 8th Army, which, as we have already seen, had been detailed for the defence of East Prussia, comprised four army corps, one reserve and one cavalry division and some *Landwehr* elements. Against them, as we have also seen, were ranged the forces of Rennenkampff in the north, and Samsonov in the south. Conrad von Hötzendorf had begun his offensive in Galicia and was endeavouring to press with four armies over the Bug and the Vistula into Poland, but after a few encouraging initial successes this effort soon proved abortive. An Austrian offensive in Serbia had a similar fate. It was not long before von Hötzendorff was pressing for a diversionary offensive to be carried out from East Prussia. Moltke, already under terrible tension because of developments in the west, saw before him the dangerous possibility of Russia and Austria concluding a separate peace, the prospect being rendered all the more ominous by the fact that new army corps from Turkestan, Siberia and the Caucasus were known to be arriving in Eastern Poland, so that a huge force was gradually being assembled. An ill-advised advance by one of Pritt-witz's corps produced the reverse of Gumbinnen, and, now that the Austrians were faring badly in Galicia, the danger arose that the whole frontier from Lyck to Kattowitz might soon be lying open to Russian attack.

Moltke now thought of Ludendorff, whose prestige had increased so enormously through his victory at Liège. He summoned him on August 22nd and disclosed that he had a much bigger task in mind for him than the one he had already accomplished. He was to go east. Von Stein, the Quartermaster-General, sought to forestall a possible refusal by urging that "reasons of state" demanded his compliance.

Now Prittwitz and his Chief of Staff had been removed from their posts, but Ludendorff was only a major-general, and could therefore not aspire to be more than a Chief of Staff to a new commander. To fill this latter post, therefore, Moltke chose Paul von Beneckendorff und von Hindenburg, who had at one time commanded the 4th Army Corps, and was now, in his sixty-eighth year, living in retirement in Hanover. Moltke telegraphed, asking Hindenburg whether he would be ready to undertake an important task immediately; the old man replied laconically, "Am ready". Ludendorff travelled east via Hanover, and stepped into the train that was carrying his new commander to Marienburg. The two men had till then been strangers.

Writing his memoirs later in life, Hindenburg compared his relation with Ludendorff to that of a happy marriage, but these memoirs were written to serve a definite purpose. They were written to rekindle patriotism and above all to present an edifying picture to the youth of defeated Germany, and no inconsiderable arts of persuasion were necessary before the old gentleman would consent to these pleasing embellishments. In actual fact, the relations between the two men were rather different. Ludendorff held himself to be the inspired general, and was bitterly envious of the credit which Hindenburg received for their joint victories. Here was by no means that perfect military wedlock which had subsisted between Blücher and Gneisenau.

When, on August 23rd, Hindenburg and Ludendorff reached Marienburg, they found themselves faced by an enormous superiority of men and guns, with German forces retreating to the Vistula. Samsonov was threatening that retreat, but, as against this, Rennenkampff was exploiting his success at Gumbinnen with remarkable slowness. The two men came to an exceedingly bold decision. They withdrew all units facing Rennenkampff, leaving only a cavalry screen to conceal the movement, and threw all available forces into the protection of their threatened flank. Their aim was to envelop Samsonov, and having disposed of the Naref army, to use all their forces for an annihilating blow against Rennenkampff. The feasibility of the plan was enhanced by the fact that the chain of the Masurian lakes separated the two Russian armies. Despite this, both French and German critics have called Ludendorff a gambler for his decision on this occasion. He was certainly not that. Gambling was wholly alien to the operational methods of the General Staff, and it was in these that Ludendorff had been trained.

The first preliminary engagements took place on August 26th, and it was about this time that Rennenkampff took the decision to push on to Königsberg, while two new Russian armies assembled in Warsaw which were to strike at Berlin, but Rennenkampff was too slow, and Samsonov's fate was sealed between the 27th and 30th. The 13th Corps appeared in his rear and a diversionary effort ordered by Shilinski came too late. Samsonov shot himself when he realized the position was hopeless; thirteen generals, 92,000 men and 350 guns fell into German hands. Ludendorff gave the battle the name of Tannenberg, after the village behind the German lines where in 1410 King Jagiello of Poland and Grand Duke Witowt of Lithuania had inflicted such a crushing defeat on the German order.

Though the lustre of Tannenberg put even Sedan in the shade, it did no more than stabilize the north-eastern front, for it was, after all, no more than a local victory in a war that was being fought on several fronts at once. A particularly unhappy fact connected with it is that two corps (which neither Hindenburg nor Ludendorff had asked for, and which proved to be so sorely needed in the west) arrived too late to take part in the action. On September 9th, the west's day of destiny, the two generals were scoring another victory at the Masurian lakes, this time over Rennenkampff. In Galicia, however, the Austrian Army was collapsing. The ring of the multi-front war was closing around Germany.

VIII

Meanwhile, in the west, Falkenhayn was unwilling as yet to abandon the traditional strategy of envelopment. The German right was hanging in the air, so to speak, and the possibility still existed of resuming the initiative. The British Expeditionary Force could be cut off from its supply bases on the Channel; the enemy left could then be outflanked and his whole front rolled up. Thus, despite the successes in the east, and despite the fact that Russia with her latent unrest was the weakest of Germany's enemies, Falkenhayn's gaze remained fixed on the west.

Four reserve corps of war-volunteers were more or less ready for active service. They contained the flower of the educated youth of Germany, the main source from which new officers should have been drawn. These corps were formed into a new Army Command and thrown as fuel into the fire of a new offensive. In October these young, hastily-trained troops attacked across the Yser in the area Ostend-Menin-Ypres. The enemy made the maximum efforts to hold the deadly onslaught. Above all, the British fought, one might say, with their backs to the wall, and displayed the toughness characteristic of this race in such a situation. Further, that very thing occurred which the General Staff had believed impossible. Indian troops appeared in Northern France; troops also came pouring from their garrisons in other parts of the Empire, while Canada, Australia and New Zealand immediately organized formations of volunteers to aid the mother country in her need. Even so, the capture of Ypres, paid for by enormous losses, drew steadily nearer, but the Belgians had opened the sluice gates, so that a part of the battlefield was flooded, and at the beginning of November the last German offensive stagnated in a sea of blood and mud. An unknown volunteer was at that time fighting in one of the German regiments. His name was Adolf Hitler.

IX

The Chief of the General Staff now came to look upon himself as the Commandant of a huge beleaguered fortress. This meant that he would have to use his available forces with the utmost economy, since the duration of the siege could not be foreseen. It also meant that he must hold on to every inch of ground that he had occupied. In his memoirs he tells us that it was never his ambition to bask in the glory of some spectacular victory. His aim was to make possible the indefinite prolongation of the war, and at the same time to continue directing a series of effective but localized blows at each of his enemies in turn. He did not dream of surrendering, but he knew very well that there was a limit to his resources. Militarily speaking, his only hope was that his enemies would exhaust themselves by their attacks, or ultimately simply weary of the strain of the siege.

Thanks to the fact that War Ministry and General Staff were now united in Falkenhayn's person, the Supreme Command, whose headquarters had now been transferred to Charleville-Mézières, enjoyed enormous power. The Emperor was now confining himself to the part of a crowned observer, while the Chancellor in Berlin withdrew increasingly into the background. The Supreme Command had not consciously sought this eminence; it had been thrust upon it because all other traditional sources of authority had proved themselves too weak for the occasion.

Falkenhayn's new plenitude of power was, on the whole, as little disputed as was the new strategy of economy, though that does not mean that he was immune from criticism. This was led by none other than Moltke, who, as Deputy Chief of General Staff in Berlin, was making desperate efforts to make up for his own mistakes, the seriousness of which he now recognized. Moltke no longer believed in the possibility of a decision in the west, and saw hope only in the annihilation of the Russian Army, which would then be followed by a separate peace. Once that was accomplished, the neutrality of Italy and Rumania was, of course, assured.

This "Eastern Party" enjoyed the support of Hindenburg and Ludendorff, whose prestige had enormously increased since Tannenberg, and also of the Crown Prince and the Empress. Moltke pressed his case with vigour—he was one of those who took exception to Falkenhayn's dual function, and in this he was warmly supported by the Chancellor—and he attacked Falkenhayn's inelastic defence in the west, which was defending every yard of trench and spending rivers of blood for no adequate reason. He pressed for a defence policy that thought in terms of large areas. Falkenhayn, he wrote, was just "fiddling around", he had neither the courage nor the vision for great and vital decisions. In a letter to Hindenburg he referred to Falkenhayn as the man who was hurling both country and dynasty to ruin. If a separate peace could not be made with Russia, the war was lost.

Falkenhayn began to prick up his ears. He formally forbade the submission to himself of further memoranda by Moltke, and also tried to forbid that officer to express his views in public without permission of the General Staff. Moltke, however, was not deterred, and even began to cast his eyes further afield. Turkey had thrown in its lot with the Central European powers in the autumn of 1914, and in November the ageing Field-Marshal von der Goltz was sent to Constantinople as military assistant. To the "eastern solution" there was now added the "oriental solution". Goltz was planning an alliance with Rumania and Bulgaria to form part of a Balkan coalition against Russia and Serbia. He had also other projects in mind—an attack on the Suez Canal with combined Turkish and German forces, and an undertaking in Persia. Count Kanitz, the military attaché in Teheran, had been working on this last with the assistance of German agents and of the Swedish officers of the Persian *Gendarmerie* who were friendly to Germany. Events, however, were to show that there was no adequate diplomatic or military, and, above all, no financial basis, for Goltz's "Alexander campaigns", as they came to be called, and there was some justification for Falkenhayn's calling their author a visionary.

Taking one thing with another, the policy of making a maximum effort against the Russians would probably have offered Germany the best hope of escaping from the paralysing embrace of her enemies, and, what with the Austrian collapse and the consequent threat to the industrial centres of Silesia, circumstances actually compelled Falkenhayn to make some effort in that direction. In mid-September, he created the 9th Army out of reserve formations from the 8th. This was placed under the command of General von Mackensen, who had already distinguished himself at Tannenberg, Hindenburg and Ludendorff being given command of the whole eastern front. Beyond this Falkenhayn would not go. He made dozens of useless attacks in Flanders, but denied the eastern front any decisive accession of strength. The result was that, despite some very hard fighting and some spectacular successes, Hindenburg could do little more than fight his enemy to a standstill. He certainly was unable to destroy him.

X

In the winter of 1914/15, Falkenhayn was concerned to fill the gaps in the Army by creating new formations. Between eighteen and twenty fresh divisions were formed, and the establishment of infantry divisions was reduced from four regiments to three. Also, every battalion was now furnished with a machine-gun company. There were increases in artillery; new weapons, suitable to the requirements of trench warfare, such as trench mortars, began to be produced, and there were experiments with poison gas. Siege warfare made vast new demands on industrial and engineering potentials, so much so that the main business in the conduct of war was largely transferred to an altogether new sphere. It had to concern itself more and more with maintaining the productive powers of labour and its determination to keep up the struggle. In this connection there was a significant development. A raw materials department had been attached to the War Ministry in the autumn of 1914, and its direction was entrusted to Walter Rathenau, a Jew. Rathenau was the son and heir of the founder of the *Allgemeine Elektrizitätsgesellschaft*. He was a man who united the abilities of a great business leader with real qualities of philosophic wisdom. His appointment to the War Ministry, however, was nothing less than a silent revolution. It was followed by another. Despite the efforts made, the British blockade caused stoppages in the supply of munitions, and the shortage of Chilean nitrates threatened to become disastrous. Science came to Germany's aid, and it was Professor Haber, a Jewish scientist, who succeeded in deriving synthetic nitric acid from ammonia and so made possible the continuation of the war. Haber laid the foundation of the War Ministry's chemical department. It was the second great silent revolution.

While these preparations were being made at home, Hindenburg and Ludendorff were, for the winter, planning a grandiose pincers movement against the Russians; but the unfavourable distribution of forces between west and east would only permit a limited offensive which was launched in the Masurian region. This was, of course, wholly in keeping with Falkenhayn's policy of striking limited but effective local blows. By this strategy he hoped to paralyse Russia's offensive power and stabilize the eastern front, his aim being the creation of a strategic glacis, behind which Silesia, Hungary and Moravia would be secure.

Certainly some kind of drastic action was necessary. It was becoming more and more evident that Italy would soon be going off into the Allied camp, since Austria obstinately refused to pay the price of her neutrality, that price being the Italian Tirol. Falkenhayn vainly tried to influence Austria into adopting a more accommodating policy, but the aged Francis Joseph had had to hand over too many provinces in his long life. In the Balkans the outlook was equally unsatisfactory. Serbia barred the way to Turkey. The attitude of Bulgaria and Rumania depended largely on the way the fortunes of war were going in Russia. British warships were attempting to force the straits of Constantinople—they were to land troops at the Dardanelles later in 1915—and even Falkenhayn ultimately realized that the main theatre of war lay in the east.

At the beginning of 1915, at Falkenhayn's suggestion, Imperial Headquarters were transferred to the Prince of Pless' castle in Upper Silesia—the Prince had been a shooting companion of the Emperor's —and Falkenhayn began planning to roll up Russia's whole Carpathian front by breaking through at its hinge in the Gorlice-Tarnow area. For this purpose, a new 11th Army was created and placed under Mackensen. It consisted of three German and one Austrian corps, together with two German infantry and one Hungarian cavalry divisions. It received as Chief of Staff, Colonel Hans von Seeckt, whom Ludendorff considered one of the ablest among the younger Staff officers. Hindenburg and Ludendorff were to assist the break-through by an offensive in Courland and Lithuania. Before Ludendorff's eyes there arose the picture of a new Cannae with one of the enveloping arms striking through Northern Poland, but Falkenhayn withheld his consent to a manoeuvre carried out over so vast an area. His aim was to do no more than to make secure a front which would extend from Lithuania to Eastern Galicia.

Seeckt wrote of Mackensen's attack, which started on May 2nd, 1915, that before the war such break-throughs had been *verboten*; Mackensen, however, from a purely military point of view, was completely successful. He pushed forward to Przemysl and Lemberg, while, in the north, German divisions marched on Warsaw and Brest-Litovsk. Victory followed victory. The only trouble was that none of them brought a decision. Falkenhayn had hoped that the shattering of the Russian armies would give diplomacy the chance, by offering generous terms, to secure a separate peace. Seeckt even contemplated the possibility of the traditional friendship between the two countries being renewed. But though feelers were put out in Stockholm, nothing came of the matter. Germany lacked diplomats of the quality she had had in Bismarck's day. Apart from the weakening of the Russian armies and the capture of a number of fortresses, including Warsaw, the only visible gain from the offensive was that Bulgaria joined the Central Powers—a gain, as Ludendorff coldly calculated, of twelve strong divisions. As against this, Italy declared war on Austria and started attacking in Istria, and thus the scales remained even.

XI

From now on, the German armies were never granted a breathing space, nor did they anywhere achieve a decision. All that remained was the everlasting friction between the German and the Austrian Staffs, worry about dwindling reserves of manpower, food and materials, the pressure of the British blockade, and a strategy which had the same quality of desperation as that of the captain of a damaged ship who tries to maintain leeway and stop leaks in a heavy sea.

Meanwhile divided counsels continued. Ludendorff ceaselessly pressed for his great eastern offensive, which would liberate forces for a decisive battle in the west, Goltz, the "Romantic of war", defended his "oriental solution", Hötzendorf was for knocking Italy out of the war, while Falkenhayn feared the vast Russian spaces, thought a break-through in the west impossible and considered the Italian front unimportant. Characteristic of his strategy of economy was his successful effort against Serbia in the autumn, when with a combination of Austrian, Bulgarian and German forces he reduced her military effectiveness to zero, thus opening the road to Turkey for German reinforcements. Even so, Falkenhayn was quite unable to say when the storm in which the ship of state was labouring would end, or what course should be charted to bring it safely to harbour.

Seeckt analysed the situation as follows. Germany at the beginning of the war had had the aim of destroying the military forces of her three western opponents. This aim it had been at the time within her power to realize. At any rate, there had been a reasonable prospect of her doing so. After that she had sought to destroy the fighting forces of Russia. In this, too, she had failed because of the faulty distribution of her troops and her failure to exploit her initial successes. From that point onward, Germany's forces had been insufficient for a strategy of annihilation. Apart from the new chemical weapons, the one hope for 1915 was that of using the submarine to break England at her own game of economic warfare.

Now, it was true enough that while the war for the Central Powers was mainly a question of raw materials, it was largely one of sea communications for Britain. What was doubtful was whether Germany's naval power and the productivity of her shipyards would suffice for carrying on submarine warfare in a big way. The Emperor had built a strong battle fleet but not a submarine fleet, and few submarines were available at the time. Tirpitz vainly sought permission to bring his High Seas fleet into battle. It was forced to remain idle in port—except for the indecisive engagement off Jutland in 1916.

This caused attention to be focused more intensively than ever on submarine warfare, and in due course the Admiralty sought to enlist Falkenhayn's support for the idea. Unfortunately, Falkenhayn completely lacked the equipment to form a correct estimate of its possibilities, and becoming an ardent convert, demanded its ruthless application. He does not seem to have realized how slight were its chances of success, or that, in so far as it did succeed and submarine warfare extended to the oceans of the world, that very success might bring America into the war.

Submarine warfare was, of course, closely connected with the problem of industrial production, and this in its turn touched the equally difficult problem of the social question. Relations between labour and the officer corps had for decades been bad, yet now the General Staff saw itself confronted by the task of preserving the first fine frenzy of enthusiasm that had marked the early months of the war, and in particular of preserving it among those very elements which till now it had regarded with aversion and distrust.

This, however, was only one among a number of difficulties. The epoch of so-called "War Socialism" had set in, and both War

Ministry and General Staff found themselves compelled to take a hand in the direction of armament and food production; yet "War Socialism" could only produce results if the traditional profit economy was substantially modified and made to satisfy the workers' aspirations towards an enhanced standard of life. This meant that Falkenhayn was called upon to play the part of a Scharnhorst or a Gneisenau—a preposterous notion for a man of Falkenhayn's stamp. Given the personal equation, it is hardly surprising that the General Staff should have failed completely in this department, despite its plenitude of power.

Nevertheless, throughout 1915 the General Staff steadily expanded its influence. Falkenhayn yielded to the Chancellor's pressure and agreed that the offices of War Minister and Chief of Staff should again be separated, though this did not mean that the General Staff abandoned its hold on the former vantage point, for the new incumbent was none other than General von Hohenborn, the Quartermaster-General. The fact is that one can already speak of a new power in German affairs. In the High Command the people who really mattered were not such men as the Commandant of Imperial Headquarters, or the heads of the Emperor's military, naval and civil cabinets, nor even altogether the Chief of the General Staff himself; rather did power reside with the largely untitled specialists who were heads of departments—Tappen, the head of the operations department; Colonel Bauer, head of the department dealing with the technical problems of artillery; Colonel Nicolai, the successor of Hentsch as head of Intelligence. Above all, the great Chiefs of Staff of the various army commands, the Seeckts, Kuhls, Lossbergs, Heyes and Rheinhardts, whose brains had conceived so many brilliant local actions, began to carry a weight that was actually greater than that of the Army Commanders themselves. The era of rule by the General Staff had begun.

From time to time the idea arose of giving a number of these Chiefs of Staff of the new generation a place in the general conduct of the war. The plan was to make Falkenhayn Chancellor, Ludendorff, Chief of General Staff, and Seeckt, Quartermaster-General, though considerations of seniority put difficulties in the way of such a course. However, the failure of this project to materialize was not due to any lack of self-esteem on the part of the officers concerned. Seeckt's attitude when he was Chief of Staff to Mackensen is typical in this respect. He expressly objected to being compared to Gneisenau. He was, he declared, unique. This restless and ambitious self-assertion which an affectation of economy of words and a studied aloofness made more palpable than it otherwise would have been, was something wholly alien to the Staff officer's tradition of anonymity. It was, in fact, a direct violation of it.

XII

Seeckt's political ideas are particularly interesting in this connection, for Seeckt's was the best mind of all that generation of Staff officers. For a Prussian officer and a Junker, he bore the marks of an unusually liberal education on Christian and humanist lines. His interests were wide. He had knowledge of the world, and had spent his peacetime leaves travelling in Spain, England, France, North Africa and India. Like the majority of Staff officers, he was an anti-parliamentarian and an anti-liberal, so much so that Groener, of the railway section, was in his eyes definitely suspect as a South German democrat. Democracy considered the human personality as a whole, whereas Prussia only understood the ethics of duty and of service to the State. That was why at this time Seeckt had no interest in awakening the latent powers of the nation but wished rather to constrain them through the rule of the "strong man", the dictator. Since such reflections quietly ignored the Emperor, it was assumed (some memory of Bismarck may have played a part here) that this dictatorship should be exercised by the Chancellor. That such a dictatorship would destroy the monarchy seems to have escaped him.

Of even greater interest are the ideas revealed in Seeckt's correspondence on the subject of foreign policy. He did not believe that the rivalries between the western powers, which had brought about the conflagration of 1914, would settle themselves in a single passage of arms. This conflict would have several phases. The current war, in Seeckt's opinion, would end in the temporary exhaustion of all belligerents. It would be followed by a period of economic struggle. After that would come a final and decisive armed conflict. The task of German policy must therefore be to prepare for the next war, and to establish positions from which it could be most advantageously fought. This did not necessarily mean a policy of annexations such as that sponsored by the Pan-Germans, but rather the creation between the Atlantic coast and the Near East of a system of alliances, a league of states to which would belong Holland, Belgium, Sweden, Denmark, Norway, Austria-Hungary, Rumania, Bulgaria, Greece and Turkey. In the case of Russia he hoped to reach an understanding by diverting Pan-Slav ambitions toward Asia and, above all, toward British India. As regards the Far East, Seeckt pressed for an understanding with Japan, which, as a warrior state, should be left to control East Asia. Germany's most important sphere of influence would be Turkey.

These were, of course, merely Seeckt's private opinions. They were not the views of the General Staff. For all that, however, such ideas were very much in the air at the time. In 1916, for instance, there was published anonymously a work called *The Next War*, which stressed the need for comprehensive economic preparations for a second world war, and was believed to be the work of a leading ordnance expert, Colonel Bruchmüller. Actually, Seeckt's notions were more moderate than those of many of his contemporaries. Thus, unlike Falkenhayn, who was opposed to premature annexation plans, Stresemann, who was later to become the ardent advocate of Franco-German understanding and European collaboration, was at that time positively luxuriating in such projects, and talking of a German Empire that would stretch from Flanders to Esthonia. Though, as we have seen, Seeckt did not go anything like so far as this, it is not hard to understand that Seeckt's ideas formed a link between the General Staff and the war aims of the Pan-Germans, and did much to increase the sympathy between those two bodies. The fact that Seeckt's views were shared by Ludendorff served to assist this process.

XIII

More powerful forces, however, than the speculations of individuals were creating common ground between Pan-Germans and General Staff. The numerous business leaders who stood behind the Pan-German movement had put a crudely materialist interpretation on the real meaning of the war, and had as early as the end of August, 1914, made up their minds about the purpose it was to serve. In demanding large slices of Flanders, Eastern France and of the Polish and Baltic territories, National Liberals like Stresemann and Bassermann were completely at one with conservatives like Hugenberg, and even with such a lone wolf as Stinnes (who was for annexing the whole of Normandy) or, for that matter, with Erzberger of the Catholic Centre party, who for a time voiced similar views—until their monstrous nature became apparent to him.

The disastrous thing was that the desire of big business to get hold of the iron ore of Longwy and Briey, and to obtain control of the rich mining and industrial areas of Belgium and Northern France coincided with the purely strategic aspirations of the General Staff to put a belt of territory in front of Germany's real borders. The simple acquisitiveness of business interest, and the obsessive terror which Germany's geographical position inspired in the minds of the General Staff thus tended towards the reinforcement of the same set of ideas.

If one takes this into account, and if one further allows for the absence since Bismarck's day of all genuine political leadership, one understands much of what occurred; one understands, for instance, how it came about that when Class of the Pan-German League launched his campaign against Bethmann-Hollweg because the latter vainly sought to put a brake on the more perilous formulations of war aims, he found allies in the General Staff. Yet the proclamation of war aims of the kind in question, inspired as it so largely was by big business, was the very worst answer which German leadership could give to the questioning masses. It was nothing less than a provocation to the ordinary man in the trenches, whose family at home was soon to be haunted by the spectre of hunger, while he submissively endured more than a man should be asked to bear.

XIV

After the conquest of Serbia, Mackensen and Seeckt had hoped that Falkenhayn would order a drive to the Aegean, and, in particular, to the port of Salonika, which would have made the Balkans secure against invasion. However, Falkenhayn held that this would require too large a force. Falkenhayn himself took the view, for which there was some justification, that England was the most dangerous of all his enemies. Since the Army had not the means of making a successful landing on British soil, he saw, apart from the submarine war, only one way of forcing England to abandon the conflict. This was to break France, her "continental sword". This aim he hoped to achieve by bringing the French Army to battle at a point where it could not yield ground without mortal loss of prestige, and so to bleed it to death. The point most suitable for this enterprise, which was also one of the strongest points on the French front, was the fortress system of Verdun.

Verdun was the most modern fortress in France. It was surrounded by two fortress belts, in addition to flanking defences. It made extensive use of armour and concrete shelters. An earlier strategy would have deemed it absurd to attack the enemy where he was thus in strength, but it was a principle of Tappen's, to which he had often given expression, that it was ridiculous to attack where there was nothing to be attacked. It was in vain that Seeckt, who had a much better head on him than Tappen, prophesied the certain failure of the whole enterprise.

In February, 1916, the 5th German Army under the Crown Prince began the assault. It dragged on for months with terrible artillery duels and costly storming attacks, and resulted in the capture of a few forts. France was to bleed to death, and it is true that the battle swallowed up the flower of the French infantry. Roughly seventy French divisions were completely consumed in this furnace, though German infantry suffered almost as heavily. German losses finally amounted to 282,000 men as against 317,000 on the French side, but behind France stood the British Empire and the huge armies of Russia, shaken, but still unconquered, and also potentially the vast power of the United States. Behind Germany stood a homeland threatened by hunger and social unrest, and two allies, Turkey and Austria, who were already in process of decay.

Ludendorff sought a decision in the east, and it was in the east that Falkenhayn's fate was determined. The skill of von der Goltz had contrived to shut up a British force, which had set out to take Bagdad, in Kut-El-Amara, and had compelled it to surrender, but Goltz did not survive the campaign, for a tropical disease carried the old man off. At the memorial service in the Reichstag, Moltke had a heart attack—a curious coincidence, for both men were now out of favour. A week later the British attacked on the Somme with a crushing superiority of aircraft and artillery. At the same time the Austrian front collapsed in Galicia under the last mighty attacks of the Russians which had begun on June 4th. Hötzendorf was compelled to abandon all schemes for an attack on Italy. In order to save the Carpathian line and the Danube basin, a German-Austrian army group was hurriedly formed and put under the command of the Archduke Karl, the Austrian heir to the throne.

The Russian offensive had even graver consequences. Rumania entered the war with 750,000 completely fresh troops. The Rumanian declaration of war on August 27th was Falkenhayn's death sentence. Falkenhayn had shown that he was neither a great and resourceful strategist nor the kind of man who can become a symbol and an inspiration to the masses. He was the typical General Staff officer, a man who liked to work quietly in the background, detested popularity-hunting and never in any circumstances thrust himself on the public's notice. That was why he never had the public's confidence, which went wholly to Hindenburg and Ludendorff.

Now, we have already noted the odd position of Colonel Bauer; he was, after Tappen, the most influential man on the General Staff. Cutting right through all red tape, Bauer now went direct to the War Minister and demanded Falkenhayn's replacement by Hindenburg, with Ludendorff as the latter's collaborator. He was completely successful. On August 28th, Hindenburg and Ludendorff were summoned to Pless, while Lyncker informed Falkenhayn that His Majesty had decided to avail himself of the advice of the commander of the eastern front.

Falkenhayn was too proud a man to allow himself to be kicked out. He immediately tendered his resignation, which was as promptly accepted. On August 29th, Lyncker informed Ludendorff that the Emperor had decided to appoint Hindenburg as Chief of the General Staff, while Ludendorff's post was to be that of Second Chief. Ludendorff preferred the designation of First Quartermaster-General, and this was approved.

This was the first occasion on which the appointment of a Chief of Staff resulted from the pressure of public opinion, and it was in this manner that, in the hour of greatest travail and confusion and with fearsome artillery duels thundering on all the fronts, Hindenburg assumed his office.

CHAPTER VIII

THE SILENT DICTATORSHIP

HINDENBURG AND LUDENDORFF, 1916-1918

I

DURING the First World War, all the larger cities of Germany put up wooden statues of Hindenburg, into which donors of a small contribution were allowed to drive an iron nail. The idea was a vulgarism, if you like—one of the worst that that vulgar, stunt-loving age produced—but it was also something more. Seeckt, who had an excellent instinct in anything pertaining to aesthetics, wrote somewhat later that one could not conceive of Hindenburg's statue being done in the Italian fashion in bronze or marble, but only in that material which was used by the great German artists of the Middle Ages when they portrayed kings or saints in their cathedrals.

There is a great deal in this observation, for since Moltke's day people had come to look on the General Staff as an institution from which even the impossible could be expected, and these statues really did somehow seem to people to represent something greater than the ordinary run of men. In those final years of the declining Hohenzollern régime, the big, broadly built man who was the last Chief of the royal Prussian General Staff did seem to be in some way not a mere man, but an embodiment in human form of the remaining strength of the State, a refuge to the faltering and a hope to those of little faith.

Yet Hindenburg dated; he belonged to an era that was already dead. When he said, as he often did, that he felt most at home in the Germany of Bismarck and William I, he did not speak idly, and this was the great difference between himself and Ludendorff, for the figure of Ludendorff, whose almost brutal powers of work and quite extraordinary organizing ability subserved a mind that was essentially one-sided, tends rather to suggest that essentially modern thing, the great technical expert who, if he is to function and fructify, needs the guiding hand of some person of broader and more balanced outlook. Hindenburg was not altogether capable of playing this latter part.

Even so, the two personalities were complementary to each other, so much so that, despite the fact that their human relationship was far less ideal than people supposed, it is no more possible to dissociate the two names than it is those of Blücher and Gneisenau, though that was a partnership between two men of a very different kind.

Hindenburg and Ludendorff had little in common save their background. Both were descended from uprooted and impoverished families of landowners. The Beneckendorffs had once possessed numerous estates both in Eastern and Western Prussia, and in addition had by intermarriage acquired those of the vanished family of von Hindenburg; but they had lost almost everything in the agrarian crises that followed the wars of liberation. Thus, like that of so many Junker officers, the greater part of von Hindenburg's life stood under the law of poverty, and his silent longing to re-acquire the family estate at Neudeck could only be satisfied in old age.

Apart from the fact of professional success, his career is in no way remarkable—a lieutenancy in the 3rd Foot Guards, two spells on the General Staff, headship of the General War Department of the Prussian War Ministry (this was the only occasion on which he made contact with the world of politics), after which he became Chief of Staff to an army corps, then commander of a division. Finally, from 1903 to 1911 he commanded the 4th Army Corps in Magdeburg. His world throughout his life remained that of the Prussian Army and of the General Staff. He knew no other—least of all, that of humanist culture, about which he roundly declared a man need not bother his head. Indeed, he cheerfully admitted that, apart from military works, he had in the whole of his adult life never read a decent book. He was a characteristic product of the culture from which he came, full of the consciousness of his rank, tactful and dignified, a Christian in outlook, but a Protestant Christian, sober in habit, unimaginative and marked by a certain peasantlike narrowness of mind. He was what the Germans call *ein amusischer Mensch*, a man untouched by the liberal arts, though a truly great general should surely have within him something of the creative and imaginative power of the artist.

Ludendorff, too, was *ein amusischer Mensch*. His father was a landowner who, like so many of his kind, had gone through bankruptcy in the 'eighties and ended up by earning his bread in the hail insurance business, and the son had unconsciously absorbed much of the narrow nationalism and social resentment that characterized this kind of person. In his memoirs, Ludendorff has left us a description of his father's study while the latter still possessed an estate on those

bare East Elbian plains. It was wholly devoid of any cultural equipment. The elder Ludendorff had served as an officer of the reserve
in the campaign of 1870, and the room contained, over and above
essential furniture, nothing more than a few warlike mementos of
that experience, to wit, a sword, a *mitrailleuse* cartridge and a piece
of wallpaper from Château Bellevue, near Sedan; a plaster bust of
Frederick the Great was the only other ornament.

Like Hindenburg, Ludendorff had passed through the hard school
of the cadet corps and then become an infantry officer, though, unlike
Hindenburg, he went to the line. At the *Kriegsakademie* his instructor
was General Meckel, the reorganizer of the Japanese Army, and it
was the latter who recommended him for the General Staff, with
which his connection remained much more close than that of
Hindenburg. The dark-blue uniform, with its silver embroidered
collar and the trouser stripes of carmine red, was more to Ludendorff
than the token of a successful military career. It was the symbol of
his social rehabilitation.

By 1908 he had become head of the deployment section. His world
was his work, and his work the study of every conceivable military
situation that any combination of circumstances could produce; but
the very fact that the German officer corps was a closed corporation
caused him to be more shut off from the world than would have been
the case with an officer of another country engaged on similar work.
He saw his homeland on Staff journeys, he also saw other countries—
when he visited them for purposes of military study. In this manner
he saw Russia; also, through being seconded to the Marines, he got
to see something of England and Norway; but he saw what he did
see solely through the eyes of a General Staff officer.

Ludendorff's character was marked by a burning ambition and by
an aggressive self-confidence which the sheer isolation of his life may
have done something to foster, though on occasions these traits
caused him to violate traditions which were fundamental to that very
General Staff which had kept him spiritually confined. Thus, shortly
after Tannenberg he was once heard to remark, "When *I* won the
battle of Tannenberg"—an unforgivable sin according to the General
Staff code. In Hindenburg he saw, on his own confession, nothing
but a serviceable symbol, and he believed that the masses needed
some symbol of this kind—which amounts to saying that Ludendorff
considered Hindenburg a man of straw.

Hindenburg, on the other hand, who was endowed with a generous
portion of common sense, and even with something of the slyness of

his country-dwelling ancestors, was well aware that his adviser was unequalled in sheer technical competence and needed no more than the most general supervision. Hindenburg in fact accepted the position with that humility which so often goes with good intelligence. Indeed, he displayed, and in high degree, that very quality in which Ludendorff was so sadly deficient; and it was perhaps fortunate for both men that he did so.

II

The change of régime brought about a number of other changes, some of a very drastic nature. Tappen was replaced as Chief of Operations by Lieutenant-Colonel Wetzel, a much more imaginative and nimble-witted man, who not only had wider cultural and social horizons (and, incidentally, a better military education), but also possessed a far better grasp of the principles of modern war. Further, the greatly increased Air Force, which had now begun to develop aspirations to become an independent service, was placed directly under the General Staff. Another interesting development was the addition to the political department of a special section for liaison work with the Foreign Office, an activity in which a certain Captain von Schleicher found congenial employment. It was in keeping with the general trend that Ludendorff should at this time have been at pains to re-assert the principle of the joint responsibility of General Staff officers for decisions taken by the commanders to whom they were attached. This applied particularly to the Chiefs of Staff of army group commands. A result of this was that the General Staff, by using this secondary channel, was able to impose its will even more completely than before.

Of even greater importance is the place the General Staff began to occupy in the national life as a whole, and the steady extension of its activities for the General Staff was already concerning itself with such matters as the press, films, general propaganda, armaments and food. As we have already seen, it was, or should have been, the Emperor's function to hold the balance between the different competing authorities and so keep the General Staff in its place. Nominally that function still remained with him, but, as we have also seen, he was proving himself more and more unequal to it. Much the same applied to the Chancellor, for Bethmann-Hollweg was not a sufficiently strong personality to put up effective resistance against the silent pressure of military influence. Nor did the Reichstag make a better showing. The Liberal opposition was lukewarm, the Socialists ham-strung by doctrinaire preconceptions. Moreover, despite the presence of such men as Ebert, Winnig, Noske and the trade-union leader, Legien, they were handicapped by a sad lack of outstanding person-alities. Stresemann, the spokesman of the National Liberal reformers, committed the blunder of actually seeking a partnership with the High Command and making this the prime object of all his efforts. The fact is that Bismarck's titanic figure had so cowed the Reichstag that it was no longer conscious of its authority, while the Emperor had consistently refused to seek touch with leading Parliamentarians, and had seen in the legislature nothing but a talking shop. A plant that had grown up in such adverse circumstances could scarcely be expected to flourish.

Such a situation should logically have led to a military dictatorship. In actual fact it did not do so—not that Ludendorff's domineering personality failed to assert itself. Ludendorff was bursting with plans. Nothing was being done, he complained to the Crown Prince, but somebody surely ought to do something—and so Ludendorff came out with a number of far-reaching schemes, many of which involved the most radical interference with the private lives of ordinary Ger-mans. There were schemes for raising the birth rate, and for lessening the number of those evading military service, schemes for improve-ments in housing, and for combating venereal disease, schemes for stopping the flight from the land, schemes for making provision for returning soldiers by means of rural resettlement. A *Wehrschulgesetz* was to provide for the pre-military training of youth, and a *Reichs-Aufklärungsamt* was to battle with subversive agitation (which was now dangerously on the increase) and with the brilliantly directed propaganda of the Allies. Most important of all, Ludendorff urged the introduction of compulsory service for all persons between the ages of fifteen and sixty and the mobilization of female labour for munitions.

Yet, oddly enough, Ludendorff rejected the idea of an actual mili-tary dictatorship. Despite the fact that such a man as Mackensen was pressing for a military Chancellor, while Seeckt was declaring that a military dictatorship was the simplest solution of current problems—in a word, despite the fact that circumstances were almost tossing the thing in his lap, Ludendorff persisted in treating the idea as a counsel of despair, and continued wistfully looking for his strong man, his "German Lloyd George" in the ranks of the politicians and parlia-mentarians. He could not find him. Meanwhile, by the strangest of paradoxes, parliamentarians like Stresemann were becoming increasingly convinced that military dictatorship was the only hope of salvation, and were toasting Ludendorff as the German Cromwell. This attitude of Ludendorff's had far-reaching consequences, for the younger generation of Staff officers took it to heart and when their turn came, under the Weimar republic, to occupy leading positions in the Reichswehr, they accepted the principle that a soldier's training did not qualify him for politics and that the assumption of political responsibility by the military was a mistake; in particular they came to distrust a military dictatorship, and in this their instinct was sound, for every dictatorship must be based on the mass.

Even, however, if Ludendorff rejected the idea of a military dictatorship as such, an economic dictatorship carried out by the military was for all practical purposes a fact. The various controls over food, raw materials, labour and munitions grew larger from week to week, and these were gathered together under General Groener in the *Allgemeines Kriegsamt*. Nor could it very well be otherwise, for, thanks to the enemy's prodigal use of his enormous superiority in materials, the main emergency might well be said to reside in the sector of production.

This, amongst other things, had as a result that the first great act of the Ludendorff-Hindenburg régime was concerned with the increase of industrial output. With Ludendorff's especial blessing, Groener and Bauer worked out the Hindenburg programme, which provided for vast increases in planes, guns, lorries and all the other paraphernalia of war. Almost concurrently, the *Hilfsdienstpflichtgesetz* of December 1916, though it fell somewhat short of Ludendorff's aspirations—he complained that it was neither fish nor flesh—provided for a respectable influx of female labour into the factories, to say nothing of prisoners of war and so-called "help workers" from Belgium and Poland.

Whatever his views on military dictatorship, there were no bounds to Ludendorff's enthusiasm for War Socialism—the Belgian workers might have given it another name—and that, too, was understandable, for War Socialism involved the ruthless exploitation of all human and material resources, and this was wholly in tune with Ludendorff's conception of war. Nevertheless, even War Socialism failed to solve the most essential problem of all, for it failed to effect the spiritual mobilization of the German masses.

This was, in all conscience, difficult enough. Not a finger had been laid on the Prussian's precious graduated franchise, while the financial jamboree of war contracts continued unhindered. Even Ludendorff had sufficient instinct to recognize the existence of a problem here, and urged the appointment of a Propaganda Minister; but there was little to be got from that, for the ruling class had long ago written off the patriotism of the ordinary German, and was thus incapable of pleading with him with any show of conviction.

This unhappy dichotomy expressed itself in yet another way. The pick of Germany's officers had fallen on the battlefields, and Ludendorff himself had urged that the gaps should be filled, without particular regard to background, from the more promising elements among the N.C.O.s and the rank and file, which had proved their worth in the hell of battle; but the selection of officers was the last remaining privilege of the Military Cabinet, and for the Military Cabinet social standards were still the determining factor. The only concession to which it would agree was the creation of the wretched hybrid of the *Offizierstellvertreter*, or deputy officer. Sergeants with good records were, in certain instances, permitted to perform officers' duties for the duration of the war, on the understanding that they would revert to their old rank at its conclusion.

The improvisations of the General Staff just sufficed to solve the economic problem within the limits imposed by the raw material supply. Ludendorff's ventures into politics, however, ended in a fiasco. The first of these was the proclamation of an independent kingdom of Poland, a first-class blunder, since it destroyed the last hopes of a separate peace with Russia, and this at a time when the Czar had just appointed, in Boris Stuermer, a Prime Minister who had the reputation of strongly supporting inter-dynastic understanding. Ludendorff allowed himself to be talked round by von Beseler, the Governor General of Poland, into believing that an independent Poland would furnish Germany with fifteen to twenty divisions, and since he had always been a man who was hypnotized by numbers, he became an unresisting victim to von Beseler's unrealism. Yet Ludendorff should have known better. He came from Posen, and should have known something of Poland's hatred of Germany.

In his attitude towards unrestricted submarine warfare, as in the matter of such attempts as were made to open peace negotiations with the enemy, Ludendorff's perceptions proved equally inaccurate. He held that the language used in any expression of readiness to negotiate should invariably be as strong as possible, lest the other side should imagine such overtures to be a sign of weakness, while in the matter of submarine warfare and its possibilities of success he unquestioningly accepted the sanguine estimates of the Admiralty staff. Being a man incapable of thinking except in terms of power pure and simple, he was incapable of treating President Wilson's efforts at mediation at their face value, but looked upon them as so much shadow boxing, though in his utter failure to appreciate the significance of the American factor he was equalled, strangely enough, by Seeckt. Seeckt believed that America's entry into the war, as a result of that same unrestricted submarine warfare which Ludendorff had advocated, might prolong the conflict; he wholly failed to see that it would determine it.

III

It was not long before Ludendorff realized that so long as Beth-mann-Hollweg was Chancellor his policy of total war could never be put into effect—Bethmann-Hollweg was too much of a humanitarian for that—and there were many outside the Army who shared Ludendorff's point of view. Interest in a settlement that entailed substantial annexations was widespread, so much so that not only the Pan-Germans but also members of liberal and even leftist parties were affected by it, and so brought into opposition to the Chancellor. The recurrent fight about the Army estimates had accustomed Ludendorff to dealing with political parties, so that everything was now set to assist him in his efforts to have a "War Chancellor" appointed.

Contact was now made with the many oppositional elements in the Reichstag, with Colonel Bauer acting as intermediary. Many members were for pushing Ludendorff himself into the Chancellorship, but Ludendorff felt unequal to the double burden. As against this, Stresemann and Erzberger, perhaps the two most noteworthy person-alities in politics, were pressing the candidacy of Prince von Bülow, from whose undoubted diplomatic skill they hoped for a purely political solution of their difficulties. Ludendorff himself would have preferred Tirpitz, but Tirpitz had had differences of opinion with the Emperor about the conduct of the naval war, and was out of favour.

Having entered politics, the General Staff showed an engaging readiness for the amenities of political intercourse. In 1917, for the first time in history, members of the Reichstag were received at the Königsplatz and enlightened on the details of the military situation. Soon the Imperial Family caught the fashion, and both the Emperor and the Crown Prince thought it opportune to hear what party leaders (including even social democrats) had got to say for themselves. The charm of the occasion was unfortunately marred by the Emperor's inveterate lapses into oratory and by the Crown Prince's persistence in treating parliamentary delegates as though they were corporals reporting to a company commander.

The pressure exerted was not ineffective, and at length, by threatening resignation, Hindenburg and Ludendorff secured the Chancellor's dismissal. This, however, did not serve to diminish the Emperor's distaste for the appointment of either Tirpitz or Bülow, and not even the Chief of the great General Staff could yet unrestrainedly impose his will on the Supreme War Lord. At this stage, Colonel General von Plessen suggested Dr. Michaelis, the Food Minister, whom he described as "a man who would take a grip on things" (*ein Mann der durchgreifen könne*). Neither Hindenburg nor Ludendorff knew Michaelis, but they declared themselves satisfied, and Michaelis was made Chancellor. The General Staff had at last had the deciding voice in a Chancellor's appointment.

Ludendorff, however, was not content, and sought yet further support for the strong policy he desired. He found it in the *Vaterlandspartei*, an organization founded in 1916 by Tirpitz and a high East Prussian official, Wolfgang Kapp. This was a party—Class was one of its supporters—which embodied the aims of all the annexationists and all the devotees of crude power politics. Its spirit was wholly alien to that of the masses, and if Ludendorff thought, as he apparently did, that it would help raise morale and enhance unity behind the front, he was sadly mistaken, for it did the worst possible service to that particular cause. The fact is, however, that Ludendorff's mind was set and his own annexationist pretensions were growing wilder than ever. A memorandum of his dated September 1917 on war aims not only demands strategic belts of territory in Poland, Lithuania, Courland and Eastern France, but, on top of that, asks for the incorporation into the Empire of Belgium, which was to be divided into Vlamland and Wallonia. The incorporation of Belgium, Ludendorff argued, would not leave Holland unaffected, and Holland would be bound sooner or later to seek its own incorporation into Germany. Denmark would have to be brought into closer economic unity with Germany, while further afield an alliance would have to be made with Japan and a large compact colonial empire created in Africa. Lloyd George once asked Foch what he really thought of Ludendorff. "*Un bon soldat*" was Foch's reply. It is noteworthy that he did not say "*Un bon général*". Foch's judgment was sound. Ludendorff was a

soldier and nothing more. In politics he was in territory alien to him—
and he was helpless.

Meanwhile Britain was finding the answer to submarine attack in
the convoy system, and it was not long before it was found that the
operations of a lone submarine against ships proceeding in strongly
defended convoys, and carrying in addition armaments of their own,
were too precarious and unpromising to be worth undertaking. This
centred hopes once more on the land war, and here, though the
general outlook was not encouraging, Hindenburg and Ludendorff
scored one noteworthy success. They created a unified German and
Austrian command under the nominal leadership of the German
Emperor. Unfortunately the death of Francis Joseph in November
1916 and the replacement of Hötzendorff by Lieutenant-General Arz
von Straussenburg put an end to this arrangement. The new
Emperor Charles was determined to save his Empire in his own way—
if necessary by disavowing his German ally. Charles knew that there
was no hope for the cause of the Central Powers.

IV

The last months of 1916 saw another undertaking with limited
objectives, and one which proved that, given a field of manoeuvre of
traditional size and the traditional tactics of open warfare, the General
Staff had no equal. The objective in this case was to cut Rumania as a
serious military factor out of the war. Brilliant performances were on
this occasion put up both by Falkenhayn and Mackensen, the former
driving into the Rumanian plain over Siebenbürgen, the latter invading from the Dobruja with a mixed German, Turkish and Bulgarian force. On December 6th Mackensen rode into Bucharest on a
white horse. The remainder of the Rumanian Army was pressed back
into Bessarabia. Immediately after this, Falkenhayn went as a Turkish
Field-Marshal to Palestine, accompanied by a man who was one day
to play a somewhat conspicuous part in German affairs—Franz von
Papen, major on the General Staff and sometime military attaché in
Washington. It did not, however, escape the cool perception of old
Hindenburg that all these successes were only partial successes. In
his memoirs he had occasion to point out that only in one solitary
instance did the Central Powers succeed in completely eliminating
an opponent. That opponent was Montenegro. So far, the encircling
ring of enemies had been pressed outwards; the Belgian Army
had been pushed back across the Yser, the Serbian into Corfu and

the Rumanian to Bessarabia, but the ring had nowhere been broken.

Strategically, 1917 was given over to the defensive, to "operative stagnation", as Seeckt called it—despite the fact that revolution had broken out in Russia at the beginning of the year. In the west, Ludendorff deserves credit for introducing a new tactic of mobile defence. This made possible a system of defence in depth which permitted front-line positions to be temporarily abandoned. Casualties were greatly diminished by this expedient, which, however, did not touch the main strategic problem at all.

The nature of this last, now that America had entered the war, was quite unmistakable. It was to find the means of obtaining a decision before the arrival of American forces turned the scale. For this to be achieved it was essential for the deadlock of positional warfare to be broken, and here Ludendorff's mind could not progress beyond the tactics of the break-through, and Russian military writers have discerned the utter degeneration of the art of war in the complete failure of either side to make any progress in that direction.

Yet the means were actually at hand. In 1916 the British had put into the field armoured machine-gun carrying motor vehicles, equipped with caterpillar treads, to which they were ultimately to give the name of "tank". They were designed for the destruction of trench systems and barbed wire entanglements. They still suffered from grave defects and could only move slowly across the landscape like great clumsy tortoises, but within limits they unquestionably achieved their object.

Nobody recognized the revolutionary operational potentialities of this new weapon, least of all the Prussian Army, whose powers of adaptation to technical development had never been remarkable. Hindenburg simply stated that the German infantry could get along without such things, and the only effect of the impact of the new contrivance was a concentration on methods of defence. Anti-tank rifles, light artillery, etc., were developed with projectiles capable of penetrating the tank's armour.

Colonel Bauer alone was alive to the real significance of the new weapon, and gave orders for the construction of a German model. In May 1917 an experimental tank was exhibited to representatives of the High Command, but they were dissatisfied with it, and it was only in the autumn that the Prussian War Ministry hesitatingly gave orders for the construction of a number of heavy tanks of type A7V, while Colonel Bauer on his own responsibility directed Krupps to produce plans for a light, fast model. Meanwhile, France and Britain had already gone over to mass production. In Germany, however, this was impossible, for the shortage of raw materials was already endangering the supply of aircraft and lorries. At last, in 1918, nine German tank formations appeared on the field, for the most part equipped, not with A7V's, but with captured British tanks.

In the spring of 1917, however, even this modest measure of progress had not yet been effected. One side had no tanks at all, while the other had not yet learned to make use of what it had, so that both sides stared spellbound at each other's fortifications, searching desperately for possible points of penetration. In April General Nivelle, who had succeeded Joffre as generalissimo of the French forces, made the last tremendous effort to break through the German front on both sides of Rheims by means of one great punch and a huge concentration of artillery. Thanks to Operation *Alberich*, by which German forces were quietly withdrawn to the shorter and strongly-defended Siegfried line (known to the British as the Hindenburg line) and to General Nivelle's astonishing carelessness in the matter of secrecy, this effort was partly forestalled, while Ludendorff's elastic defence did the rest. The attack broke down with appalling casualties, the offensive power of the French infantry was crippled, and mutinies followed in no less than sixteen army corps, though Clemenceau's leadership contrived to restore France's equilibrium.

In the late summer the British in their turn made a final assault *en masse* on Paschendaele ridge, the object being to capture the German submarine bases on the Flanders coast, but this, too, only resulted in a well-nigh fatal outpouring of blood and in the paralysis of Britain's power of attack. The German infantry remained mistress of the field till its supremacy there was called in question at Cambrai, for at Cambrai for the first time tanks were not only used correctly but were also used in sufficient numbers, there being some four hundred of them. But for the fact that the British commander was unable to exploit his success, much more decisive results might have been obtained.

V

Meanwhile the Bolshevik agents whom Ludendorff had deliberately injected into Russia, had seized power, and this, together with the increasing famine occasioned by the British blockade, began to cast the shadow of revolution over Germany. As the food situation deteriorated, Ludendorff's conviction grew stronger that only substantial acquisitions of territory in the east could save the Empire. The Bolshevik leaders had declared themselves ready for negotiations, but were somewhat taken aback when the full scope of the Supreme Command's territorial ambitions was made plain, for the stipulation was now made that Lithuania, Courland, Esthonia, Poland and the Ukraine should be regarded as lying within Germany's sphere of influence.

Despite the harshness of his terms, Ludendorff succeeded in neutralizing Russia, and thus released large forces for the west, but now there were new problems. In the autumn of this year, Wetzell began to speak of knocking Italy out of the war, Italy being the weakest of the great enemy powers; in secondary theatres, however, Ludendorff would only permit operations with limited objectives. Thus, though an operation against Italy was undertaken which resulted in the crushing Italian defeat at Caporetto, the success was not exploited; the idea that a secondary theatre of war could become decisive had no place in Ludendorff's mind.

Peace negotiations with the Bolsheviks were the occasion for certain developments in the relation between the Government and the General Staff. Dr. Michaelis, who had to some extent been the General Staff's own nominee for the Chancellorship, had proved himself quite unequal to his task. His proposed successor, Count Hertling, was duly presented to the High Command, and after his experiences with Michaelis, Ludendorff preferred not to put up a candidate of his own. Once in office, Hertling took up the question of political precedence in matters of state, with the result that at the Brest-Litovsk negotiations Hindenburg and Ludendorff had to content themselves with a purely advisory rôle.

The advice which they gave differed markedly from certain ideas of Seeckt, who was probably more longsighted than Ludendorff. Seeckt wrote at the time that in breaking up Russia, Germany was playing the Allied game. He envisaged Russia as the potential ally for the second phase of the great international struggle, and wished to see the beginnings of a policy of understanding in the east. He saw no obstacle to this in the Bolshevik ideology nor any danger to the social order, but Ludendorff's policy was to hold what he had—which was the reason why it never occurred to him to use Belgium and Alsace-Lorraine as bargaining counters in return for a free hand in the east, an approach that might well have led to the opening of diplomatic conversations.

Ludendorff's attitude was in sharp contrast to that of Groener, who as far back as 1916 had believed in a policy of restitution and considered such a policy to offer Germany the most favourable solution of her difficulties. One day, however, Groener was ill-advised enough to give a hint of what was in his mind in the presence of Hugo Stinnes, the coal magnate, and the latter caused him to be removed from his post as head of the *Kriegsamt*.

Under the threat of force the treaty of Brest-Litovsk was at last signed. At the same time new ventures were undertaken in the Baltic area, in Finland and the Ukraine, the greatest effort being made to get hold of the great food-producing territories of Southern Russia. Puppet governments were set up in the Ukraine and Georgia, for the most part consisting of the extreme reactionary elements of the old régime. In the Ukraine an effort was made to recruit troops, but two divisions which were created in this way had to be disbanded.

VI

Meanwhile, in the Near East there was a kind of prelude to the ultimate Turkish collapse. A mixed British and Indian force took Bagdad. The Palestine front was also thrown off balance. In December, Seeckt was attached to the Supreme Turkish Command, a typical example of the part the great chiefs of Staff were playing, for in theory at least the despatch of such a leading expert was accounted the equivalent of the provision of a sizeable body of troops.

Seeckt, whose staff in Constantinople was joined by Major Köstring, Captain Fischer and Captain Tschunke, able officers who were all to play a great part in the future, had ambitious plans in mind. One of these was an offensive across Northern Persia with the object of regaining Mesopotamia. Another concerned the penetration of the Caucasus, possibly with the ultimate objective of a Goltzian march on India. There was, however, no solid basis, for any such plans, for signs were already apparent that the strain not only on the armed forces but on the whole structure of the state, was greater than could be borne.

In 1917 the first cases occurred in which crews of the idle battle fleet deliberately refused obedience. In Graudenz a number of German prisoners of war returning from Russia broke into open mutiny on hearing that they were to be sent to the western front. Desertions behind the front showed a marked increase, and a number of large-scale strikes took place in the armament industry. Ludendorff asked for strong measures, but the expedient of sending strikers to the front was scarcely a fortunate one. Revolutionary agitators were thus brought into the fighting line. Moreover, to treat armed service as a form of punishment was an insult to those engaged in it. Scharnhorst had declared that serving one's country was a duty of honour, and that was still the theory.

VII

In the midst of these vicissitudes, German planning still went forward. Both the French and the British, however, had recognized the utter uselessness of running their heads against a wall, and were determined to await the coming of the Americans before going over again to the offensive. Ludendorff, on the other hand, was resorting with increased determination to "Buffalo strategy", as Foch designated the unimaginative expedient of continuous violent frontal assaults. He argued that, once the American divisions appeared, the factor of numbers would begin to work irretrievably against Germany, and then the last prospect of victory would disappear. The only hope appeared to lie in gathering all his forces into one mighty punch which would shatter the enemy's front and enable him to roll it up. In the east a considerable number of divisions had been released, troops were drawn from the Italian front, and the Ukrainian venture was allowed to be undertaken with forces which were actually inadequate. He even considered the idea of concentrating Austrian, Bulgarian and Turkish divisions in France—but nothing came of this.

The General Staff had had its mind full of the "Great Battle" since the autumn of 1917. That Wetzell's conception of attacking Italy was fundamentally sound is proved by the alarm produced among Allied statesmen by the Italian defeat, but in Ludendorff's view only an attack on the strongest part of the front would impart the necessary quality of moral shock to a military success. Ludendorff's "Great Battle" in the west was his last card. In a memorandum to the Emperor he declared that he would guarantee success, so long as the peace would justify the cost. Both Ludendorff and Hindenburg believed, as did also Wetzell, that the military offensive would be accompanied by a diplomatic offensive. Ever since the crises of 1916 and 1917 there had been circles both in Paris and London that were ready to negotiate. However, the diplomatic offensive came to nothing, for there was no really close co-operation between the High

Command and the Foreign Office, and neither Kühlmann nor Ludendorff had any understanding of each other's line of reasoning.

But the military offensive suffered from even more important defects than the lack of diplomatic support. Ludendorff was utterly without comprehension of the fact that an army that had gone through four years of terrible battles could no longer put up the performance of the men of 1914. He had become a typical chair-borne general who conducted operations from an office desk. Clausewitz had designated strategy as the art of applying available means. Ludendorff could no longer distinguish between what was possible and what was not. Everything was possible if you barked out the order for it in a loud, gruff tone of voice.

After considering various alternatives, Ludendorff eventually decided to attack on both sides of St. Quentin and strike at Amiens, where the French and British Armies joined. If the break-through succeeded, it should be possible to roll back the British Army to the Channel and drive it to its ships.

The preparation of the huge masses of troops and artillery required for the attack began in the early days of 1918. Nearly 7,000 light and heavy guns were concentrated for the preliminary bombardment. At last, in the early hours of March 21st, "Operation Michael" started, with a deafening crash of fire.

The attacking armies broke right through the British fortifications, the 5th British Army being completely destroyed. Unfortunately, the tank, which might here have secured a decision, had been utterly neglected and the British front was not rolled up, though Amiens seemed almost to come within the German grasp. Since, however, there was no means of moving troops forward with sufficient speed, the blow did not go sufficiently deep, but spread out laterally. The front on which the enemy was pushed back widened from the original 70 kilometres to 140, but nowhere was he pushed far enough. Approximately 90 divisions were hurled into the melting pot of this battle without achieving any decisive result. The end came on April 4th, for by then the offensive power of the overtaxed infantry had vanished; also the attacking troops had got ahead of their artillery and supplies. The attack came to a standstill. "Man's work always proceeds piecemeal," Hindenburg was later to write in his memoirs.

VIII

On April 9th, Ludendorff began the second act of the drama, and made a new attack, this time between Armèntieres and La Bassée. The chief weight of this fell on some Portuguese troops which were overwhelmed by an enormous superiority of numbers, and the German masses poured through the gap, but this attack also had lost its force by April 25th. German casualties were one-third higher than those of the Allies, and there was already considerable scepticism among such men as General von Lossberg, Chief of Staff of the 4th Army in Flanders, as to the ultimate outcome. It almost appeared as though this outpouring of blood was completely pointless, a crime against the true spirit of the art of war.

Nevertheless, Ludendorff remained undaunted in his desperate fight to break through the enemy line and secure freedom of manoeuvre, and so the third act began. This consisted of a diversionary attack on the hotly contested Chemin des Dames, which was to be followed by a blow in Flanders. Launched with immense masses of men and artillery, this third German attack succeeded in taking Soissons, and shortly afterwards German troops once again reached the fateful waters of the Marne and at Château Thierry came within 70 kilometres of Paris. German aircraft now appeared over the French capital, which also became the target for long range artillery. For a third time, the German offensive power died away, and on June 5th this third attack came to a halt. It was about this time that General von Kuhl declared that the German lack of tanks would be decisive.

About this time also, Colonel von Haeften, liaison officer between the General Staff and the Foreign Office, began again to develop the idea of a political offensive. He suggested a propaganda campaign carried on by men prominent in German public life, who were to represent Germany as the champion of the West against Eastern Bolshevism. In this way he hoped at least to save Germany's conquests in Eastern Europe. However, relations between the High Command and the Foreign Office were by this time definitely bad. Ludendorff had long looked askance at Foreign Secretary Kühlmann's pacifist trends. Meanwhile, the Emperor sat resignedly at Headquarters and complained that the High Command, the Reichstag and the Chancellor were all dragging him in different directions. Kühlmann saw clearly that the main basis of any move for peace must be a readiness to restore Belgium's independence, but Haeften, a shrewd and moderate-minded man, was at that time almost the only person to press the idea with any conviction. Ludendorff says that between May and June he urged the Foreign Office to make a conciliatory declaration in regard to Belgium, but his subsequent attitude scarcely confirms this. On June 24th, Kühlmann declared that while Germany was faced by the existing coalition of enemies some political exchange of ideas was indispensable, if there was ever to be an end to the fighting. So far from supporting him, Ludendorff was furious. He looked upon such talk as almost amounting to defeatism, and, acting together with Hindenburg, demanded Kühlmann's dismissal. Thus, Admiral von Hintze, Military Plenipotentiary at St. Petersburg, became the new State Secretary at the Foreign Office. Ludendorff still believed that Britain should only be listened to if she approached Germany of her own accord, for the extension of Germany's power through the occupation of the Ukraine strengthened his sense of power.

During all this time, things on the home front had been going from bad to worse. Hunger stalked abroad, while the ineptitudes of the *Vaterlandspartei* strengthened the impression that the war was being carried on to satisfy capitalist greed, and so further increased the unrest. Ludendorff had yet other difficulties. The fearful battles in France were depleting Germany's reserves. Ludendorff appealed for an additional 200,000 to be called immediately to the colours, but he appealed in vain.

IX

On July 15th, Ludendorff ordered another attack to be made on both sides of Rheims, this time with 2,000 batteries and 47 divisions; the object was again to divert the enemy from Flanders, where it was still intended to launch an overwhelming German attack. Information of his plans reached the enemy, and his progress was thus limited. On the 18th, Foch, who shortly before this had been put in command of all the combined French and British forces, struck into the attacking troops out of the forest of Villers-Cotterets with 350 fast new Renault tanks, and pushed back the German forces on a front of 45 kilometres, ten German divisions being completely destroyed. Actually, Ludendorff had already ordered the retreat on the 17th and the French success was accompanied by heavy rearguard actions which lasted till August 2nd. Hindenburg already anticipated what was to come.

He wrote to his wife that it would not be his fault if the war was not won. That fault would lie with the homeland which had not succeeded in imparting the necessary spiritual strength to the fighting front. He would not even concede that people had any excuse for worrying about their food, for, like Ludendorff, he had utterly lost touch with reality.

On August 8th the British 4th Army under General Rawlinson, attacked between Albert and Moreuil on both sides of the Amiens-St. Quentin road. The attack was launched by 600 light and heavy tanks. Cavalry and armoured cars were held in readiness to follow through. Six or seven German divisions were completely over-run, the armoured cars in some cases coming right up to the divisional battle headquarters and taking the staffs prisoner. It was the beginning of the end. Retiring infantry received troops coming up in support with the cry "Strike-breakers!" It was the revolt of desperate men who had expended the last vestiges of their strength. In the holding actions which followed between the Scarpe and the Somme, the German front was once more reformed, but now the German divisions, though for the most part still offering stubborn resistance, were steadily retreating toward Belgium. The Allied superiority in tanks and aircraft was becoming irresistible.

Ludendorff called August 8th the black day of the German Army, and on this day, like the impact of a blow, came the dreadful realization that the war was lost. At best, the Army must at all costs have a breathing space, an armistice, in which to summon new strength and reorder its shattered and decimated contingents. On August 13th a meeting with the Emperor took place at Spa, at Ludendorff's request, at which were present, amongst others, Hindenburg, Ludendorff, Hertling and Hintze. Ludendorff advised the maintenance of a vigorous defence, and was for holding on to Belgium. Hindenburg agreed to unofficial feelers for peace being put out, but would not go beyond this. He held that a formal offer of peace must not be made until the military situation had improved. Yet both were in agreement with the Emperor's suggestion to seek the good offices of the Queen of the Netherlands or the King of Spain.

Since Ludendorff was a man who could not conceive of people waging war with any other purpose than the utter destruction of their enemy, there can be little doubt that his intention now was merely to find out what terms the Allies would offer and then to rouse both Army and people to one last gigantic effort. The threat of such a struggle of desperation must have appeared to him an excellent means of exerting diplomatic pressure—providing one had the right kind of diplomat, a condition which at that time was unfortunately not fulfilled. There was also another difficulty. The masses were no longer in hand. The masses wanted peace. They wanted an end to the torture, however that end might come. Ludendorff would even have been ready for that precious reform of head and members—he would actually have co-operated with social democrats, if they would only whip up the masses for that last battle of all. Neither Ludendorff nor Hindenburg had as yet realized that they had no longer control over events but that they themselves were being controlled by forces which were wholly new to them.

X

Ludendorff now abandoned his system of elastic defence in favour of the slogan, "Where we are, we stand", but well before August was out, the enemy had made nonsense of it. The French attacked between the Oise and the Aisne, and the British in the direction of Bapaume and Cambrai. In each case large numbers of tanks were used, and though their use lacked any kind of plan, the attacks were successful. In September the Americans launched their first great offensive, and Ludendorff began now to think of a stand on the Maas or the Rhine, while holding the fortifications of Alsace-Lorraine in the south. During all this time, disintegration was spreading rapidly behind the front, with desertions mounting as drafts went up the line. Even so, the old battle-hardened divisions still compelled the respect of British generals, many of whom thought that it would take a year, or possibly two, before final victory was achieved.

But there were weaker fronts than that on the west, and while the latter still held, Marshal d'Esperey broke through from Salonika. On September 15th, the Austrian Emperor formally petitioned for peace, while the Bulgarian Army mutinied. On the 25th Bulgaria also sued for peace. Before that, on the 18th, the Palestine front had cracked, preluding the collapse of the Ottoman Empire. Seeckt, as Chief of Staff of the Turkish armies, still believed in the possibility of a "Hubertusberg Peace", by which the *status quo* might be restored, and again raised his voice for an understanding with the existing Russian government, but, like Hindenburg, Seeckt no longer controlled events.

The news from the Balkans caused a wave of pessimism to sweep over the High Command, and quite suddenly Ludendorff seems, at least temporarily, to have lost his nerve. He started to clamour for the immediate conclusion of an armistice. Hindenburg still wanted to hold on to the iron ore of Briey and Longwy, whereupon Ludendorff told him with some heat that it was too late for that. Ludendorff was at this stage ready to propose Wilson's fourteen points as a basis of negotiation. These not only stipulated the freedom of the smaller nations, but also the freedom of the seas, a dangerous factor in Anglo-American relations. He had now fled completely into the army of the politicians, his last-ditch battle being held in reserve only for the most extreme eventuality. He still believed that negotiation might save the conquests in the east. The hostilities, however, must be broken off. The idea of bombarding London and Paris from the air with a new light incendiary bomb which was just going into production was rejected. Allied superiority in the air was too overwhelming. So it was both Hindenburg and Ludendorff thought it not inconsistent with their honour to associate themselves with a request for an armistice, Major von den Bussche-Ippenburg being sent to explain to the Reichstag the likelihood of a possible collapse in the west.

Meanwhile Hertling had resigned, and the Emperor called upon Prince Max von Baden to succeed him. It was on the Prince, a man of humane and liberal views, that there fell the double burden of introducing at the eleventh hour, under the threat of revolution, a Parliamentary constitution and of translating Ludendorff's now almost precipitate demands for an armistice into reality, for Ludendorff was insisting that there was not an hour to lose, since the collapse in the west might occur at any moment. All this while, the great battle was continuing. The British occupied the submarine bases on the Channel coast, while the Franco-American offensive in Eastern France made steady progress. Mackensen received strict orders to hold Rumania and its oil at all costs, but he had scarcely received the order when General d'Esperey's troops appeared in Belgrade.

At length, at the end of October, after various interchanges of notes, President Wilson made his terms clear. They virtually amounted to the surrender of all military means of defence. This was too much for Ludendorff, and an appeal to the Army over Hindenburg's signature denounced the terms as unacceptable. The new Chancellor considered that his own authority had been disavowed by this, and demanded the withdrawal of the appeal. Hereupon, Ludendorff wrote out his resignation. For the last time the Emperor received him in Berlin and told him that he would actually look on his resignation as a favour, since he had now to rebuild his Empire with the help of social democrats. Ludendorff then again offered his resignation verbally, and the Emperor nodded his head. Deeply wounded, but with his head still held high, and as obstinate as ever, Ludendorff returned to Spa to take leave of his colleagues.

Hindenburg, however, remained, and the fact that he did so was of great consequence to the future of the General Staff, but after having his appeal thus countermanded Hindenburg made up his mind that from now on armistice negotiations should be left wholly to the Government, and refused to allow the High Command to have anything to do with them. If anybody surrendered, it was not to be the leaders of the Army.

XI

The story of the Emperor's abdication under pressure from the American President and under the shadow of revolt in the interior has been told too often for any detailed account of it to be given here. In strict theory, the destruction of the monarchy entailed the end of the Prussian Army, the General Staff, the Military Cabinet and all the other extra-constitutional institutions dependent directly on the Crown. But though the monarchy ended, continuity was maintained by the Army, which found a means of adjusting itself to the new age.

One man stands out particularly at the moment of this difficult transition. The Central Department of the Great General Staff proposed several names for the vacancy created by Ludendorff's departure. Those of von Kuhl, von Seeckt, von Lossberg and Groener were all put forward. Colonel Heye, with whom Ludendorff had replaced Wetzell as Chief of Operations, thought Seeckt was the best man, but Seeckt was difficult to reach, and it might have been several days before he could have put in an appearance—particularly as the Straits were in the hands of the Allies. Of the remaining three, Groener, as a South German, was especially acceptable to the democratic parties. So Groener became the new Quartermaster-General and Hindenburg's adviser; he was the first convinced democrat who had ever held a leading position on the General Staff.

It was Groener who on that fateful November 9th uttered that one dramatic sentence which showed that a new epoch had begun. On the previous day, the 8th, the red flag was already flying in all the principal cities, soldiers behind the front were electing soldiers' councils Russian fashion, while General von Linsingen was preparing half-heartedly to try conclusions with the workers in Berlin. On this occasion, to be ready for all eventualities, Groener, acting through Heye, put two questions confidentially to army and army-group commanders on the western front.

The first of these questions was whether troops would fight for the Emperor against the homeland. Twenty-three replies were negative and fifteen uncertain; only General von der Schulenburg, the Crown Prince's Chief of Staff, gave an unqualified affirmative and pressed for action. The second question was whether the troops would allow themselves to be used to quell a Bolshevik attempt at subversion. To this twelve replies were affirmative, nineteen uncertain and eight definitely negative. Colonel Heye, who with his big moustache looked like a sergeant-major of the old school and could on occasion talk like one, communicated the result to the Emperor. It will be remembered that Waldersee had looked upon the mere raising of the question of the soldier's obedience as a mortal sin, but Groener, Heye and Schleicher, who was now Groener's assistant, were men who felt they had more at stake than the Imperial crown. They were thinking of Germany and the German Army. At the historic Crown Council on the 9th, Schulenburg again pressed for action, but Hindenburg gave him no support, and for many years afterwards the question was to torture him whether he could not after all have carried the Emperor through the revolution as the weak romantic Frederick William IV had been carried through that of 1848. When the discussion turned on the doubtful reliability of the troops, the Emperor made a reference to the duty imposed by the soldier's oath. It was then that Groener told him that in prevailing circumstances this must be looked upon as a fiction.

With these words the whole world of Prussia and particularly the world of the Prussian Army was shattered—and yet the General Staff did not perish. On the contrary it continued. While Scheidemann, the social democratic deputy, was proclaiming the Republic in Berlin—the Chancellor had already without his master's knowledge announced the Emperor's abdication—the General Staff continued to stand like a rock under its giant Chief of Staff and his most adept Quartermaster-General. Hindenburg's policy of taking no part in the armistice negotiations was strictly adhered to, the only officer attached to the armistice delegation being the sometime military attaché in Paris, General von Winterfeld. Erzberger, who headed the delegation, a quick, keen-witted man, insisted that the Allies would prefer to negotiate with civilians. In acting on this principle he really did the General Staff a great service. Whether he did his country a service is another matter, for the theory that the Army had never capitulated led to the inference that the laurels of victory had been snatched from its pure brow by the dirty fingers of democracy. None knew better than the younger generation of Staff officers that this was nonsense—which did not prevent it from becoming the standby of unscrupulous nationalist demagogues who sought to profit by their country's misfortune.

It is true enough that to all Staff officers the news of the Emperor's abdication seemed at first like a mortal blow. Seeckt, on whom the hopes of all those were centred who had any real inside knowledge, heard the news on the train that was carrying him home from Constantinople through the Ukraine. For hours this self-controlled and apparently unemotional man sat in his compartment with tears in his eyes. The Army had lost its "Royal Shield", as Seeckt himself had once put it, and all such people as Seeckt began in this hour to search for a new symbol and for some new thing to prop that state which in the eyes of all officers must of necessity repose on the pillars of order and authority. That was why at a later date General von Rabenau, one of Seeckt's closest collaborators, was to speak of the "vileness of the November revolt" by which those pillars had been destroyed.

Ludendorff, the fallen Titan, heard the news in a modest boarding establishment in West Berlin. It did not altogether come as a surprise, and the feeling it excited was not grief but rage. Being a man incapable of entertaining any doubts about himself and certainly incapable of self-accusation, he began immediately to search for hidden powers which must in some sinister way have made his perfect plans ineffective. Thus it was that he turned his back on the civilized tradition of his time and began those dark meditations on the secret behind the secrets, the hidden powers of Jews, Freemasons and Jesuits. He began to concern himself with mystical numbers and similar things to an extent that soon reached pathological dimensions. He immediately began to write his reminiscences, because the true German had in his belief something to learn from what had occurred. With typical effrontery he declared that the stupidest thing the November revolutionaries had ever done was to let him stay alive. When suspicious looking characters began to hang around his Berlin residence, he found it preferable to take refuge on the estate of some old friends in Sweden.

Shortly before he left Berlin he was visited by Sir Neill Malcolm, one of the English Generals. Ludendorff began indulging in the most violent abuse both of government and people, who, he claimed, had left him in the lurch, and declared that Germans had proved themselves to be no longer worthy of their warrior ancestors. General Malcolm thereupon asked, "Are you endeavouring to tell me, General, that you were stabbed in the back?" Ludendorff was delighted with the phrase. "That's it!" he shouted. "They gave me a stab in the back—a stab in the back!"

CHAPTER IX

THE SPHINX

SEECKT AND THE "TRUPPENAMT"

I

WHEN at 11 o'clock on November 11th the guns suddenly grew silent along all the front, there were in Germany four active centres of power. There was, first, the Prussian General Staff, which was embodied in the Supreme Command. Next, there were the vast but gradually dissolving armies of Germany's fighting men; both at home and behind the fronts these had nearly everywhere hoisted the red flag, abolished the privileged status of the officer corps and elected soldiers' councils. Then there was the Council of People's Deputies, which was acting under the leadership of Ebert and Scheidemann and formed a sort of gathering point for the forces of moderation and democracy. Finally, there were the out and out revolutionaries. These last included the Independent Social Democrats, various Bolshevik groups who were trying to organize themselves in one way or another, and the sailors of what had previously been the Imperial Navy, who now formed a sort of armed guard for the extremists. Each of these four great groups had achieved a considerable measure of cohesion and thus stood in contrast to the great mass of Germans; for the great mass of Germans remained passive and helpless, while the nobility sat apprehensively on its estates with the Russian partition of great landed properties all too vividly before its eyes.

In this general picture the General Staff stood out as a factor of decisive importance for all those forces that had any real belief in order. Its members were still united by personal inclination, common educational background and a habit of discipline. Moreover, despite accusations that it was a centre of war-mongering and "Prussian Militarism", the General Staff was still surrounded by an aura of mystical respect—and this not wholly without cause; for the last battle had never been fought, the front was still unbroken—at least it was unbroken in Belgium and Eastern France—and large forces still stood in Poland, the Ukraine and the Baltic territories. It was the politicians who had signed the terms of surrender, it was the Chancellor and his associates who had prematurely proclaimed the Supreme War Lord's abdication. The General Staff had had no hand in these things. Its prestige was therefore still apparently unimpaired, and when Hindenburg stolidly continued at his post as Chief of the General Staff, even Liberal politicians like Stresemann began to recognize this as a fact of prime importance, so much so that beside it changes in the external form of the State became comparatively irrelevant.

It was not long before even the People's Deputies realized that the General Staff was indispensable, for the People's Deputies were beginning to feel the masses slipping from their hands and needed an effective power instrument if they were to direct the revolution into the paths of moderate reform. Further, if they were to satisfy the Allies' demands for evacuation of the occupied territories and speedy demobilization, they needed a suitable apparatus of military control.

The situation created by the armistice had to some extent been anticipated and, with Hindenburg's approval, Groener, Schleicher and Heye had at the beginning of November drawn up their plans. The Army was to be withdrawn behind the Rhine, where a strong defensive line was to be created; to restore order and military discipline, reliable troops were to be sent to the larger cities and, above all, to Berlin; finally, strong forces were to be despatched to the east with the double purpose of holding the territories in the Ukraine, Poland and the Baltic area, and of setting up a protective barrier against Bolshevism. These preparations were overtaken by events. As already indicated, the terms of the armistice laid down that all occupied territories were to be evacuated and the whole Army demobilized in the shortest possible time.

Meanwhile, new problems had arisen. The puppet régimes of Hetman Skoropadski and of the Georgian republic collapsed while German troops in the Ukraine began in many cases to be infected by Bolshevik propaganda. In Hungary a red government was formed, the Czechs proclaimed their independence, as did the Poles, and similar movements towards autonomy appeared in Lithuania, Lettland and Esthonia. The Polish population of Posen rose up against the German authorities, while their fellow nationals in Western Prussia and Upper Silesia grew distinctly restless. Meanwhile, of course, the Allied Salonika Army had forced the abandonment of

Rumania. Thus the whole German position in the east was already endangered.

II

While these developments were proceeding, new dangers threatened at home. Some ten thousand soldiers' councils had been created in the Army. At the end of November there came into being a Central Soldiers' Council, a sort of Army parliament, a thing wholly without precedent in the annals of the German Army. The soldiers pressed for immediate demobilization, the abolition of all differences of rank and the right of the troops to elect their own superiors.

The question now arose whether the Soldiers' Council or the General Staff was to be put in charge of things, but the Council of People's Deputies had no more interest than the Army itself in allowing the troops to return in disorder. Even the Allies did not wish to see chaos appear on German soil, while for the social democratic republic, which the great personalities among the moderates were striving to create, and which was in point of fact slowly coming into being, orderly demobilization was a matter of life and death. Thus it was that in that very Berlin which Scheidemann himself had designated as a madhouse during the turbulent days of November, the idea of order contrived to assert itself—and for the achievement of order the General Staff was indispensable.

In the eyes of the General Staff, it is true, the People's Deputies had incurred the odium of signing the armistice terms, but the more shrewd of the General Staff officers had already recognized that Germany could never really have been expected to carry the burden of a war on several fronts. They thus felt that their defeat had occurred in the political and economic rather than the military field, and had therefore done nothing to impair their self-respect as soldiers. To people who harboured such sentiments as these, the signing of the armistice might well appear as something other than a purely criminal act—but an even more powerful consideration that drew the parties together was that Hindenburg, Groener and Schleicher were haunted by the spectre of Bolshevism. Thus was born the strange alliance between the General Staff and the People's Deputies which guarded the cradle of the German republic. Already on the evening of November 9th, Ebert, who held the portfolios of internal affairs and the Army in the provisional government, had telephoned to the Supreme Command and asked whether he could count on its help in his battle with Bolshevism. Schleicher answered in the affirmative and on the 10th the partnership was complete, though neither side felt too comfortable about it and each was somewhat suspicious of the other. The thing was accepted as a necessary though somewhat embarrassing evil.

Hindenburg kept somewhat in the background during these proceedings. It was Groener and Schleicher who on this occasion acted as the General Staff's spokesmen, Groener acting in his character of a friend of bourgeois democracy, while Schleicher was alert enough to see a chance for the Army's survival in new clothing. The head of the First Quartermaster-General's department now gained a new importance as a sort of political Chief of Staff, so much so that he quite overshadowed the old Operations section of the General Staff which hitherto had been accounted the real brain of that organization.

Kurt von Schleicher who came from much the same kind of social background as Waldersee, also resembled the latter in his political ambition. Indeed he possessed rather more of that quality than had hitherto been considered customary for a Prussian Guards officer. There was however this difference between the two men that Schleicher really understood the forces of his age, while Waldersee did not. Schleicher's weakness was that the curious hybrid position which he occupied caused him to pay too much attention to mere lobbying and intrigue. The personality of Groener, however, may in this respect have acted on him both as an example and a corrective, for Groener was a man of principle who was sincerely concerned to put an effective power instrument into the hands of the young republic, and who thus had no occasion to concern himself with the seamier side of politics. Yet as soldiers both Groener and Schleicher were of one mind in this: both knew that the ability to make good alliances was the basis of any successful conduct of international affairs, and both wanted to put Germany in a position where she could make such alliances.

Although the essentially unmilitary phenomenon of the soldiers' councils filled both men with resentment, and though the affair of a central congress of such councils suggested an unpleasant parallel with recent developments in Russia, they had, if they had known, no real cause for apprehension, for the German soldiers were not Russians. Most of them were far less concerned with revolution or with the extirpation of the officer corps than with getting out of uniform as quickly as they could. As a result the General Staff had very little trouble with such delegates from the councils as were sent to Spa. All that was necessary was to explain the difficulties which the withdrawal demanded by the Allies entailed, and to ask them whether they were prepared to take the responsibility for a complete breakdown in the arrangements. If, as was nearly always the case, they were ready to co-operate with the General Staff, they were given an office and thereafter gave no trouble at all. Indeed the councils were themselves soon sending out appeals for obedience.

It was the General Staff's first victory. It had once again been saved by its mastery of the art of leadership. It was saved yet a second time, though unwittingly, by Marshal Foch. When in December negotiations were begun for continuation of the armistice, which was originally limited to four weeks, Erzberger reversed his previous position and asked for representatives of the General Staff to be present. Foch refused to have any dealings with them, however, and so completed the work of shifting the stigma of submission from the General Staff on to the politicians.

III

While the withdrawal from France and Belgium was being completed the General Staff transferred its headquarters to Bad Homburg. From thence in December it finally moved to Cassel and established itself in Schloss Wilhelmshöhe. In Berlin the Deputy Chief of Staff of the Home Forces began to go about his work in civilian clothes, and on February 1st, 1919, the General Staff was placed on a peace footing. Meanwhile Colonel von Haeften had gone to Berlin as a go-between, to be followed shortly afterwards by Schleicher.

With his forces thus in position, Groener now made certain concrete demands. A properly elected Constituent Assembly was to be called together to draw up a constitution. The civilian population (which had got possession of large quantities of weapons) was to be disarmed. All soldiers' and workers' councils were to be forbidden. When Groener made these demands the General Staff was still, even in the matter of mere numbers, a very real power. It still had behind it the fighting divisions that were returning from the front, and these had up till now largely maintained, and even shown pride in, their traditional Prussian discipline. Even so there was the home front to be dealt with. Ebert might well approve Groener's plans, but the power-issue between the workers' and soldiers' councils on the one hand and the People's Deputies on the other was still undecided.

In Berlin the soldiers' and workers' guards, which were supposed to be responsible for the safety of the deputies, were purely ephemeral bodies, the police presidency was in the hands of an Independent Socialist, while radical elements were in control of various highly pugnacious and determined bodies of irregular and self-recruited shock troops such as the *Volks-Marine-Division*, or People's Naval Division, and against these the provisional government could in the long run set nothing but its good intentions. In these circumstances the fate both of the revolution and of the republic would be decided by the return of the Army, and that the Army did contrive to return without any very great difficulty—despite occasional local friction with the soldiers' councils—was the last military achievement of the Prussian General Staff.

IV

Groener and Schleicher had both recognized that a real decision could only take place in the capital. Whatever else happened, Berlin must be firmly in the hands of the new government, for in Groener's eyes Ebert was for all practical purposes the new Chancellor whom it was his duty to support. Nor was he slow to recognize that this man of humble birth had the qualities of a true statesman, despite the fact that the resentful remnant of the old society covered him with ridicule and contempt. Immediate action was essential. Disturbances were taking place in Bavaria, in the Rhineland and in Westphalia, Centrifugal tendencies, which the French were endeavouring to stimulate into open Separatism, were becoming apparent in various parts of the country, and the Polish revolt in the eastern provinces was a further source of danger.

These considerations led Groener to have a plan drawn up for Ebert, according to which Berlin was to be occupied by nine trustworthy divisions of front-line troops, General Lequis being sent to the city as town commandant. Lequis insisted on the immediate dissolution of the *Volks-Marine-Division*. Schleicher too was pressing for immediate action against the irregular possession of arms, while Major Meyn, an officer of the General Staff, was already organizing those five "Centuries" of shock troops for street fighting which were ultimately to become the nucleus of the Prussian *Schutzpolizei*.

But Ebert could not make up his mind. He was, after all, a labour leader, and it was under his leadership that the workers had fought and suffered to bring about the revolution which had just taken place.

Yet now the officers were seeking his permission to fire on those same workers if the necessity arose, and Ebert began to foresee that civil war which the General Staff had always held to be unavoidable if clear power relations were ever to be established. It was a terrible moment.

On December 11th, the first returning troops reached Berlin. They included regiments of the Prussian Guard. Ebert received them at the Brandenburg Gate and called out to them that they had been "unconquered in the field". Up to that hour the victory of the General Staff had been complete. Now there was a change. The desire for rest and quiet began to assert itself, the propaganda of the soldiers' and workers' councils began to take effect, and the General Staff completely lost control of the demobilization.

The General Staff had planned for the men to be demobilized by divisions, whereas the soldiers' councils had pressed for demobilization to be by age groups, and it was now the soldiers' councils that contrived to impose their will. Those same regiments which had proudly marched in parade step down Unter den Linden began to disperse, the old Army finally dissolved. Once more huge quantities of weapons and ammunition were thrown, and even traded away, and subversive elements were thus given another opportunity to re-arm. The Central Soldiers' Council now renewed its demand for the abolition of all distinctions of rank. It also insisted that Hindenburg should go and that the supreme military authority should be vested in itself. The General Staff refused these demands—it was now for that organization a matter of life and death—so that a situation arose in which the General Staff, the Council of People's Delegates and the Central Soldiers' Council were left facing one another without any of the three possessing the effective means of power.

On December 16th all General Staff officers who were in Berlin at the time assembled at the old red house in the Königsplatz to discuss the position. Four days later a second meeting took place, and on this occasion Schleicher put forward certain very definite ideas. The government, he claimed, was without effective means of power. Such means had therefore to be created, and he proposed that this need should be met by the organization of bodies of volunteers.

Now as far back as November 24th Hindenburg had sent out orders from Wilhelmshöhe for the Army staffs to help in the setting up of volunteer border guards in the east, but it was not till January 9th that the provisional government sent out an appeal for the formation of yet further bodies of volunteers. When it did come, however, it had immediate effect. Within a very short time the first new *Frei-korps* had come into being, for the most part under the leadership, not of officers of the General Staff but of young impatient combat officers who had got the war into their blood. Soon, all over Germany —in the south Bavaria was particularly conspicuous in this respect— one new formation was coming into being after another, composed largely of men of the *landsknecht* type (of the kind of professional military adventurers, that is to say, whom every long war tends to breed), though these were mixed with men who were honestly concerned to re-establish law and order and wanted the revival of a properly constituted political authority of the traditional kind.

These volunteer groups varied greatly in strength and equipment, some possessing heavy artillery, tanks, armoured cars and aircraft, others being much more modest affairs, but there was one thing they certainly had in common. Although it was the General Staff that had originally called them into being, they were soon to bring to the fore a certain type of leader—Captain Ehrhardt, General von Epp, Captain Röhm and Lieutenant Rossbach are excellent examples—whose whole outlook was a menace to the General Staff tradition; for these *Freikorps*, and particularly their leaders, tended more and more to be centres of political unrest, and it was not long before there was born among them a new radicalism of the right which drew its spiritual nourishment both from the comradeship of the fighting line and from the resentment of a generation of uprooted young men in officers' uniform, who felt cheated of their deserts by the ruin of the middle class. Here for the first time was to be found that fatal fusion of nationalist and socialist ideas. Here the legend of the stab in the back was to gather its most impassioned propagators. Here too was to originate that underground system of gang justice known as the *Feme*, by which those considered treasonable or disloyal were despatched. It was for such formations that in the early months of 1919 Corporal Adolf Hitler was working as an "Education Officer", in vulgar language a political agent, his task being to gather information about all political parties. It was also out of the ranks of the *Freikorps* that there were to originate such organizations as *Consul*, the *Reichsflagge* and the *Sportvereinigung Olympia* which were chiefly concerned with political violence of one kind or another, and it is in such company as this that we must seek the murderers of Rathenau and Erzberger. A hard battle was to be fought before it was decided whether the spirit of the *Freikorps* or that of the General Staff was to mould the new army.

If we are to do justice to the story of the General Staff during this critical period there is one thing of which even at this stage we should take careful note. It is that the General Staff was not primarily concerned to uphold any particular form of State but simply with the principle of authority and order, a principle that could be incorporated equally well in a democratic, monarchial or socialist form of society. Coupled with this conception of order was the preservation of the *Reich*, the German commonwealth, which, in Seeckt's mind, now replaced the "Royal Shield" as a symbol. It would be wrong to say that the form of State was to such men a matter of complete indifference, but it certainly was secondary. Even so, however, there were differences between the General Staff and Ebert, and it was impossible to get his agreement to all the stern measures which Groener and Schleicher proposed or to convince him of their necessity. Indeed so obstinate was Ebert that Schleicher finally lost his patience and returned to Wilhelmshöhe.

The breach however was short-lived. On December 23rd the *Volks-Marine-Division* revolted against the People's Delegates and Ebert found himself blockaded by the rebels in the Wilhelmstrasse. He telephoned for help to Schleicher who promised relief. Lequis' forces were, however, insufficient and the first attempt to effect a military occupation of Berlin came to nothing. When in January matters were made worse by a Communist uprising organized by the Spartacus League, the Council of People's Deputies was itself forced to call on the *Freikorps* for aid. The result was that the rising was successfully put down with the help of mine throwers, artillery and armoured cars.

V

It was in this hour of direst need that Ebert resolved to turn over the conduct of all military affairs to Gustav Noske, the governor of Kiel, though General Reinhardt who had been in charge of demobilization at the War Ministry was given the post of Minister of War. Noske, a sometime woodworker and later the editor of a social democratic paper, had contrived to keep the Kiel sailors under control. It was presumed that he would be able to settle with the Spartacists. Indeed his personality was so much to the liking of the officers, that Captain Pabst, Chief of Staff to a Guards Cavalry division, conceived the idea of proclaiming him dictator, a project of which Noske had no knowledge and which came to nothing. With the assistance of the *Freikorps* the defenders or order triumphed under Noske in the early months of 1919, though not without heavy fighting.

Even now, however, neither Noske nor Ebert was wholly prepared to drop the idea of soldiers' councils, but the forces of the old officer corps were steadily gaining in strength and a new type of soldiers' organization began to come into being. The year 1919 became the year of the *Soldatenbünde* or ex-soldiers' unions. In Central Germany, the one-armed Captain Seldte, an officer of the reserve, and in civil life a manufacturer of soda water, and Lieuteanant-Colonel Theodor Düsterberg, a sometime officer of the General Staff, founded the *Stahlhelm* organization, while ex-officers formed the *Bund Deutscher Offiziere* and the strongly monarchical *Nationalverband Deutscher Offiziere*. Ludendorff came back from Sweden. The tide had turned.

The centre of military interest had now shifted to the east, a fact which resulted in the Supreme Command transferring its head-quarters during the course of 1919 to Kolberg. Here, as the German forces were withdrawn from White Russia, Poland and the Ukraine, the foundation was laid for an organization of frontier guards to defend those regions where Germany was still asserting her power against any pretensions on the part of the new Polish republic. Two new commands were created at this time, "Frontier Defence North" and "Frontier Defence South", but the situation was further complicated by the fact that German detachments under Major Rüdiger von der Goltz, who had liberated Finland from the Bolsheviks, were carrying on a more or less independent war against them in the Baltic region, an enterprise in which they were assisted by Russian "White Guards" and elements of the Baltic bourgeoisie and nobility.

Seeckt, who was appointed Chief of Staff to "Frontier Defence North", was thus confronted with a very delicate situation, not the least delicate element of which were Goltz's *Freikorps*. Seeckt tended to view these bodies as a possible bridge between Germany and a new firmly constituted government in Russia, yet he had to recognize that the possibility of their undertaking some counter-revolutionary coup against the Reich was not to be ruled out. Seeckt set his face against any such scheme, in the success of which he had in any case no confidence. In due course, as a result of Allied pressure, this force had to be withdrawn, though hopes had for a time been entertained that it would play a part in Allied policy.

VI

While Seeckt was preoccupied with affairs in the east, where he had, at the bidding of the Allies, to cut short an all too successful operation against Polish rebels in Posen, the Peace Conference was deliberating in Paris, and in April it looked as though the German government, which Scheidemann had now taken over, would be given the opportunity of submitting its views. At the instigation of the General Staff, Seeckt had drawn up in the early part of the year a memorandum on the Army question. The future Army of the Reich was, according to this scheme, to consist, as of old, of contingents from Prussia, Bavaria, Württemberg, Baden and Saxony. These contingents, by virtue of treaties to be drawn up between the States concerned, were to be formed into a homogeneous Army under the command of a Reich War Minister and a Reich General Staff. The standing Army, which was, according to Seeckt's plan, to consist of 24 divisions together with specialist troops, was to be composed of volunteers who were to engage themselves for a period of two years. This Army was to have behind it a militia, based on a three months' training period and yearly exercises. The various excrescences of democracy, such as soldiers' parliaments and election of officers by the rank and file, were considered damaging to the troops and ruled out. This general conception is clearly influenced by the experience which the General Staff had now gained of the character of mass armies. Seeckt had by now developed a profound distrust of their reliability.

In March a new law was promulgated for a provisional *Reichswehr*. By its provisions the President of the Reich, Ebert, was Supreme Commander of the Army, while Noske as *Reichswehr* Minister would act as its representative both at home and abroad. The function of the Army was declared to be the protection of the Reich's frontiers and the maintenance of order. Such *Freikorps* as had grown up to date were to be incorporated in the *Reichswehr*, which was to be equipped with heavy arms and was now to attain as high a figure as 400,000 men. The exact position and function of the Supreme Command which was still at Wilhelmshöhe and of the General Staff was left undecided. The old Prussian War Ministry was still allowed to remain in being for winding up purposes.

The law embodied certain decisive new departures. Not only did such strongholds of the old princely power as the Military Cabinet disappear, but military justice was abolished. Henceforward both officers and men came under the jurisdiction of the civil law. Further, no military personage was to be allowed to hold the post of War Minister. Also, contrary to Seeckt's proposals, delegates from the various barracks garrisons and from the larger formations were to form a *Heereskammer* or army chamber; this was to replace the soldiers' councils which were finally to be abolished.

In due course the Prussian War Ministry and the General Staff organized two Peace Commissions which were to accompany the German delegation to Versailles. Groener appointed Seeckt to the General Staff commission which was ultimately united with that of the War Ministry. Seeckt now reformulated the General Staff proposals for the *Reichswehr*. Presumably anticipating objections to an Army of 400,000, he now proposed one of 300,000 composed of long service volunteers who were to be equipped with aircraft, tanks and heavy artillery. A militia, based on compulsory service, was again to be in support. Seeckt also urged in advance that no undertaking of unilateral disarmament should be given nor should Germany commit herself to the unilateral demilitarization of the left bank of the Rhine. Groener fully expressed Seeckt's mind when he declared to the National Assembly that the maintenance of Germany's most important political problem was to ensure her capacity to make alliances. He even went so far as to say that an attempt should be made to retain at least the western part of Alsace-Lorraine as a strategic glacis.

However when in May 1919 the German peace delegates arrived in Versailles, they found that all essential decisions had already been made; they were handed a complete draft, and told that they had only a limited time in which to make their observations. The Allied terms provided for what was in effect the complete disarmament of Germany. The strength of the Army was to be reduced to 100,000 men, universal service was to be abolished, and the Great General Staff forbidden. The new German Army was not permitted to have aircraft, tanks or heavy artillery, and in order to prevent reserves from coming into being, the period of service was laid down as twelve years in the case of men and twenty-five years in the case of officers. The fleet was reduced to a few cruisers and a few old ships of the line, the personnel was limited to 15,000 men and all underwater craft were forbidden. In addition to the above, the Emperor and a number of well-known generals were to be handed over as war criminals.

Apart from its military provisions, the proposed Treaty entailed the cession to Poland of the province of Posen and of a great part of West Prussia, East Prussia being cut off from the Reich by a land corridor. Danzig was to become a so-called "Free City". The left bank of Rhine and a strip of territory on the right bank were demilitarized, while British, French, Belgian and American troops remained in occupation in the Rhineland. A Control Commission was to supervise the execution of the disarmament.

It was useless for Seeckt to reproach Count Brockdorff-Rantzau, the Foreign Minister who led the delegation, for insufficient vigour in defending the Army's interests. The decision to disarm Germany was irrevocable. Seeckt vainly endeavoured to get agreement to an Army of 200,000 men, equipped with aircraft, while Groener insisted that 350,000 was the minimum that could be considered; Brockdorff-Rantzau refused to put any such proposals forward.

VII

Before the German delegation left Versailles the question naturally arose as to what would happen in the event of Germany's refusing to sign, and during May Groener discussed the possibility of further German resistance in such an eventuality with Seeckt and Reinhardt. General von Lossberg, Chief of Staff to *Reichswehr* Group Command I, and Major von Stülpnagel, Chief of the Operations Section, were for raising a popular revolt against Poland in the east, but neither Seeckt nor Groener had any illusions about Germany's defencelessness in the west, or her inability to hold the Ruhr, the Rhine, Hessen or Baden. At the very utmost, in Groener's view, the Elbe might be defended.

Hindenburg was now formally approached by the government and asked his views on the prospect of successful armed resistance. He replied that success was possible in the east but that the west could not be held, closing his observations with the remark that as a soldier he preferred to perish with honour rather than to surrender. In this way Hindenburg once again put the responsibility on the politicians. Groener was more honest. He refused to sanction the destruction of his country, and since destruction was the only alternative, recommended signature. When the matter finally came up for full discussion in Kolberg, Hindenburg left the room.

According to the strict Prussian code of honour Hindenburg was right, Germany should have gone down fighting, but there were those who thought there was something more important than the Prussian code of honour. Seeckt in particular thought it more important to keep the Army in being and preserve the possibility of a military resurrection; it was not long before Seeckt could make a beginning on that work.

As we have already seen, the Treaty of Versailles forbade the Great General Staff. It did not, however, forbid the *Truppengeneralstab*, called here the 'Operational General Staff'. When therefore on the day on which the treaty was signed, Reinhardt summoned Seeckt and asked him to take over the affairs of the Great General Staff (in place of Hindenburg who had resigned) pending its final dissolution, Seeckt accepted the task, but a letter which he addressed to Hindenburg on July 7th shows clearly what was in his mind. In this he said that if he could preserve, not necessarily the form, but the spirit of the General Staff, he believed that his present activity would be accounted as something more than that of a gravedigger. Wetzell, the sometime Chief of Operations, may have been nearer the mark than he knew when he adjured Seeckt at least to save the kernel of "the fine and nobly conceived institution of the Great General Staff", and transplant it in some form or other into the new Army. That precisely was Seeckt's intention.

The German government refused categorically to hand over Hindenburg, Ludendorff, or anyone else, as war criminals. Instead of this, a German Parliamentary Commission was set up to enquire into the causes of the collapse, and to examine the conduct of the German statesmen and high ranking officers concerned. Hindenburg, who was invited to appear before this body, showed plainly by his disgruntled and resentful bearing that he considered himself a victim of the "stab in the back", a victim, that is to say, of those very men who were now sitting on the Commission of Enquiry. He refused to shake hands with the Chairman of the Commission, and was very soon making his listeners feel that he was an accuser rather than an accused. His huge figure probably made it easier for him to create this effect, as in his deep growling bass he expounded to the Commission that Germany would have won the war if there had been no *Flaumacher und Aufwiegler* (creators of discontent and despondency). This was Hindenburg's sincere conviction—an astonishing example of the powers of illusion.

VIII

Until January 1st, 1920, when the Treaty was actually to come into force, the Supreme Command was permitted to maintain its headquarters in Kolberg but there was now little point in doing so, and the same applied to the old Prussian War Ministry. It was obvious that the most pressing task of the hour was to create a firm and effective organization for the new Army. Seeckt now planned a somewhat novel horizontal organization under which the different departments of the *Reichswehr* were on one level of authority, and all came immediately under the *Reichswehr* Minister. These departments included the *Heeresamt* or Army Office which took over the tasks and powers of the old War Ministry, and in particular the *Truppenamt* or Troop Office",* which was to carry on what had hitherto been the work of the General Staff. Both *Heeresamt* and *Truppenamt* remained part of the permanent organization of the *Reichswehr*. Seeckt further sought to copy the English model by creating an "Army Council" of the highest ranking generals, and by providing for a parliamentary Secretary in the Reichstag to safeguard the Army's interests.

At this time things were made more difficult for what may be called the traditionalist party, by the circumstance that Seeckt became seriously ill with heart trouble and was only able to return to duty in the autumn. On October 1st, however, a complete reorganization of the *Reichswehr* Ministry was carried into effect. The Ministry was moved to new quarters in the Bendlerstrasse, the old Prussian War Ministry was finally closed and the old Supreme Command wound up. Groener retired and went into politics.

Seeckt's horizontal arrangement of departments was now changed to a vertical one by the creation of the post of *Chef der Heeresleitung* or Chief of the Army Command, who came directly under the *Reichswehr* Minister. This officer had a number of departments under him of which the *Heeresamt* and the *Truppenamt* were the most important. The most promising candidate for the new post was obviously Seeckt himself, but Noske succeeded in persuading Ebert to appoint General Reinhardt, for he believed, not without some justification, that as a South German Reinhardt would be more in sympathy with the new form of State.

Seeckt was given the *Truppenamt*, the strength of which ran to about sixty officers. He incurred a slight setback however. It had been Groener's wish to preserve for the *Truppenamt* the General Staff's old *Immediatstellung* (i.e. its right to approach the head of the State direct), but with the new vertical and centralized organization this became impossible. The right in question had necessarily to lapse, as

---

* The *Truppenamt* plays so large a part in history from now on that it is thought best to use its characteristic but deliberately misleading German name throughout. (B.B.)

did the theory of the "co-responsibility" of General Staff officers, for a very considerable part of the old tasks of the Chief of General Staff now devolved, not on the *Truppenamt*, but on the *Chef der Heeresleitung*, who united the functions of Supreme Commander and Senior General Staff officer in his person.

Even so Seeckt in his new post was able to carry out three important measures. He secured the foundation of the *Reichsarchiv*, or department of State archives, the function of which was to collect all documents relating to the war, and carry on the business of research into military history. He contrived to preserve the *kreiskommissars*, the recently created district commissioners concerned with frontier defence, and also succeeded in putting through a new Army law. This last was actually promulgated in 1921 and was so framed as to keep the Army away from any kind of political activity, with the result that the Army was immunized not only against Communist but also against democratic influences.

IX

As yet the authorities in charge of the new Army no more constituted a true unity than did the Army itself, for their relations were charged with latent tensions—tensions between Reinhardt and Seeckt, tensions between democrats and conservatives; to these was added the antagonism between General von Lüttwitz on the one hand—Lüttwitz was in charge of *Reichswehr* Group Command I in Berlin—and both Seeckt and Reinhardt on the other. Yet another source of trouble was the fact that the *Reichswehr* authorities tended to be at loggerheads with the *Freikorps*. These bodies were supposed to be in process of dissolution, but were, in point of fact, very far from being dissolved, and in the autumn of this year the *Baltikumer*, or men from the Baltic, as they called themselves, came home to swell the ranks of the Republic's disgruntled Praetorians.

Military adventurers of this kind, who felt that the Republic had betrayed them, usually gathered together in one of those numerous secret organizations in which nationalism and revolution were so characteristically blended. There was, however, at this time also a movement in progress, organized by members of the late *Vaterlandspartei* for general reform on what purported to be a "Prussian" basis. The centre of this movement was a certain *Landschaftsdirektor* Kapp. Kapp's plans were based on the circumstance that no properly constituted Reichstag was yet in being, but that, instead, the National

Assembly was still carrying on the government, and that, further, the President of the Republic had merely been elected by the Assembly and not by the people as the constitution provided. More grist for Kapp's mill was provided by a scandal which involved Erzberger, who was now Finance Minister, and which to some extent brought the whole Republican system of government into disrepute.

Kapp now began to plan a *coup d'état*. The whole government was to be taken by surprise and with military help put under lock and key. An authoritarian régime under a *Reichsverweser* was then to be proclaimed and the old Prussian values of duty and obedience reestablished. In due course, Kapp and his friends—their ideas seem to have been quite singularly out of touch with their times—were approached by Lüttwitz. Ludendorff and Colonel Bauer also threw in their lot, as did a number of other personalities of the Junker caste, while some of the subordinate *Reichswehr* commanders were not disinclined to put their troops at the venturers' disposal. Lüttwitz, however, believed the disgruntled *Freikorps* to be the ideal instrument for the job, and on March 13th, 1920, the attempt was ultimately made.

Experienced General Staff officers such as Fritsch and von Lossberg could see in such a *coup d'état* nothing but a weakening of the authority of the State, an authority which it had taken so much labour to establish, but Seeckt was influenced by somewhat different considerations. At the beginning of 1920 there had been grave communist-inspired unrest in Saxony, Southern Germany and particularly in the Ruhr, which glaring local social contrasts made particularly rife for trouble; indeed there were a number of signs that a general revolt was being planned. Seeckt, however, opposed the use of troops for police purposes. It was, he held, not the Army's function to suppress disturbances. The Army's purpose was to provide the kernel of a greater Army, it must not allow itself to be torn asunder in struggles between the classes, it must not become an instrument of civil war. The Army—such was Seeckt's intention—was to become a new *imperium in imperio*, which would maintain touch with any organization that had the defence of the country at heart, but would not commit itself politically one way or the other.

In the days following March 13th Seeckt maintained his characteristic attitude: Lüttwitz, with a certain chivalrous blindness to reality, had committed the blunder of sending the government an ultimatum, so that its members were warned and thus able to escape arrest by flight. Seeckt was more cautious. Actually the attempt at a *coup d'état* by the *Freikorps* was as much a revolt against the authority of the General Staff as against that of the government; but for Seeckt the issue was not so simple. It is true that, ill-considered and ill-prepared as it was, this rash venture of Kapp and his friends might seriously endanger the internal cohesion of the Army, but it must not be forgotten that the *Freikorps* were in Seeckt's eyes the precursors of the *Reichswehr* and to some extent represented the source from which it had sprung. It was this that was at the bottom of Seeckt's attitude. When the insurgents marched into Berlin, Noske and Reinhardt raised the question of using the *Reichswehr* against them. Seeckt's remark on this occasion was a model of terseness: "*Truppe schiesst nicht auf Truppe*", which may be loosely rendered, "German soldiers don't shoot at each other". Pressed further, he asked Noske whether he wanted a battle at the Brandenburg Gate. When Noske burst out that he was being deserted by everybody and saw no possibility ahead but suicide, Seeckt's only answer was a mocking smile. The Chief of the *Truppenamt* elected to wait, though he could on this occasion already have turned the scale.

The entry of the *Marinebrigade Ehrhardt* and the other *Freikorps* into Berlin in full field-service kit caused the government to retire first to Dresden and then to Stuttgart—all, that is to say, except Vice-Chancellor Schiffer, who remained behind as a go-between. Kapp proclaimed von der Goltz as Chief of General Staff. Seeckt quietly handed in his resignation, leaving Heye behind as his deputy in the *Truppenamt*.

Goltz never took over his new post, for the government now displayed commendable energy; it proclaimed a general strike. Most of the *Reichswehr* commanders maintained a watching attitude. In four days the military dictatorship was at the end of its resources, and the General Staff had had a new object lesson to demonstrate the absurdity of a military dictatorship without a mass basis.

Seeckt had understood that absurdity in advance. When he was asked why he had not joined in, he replied that a Prussian General did not break his oath—a strange observation indeed, since he had singularly failed to perform his sworn duty. The truth is, of course, that all Seeckt cared for was the preservation of the Army's integrity, the integrity, that is to say, of his own special instrument. Apart from that he did not feel very deeply on the matter.

Very characteristically Seeckt prevented the imprisonment both of Ehrhardt and Lüttwitz and procured immunity for all other high military personages that had taken part in the affair. All this is typical, as typical of his latent anti-Republicanism, as was his attitude towards the Republican flag. He accepted the latter because, in his own words, he did not wish to see the old Imperial colours of black, white and red besmirched by the Republic, but he sabotaged any attempt to introduce republican decorations with a red, black and golden ribbon into the Army. The Republic was to be strictly prevented from having any attraction for that body.

On March 17th, the same day on which Kapp had withdrawn from Berlin in the morning, followed by Lüttwitz in the afternoon, Noske handed over by telegraph to Seeckt the command over all Troops in Group Command I. At the same time Vice-Chancellor Schiffer entrusted him with the office of *Chef der Heeresleitung* (from which Reinhardt retired) and, Noske having also been dismissed, with the *Reichswehr* Ministry. Some of his colleagues held that Seeckt had sold himself to the Republic. Colonel Bauer declared that in the eyes of all officers Seeckt stood as one judged and condemned. Such an attitude, however, did nothing except reveal the hopeless political shortsightedness of those who adopted it.

The Kapp *Putsch* had dealt a mortal blow to the workers' confidence in the new democratic state. It produced a number of disturbances, those in the Ruhr, which were again Communist-inspired, being particularly grave. In the latter district several *Freikorps* were disarmed and in part massacred. Moreover artillery mine throwers and armoured cars came into the hands of the insurgents. A regular red army came into being and this time the use of troops could not be avoided. During the course of operations *Reichswehr* units in several instances violated the demilitarized zone, whereupon France, by way of sanctions, pushed forward its occupation troops towards Frankfurt and Darmstadt.

X

It was under these unpropitious auspices that Seeckt finally set about the task of rebuilding the Army. Actually the position of *Chef der Heeresleitung*, which he now held, was contrary to the Treaty, for the provisions of Versailles not only forbade the Great General Staff, they forbade the existence of a generalissimo. They laid down that the command of the *Reichswehr* was to be in the hands of a parliamentary War Minister who was to be a civilian, and of two Group Commanders, each of whom was to have equal authority with the other. Seeckt's first problem was therefore to maintain his position as Commander in Chief.

That he contrived to hold on to that position was not due to any special aptitude for ingratiating himself with his late enemies. A number of conferences took place after the signature of the Treaty and Seeckt accompanied the German delegation to the first of these conferences at Spa, since the final reduction of the Army to 100,000 men was to be discussed there. It is possible that a more skilful touch could have secured for Germany an Army of 200,000 or at least 150,000 men, for in English eyes France was already beginning to assume that invidious position of military predominance which till then had been occupied by Imperial Germany, so that Lloyd George was not wholly averse to concessions. Lloyd George, however, had on the whole little use for generals, having quarrelled with too many of them during the war, and Seeckt's haughty manner was not calculated to convince him that Prussian generals were any better than their opposite numbers in Britain.

So Seeckt had to make shift as best he could and the essence of what was in his mind is well revealed by a French writer who spoke of him as trying to create *"une grande armée en miniature"* for the *Reichswehr* as the kernel of a future national Army—and this was at least one of Seeckt's objectives—had to contain in embryo more or less all the elements of such an army. The *Reichswehr*, however, had yet another purpose, for this *Führerarmee* or "Leader Army", besides supplying the necessary instructors to a larger Army, was itself to provide the core of a mobile shock force. In so far as Seeckt distrusted the mass army, this latter function of his *élite* Army was probably uppermost in his mind, all the more so since such a conception implied that the curse of positional warfare, which Seeckt's biographer so aptly called an "operational perversion", had at last been overcome. Incidentally this same train of ideas with their emphasis on mobility caused Seeckt to have a high esteem for cavalry. The Allies, believing the cavalry arm to be outdated, had allowed Germany quite a sizeable mounted force and, in a sense, Seeckt made a virtue of this necessity. Certainly the essence of his plan was to offset the weakness of his numbers by the maximum of mobility, and as early as 1921 he was ordering exercises in the difficult country of the Harz mountains in which he employed motorized infantry loaded into lorries.

The distrust which Seeckt and many like him felt for mass armies was, as we have seen, one of the grounds in which his genuine preference for a small *élite* Army was founded, but needless to say smallness was not in every respect an unqualified advantage, even if one made the assumption that Germany would not again engage in a multi-front war. So diminutive a force as Germany was now allowed made the problem of frontier defence highly intractable, and that problem was a pressing one. In the east, Poland and Czechoslovakia, the two new States which stood under French protection, each thrust a wedge into German territory, and though relations with Czechoslovakia gradually became comparatively friendly, Poland was claiming more territory in East Prussia and Upper Silesia than the Treaty had so far allowed, and there was real danger of conflict. The question of Upper Silesia's fate had not yet been settled. It was to be decided by a plebiscite, and there were a number of Polish attempts to anticipate that decision by stage-managed revolts. In these circumstances a force of 100,000 men was definitely too small and that was why the idea of universal service was never abandoned, and why his ideal remained that of the mobile *élite* Army which would be supplemented by a conscript militia. At present the nearest approach to the latter was only the illegal *Grenzschutz Ost*.

Though provisionally confined to 100,000 men, Seeckt continued to aim at a figure of twice or three times that number, even for his *élite* Army; increases in the latter, however, were only to take place by slow stages—a method of procedure which was one day to clash violently with the dynamism of Hitler. The germ of the preparatory measures designed towards this end are already observable in 1921 in the elaborate training schemes by which troops learned the use of every weapon available to them. Thus, from September 1921 onwards all members of transport units were unofficially trained as artillerymen.

The function of the *Reichswehr* as the kernel of a National Army of the future implied for Seeckt, as we have seen, that it must in no circumstances be used in any kind of civil war. The use of troops for police purposes involved the danger of an alienation between Army and people which had at all costs to be avoided. This was an additional reason for insisting that officers should be strictly unpolitical beings. Seeckt's officers were not to be counter-revolutionaries—nor, on the other hand, were they to be republicans.

Not all social democrat politicians were as friendly to the Army as Ebert and Noske, but Seeckt preserved the gulf between Army and State even when the latter's representative made real efforts on the Army's behalf. It was Ebert's conviction that the Head of the State should concern himself about its armed forces and take an interest in their wellbeing. He expressed the wish to be present at parades and manoeuvres. Yet precisely because he knew that this simple dignified man had qualities which drew men towards him, Seeckt set his face against all Ebert's attempts to participate in Army affairs—much as he had set his face against Republican medals and decorations. The President of the Republic was no concern of the *Reichswehr*. The *Reichswehr* was not even to know him.

In this respect Seeckt differed markedly from Schleicher, who was always declaring that the officer corps should be wedded to the spirit of its age. This should not, as a matter of fact, have presented insuperable difficulties, for the officers of the *Reichswehr* showed a strong preponderance of bourgeois elements, though the 9th Infantry Regiment in Potsdam, the so-called *Traditionstruppenteil* of the Prussian Guard, and certain cavalry regiments formed exceptions to this rule. Members of the princely houses however were conspicuous by their absence; their presence would undoubtedly have provoked sharp criticism in the Reichstag.

XI

The first *Army List* of the new Army which was published in 1923 showed that there had been a successful attempt to bring over as many competent General Staff officers as possible from the old Imperial Army into the *Reichswehr*—a fact which helped to preserve that continuity of tradition which to Seeckt was a matter of such vital importance. Seeckt had arranged that every contingent of the *Reichswehr* was to be regarded as the successor of a number of famous regiments of the old Prussian, Bavarian, Saxon and Württembergian armies. In this sense the *Truppenamt*, as already indicated, was unofficially the carrier of the Great General Staff's tradition, and it was in point of fact not long before it turned into much the same kind of school of uniform operational thought, though as the result of the smallness of its numbers it could not command quite the same influence as its predecessor.

Officially the designations "General Staff" and "General Staff officer" were dropped, the terms *"Führerstab"* and *"Führerstabs-offizier"* (Leader Staff and Leader Staff officer) being substituted. But the spirit remained the same. In Seeckt's new instructions for General Staff officers we find the following: "The form changes, the spirit remains. It is the spirit of silent selfless devotion to duty in the service of the Army. General Staff officers have no name. We have now no time either to lament or to accuse—we certainly have no time to be weary. As long as we do our duty, our honour is unimpaired."

The *Truppenamt* was, of course, only one of a number of offices that came under the *Chef der Heeresleitung*, the others being the *Allgemeines Heeresamt*, the *Heerespersonalamt, Heeresverwaltungsamt*, and *Heeres-Waffenamt* (General Army Office, Army Personnel, Army Administration, and Armaments Office), and the *Truppenamt* was composed of four departments. T.1 under the title of "Home Defence" represented the old Operations and Deployment section of the General Staff. T.2 was the Organization section, T.3 dealt with foreign armies, T.4 with training. We have already seen that the old and very characteristic department of the General Staff which dealt with research into military history had been turned into a separate civilian department though under the control of leading experts of the General Staff. Similar dispositions were also made in the case of the equally vital mapping and survey department. The old Central Department of the General Staff which dealt with personal records was not resurrected, its functions being taken over by a section of the *Heerespersonalamt*. Meanwhile, of course, the old *Truppengeneralsstab*, or Operational General Staff, continued to live on in the staffs of the Group Commands, Military Districts and in those of the artillery and infantry commanders.

All this is in line with a phenomenon which we may usefully note here—namely, the persistent duplication of staffs. Seeckt himself, as *Chef der Heeresleitung*, had under him not only the *Truppenamt*, in which the Great General Staff had been preserved, but also in addition a Chief of Staff of his own. We have just seen that groups, military districts and other formations had their General Staff, but they had an ordinary staff as well. Thus, in the 2nd Infantry Division at Stettin, the Divisional Chief of Staff had under him a General Staff of nine officers in addition to a divisional staff of ten officers, and even the *Infantrief'ührer II*, the second in command of the infantry, had a General Staff of two officers and a staff of one officer. This method of hoarding experienced General Staff officers had to be dropped in the years that followed—presumably as a result of representations by the Control Commission.

Even so the foundations were being laid, and even at this early stage, the officers who were to lead the great armies of the Third Reich had already begun their careers. Von Blomberg, von Leeb, von Bock, von Falkenhausen and von Rundstedt were in 1923 serving as lieutenant-colonels and Divisional Chiefs of Staff. Von Brauchitsch and Kesselring were in the *Truppenamt's* training section. Kress von Kressenstein was an artillery commander, while Beck and Von Fritsch were each on the staff of an artillery regiment, and Halder on that of an infantry division. Colonel General Guderian, the last great Chief of Staff in the Second World War, was serving with the rank of captain as an inspector of motor transport, and we can also at this juncture note among the Staff officers of the 7th Infantry Division the name of Ernst Röhm.

There remained the problem of ensuring for the General Staff a suitable supply of recruits. Since the old *Kriegsakademie* had been abolished, so-called military district examinations were instituted. The attainments required for these included not only the military sciences, but languages, political science, history, a knowledge of railways and communications, and other subjects. Seeckt insisted not only on suitability of character but on a good general education together with a most thorough professional training.

The small number of vacancies made for a ruthless process of selection. Thus, in the spring of 1922, a hundred and sixty-four officers sat for examination in the 4th military district. In the autumn, twenty of these were ordered to undergo the *Führergehilfensausbildung*, or training as "Leader's Assistants". Six of these passed on to the next stage of training. At length, in 1925, one single officer was posted to the *Truppenamt* in Berlin. When Hitler ultimately undertook the creation of a large Army, the shortage of trained General Staff officers was distressingly apparent.

Whether this system really did succeed in ensuring that only the very best officers reached the General Staff seems debatable. The fact that there were so few posts had other consequences than the one described. Circumstances being what they were, it lay in the nature of things that the choice of candidates was sometimes dictated by all too human rather than by purely objective considerations. To this must be added the fact that the policy of selection tended to be controlled by a comparatively small group of officers in the *Allgemeine Heeresleitung*, who had all worked together in the old Supreme Command.

This made the chances of efficient and independent-minded outsiders somewhat slim in comparison with those of highly qualified men who were sufficiently humble and adaptable to fit themselves into the system. There was more than one example of downright undeniable favouritism. An instance is provided by the promotion of von Hammerstein-Equord's exceedingly mediocre brother to the post of Inspector of Infantry. Also the palpable tendency to favour artillery officers in selecting candidates for the higher General Staff posts had nothing to do with the decisive character of this arm, but was due to the very human circumstance that General Staff officers who happened themselves to be ex-gunners inclined more or less automatically to favour their old comrades.

Attention has already been drawn to the fact that owing to its diminished size the *Truppenamt* did not have the same influence as the old Great General Staff. It also lacked much of the latter's glamour, and this because its activity was necessarily circumscribed. The opportunities for large-scale military planning were limited to frontier defence. Moreover, the rapid changes of Chiefs of Staff from Seeckt to Heye, then to Wetzell, Blomberg, Hammerstein-Equord, and finally to Adam, constituted an unfortunate break with the old tradition. Yet the thing which principally marked this new generation of General Staff officers was that all these officers had somehow to learn to do two somewhat contradictory things at once, namely, to preserve the ethos of the Prussian officer and at the same time serve a political order which was in reality alien to their inmost selves. Moreover, all were trained to use the methods of conspirators in order at least to provide the basic minimum of protection for their country's frontiers, and all nurtured a double resentment—against their own government on the one hand, and on the other against the foreign signatories of the Treaty by which restrictions that so hampered them had been imposed.

XII

The chief problem of the young republic was Poland. It was a problem that was both military and political; it was also one that, at any rate in Seeckt's eyes, called for Staff work of a particularly cool and objective kind. Poland, whose corridor to the sea now separated East Prussia from the Reich, had a strong French-equipped army and in French eyes had the dual function of providing a control post against Germany and a barrier against Bolshevism. It was in 1920 and '21 that matters first began to come to a head between Poland and Germany, and it was with the breakdown of the Polish offensive in the Ukraine—Seeckt was at Spa at the time—that the story may be said to commence. When the Polish collapse occurred, Pilsudski, at that time Prime Minister of Poland, appealed to his French ally, with the result that a French military mission was sent to Warsaw under

Weygand. Weygand succeeded somehow in putting a new strength into the Poles. The decisive battle before the very gates of Warsaw went against the Russians, and men spoke of the miracle of the Vistula.

For Seeckt however this 'miracle' was something of a blow. Friendship with Russia was integral to his whole political outlook. As he saw things, such friendship was not only in line with Prussian tradition—the memory of Tauroggen died hard—but rested on an obvious community of interest. Soviet Russia, like Germany, was an outcast who had been shut out from the League of Nations. Also Soviet Russia had not signed the Treaty of Versailles.

When on September 9th, 1920, General Zeligowski seized Vilna by a *coup de main*, the thought not unnaturally occurred to those in Germany whose business it was to entertain it, that Poland might be tempted to equally arbitrary acts against German territory. Seeckt turned his gaze towards Moscow. A system of new alliances was for him the cornerstone of successful foreign policy and communist-inspired social unrest in various parts of Germany suggested that her position was too precarious for delay. In August 1919 German troops had suppressed the first Polish rising in Upper Silesia; then in August 1920 the Poles had risen again. If one could only unite with Russia, one could not only take the wind out of one's own Communists' sails but cover one's rear against Poland as well.

In May 1921 came the third Polish revolt, which coincided with a crisis in the Reparations question, and Seeckt began seriously to reckon with the possibility of war with Poland. Seeckt had, needless to say, already given thought to that eventuality. Plans involved the immediate expansion of the seven infantry divisions which he was allowed to twenty-one, and the taking up of a defensive position on the Weser against the west. Meanwhile what was perhaps, in view of his numbers, an over-ambitious pincers movement was to be undertaken in the east. This general plan was in this year used as the basis of a war game at the *Reichswehr* Ministry under the direction of Heye.

Although however Seeckt regarded it as intolerable that Poland should continue indefinitely in her present form, he had enough sense to see that Germany would for a long time be incapable of solving this problem by force. Certainly for the moment the presence in Upper Silesia of the Allied Plebiscite Commission and of French, British and Italian troops, which were to ensure the carrying out of its decisions, prevented Germany from using any regular forces. With the concurrence therefore of the Chancellor, Dr. Wirth of the Centre Party, Seeckt confined himself to giving unofficial support to the local volunteer formations by giving them arms and also the assistance of a number of General Staff officers, who did their work in mufti. By mid-May, roughly twenty volunteer battalions were in the field, equipped with field artillery and mine throwers, a further nine being in process of formation. The former Generals von Hofer and von Hülsen were in charge of the operation. On May 21st the Annaberg was stormed.

This kind of thing provided a happy outlet for members of the now dissolved *Freikorps*, and as the new volunteer units gradually dispersed, many of the men who had fought in them organized themselves into what were called "Workers' Associations", and found a hide-out on the estates of the great Silesian magnates. Others were ultimately absorbed into the Army's *Grenzschutz Ost*. Meanwhile, the League of Nations decision saved a very modest part of Silesia for Germany.

The Polish revolts, Zeligowski's *coup de main* at Vilna and the territorial aspirations of various chauvinist bodies like the "Westmark Union" (which claimed East Prussia and Pommerania for Poland) put the *Heeresleitung* and the *Truppenamt* in rather a strong position against the Reich government and in particular against the very distrustful government of Prussia. As a result it was possible to secure the retention in the eastern provinces of a number of illegal formations. To keep them supplied with men the military authorities relied chiefly on the *Stahlhelm* and the ex-officer organizations—a circumstance which kept Severing, the Prussian Minister of the Interior, in a permanent state of apprehension. The bodies in question were all fundamentally monarchist and anti-republican, and one could never be certain whether the weapons which the *Reichswehr* Ministry had supplied, and which were secretly dumped on the estates of East-Elbian landowners, would not one day be turned against the government itself.

XIII

The Polish question was the godmother of that alliance between the *Reichswehr* and the Red Army which was to have such far-reaching consequences for the officer corps, though it was also, to some extent, Seeckt's answer to the whole French system of alliances in Eastern and South-Eastern Europe. For the social and psychological aspects of Bolshevism Seeckt had very little critical understanding, and he listened quite cold-bloodedly to the proposal of the Bolshevik negotiators that he should co-operate in preparing world revolution. The idea that Russian armies might one day appear on the Rhine was in his eyes nothing more than a story to frighten children.

The *rapprochement* was made all the easier by considerations of economics. To realize their plans for the industrialization of Russia, Lenin needed the support of a country that was itself highly industrialized. Normal diplomatic relations had ceased to exist with France, Britain and the United States. As against this, excellent relations had developed with Turkey, and though Turkey could not supply Russia's needs directly, it was Enver Pasha, who had got to know Seeckt well during the war, who first brought the two parties into touch.

In March 1921 negotiations were opened for the transfer to Russia of prohibited German industries, and Trotsky who in 1920 had been contemplating the over-running not merely of Poland, but of the whole of Germany, now declared himself prepared for an understanding with the German government and the German Army. Seeckt saw the great chance for German industry, which could now guarantee Russia's rearmament; Radek, Krassin and other leading Russians came to Berlin. Seeckt won over both Wirth and von Maltzahn, the Foreign Secretary, to an eastward orientation. He personally received Radek, who in 1920 had been one of the organizers of the revolt in the Ruhr, and entered into an embittered controversy with Brockdorff-Rantzau who was prepared to approve an economic *rapprochement*, but urgently warned against any further commitments.

With the help of Tschunke, who had been his colleague in Turkey, and that of von Schleicher and Major-General Hasse the head of the *Truppenamt*, Seeckt now organized the "Special Branch R" in the *Reichswehr* Ministry. Schleicher allowed his residence to be used for meetings with Soviet politicians, while Nicolai, the some time head of the Great General Staff's Intelligence Department, and shortly afterwards Lieutenant-Colonel von Niedermayer, the leader of an expedition to Afghanistan, went to Moscow as the secret representatives of the *Reichswehr*. Later Hasse paid several visits to the Red Army Staff.

In the autumn of 1921 Radek asked Seeckt whether he would support Russia in the event of a Polish attack on her. Seeckt made it clear that such action would be impossible for Germany, since any conflict with Poland would immediately result in the intervention of Czechoslovakia and France; he did however promise benevolent neutrality and military advice on the understanding that such military advice would be reciprocated. In this way it was possible for Russia to apply the methods of the German General Staff in the construction of her own apparatus of command, while the *Truppenamt* obtained the opportunity to study forbidden weapons and, in particular, tanks and aircraft, on Russian soil, and to train its specialists on the spot. Relations grew closer. Already in 1922 the Russian Staff was inviting Seeckt to report on the military situation in the Dardanelles, and the Russian Field Service Instructions of 1925 bore a remarkable resemblance to German models.

In order to further this military and economic co-operation two organizations were created. One of these was the GEFU, or *Gesellschaft zur Förderung gewerblicher Unternehmungen* (Society for the furthering of Industrial Enterprises), which was under the direction of Tschunke and had offices in Moscow and Berlin. The other was the *Bersol-Aktien-Gesellschaft* which operated in Russia and was concerned with the manufacture of poison gas. German specialists now supervised the production of shells for the *Reichswehr* in Russian factories, and Professor Junkers opened branch factories in Fili near Moscow and in Kharkov, and began to construct military aircraft. The Treaty of Rapallo, so startlingly signed between Tschitscherin and Rathenau at the Genoa Conference, put an official stamp on the new relationship, and Seeckt, who, though he could never forget that Rathenau was a Jew, was nevertheless delighted with his achievement, began to talk of a "positive policy". It is at this point that the General Staff may be considered to have turned against the West.

In 1922 Special Branch R sent the first officers to be trained in Russia. In the following year a tank school was opened in Kasan, and a school for fighter pilots came into being at Kharkov. An anti-gas training centre was organized, and on the manoeuvre grounds at Kiev and Lipetsk in Russia and at Arys in East Prussia German and Russian officers carried out exercises together. At home on manoeuvres, wooden dummies had been used to represent tanks for training purposes, and the value of this expedient seemed to be distinctly enhanced when it was known that dispositions were being made to equip the Army with real tanks in an emergency.

There were reciprocal advantages for the Russians. A number of high ranking Russian officers, among them the future Chief of Staff of the Red Army, Tuchatschewski, and Zukov, the future Deputy Minister of War, came to Berlin to study the way the *Truppenamt* trained aspiring Staff officers. It was not long before Schleicher too went secretly to Moscow.

At length in 1923 definite arrangements were completed between Hasse and his Russian opposite number Lebedev which ensured Russian aid in the event of a Polish *coup de main* against Upper Silesia, and in conformity with this agreement two army groups, one of seventeen and the other of nine divisions, were kept massed in White Russia and the Ukraine. To these in due course were added three cavalry corps. Undoubtedly the arrangements with Russia had a sobering effect on the chauvinists of Poland, for rumours of what was happening trickled through to that country; the military alliance between Poland and Rumania of 1926 was signed, among other things, for the express purpose of guarding against a Russo-German attack.

The Russian Army had, of course, a special interest for Seeckt's officers because it too embodied the idea of an *élite* army, based on a militia, the *élite* army being well equipped with cavalry and motorized units. But Russia also provided the example of a unitary political party which educated the masses in discipline and stimulated their military zeal. It is true enough that Schleicher, Blomberg, Hasse and the other generals who went to Russia had little use for Bolshevik ideology. Yet Blomberg once admitted in a conversation with Rauschning that the example of mass discipline which he had got to know in Russia had nearly made a Bolshevik of him, and had certainly turned him into a National Socialist.

XIV

When Stresemann took over the office of Chancellor, the official Russian policy of the Treaty of Rapallo, and the secret Russian policy of the Army were the only hopeful things in the whole of Germany's foreign relations. All her dealings with the West were hamstrung by the Reparations question. Internally, Germany shared with her victors the universal economic malady. Currencies were collapsing everywhere, and everywhere the social order was shaken to its foundations. In October 1922 Mussolini had marched on Rome, and achieved victory for the first of those revolts of the *petit-bourgeoisie* which were to mark the history of the declining Central Powers. Meanwhile Hitler was preparing for his first (and unsuccessful) coup.

It was while such tensions were charging the atmosphere that

France decided to settle the various current differences on the Reparations question by seizing the Ruhr as a pledge. On January 11th, 1923, a French army, fully equipped for war, marched into the Ruhr territory under General Degoutte with heavy artillery and tanks. A violent and more or less officially legalized campaign of sabotage started in the Ruhr, with the *Heeresamt* standing as a general directing force behind it. Bridges were blown up, bombs were thrown, and there were some attempted murders. Fritz Thyssen, the industrialist, together with the retired General von Watter, who had subdued the "Red Ruhr Army", drew up plans for armed resistance by volunteer formations to be known as the *Ruhrfreischaren*.

These ideas, however, did not meet with Seeckt's approval, since they might mean war with France who would, in due course, be supported by her Czech and Polish allies; Germany was not strong enough for that. Seeckt and Hasse both made up their minds to avoid anything in the nature of armed resistance, so long as French troops refrained from entering Central Germany. Even so, that eventuality had to be borne in mind, and to provide for it Seeckt set himself to find out what paramilitary formations he could count on to co-operate.

Now, Ludendorff was at that time living, greatly respected, in Munich, while Hitler's "*Sturm-Abteilungen*" constituted an efficient private army. Seeckt got in touch with both of these men. Ludendorff was prepared to lend what he called his "world historic" name on the understanding that in the event of war he would be given the supreme command. Seeckt did not officially reject this condition, though he accepted it with considerable mental reservations. His conversation with Hitler, which took place in Munich on March 11th, is of somewhat greater importance, for it left a very strong impression on him, and Seeckt was a man whose manner usually suggested that he was not greatly impressed by anything; as against this, the fanaticism with which Hitler claimed the leadership of any nationalist movement for himself and his party inspired Seeckt with some misgivings. It was the first meeting between the leader of the coming National and Socialist mass party and the leader of the Army, and it was to have far-reaching consequences.

For the moment, however, these were not apparent. Hitler did not refuse his service in the event of an actual armed conflict with France. Shortly after the meeting, however, he forbade his followers to take part in any passive resistance scheme of the republican government. Somewhat later, a certain Kurt Luedecke, one of Hitler's "S.A." men who had fled abroad, declared that about this time

French money had flowed into the coffers of this permanently embarrassed saviour. So far, however, no confirmation of this has come to hand.

XV

Seeckt took more concrete precautions. Immediate arrangements were made to train so-called "Temporary Volunteers" in the *Reichswehr*, so as to increase the number of available reserves. In March secret mobilization instructions of a rather imperfect kind were circulating in all military districts. Orders were placed abroad for a hundred fighter aircraft, though delivery failed to be effected by due date. The *Truppenamt* again drew up plans for a defensive position on the Weser.

Meanwhile new trouble arose with Severing who was made apprehensive by the growth of combat organizations with leanings towards radicalism of the right. Severing began to call for a police enquiry into the number of *Reichswehr* officers employed in *Grenzschutz Ost*, an institution which was becoming more and more surrounded with an air of sinister legend. In this twilight atmosphere a saying of von Blomberg's gained some currency: "With Prussian officers correct behaviour had been a point of honour. With German officers it must be a point of honour to be sly."

Certainly conspiracy was in the air, and in view of the permanent conflict with the Prussian government in the matter of the frontier guard, it is hardly to be wondered at that there was increasing talk among officers of a *coup d'état* against an institution with so little appetite for the business of defence. The air was charged throughout the summer. German business threatened to perish in the vortex of devaluation, the financing of the struggle in the Ruhr consumed the Reichsbank's last reserves. Social unrest, intensified by rising prices and hunger, was everywhere on the increase. The Communist party worked for a new general uprising, but discontent was as rife on the right as on the left and everywhere men yearned for a saviour who would free them from their misery. Bavaria began to become a centre of right radicalism, and also of certain growing separatist tendencies, and the idea began to circulate of calling an "Angora" government into being there against the "putrid" socialist government of Berlin, much as Kemal Pasha had called his government of national resistance into being against the moribund and corrupt régime of Constantinople.

Two circles of conspiracy began to crystallize in Munich: one, which was clerical-conservative, centred round the Bavarian *Regierungspräsident* von Kahr with Crown Prince Ruprecht of Bavaria and his able lieutenant Count von Soden-Frauenhofen hovering in the background. The other centred round Hitler and his National Socialists. From Hitler connections extended through Colonel Haselmayr and Captain Röhm to younger members of the officer corps. In particular the officers of the Infantry School at Munich seemed ready to be won over.

In August the Cuno Cabinet was at the end of its resources, and Ebert called on Gustav Stresemann the leader of the *Deutsche Volkspartei* to save the country. Stresemann formed a coalition government representing all republican parties from right to left. He was the first Chancellor with real statesmanlike qualities who had ever crossed Seeckt's path. Stresemann had filed his political petition in bankruptcy as an annexationist of the Ludendorffian observance, and had concluded from the obvious fact of its collapse that the old German brand of power politics had been mistaken. He saw the lamentable position of all the great belligerent powers and concluded that co-operation was the only thing by which their difficulties could be resolved. His great aim was a reconciliation between France and Germany and this was to be the corner-stone of the future edifice of Europe.

Seeckt's view of the matter was very much the same as that ascribed by Stresemann to Hindenburg. "He was not in principle against a policy of understanding but as an old soldier did not believe that there was any practicable substitute for war." Such an attitude was not uncommon among Seeckt's kind. When the democratic Deputy Eugen Fischer-Baling during these years made the "Policy of Understanding" the subject of some lectures before high ranking officers of the *Reichswehr* Ministry, one of these remarked at the conclusion of a discourse: "Gentlemen, this simply won't do. After all *somebody's* got to be our enemy." (*So geht das doch nicht, meine Herren, einen Feind muss man doch haben*).

Thus it was that a tension grew up between Stresemann and Seeckt which was much more acute than that which had subsisted between himself and Wirth, for Seeckt now began to fear for his Russian policy. Soon Stresemann was saying that Seeckt was his "unrequited passion", while Seeckt's letters were punctuated by the recurrent refrain that the most important job of the moment was to push off "Herr Str." Nor did the fact that at this time the *Reichswehr* was more indispensable than ever to the government cause Seeckt to change his attitude. Once when Ebert asked him behind whom the *Reichswehr* really stood, Seeckt answered him with the words, "The *Reichswehr* stands behind *me*." It was a triumph of Seeckt's special brand of isolationism.

XVI

In the previous year Seeckt had declared at a Cabinet meeting that there was only one man in Germany who could make a *putsch* (slang for *coup d'état*) and he was not going to make a *putsch*. Events on the whole were to bear out this statement, but Seeckt's self-denial could not prevent the crisis. It broke out when the final collapse of the mark forced Stresemann to call off resistance in the Ruhr. The Prime Minister of Bavaria promptly proclaimed a state of emergency and called on Kahr, the proxy of "King Ruprecht", to act as "General State Commissioner". The Reich government replied by proclaiming a state of emergency for the Reich. Thus considerable power passed into the hands of the *Reichswehr* Minister. East-Elbian land-owning circles pressed Seeckt to take complete charge, but Seeckt replied that he knew what he was about and would not be pushed.

The situation continued to become more dangerous. In the Rhineland a separatist movement broke out with the warm approval of French generals. In Saxony Dr. Zeigner, the radical Prime Minister, began arming the workers. At last in October a number of "Temporary Volunteers" who were warm sympathizers with National Socialism rose at Küstrin under Major Buchrucker, and proclaimed their intention of marching on Berlin to arrest the government. Seeckt immediately ordered counter measures. Before however these could take effect, the whole affair collapsed thanks to prompt action by Colonel Gudowius, the fortress commandant. Shortly afterwards Communist disturbances in Hamburg necessitated the employment of naval personnel. Chaos seemed to be breaking in from all sides.

Hitler's paper, the *Völkischer Beobachter*, now attacked Seeckt whom it accused of planning a reactionary dictatorship together with Count von der Schulenburg, the Crown Prince's late Chief of Staff. It also asserted that his wife was a Jewess. This nonsense moved Seeckt to order General von Lossow, who commanded the 7th military district in Munich, to forbid the paper to appear. Lossow refused. Hitler, who was now declaring that it was his mission to save Germany, had too many adherents among the younger officers. On October 19th Seeckt removed Lossow from his post. The Bavarian question had now become for him a question of military discipline. His somewhat overweening utterance that the *Reichswehr* would obey him was being called in question.

On the 22nd Kahr ostentatiously commandeered the 7th Infantry Division with Lossow at its head for the service of the Bavarian government. However, the attitude of the artillery commander, Major-General Kress von Kressenstein, remained doubtful. On the same day the 4th Infantry Division with detachments from the 3rd Cavalry Division marched into Saxony on orders from the Reich government to arrest the Saxon government and to prevent the arming of the workers. Zeigner in Dresden yielded before the threat of machine-gun detachments who were quite ready to shoot. In Freiburg there were casualties when the military fired into the crowd. Ebert complained that the confidence of the workers in their government had been destroyed. Stresemann's grand coalition collapsed.

Hasse, von Stülpnagel and von Schleicher now told Seeckt that there was only one thing to do. This was to proclaim a military dictatorship. Otherwise a radical revolution from the right was a certainty, and if that happened, the *Truppenamt* feared intervention by France and her allies with consequences that no man could foresee. But Seeckt had learned the lesson of the Kapp *Putsch*, assuming that he ever needed that instruction, and shared Talleyrand's view that one could do everything with bayonets but sit on them. The utmost which he was prepared to do was to form a Cabinet, if the President called upon him, or if necessary to support a National Directorate. He even drew up a sixteen-page programme, but that was as far as the matter went.

On the day following the move of Hasse, Schleicher and Stülpnagel, Seeckt went to see Ebert but that cautious and intelligent statesman convinced him that a "Seeckt government" would make no appeal whatever to the masses; he conveyed this information very tactfully by telling Seeckt that he could not dispense with him as *Chef der Heeresleitung* and that was why he could not make use of him as Chancellor.

In that moment there began Seeckt's quest for a political leader who could act as a medium for the Army's wishes. It was now clear to him that he would never play that part himself. Major von Rabenau, who at that time was working in the *Truppenamt*, relates how he heard officers in the *Reichswehr* Ministry say that if Seeckt did not seize power he would have to go—but Seeckt stayed. He summoned the commanders of the two Army group commands, General von Tschischwitz and von Behrendt, to Berlin. Both thought it was a matter of proclaiming him as a dictator, and were prepared to act, but Seeckt merely gave them a cool and objective review of the situation, and they returned disappointed. It was not till much later that at least one of them, von Tschischwitz, saw that Seeckt was right.

CHAPTER X

THE KING MAKER

KURT VON SCHLEICHER—HAMMERSTEIN-EQUORD

I

THE political *impasse* ended in the formation by Stresemann of a kind of bourgeois rump-cabinet. In Munich, however, Hitler took more drastic action. Fearing that Kahr might beat him to the post and proclaim Ruprecht King of Bavaria, Hitler, on November 8th, proclaimed a national dictatorship. Ludendorff, with perceptible distaste for the donor of such favours, accepted from Hitler the command of the National Army. Von Lossow, Kahr and Colonel von Seisser, the head of the State police, acting under threat of force, declared themselves ready to co-operate, while the Infantry School mutinied and proclaimed its allegiance to Hitler.

The Reich government reacted quickly to these developments. On the night of the 8th, Ebert and Stresemann conferred full executive power on Seeckt, who instructed Kress von Kressenstein to act. Meanwhile, however, Kahr, Lossow and Seisser, having recovered from their surprise, had taken action on their own account. As a result, a demonstration of the National Revolutionaries came up against a cordon of State police at the *Feldherrnhalle*, and these opened fire.

A number of Hitler's adherents fell. Hitler himself fled. It seemed the end of a nightmare.

The fate of the Republic was now wholly in the hands of Seeckt, whose first act was to ban both the Communist and National Socialist parties. The Infantry School was removed from Munich to Dresden, and "unreliable" members of the officer corps, such, for instance, as Captain Röhm, were removed from the service. Even so, something of Seeckt's mind is revealed in a remark he made to his adjutant, Captain von Selchow. Speaking of the young officers who had taken part in the *Putsch* and whom he had dismissed, he said that if they had stood aside he would have despaired of the future.

Naturally, Seeckt had now made enemies. There was a plan by

National Socialist fanatics (it came to nothing) to shoot him while he was on his morning ride, and Colonel Hierl, a National Socialist writer, was in the years to come to attack him in his *Grundlagen einer Deutschen Wehrpolitik* for making himself a tool of politicians who were enemies of their country in disguise. To maintain detachment in the prevailing circumstances was anything but easy. Class, of the former Pan-German league, sent him a message inviting him to assume the rôle of General Monk and restore the monarchy. Seeckt replied that he would fight any disorder to the last round. Then, when the *Deutschnationale Volkspartei*, the successor of the old conservative party, enquired through Tirpitz whether there was anything it could do for him, Seeckt answered with a brief "Nothing".

II

Under the protecting wing of Seeckt and his extraordinary powers, the currency was stabilized, while Stresemann as Foreign Minister in the Cabinet of Marx took the first steps to solve the Reparations question and to improve Franco-German relations. Since it involved a revival of the Control Commission, the last-named part of his policy found little favour with Seeckt. Quite apart from this, however, Seeckt felt that the time had come for him to relinquish his powers, and even Schleicher concurred in this and was for ending what was virtually a dictatorship.

On February 13th, 1924, Seeckt informed Ebert that the task which the original emergency had rendered necessary was now complete. The issue of the new and stable currency, together with the imprisonment of Hitler and the consequent set-back to the radicals of the right, had caused a perceptible release of tension. Seeckt was once asked whether he thought he might not have made a mistake in abandoning power, but he would give no reply beyond an Eleusinian "Perhaps".

In 1924 Stresemann's "Policy of Understanding" resulted in the Dawes Plan, which not only produced a provisional solution of the Reparations question, but paved the way for the granting of extensive American credits to German industry. In 1925 there followed the Locarno Pact. By this all claims to Alsace-Lorraine were relinquished and Germany's existing western frontier was formally recognized by Germany and guaranteed by England and Italy. In the following year Germany was received into the League of Nations.

This latter circumstance introduced what was more or less a rival factor to Seeckt's Russian policy. It is true that Stresemann to some extent completed the Locarno system by signing a Treaty of Friendship with Russia in 1925, but his main objective remained reconciliation with France, and anything that was conducive to that end had an immediate priority.

Despite his misgivings, Seeckt, who was in his way as shrewd a tactician as Stresemann, always fell in for the time being with Stresemann's line, though there may be something in Rabenau's anecdote of an unnamed officer in the *Truppenamt* who remarked apropos of the League that the best way of ruining a club might well be to join it. This may possibly have been the attitude of Seeckt.

As regards the Control Commission Stresemann had argued that this concession was merely a matter of tactics, and indeed the infliction did not prove to be a heavy one, for the Control Commission was disbanded in 1927, the admission of Germany to the League of Nations having turned it into an anachronism. It was much the same with the army of occupation in the Rhineland, to the provisional retention of which Stresemann had agreed. This too was gradually withdrawn—the Ruhr had been vacated at the time the Dawes Plan was signed. Even so, some of Seeckt's colleagues were not really happy. Stresemann's bloodless victories were something to which soldiers were unaccustomed. As Fischer-Baling's questioner had remarked, "After all, *somebody's* got to be your enemy."

From now on there were really two schools of foreign policy in Germany, a West-European school represented by the Democrats and the Socialists, and an East-European school represented by the military. A very remarkable circle of men now began to gather around Arnold Rechberg, the sculptor and nitrate king, who had lived for a long time in Paris, and General Max Hoffmann. These men began to take up the idea, to which Marshal Foch and his successor in the General Staff were reputedly parties, of developing the new Franco-German understanding into a military alliance against Soviet-Russia and organizing an anti-Bolshevik crusade.

Both the *Heeresleitung* and the *Truppenamt* rejected all such ideas with vehemence. Seeckt expressed the general feeling when he said that Germany must not be debased to the level of a mercenary for the western powers. Stresemann was equally opposed; his policy of understanding did not extend as far as alliances of this kind. Equally unacceptable were certain proposals which Mussolini communicated to General von Cramon, the German representative on the Control Commission. Rivalry in the Mediterranean was at this time causing considerable tension between France and Italy, and Mussolini wondered whether the *Reichswehr* was to be had for a war of revenge in alliance with Italy against France. This proposal aroused some interest in the *Stahlhelm*, but left the *Heeresleitung* cold, for the latter considered the whole notion Utopian, and furthermore estimated the value of the Italian Army at zero.

III

In February 1925 Ebert died very suddenly. Seeckt had for a time toyed with the idea of offering himself as a candidate for the Presidency, and had even instructed Schleicher to prepare his campaign. Ebert's death, however, cut short all such plans. The first ballot proved ineffective, owing to the multiplicity of candidates. In the second ballot the bourgeois parties and the parties of the right united behind Hindenburg, who still possessed a certain hold over men's minds as a symbol. A left-wing paper once wrote that the Republic was the continuation of the Empire by other means, and in a limited way Hindenburg's Presidency did revive certain features of the past. The authority of the State was perceptibly increased, and the position of the Army, which now had a substitute for the old "Royal Shield", made more secure.

As soon as Hindenburg was made President, Schleicher hit on the idea of having Hindenburg's son, who was serving as a colonel in the *Reichswehr*, appointed as the President's adjutant. Colonel von Hindenburg had been a brother officer of Schleicher in the Guards. By this move a strong personal link was immediately created between the Army and the Head of the State. This kind of thing caused the idea of democracy to suffer a relative eclipse, though there proved to be no justification for Stresemann's fear that the new President's many ties with the old Prussian nobility would cause him to become the centre of a Monarchist Vendée. The opposite was the case. Hindenburg's conscience was always burdened by the thought that in 1918 he had failed to comply with his oath, and this made him all the more determined to fulfil the oath he had sworn to the new constitution. For all that, his background and training caused his outlook to be that of the age of Bismarck. He had little understanding for the more democratic age in which he lived—which was probably why he only accepted the candidacy after considerable hesitation.

It may be something more than mere chance that the year 1925 saw the first serious attempts to evade the disarmament provisions of

Versailles over the Reich as a whole and not merely, as hitherto, on its eastern frontier, though the fact must never be lost sight of that even such nationwide evasions all had their origin in the problem of the Polish frontier.

In 1926 this was rendered more acute by the creation of Pilsudski's military dictatorship and a consequent considerable strengthening of the Polish Army, a circumstance which rendered the disquiet caused by the existence of the Polish Corridor more acute. Speaking under oath at Nuremberg, Generals von Blomberg and Blaskowitz explained how much the military thinking of *Reichswehr* officers was at this time dominated by fear of a Polish invasion. It is, of course, true that the Locarno pact had ensured the security of Germany's western frontier, and that this guarantee was worth far more than a few tens of thousands of imperfectly trained troops, but it was some time before Seeckt or Wetzell, who had succeeded Hasse in the *Truppenamt*, could bring themselves to repose much confidence in that, and their sense of helplessness was increased by the fact that under pressure from the western powers a great deal of the power of the *Chef der Heeresleitung* passed to the (civilian) *Reichswehr* Minister.

IV

The new treaty evasions were concerned primarily with the illegal increase of military effectives, with preparation for a possible mobilization and with the development of forbidden weapons such as heavy artillery and tanks (to say nothing of weapons that were entirely new) and with the creation of a secret Air Force and cognate activities on the part of the Navy.

The organization which was primarily concerned with the first of these activities, namely the problem of increasing effectives and supplying the weak regular forces with some kind of a trained reserve, was the *Grenzschutz Ost*, which, as we have noted, owed its origin largely to Seeckt's own activities in 1919. The existence of this institution enjoyed the moral support even of Socialists and left-wing Catholics. Wirth repeatedly defended it, while Stresemann knew what was happening and approved it by his silence, nor had he any intention of changing his attitude so long as the Polish question remained unsolved.

The backbone of the whole system of frontier defence in the east was formed by the so-called "black staffs" who worked, ostensibly as civilians, under the eastern military district commanders, and by the

Kreiskommissars, who were also supposed to be civilian functionaries and whose chief concern was the keeping of muster-rolls and the care of concealed arms. All these worked in co-operation with the Prussian governmental machine, although the Prussian government itself periodically sought to put a stop to these proceedings.

Schleicher, who for a long time was concerned with the organizational direction of this frontier defence, replied to all protests with the stereotyped assurance that the measures in question were about to be discontinued—though, needless to say, they were not discontinued at all. The strength of this irregular defence force came to about 30,000 men, and to this must be added the so-called "Workers' Associations" (generally ex-*Freikorps* men or members of the *Stahlhelm*) who guarded the arms dumps. Usually these dumps consisted of nothing more than small arms and small-arms ammunition, though in a few isolated cases some pieces of artillery and some armoured cars were also hidden away.

Further measures taken about this time dealt even more directly with the *Reichswehr* itself. Seeckt had on no less than three occasions drawn up lengthy memoranda emphasizing the importance of the *Reichswehr's* function as a protectress of the national frontiers, and he now was quietly permitted to raise the ratio of discharges from 13 to 25 per cent, the aim again being gradually to build up a modest body of reserves. The *Truppenamt* during this period also acted as adviser to the Navy, which set about the illegal training of volunteers. In this case the results were not spectacular, since not more than 600 men were raised.

Schleicher took over the political end in these affairs, a task of some delicacy, for though Stresemann was content to be blind in the matter of the frontier irregulars in the east, he did not wish to endanger Franco-German relations by going too far. However, the *Reichswehr's* rear was silently but effectively covered by the personality of Hindenburg, while evasive tactics did the rest. From 1920 onwards the Reichstag had sought by means of parliamentary committees of enquiry to get some notion of what the *Reichswehr* was really doing, but on all such occasions both Seeckt and Schleicher proved themselves experts in sabotage, an art in the exercise of which they were noticeably assisted by a nice discretion in the choice of Army personnel. This choice was made with the aid of confidential agents who were usually members of the *Stahlhelm* or of one of the officers' associations, and if there was reason to believe that the aspiring recruit was actively sympathetic to the republican cause, say if he was a member of the *Reichsbanner*, the republican defence organization (a sort of republican version of the *Stahlhelm*), his military ambition would receive scant encouragement. Such situations were, however, in the main rare, for would-be recruits were rarely to be found in republican circles.

Militarily, all these measures amounted to very little. There were, however, others. The General Staff had learned its lesson in the Great War and realized the importance of industrial production. It was thus concerned to busy itself with certain preparations in the sphere of defence industry. This work was allotted to a section of the "Weapons Department" in the *Heeresleitung*, the section being first designated by the term *Nachschub* (replacements) and later by that of *Wirtschaftsstab* or "Economic Staff". This Economic Staff received considerable assistance from the *Reichsverband der Deutschen Industrie*, which was certainly actuated among other motives by the prospects of profits which a revival of the armaments industry held out to it. The Staff's function was, broadly, a double one. It constructed a scheme which was to come into effect on the outbreak of war for all matters relating to the provision of raw materials, design and the manufacture of finished goods. It also organized forthwith a number of "black" production centres for war materials, i.e. production centres the existence of which was kept hidden from the Control Commission. Thus in the firm of *Rhein-Metall*, the railway carriage department took over the business of developing artillery construction.

Needless to say, the firm of Krupp played an important part in all these affairs. These new developments naturally gave rise to some innovations within the *Reichswehr* itself. From 1926 onwards, industrial specialists were attached to the staffs of all military districts. They also caused the Weapons Department to call into being something named a "statistical society". This was an organization of German industrialists acting under the leadership of *Geheimrat* von Borsig, with the general aim of furthering the efforts here described.

Those who conducted the *Reichswehr's* affairs were not men who were deterred by so pedestrian a circumstance as inadequate appropriations, and so when that contingency seemed imminent, Schleicher founded the "Society for *Militär-Politik*" (these German hybrids are often untranslatable) "and Military Sciences", which he duly registered under the innocent semblance of a limited company and which succeeded in winning most gratifying financial support for the cause from a number of leading industrialists.

The fact that many types of weapons were forbidden did not hinder their appearance on German drawing boards. As far back as 1922 the *Reichswehr* had signed a contract with Krupps concerning the further development of German artillery. Now Krupps had before the signature of the treaty made contracts for the delivery of various types of guns with the government of Holland and of a number of South American states. Thanks to their connection with the Swedish firm of Bofors, they were able to make delivery. Through the good offices of Krupps, officers of the *Reichswehr* were thus able to be present on Swedish artillery ranges and watch the performance of new types of guns. These included a new type of howitzer for mountain warfare which had been ordered for the Dutch Army in the East Indies, a new self-propelled gun, a new type of 21 cm. mortar and a new type of sprung gun carriage. It was, of course, a disadvantage that for Germans only a few experimental models of such weapons were available, and often even these were not forthcoming, but nevertheless essential knowledge concerning them was now obtained. In 1925, however, matters progressed a little further. Krupps received certain new orders, including one for a 7.5 cm. gun suitable for mounting on a "large size tractor", the code designation for a tank; but the story of Krupps' secret assistance to the development of the tank arm must be told somewhat later.

Meanwhile, the Navy did not lag behind its sister service either in energy or discretion. The development of the submarine, the M.T.B. and of naval aircraft was studied with a zeal that was augmented rather than diminished by the fact that officially Germany was not supposed to be engaging in such activities at all. A mysterious office in Holland went so far as to supervise the construction of submarines on the spot, and the building of other submarines kept Spanish shipyards busy under the benevolent gaze of Primo de Rivera and the King of Spain. Admiral Canaris, who was later to achieve considerable fame, and who was at that time diligently building up a foreign naval intelligence service, conducted negotiations in these affairs.

Meanwhile, German naval advisers were gaining invaluable experience in Turkey and Finland, while the despatch to Japan of the plans for new underwater craft served to keep the designers' hands in. To complete the picture one should in no wise omit the various commercial enterprises in which Captain Lohmann of the Navy's sea transport department, the son of one of the managers of the North German Lloyd, called into being. The object of these ventures was to provide the money for further secret construction of submarines and M.T.B.s. Actually it was Lohmann who made the first contacts with Spanish shipbuilders like the millionaire Echevarrieta. All his commercial and shipping companies, such as the Navis Company, the *Baltische Segelschiffsreederei* (Baltic Sailing Ship Company) and the *Fischdampferreederei Sirius* (Sirius Trawler Company) and the *Travemünder Flughafen Gesellschaft* (Travemund Sea-Plane Harbour Company) served the purposes of secret rearmament, and in all these ventures Lohmann scrupulously refrained from obtaining any personal advantage for himself. In addition to the above, Lohmann also got control in 1924 of a large film company, the Phoebus A.G., which he used for propaganda purposes. In these various developments the Navy was chiefly concerned about a possible conflict with Poland. Should that occur, it was hoped at least to keep the Baltic clear of French ships.

Germany's secret rearmament served to create the basis for a possible enlargement of her fighting forces, though such enlargement would necessarily have had to be of extremely modest dimensions and would necessarily have to proceed by slow stages. Its peculiar danger did not lie in the military sphere at all, but rather in the circumstance that it accustomed people to the idea of engaging in violations of a duly signed treaty.

V

The policy of secrecy and subterfuges had not served to make the relationships between Seeckt and Gessler, the *Reichswehr* Minister, an altogether happy one. Gessler, immune apparently to the normal vicissitudes of politics, had continued to hold his post through a long succession of cabinets, and was now with increasing frequency forced to become a Parliamentary apologist for Seeckt's departmental escapades. The fact that Seeckt combined his undoubted adroitness with a persistent and distinctly unco-operative hauteur in most of his personal dealings did not make collaboration easier.

The persistence of Seeckt in his arbitrary acts at length induced Gessler to conceive the idea of gathering about himself a special staff with an office of its own. He thus hoped to have a more direct influence on the general attitude of the Army. Now, this intention of Gessler's coincided with an increasing disgruntlement on the part of Schleicher. Since the abandonment of Seeckt's candidature for the Presidency, in which he had been actively concerned, Schleicher complained that he had been shabbily used. He therefore greeted Gessler's plan to establish this new office, which would be independent of the *Chef der Heeresleitung*.

In 1926, such an office was opened in the *Reichswehr* Ministry under the designation "Political Department" (*Wehrmacht*); and Schleicher was put at the head of it and thus became unofficially the Minister's all-powerful deputy and adviser. In normal times the head of such an office would probably have been no more than a mere intermediary between Minister and Army, but in this age of backstairs politics it was inevitable that a capable and ambitious man who occupied the position which Schleicher now held should turn into a kind of political Chief of General Staff. Schleicher, who was both ambitious and capable, was not slow in charging himself with the care of a whole array of questions including matters relating to the League of Nations, the press, espionage and departmental appropriations, and had soon educated the Army staffs into short-circuiting the *Heeresleitung* and informing him directly of any unusual happenings, particularly when these were of a political nature. Thus it was that Schleicher began his slow rise towards the summits of power. It was not altogether unfitting that the device on his family coat of arms should have been a ladder.

It was unfortunate for Seeckt that he should at this juncture have made a number of tactical blunders. He issued an order concerning the manner in which officers should conduct duels—and failed to tell Gessler about it. He also approved an application by the Crown Prince to allow his son, Prince William of Prussia, to take part in uniform in the exercises of the 9th Infantry Regiment. This was more serious, especially since towards the end of September the leftist and democratic press got wind of the matter and there was a storm of indignation. The distrust of the old ruling house was far greater than Seeckt had suspected and, incidentally, far greater than the Hohenzollerns had deserved.

Gessler had now had enough. Schleicher wanted first to take the bull by the horns and issue a flat denial of everything. Then he began to see that the crisis provided an excellent opportunity for getting rid of Seeckt, and so threw in with Gessler, being careful all the while to leave Seeckt without any information on the real state of affairs. There was now a public demand for Seeckt's removal, and Gessler began to say openly that he was sick and tired of acting as a whipping boy for Seeckt, also that the Army had encountered enough difficulties from the republican press without Seeckt adding to them by a piece of folly which served no purpose whatever. The Chancellor, Marx, warned Hindenburg that a Cabinet crisis was approaching.

Things began to look bad for Seeckt, and Fritsch was for armed resistance should the politicians really demand Seeckt's head, but Seeckt was too much of a realist not to know that a *coup d'état* on behalf of his own person carried out against the will of Hindenburg was unthinkable—and there were no grounds for supposing that Hindenburg would will anything of the kind.

Actually, Hindenburg as a constitutional President could not act against the Chancellor's advice, and the Chancellor did not think Seeckt's retention worth the Cabinet crisis which he had already declared to be imminent. Thus, at noon on October 8th, Hindenburg received Seeckt in what proved to be a valedictory audience. The *Vossische Zeitung* wrote that there was a limit to the patience even of republicans, and that this applied even to so important a person as Seeckt.

VI

It looked as though the question of Seeckt's successor might become a matter of some contention. The names of Hasse, Lossberg, Kress von Kressenstein and Reinhardt were all mentioned. Seeckt had himself, when planning to contest the Presidency, named Heye, late chief of the Operations department, as the most suitable candidate for his post. Heye was at the moment commanding the 1st military district in East Prussia which was accounted the most difficult and important of all commands—in itself a recommendation. What was even more important was that Schleicher backed him, for not only was Heye an old colleague of Groener's but he had also had the reputation of being a more accessible man than Seeckt and far less of a hidebound conservative.

And so it was that this son of Frisian farmers with his fierce-looking sergeant's moustache became Germany's second *Chef der Heeresleitung*. A certain air of greatness still attached to Seeckt, and there were many for whom he still held the promise of mysterious political possibilities—this despite the fact that Schleicher was diligent in defamation and even stooped to such expedients as forbidding his presence at manoeuvres. It was left to others to complete the design the broad outlines of which Seeckt had indicated, but they did so with a purpose other than Seeckt's. By the time that had happened, however, Seeckt was old—and helpless.

VII

Few men in Germany were for the moment more disturbed by the fall of Seeckt than the Russian Ambassador, Krestinski; it was, however, not long before Schleicher succeeded in reassuring him. Nor was this too difficult, for the *Reichswehr* continued to lean towards the east, though this policy tended to be handicapped by the awkward circumstance that those who were ignorant of the policy's existence frequently execrated the *Reichswehr* for not pursuing it, while the initiated all too often disapproved of them for pursuing it too well. In 1926 the Communist dock workers in Stettin refused to unload munitions for the "advance guard of the German bourgeoisie" in happy ignorance of the fact that it was "the shock troops of the revolution" that had despatched them, while in December of that year an impassioned meeting took place at the Foreign Office at which, in the presence of a number of embarrassed Cabinet Ministers, leading socialists inveighed against the iniquitous liaison between the *Reichswehr* and the Red Army.

It was a delicate situation, and it was all Gessler could do to reassure Stresemann on the one hand and the socialists on the other that there would be no more munitions from Russia. They would, he also assured them, find Heye a much more co-operative sort of person than the late holder of his office—and in any case one would strive earnestly to provide younger generals.

There were also other sources of trouble. *Grenzschutz Ost* was becoming more than ever a thorn in the socialist flesh, though here Gessler held his ground, while the violent differences on the subject *Panzerkreuzer A* (Germany's first pocket-battleship, which according to treaty Germany was now permitted to build) betokened a growing distaste for the whole business of defence. All these things tended to produce one result, namely that the *Heeresleitung* and particularly the *Truppenamt* became more circumspect in their dealing with a State that was only prepared to concede the *Reichswehr* so modest a place, and also more determined in their opposition to it.

Schleicher, who was now the main inspiration of the *Reichswehr's* new line, was thoroughly in his element. The congenial tactics of evasion and *démentis* were perfectly suited to his talents, so that in the main things went on very much as before. In the years 1927 and 1928 a number of Russian officers came to Germany for training in the *Truppenamt*, and this happy relationship continued, so that when in

1931 the first experiments with airborne forces and paratroops were made in Russia, those proceedings were appropriately graced by the presence of Hammerstein-Equord, who was *Chef der Heeresleitung* at the time.

In this situation the peculiar characteristics of Heye's personality were by no means without their value. Though Heye was a product of the old-fashioned cadet school and a member of the old General Staff, he was within limits genuinely ready to be reconciled to the spirit of his time, and at least outwardly he was a democrat. At an inspection in Stettin he on one occasion brought himself to shake hands with some of the men, to enquire then and there whether they had any complaints, and to assure them that if they had anything on their minds they could at any time refer it to himself in Berlin. Needless to say, such conduct, which made hay with the rules of official procedure, inspired officers of the older tradition with a certain nervous apprehension.

However, these delightful gestures so far from betokening a change in the *Reichswehr's* general policy, served only to facilitate that policy's smooth execution, and serious attention now began to be given to a discreet though necessarily modest development of the prohibited tank arm. In October 1928, the *Heeresleitung's* Weapons Department invited Krupps to deliver two experimental "light tractors", i.e. light tanks armed only with machine guns—a "medium tractor" equipped with a gun was to follow in 1932. These orders formed part of an effort to create with Russian help the nucleus of a motorized force, the *Reichswehr* being for the moment wholly without useful experience in that department.

A number of difficulties were encountered here. The Allies had sanctioned the provision for the police of armoured cars equipped with machine guns, but it was only after long negotiations that the *Reichswehr* were permitted 150 four-wheeled armoured troop carriers, which, however, were to have no weapons mounted, and even this modest number proved unattainable for financial reasons. Since the manufacture of caterpillar treads for tanks was forbidden, experiments were made with multi-axled armoured vehicles suitable for cross-country travel, though here the stipulation that the vehicles should be amphibious proved something of an obstacle. In Russia, the Red Army gave facilities for experimenting with such six- and eight-wheeled vehicles and with small cars of the British Carden Lloyd type, which were copied from foreign models. In due course, Krupps were instructed further to develop vehicles with caterpillar

treads, and here Krupps introduced an important innovation by sub-
stituting welding for rivetting, a procedure which made possible a
noticeable saving of weight.

General von Vollard-Bockelberg, one of Hindenburg's and Ludendorff's old wartime assistants, who was inspector of motor transport
troops, brought about a separation in the seven motor transport units
between the *Panzerkampfttruppe* (the section concerned, largely
theoretically, with tank warfare), the armed motor-cyclists and the
transport section proper. Efforts were made to study tank tactics with
the aid of ordinary commercial tractors of the kind now widely used
in agriculture. In order to familiarize the troops with the appearance
of tanks, a dummy wooden tank, complete with turret, was constructed for Army manoeuvres, and armed motor-cyclists, together
with infantry in armoured troop carriers, appeared in these manoeuvres in 1928.

A so-called "Motor Transport Staff" was called into being for the
study of the tactical and other problems of tank warfare; it was the
stem from which was later to spring the School of Armoured Warfare. Vollard-Bockelberg's successor, Otto von Stülpnagel (a cousin
of Seeckt's collaborator), developed his predecessor's work still
further and divided every contingent into four sections: armed motor-
cyclists, tanks, armoured cars and an anti-tank company. The idea of
thus creating a special anti-tank company originated with the Chief
of Staff of Motor Transport troops, Lieutenant-Colonel Guderian.
While officially all these units only worked with dummy tanks, the
instructional staffs obtained practical training in Russia.

In 1931 the post of Inspector of Motor Transport troops was taken
over by Major-General Lutz, an old specialist of the Great War in
that particular department. Lutz went on with the work, and the
autumn manoeuvres of 1932 were to show whole battalions of armed
motor-cycle troops and special motorized reconnaissance units. In
addition, several cavalry detachments were motorized. Multi-axled
vehicles made their first official appearance.

The development of completely new weapons constitutes yet
another phase of Germany's rearmament activity. In this the application of the rocket principle to the problem of missile propulsion was
of particular importance. Encouraged by the experiments with rocket-
driven cars by such men as Max Vallier and Fritz von Opel, and at
the special instigation of Doctor, later Lieutenant-General, Dornberger, the Weapons Department in 1930 opened a special section
for rocket development, the original idea being to construct a powder

rocket; but Dornberger, at that time an ordinary artillery officer, interested himself further in certain experiments with rockets propelled by liquid fuels which were being carried on privately at the time. From this derived the so-called "A" models, from which certain types of V-weapons were developed. At this stage no very encouraging results were obtained, and Dr. Becker, the head of the Ballistics section of the Weapons Department, declared in 1932 that the time for such things had not yet arrived.

Naturally enough, a major concern of the *Reichswehr* Ministry had been to preserve the nucleus of a future Air Force. When reorganizing the Army in 1919 and 1920, Seeckt had taken pains to ensure that a number of officers of the Air Force were taken over into the new Army, among them the old Chief of Staff of the air forces, Colonel Thomsen. Seeckt's own personal Chief of Staff, Major-General Ritter von Haack, had been the last inspector of the Bavarian Air Force. Thomsen, who was followed by Captain Wilberg, became the head of the *Fliegerzentrale* or Air Force office of the *Reichswehr* Ministry; this office contained at first three, and finally about fifteen, officers, and in accordance with the organizational principle obtaining in the Great War, was attached directly to the *Truppenamt*. Here Captain Student, who was later to organize German paratroops, acted as technical adviser. Field-Marshal Sperrle, as he was later to become, also put in a certain amount of service. Training centres were set up within the various military districts, and their staffs were all provided with an Air Force expert. It was at this time that Douhet, the Italian Air Force general, was making his sensational prediction that the decision in any future war would be made in the air—an opinion by which Seeckt, Stülpnagel and others were definitely influenced.

The Treaty of Versailles only permitted an infinitesimal number of officers to receive flying instruction, but with Russian help this figure was substantially raised. In 1923, certain concessions were made in regard to civil aviation; further, as we have seen, Seeckt ordered 100 fighter planes from abroad during the Ruhr crisis, though these arrived too late to be of any service at the time. The first main object of Seeckt's striving, however, had been the abolition of the civilian Reich Air Office, which directed all matters concerned with aviation. In its place he got an air transport department grafted on to the Transport Ministry and had Captain Brandenburg, who was in his confidence and who had led the raids on England, put in as its head. The Transport Ministry allotted the *Reichswehr* 27 million marks in all for purposes of military aviation.

In 1926 the Paris Air Convention put an end to the International Committee of Guarantee's supervision of the German aircraft industry. The number of officers who were permitted to be given flying training for meteorological and police purposes was now raised to 72. Needless to say, the leading aircraft firms, Junkers, Heinkel, Dornier, and the rest, had long been having aircraft built in Russia, Switzerland and Sweden. Thanks to the fighters that had been bought during the crisis of 1923 and the secret production of the German aircraft industry, it was possible to build up a small air force within the framework of the civilian air transport company *Luft-Hansa*, which in course of time came to possess no less than four flying schools. At all of these secret military training was carried on. A man of great energy was the manager of this concern. His name was Ernst Milch. German efforts were further assisted by a military test aerodrome which had been in operation at Reuchlin since 1925, and a military department which existed within the *Versuchsanstalt für Luftfahrt* (Experimental Institute for Aviation). In 1926 Germany's Air Force consisted of two fighter squadrons, one bomber squadron and one auxiliary bomber squadron. By 1931 the numbers had increased to four fighter squadrons, eight observation squadrons and three bomber squadrons. The whole flying personnel had also been organized by Captain Wilberg in the *Ring der Flieger*, a branch of the Aero Club. This later joined with a fliers' section that had been organized by the *Stahlhelm* and became the *Wehrflugorganisation* (Defence-Fliers' Organization). In this manner the small Air Force nucleus was gradually expanded.

VIII

In December 1930 Heye retired on grounds of age. His successor was Major-General von Hammerstein-Equord. This officer had served with Schleicher in the Guards, and his appointment was one among a number of interesting changes that took place about this time. Towards the end of 1927 news had got around of the unusually multifarious business activities of Captain Lohmann, and there was an outcry concerning the use to which he was said to be putting the Navy's secret funds. There was something of a scandal. Lohmann had to retire, and Schleicher used the opportunity to disavow Gessler and to put in Groener as *Reichswehr* Minister. This gave Schleicher a vast increase of power, and enabled him to establish himself as something in the nature of a permanent secretary. Thus, in 1928, the world had been confronted with the curious spectacle of a President who was the ex-Chief of General Staff and was now served by his last Quartermaster-General in the capacity of *Reichswehr* Minister. It was at this point that Hammerstein-Equord began to come into prominence, for when, in 1929, Blomberg, who till then had been Chief of the *Truppenamt*, was given command of the 1st military district, it was for his old brother officer, at that time Chief of Staff to the first group command in Berlin, that Schleicher secured the post.

The appointment was almost as interesting as that of Groener, though in a different way. Both Schleicher and Hammerstein-Equord held the view that the problem of the masses would continue to remain insoluble to them unless they sought to gain touch directly with the workers. Yet while Schleicher showed occasional vacillation in this admirable attitude, Hammerstein-Equord, to the horror of many of his brother officers, set his course boldly toward the left and sought to make contact with a number of leading Social Democrats. Indeed, so diligent was he in these unusual activities that he began to be known in the *Reichswehr* Ministry as the Red General, nor did he appear to be unduly disturbed when both his daughters openly joined the Communist Party. However, this kind of dalliance, not uncommon among descendants of ancient families, was not in 1930 held to be an obstacle to his appointment as *Chef der Heeresleitung*, and *Chef der Heeresleitung* in due course he became, while Major-General Adam took over the *Truppenamt*.

In the meantime, however, the sky had begun to darken. In the autumn of 1929, at the very moment when Stresemann had contrived in the teeth of right-wing opposition to get the Young plan through and so had finally ensured the settlement of the Reparations question and the evacuation of the Rhineland, the great economic crisis broke in upon the world. Nor was this at that time the only catastrophe by which Germany was visited. Stresemann, already sick unto death, suffered a stroke on October 3rd. This proved fatal, and so there passed away the only German statesman who had truly built up a capital of international esteem.

Round about the turn of the year, Seeckt published an article entitled "Flood-tide", in the *Kölnische Zeitung*, in which he called for the appointment of a Dike-reeve. A little after this he joined Stresemann's old party, the *Deutsche Volkspartei*, and made an effort to get into politics. Possibly he still thought that the part of the Dike-reeve would be his own.

IX

The fate of the Army and to a large extent the fate of Germany, lay now more and more in Schleicher's hands, and Schleicher, now a major-general and with the reputation of being the ablest political general Germany had, could devote himself with increasing zest to the congenial business of kingmaking. Hermann Müller's grand coalition Cabinet of Republicans and Social Democrats had disintegrated in March 1930, but before its final dissolution Schleicher had further strengthened his position. Muller's frequent illnesses virtually made Groener acting Chancellor, and in this situation Groener, who found the load more than he could bear, depended more and more upon his friend. Soon Schleicher was personally attending Cabinet meetings and was acting increasingly as a go-between between party leaders and the government.

It was about this time that Schleicher's eye fell upon Brüning, and in the rather devious manoeuvres on which he now embarked (of which Brüning's instatement marks the beginning) he must in the absence of evidence to the contrary be credited with a sincere desire to serve his country. Just then the country was faced by a double crisis. The Young plan had been passed, but by a fractional majority, and in the teeth of the opposition of Hugenberg and his Nationalists, and these had now turned bitterly against Hindenburg, who did what undoubtedly was his constitutional duty and supported the policy which, however precariously, had been ratified by the legislature.

The other crisis was monetary. The Müller administration was heading straight for bankruptcy, and it was becoming evident that it would soon no longer be able to pay unemployment insurance at the statutory rate. This might mean grave disturbances and possibly revolution, and it became obvious that the services of the *Reichswehr* might be required to restore order, a situation which the whole tradition of that body made it anxious to avoid.

It was in these circumstances that Schleicher conceived the idea of a government ruling by protracted use of paragraph 48 of the constitution, for this permitted the suspension of the Reichstag's rights when there was a threat to public security, and the carrying on of government by means of emergency decrees. Schleicher contemplated the use of this provision to a far greater extent than was constitutionally warranted, and since the Left was discredited and the Right, since the Young Plan's adoption, was sitting sulking in its tents, selected Heinrich Brüning of the Centre Party to be the instrument for his plan.

Schleicher had had dealings with Brüning in discussions over the estimates, and had been genuinely impressed by his patent honesty and excellent political instinct. What really counted, however, was something else, and it shows the part that the sentiments of ex-servicemen were beginning to play. What counted was that Brüning had served as an ordinary lieutenant at the front. Also he had won the Iron Cross First Class, and there really were men—and high-ranking officers were among them—who were ready to make that a prime consideration. Anybody who had won the Iron Cross First Class must be a sound fellow. It was not long, however, before Brüning was finding it impossible to get a majority for his policy of deflation, and (though never using them to the extent that Schleicher had originally proposed) he actually did begin to govern by means of Presidential decrees, and was duly backed by the bayonets of the *Reichswehr*, which Schleicher was ready to put at his disposal. Brüning's aim was to master the crisis by ruthless economy, and this line was by no means unacceptable in high quarters, for the ageing President was tired of Parliamentary horse-trading, and the idea of economy appealed to the old gentleman for sentimental reasons. It reminded him of 1813 and iron wedding rings.

Brüning's policy nevertheless added greatly to the general unrest and enormously increased his own mounting unpopularity. Also, there were new forces on the horizon. Since 1923, the National Socialist Party had lapsed into relative obscurity, but the hour of economic collapse was the hour of Hitler, who was now promising heaven and earth to all who were bewildered and disappointed. As far back as 1929, Schleicher had expressed his misgivings to Brüning concerning the growth of this party, which was gaining particularly large numbers of adherents among young naval officers and among the workers at the naval stations at Kiel and Wilhelmshaven. Now, Germany already had her Communists, and Schleicher feared that if the National Socialists came along to add further to her internal disorders, Poland might be tempted to that *coup de main* against Silesia which was known already to exist on paper. This last consideration impelled him to ask Brüning to enquire confidentially in London and Paris whether in view of the danger of civil war some increase in the *Reichswehr* might not have the formal approval of the late enemy powers—but Brüning's enquiry elicited a negative reply. Being a man who always believed in having two strings to his bow, Schleicher at this time sought to reinsure himself by having an interview with Hitler, who made a much less favourable impression on him than he had on Seeckt. Hitler's habit of communicating his ideas in thunderous monologues of unlimited length, during the course of which his interlocutor could never get a word in edgeways, convinced him, Schleicher, that the man was a monomaniac. Whenever, after that, mention was made of Hitler's pretensions to unlimited power, he would invariably say that anybody might become Chancellor, as far as he was concerned, but not "that fellow". Hindenburg made it plain that he shared Schleicher's aversion to "the Bohemian corporal".

And yet, despite all this, there were things about Hitler's party which drew Schleicher's interest. The S.A. and the S.S., the Storm Detachments and the *Schutzstaffel* or "Protection Detachments" had provided a haven for large numbers of officers and men who had fought at the fronts. Röhm, the S.A.'s Chief of Staff, who for a time had had to leave Germany because of his homosexual propensities—he had in the meantime become a lieutenant-colonel in Bolivia—had been a captain, while the leader of the S.S. was an ex-ensign named Heinrich Himmler. Also, there were large numbers of ex-*Freikorps* men in the S.A. Such men were too valuable to lose.

While Schleicher hesitated on the brink, however, others had taken the plunge. In *Grenzschutz Ost* in East Prussia, a very close collaboration had begun to develop between General von Blomberg, the commander of the 1st military district, and his Chief of Staff, General von Reichenau, on the one hand, and the *Standartenführer* of the S.A. on the other. Both Blomberg and Reichenau thought that the *Reichswehr* should associate itself with whatever faction could show the most marked patriotic up-surge. There was no question that the National Socialists fitted that specification, for the *Stahlhelm*, once the main centre for illegal military activity, had become painfully respectable in its old age and was losing its hold over youth. Thus it was that in 1930, in a number of training centres such, for instance, as Döberitz, S.A. units began to receive illegal military training. Röhm was encouraged by this to demand that the S.A. should become admissible to the *Wehrflugorganisation* which was threatening for a time to be the privileged preserve of the *Stahlhelm*. Suddenly, however, Hitler to the indignation of Hindenburg, forbade the Pommeranian S.A. all participation in the activities of *Grenzschutz Ost* on the ground that the latter was co-operating with republican government authorities, though just what else it could have been expected to do was never explained. This somewhat startling *démarche* caused the whole picture to become even more confused than before. It also considerably diminished any inclination Schleicher may have had to throw in with the movement and his ingenuity was now directed to the problem of seducing the elements in it that were genuinely anxious to bear arms for Germany from their present regrettable party allegiance.

Meanwhile, to complicate the tangle of cross purposes still further, certain *Reichswehr* officers, including the *Chef der Heeresleitung* himself, had progressed as far as National Socialism was concerned from a contemptuous neutrality to a very determined opposition. When two young officers of the 5th Artillery Regiment in Ulm, commanded at that time by Colonel Ludwig Beck, tried to found National Socialist cells, Hammerstein-Equord took a hand in the matter and ordered them to be punished and dismissed from the Army.

X

In the Reichstag elections of 1930, the National Socialists obtained 107 seats and emerged as the strongest of the right-wing parties. In the *Deutschnationale Partei* a more moderate opposition of men who still were genuinely conservative in sentiment had begun to form against the party leader, Hugenberg. The result was that the party began to disintegrate. The *Deutsche Volkspartei*, on which Seeckt had staked his political fortunes, fared no better. It dwindled almost to nothing. After the elections Schleicher had a meeting with Arnold Rechberg, who was still championing a Franco-German alliance, and confessed that money from his secret funds had played a part in the National Socialists' victory—a strange confession, when one remembers his utterances to Brüning. When Rechberg remarked that this was a dangerous line to pursue, Schleicher said that he was, if anything, a saner man than Rechberg. It was part of his policy to establish centres of influence wherever he could, and in fact his attempt to entice the party by means of a financial bait was part of his effort to master it and direct it into ways more agreeable to himself.

It was in the general trend of the time that in the spring of 1931 Seeckt should again get into touch with Hitler. After the meeting he was ready to declare that the National Socialist Party must undoubtedly be regarded as a "saving element" and allowed to play this beneficent part in the general scheme of things. This comforting conviction did not prevent him from stipulating that whatever part he played in that scheme, he (Seeckt) must remain "Seeckt" and he must be allowed to maintain his own distinctive style. Needless to say,

Hitler gave his usual sweeping assurances. What Seeckt had in mind was, of course, to capitalize on the patriotic fervour of the National Socialists while at the same time preserving the distinctive identity and independence of the Army. He also had some notion of uniting Hitler's party with the forces of conservatism into a government of national concentration. Such notions only show how the old Prussian type of mind had completely lost all clarity of vision.

Perhaps it was the wisdom of age that in this respect gave Hindenburg a somewhat greater perspicacity. He saw that any seizure of power by Hitler might lead to warlike complications with France, Poland and Czechoslovakia, and he was determined to save his people the horrors of another war. Moreover, he hoped that a satisfactory settlement of the disarmament problem and a relaxing of the economic crisis would gradually cause the human driftwood that was gathered in Hitler's party to disperse. Nor, indeed, was the outlook too bad—if for a moment one could ignore the huge unemployment totals and the drastic wage and salary cuts. Brüning had been steadily working for the suspension of all Reparations payments and for the recognition of Germany's moral right to rearm, should the disarmament negotiations break down—and he had not been unsuccessful in making headway in that direction, though thanks to the shortsightedness of France, the attempt to bring about an *Anschluss* with Austria proved abortive.

In the short run, however, Hindenburg had little power to arrest the trend of events, and Hitler's numbers and influence continued to grow, while his utterances showed all too clearly which way his mind was working. The increasing rivalry between the *Stahlhelm* and the S.A. caused a meeting to be held between Hitler, Seldte and Düsterberg. At this meeting Hitler declared that when he came to power, he would send for the Minister of War and ask him how much in all rearmament would cost "... and if he says 20, 40, 60, yes 100 milliards of marks, he'll get the money ... and then we'll rearm, rearm, rearm till we're ready and then ... and then ..." "Then," interjected Düsterberg, "the world will again close its ranks against us. You'll have a second world war on your hands, and you'll lose it for us, as we lost the last." Hitler said: "I'll have anybody shot who breathes a word of rearmament!" Düsterberg here tried to make an objection, but Hitler merely screamed, "Have him shot ... Have him shot!" At this point the leader of the *Stahlhelm* broke off the interview, and doubts began to come to him whether the man whom he had been confronting was not some kind of neuropath.

One year later, Hermann Rauschning, the President of the Danzig Senate, at that time still a supporter of the movement, was to be a witness when Hitler, over tea and cakes at his country estate, made the wildest utterances about a war of revenge that he would conduct when he came to power. He was careful to point out that *he* would conduct the war. He needed no generals. If the war was lost, then he would drag down the world in his own catastrophe. Germany would never again surrender. When he said this he began to hum the motif of the grand final conflagration from *"Götterdämmerung"*. It was impossible to say at the time whether such utterances were really part of a serious plan, or whether they were no more than the product of a lively but moody imagination.

XI

And still the skies grew darker. In that same autumn of 1931, the Conservatives, thinking the moment had come to make political capital out of the enmity with which the Chancellor was surrounded, threw all caution to the winds and at a convention in Bad Harzburg allied themselves with Hitler. Seeckt was present on this occasion, as were a number of Prussian princes, and great industrialists like Thyssen began from now on to supply the movement with funds. Certainly conditions were critical, for there were others besides Hitler who could capitalize on misery, and as Hitler's numbers multiplied, so did those of the Communists.

Fights now began to take place in the streets of all great cities between the S.A. and the "League of Fighters for the Red Front", for the Communists, too, had their propaganda. Relations between the Red Army and the *Reichswehr* continued to be excellent, but this did not in the least prevent the subversive agitation of the Communist Party. On the contrary, it grew daily more violent. The Reich was thus rapidly dividing itself into two opposing camps of desperate humanity.

As it was difficult to hamstring both factions at once, or possibly because left-wing activity was to some extent merely a reaction against the dynamism of the right, Schleicher, Brüning and Hammerstein-Equord weighed the possibilities of suppressing the National Socialists by force. Since Hammerstein-Equord was convinced that support from republicans was now indispensable wherever it could be obtained, Schleicher got into touch with Major Mayr, a retired *Reichswehr* officer who had become one of the leaders of the

Reichsbanner. Unfortunately, generals were suspect in this quarter, whatever their professed political opinions, so that the results of this move were exiguous. This, however, did not prevent him from communicating to the Pres:dent the suggestion that common action should be taken with trade unions against the growing radicalism of the right. Hindenburg, however, took the view that National Socialism could not be suppressed.

This embarrassing impartiality seems for the time being to have ended the matter, and further action was made difficult by the circumstance that about this time Hindenburg suffered a severe mental breakdown. Brüning tells us that periods of mental freshness and clarity now began to alternate with phases in which Hindenburg's mind seemed hardly to be working at all. Hindenburg had obviously been aware of what was coming. When elected President he had told Luther, the Chancellor, that he hoped he would not be left in his post till he had gone senile, for one never realized oneself that that was happening. It was unfortunate that Hindenburg's foreboding should have been justified at that particular moment, for this old and failing man who had been the last Chief of the old Great General Staff was in reality the only remaining bulwark against Hitler's twentieth-century Anabaptists. There was nothing else to hold the flood.

Hindenburg still had the Army behind him. Generals and General Staff officers were, of course, in the main conservative. It was, of course, difficult to say what influence these men still carried among the younger officers who were instinctively sympathetic for the nationalism of the new movement, and most certainly when Hitler visited the cruiser *Köln* about this time, the officers received him with enthusiasm. Yet there can be no doubt that a firm order which had the authority of the venerable President behind it would have been implicitly obeyed—even an order to act against the National Socialists. Prussian tradition was too strong to permit of anything else.

Not that the Army during these months was wholly at one with itself, or that it did not in some cases come to play a part out of keeping with its classical rôle. Brüning, as we have seen, was, thanks to his determined efforts, making steady progress in the field of international relations, and this raised the question of what should be done in the event of a recognition of Germany's right to military equality. Schleicher's plan was to renounce all heavy offensive weapons and transform the Army into a militia of the Swiss pattern. Schleicher's discussions with Major Mayr had adumbrated this idea, and at least in this department found a sympathetic response. Höltermann, the chief of the *Reichsbanner*, was definitely favourable to a militia. However, this departure of Schleicher's still ran completely counter to the views of the General Staff, and when, as happened in 1932, military writers began to broach the idea of a militia, they encountered in the *Truppenamt* the firm opposition of the Seecktian school. For in the Bendlerstrasse that school was still supreme. The Blomberg-Reichenau clique was in a minority, and even Blomberg was soon to go. Blomberg had had a fall from his horse and sustained concussion of the brain, and Brüning, who distrusted Blomberg's National Socialist proclivities, contrived to get him removed by transferring him to the post of Chief of the Disarmament delegation in Geneva, where his adroitness and charm embarrassingly enhanced his prestige.

At home, however, the Seecktians remained exceedingly strong, as is clearly shown in the *Army List* of 1932. Incidentally, this *Army List* shows the names of most of the principal actors in the coming tragedy, such as Manstein, Sodenstern, Jodl, Krebs, Speidel, Model, Keitel and the rest. All these were working in the *Truppenamt*. Brauchitsch was an inspector of artillery; Guderian, now a colonel, was Chief of Staff to Major-General Lutz, the Inspector of Motorized Troops, while Bock, Rundstedt, Ritter von Leeb and von Fritsch were commanding divisions. Beck was still an artillery commander, Halder, Chief of Staff to an infantry division. Joachim von Stülpnagel had retired to become business manager of the *Berliner Börsenzeitung*, a staunchly conservative organ. Such is the story told by the *Army List* of 1932. It was the last German list ever to be accessible to the general public.

During 1932, various attempts were made outside the Army to extend military training by means of Labour Service Camps and so-called *Wehrlager* or Defence Camps which were organized on a party basis. With this strong conservative bias predominating, it was naturally with mixed feelings that the *Heeresleitung* felt it politic to give their moral support to such ventures, which, however, for the most part remained outside the Army's control. The *Reichskuratorium für Jugendertüchtigung* which was set up about this time—the name denotes devotion to the physical hardening of youth—was presided over by General Edwin von Stülpnagel, then in retirement, but the Volunteer Labour Service which both the *Stahlhelm* and the S.A. now began to organize were kept wholly independent of the Army and the type of training that young men underwent in these bodies rarely met professional requirements.

XII

An account of the fall of Brüning and Groener his lieutenant need hardly be given here. The facts are well known, though recent disclosures seem to show that the part played by Brüning's attempt to partition the great estates was of little historical significance.*

Brüning had made plans, as Schleicher himself had done and was to do again, for the breaking up of large unprofitable estates, but actually Brüning's schemes had the approval of some of the more farsighted of the great landowners, among them some of Hindenburg's personal friends, such as Count Brünneck-Bellschwitz. Incidentally much the same applies to the scandals concerning the administration of the *Osthilfe*, the state funds which had been put at the disposal of the East-Elbian landowners for the assistance of agriculture.

* For the benefit of English readers, a brief résumé of the facts had better be given.

As the Hitlerite menace grew, Brüning saw only one method of countering it. Observing that Hitler was already far stronger than his temporary allies on the right, Brüning determined on seeking a restoration of the monarchy, though this time the monarchy was to be a constitutional one. To achieve this it was essential that Hindenburg should stand again as President to carry through the change. The old man gave his reluctant consent, and Brüning now sought to gain the backing of the opposition parties and since he wished, as did Hindenburg himself, to avoid the turmoil of a presidential election, offered his own resignation if they would enable him to attain his object by the method of a parliamentary two-thirds majority. The effort failed and Schleicher, for whom Brüning had almost outlived his usefulness, could probably now have struck him down; but Brüning was still needed to help Hindenburg through the detested business of public re-election, and Schleicher wanted Hindenburg re-elected quite as much as did anybody else. Once the old man was back in office, however, that consideration no longer prevailed, and Schleicher could strike out on a line of his own. During Brüning's absence on campaign for Hindenburg, he had borne heavily on Groener, who had taken over the Ministry of Home Affairs in addition to his own, and again urged the latter to secure the prohibition of the National Socialists. Brüning on his return was confronted with this demand, to which, after some hesitation, he agreed, and was successful in obtaining the President's signature. Schleicher thereupon immediately reversed his position and let it be known that he was not in agreement with his chief, but persuaded Hindenburg that if Hitler's storm troopers were banned the prohibition should also extend to the *Reichsbanner*, which he described as a most insidious organization. He was, however, careful to avoid all mention of the *Stahlhelm*, of which Hindenburg was President. Hindenburg thereupon addressed a letter to Groener on the subject of the *Reichsbanner*, of which copies appeared in the press.

Groener's reaction was immediate. He recognized that the thing was a put up job, went to Hindenburg and proved to him that the charges against the *Reichsbanner* were baseless. However, although no action was taken, the President's letter could not be withdrawn, and the Nazi party, now proscribed, made all the capital out of it that they could, and were greatly assisted by it in the elections which now fell due in Prussia and other German states. In Prussia their numbers rose from 9 to 162.

Brüning had yet one hope left of countering the Nazi menace. This was a spectacular success in the field of foreign policy, and this he nearly achieved. In

Undoubtedly there had been suspicion of nepotism by the Commissioners who often came from East-Elbian Agrarian circles themselves, and old *Kammerherr* von Oldenburg-Januschau has confessed in his memoirs that he acted on the principle:

> *"Da sprach der alte Pelikan,*
> *Kinder lasst mich auch mal ran."*

But for all that, the historical importance of the whole affair has been grossly exaggerated.

Schleicher had long had Brüning's successor in readiness, and introduced him to Hindenburg, who had been delighted with him. Herr von Papen had been a major on the General Staff and belonged to the right wing of the centre party. He had married the daughter of an industrial magnate of the Saar, and had excellent relations with France. In the general confusion it seems to have occurred to nobody to enquire what other qualifications he possessed, but the nobility, which had begun to feel how deeply not only the great landlord class but Germany itself had been undermined, began now to act like men

conversations at Geneva, Brüning secured the agreement of MacDonald, Stimson and later of Grandi to a formula whereby, against an undertaking by Germany to abstain for five years from increasing her armaments, the Saar was to be restored, the service period of the *Reichswehr* was to be reduced from twelve years to three, and Germany was to be allowed a militia with a training period of eight to twelve weeks annually for 100,000 men and was to be permitted the possession of all weapons possessed by any other power. Tardieu, then fighting an election in France, was telephoned to and urged to return at the earliest possible date to Geneva.

Considerable as was this achievement, the fact remained that Brüning was compelled to return to Berlin without an agreement in his pocket and was therefore still vulnerable. Even so, Schleicher still needed him to perform one service. The Reichstag was to reassemble on May 9th and the finance bill which would make any government secure for a year had to be piloted through the Reichstag. Immediately this was done, the Nationalist deputies started a violent attack on Groener, whom they sought to drive into a suppression of the *Reichsbanner*. Groener, already a sick man, rose magnificently to the occasion, and despite continuous interruption hurled defiance in the face of his enemies. Immediately he had concluded, Schleicher and Hammerstein-Equord appeared before him in the chamber and coldly informed him that he no longer possessed the confidence of the *Reichswehr* and must resign.

With Groener fallen, the political death of Brüning was not difficult to achieve. Despite his success in foreign policy, there were many counts to be worked up against him, particularly his failure to achieve a working coalition in the Reichstag to slip Hindenburg back into the Presidency, and his inability to effect a reconciliation between Hindenburg and the latter's own party, the Nationalists. All this counted against Brüning and Brüning was forced to resign. A few hours before that resignation was formally accepted, but when Hindenburg had already made his position impossible by declaring his intention of appointing an entirely new Cabinet, the American Ambassador sought an interview with Brüning. At 9 o'clock the Ambassador was with him and told him that Herriot, who had replaced Tardieu, accepted his disarmament proposals as a basis of negotiation. When Brüning's successor sought to continue the negotiations where Brüning had left them, the climate had changed and Herriot was no longer willing to extend his confidence. (B.B.)

in a panic. The creation of an authoritarian Cabinet of Conservatives with a ring to their names was somehow satisfying to these insecure people, and such a Cabinet was now formed—with Herr von Papen at the head of it.

The new Cabinet, in which Schleicher took the post of *Reichswehr* Minister, took the view, though there were dissentient voices, that the National Socialists should be persuaded into some kind of practical collaboration. Schleicher was at first among the dissentients, yet he was hesitant in that dissent. For one thing, he was genuinely concerned about what the Poles might do if the *Reichswehr's* whole effort had to be devoted to the quelling of civil disturbance. Then there was the purely technical problem whether the *Reichswehr* was strong enough to fight off two simultaneous revolts, one from the right and one from the left. It was better to have one enemy than two, for apart from the *Reichswehr* he had only the gendarmerie who, it is true, had armoured cars and had been trained in street fighting, but who numbered only sixty thousand men.

While Schleicher was hesitating, Papen made his first coup. He got rid of the social democratic government of Prussia on the pretext of alleged subversive activities, of which Schleicher himself had heard, but really because he needed control over the Prussian police before the Nazis could obtain it. Schleicher had had a state of emergency proclaimed in the 3rd military district and given General von Rundstedt plenary powers. Thus it was that the Prussian government was actually removed by a captain of the 9th Infantry Regiment and a handful of men. Schleicher had given his approval to these proceedings because the strong National Socialist minority in the Diet held a key position, and could have brought pressure to bear on a government which had long ceased to command a majority.

In the elections which followed shortly after Papen's coup, Hitler swept the polls, the National Socialists returning as by far the strongest party in the Reichstag. Since this circumstance could not be permanently ignored, Hindenburg in August received Hitler, and after listening to his verbose expositions, sought to enlighten him on the political facts of life. External complications, he insisted, had at all costs now to be avoided, and for this reason it was impossible fully to satisfy Hitler's demands for office. The most that could be considered would be to allow Hitler a place in a right-wing coalition Cabinet, assuming he would consent to accept it. Hitler rejected this offer, believing as he did that as leader of the strongest party in the country he was bound sooner or later to attain full power. A few weeks later, Papen was disavowed by his "Cabinet of Barons", all parties falling away from him except the handful of *Deutschnationalen* under Hugenberg.

The Reichstag was dissolved. New elections were held in which the National Socialist figure slightly declined, though the general picture remained fundamentally the same. Papen now realized that there was only one thing left to do: it was to govern without the parties, and to effect a reform in the constitution. This solution involved the risk of civil war; it certainly meant a fight with the National Socialists, even if the Communists and trade unions did not join in. The only remaining solution was one which neither Schleicher nor Hammerstein-Equord would face.

Schleicher (who had been quietly getting rid of generals with Nazi sympathies, though of course he could not touch Blomberg and Reichenau) now developed an idea. It was inspired by both his personal aversion to Hitler and his old ambition to capture the valuable elements in the National Socialist movement for himself. There were three groups distinguishable among the uprooted personalities who made up the leadership of Hitler's party. There were those in Hitler's immediate *entourage*, there was the clique of adventurers and *Freikorps* men gathered round Röhm (who made fun of "Adolphe legalité" for shrinking back from seizing power by force) and there were the convinced doctrinaire National Socialists gathered round Gregor Strasser. Tensions within the party were on the increase since Hitler had failed in his candidacy for the Presidency and taken the outlawing of his party lying down. Strasser had begun to suspect that Hitler was much less concerned for the cause of National Socialism than he was for his own personal power. Schleicher now made up his mind to turn these difficulties of the Nazis to his own account and to draw the Strasser wing and with it the great mass of Hitler's working-class supporters and also those elements which were really ready to fight. He would then endeavour with the help of Strasser and representatives of the Social Democratic and Christian trade unions to form a government on a mass basis. This was undoubtedly the greatest of all Schleicher's plans.

It was because he had such plans as these in mind that when in November Papen asked him to take up the fight with the Nationalist Socialists, Schleicher deliberately backed out. His excuse was that the *Reichswehr* was insufficiently motorized to risk being involved in a civil war which might at one and the same time have to be carried on against left and right. Schleicher's refusal, needless to say, still further weakened Papen's position, though that was already precarious, for Hindenburg was in some doubt whether Papen's proposed "constitutional reform" did not amount to a breach of the constitution which he had sworn to protect. Also, with death so near, he dreaded the thought of involving his country in the horrors of civil war. Nor did there really appear to be any need for this. Communists and National Socialists had already worked together during a recent strike of transport workers, and so Schleicher, who at least seemed to promise the possibility of a pacific solution, became the man of the hour.

Papen was forced to retire, though he retained an office in the Chancellery as the President's unofficial adviser, and on December 1st, Lieutenant-General von Schleicher, till then *Reichswehr* Minister, was appointed Chancellor.

XIII

Schleicher now came out with a very comprehensive programme which included the strengthening of good relations with the Soviet Union and various bold schemes relating to the creation of employment and rural resettlement. It also included the expansion of the armed forces by means of a militia. This was indeed putting the cat among the pigeons, for the generals were antagonized by the notion of a militia, while the East-Elbian nobility was once more up in arms about the resettlement proposals which might involve the partitioning of their estates; like all dying societies they clung to the belief that they could still save everything, which only made it more inevitable that they would ultimately save nothing at all.

Schleicher did not increase his popularity in these circles by designating himself as a "social general". Hammerstein-Equord, who now followed him implicitly, had long been known as a "Red". Everything now depended on the two reforming generals being able to find mass support. Schleicher spent his time feverishly negotiating with pretty well everybody. He negotiated with Strasser and his followers, with Hugenberg, Dr Dingeldey and Dr Kaas (who respectively, led the *Deutschnationale Partei*, the *Deutsche Volkspartei* and the Centre Party) and also with Adam Stegerwald and Wilhelm Leipart, who led the Christian and Social Democratic trade unions. However, these negotiations took time, and time was the one thing Schleicher had not got. To make matters worse, the leaders of the Social Democrats committed the blunder of refusing to negotiate with a "reactionary general". Men of vision, such as Noske, were horrified; Schleicher was far from being Noske's ideal of a statesman, but Noske had the sense to see that it was now all or nothing. Noske, however, was helpless.

So Schleicher's chances slipped away, for he soon found that he had grossly overestimated Strasser's influence in the National Socialist Party. By January it was obvious that Schleicher's plan to split that party was Utopian. Hitler's daemonic personality was far too strong for that.

In the meantime, Papen had returned to the idea of a coalition, and got the Cologne banker von Schröder to arrange a meeting with Hitler. A further factor in the affair was that the National Socialists had contrived to bring about a personal interview between Hitler and Oscar von Hindenburg, the President's son and adjutant, who till now had objected vehemently to Hitler's being Chancellor. The meeting took place in the house of Joachim von Ribbentrop, Hitler's expert on foreign affairs. Herr von Oldenburg-Januschau, that old crony of Hindenburg's who had so persistently endeavoured to persuade the President into sanctioning some kind of a Junker dictatorship, took up Papen's idea that it would be possible to "hedge Hitler round" with sound Conservatives. In the end, however, Schleicher made up his mind to fight. Hammerstein-Equord was ready to use the *Reichswehr* against Hitler, and Schleicher went to Hindenburg to ask for powers to carry on the government under a state of emergency.

Now it is quite true that just at this time the older parties in the Reichstag were asking for an accounting of the *Osthilfe* moneys, to which allusion has already been made, and there can be little doubt that this was not too welcome in agrarian circles; echoes of the resulting exchanges may have reached the ears of Hindenburg, but there is no ground for supposing that it was the fear of some damaging revelation in this department that caused him to be hesitant in provoking potential critics by acceding to Schleicher's demands. Those demands, however, were refused. The fact is that Hindenburg was getting very old and the necessity of taking any drastic decision merely produced a state of excessive fatigue.

The upshot of the whole affair was that Hindenburg dropped Schleicher altogether. He seems before doing so to have suggested a Cabinet with Papen and Hugenberg, but neither Schleicher nor Hammerstein-Equord would consider that, since it would lead to civil war.

What was now to be done? A "cold *coup d'état*", such as Schleicher had actually suggested was not in Hindenburg's line. Apart from anything else, he feared that the National Socialists might indict him before the Supreme Court for unconstitutional conduct. The party had already threatened to make the suppression of the government of Prussia the occasion for such a charge. Such notions were ruled out, nor was Hammerstein-Equord more successful when, just after this, he sought out the old gentleman and warned him of the danger that Hitler might seize power. Hindenburg sullenly retorted that Hammerstein-Equord had better confine his attention to his autumn manoeuvres. However, in due course Hammerstein's quiet and objective exposition convinced him that Hitler and his followers were men who would stick at nothing, though he ended by saying rather lamely that surely nobody would suppose he would make a Chancellor of the Bohemian corporal.

It was at this moment that Papen came forward with the idea of a National Government with Hitler as Chancellor, himself as Vice-Chancellor and Prussian Prime Minister, and a phalanx of Conservatives in the principal offices of state. Hindenburg gave in, and on January 28th, 1933, Schleicher resigned, though he continued to conduct the country's business till his successor was appointed. Thus an end came to this strange new mixture of the *Reichswehr's* in which authoritarianism and social justice were combined. It ended like all the other political ventures of the military. It ended in failure.

Papen's chief candidates for office were Neurath for Foreign Affairs, Blomberg for the *Reichswehr* Ministry, Hugenberg for Commerce, Count Schwerin von Krosigk for Finance—he had held that portfolio under Schleicher—and Gürtner for Justice. All these men were known to Hindenburg. Papen also planned to give Düsterberg a post, but Düsterberg refused.

One hope still remained for Schleicher. That hope was Blomberg. On January 30th the government was to be sworn in by Hindenburg. Blomberg, who had again resumed command of his old military district, was summoned to Berlin, and Schleicher and Hammerstein-Equord thought they saw a last chance. They could try and bring Blomberg round to their side, and through Blomberg inform the President that the *Reichswehr* would not sanction the new government. Schleicher sent his adjutant, Captain Noeldechen, to the railway station with orders that Blomberg was to report to the *Chef der Heeresleitung* forthwith.

Meanwhile, Papen was still at the Chancellery arguing furiously with Hitler and Hugenberg about the composition of the new Cabinet. Düsterberg was present, as was also the sometime Air Force Captain Göring, who was marked down for the Ministry of the Interior and for the proposed Aviation Commission. According to Düsterberg, Papen was working under the threat that if a government was not formed by 11 o'clock, the *Reichswehr*, under Schleicher and Hammerstein-Equord, would march. Düsterberg asked him where he had got his information. Papen replied, from the younger Hindenburg. Düsterberg went to see the latter, and found that he had had a sentry posted outside his door. Oscar von Hindenburg was in a state of frantic excitement. Obviously he had hitherto assumed that Schleicher would be satisfied with Papen's idea of "hedging Hitler round", but had now received some report of what the fallen Chancellor intended. He said he would himself meet Blomberg at the station and would certainly pay the "traitor" Schleicher out. So when Blomberg arrived at the railway station he found both Noeldechen and Oscar von Hindenburg there to meet him.

The question was now which of these two men Blomberg would accompany. Custom dictated that he should first report to his immediate superior, in this case the *Chef der Heeresleitung*, Hammerstein-Equord. He did not, however, go to the latter, but straight to his supreme commander, Hindenburg. Schleicher had lost his last battle.

At 11.15 on January 30th, 1933, the new Chancellor, Adolf Hitler, the son of an Austrian customs official and the grandson of a tramp, presented himself to have the oath administered in the company of his Conservative colleagues. A little later Papen was to remark to some of his friends that it was quite a mistake to suppose that Hitler had seized power. "All that has happened," he said, "is that we've given him a job."

CHAPTER XI

THE UNEASY PARTNERSHIP

LUDWIG VON BECK—REICHENAU

I

THE "Brown Affair", so most German officers thought, was no concern of theirs. They were pleased, of course, at the prospect of being free to rearm, and, when all was said and done, the Revolution—the National Upsurge, that was what most people called it—had been sanctioned by the generals. That did not mean that the Army was going to abandon its traditional detachment, but there was a factor here which it could not ignore. The drama that was unrolling before its eyes was a real revolution—and a psychological release of a quite unprecedented kind. The enthusiasm which it had generated was perfectly genuine, and in many cases it was just those men and women who really wanted order who were pleased, for they saw here a return of the typical German values of order and discipline.

But above all Hitler had mastered the art of giving hope back to the hopeless, and, more important, of providing illusion to a people that wanted illusion almost more passionately than they wanted anything else. Hitler had thus accumulated a capital of love and reverence that made him a popular idol, and it is this fact that became a determining element in the policy of the *Reichswehr*.

And for the moment the Army had no cause to grumble. With the appointment of von Blomberg to the post of War Minister, there began for his ministry a new chapter in which it started to enjoy an amplitude of power such as the old Prussian War Ministry had certainly never experienced. As soon as he was installed, Blomberg summoned his old Chief of Staff, von Reichenau, to act as *Chef der Ministeramtes*, i.e. as his second-in-command. Reichenau was immediately made a general, and of Reichenau it may be said that he was the first military expert of real importance who placed himself entirely without reservation at the dictatorship's disposal.

It was an important gain for the new order. To the small people who had been pitchforked into prominence in the party, Reichenau with his well-bred appearance and glinting monocle, must have appeared as the typical Junker, but Reichenau was something more than a typical Junker. He was a man of Napoleonic ambition, and, possibly in his own estimation, of Napoleonic abilities. He was, of course, the son of a general, but even in this respect he was out of the ordinary, for he had something of Waldersee's sparkle and dash. What distinguished him chiefly, however, was that he understood the forces of the modern age. He also made a name for himself as a ballistics expert and knew the importance of technics, but he also knew the importance of the mass. Hitler understood these things, too, and it was because he believed that Hitler would use that understanding for the benefit of the military that Reichenau so greatly admired him. Only in one particular did the ghost of misgiving dim his devotion, for Reichenau did not altogether like the party. The "Lads in Brown," he held, had really got to be taught discipline.

II

Scarcely was Hitler in the saddle before the Army became the object of a number of congenial attentions which followed one another in rapid succession. The *Truppenamt* received orders to treat its proposed paper mobilization strength of 21 divisions as a peacetime establishment. It was also instructed to make preparations for a second-line organization and to set about the procurement of heavy artillery and tanks. The first plan that was evolved provided for an Army of 300,000 men equipped with heavy weapons and an Air Force. In 1933, Krupps were able to start their first regular programme of tank production under the designation of an "Agricultural Tractor Scheme". Plans were already in existence, and it was possible to make delivery in August of five units. A further hundred followed in 1934. It was not long before the first tank battalion had been set up under the designation of "Motor Transport Training Unit".

Further, a War Industries Staff, to succeed the old Economic Staff, was called into being and put under the command of General Thomas, with an armaments production section, a raw materials section and a price-checking section. Every military district now had attached to it an Inspectorate of War Industries under a general with the standing of a divisional commander. All this had, of course, to be kept secret, for the Treaty of Versailles was still nominally in force, though now that the disarmament conference had broken down it was being persistently declared that Germany could not observe that Treaty's provisions for ever.

Progress was as rapid in the air. An Air Department was formed in the *Reichswehr* Ministry, though it did not stay there for long, for it was soon taken over by the new *Reichskommissar* for Air, Hermann Göring. This was the beginning of a new Air Force which strove with some measure of success to exist as an independent fighting service under the command of a man who had never belonged to the old caste of generals at all, though he got Hindenburg to give him an infantry general's rank.

It fell to the regular General Staff officers of the *Fliegerzentrale* to do the organizational spadework in the new service. After that, new men, like Milch, appeared on the scene who rapidly rose to be generals. The status of the Air Force now became a matter of ever-growing controversy, for the old General Staff officers were all for concentrating on the formation of an Army Air Arm, while the new men who had been taken direct from civilian life and who were for the most part old wartime fliers (and, of course, ardent National Socialists) stood out for complete independence from the Army.

The matter tended, however, to be fought out at a considerably higher level. Göring, Himmler and Röhm were at the moment the Big Three of the party, and each one of these in the hidden struggle for power was striving to equip himself with a private force of his own. As Prussian Minister of the Interior, Göring had under him the police force, which was organized on a military basis. Röhm had the S.A., and Himmler the S.S. It was soon evident that Göring meant to add the German Air Force to what was already really his private army.

To the further satisfaction of the military, a number of the distinctive arrangements of the Republican era were now abolished. The confidential delegate from the rank and file disappeared, military justice was re-established, the Army from now on being withdrawn from the jurisdiction of civilian courts. Military attachés were appointed to London, Paris, Rome, Moscow and Washington. Further, military science itself made great strides. The retired General von Cochenhausen, who had gone to the *Luftwaffe*, called the *Deutsche Gesellschaft für Wehrpolitik und Wehrwissenschaft* (German Society for Military Policy and Military Science) into being, deliberately choosing June 28th, the anniversary of the signature of the Treaty of Versailles, as the day of its foundation. In this society were gathered a body of men, all leaders in their respective fields, who made it their task to study all the problems of total war, psychological, technical, geographical and the rest. Here the geopolitical doctrines of General Haushofer fell on fruitful soil.

III

The innovating spirit of the time was not without its dangers for the General Staff, which was naturally aspiring to recover its ancient place in the scheme of things. Had the General Staff been certain of achieving that, it would have been quite ready to close an eye to some of the régime's less pleasing features, but time was to show that there were deeper contradictions between the party and the General Staff than were apparent on the surface. It was only gradually that the General Staff was to realize that the new "Leader" principle was wholly incompatible with their own tradition which made the subordinate take responsibility for advice offered to a superior. In addition to this, Hitler's desire to stamp a new Army out of the ground involved a number of serious technical headaches. If the re-introduction of universal military service was to be taken as a serious project, the question would arise of finding instructors for the training of no less than fourteen year groups. There just were not enough instructors for that figure. Also, funds were short, so short that in 1933 the autumn manoeuvres had to be suspended. And, finally, there was Göring.

Göring was driving ahead with the *Luftwaffe* without the least regard for the Army's requirements. Among other things, he denuded the Army of quite a number of first-rate experienced General Staff officers such as General Wever, the *Luftwaffe's* new Chief of Staff, Colonel Stumpff, head of its personnel department, Colonel Kessel-ring, who became administrative Chief, Generals Felmy, Wilberg and others. Unfortunately these men were quite unable to communicate to this new body of officers in all its motley of novel uniforms anything of their own tradition and spirit.

If there was a certain lack of sympathy between the new types of officer and the old, a much more violent antagonism was soon to develop against the S.A., which was full of the worst kind of *Freikorps* adventurer, the kind which the General Staff had sedulously sought to eliminate in 1919 and 1920. The new political army which did not serve the State but professed rather to serve an idea, a new socio-religious doctrine of salvation, counted some 400,000 armed men, and was divided into 24 S.A. Groups, corresponding roughly to army corps. In the days of seizure of power, the S.A. had on occasion been used as a kind of auxiliary police. Since then they had evolved into an instrument of terror. A number of wild S.A. leaders of the *Landsknecht* type, who had served sentences for *Feme* murders and were bound to one another by their homosexual proclivities, organized heavily-armed bodies of "Staff guards" about their persons, and became a law unto themselves. Karl Ernst in Berlin and Edmund Heines in Breslau were the most notorious. Röhm organized his own cavalry, sapper and intelligence units.

One of the first things to happen under Hitler was the breaking up of the *Stahlhelm*. Till now, the *Stahlhelm* had been regarded almost as an extended arm of the *Reichswehr*, but Hitler's followers considered it too conservative in sentiment and brought it under the control of the S.A. Seldte, the original head of the *Stahlhelm*, who had become Reich Labour Minister, raised no objection to this. Düsterberg, who protested to Blomberg and Reichenau against old front-line soldiers being put under a paederast, was told that nowadays that kind of thing was no longer material.

Much of this recalled what happened in Italy in the early days of Fascism. Here, too, the *Squadristi*, the equivalent of Hitler's Storm Troops, had consisted largely of front-line officers who had lost their social bearings. These men who made up the kernel of what was later to be the Fascist Militia, for the most part encountered the vehement opposition of the Italian generals. Incidentally, the parallelism went further, for Göring's creation of a National Socialist Air Force merely repeated Balbo's creation of a Fascist Air Force, which claimed the leadership of the other fighting services.

Ludendorff had taught that the true distinguishing mark of Germany's rearmament would not be universal service but the attainment of a German *Weltanschauung*,* and it was precisely the Nazi *Weltanschauung* that came up against the tradition-bound Prussian officer, whose ideas were still more or less rooted in Christian values. It was natural enough that Hitler should endeavour to penetrate this phalanx of the officer corps, for every totalitarian State had sooner or later come up against a similar problem. In Russia it was not solved till 1937 when the Army was finally brought into gear with the one-party State at the cost of some ten thousand higher officers' lives. The Italian story is somewhat different, because the Italian officers had the Crown at the back of them. In Germany this inner conflict was never really resolved at all. Hitler scored some partial success, but in

---

* The word means literally "World Outlook", but is really untranslatable, the commodity being (perhaps fortunately) rare on English-speaking markets. (B.B)

the end the tradition-conscious part of the officer corps revolted against him.

As the less pleasing sides of the revolution grew apparent, the officer corps became increasingly conscious of its helplessness. Schleicher raged, but Seeckt, when reports came to him of Schleicher's outbursts, could only remark with melancholy resignation that all he and his colleagues had stood for was now *vieux jeu*. Hammerstein-Equord endeavoured to pick up the threads of the past and tried to take counsel with Schleicher and Brüning. Brüning, who had sought safety within the walls of the Hedwig Hospital in Berlin, remained passive, though he seems to have been privy to some kind of rather futile plan against the régime which got nowhere at all.

Schleicher, however, was as little prepared as Hammerstein-Equord to let things drift. He simply could not be shaken in the belief that he could once more regain the President's confidence and so get the fetters off his hands. It was not a wholly preposterous conviction, for the Nazi terror which had already attracted the world's attention had hitherto confined itself to the Jews and to the parties of the left. It was now rapidly extending to Hitler's old allies on the right. Hindenburg could thus hardly remain disinterested—at least, so Schleicher thought.

What would be the attitude of the military district commanders? That was the great question. Rauschning, who was becoming very concerned about the turn things were taking, had interviews with both von Brauchitsch, who had succeeded Blomberg in the command of the first military district, and with Blomberg himself. Brauchitsch insisted that the Army could not rearm unless it was kept free from disturbances. The *Reichswehr*, he insisted, must remain neutral.

Blomberg made much the same reply, and once when Herbert von Bismarck-Lasbeck, the Conservative State Secretary in the Prussian Ministry of the Interior, also made representations on similar lines, Blomberg simply replied that he was an officer and had to obey. Bismarck rejoined that he had no wish to speak to Blomberg the General, but to Blomberg the Minister, who as a minister could not evade political responsibility. Blomberg banged his fist on the table, and cried that he forbade such talk in his office.

IV

Till now, all the *Truppenamt's* calculations had depended on maintaining good relations with Russia and had assumed Germany's continued membership of the League of Nations; but, thanks largely to Hitler's ideological predilections, that whole basis was on the point of crumbling. In 1933, General Thomas went to Russia and afterwards tried to impress Hitler with the importance of maintaining good commercial relations with the east as a basis for German rearmament. Hitler replied that those were nothing but "Potemkin villages" and that Russia could never be anything but a destructive force.

When on another occasion Thomas brought up the subject of commercial relations with China, whither Seeckt had gone to reorganize the Army (now almost wholly controlled by German advisers), he was told that he (Hitler) was only concerned with *Realpolitik*. Hitler's ideas on *Realpolitik*, however, had been entirely formed by his early impressions of the conflict between Slav and German within the Dual Monarchy. Slavdom was the great enemy; England, Italy and Japan the ideal allies. Beyond that his thought did not go. So the "Russian line" of the *Reichswehr*, which had recently been developing into a "Russo-Chinese line", was abandoned, though the Soviet Union was quite ready to forget all ideological differences between itself and Germany. In November 1934, at the customary banquet commemorating the October Revolution, Blomberg gave the toast, "The Red Army", for the last time.

The League of Nations policy was also abandoned when the Disarmament Commission refused to accept without reserve the principle of equality of armaments. Hitler withdrew from the League in the autumn of 1933, and it may have been some foreknowledge of this step that caused Blomberg, in the spring of that year, to issue secret orders for the event of an application of sanctions by France. In such a case resistance was to be offered, even if there appeared to be no prospect of military success.

After Germany had actually withdrawn from the League, the *Truppenamt* issued orders for "Enterprise Schulung". The line of the Rhine and the Black Forest was to be held in the west, and the Obra-Netze line in the east. Militarized police, railway guards and the customs service were to be placed under the military to assist in evacuation in the west. Blomberg, however, insisted that his special sanction must be obtained before any troops were actually committed. He knew the Army was too weak to risk any serious international complications.

Meanwhile, Hitler took the matter of Poland in hand. Without consulting the Army, he opened negotiations with Pilsudski with a view to concluding a Treaty of Friendship, which was ultimately signed early in 1934. This was to compensate for the loss of the friendship of Russia, with whom he intended to break. Strangely enough, it was just at this time that Captain Sosnowski, a Polish secret agent, got hold of certain plans for Russo-German co-operation in the event of a Polish attack. Sosnowski secured these with the help of certain titled lady secretaries of the *Reichswehr* Ministry. It was not an opportune happening from any point of view, for it showed Germany's new friend all too clearly just what German friendship was worth.

V

While Polish-German relations were being so felicitously re-established, certain changes were taking place in the High Command. Adam was considered inimical to the new dispensation and was removed from his post as head of the *Truppenamt* and given command of the 7th Division in Munich. He was succeeded by Lieutenant-General Beck, at the time commanding the 1st Cavalry Division. A little afterwards, Blomberg was raised by Hindenburg to the rank of colonel general and given command over all three fighting services—Army, Navy and Air Force. This made Göring Blomberg's subordinate in his capacity of Supreme Commander of the *Luftwaffe*, though not in that of *Reichskommissar* for Air.

The extension of the *Reichswehr* Ministry's authority, however, carried certain implications on which Blomberg was not slow to seize, and he now set about turning the *Ministeramt* into a kind of working and co-ordinating staff to which the *Truppenamt* and the naval and air staffs would be subordinated. Reichenau, who under the new arrangements became something like the Chief of a Wehrmacht General Staff, was naturally enough delighted with them, and it must be admitted that they did not wholly lack justification; the failure during the late war to co-ordinate the Great General Staff with the Staff of the Admiralty was still remembered.

Among other changes was a change in the *Ministeramt's* name. It became the *Wehrmachtamt*, and, what was even more important, furnished itself with a department that was virtually, though not in name, a commander-in-chief's office. It was called the Department of National Defence and was made up of Staff officers from all three fighting services. This arrangement, which was ultimately to subordinate the General Staff to what was in some respects a kind of duplicate of itself, was the beginning of its progressive abasement.

It was under these not too favourable auspices that on October 1st Lieutenant-General Beck, long accounted one of the best strategists in the Army, assumed the headship of the *Truppenamt*. Beck was not a son of one of the old Prussian landed families, his background being that of business and the learned professions, and his father a leading ironmaster. His picture shows a finely chiselled, highly spiritual face, and as a type he seems rather like a reversion to the elder Moltke, though the circumstances in which he was called upon to act were tragically different. Moltke had raised the General Staff to a wholly unique level of excellence. Beck was faced by the hard crude fact of its already inevitable decline.

The *Truppenamt* when Beck took over was already only on the fourth level of authority, the *Reichswehr* Minister, the *Ministeramt* and the *Chef der Heeresleitung* representing the steps to the top level of departmental power; for all that, Beck saw himself faced by the inevitable conflict between the General Staff tradition in which he had been trained, and the so-called "political soldiers" of the revolution, of whom the madly ambitious and undoubtedly able Reichenau was merely a variant in orthodox military guise. There was also that other latent struggle with Göring who, though himself now technically a subordinate like Beck to higher powers, still tried to claim priority over the Army.

These battles were difficult to fight, now that the old privilege of *Immediatstellung* had lapsed. The best he could hope for was to be championed by the man whose chief adviser he was supposed to be—the *Chef der Heeresleitung*. But Hammerstein-Equord, being an opponent of National Socialism, was now wholly without influence. Indeed, he was under police supervision and certainly did nothing— at least, not openly—to back Beck up. Perhaps this was because he had confidence in Schleicher's ability to get rid of the régime. Perhaps, on the other hand, it was just his love of taking things easily, which he often said was his besetting sin.

A further loss of influence resulted from Blomberg's determination to get complete control of the Army into his own hands. The War Industries Staff was now attached to the *Wehrmachtamt*, as was also the secret service, which, since the Sosnowski affair, had been put under Canaris. There was also the chairmanship of the *Reichsverteidigungsrat* (the Council of Reich Defence).*

This *Reichsverteidigungsrat* was an organization concerned chiefly

---

* Not to be confused with *Abteilung Landesverteidigung* or "Department of National Defence".

with mobilization problems, which Blomberg and Reichenau had caused to be called into being in April, membership being extended to representatives of all departments concerned. Originally the Chief of the *Truppenamt* in his capacity of Chief of General Staff was to have been its chairman, but now the chairmanship to passed Reichenau, who in this and other matters always enjoyed the sympathy and confidence of his chief—another political soldier like himself.

VI

Hammerstein-Equord, of whom Hitler was later to say that he looked upon him as one of his most dangerous enemies, was retired at the end of 1933, and Reichenau might well have thought that as a "Party General" his hour had now come; yet, as a matter of fact, the Seecktian tradition was stronger than he. Of the two group commanders, Rundstedt and Leeb, neither was willing to work under him, so the man chosen as Hammerstein-Equord's successor was the commander of the third military district, Lieutenant-General von Fritsch.

Fritsch was something of a paradox. Outwardly he seemed a robust and soldierly type, a typical officer of the old school. Needless to say, he wore a monocle; his outlook was fundamentally Christian and conservative. Yet in reality he was a man of very delicate sensibility, something of an epigone, and his outward bearing was a triumph of self-mastery.

Politically he had just about as much wisdom as the other generals. Christian and Monarchist though he undoubtedly was, he was, like so many others, impressed by the gigantic fact of Hitler's popularity, and once asked Rauschning what could be put in the place of National Socialism if Hitler were ever destroyed. It was a revealing observation.

It is perhaps unjust to criticize such sentiments too harshly. Hitler at that stage had given no grounds for supposing that his policy was aimed at anything but peace—his friendship pact with Poland certainly led one to that conclusion—and most certainly neither Fritsch nor Beck had any wish for war. Fritsch knew well enough that Germany was not strong enough to fight a multi-front war, while Beck was particularly insistent that no war in which Germany was involved could be anything else.

Unfortunately the generals were not privileged to hear Hitler expounding over the tea table. Generals were not too welcome there, for it almost seems as if the ex-corporal could never master his feeling of inferiority in their presence. That might perhaps explain why some-what later Hitler should have chosen to tell Keitel and Halder that he had been a lieutenant in a Bavarian Infantry Regiment—surely a somewhat euphemistic description of his activity as a so-called "Education Officer" and political agent.

In the main, Fritsch had little time to concern himself with ex-ternal problems. He tended to be kept too busy by problems at home, where the S.A. gave him quite enough to think about. It was not Fritsch's fate, as it was that of Scharnhorst and Gneisenau, to in-fluence the Army's political development, as he was building that Army anew. All he could do was to deal with that political develop-ment's excrescences.

On the other side, it was in a way natural enough that the S.A. should regard the Army with jealous suspicion. The Army had been the real basis of Germany's mass education, and now that universal service was returning, its educational influence might once again be considerable. But it was precisely the S.A. and the Party on which, in the opinion of those bodies, the task of education properly devolved—the very special kind of education of which they had a monopoly, which was education in *Weltanschauung*. The battle about the Army chaplains, whom Fritsch and Beck (and even more so, the Catholics Leeb and Kress von Kressenstein) wanted to keep on, and whom the S.A. wanted abolished, was only the first of many conflicts in the spiritual field.

Fritsch's task was no easy one. In a document which he drew up at the time of his fall in 1938, he wrote that when he took up his appointment he had found a heap of ruins. Hammerstein-Equord did not move a finger, while Reichenau seemed to be following a policy of his own which consisted in trying to counteract the S.A. by keeping in with the party. For Reichenau, to do him justice, really did stand up to the S.A., and it was with a view of making a counterweight to S.A. influences that he created the "soldiers' unions" for ex-Army men, which were to form the basis of a sort of reserve militia. That went flat against Röhm's idea of welding S.A. and Army together into one great militia force, so that in the end it would be only the political soldier who would bear arms at all.

Even so, Reichenau's everlasting flirtations with the party, however laudable their object, made the Army feel perpetually insecure, since nobody could ever tell which way the ministerial cat was going to jump. As to Blomberg, Fritsch had served under him when acting as chief of the *Truppenamt's* T.I. On the whole, he had a high opinion of

Blomberg, though he considered him in his capacity of *Reichswehr* Minister too prone to take up newfangled ideas—and also too easily influenced.

Thus the problems presented by the S.A.'s existence went largely unsolved and they were often of a very disturbing kind. *Grenzschutz Ost*, for instance, had been largely built up with the help of the *Stahlhelm*, but now that *Stahlhelm* had been broken up and incorporated in the S.A. The result was that *Grenzschutz Ost* had become an almost totally unserviceable instrument. That was only one among a number of counts. The S.A. was continually asking for instructors who could ill be spared from the Army. On Berlin-Brandenburg S.A. Group's Beer Evenings, Group Leader Ernst, a former hotel page and later a bouncer in a Berlin café frequented by homosexuals, would regularly expound his ideas on a "People's General Staff". It may have been a confused notion of something of this kind that caused an S.A. leader to present himself to Colonel Halder, Chief of Staff of the ninth military district, with a demand to be initiated into the work of his office. Halder reported the matter, which turned out to be by no means unique, personally to Fritsch. Eventually, Fritsch felt constrained to set up a brigade at Döberitz at full war strength with orders to take immediate action against the S.A. should the latter engage in acts of violence. In Stettin, things came to such a pass that von Bock, the commander of the second military district, forbade anybody in S.A. uniform to enter any military building.

VII

Its character being as here described, it was hardly to be expected that the S.A. would reach a *modus vivendi* with the *Reichswehr* or any other legal and established institution, nor did it show any signs of doing so. Throughout the year 1933, negotiations had taken place between the *Wehrmachtamt* in the *Reichswehr* Ministry, the *Allgemeines Heeresamt* and *Obergruppenführer* Krüger of the S.A. concerning the training of the S.A., though in the main nothing better had resulted from them than vehement differences of opinion. Reichenau, despite some friction, did get agreement on a scheme of pre-military training for the young, and for this made use of the Hitler Youth. He further in this general connection organized courses of military training for university students, and General Staff officers were sent off to the leading universities as instructors in so-called

"Military Sports" and in that branch of learning for which the word "Defence Politics" (*Wehrpolitik*) had been coined.

However, the introduction by the S.A. of compulsory labour service, of yet more "Defence Camps" and of so-called "*Geländesport-schulen*" or "Cross-country sport schools", had the effect, already previously noted, of interfering with a uniform military training. On top of everything, the S.A. organized an "Office of Defence Politics" (*Wehrpolitisches Amt*) which was the nerve centre of a special National Socialist defence policy.

This raised fundamental issues and on these and other matters Reichenau really made the quarrel with the S.A. his own, more so, indeed, than the Army itself. Both he and Blomberg demanded the abolition of the *Wehrpolitisches Amt* and full control over all funds allotted to any kind of military training by the S.A. They also took steps to elaborate the training programmes of Reichenau's "soldiers' unions" for ex-Army men.

Now, Röhm, as we have seen, was particularly inimical to these "soldiers' unions", for he saw in them an instrument which might one day make the S.A. superfluous. Röhm had, as a matter of fact, long begun to see himself as the commander of a revolutionary German army. What was more, certain circumstances appeared to be not unfavourable to that ambition. The more desperate and adventurous of the S.A. leaders were coming round to the view that the seizure of power on January 30th had been no true revolution at all. There had been too little bloodshed. The Communists and Social Democrats had been the only ones among their enemies with whom they had settled accounts. The upper class reactionaries had escaped, and after the manner of men who, as was often the case, have sunk beneath their own class, they hated these last much more intensely than they hated the left.

Things really came to a head when a demand was openly made that the *Reichswehr* should henceforth only be recruited out of the S.A., which would have meant that the whole Army was gradually to be "revolutionized". The S.A. group leaders would then move in and take over the posts of the commanding generals.

Nor was it by any means certain that in pursuing this aim the S.A. would observe the niceties of constitutional procedure. At Nüremberg, Jodl declared that Röhm was anything but a "Morning coat revolutionary". This seems to mean that the *Truppenamt*, where Jodl was serving at the time, was quite prepared for Röhm to resort to force to achieve his ends, and in point of fact it was just about this time considered advisable to put on extra guards in the Bendler-strasse.

Again, however, the powers which could decide these things were on a higher level, for the clash between *Reichswehr* and S.A. was only the reflection of the conflict between more exalted personalities. The real tussle was not so much between Röhm and Beck, or even between Röhm and Fritsch, but was a sort of quadrilateral one between Röhm Reichenau, Göring and Himmler. Göring saw in Röhm a rival in the race for control of the *Wehrmacht*, while Himmler resented his own nominal subordination to the S.A.

Hitler seems, for a time, at least, to have been the plaything rather than the master of these forces, and yet Hitler was under the urgent necessity of making up his mind. Hindenburg would not live much longer, and it would be as well for Hitler to put his own house in order before the question of a successor to Hindenburg had to be answered.

The first indications of the manner in which Hitler would deal with the problem of the S.A. came in March. In that month he made a speech in the *Reichswehr* Ministry to the military district commanders and S.A. group leaders, in which he described the Army as the bearer of the nation's arms, while the S.A. was charged with the more nebulous duties of being the "Shock troops" of the new *Weltanschauung*. This, however, hardly served to lessen the tension, nor did it curb Röhm's importunity, though, according to his own account, Hitler spent several hours endeavouring to make him see reason.

VIII

In June Papen delivered a sensational speech to the Marburg students in which he said that there must ultimately be an end to every revolution and that the time must always come when right and justice have to be restored. Despite the fact that Papen no longer counted for anything and, unlike Göring, Röhm, Himmler and Reichenau, had no concrete power behind him, the answer was not slow in coming. Goebbels forbade the dissemination of the speech. Jung, Papen's collaborator and the moving spirit in the group around the latter, was arrested, while both Goebbels and Hitler's deputy, Rudolf Hess, issued warnings to the people who thought they could start a drawing-room opposition to the régime.

If Papen's speech seemed strange, which it did, since there was no possibility whatever of his following it up by deeds, the conduct of Röhm was stranger still. After the S.A. had been sent on four-weeks' leave towards the end of June, he sent a message to Fritsch saying that he hoped for an amicable settlement of the conflict. Then he went off for a holiday to Bad Wiessee, whither the S.A. Group leaders were summoned for a conference.

All this hardly suggests that Röhm was preparing a *Putsch*. Hitler afterwards stated that he had had reports according to which the S.A. were preparing a mutiny, and no doubt such reports had been put into Hitler's hands by those most interested in pushing that essentially dilatory man into a decision, for whatever might be the case with Röhm, neither Reichenau, Göring nor Himmler could afford to wait. So Hitler was compelled to make his choice, and, since the S.A. despite its numbers had little chance against artillery and machine guns, Hitler chose the Army.

Not that there had not been some concessions by the latter. Blomberg some months previously had ordered the Swastika to be worn on all military uniforms. Now, on June 30th, an article of Blomberg's appeared in the *Völkischer Beobachter* on the fusion of the Army with the State. That represented a final retreat from the old Seecktian ideal of isolation. Formally, at any rate, the idea of an *imperium in imperio* had been abandoned.

On the day on which that article appeared, Hitler personally arrested the S.A. leaders in Wiessee with Röhm, his personal friend, whom he addressed as "*Du*", at the head of them. Göring and Himmler took simultaneous action in Berlin. The executions began. There fell on this day not only the old guard of S.A. leaders, but all who had at any time opposed Hitler, or were privy to such scandals as the mysterious death of Hitler's niece, who was believed by some to have been his mistress. Schleicher and his wife were despatched in their home in Lichterfelde by a six-man execution squad of the S.S. Von Bredow was killed in similar circumstances. Papen was put under house arrest in his home. Von Bose, his first assistant, was shot in his office. Jung was also executed that day and Papen's secretaries were put in prison. Düsterberg escaped. His wife contrived with the aid of Major-General Groppe to get in touch with old Oldenburg-Januschau, who informed Hindenburg. Hindenburg ordered Blomberg to save him. Among those who had acted against Hitler in the Beer-hall *Putsch* Kahr was slaughtered and von Seisser sent to a concentration camp. Brüning had contrived with some difficulty to escape abroad.

Little, if anything, of all these happenings was known in the *Heeresleitung*. Fritsch and Beck sat in their offices in complete ignorance of the fact that Schleicher, the sometime *Reichswehr* Minister, had been shot. They heard that shootings had taken place in what had once been the Cadet School at Lichterfelde, but on enquiry at the *Wehrmachtamt* were told that it was a purely internal affair of the party from which it was desirable for the *Wehrmacht* to keep entirely clear.

This seems to have been a very widespread impression. When General von Witzleben, the commander of the third military district, heard that the "wild and degenerate S.A. leaders" were being shot, he was delighted and remarked that he wished he could be there.

Fritsch, however, had begun to grow restless and tried to find out through the secret service what was really afoot. He lunched that day with the Foreign Minister, von Neurath, who was entertaining Prince Takamatsu, the Japanese Emperor's brother, at lunch. The Prince was nearly an hour late and explained that he found the road in which von Neurath lived cordoned off by chains. At Nuremberg von Neurath still was under the impression that the whole matter was concerned with an S.A. revolt. He had concluded at the time that the S.S. had taken the precaution of isolating him. Fritsch was later to tell Neurath that a "black list" containing his own name had been found in Röhm's papers.

All this may well serve as an indication of the way everybody outside the charmed Nazi circle was led by the nose. Alarm was soon widespread, however, and an incident at the Ministry of Transport served to put most Ministers, especially the less exalted ones, in terror of their lives. In that Ministry, *Ministerialdirektor* Klausener, the leader of Catholic Action, was liquidated on the spot by the S.S. When the Minister, von Eltz-Rübenach, came hurrying along to see what was happening, he was told to mind his own business if he didn't want a bullet too.

Three days later, when he had been released from internment, Papen visited Fritsch, who had been at the *Kriegsakademie* with him, and asked him why he did not intervene. Fritsch said he could do nothing except on orders from Hindenburg. Fritsch had heard of the murders of Bredow and Schleicher. He had protested to Blomberg and Reichenau but got surprisingly little sympathy. Reichenau took the line that Schleicher had really ceased to be a soldier, it was regrettable that he had been shot, but every revolution had its imperfections. Papen now tried through a mutual friend to make contact with Hindenburg, but was unsuccessful. Neudeck had been sealed off hermetically from the outside world.

IX

The fact that two of its leading personalities had been murdered was accepted quite passively by the Army, nor did it lift a finger when these murders were publicly declared to be justified, or when Hitler claimed the right, in cases of mere suspicion of treason, to order executions without even the pretence of a trial. An effort was made by Rundstedt, Witzleben and by Witzleben's Chief of Staff, von Manstein, to have a court of enquiry investigate the actions of the murdered men. Blomberg and Reichenau, however, remained silent. Eventually the aged Field-Marshal von Mackensen went to Hitler with a general plea for the re-establishment of common decency in public life. Hitler actually showed some concern and was silent for a moment before replying. Then he said, "It may be as you say, but I cannot help myself."

There was also a resolution passed by the Schlieffen Society, of which Mackensen was president, the meeting being attended by some 400 Staff officers. The resolution declared that Schleicher and Bredow had fallen upon the field of honour. The press was not allowed to carry the story, however, and the names of Bredow and Schleicher were soon shrouded in silence—unless, of course, anyone thought it opportune to raise his voice in further detraction. The *Reichsverband Deutscher Offiziere* achieved that doubtful distinction. It hastened to declare its intention of drawing away from the murdered man, who, it was asserted, had by his everlasting intrigues forfeited the confidence of all decent officers.

For a time Reichenau might well have thought that he had achieved a political triumph, and one made all the more remarkable by the fact that the Army had never been committed; the revolutionary army, which had been the rival of his own, had been completely eliminated, and indeed the S.A. never recovered from this blow. Its numbers still remained large but it ceased altogether to play any real part in affairs.

However, if Reichenau felt he had cause for self-congratulation, he was soon disillusioned. On July 20th the S.S. under the leadership of Heinrich Himmler was declared an independent organization and so a new rival to the Army came into being and one that was more powerful and more ready to strike than the S.A. had ever been.

Himmler now set out in earnest to turn the S.S. into the armed force of the revolution.

The S.S. had begun with the setting up of certain permanent armed detachments which were to serve certain specific institutions or personalities. Among the latter were Hitler's bodyguard the *Leibstandarte Adolf Hitler* and the Death's Head Contingents which guarded the concentration camps. The whole of the *Allgemeine und Waffen S.S.* (General and Weapon S.S.) was now organized into 24 S.S. *Oberabschnitte*, which corresponded roughly to corps districts, and it was not long before the first clashes took place. There was trouble with the troops at Alengrabow when the S.S. started to shout insults against Fritsch, and more trouble at a higher level when von Brauchitsch in East Prussia tried to prevent the S.S. being equipped with heavy weapons.

Hitler at first took the Army's part, and forbade the equipping of S.S. with artillery and also conceded the Army the right to inspect S.S units in order to ensure uniformity of training. But Himmler was tough and did not give up the fight, and what was more, Himmler's power began to grow enormous, for beside the S.S. he was soon to control both police and Gestapo. So for Blomberg and Reichenau the S.S. remained as dangerous a thing as it was for anybody else.

While these struggles were at their height Hindenburg died. Hitler had a law passed forthwith uniting the offices of Chancellor and President in his own hand. Blomberg was not slow to take his cue. Immediately after the news of Hindenburg's death, on August 2nd, he ordered the Army to take the oath to the 'Führer and Chancellor'. It was for many officers a crucial moment, and for years afterwards Beck continued to debate with himself whether he had not been in duty bound to refuse that oath. He would often hereafter speak of August 2nd as the black day of the Germany Army. However, black day or no, the oath was taken, and the power of the oath was great— particularly where those officers were concerned who were still rooted in the Christian and traditional way of thought.

X

Hitler's new orientation in foreign affairs, his ending of the *entente* with Russia and his courting of Poland, his clumsy attempts in the spring of 1934 to initiate an understanding with Italy, these together with the murder of Dollfuss by the National Socialists of Austria, were not without effect in the international field. Barthou now began his attempt to weld together Czechoslovakia, Jugoslavia, Rumania, Poland and Russia into a common system of alliance.

Early in 1935 Hitler in his turn decided that the time had come officially to introduce compulsory universal service and to announce publicly that an Air Force was in process of creation. Contrary to the practice that he had so far followed, he failed to notify the military authorities of his epoch-making decision until the very last moment. Actually Hitler communicated his intentions to his military adjutant, Colonel Hossbach, on March 14th and the information was passed on to Blomberg, Fritsch and Beck on the following day.

Blomberg was horrified, he feared international complications, and the Army in its present state of disorganization was quite unfit to deal with anything like that. Fritsch and Beck took the matter more calmly, though the former was at pains to make it perfectly clear to Hitler that putting the Army on a universal service basis would take time and was not a thing that could be rushed. Even so, he was not averse to the idea. He looked upon the Army simply as a means of asserting Germany's integrity and honestly believed that this motive was at the bottom of Hitler's policy.

On the 16th Hitler publicly announced his plan in one of his enormous, wide-ranging speeches. The new Army which he then described was to have 36 divisions and 12 corps. The measure was accompanied by some significant changes in nomenclature. The *Reichswehr* Minister became the Reich War Minister and Blomberg was given Field-Marshal's rank as being more appropriate to the dignity of the commander of all three fighting services. The *Chef der Heeresleitung* was transformed into *Oberbefehlshaber des Heeres* (Supreme Commander of the Army), the term *Heeresleitung* being changed to *Oberkommando des Heeres* (O.K.H.) while the *Truppenamt* threw off its disguise and overtly assumed the title of General Staff of the Army.

France, in addition to increasing the period of military service, answered the new German move by signing a Treaty of Mutual Assistance with Russia. Hitler's rejoinder was to re-emphasize Germany's readiness to enter once more into disarmament negotiations. Aside from this, he made a naval pact with Britain imposing a limit on the naval armaments which technically he was still forbidden to have at all. This agreement, which was not negotiated through the Foreign Office but through Ribbentrop, his private adviser on international affairs, derived from a belief that it was possible to buy a free hand in the east with an accommodating gesture in London.

In these diplomatic ventures Hitler sedulously avoided consulting
his military advisers. Indeed he seemed almost apprehensively concerned to keep each province of responsibility strictly circumscribed
in order to secure the maximum freedom of action for himself. This
really explains his failure to consult competent professional soldiers
before announcing his scheme for universal service. Actually Fritsch
and Beck thought that 36 divisions were quite impracticable and preferred to continue with Seeckt's old plan for 21 divisions, which, in
a rudimentary fashion, was already being realized. At length they
were able to carry their point sufficiently for the scheme to be cut
down, at least for the immediate present, to 24 divisions, to which
were to be added two cavalry divisions, one mountain brigade, one
independent cavalry brigade for East Prussia and some experimental
tank units. These were to be organized into 10 corps and distributed
among three army groups with headquarters at Berlin, Cassell and
Dresden. One further development was still to follow in that year.
The inspector of motorized troops was made the Commanding
General of tank troops.

XI

The retransformation of the *Truppenamt* into the General Staff
presented Beck with a tremendous problem. It was now his task to
try and put back that institution into the position it had once held in
the military hierarchy—and, as we have seen, there was already a
disposition to exclude it from that. In actual size the General Staff
now increased considerably, and eight new departments were added
to the existing four. The old Central department, which dealt with
personnel matters, with postings to the General Staff and with all
appointments down to the rank of divisional commander, was completely reorganized. The Training department and the Foreign
Armies department were each divided into two, while new departments were created for technical questions, transport, mapping, military history, fortifications and supply services. The various departments of the General Staff were distributed among five *Oberquartiermeisters*. Further, the General Staff had put under it the 19 military
attachés, various subsidiary organizations such as the Army Film
Office, and a number of institutions dealing with records and military
history.

In all, 190 officers were employed. A little less than a third of these
were officers recalled from the retired list, so-called "E" officers. The

Army List of 1938 shows that out of 187 officers no less than fifty were titled, a remarkably high percentage, considering that the proportion of titled officers in the Army as a whole had by then fallen to ten per cent.

There was a danger that in this hurried reorganization the General Staff might lack a clear grasp of its tasks. Beck was alive to that danger, and made provision for it by creating a special section for the scientific study of any new military problem that recent developments had called into being. It was an undertaking that neither Hitler nor Blomberg adequately appreciated and one which remained unnoticed.

It was not long before Beck was tackling one problem which was cardinal. It was the question of the old theory of co-responsibility. The issue was whether under an authoritarian State that theory could still be upheld, and Beck called upon the Department of Military Science to study it. He received a negative answer, but in spite of it gave orders for the principle to be re-established. It was a most significant departure. When later the occasion arose for a revolt against Hitler and his insane method of waging war, it was essentially this conception of co-responsibility that was the driving force behind the officers concerned. Major-General Stieff, Chief of the General Staff's Organization Section, has, in his own case, explicitly testified to this.

Beck in fact now set himself once more to produce a generation of General Staff officers trained in the tradition which the elder Moltke had laid down. It was not an easy task. Nevertheless, there were a number of able officers available to help him in this work. These were von Manstein, looked upon as one of the most promising of the younger strategists, acting as *Oberquartiermeister I*, and Generals Halder and Karl Heinrich von Stülpnagel, who were acting as *Oberquartiermeisters II* and *IV* respectively. To these names must be added that of Colonel Hossbach, who as *Wehrmachtadjutant* was the Army's personal representative to Hitler.

Stülpnagel, by the way, deserves a special passing mention here as being co-author with Beck of the new Battle Instructions which were now drawn up. These instructions are noteworthy because they embody a drastic change of principle. The cardinal idea developed by the *Truppenamt* had been that of "delaying defensive action". Fritsch designated this doctrine of the transition period as "organized flight" and insisted on its being superseded by the traditional tactics of attack. The future was unfortunately to show that neither he nor Beck was prepared to translate that principle into the political sphere.

Unfortunately, too, Beck's wish to recreate in the General Staff a uniform and coherent school of thought on traditional lines encountered obstacles which in the long run were to prove well nigh insurmountable. A number of General Staff officers, at the head of whom stood Jodl, now began to take the view that the only justification for the General Staff's existence in a modern "Leader State" was its study in peace-time of the problems that would arise in war. Once war had broken out, the "Leader" principle must be unwaveringly applied, the task of the General Staff officer becoming that of a "Leader's Assistant" pure and simple, and not that of a responsible adviser with an independent judgement of his own. This went, of course, flat against Beck's cardinal doctrine, and his difficulties were increased by the fact that the number of officers on the General Staff (and among the commanding generals) who had passed through the school of the old Great General Staff was becoming progressively smaller, though it was still large enough to provide the principal commanders of the first years of the Second World War. Their successors were by no means all of one piece.

At the reopening of the *Kriegsakademie* in October 1935 under the title of *Wehrmachtakademie* Beck made a rather noteworthy speech. Taking Moltke's words "Genius is work" as his text, Beck formulated the principles of the General Staff's work roughly on these lines. First, logical and systematic thought, careful working out of all situations, and avoidance of the *'coup d'oeil'*—Hitler's favourite method. Then, after good planning, decisive action. The principles underlying the successful waging of war, he continued, had not been changed by the technical revolution. Human beings and not machines were still the real instruments of war.

The speech must surely have evoked much criticism on the part of Hitler's friends, for, unlike that of Blomberg on this occasion, it avoided any fulsome flattery of the new Supreme War Lord and was full of that "accursed objectivity" with which the Party was everlastingly reproaching the General Staff. No doubt it also confirmed Hitler, who was present on this occasion, in the belief (expressed to his intimates) that the General Staff was "just a club of intellectuals".

Beck's tragedy had really begun on the day he assumed his office, for the subordinate level of his authority ensured his isolation. Apart from the occasion of Fritsch's fall—and here the issues were purely political—he had only one short conversation with Hitler during the whole period between 1934 and 1938. Probably Hitler never felt the

need of having a talk with his Chief of General Staff, and this may
not only have been due to his dislike and distrust of the General Staff
as an institution. Perhaps Hitler really believed in the years from 1933
to 1937 that he could attain his aims peacefully by means of an
entente with Britain and Italy. Or again he may have thought that the
time for carrying out his tea-table phantasies had not yet arrived.

In the main the world heard little of Beck. The names of Moltke,
Waldersee, Schlieffen and Hindenburg had represented something
clear and concrete to the German public. Not so that of Beck. The
reorganization of the Army and the whole rearmament programme
was carried out under the mantle of secrecy, and this alone served to
keep Beck's name obscure.

Here was, perhaps, Beck's most severe disadvantage in his battle
with Hitler. He sought and found contacts with some of Hitler's
opponents. Hammerstein-Equord helped him in this by putting him
in touch with old trade union leaders like Wilhelm Leuschner, who
had once been Minister of the Interior in Hesse. Even more important than this were his connections with Dr. Goerdeler, lately
Price Commissioner for the Reich and Lord Mayor of Leipzig, who
had retired from these posts because he refused to have any part in
Hitler's policies. Yet all these connections were precarious and had
necessarily to be kept dark, and so the masses on whom so much
depended continued to know nothing of the Chief of General Staff.

XII

Actually the real centre of military opposition to the régime was
not the General Staff but the Secret Service Office of Admiral
Canaris and his Chief of Staff, Hans Oster, later a major-general.
This office was in charge of intelligence, sabotage, counter-espionage
and similar activities. It was primarily concerned with foreign
countries but it also had agents working at the various Corps headquarters. In all some 15,000 persons were in its employ and it was
thus in a better position than anybody else to cut across Himmler's
net of secret agents.

Canaris, however, was rather a strange kind of man who could only
do his job properly if he was playing some kind of a dangerous double
game. He was at heart such a passionate enemy of any kind of violence that he was opposed to all overt resisting of Hitler, and was
content to try and spoil the latter's plans by quiet but determined
sabotage. However, he served as a useful cover for more active spirits

like Oster and was careful only to employ such General Staff officers as were convinced anti-Nazis. He also achieved one other thing: he supplied Beck with an efficient intelligence service.

Thus for some time there were no open tensions between Hitler and the Army. Hitler's attitude in this matter during these early years is excellently exemplified by the manner in which he received Seeckt on the latter's return from China in 1935. He sent a general to meet him at Basle, and then received him at the Chancellery in the presence of Neurath, Blomberg and Schacht. He listened quietly while Seeckt dilated on the necessity of pursuing a clear cut policy in China. Seeckt was agreeably impressed. He found Hitler objective, human, polite and self-assured. For a time he was under the illusion that he possessed Hitler's ear. Then suddenly something happened which was altogether different from what he had been led to expect. Ribbentrop signed an anti-Commintern pact with Japan.

Though Hitler privately made fun of Seeckt's Chinese army, he did not prevent General von Falkenhausen, a very able soldier, from going out to China as Seeckt's successor. In 1938 a Chinese army group under Falkenhausen scored a notable victory over the Japanese in Shantung, whereupon the Japanese made urgent representations in Berlin for Falkenhausen's recall and Hitler compelled that reluctant officer to return—under the threat of reprisals against his family.

In 1935, however, the High Army Command had not yet shed its belief in the possibility of loyal co-operation with Hitler, so that the early phase of Beck's struggle was merely concerned with trying to regain for the General Staff something like the position held by its Imperial predecessor. There was as yet no vital conflict of principle with the régime. The differences concerned matters of organizational arrangement. In a series of memoranda which he prepared for Fritsch, Beck stressed that since Germany was a continental power, the Army was her most decisive arm, and the General Staff was the Army's proper leader. This being the case, it was incumbent on the Navy and the Air Force to subordinate their own operational designs to the Army's planning.

These expositions were mainly directed against Blomberg and against the *Wehrmachtamt* and its "Department of National Defence". However, certain changes were to take place in that very quarter which were adverse rather than favourable to Beck's ideas.

On October 1st, 1935, Reichenau was given command of the new 7th Army Corps in Munich. His successor as Chief of the *Wehrmachtamt* was Wilhelm Keitel, whose son had married Blomberg's daughter. Keitel, who like so many others was an ex-artilleryman, wholly shared Blomberg's view that the "greatest revolution in all world history" had just taken place in Germany, and that it was now for the Army to seek to reconcile itself with the new forces of the age.

Now it was under Keitel that there began the advance of another man to whom reference has been made and who was to play a significant part in events. This was Alfred Jodl, who, in 1935, became head of the Department of National Defence, and proceeded most energetically to build it up into what was really an operations department of the Reich War Ministry. Jodl was undoubtedly an exceptionally able officer—that was certainly Fritsch's opinion, though Fritsch also observed in him an almost pathological personal ambition. Perhaps it was this last that drew him to Hitler, for there can be no question of the greatness of Jodl's admiration for him, though even Jodl was to have his misgivings. He was the son of a middle-class family and could not but be estranged, as he confessed to the American doctor at Nuremberg, by Hitler's outbursts of hatred against the officer corps and the middle class.

As we have seen, it had been Blomberg's original intention to create his own working staff which could represent the ideas of all three fighting services. Jodl, however, openly aimed at creating, with the aid of the Department of National Defence, a kind of Super General Staff which would be placed in authority over the General Staffs of the Army, Navy and Air Force. Beck in a memorandum dated December 5th sought to counter these pretensions by sketching out a sphere of authority for the Army's Commander in Chief. He declared that the latter should be treated as the authoritative adviser of the Cabinet and the War Minister in all questions concerning war on land. In the event of war he should be in command of all armies and given complete independence. It was thus the Commander in Chief of the Army who was to have the ultimate authority in an emergency, and not the War Minister. The latter was a mere co-ordinator, whose task it was to see that the operations of the three services were in harmony with one another.

What was written in this memorandum concerning the powers of the Commander in Chief was also to be taken as applying to the Chief of Staff, in so far as Beck wished to see the old relationship between these two officers re-established. There were some differences of opinion between Beck and Fritsch on this latter point, however, for the curtailment of his own authority made Fritsch disinclined to allow Beck any more power than was enjoyed by any of the other departmental chiefs.

The thing was finally settled when Fritsch signed an order of Beck's own drafting, according to which the Chief of the General Staff was charged with the investigation of all questions relating to the preparation of war and its conduct, but was declared to have no power of command. This was a compromise, but it did in some measure succeed in establishing the General Staff's position as the brains of the Army.

With this difficulty out of the way, Fritsch naturally identified himself with Beck's proposals, and this brought him into collision with Blomberg. Blomberg saw in Fritsch's aspirations a threat to his own position, and Blomberg had already enough trouble on his hands. He had already got to fight Göring, who theoretically was his subordinate as head of the Air Force, but was nevertheless his equal as Reich Minister for Air. It was a losing battle, for Göring was able to use this curious hybrid status to secure preferential treatment for the *Luftwaffe* and showed no consideration whatever for the claims of anyone else.

None of this served to make Blomberg more accommodating. Nevertheless, for the time being at least, Fritsch was able to convince Hitler that the Army's position needed strengthening, and by an order of April 20th, 1936, the Commander in Chief of the Army was recognized as the Government's authoritative adviser on all matters relating to land warfare, and both Fritsch and the Commander in Chief of the Navy, Admiral Raeder, were given the status of Ministers and could be summoned to Cabinet meetings either by Hitler or Blomberg. The only trouble was that there were no Cabinet meetings, at least not in the sense of meetings at which formal decisions were taken. Hitler's imaginative but completely untrained and undisciplined mind was incapable of anything in the nature of systematic work, also he was in perpetual fear that in a properly conducted Cabinet meeting he might encounter opposition. So this part of Fritsch's victory was purely nominal.

Curiously enough, this unfortunate idiosyncrasy of Hitler's and his persistent predilection for resorting to extra-constitutional methods of government affected Blomberg quite as much as it affected Fritsch, and in Blomberg's case there was a certain irony in the situation. The post of Reich War Minister had long been a dream of constitution builders. Now that it had become a fact, the circumstances of the case were such that the office was purely decorative, and Blomberg was completely unable to exercise any true ministerial function or to have any influence on the course of policy. Fortunately for himself, he had no particular ambitions in that direction and confined himself to the rôle of a simple soldier carrying out the orders of his superior.

XIII

Such were the conditions in which the rebuilding of the Army was undertaken, and few could have had any illusions about the size of the task. Beck himself estimated the time necessary for its completion at seven to eight years. He was convinced that the new Army could not be looked upon as a reliable military instrument before 1942 or 1943. Even Keitel held any kind of military action to be out of the question till then.

Certainly in mere matters of numbers the Army was for some time bound to be in a position of hopeless inferiority. France, Poland and Czechoslovakia had some ninety divisions between them, while Germany was experiencing the most formidable difficulties in setting up twenty-four. At the end of 1935 not a single one of them was ready. Jodl declared at Nuremberg that the years 1935 and 1936 were the most dangerous period of German rearmament. Almost the whole of the old Army of 100,000 were dispersed in small instructional groups.

The work which now began to fall on the shoulders both of the General Staff and the officer corps was enormous. Normally every company of infantry in the *Reichswehr* was being turned into five, the twenty-one infantry regiments together with uniformed police units were being converted to a total of one hundred and five. Meanwhile the lack of trained General Staff officers was proving nothing short of disastrous, nor could the General Staff hope to maintain the high standard of requirements for new aspirants. But then the officer corps was suffering as a whole. It was ceasing rapidly to be the closed tradition-conscious corporation of Seecktian days. Large numbers of officers of the old Imperial Army were recalled from the retired list, others were taken from the uniformed police and from the ranks of the N.C.O.s. Generals in particular suddenly increased prodigiously in number. There had been 42 of them in 1932. The number now rose to 400.

The officer corps now began to present a most variegated picture. Its members differed increasingly from one another in education, social background, political orientation, and above all in general suitability for commissioned rank, and naturally large numbers of out and out Nazis were now to be found here. It was not long before complaints were being made that Reinhard Heydrich, an ex-naval officer who had been dismissed the service for dishonourable conduct, and was now head of the Security Service, was slipping his confidential agents in among the officers in order to bring the Army under supervision by the secret police. There were even generals now who held high rank in the S.S.; one of these, a major-general was among those who had been removed by Schleicher from the Army because of his National Socialist sympathies.

All this meant yet further isolation for the General Staff, which had to battle with problems of its own. Not only was it so overloaded with work that it was impossible for officers to take a turn at regimental duty, as had once been the practice, but it was also confronted with questions as controversial as any personal issue. These concerned the rôle of the Air Arm and of the tank. As regards the first, the part it had to play in the defence of German territory was still obscure and for Beck the defence of that territory was the basis of all the General Staff's planning; Göring and certain other Air Force commanders believed that in any new war the Air Force would be the decisive arm, while Guderian and General Nehring based their ideas on Fuller, Martel and de Gaulle and believed that the decisive rôle would fall to the tank, which they held should be employed in large, more or less self-sufficient, formations—Guderian was soon to express these views in an authoritative work *Achtung, Panzer!* which appeared in 1937.

Both Beck and Fritsch were more conservative, however, and in the main the General Staff tended to be sceptical, or at best to reserve its judgment, till a host of questions dealing with weapon efficiency, fuel supply and methods of organization and command could find satisfactory answers. Moreover cavalry was still far from lacking a champion, and von Pogrell, the last Inspector General of that arm, which it will be remembered had found special favour with Seeckt, fought doggedly for its retention.

At the moment the 1st and 2nd Cavalry Divisions had been organized into a Cavalry Corps with motorized and armoured reconnaissance units, but in 1938 the decision was finally made to convert the great majority of cavalry regiments either into tank regiments or into what were called motorized *kavallerieschützregimenter* and to set up three tank divisions and a number of so-called "light divisions". The rest of the cavalry was allotted to the different corps by regiments, to act as reconnaissance troops.

Now Hitler loathed anything to do with horses, and had an unshakable faith in the internal combustion engine. So Guderian's idea of forcing a lightning decision by committing vast masses of tanks in combination with motorized infantry, self-propelled artillery and aircraft, fell on fruitful soil. English observers later spoke of a revolutionary "tank-school" represented primarily by Guderian and of a rival school championed by Fritsch and Beck which put its whole faith in infantry and artillery combat. This was only correct within certain limits. It is true that Guderian once said that "the penny had only dropped the right side up" on the Staff journey of 1939, when for the first time the employment of large numbers of tanks had formed part of the exercise. But it is untrue that the General Staff was ever hostile to the tank in principle, it merely did what was its duty. It quite dispassionately weighed up both sides of the case before making up its mind. Even so, Guderian continued to entertain a certain bitterness against the military orthodoxy of the General Staff, while the fact that most of its officers were ex-gunners caused the tank enthusiasts to speak of them as the "gentlemen of the Horse Artillery".

Meanwhile the development of the rocket, in so far as it was to some extent a thing apart, followed a more or less uncontroversial course under the care of General Dornberger and of the Weapons department. Experiments with rockets propelled by liquid fuel were resumed on the Kummersdorf range in 1933, and in the following year the so-called "A.2's" were tried out at Borkum. A "special devices" department was in due course organized, and in 1936 the *Luftwaffe* started taking a hand in the business and set up the Peenemünde testing ground. The problem set was to build a rocket with a range of 500 kilometres.

XIV

In the light of all these innovations Beck's purely strategic ideas strike us as remarkably sober and conservative. They were nevertheless based on clearly thought out principles. Beck knew as well as anybody else that he was living in an age when wars tended to be waged by coalitions, and the economic factor played a decisive part. When those facts were taken into account it was obvious that Germany's strategic position was not better than it had been in 1914, but a great deal worse. There was nothing now to cover her south-eastern flank, since little rump-Austria counted for nothing either as an enemy or an ally. Hungary had been subjected to disarmament provisions similar to those which had originally been imposed on Germany. As against this Czechoslovakia, which had been armed by France, thrust a wedge deep into Germany so that the industrial regions in the centre of Germany were under continual threat of attack from the air.

In 1914 German strategy had been successfully conducted on internal lines. It was on that possibility that Schlieffen had banked when he drew up his great plan. Beck saw clearly that aerial warfare had changed all that. Nor was much to be hoped from Italy and Japan whom, in 1935 and 1936, Hitler was winning over as potential allies. Beck considered them worthless. Worst of all, apart from one year-group numbering 250,000 to 300,000 men, he had no reserves. In 1914 the German Army had had twenty-five year-groups at its disposal.

Now there were two possible policies to choose from in that situation. Beck decided that only one of them was right. His view was that, having regard to Germany's prevailing geographical situation, it was now the statesmen's duty to avoid any kind of armed conflict. Hitler thought otherwise. If the geographical situation presented difficulties, then the thing to do, according to Hitler, was to change the geographical situation. Hitler's policy, that is to say, was to push Germany's frontiers outwards to such a degree that a strategy of internal lines would again become practicable. Thus the champion of power politics and the champion of common sense and moral responsibility at last stood openly face to face.

In 1935, Ludendorff had published a book on total war which greatly strengthened Hitler's convictions. It pressed for the full application of the principles of a war of ruthless annihilation waged by one people against another and using up the last ounce of each people's strength; such a war would necessarily require a dictatorship to carry it on. This book was carefully read by the General Staff, for, despite his inanities on the subject of malevolent secret powers, Ludendorff still enjoyed great respect in military circles. Nevertheless, the General Staff rejected the book root and branch.

Beck's deployment plans argued a very different outlook from Ludendorff's. They were the plans of a commander using all the defensive possibilities of his position and restrained by a realistic estimate of his own resources. Till 1935, the only provision that had been made for the west were the plans for "Operation *Schulung*", which were to come into effect in the event of France applying sanctions. They were little more than an evacuation scheme.

In 1935 Beck ordered the drawing up of a "Red" defensive deployment plan for the west, according to which three weak armies were to cover the Rhine, while a fourth was to provide cover against Poland in conjunction with the forces already available in Silesia. The Czechoslovak frontier was to be made secure largely by *Landwehr* units and finally a further army was to be organized in Central Germany and held in reserve. Plans were also made for the evacuation of Silesia and if necessary the Baltic coast. Some years later a "Green" plan involving slightly larger commitments of forces was drawn up for defence against an attack by Czechoslovakia.

Poland, despite the Friendship Pact, continued to be a source of apprehension. For some time during the earlier part of his period of office, Beck possessed an excellent purely personal source of information in the Chief of Protocol at the Foreign Office, von Bülow-Schwante. Ultimately, however, Blomberg forbade these somewhat irregular communications. Also von Bülow-Schwante got into Hitler's bad books. However, there were other sources of information and at length the General Staff thought it advisable to reorganize the security arrangements in the east. In 1936, therefore, *Grenzschutz Ost* was done away with and work begun on a line of fortifications on the Oder-Warthe region. In due course these were followed by a fortification of Germany's western frontier, so that she had an adequate defensive shield on both these flanks. In an emergency the former was to be manned by twenty-one *Landwehr* divisions. Meanwhile, by a strange and eloquent coincidence, Jodl, in the Department of National Defence, was drawing up quite separate plans for the security of East Prussia.

XV

Until 1937 there had been no clear indication in any of Hitler's utterances that his mind was occupied with military plans of a very different kind. Such remarks as reached Blomberg and Jodl about a settlement with Russia being unavoidable, seemed hardly worth taking seriously. Certainly, Hossbach, Hitler's adjutant, who was Chief of the Central Department and often had occasion to speak to Beck, did not have the impression that Hitler in 1937 was entertaining any ideas of war. The remarks made in Hitler's circle of intimates, of course, did not reach Hossbach or any other officer; yet Hitler had already remarked to those intimates that every generation needed a war, and that he would see to it that the present generation got what it needed.

CHAPTER XII

THE STRUGGLE AGAINST WAR

FRITSCH—BLOMBERG—BRAUCHITSCH

I

THOUGH both Blomberg and Keitel continued to work for some kind of reconciliation between the fighting services and the revolution (in contrast to Beck and Fritsch who still endeavoured to preserve the Seecktian ideal of neutrality) the tension with the Party was not perceptibly relaxed. The Party continued in its efforts to extend its influence over the Army. Every year now, political courses were arranged for officers, at which Hitler, Himmler and other Party leaders would speak, and the Party occasionally succeeded in obtaining the removal of unco-operative generals; thus Julius Streicher secured the removal in 1935 of the commander of the Nuremberg division, Lieutenant-General Stephanus.

Support for the Army from the left was naturally for all practical purposes non-existent. Except in a very few instances, the few Social Democrats that remained avoided all contact with it, while isolated attempts by the members of the old right to woo one of the generals (as *Regierungrat* Gisevius tried to woo von Kluge, at that time commander of the 6th Corps) were treated as unwelcome distractions from the serious business of rearmament. Apart from the latter consideration, anything in the nature of a pronunciamento by an isolated general, or even a group of generals, held out little prospect of success, since generals could never be completely certain of their troops.

Despite this, the illusion continued to prevail in conservative circles that Fritsch was lying in wait for the S.S., though the truth was that the S.S. was lying in wait for Fritsch and was taking every opportunity of discrediting him. Meanwhile, the S.S. was steadily endeavouring to build up its own strength. At the beginning of 1937, Himmler's armed forces, including Hitler's bodyguard, consisted of eleven battalions and some 5,000 Death's Head guards for concentration camps, but his plans continued to be for nothing less than a regular S.S. Army and an S.S. Air Force.

II

Since the summer of 1935, the General Staff had as a routine matter tried to determine the prospects of success, if the occasion should arise, for remilitarizing the demilitarized zone. The fact that such action would violate the Locarno Pact, and the unprepared state of the Army, caused Beck to set his face against any such project. Nor were Blomberg and Fritsch disposed at this stage to favour military adventures, being much more concerned to go on quietly with the reorganization of the Army.

In 1935, affairs in Europe took a turn by which the grave weakness of the West was made painfully obvious. Abyssinia was attacked by Italy and signally failed to obtain the protection for which she appealed to the League. The League imposed sanctions, but this merely drove Italy into Germany's arms, since Germany was not among the powers by whom sanctions were applied. Thus Austria was deprived of her last potential protector.

Then, in January 1936, Laval announced his intention of asking the Chamber to ratify the Franco-Russian Mutual Assistance Pact, and this gave Hitler his cue. Outwardly Hitler made a great show of courting France. He showed courtesies to French ex-servicemen and granted a number of cleverly staged interviews to the French press. In the meantime, however, he informed Blomberg that in his opinion the proposed Franco-Russian treaty was a violation of the Locarno Pact, and that this left Germany free to reoccupy the demilitarized zone. Needless to say, he did not go through the formality of denouncing the Locarno Pact, his real intention being simply to present the West with a *fait accompli*.

Blomberg did not see fit to say anything to Fritsch or Beck, but in February Hitler himself let Fritsch know what was in his mind. Fritsch was anxious enough for security reasons to reoccupy the zone, but told Hitler that he felt it would be utterly wrong to accept the risk of war on that account. Hitler definitely engaged himself on this point, having just received encouraging reports on the probable attitude of Italy and heard Neurath's opinion that the West would not march.

It was not till March 6th, one day before the actual operation, that Beck and the General Staff were informed. Jodl has described the effect of this information. He says that the atmosphere was very like that of the roulette table when a player stakes his fortunes on a single number. At length it was decided to use as weak a force as possible so as to cut losses to a minimum in case of French counter-measures, and in point of fact only a single division was employed. Beck was even at this stage asking for the assurance that the left bank of the Rhine would not be fortified.

France in her first moments of alarm mobilized 13 divisions, manned the Maginot line and made enquiries in London as to the possibilities of joint action. Meanwhile, in London the military attaché, Geyr von Schweppenburg, seems quite needlessly to have taken alarm. He quite irregularly wired his apprehensions to Berlin, where it soon appeared that the nerves of Hitler and Blomberg were as bad as his own. Blomberg, on receipt of the news from London, clamoured for the immediate evacuation of Saarbrücken, Treves and Aix-la-Chapelle, and Hitler, though he reprimanded Blomberg for losing his head, confessed afterwards that he hoped he would not have to go through another such ordeal for at least ten years. Von Schweppenburg was recalled, though Beck seemed to think that as an officer of the General Staff Schweppenburg had the right to communicate his views.

It was not long before it became apparent that neither France nor Britain was prepared to act. Apparently public opinion in England did not take the view that the demilitarized zone was worth fighting about. Hitler achieved a triumph of misinterpretation by ascribing this attitude to the influence of Edward VIII, who as Prince of Wales had taken some interest in the achievements of National Socialism, nor could he rid himself of the illusion that this monarch would have been pleased to arrange an Anglo-German pact. Hitler for his part sought to embellish his coup by vehemently propagandizing his desire for peace and a new Locarno. At this stage no documents are available to show how much of this expressed a genuine intention and how much was pure bunkum.

III

In the summer Hitler permitted himself another adventure. When Franco asked for German help in a revolt against the existing Spanish government and for the provision of tanks and aircraft, Hitler agreed. Possibly he was genuinely concerned about the Bolshevik danger to Spain. However, responsible military authorities opposed him in this matter, and thanks to Fritsch and Blomberg, Franco's request for the despatch of three German divisions was flatly refused.

Blomberg sent Colonel Warlimont, of the *Wehrmachtamt*, as military adviser; General von Thoma went as an observer; further, a few tank training units were put at Franco's disposal. That was the limit of the Army's contribution, for neither Thoma, himself a tank officer, nor Guderian set much value on the possible lessons to be learned in Spain so far as tank warfare was concerned.

Military niggardliness, however, only served to inflame the enthusiasm of Göring, who saw a wonderful opportunity for trying out the new *Luftwaffe*. So the "Condor Legion" was sent off to Spain, consisting of four fighter-bomber, four fighter, one reconnaissance and two seaplane squadrons, together with ground staff, a number of heavy anti-aircraft batteries and radio units. Members of the Condor Legion occasionally encountered their own countrymen fighting on the opposite side in the International Brigade. A few deserted the Swastika flag. If there was any lesson to be learned from this, it was not taken to heart.

The year 1936 was marked by two further events, the introduction of the two-year period of service for the Army, which made it possible for two additional army corps to be set up, and the death of Seeckt. Seeckt died in December of sudden heart failure. He was the only German soldier who at that time had truly won international respect. Certainly he was the only man whom, despite its fatal fission, the officer corps might still have been ready to follow. Hitler was present at his funeral, but left during the service, at the moment when the chaplain was beginning his sermon. It was perhaps an omen of those coming events by which the dead man's work was to be destroyed.

IV

The matter of the Red Army and its relations with the *Reichswehr* was once more to become topical in the following year. In London, at the funeral of George V, Blomberg had had a meeting with the Russian Chief of Staff, Tuchatschewski, an old acquaintance of his. Each of the two men was representing his government on that occasion. This may have led indirectly to the invitation to attend the autumn manoeuvres which Fritsch subsequently extended to General Uborewitsch, who had under Blomberg passed through the *Truppenamt's* instructional course. A small but significant incident arose out of this. When entertaining Uborewitsch at a dinner, Fritsch had ostentatiously raised his glass to the Red Army. Hitler obviously got to hear of the matter and in his address on January 30th, the birthday of his revolution, remarked with a considerable show of anger that if he had the right to expect an anti-Communist attitude from the German worker, then no one was entitled to "carouse and swill" (*"pokulieren und zechen"*) with Communist functionaries. Needless to say, that shaft was aimed at Fritsch.

In the spring of 1937, Tuchatschewski visited Prague in his capacity of Deputy Commissar for War, to discuss questions of military co-operation with the Czech government, and on his return passed through Berlin. A short time afterwards the Czech secret service learned that the substance of the Prague conversations had been made known to the German counter-espionage. Benes was profoundly shocked and communicated this intelligence to Stalin. Soon the world was to receive the astonishing news that Tuchatschewski and a whole number of other high-ranking military officers had been shot for high treason. A whole host of further executions followed almost immediately. What struck the people most concerned in Germany was the fact that the high-ranking officers were nearly all men who had passed through the *Reichswehr's* instructional courses.

The rumour spread that Tuchatschewski, whose overmastering ambition was notorious, had been planning a *coup d'état* with German help. As against this, Heydrich was boasting to Canaris that it was he who had delivered the commanders of the Red Army to the executioner, and that he had done this on the Führer's orders by means of forged evidence—which sounds a little too much like a thriller to be true. German officers tended on the whole to believe that Tuchatschewski had really been planning a military coup, and the story went round that he had been betrayed by a dubious intermediary in Paris, a certain General Skoblin. Whatever may be the real facts, these executions were a sort of "Mene Tekel", for here a dictator had put his heel on a refractory officer caste. Nobody as yet believed that such methods could ever come to be used in Germany, yet it was not long before the Tuchatschewski affair was to be followed by the case of Fritsch.

Russian generals were not the only ones who paid courtesy visits abroad at this time. In June of 1937, Beck, on his own initiative, went unofficially to Paris, where he called on General Gamelin and on Daladier, at that time French Minister of War, and also met the French General Staff. His purpose was to assure them that he considered a new war chimerical and that the new German rearmament served no other purpose than the security of the country. Beck undoubtedly believed that his action would produce tangible results, and similar hopes may well have animated von Schweppenburg in London. Certainly that officer took pains to keep on friendly terms with high-ranking officers in Great Britain. Within a month of Beck's Paris visit, however, there were plain indications that Hitler was changing course, for in June Blomberg received orders to keep the forces in a state of permanent readiness for immediate mobilization and to issue the instructions contained in the celebrated Blomberg directive.*

Four months later, on November 5th, Hitler quite unexpectedly summoned the commanders of the three fighting services to the Chancellery, together with Blomberg, Neurath and Hossbach, and disclosed certain views on the situation which he had never previously expressed. His remarks seemed so important to Hossbach that he made notes of them immediately after the conference, and in this way preserved them for posterity. These so-called "Hossbach Minutes" were produced in evidence at Nuremberg.

According to these minutes, Hitler stated that force alone could provide a solution to the German question, and there were three sets of circumstances in which it might be applied with good prospects of success: (1) on the completion of German rearmament, that is to say, not before 1943; (2) in the event of France suffering such serious internal trouble as to render her powerless; (3) in the event of France being tied down through war with another power, such, for instance, as Italy, with whom she might be involved over the Spanish question. Hitler further declared that before any military action could be taken it was essential for Germany to secure her flank (that is to say, eliminate Austria and Czechoslovakia) and that Japan could be made to play the part of a counter-weight to Russia.

It is true that the substance of his intentions must have already been known to the greater part of his hearers, but the realization that what hitherto had been made to look like a scheme for a hypothetical eventuality was now a fixed and definite resolve had a terrible effect on most of those present. Both Fritsch and Blomberg declared immediately and with great emphasis that a war against England and

* The declared purpose of the measures in question was to guard against sudden attack. Its real purpose was the speedy exploitation of any opportunity that a changing political situation might produce, and it enjoins that to parry the imminent attack of a superior enemy coalition, of which the directive admits that there was at that time no prospect whatever, preparations were to be made for a surprise pounce on Czechoslovakia with the great bulk of Germany's armed forces. The necessary conditions in the field of politics and international law were to be created beforehand. (B.B.)

France was out of the question and that they also held it to be highly improbable that situations (2) and (3) would ever arise. As regards Germany's flank, Blomberg insistently drew attention to the strength of the fortified line in Northern Bohemia. Fritsch was sufficiently disquieted by what Hitler had said to offer to give up a trip to Egypt which he was about to make, but Hitler did not wish this and declared that there was no question of any immediate complication. It is possible that there was an element of apprehension in that re-assurance, and that in that hour he had made up his mind that Fritsch might possibly be dangerous.

However that may be, one result of the discussion was unmistak-able. Everyone knew where they stood. Hitler had plainly declared his wish for another war, while his War Minister and the Commander in Chief of his Army made it equally clear that they wanted nothing of the kind. Göring alone of all those present on this occasion appeared to preserve his equanimity. No doubt Hitler had said nothing that was particularly new to him, but all the rest were profoundly dis-turbed. The effect on Neurath was to produce several heart attacks, for Neurath remembered the so-called will of Hindenburg all too well, and had not forgotten the dead man's adjuration to his successor to spare Germany another war.

After the meeting Neurath joined Beck and Fritsch in the Bendler-strasse, to discuss what could be done to try and dissuade Hitler from his intention. It was ultimately decided that Fritsch should approach Hitler and explain the military impracticability of his plans, while Neurath, as the responsible head of the Foreign Office, would have to do whatever he could to safeguard peace. None of these men knew Hitler, however, or appreciated the difficulty of the task they had undertaken, which was in any case rendered impossible by Hitler, who refused to see them at all. At length, Fritsch went on his trip to Egypt. As an old Prussian officer, the notion never occurred to him that Hitler, whose suspicions of him were now thoroughly aroused, was having him followed by a number of Gestapo men, by the agents, that is to say, of Himmler, his worst enemy.

Fritsch's next move was to order the General Staff to re-examine "Case Green" from a new angle, the purpose of the enquiry being to form a judgment on the possible military success or lack of success of a surprise attack on Czechoslovakia, assuming that the western frontier was screened off against France. Fritsch hoped in this to forestall Hitler's intentions by producing definite evidence that proved his plan untenable.

What it was that induced Hitler to disclose his intentions at that particular moment, we do not know, though we can make a pretty good guess as to their origin. As Keitel was later to disclose, Hitler had a very comprehensive knowledge of German military literature, and the notions which he expressed on November 5th sound like a rehash of the wholly superannuated notions of Goltz and Bernhardi seen through the eyes of an Austrian who had grown up under the dual monarchy and so tended, as we have already seen, to treat the conflict of German and Czech as questions of primary importance. The creation of the succession states would naturally have put ideas into the head of a crude advocate of power politics, who was wholly devoid of moral restraint and whose claim to wisdom rested on his assertion that he had been sent to rid the world of the burden of conscience.

Till now Hitler had looked upon Fritsch as a distinguished military expert and had left him a free hand in building up the Army. Indeed, he had frequently rejected requests of the Party when these were to the Army's disadvantage. In doing so he may well have been influenced by the ingenuous layman's belief that the General Staff was a sort of witch's cave in which schemes for the wildest kind of aggressive wars were continually on the brew. Now he was made to realize that war was the last thing the General Staff wanted, and that he himself must forge the instrument to carry out his fantastic plans. This may explain his sudden enmity to Fritsch.

Unfortunately there were those to whose profit that enmity could be made to redound. Three other men, each a rival of the other, saw in Fritsch an obstacle to the realization of their aims. Reichenau, even after he had left the War Ministry to take command in Munich, still hoped to become the Army's Commander in Chief. Göring, who saw himself in the part of a German Douhet, considered that the other fighting services should be subordinated to the *Luftwaffe*. Himmler dreamed of an S.S. Army and of opening up Eastern Europe by colonizing it with a new race of warrior farmers. In addition to all this, Göring believed Fritsch quite capable of undertaking a military coup against the Party.

V

Ludendorff had once warned Fritsch against Hitler and had prophetically declared that he kept faith with no man and would betray Fritsch as he had betrayed others. Ludendorff had certainly had his experiences with "Herr Hitler", as he persisted in calling him despite Hitler's title of *Führer*, and yet it may be questioned whether even Ludendorff had fully summed him up. In any case his wisdom on that subject, if he had any, was on this occasion of little avail to Fritsch, for in December, 1937, Ludendorff died.

Now Ludendorff's funeral was marked by a small incident which was to be the beginning of something more important, for at that funeral Blomberg confided to Hitler, who was of course present, as were large numbers of generals, that he intended to marry again—he was a widower—but that the lady he proposed to marry had what is called "a past". Hitler was not unduly perturbed by this, and gave the thing his blessing. Blomberg also went to Göring and confessed to him that the lady in question was not of his own rank. Göring replied that in the new Reich people were pretty large-minded about that sort of thing. After all, he had himself married a divorced actress.

The marriage took place on January 12th, 1938, Hitler and Göring being present as witnesses, and Jodl, in the Department of National Defence, made the entry in his service diary, "The Field-Marshal surprisingly marries Fräulein Gruhn". Very shortly after this, Göring put into the hands of Count von Helldorf, the president of the Berlin Police, a document from which it was evident that "Fräulein Gruhn's" past was, to say the least, dubious. Helldorf took the document to Keitel. Keitel's first impulse was to try and have the whole thing hushed up. It did not occur to him to speak to Fritsch or Beck, let alone to Blomberg. Rumours were, however, already circulating concerning the new Frau von Blomberg, the wife of the first soldier in the land, and an anonymous telephone caller asked Fritsch whether he knew that the War Minister had married a whore.

Meanwhile Neurath had at last contrived to get an interview with Hitler, and had told him of the uneasiness with which the generals had been inspired by his plans. He sought to persuade him that if he would be patient the main aims of his policy could be achieved by peaceful means. Hitler replied that he could not wait, whereupon Neurath said that he did not wish to incur the guilt of co-operating in the kind of thing Hitler had in mind. It is on the whole probable that this conversation made Hitler decide to take action against the revolt which he felt was spreading both in the Foreign Office and in the General Staff.

If Hitler at this stage already intended to strike, circumstances certainly played into his hands. First of all, towards the end of January the generals were for the most part absent in East Prussia, where they were taking part in a Staff journey under von Rundstedt, while the energetic General von Witzleben, the commander of the 3rd military district, one of the few men who was completely undaunted by Hitler, lay ill in Dresden during the whole of this period. There was, however, more to come.

On January 24th, Göring laid before Hitler the documents relating to Blomberg's wife. It is possible that at the same moment he showed Hitler certain documents relating to Fritsch. Fritsch had returned from Egypt still shadowed by the Gestapo. For some reason he was ill at ease about things, and remarked that he had only just returned in time. The truth is that he should never have gone away at all. The documents concerning Blomberg's wife showed that she had been a prostitute on the books of the *Sittenpolizei* (the department of the police that was concerned with the regulation of prostitution) and had on one occasion been punished for selling indecent postcards. This, of course, settled Blomberg's business, and at first Hitler seems to have entertained the notion of appointing Fritsch as his successor. It was, however, precisely for that eventuality that Göring and Himmler had been prepared, and this was the reason why they had armed themselves with the documents relating to Fritsch; for these documents adduced the evidence of one Schmidt, a well-known homosexual blackmailer, to show that Fritsch had committed a criminal act in November 1934 at Potsdam Goods Station. It is stated that Hitler had already seen these documents once before—in 1935—and had ordered them to be burned. Needless to say, this was not done, nor were Himmler and Heydrich the kind of men who would have committed such a criminal act of folly.

On the following day, Hitler told Hossbach of the evidence he had in hand in reference to both Blomberg and Fritsch. Hossbach knew enough of the serpentine intrigues behind the régime to recognize that this was nothing but a very dirty attempt to discredit the Army's commander. When, therefore, Hitler instructed him to invite Fritsch to the Chancellery for the following evening, but to refrain most strictly from disclosing the object of the summons, Hossbach decided to warn Fritsch in advance.

Fritsch's first words were, "A lot of stinking lies" ("*Erstunken und erlogen*"). He had, of course, no notion what was behind the business. Being a gentleman of the old school, it never entered his mind that the head of a country of sixty millions would resort to gangster methods to achieve a political end. All he could think of for the moment was the attack on his personal honour.

Hitler was now in the agreeable position of having a handle

against both of the two troublesome leaders of the Army. Yet although Hitler so often boasted of his ability to make lightning decisions, he was in reality far from being endowed with that faculty, being a man who depended on intuition rather than on reason. Quite obviously at that particular moment he had formed no clear notion of how to proceed. However, on the 26th he did summon Blomberg, and at noon on that day Jodl was informed, through Keitel, of Blomberg's dismissal. Keitel told Jodl that Hitler wanted to announce the fact to the nation on the 30th, though the form the announcement would take had still to be decided on, for the Blomberg scandal touched those who had been witnesses to the marriage.

After Keitel had spoken to Jodl—he had tears in his eyes when he did so—he visited Fritsch and Raeder to discuss the question of Blomberg's successor. Actually, Jodl knew at that time that Blomberg had on a previous occasion suggested Göring as that successor, and that Hitler had refused that suggestion. Even Göring must not be given too much power.

However, others besides Jodl had already put forward their views. Hossbach had proposed the creation of three separate ministries for the three fighting services, with the proposed Army Ministry at the head of them. But that, too, had not been to the taste of Hitler, Göring or Himmler. As a matter of fact, it was to be left to Blomberg to propose the solution which Hitler liked best. On the following day, when he called to take his departure, he was to suggest that Hitler himself was to be his successor. It was really the logical outcome of Blomberg's previous policy, though in the eyes of the generals of the Seecktian school it was treason. Blomberg was also to distinguish himself on this occasion by telling Hitler that Fritsch might quite possibly be a man of abnormal tendencies. Fritsch, he declared, had always been an odd fish. He had never married and would have nothing to do with women.

However, Fritsch's fate was already sealed. On the evening of the 26th, Fritsch appeared at the Chancellery, trembling with rage, but also badly shaken, for he had always believed that he possessed Hitler's confidence. He gave Hitler his word of honour that all reports of alleged moral offences were lies, but the word of honour of a Prussian general and nobleman meant nothing to Hitler, and he personally confronted him with the blackmailer, Schmidt, with a man, that is to say, who already had a prison record. When Schmidt professed to recognize Fritsch, that finished things so far as Hitler was concerned. Göring, who was present on this occasion, naturally believed Schmidt and not the general. Fritsch left the Chancellery outwardly calm but inwardly a broken man. He still could not believe that such things could really happen in Germany.

Colonel Hossbach now proposed that the Chief of the General Staff should be heard in the matter, and that same night Beck was called to the Chancellery. Hitler showed him the documents and asked him whether Fritsch had ever borrowed money from him. Hitler assumed that an officer would hardly be in a position to meet the demands of a blackmailer without making some special provision. Beck indignantly denied that Fritsch had ever done anything of the kind. Yet even Beck, shrewd, kindly and decent-minded man that he was, showed signs of being impressed by Hitler's evidence. It was only with difficulty that Hossbach could make him grasp the true nature of the shabby gamble that was being indulged in with the honour of a blameless officer.

The next question was how Fritsch was to be tried. Hitler and Göring wanted a special tribunal, the alternative being, of course, a court martial. Here Fritsch committed a bad blunder. Strictly speaking, he was only amenable to military jurisdiction, the restoration of which he had himself emphatically welcomed. Nevertheless, in the consciousness of his complete innocence, he quietly answered a summons to appear at the headquarters of the Gestapo in the Prinz-Albrecht-Strasse. In doing so, he was tacitly admitting the latter's jurisdiction over the Army. It was to some extent a consequence of this that Gestapo agents now ventured to force their way into the various barracks in the middle of the night and arrest any man who had at any time acted as Fritsch's batman. The object was to get witnesses who would support a charge of unnatural vice. Nowhere did the orderly officer dare to intervene. It was ominous that the same police official had charge of these arrangements as had sent out the execution squads for Schleicher and Bredow.

The fact is that by now the generals had a huge amalgamation of power ranged against them, and though most of the commanding generals still belonged to the old school, they could no longer be certain of the Army's obedience. The Navy, on the other hand, was at best neutral, while the *Luftwaffe*, with which all A.A. units were incorporated, stood directly under Göring. In addition to these, there was the mighty apparatus of the Party with all its interlocking organizations, there was the police and there was the Gestapo. The Dictatorship was, moreover, master of the whole network of communications, including press and radio. There was thus no way for the generals to make their case known to the public, and in any case how were they to justify themselves to the working masses, whom Hitler's rearmament programme had at last given work and bread? Yet perhaps the greatest element of weakness lay elsewhere. To carry out a successful coup, something more was necessary than mere personal pluck. There was need of a truly great and inspiring personality, a man who called up a clear and definite picture in the public mind, and there was no such man among the generals.

VI

On January 27th, after Blomberg had gone off to Italy, Hitler summoned Keitel. Hitler at this stage knew so little of the Chief of the *Wehrmachtamt* that he quite wrongly spoke of him as "General von Keitel". He complained that he was getting ever lonelier, and Keitel would have to stick it out with him. Keitel, who was a very simple soul, was touched by this remark, and indeed in that moment Hitler had won him over. Thus began that personal association between Hitler and Keitel which lasted till the end.

Naturally enough, the question of Blomberg's successor was brought up between the two men, and the name of the Crown Prince's Chief of Staff, von der Schulenburg, was put forward. Schulenburg was a member of the Party, though still a conservative at heart. Rundstedt, Stülpnagel, Leeb and Reichenau were also mentioned. Hitler thought Rundstedt too old and tired, Stülpnagel was hostile to National Socialism and Leeb was a Catholic. Reichenau seemed the most promising candidate, but to Keitel's relief Hitler declared that he was shallow and unstable. After the talk, Keitel told Jodl that the *Wehrmachtamt* was not only secure but that its status had actually been raised. Keitel also told him that Fritsch would have to go, and claimed to have known for two years that he was a pervert, which seems to prove that the intrigue against Fritsch had been going on for a very long time.

For Fritsch's successor Keitel put forward the name of von Brauchitsch, who since 1937 had been commanding the newly formed 4th Army Group, and von Brauchitsch was summoned to Berlin, where, much to Beck's annoyance, he failed to report to that officer, though this was what regulations demanded, Beck being for the time being the senior officer in Army Command. Actually, though von Brauchitsch may not have known this, Beck had become rather inconvenient to Keitel (now the most powerful man behind the scenes of the War Ministry) since Beck had been pressing for the status of the General Staff to be raised and for the incorporation into it of the Department of National Defence, but this did not suit Keitel's book, since Keitel cared much more about the safeguarding of his own position than about the General Staff. Thus it was that when he saw Brauchitsch he asked him not only whether he would as commander of the Army be willing to integrate the latter with National Socialism, but whether he would do this in association with a new Chief of Staff.

Now Brauchitsch was at that time burdened with divorce proceedings, and asked for time to think it over. Apart from his personal complications, he was at that time a great admirer of Beck's and did not like the idea of changing the Chief of Staff. At length, however, he agreed. Before doing so, he had a talk with Hitler in the presence of Rundstedt, which is remarkable for one small incident. Hitler on that occasion made a reference to the honour of the Army, whereupon Rundstedt brusquely interrupted him to say that the Army needed no instructions from him in matters of honour. Hitler silently accepted this rebuff.

The question of a successor to Blomberg was still unsettled. Reichenau still seemed a possible candidate, though Rundstedt frankly declared that as a Party general he would be unacceptable to the Army. After a good deal of further discussion, Hitler at last let the cat out of the bag, and informed Keitel with a certain amount of circumlocutory verbiage that he intended with Keitel's help to take over the command of the armed forces himself.

Even putting the *Wehrmacht* under Reichenau would have been better than what now occurred, for the War Ministry virtually lapsed out of existence, while Hitler, with the aid of the *Wehrmachtamt*, which was now transformed into the *Oberkommando der Wehrmacht* (Supreme Command of the Armed Forces), took complete charge of everything, Keitel being made the new *Oberkommando der Wehrmacht's* or O.K.W.'s Chief of Staff. After some hesitation on Hitler's part, Beck was allowed to remain on as Chief of General Staff, thanks largely to Jodl's intervention. For a time Hitler had entertained the idea of appointing Halder in his stead. Halder, however, was a Catholic, and this in Hitler's eyes was quite as objectionable as the possession of the traditional Prussian outlook.

Though the original plan had been to make an announcement on January 30th, it was not till February 4th that the new arrangements were proclaimed. On that date the astonished public was informed that the War Minister and the Commander in Chief of the Army had retired on grounds of health; nor were these the only ones who appeared to have been visited by unsuspected bodily infirmities. Indeed, a detached observer could not but conclude that an epidemic of some kind had broken out among high-ranking officers, so numerous were the older generals whose health had become suddenly afflicted. All the remaining members of the Seecktian dispensation succumbed to this prevailing malady—Ritter von Leeb, the commander of the 2nd Army Group, the commander of all tank troops, General Lutz, the inspector of military schools, General Niebelschütz, the commander of the 8th Army Corps, von Kleist, together with Pogrell and Kress von Kressenstein, of whom the one was inspector of cavalry while the other commanded the 12th Corps. There were dozens of other victims, including a number of members of Seeckt's old *Fliegerzentrale* in the *Truppenamt*. Some of these retirements were a revenge for the part the men concerned had played at the time of the Munich *Putsch*. On the other side of the account, Guderian replaced Lutz with the title of "Chief of Fast Troops in the O.K.H.", while Göring's elevation to the rank of Field-Marshal was meant to provide a sop to his ambition.

In the ranks of diplomacy, Neurath was replaced by Hitler's crony, von Ribbentrop, while Ulrich von Hassell and Herbert von Dircksen, Ambassadors at Rome and Tokio, had their places taken by a son of Field-Marshal Mackensen and Major-General Ott. In Neurath's case, his dismissal was camouflaged by his appointment to the chairmanship of a new secret Cabinet Council, which, it was stated, the Führer had decided to form. This secret Cabinet Council, of course, never functioned at all.

Needless to say, foreign newspapers vied with one another in sensational reports. According to one story, Fritsch had planned a coup to restore the monarchy and Prince Ferdinand of Prussia was to be proclaimed German Emperor. According to a further report, one company had already marched on the Wilhelmstrasse, while a mutiny of the 5th Cavalry Regiment in Stolp and the alleged flight of ten generals to Prague accompanied by the corpse of Ludendorff all formed part of the news. These things were too beautiful to be true, but they were not so very much more inaccurate than the official announcement, towards which news reporters continued to maintain their congenital scepticism, so much so that an official of the Propaganda Ministry lost something of his equanimity and was moved to declare to a group of foreign correspondents that anyone who refused to believe that the generals had retired on grounds of health would just have to get along with his unbelief as best he could, for the Propaganda Ministry had every intention of sticking to its story.

On that same February 4th Hitler invited the leading generals to the Chancellery and acquainted them with the misdeeds of which Fritsch and Blomberg had made themselves guilty. The generals listened to him in silence—to the immense relief of Hitler, who had feared this day would be one of crisis, perhaps of fatal crisis. Later that day, in the relaxed atmosphere of a circle of old S.A. friends, he declared that he now knew every general to be either a coward or a fool. Goebbels disclosed later that what the Party had really feared was not a Monarchist *Putsch*, but the collective resignation of all high-ranking officers.

Now, according to the Prussian code, this would have been mutiny. The fact that Goebbels thought it possible that such a step would be taken showed how little this wholly amoral cynic understood of the importance of the military oath to the older type of soldier. Yet the generals were equally out of touch with reality. Most of them thought that what had happened was a mere reshuffling of posts. They did not realize that what had actually come to pass was the complete subjection of the Army to the will of Hitler. Pogrell was later reported to have said on this occasion that there was nothing left for the Army except to march, but if he said this, he stood alone.

The successful exposure at the court martial of the tricks of the Secret Police by Fritsch's counsel, Count von der Goltz, the proof that the men behind the plot had brought pressure to bear on Schmidt to give perjured evidence and Fritsch's subsequent acquittal —all these things had now become little more than an epilogue to the main drama. The public heard nothing of them. They also did not hear that before the trial the Gestapo tried to murder Fritsch and had planned to fake up this murder as a suicide, nor did they hear that the Chief of the General Staff saw fit to provide Fritsch with a bodyguard of young reliable officers, and that the attempt to murder Fritsch was only frustrated by having a company of infantry somewhat ostentatiously do their drill near the deserted villa where Fritsch's examination by the Gestapo had been arranged.

Even the Army did not hear about these things, for it was not considered prudent to disclose them. Men like Beck had in these days to walk very warily, if they were to continue in their posts, and Beck himself thought he had excellent reasons for not leaving. So long as he was Chief of Staff, he could at least try to avert the catastrophe of another war. He still believed that the General Staff would succeed in changing the régime's policy. He still did not want to fight against Hitler, he merely hoped to capture him. Yet Beck was already isolated. Rundstedt hoped at first that after Fritsch's acquittal it might be possible to put Fritsch in Keitel's place, but there was no hope of Fritsch's power being restored. Things had gone much too far for that to happen.

The result of Hitler's taking control of the armed forces was a complete reconstruction of the departmental hierarchy, so that it came to take a form not very dissimilar to that of the earliest days of absolutist power. The transformation of the *Wehrmachtamt* into the *Oberkommando der Wehrmacht* involved the formation of a personal working staff around Hitler, and the general effect was not unlike the military cabinets of the Prussian kings and German emperors. Once Blomberg had vanished, the Department of National Defence, which in the war received the designation of *Wehrmachtführungsstab* (Wehrmach Leader Staff) had the ground more or less cut away under its feet before, in General Warlimont's opinion, it had recognized its true function. Hitler turned it into an office that supplied him with information and circulated and supervised his orders. This created a most unhealthy atmosphere, half military, half political, which had no kind of relation to real General Staff work.

This new Military Cabinet contrived to achieve a position which would have been quite impossible had a constitutional War Minister been in existence, for here again the congeries of departments, if those of the *Wehrmachtführungsstab* are included, represented something like a super General Staff, for in addition to a host of departments in *Oberkommando der Wehrmacht* itself as a whole, the *Wehrmacht-führungsstab* had its own operations department and a quartermaster-general's department with sub-sections for all three services and liaison officers from the S.A., the S.S. and Labour Service.

When Brauchitsch repeated the old proposal for the raising of the status of the General Staff proper, Keitel got Jodl to answer him that modern war was no longer a purely strategic question, but in great measure a matter of economics and propaganda. The decisive thing was the exploitation of the entire human potential, not the deployment plan. Thus it was necessary for the *Wehrmachtführungsstab* to exist alongside of the General Staff proper.

Much, perhaps everything as far as the Army was concerned, now depended on the man who was the new Chief of the O.K.W., or, to be more exact, its new Chief of Staff. Wilhelm Keitel was the son of a family of landed proprietors in Brunswick. He had passed through the Artillery and had entered the General Staff in 1915. The end of the First World War found him holding the position of G.S.O.1 to that somewhat savage officer, Admiral von Schröder, the commander of the Naval Corps in Flanders. In the *Reichswehr* he had done both regimental and staff duty, and since October 1935 had held, as we have seen, the position of Chief of Staff to the *Wehrmachtamt*, a position which he himself defined as Chief of Staff to the Minister of War. He was an industrious and careful worker.

Before the Nuremberg tribunal Keitel described himself as an ordinary soldier who had sought to do his duty and placed his abilities at the service of the State. He had served under the Emperor, Ebert, Hindenburg, and Hitler, and repeatedly answered the charges preferred against him at the trial with the statement that the soldier must have confidence in his government, and he did this in a tone of injured innocence that almost suggested that he himself was the accuser. Keitel thus drew a picture of himself as a military expert pure and simple, and as a man wholly devoid of any principles or postulates relating to matters outside his specialized field. He pictured himself, in a word, as that very type of man which the General Staff had so frequently produced. There is no need to doubt his sincerity. Being completely ignorant of politics, he had simply formed the conviction that the National Socialist revolution was the greatest event that had ever happened in the history of the world.

To all this there was, of course, added the influence of a normal ambition. Moreover there were the gifts of money, with which Hitler was more lavish than all the Prussian kings put together. One of Keitel's sons declared in captivity that it was his father's hope to found something in the nature of a dynasty, and, in point of fact, no less than three men who bore Keitel's name became generals. For all that, to picture Keitel as a mere time-server would be unjust.

Yet Keitel could never rid himself of a certain feeling of inferiority, one might almost say of embarrassment in regard to Hitler. There was for the soldier and General Staff officer something incomprehensible about this revolutionary. At Nuremberg he referred to Hitler as having more comprehensive plans of military reform than any man he had ever met, though he also said that he never really felt that he possessed his confidence as a human being. Despite this, however, he had tried to give him loyal service, and it was a type of service that suited Hitler's needs. Hitler had no use for a General Staff as Moltke had conceived it, for in such an organization he was bound to meet men whose judgment was not influenced by his reverberating monologues. He did, however, require a Berthier, an indefatigable office manager that is to say, and Keitel most certainly fitted the part.

When the Russian prosecutor, General Rudenko, asked Keitel whether as a thoroughly trained soldier he could not have influenced Hitler, Keitel replied that Hitler had studied military literature and works of the General Staff to a degree which would have been almost unbelievable even in a professional officer and that he had quite an astonishing knowledge of military matters in general. He told how at headquarters Hitler had read Moltke, Clausewitz and Schlieffen till late into the night. He regarded Hitler as a genius, and in relation to him felt himself to be a pupil rather than a teacher.

Hitler's prejudice against the General Staff may have been instrumental in causing him, after a time, to short circuit even his own private staff and to work through the *Wehrmachtadjutant*. Colonel Hossbach had acted as a kind of military watchdog for the General Staff, but Colonel Hossbach was no longer there. He had confessed to Hitler that when he had been sent to invite Fritsch to the Chancellery on that memorable January 26th, he had felt it his duty as an officer to disobey Hitler's orders not to reveal the cause of the summons. That had, of course, made his position untenable. With Hossbach gone, it was not difficult to make certain changes. The linking of the post of *Wehrmachtadjutant* with that of the Chief of the Central Department of the General Staff had been designed to prevent the post of adjutant becoming another channel of independent action, but it was precisely this connection between the adjutancy and the General Staff that was unwelcome to Hitler. For this reason a new organization consisting of four adjutants was created, two of whom were supposed to represent the *Wehrmacht*, the other two the remaining services. Lieutenant-Colonel Schmundt was Adjutant in Chief, the other adjutants were largely young men personally devoted to Hitler. The general tendency of things from now onwards is made clear by the fact that in the war the *Heerespersonalamt* was united in Schmundt's person with his adjutancy. This really amounted to reviving the old Department of Personal Affairs and with that the old rule of the Adjutant-General's department that had obtained under Witzleben and Manteuffel.

No one could now help noticing a steady diminution in the General Staff's influence and prestige, and with it, after a brief period of expanding power, a lowering of the status of the O.K.W. These developments were counterbalanced by a corresponding rise in the power of Hitler's new adjutants. Schmundt managed to earn the good opinions of Hitler and gained an influence over him which was sometimes difficult to control.

VII

Even if Beck had not already drifted into opposition on political grounds he would now have been compelled to do so on technical ones, for there were now no less than four General Staffs, the *Wehrmachtführungsstab*, the General Staff of the Army, the General Staff of the *Luftwaffe* and the *Kommandoamt* of the Navy which in war became the *Seekriegsleitung* and to all these was added Hitler's new version of the Adjutant-General's Department, which has just been described. At first it seemed as though Beck might find an ally in Raeder, in his struggle to get the position of the Army's General Staff improved, for Raeder objected to having the Navy run by the land-lubbers of the *Wehrmachtführungsstab*. But Raeder soon gave up the struggle, and Beck was driven to try and solve his problem as best he could.

Beck's first expedient was to have an old tried General Staff officer, General von Viebahn, pushed into the post of Chief of the *Wehrmachtführungsstab*, but it soon became all too obvious that Viebahn was no match for the wire-pullers in the O.K.W. The headship of *Wehrmachtführungsstab* thus passed to Jodl, who was of course entirely in Keitel's confidence and with it in that of Hitler. Now Jodl saw in Hitler, above all, the man who had re-established Germany's influence in the world and for this reason he was ready unquestioningly to follow him and place his not inconsiderable talents unreservedly at his disposal. Thus he made Hitler's ideas increasingly his own, and came to hold the view which Hitler held in an even more extreme fashion than Ludendorff, namely that war was not the last expedient of policy but its very essence.

It was this development which now made Beck's opposition quite open and caused him to break off all relations with Jodl and Keitel, nor was the General Staff the only breeding ground of discontent. Tendencies to oppose the régime were increasing in the O.K.W. itself. Of all the departmental chiefs, General Reinecke, the head of the *Allgemeines Heeresamt*, was the only wholehearted follower of Hitler; General Thomas of the War Industries Department, Admiral Canaris, head of Counter-Espionage and Admiral Bürkner of the

Foreign Department, followed Hitler's policy with increasing misgivings and even with increasing anger. Canaris' colleagues, who were
for the most part General Staff officers, were all more or less convinced anti-Hitlerites. Among the latter Oster was especially determined and kept up contact with Hitler's underground enemies,
particularly with Goerdeler.

The repercussions of the Fritsch affair continued to be felt. When
Canaris gave the full facts of the part played in it by the Gestapo to
von Viebahn (and Canaris made a point of doing this), von Viebahn
said that if this were known there would be a revolution—which may
well have been exactly what Canaris was hoping for. Even Jodl was
asking in March whether there had not been an element of malice in
the Fritsch business.

The thing that Beck was chiefly weighing up in his mind, when
considering how far he should carry the fight, was the attitude of
Brauchitsch. Brauchitsch unquestionably belonged to the old Seecktian school and he was reconciled neither to the treatment of Fritsch
nor to the general reshuffle that had taken place. He was by no means
a convinced National Socialist, but like all the generals he had to
accept the fact of Hitler's enormous popularity, for at that time
Hitler was not relying on terror alone to maintain his power; he still
had the love and confidence of the great mass of people. Gisevius
states in his memoirs that Brauchitsch had promised the opposition
that the Army would take action on Fritsch's behalf once that officer
had been duly acquitted by the court, but how far Gisevius had
misinterpreted some remark of Brauchitsch's it is impossible to say,
for the fact is that Brauchitsch was as helpless before Hitler's unprecedented rule of force as Fritsch had been before the machinations of
the all-powerful Chief of Police. He was not unacquainted with
Goerdeler's desire to restore a Christian State founded on law.
His remarks to Rauschning, however, show how deeply he had been
impressed by the problem of the mass and yet how in the last resort,
as an officer, Brauchitsch was utterly at a loss to find a means of
dealing with it.

VIII

Schacht had always had a feeling that the Fritsch affair had been
a sort of hint or signal of coming war. Beck too realized in February
that Hitler's assumption of command meant that his war plans were
approaching nearer to realization; it seemed as though Hitler were the

victim of a kind of maniac possession and were driven by the fear that the time for carrying out his designs might slip through his hands.

In February he set about the elimination of Austria, a step which he had treated in November as one of the pre-conditions for offensive action elsewhere. No doubt he also thought that a success in Austria might serve to dispel the dissatisfaction which he knew to exist among his generals. Moreover such a success meant the realization of his old dreams, it meant among other things the wiping out of that sense of disgrace which he had experienced when, in Vienna, he lived in a shelter for the destitute and when the Vienna Academy of Arts had refused him admission.

Schuschnigg at that time Chancellor of Austria was invited to a meeting at Obersalzberg, where Hitler presented him with an ultimatum and compelled him to accept National Socialist Ministers into his government. Schuschnigg stated later that he had the feeling of sitting opposite a maniac, but he was not yet ready for surrender. A plebiscite should prove that the majority of Austrian people desired to live on as an independent German nation. Mussolini, who had hitherto acted as Austria's protector, was unfriendly towards the plan, but Schuschnigg could still not believe that England and France would let little Austria fight her last desperate battle alone.

Schuschnigg proclaimed March 13th as the date for the plebiscite. Hitler replied by a resort to force. At half past six on the evening of March 10th the 8th Army, which it had been arranged for von Bock to take over in an emergency, received orders to mobilize. It is typical of Hitler's distrust that he gave orders that von Bock was not to be given plenary powers during the invasion. The news of the mobilization order shook Brauchitsch badly, for he feared war with Italy which had mobilized numerous divisions when Dollfuss was murdered and thrown them on to the Brenner Pass. He also feared war with Czechoslovakia.

There was no war with Italy and none with Czechoslovakia. The Austrian National Socialists organized a revolt and Mussolini left the Austrian government in the lurch. Prague did not want to act, unless London and Paris were prepared to do the same. London and Paris, however, confined themselves to protests.

Schuschnigg retired. Göring by means of an underhand intrigue forced the new Austrian Chancellor, Seyss-Inquart, who in reality was already Hitler's Deputy, to request the entry of German troops as a means of averting civil war whereupon the Inspector General of the Austrian forces announced that he was incapable of putting up effective resistance.

On March 13th German troops entered Vienna. There were scenes of wild enthusiasm on the streets, and in the corners scenes of utter despair. No less than eighty leading Austrian personalities committed suicide. Hitler made a triumphal entry into the city which had once rejected him.

On the military side the invasion had shown up a number of defects. In many cases mobilization had not been smoothly carried out and it was clear that there was lack of experience in the handling of motorized troops. Many tanks and motor transport vehicles had broken down on the road to Vienna.

The Austrian invasion completely overshadowed Fritsch's acquittal. Fritsch's trial began on March 11th with Göring acting as President of the Reich Court-Martial, though in reality he had nothing whatever to do with that institution whose proper President was General Heitz. The acquittal followed on the 18th. Schmidt, the perjured blackmailer, was subsequently shot by the S.S.

Hitler could now well afford that acquittal, for Hitler was in the ascendant. The "battle of flowers" against Austria as the officers called it, had been, as far as he was concerned, a wonderful success. A plebiscite on the union of Austria with the Reich had produced a vast majority in favour of that measure. A few public personalities who dissented were dealt with by the Gestapo. Any attempt now at a pronunciamento by the Army had become senseless.

When Erich Lahousen, head of Intelligence in the Austrian General Staff, reported for duty to Admiral Canaris—Lahousen had now become a German officer—Canaris received him with the words, "Why didn't you people shoot? Then the Corporal would have known that things can't go on like this for ever. However else is the man to learn any sense?" It was a fairly representative sentiment for the circles in which Canaris moved. In the General Staff Hitler was compared to Charles XII of Sweden, who took his country from one warlike venture to another and at last led the Swedish Army to its deadly defeat on the Steppes of Russia.

Nor did events suggest that the parallel was wholly defective. On March 10th Jodl noted in his service diary that the General Staff had received instructions to prepare "Enterprise Memel", that is to say to prepare for the reoccupation of the city which had fallen to Lithuania after the war. He also states that time must be allowed for Austria to be digested, nevertheless "Case Green" must be worked over afresh. This was certainly necessary from a technical point of view, for now that she had occupied Austria, Germany's military position so far as a conflict with Czechoslovakia was concerned was much more favourable.

The invasion of Austria had been accompanied by reassurances in Prague whose very fulsomeness excited suspicion, nor did Hitler wait any longer than April before setting to work on the Czecho-German question. Towards the end of that month he drew Keitel into discussion and asked how a conflict with Czechoslovakia could be provoked. Schmundt was a witness when the question was solemnly debated whether a stage-managed incident, or a sudden unprovoked full-scale attack was more suited to the circumstances of the case. Hitler remarked in an undertone to Keitel that after all a murder had started the 1914 war. Keitel at first was quite incapable of understanding what was in Hitler's mind. He did not realize that he was contemplating having the German Ambassador in Prague murdered by the Gestapo, and then putting the blame on the Czechs.

Keitel was convinced that Germany's available military resources were quite insufficient for a war against Czechoslovakia which would bring France and possibly England on to the scene. The war strength of the Czech Army was 45 divisions, while the German on April 1st, 1938, could count 24 infantry divisions, one tank division, one cavalry division and one division of mountain troops. All remaining tank and 'light' divisions existed only on paper or in skeleton form, and the same applies to the *Landwehr* divisions, which were earmarked for the West Wall and the Oder-Warthe line. Only seven or eight reserve divisions could actually be formed. The most that could be hoped for, if mobilization were ordered in the autumn, would be 55 divisions of most varied value and in the most varied stages of training.

Beck was particularly disturbed by another aspect of the matter when he realized Hitler's plans. Although Czechoslovakia had long been a disquieting factor for the General Staff, yet now that Germany had occupied Austria on that country's flank, the old danger had virtually disappeared. Thus not even the most specious plea of necessity could now justify the attack.

In May Hitler made a speech to a number of high-ranking officers, which was supposed to be devoted to the rehabilitation of Fritsch. In the main, however, he chiefly used the occasion to declare his unshakable determination to eliminate Czechoslovakia. Here a fortunate accident played into his hands, for at the end of that same month a false report caused the Czechs to mobilize. Hitler, of course, used the occasion to bring Czechoslovakia's aggressive intentions to the notice of the entire world.

Instead of the customary annual Staff journey, Beck ordered a written enquiry into the question whether it was possible to defeat the Czech Army by means of a lightning campaign before France could attack on the west. The enquiry was to be based on the assumption that an attack on Czechoslovakia would bring in not only France but England and possibly the United States. There could only be one conclusion, since a multi-front war inevitably spelled the end of Germany.

Beck was not slow to expound his views to Hitler who sought to fob him off with a vague (but surprising) assurance that he had no intention of starting a new war. Beck demanded specific guarantees. Hitler rebuffed him by telling him that the Army was the instrument of the statesman, and that its duty was to find a way of carrying out the tasks with which the statesman charged it—not to discuss them. Beck then declared that he would take no responsibility for orders which he did not approve and thereupon decided, as Chief of the General Staff, to sound the alarm both for Germany and for the world.

His plan was to persuade all generals to act in unison and make it plain to Hitler that his war preparations had got to be stopped, or at any rate postponed until the military and political situation had fundamentally changed. Beck drew up a document in this connection showing the danger a war in Czechoslovakia would unquestionably involve. Beck was still unwilling to take positive measures against the régime, although he commissioned Stülpnagel, with whom he had very confidential relations, to examine the possibilities of supporting collective action on the part of the generals by military means. He was nevertheless determined to force Hitler into a fundamental change of course, the watchword being "An end to warlike policies, boss-rule and Tcheka methods" ("*Gegen Kriegspolitik, Bonzokratie und Tschekamethoden*"). All the *Oberquartiermeisters* and heads of departments in the General Staff supported Beck's resolve, though Halder, who had succeeded Manstein as *Oberquartiermeister I*, doubted whether such a memoranda campaign would lead to much. He had already in 1937 tried to make Fritsch see the need for the use of armed force, and saw no reason to change his views.

Now the Chief of the General Staff had no direct power of command. The decision therefore lay with the Commander in Chief. On

July 16th, therefore, Beck wrote a letter to Brauchitsch which contained the following passage:

> The leaders of the *Wehrmacht* will incur the guilt of shedding human blood unless they are guided both by their expert knowledge and their conscience. The limit to their soldierly duty of obedience is set at that point, where their conscience and sense of responsibility forbids them to carry out their orders.

Brauchitsch at first seemed to be won over, for, like the rest, he held the armed forces in their existing state of unreadiness to be quite incapable of carrying on a war. But in the end Brauchitsch shrank back from decisive action even more completely than Beck and was less capable of forming any kind of plan. Beck had asked him to call a secret meeting of all the generals and at this meeting apprise them of the contents of his memorandum. Such a meeting was called by Brauchitsch at his home on August 4th, all the Corps and Army group commanders being present, but the results were very different from those for which Beck had hoped. Beck's memorandum had contained the following words:

> In order to safeguard our position before history and to keep the repute of the Supreme Command of the Army unstained, I hereby place on record that I have refused to approve any warlike adventures of the National Socialists.

These virile words, however, were not read out, nor did Brauchitsch personally address the assembled officers in the sense that his Chief of Staff had desired; he confined himself instead to a general review of the situation, which, it must be admitted, he described as serious.

Despite Brauchitsch's caution, Hitler got to know of the existence of Beck's memorandum, and his reaction was characteristic of the man. He asked how many people knew about it, and when he was told that only the top commanders were concerned, he more or less dismissed the whole matter from his mind. He was now satisfied that he knew his Brauchitsch.

Even so, however, Hitler thought it prudent to try and influence the general feeling of the officer corps, and with this end in view he made another very typical move. He ordered the Chiefs of Staff of the various Army groups and Corps to come to him at Obersalzberg, his object being to drive a wedge between the older and younger generation of Staff officers. On August 10th he addressed the officers whom he had summoned for three hours while a barrage of stories was released by the press, all telling of the oppression to which the Sudeten Germans were being subjected by the Czechs.

Hitler's remarks, however, did not remain entirely unanswered. General von Wietersheim, Chief of Staff to the 2nd Army Group, pointed out that the defences in the west could at best be held for three weeks. Hitler screamed at him that those defences would not be held for three weeks but for three years. In the main Hitler's attempt to bring the younger Staff officers round to his views must be held to have ended in failure. Jodl noted angrily in his service diary that the General Staff was the "*Zentrum des Miesmachens*" ("Centre of the dismal Jimmies")—and apparently the General Staff still counted for something.

Yet Hitler knew well enough that the General Staff could not make its views known to the public. It was he who had the obedience of the masses, not a certain General Beck, of whom they hadn't even heard. When he spoke to those masses he could still leave them in a kind of daze of blind obedience, in which they were prepared for any sacrifice, and it was the experience of human beings thus deprived by him of any will of their own and filled with any phantasy which he cared to inspire, that gave security to his shabby little soul.

IX

When Beck saw that his memorandum had got him nowhere and that it was impossible to change Hitler's policy, he did the only thing that was left for an officer of the old school to do—he resigned. He did this on August 18th. Hitler accepted his resignation three days later but gave the strictest orders that no mention of this resignation was to be made in the press. For reasons of patriotism Beck submitted to this, nor did a word appear in the *Militär-Wochenblatt*, though in earlier days such an event would have been considered far too important to ignore. Even Jodl refrained from noting the matter in his diary.

The General Staff now had no leader and Brauchitsch invited Lieutenant-General Halder, who was *Oberquartiermeister I*, to take Beck's post. It did not appear to occur to Brauchitsch that the honour of his order now demanded that he too should resign, for he was as little reconciled as Beck to Hitler's plans, but Brauchitsch clearly took the view that the thing for people like himself to do was to hang on to any position that they had got, and Halder apparently thought so too. Halder had on a previous occasion told Beck that it was no good just walking out. What they had got to do was to fight. He told Brauchitsch that if he accepted the post of Chief of the General Staff it was simply with the object of fighting against Hitler's war policy and that he was no more enamoured of the régime than Beck. Brauchitsch replied that Halder's attitude didn't worry him. Halder asked for a few days to think it over and had a talk about things with Beck. At length he accepted, entering on his appointment on September 1st. As to Beck, it was arranged that in the event of mobilization he was to be given the 3rd Army Group.

With the exception of General Adam, who had been Chief of the *Truppenamt*, Halder was the first Bavarian and the first Catholic ever to be Chief of the General Staff—a circumstance which, the old Prussian officers' tradition being what it was, did not make his position any easier. Halder, too, was an Artilleryman and had served together with Leeb on the staff of that most gifted soldier Crown Prince Ruprecht of Bavaria. He was a believing Christian and a man of wide intellectual interests, whose favourite subjects were botany and mathematics. Beck thought a great deal of Halder though he shared Hossbach's view that he would never be able to erect an impenetrable dam against the schemes of Hitler.

Halder's way was bound to be hard, precisely because he was a Christian and a descendant of an old officers' family, for whom the military oath had for generations been almost a sacrament. This made him all the more reluctant to admit, as admit he did, that duty compelled him to fight against his Supreme War Lord and might, in certain circumstances, even compel him to be the first Chief of the General Staff in German history to plan a *coup d'état*.

Halder was undoubtedly strengthened in his resolve by his intimate knowledge of Hitler's personality, for as Staff officer to a Bavarian division in Munich he had been a personal witness to the early stages of Hitler's career. In the notes which he provided for the American investigators of Munich he described Hitler as a very extraordinary personality, part genius and part fool, a man who seemed at times inspired and at others a mere criminal. He saw in him a man with certain feminine leanings, a man full of cruelty and lies and lacking in all restraint, and yet he had always had the feeling that he had not solved all the riddles of this man's soul. On another occasion he remarked that he had always looked for the workings of genius in Hitler, but had only succeeded in finding the diabolical in him.

When Halder took over the post of Chief of the General Staff, there began that strange duplication of plans which as far as the General Staff and most other responsible authorities were concerned, lasted right up to the final collapse of 1945. This double character had already marked the dealings of the magnates of War Industry. Gustav Krupp von Bohlen, for instance, who publicly boasted that without the preliminary work of his firm, Germany's speedy rearmament after 1935 would have been impossible, was at that same time financing a man like Goerdeler and enabling him to take long journeys abroad. In much the same way every plan of the General Staff between 1938 and 1940 had a sort of counter-plan, devised by that same General Staff, designed to cut across the first plan's provisions and thus to sabotage Hitler's conduct of the war.

The General Staff now received orders to work out a plan of attack against Czechoslovakia, an order which Beck had proved to be impossible of execution once France started to move. Deployment plan "Green" was based on the idea of a sudden overwhelming of the enemy. The great mass of the Reich's forces and particularly its armour and motorized troops were to advance from the direction of Silesia and from the Austrian and Bavarian flanking positions and break into Bohemia in such a way as to prevent the Czechoslovak forces retreating into Slovakia and the Carpathian Ukraine.

A decision was to be achieved within four days, and four armies with ten army corps were made available for this purpose. These were the 2nd Army under Rundstedt in Silesia, the 10th Army under Reichenau, which had the bulk of the tanks and motorized infantry, its task being to strike at the joint in the enemy's line at Pilsen, and the 12th and 14th Armies under von Leeb (who was now recalled) and List. These last were on the flank—in Austria. The plan was for the 2nd and 14th Armies to work together in a pincers movement.

The west was to be held by five weak divisions. The fourteen *Landwehr* divisions marked down for the West Wall (which was being hurriedly strengthened) existed, as already indicated, for the most part only on paper.

General Adam, Commander in Chief in the west, was profoundly pessimistic, but Hitler's plan was to overrun Czechoslovakia in four days and then throw all forces to the western frontier. An extended "Green" plan had been devised for the eventuality of joint intervention by France and Russia. In this plan it was assumed that France would do no more than occupy the Maginot line, while Poland, Italy and Hungary remained neutral.

These assumptions may not have sounded very realistic, but what

Hitler knew and the General Staff didn't, was that the despatches from von der Schulenburg, German Ambassador in Moscow, were describing Russia as being sick and tired of the Allies and of their inability to make up their minds. Schulenburg was even reporting that economic agreements might well provide a basis for further co-operation with the Soviet. In these circumstances the Soviet's public assurances that they would honour their commitments to Czecho-slovakia if France and England would do the same, did not inspire undue alarm.

England had despatched an intermediary to Prague to try and settle the racial conflict. Hitler, however, made every effort to under-mine this multi-national State, supporting the pretensions not of the Sudeten Germans alone but of the other minorities, while the revi-sionist aspirations of Hungary and Poland were lent a willing ear in Berlin. The propaganda reached its raging climax at the Party day celebrations in Nuremberg, in which, of course, formations of the *Wehrmacht* were compelled to take part.

X

A counter-plan, however, had been prepared, and prepared with an equal degree of meticulous care and was to be put into force concurrently with deployment "Green". Halder had actually drawn up this plan, though Halder acted in conjunction with Stülpnagel who had further disclosed the matter to Hammerstein-Equord.

This plan (of which more in a moment) had the support of the Chief of the Berlin police, Count Helldorf, who since the Fritsch crisis had recognized the evil of the system and now placed the police forces at the conspirators' disposal. Further, amongst those ready to act were General von Witzleben, commanding the 3rd military dis-trict, and Major-General von Brockdorff-Ahlefeldt, commanding the 23rd Infantry Division in Berlin. Von Stülpnagel acted as Halder's deputy in making the final arrangements.

The ramifications of the plot extended far beyond military circles. Agents of the Conservative opposition and in particular *Regierungsrat* Gisevius established connections between Schacht and Halder, the former of whom had been pressing for action ever since February. General Oster played an important part in this contact work, and both he and Gisevius were anxious for a meeting between Halder and Goerdeler. However, the constant supervision of Goerdeler by the Gestapo made that too dangerous.

Halder's first intention had been to wait till war had broken out because he feared Hitler's enormous prestige with the masses. The others persuaded him that action must necessarily be taken at that moment when "Case Green" was in process of execution. The plan was then for Witzleben's troops to occupy the quarter where the government offices were situated, arrest Hitler at the Chancellery and hand him over as a warmonger to the judgment of the German people. Now the 1st Light Division in the Wuppertal would, during the critical days, be marching through Thuringia to its assembly areas on the Czech border, accompanied by its motorized units and would be in a position to bar the *Leibstandarte Adolf Hitler's* way to Berlin. Its commander, Major-General Hoepner, a very talented soldier, and Guderian's chief rival for the leadership of the tank arm, was initiated into the plot. The conspirators at length very cautiously took Brauchitsch into their confidence. Brauchitsch was not himself prepared to act, but was prepared to "acquiesce".

What was to happen afterwards does not seem to be very clear. Rauschning, who in the meantime had had to flee from Danzig to escape arrest, learned that autumn in Switzerland something of the plans of the "Military Peace Party". According to Rauschning's information there was to have been a transitional military dictatorship. After that there was to be some form of government which would restore a constitutional State. There seems to have been no intention of restoring the monarchy though that was one of the points on Goerdeler's programme. What was contemplated seems to have been the appointment of a *Reichsverweser* (or Reich Administrator). Among the proposed candidates for this post were Rauschning, Göring, Neurath, Noske and Gessler. This list of names shows that the people concerned can hardly have thought far ahead. Göring would have been quite as intolerable as Hitler.

Never before had the general mood been so favourable to the success of a *coup d'état*, as it was in the close and thunderous atmosphere of that autumn, nor was it ever to be so favourable again. Hitler's frantic speeches, his wild threats against Czechoslovakia, the sinister propaganda on behalf of the Sudeten Germans, with whose problems the German public had hitherto had only the most negligible acquaintance—all these things produced among the masses nothing but the vague foreboding of war. The ordinary German could not understand how the imperfectly apprehended problems of Northern Bohemia could justify the horrors of another conflict. For the first time—and it was to be the last—the General Staff had the chance of striking a blow, and discontent with Hitler was so wide-spread as to promise such a venture an excellent chance of success. The masses had cheered Hitler rapturously when he brought them peace and bread. The masses were now wavering, for he was bringing them peace no longer.

While all this was happening, while mobilization was being prepared in secret, while the generals were conspiring and the drum fire of propaganda was growing ever louder, the West Wall was being strengthened in feverish haste. Since June thirty-six infantry battalions, thirty battalions of sappers, ten batteries of artillery, twelve anti-tank companies, in short any detachments that could be spared from any part of the service, had been at work on this line of fortifications—in addition to one hundred and ninety sections of the labour service. Hitler came to survey the work and said to General Adam's face, *"Ein Hundsfott wer diese Stellung nicht hält!"*, which, being one of the Führer's less urbane remarks, had best remain untranslated. It expressed what was perhaps an unreasonable confidence that the enemy could and would be kept out.

As was his custom, the Führer busied himself with endless details about the work, just as he busied himself with endless details concerning the Czech fortress line—details which General Staff and *Wehrmachtführungsstab* had unremittingly to supply. Meanwhile he gave his attention to the construction of a mobile headquarters, a Führer Headquarters containing the O.K.W., the *Wehrmachtführungsstab*, the *Wehrmacht* adjutants, Party and S.S. adjutants, press and the rest, together with special detachments of the Gestapo, guards and detachments of the *Leibstandarte Adolf Hitler* complete with anti-tank unit, motor-cylists and armoured cars.

Two noteworthy events occurred in August. By Hitler's command Brauchitsch, in Schwerin, had in all solemnity to hand over the 12th Artillery Regiment to Colonel-General von Fritsch (retired) for Hitler had appointed Fritsch to command it. It was Hitler's answer to Fritsch's repeated requests for rehabilitation. In his address Brauchitsch declared that Fritsch's departure was a matter of deep sorrow to the Army. Fritsch accepted this homage, sent Hitler "his most respectful thanks" and then on horseback in front of the men of his new regiment called for a 'Heil' to the Führer. When Halder, a little after this, asked him whether he would take over the leadership of the proposed coup, Fritsch refused.

It was in this same month of August that a most significant order of Hitler's was sent out. It concerned the special position of the police, of various S.S. formations, including the 'Junker' schools and the *Leibstandarte Adolf Hitler*. It provided that in the event of mobilization they were no longer subject to the military, and that Hitler retained their services for his own requirements. The arrests carried out by the Gestapo when German troops entered Vienna had already explained why von Bock's powers had been limited. This new order, however, started a wholly new line of development. It legalized the existence, side by side, with the Regular Army, of Himmler's S.S. Army. Himmler had won all along the line.

XI

Tension continued to mount in September till it became well nigh intolerable. Discontent spread even to the younger officers. The military attaché in Prague, Colonel Toussaint, who had an interview with Jodl about this time, expressed his astonishment over the lack of any desire for war in the officer corps, and Jodl himself was getting anxious about a possible intervention by the West. Meanwhile the civilian conspirators were pressing the military to act by mid-September.

On September 8th von Stülpnagel, who was an *Oberquartiermeister* at the time, requested that the office of the Commander in Chief of the Army be notified in writing five days before "Case Green" was to come into effect so that the necessary steps could be taken. Jodl had no idea that this advance information was required in order that the *coup d'état* might take place at the exact moment required.

Actually dates for the attack were already being arranged. In a conference with Keitel and Brauchitsch at Obersalzberg, Hitler had fixed on the 28th as the day on which the troops were to enter the "Green Manoeuvre ground". In other words the 28th was fixed as the day on which preparations for the attack were to begin.

The attitude of Jodl and Keitel during these tense days towards their more lukewarm brethren was one of sorrow rather than of anger. Jodl had designated Hitler's address on Party Day relative to the "settling of accounts" with Czechoslovakia as "grandiose" and hoped that the officer corps would blush for shame. Keitel declared himself "deeply disturbed" by the failure of Brauchitsch to overcome the hostility to Hitler among the General Staff, whereupon Jodl wrote that he was "profoundly sad" ("*tieftraurig*") that the Führer had the whole nation behind him, but not the generals. The generals still saw in Hitler the mere corporal and not the greatest statesman that Germany had had since Bismarck. He concludes by saying that as in 1914 disobedience in the Army was becoming distressingly evident, though the point of this last observation is obscure.

On a more pedestrian level were the technical problems which tend on occasion to bedevil even the best of plans. Owing to the transport of materials to the West Wall there was a shortage of rolling stock. It became necessary to shut off supplies to the west. Other headaches arose over motor transport and, in particular, over the problem of petrol supply. Moreover the secret mobilization re-awakened old rivalries between the Army and the S.A. and, in many cases, the latter refused to obey orders to hand over weapons and stores. Then in the middle of all this came the news that Neville Chamberlain, the English Prime Minister, had decided to negotiate personally with Hitler.

Chamberlain was already an old man and was moved by the conviction that there was no problem in the world that could not be settled by two decent, sensible men in a decent, sensible, heart-to-heart talk. Hitler, of course, was not concerned with the honest solution of any problem at all, nor even in a compromise. Hitler simply wanted the destruction of Czechoslovakia.

The negotiations were not too satisfactory though Chamberlain followed his first visit by a second, but the interviews served to convince Hitler that the British Prime Minister was a weak old man, that France and Britain were similarly weak and similarly ageing, and that the Western powers could not summon up the strength to act. The General Staff had even to reckon with the possibility that, thanks to these negotiations, an entry into Czechoslovakia might be quite peacefully effected, and preliminary studies of the problems connected with such an entry were officially ordered.

Then the sky suddenly darkened again. On September 22nd A.A. batteries were put in a state of readiness in Greater Berlin and all along the Czech frontier. Also there was a call-up of the aircraft observation service, which had been organized for some time past. On the 24th the arrangements for closing the French frontier were ordered to come into effect. At last on the 27th at 13.30 hours Halder received the decisive telephone message that the attacking waves were to be at their assault points. That meant that Berlin intended to act on that date.

On that same 27th Hitler, who had returned to Berlin, ordered a propaganda march through Berlin by Witzleben's troops in full battle order, the object being to raise the spirits of the population. The crowds, however, thought the regiments and batteries which they saw marching past were going to the railway station to entrain and concluded that war was already at the door. As the troops went by there was no cheering, only an uneasy and sinister silence. When Hitler, who was watching, saw the scene, he went mad, and cried to Goebbels that with people like that you could never carry on a war. There was equal resentment on the other side, General von Witzleben later confessed that he was tempted to unlimber his guns right there before the Chancellery, and then go in and lock "that fellow" up.

Then came the 28th. "Black day" Jodl sententiously noted in his diary. It was an even blacker day for Halder, who in a bitter conflict of conscience now sent out the order for the coup. A part of Witzleben's troops were already on their way to the Czech frontier, but Hoepner, the tank Commander, stood two days' march from Berlin waiting for the signal to move. Brauchitsch had approved Halder's action, but also went to Keitel and told him that if Czechoslovakia was attacked, there must be no penetration beyond the Sudeten territories, and that Hitler must have that made thoroughly clear. Meanwhile there was a wave of fugitives from the west and the O.K.W. set up a special force, the "Siegfried" force, to canalize such wholesale population movements.

From hour to hour the state of apprehension grew. At midday Brauchitsch went to the Chancellery a second time to get the lie of the land before the troops began to move on Berlin. There he heard that Mussolini had made a mediation proposal and that Chamberlain and Daladier had agreed to come on the following day to a conference with Hitler and Mussolini in Munich. Brauchitsch immediately knew that a *coup d'état* was out of the question. One really could not arrest a man and have him tried as a war criminal when he was on the point of winning a completely bloodless victory. It is said that von Halder utterly lost control of himself: "What can we do?" he was said to have cried out. "He succeeds in everything he does."

On the 29th the Munich agreement was signed and the Sudeten territories ceded by the Czechs. Jodl made the not over-recondite observation in his diary that Czechoslovakia had ceased to play any part as a power factor. The genius of the Führer had won a new victory without the application of force. "It is to be hoped that the unbelieving, the weak and the doubters will be both converted and instructed."

In Hitler's eyes, however, the refractory generals and the sceptical, cautious General Staff had lost all standing. He could not expect, he now brought himself to say, that his generals should understand him. What he could expect was that they should obey him—a touch of poor William II here. *Regis voluntas suprema lex.* Once again a number of generals were retired with Rundstedt and Adam heading the list. On October 18th this fate overtook Beck. Hitler had him informed that as the possible commander of an army group in war, he had lost confidence in him. Fritsch meanwhile had been forgotten. Ulrich von Hassell saw him in December of that year living very quietly near Hanover. He was quite resigned. There was, he said, nothing more to be done. Hitler was Germany's destiny both for good and evil.

XII

In a document which he drew up after his retirement under the title "Germany in a Future War", Beck sought to render a kind of account to himself for his conduct. In a true Clausewitzian spirit he asks that in the planning of any war the political purpose of that war must be clear, and that political leaders must never be in any kind of doubt that the aim of war is peace.

> Germany [he writes] will never be exposed to the use of force by other States, so long as she does not resort to force herself, for Germany, thanks to her geographical position, will always have to risk more in a war than states that have only one frontier to be threatened and are united to the rest of the world by routes which cannot be blockaded. If in the World War, Germany could be compared to a beleaguered fortress, despite the fact that she was comparatively favourably situated in regard to the terrain she could command, then this comparison would have an even more fateful significance in any future multi-front war which Germany would have to wage alone. A war begun by Germany will immediately call into the field other states than the one she has attacked, and in a war against a world coalition she will succumb and for good or evil be put at that coalition's mercy.

CHAPTER XIII

HITLER TRIUMPHANT

I

THE Munich conference, which represents the summit of Hitler's political success, begot in him that ultimate overweening self-confidence which was to prove his undoing. Like all the other signatories of the Munich agreement, Germany had solemnly engaged herself to respect the integrity of what was left of Czechoslovakia. During all his drumfire propaganda against the latter, Hitler had always insisted, one might almost say ecstatically insisted, that the Sudetenland represented his final territorial aspiration.

Yet if Hitler regarded himself essentially as the liquidator of the Treaty of Versailles, and Rauschning's evidence suggests that that is just what he did, he could hardly have overlooked the fact that the most important losses of German territory still remained unrectified. Nor can we suppose that he had any intention of overlooking it. He had, of course, officially renounced his claim to Alsace-Lorraine, but there was still the East, and it was in this quarter that he began to prepare for that main work of revision, to which his exploits to date had merely been preliminary.

Hitler was now wholly the autocrat. He was short-circuiting both the customary diplomatic channels and the General Staff, the latter having now perforce abandoned its advisory function and sunk to the level of a mere executive tool. For Halder, this last held certain terrible implications. It meant that all those who were now secretly Hitler's enemies and yet were determined to remain at their posts for fear they should be replaced by men more pliant than themselves, would, because of that very persistence, one day be held responsible for the very acts which they abhorred. These considerations seemed to have carried particular weight with Admiral Canaris, the head of counter-espionage, and to have filled him with a sense of inexpiable guilt. Yet Canaris remained at his post, since there was no other way in which he could hope to cut across Hitler's plans.

The curious position of all these men, Halder in the General Staff,

Weizsäcker in the Foreign Office, Canaris, and the rest, and the strange double-mindedness with which they had to approach their work, was entirely without precedent in Germany history. To the younger Moltke, the war of 1914 had seemed a terrible and tragic event, but in the last resort he never thought of it otherwise than as a just war of defence. How different was the fate of Halder, who saw the threat of a war drawing ever nearer which he could never regard as a just war at all. Ultimately the General Staff was to be wrecked by this dilemma from which there were only two escapes, a *coup d'état*, which had now become progressively impracticable, and the collective resignation of all officers, which the whole tradition and education of these men made unthinkable.

What was true of the General Staff was even more true of the officer corps as a whole. Till 1933, the officer corps had been an essentially homogeneous body, yet Jodl at Nuremberg dwelt on the profound political and ideological differences by which from 1933 onwards it began to be divided. These differences tended to extend even to purely military matters, for it would be incorrect to say that Beck's theory of the pure defensive was never criticized, particularly by the younger generation. To youth, after all, an aggressive policy is bound to make an appeal.

The Commander in Chief of the Army and the General Staff now found that their spheres of authority were being further contracted, nor was there anything that either Brauchitsch or Halder could do about it. Hitler's prestige after his bloodless victories in Austria and Czechoslovakia was too enormous. Thus, despite the fact that the Army had an Inspector of Engineers and Fortresses and the General Staff a special Fortifications Section, Hitler rejected a carefully worked out programme of Brauchitsch's which was spread over several years, for the completion of the West Wall. Instead the supervision of the work of fortifying the west was handed over to a Party member, Dr. Todt, the creator of the *Autobahnen*, who till now had held the post of inspector of roads. Todt's organization, the "O.T." ("Organization Todt"), grew up to become an army of engineers which existed side by side with the sappers of the Army proper— another instance of the splitting up of authorities.

Yet this step of Hitler's was quite in keeping with his policy of preventing any organization from becoming too powerful by paralyzing it through the creation of a duplicate and rival. Apart from this, of course, Brauchitsch's programme was not attuned to Hitler's restless frame of mind or to his dark foreboding that time was short and that, as he told Neurath, "he could wait no longer". Actually, the construction of the West Wall involved yet a further subdivision of authority, for the laying out of the rearward areas and of the so-called "Anti-Aircraft Defence areas" came under Göring, as the *Luftwaffe's* Commander in Chief.

All Brauchitsch's protests were of no avail, and indeed Hitler took steps to make protests more difficult than they were already. First, the principle of co-responsibility, which Beck had reintroduced, and the General Staff's right of direct approach to the head of the State were the foundations on which in Gneisenau's plan the General Staff had been built. Both these things, however, were done away with. The General Staff officer was deliberately restricted to normal service channels for any communication he wished to make. Also done away with was Moltke's old rule that officers of higher rank could always minute a dissentient opinion. The General Staff handbook for 1939 laid it down that the rôle of the General Staff officer was that of an adviser, helper and executive, but that he did not participate in the Commander's responsibility. It was expressly laid down that the Commander in Chief must seek the counsel of the Chief of the General Staff before making an operational decision, but that the latter, even if he disagreed with the former's plan, must give him the most whole-hearted co-operation in carrying it out.

II

On October 21st, O.K.W. received instructions from Hitler to prepare plans for the occupation of what remained of Czechoslovakia. It was a most significant event, since this was a clear invasion of the authority of the General Staff, which even Hitler had hitherto respected in this connection. Originally, the Department of National Service in the O.K.W. had simply received and passed such plans on after the General Staff had prepared them, a function which had caused Halder to nickname them "Plagiarists", but jokes about the O.K.W. as "Corporal Hitler's writing room" were rapidly getting out of date.

During the winter of 1938, Hitler further ordered the General Staff to abandon all preparations of plans for a future war and to concentrate on the training and organization of the Army. The General Staff at first saw in this order an indication that Hitler genuinely wanted peace. In reality, it was a result of Hitler's distrust and of his consequent desire to sidetrack the General Staff as much as he could. Strangely enough, the plan for a *coup d'état* had remained undiscovered, and Hitler never knew how near he had been in 1938 to his fall, but he had something like an animal's instinct for the presence of danger, and he now was achieving what he had always wanted, the relegation of the General Staff to certain purely technical fields where he still believed it to be indispensable.

All this was in the general trend of the time. As every official was now tending to be more and more effectively shut off from every other, and every department to be isolated by walls of increasing impenetrability, and since in particular no high-ranking officers were among Hitler's intimates, it was extremely difficult for responsible service chiefs to form any picture of what was in Hitler's mind. Keitel complained later that Hitler had deceived them all, while Raeder at Nuremberg declared that Hitler had always known what he wanted though nobody else had ever had that privilege. However, the events of March 1939 dispelled any mystery in this matter as far as the immediate future was concerned.

These events were swift and in essence simple. By professing to espouse the cause of Slovak independence, Hitler, under cover of the threat of blowing Prague to ashes from the air, proceeded to the annexation of Czechoslovakia. Benes' successor, Dr. Hascha, was summoned to Berlin and was forced to sign an agreement whereby Bohemia and Moravia became a protectorate of the Reich. The President of the non-existent secret Cabinet Council, von Neurath, assumed the office of Protector, and Slovakia was allowed to enjoy her independence under the wings of the German eagle, a precarious privilege and one of very doubtful value, even while it lasted.

III

Shortly before the Czechoslovak affair reached its melancholy conclusion, the instructors of the *Kriegsakademie* were entertained by Hitler at the Chancellery. One of those present on this occasion observed that Hitler, who at first seemed tired and nerveless, took a stimulant of some kind, presumably one of those which his doctor, Professor Morell, so liberally administered. Hereafter his face grew livelier, and he declared to those present that if something lay ready to his hand—he was referring to Czechoslovakia, of course—he naturally took it. That is what anybody would do. On another occasion he described to a circle of intimates with obvious glee—he slapped his thigh as he spoke—how he had bullied and intimidated

Hascha into accepting his terms. That, he said, was how he would treat any statesman who opposed his will. He would "Hascha-ize" him.

When, on March 15th, the 3rd and 5th Army Groups under Blaskowitz and List, marched from Saxony and Austria into Bohemia, and the German tanks rolled over the frozen Bohemian roads into Prague, the final act of the drama may be said to have begun. It was now plain to the whole world that Hitler's most solemn promises were entirely worthless, for it was but five months since he had guaranteed the independence of the State he had now overrun.

Events now moved with a terrifying rapidity. Italy seized Albania, and Poland rejected Hitler's offer to partition the Ukraine in return for a settlement regarding Danzig and the Corridor. From the side of England, which had speedily learned the unwisdom of Munich, began a series of guarantees—to Rumania, to Greece and, above all, to Poland. There followed on April 28th the determination by Germany of the Anglo-German naval agreement.

On that day Hitler made a long speech in the Reichstag in which he collectively denounced Poland, England and the President of the United States, who had been tactless enough to appeal to him to respect the liberties of small nations. In fact, however, these civilities were secondary matters, for the determination of the naval agreement paved the way for a huge rearmament project, the so-called "Z" plan, which provided for the building of ten capital ships, four aircraft carriers, one hundred and fifty-eight destroyers, some two hundred and fifty submarines and about sixty other vessels of war.

IV

On April 3rd, Keitel had received instructions from Hitler to prepare an attack on Poland, the enterprise being given the name "Case White". Immediately afterwards similar instructions were sent to the Supreme Commander of the Army and to the General Staff. Keitel was full of misgivings. He believed the munitions supply to be insufficient for any warlike enterprise. In fact, even Keitel did not personally think the time when Germany could wage war had come at all. At Nuremberg he declared that none of the generals wanted war, but that they had nevertheless carried out Hitler's orders, since Hitler's success at Munich had made it quite impossible to oppose his will.

The General Staff was completely dumbfounded when these directives were received, remembering as it did Hitler's instructions at the end of 1938 to refrain from preparing any further campaigns. It was also resentful. Halder had considered it a degradation of the Army to use it for purposes of blackmail—as Hitler had done in the case of Czechoslovakia. Now it began to be said that it was to be used in much the same way to put pressure on Poland.

Actually it was soon evident that Hitler intended to go further than that. During the course of April he addressed a number of high-ranking officers and told them that in the event of a conflict with the Western powers they could not be assured of Polish neutrality. There was therefore nothing to be done except to eliminate Poland by means of a lightning campaign, before England or France could intervene. It would mean bloodshed, since there was no chance of another Munich, but it was most improbable that such an enterprise would lead to another world war.

Hitler's proposed elimination of Poland obviously made the attitude of Russia a matter of prime importance, and there now began an ardent competition for her favours. Yet there was no lack of warning that a bargain between Germany and Russia at Poland's expense would have disastrous results. Papen, now Ambassador to Turkey, expounded his fears to Keitel and Brauchitsch in Berlin, insisting that any attempt to solve the corridor question by force could only lead to a world war, in which Germany's position would be hopeless.

Papen's was but one amongst a multitude of voices, both civil and military, and more attention might perhaps have been paid to them but for Keitel's and Brauchitsch's quite singular obduracy. Düsterberg contrived to get an interview with the latter and tried to make him see the truth on the subject of Hitler and the Party, but Brauchitsch observed an icy silence. Obviously he considered any talk about attempts to overthrow the government suicidal, or at best useless. General Thomas in the O.K.W. tried repeatedly to arrange a meeting between Keitel and Goerdeler, and as the Chief of the *Wehrwirtschaftsamt*, the department of defence industries, sought to put data on record showing the difficulties with which a war was bound to saddle the country. It was all in vain—especially where Keitel was concerned. Like Blomberg before him, Keitel was convinced that Hitler was a genius and could somehow make possible things which were not possible at all.

It was on May 23rd that Hitler reversed his former attitude and for the first time gave the commanders of all his fighting services some insight into his long-term plans. On this date a meeting was called at the Chancellery, and the following were summoned to attend: Göring, Raeder, Brauchitsch, Keitel, Halder, Warlimont, the *Wehrmacht* adjutants, Vice-Admiral Schniewind, Chief of the Admiralty Staff, Generals Milch and Bodenschatz of the *Luftwaffe*, and Colonel Jeschonnek of the *Luftwaffe's* General Staff. To this gathering Hitler frankly confessed his intention of disrupting the whole European system. He made it plain that the real question was not Danzig but the securing of Germany's *Lebensraum*, her "living space", in other words, the forcible acquisition of territory in the east. This, too, could not be achieved without bloodshed. As a preliminary, he again pointed out, Poland must be isolated and attacked. Poland had always been an enemy of the German cause, but the chief enemy to Germany's continental aspirations was England, and a war with England, that is to say, with England and France, would be a struggle for life or death.

To fight England, it was essential to gain command of the Dutch and Belgian coasts, from whence her life lines could be cut by air and submarine attack. Though the *Wehrmacht* must strive for a short war, the government was envisaging a struggle that might last for ten or fifteen years.

This speech, in which the first hint was given of an understanding with Russia, contained another passage very significant of the mind of Hitler. In this passage he said that the study of the enemy's weak points was not a matter which could be left to the General Staff. Instead, a "Study Staff" must be formed from among the officers of the three services, "to prepare operations at the highest intellectual level". It must consist of men who combined "great imagination with the best technical knowledge". Had this idea been carried into effect, it would have meant that yet a fifth General Staff had been called into being.

V

At the end of that same month of May, the General Staff began preparing the deployment plans for "Case White". The date by which all plans were to be complete was August 20th. The essence of the plan ultimately evolved was a rapid advance with the great mass of motorized and armoured divisions. Two army groups were to be formed, the Northern group of two armies, based on Eastern Prussia and Eastern Pommerania under the command of von Bock with General von Salmuth, an ardent disciple of Beck's, as Chief of Staff, and a Southern group of three armies based on Silesia under von Rundstedt with von Manstein as Chief of Staff. Both groups were to close in concentrically on the Polish forces in Western Poland.

The General Staff had no information concerning the provision Poland had made for the event of an attack. It was assumed that she would resort to delaying tactics and hope for help from England, France or Russia. It was therefore further assumed that she would have two strong armies on the flanks and a weak centre. The possibility that she might resort to a spoiling attack on East Prussia or Upper Silesia could not, however, be ruled out. Even so, the fact that Poland was really already encircled, since she could be attacked from East Prussia on one side and Slovakia on the other left little doubt that the Polish Army could be annihilated. Hitler was especially insistent on the fullest use being made of the circumstance that East Prussia already constituted a wedge in Poland's flank, and on large troop concentrations in this area. German plans in this connection were aided by the singularly fortunate circumstance that the festivities connected with the twenty-fifth anniversary of Tannenberg could be made an occasion for disguising the transport of a certain number of troops by sea.

Brauchitsch told Hitler quite frankly that he thought the subjugation of Poland quite feasible, and that there was even a chance of a victory over France and England, but that the position would be hopeless if Russia intervened on the side of the West. He had no notion, of course, that secret negotiations were already in progress between Russia and Germany. Hitler had not thought it necessary to say anything about that either to Brauchitsch or to the Chief of the General Staff. Nevertheless, Brauchitsch's remarks served to strengthen Hitler's conviction that the Polish problem could be successfully solved so long as Russia maintained a benevolent attitude. But there were other considerations. Unfortunately, crude power politician that he was, and lightheartedly prepared, at that, to conjure up a world conflict, Hitler simply would not admit that the Army, the instrument of his policy, was totally unready for a major war. Yet neither the vast debt which he had piled up with his rearmament programme, nor his prestidigitation with new weapons and new methods of war, dive bombers, parachutists, airborne troops and the rest, could disguise the hopeless insufficiency of his military means. Only six divisions were at that moment available for covering the western frontier, and even the talents of von Leeb, who as Germany's leading defensive strategist, had been given command of those forces, could hardly have made up for his grave, even if only temporary, inferiority of numbers in the event of a determined French attack. Nor could the taking over of the Czech Army's equipment or of the Skoda works at Pilsen make good the serious deficiencies in material.

General Warlimont said on a later occasion that no German Army had gone to war so ill prepared. There was a lack of munitions, efficient heavy tanks (the design of the latter had still not been finally decided), of radio and telegraph units and motorized and railway troops. Above all, there was a shortage of trained reserves, both officers and men.

Hitler now suddenly changed his tactics towards the Army command. Everybody, whether he asked for it or not, was suddenly assured that he (Hitler) would be "an idiot" were he to allow himself to "slither into a world war" ("*in einen Weltkrieg hineinschlittern*") like the incompetents of 1914—and all for the sake of the Polish Corridor. Raeder's fears that a world war was the very thing to which an attack on Poland would lead were countered by an inept pun. Amongst others, Lieutenant-Colonel von Lossberg, *Wehrmacht-führungsstab's* G.S.O.1, who had previously worked in the General Staff's Operations Section, was about this time given a particularly emphatic undertaking. Hitler received him at his home in Munich and in the presence of Keitel insisted that "Case White" could "never, never, never" become the cause of a world war.

Hitler improved this occasion by expressing his utter contempt for the Western statesmen. He had, he said, thoroughly taken the measure of Daladier and the "Umbrella-man" Chamberlain. They were nothing but a couple of tea-swilling old women (as near as the translator can get to "*Alte Kaffeetanten*" though it scarcely does justice to the terseness and pregnancy of the original) and they would never dare to lift a finger for their Polish allies. Halder was also amongst those who heard him say that there was no fear of Franco-British intervention.

There is no doubt that by this time Hitler had come round to believing his own story; he had certainly got to the point where he thought himself to have a monopoly in accurate forecasts. He was visualizing, as we have seen, a lightning war against Poland, and this, he thought, would be followed by a pause in which he could get his breath. He could then proceed against the West as soon as circumstances were favourable. The trump which he had up his sleeve was, of course, the negotiation he was conducting with Stalin.

Where he was completely mistaken was in his estimate of the British character and of the quality of British policy. In particular he hopelessly misread the mentality of Neville Chamberlain. That old man had returned from Munich with the words "Peace in our time" and now felt that he had been personally cheated by Hitler when the latter raped Czechoslovakia. Chamberlain had then seen that any further surrender was impossible, and had begun to come round to the views of Churchill and his circle, who had always been violent critics of Munich. England had always resisted any power that sought to dominate the Continent, and Chamberlain was firmly resolved to resist Hitler if he attempted to solve the Polish problem by force.

France might have been less determined, but was bound to be influenced by any decision in London, and London was convinced that it could at least rely on the moral support of Roosevelt, whose appeal had been so cynically dismissed by Mussolini as one of the symptoms of infantile paralysis. In Germany, however, the belief was now at last unfortunately gaining ground that a further bluff by Hitler might still succeed.

VI

In August, German preparations were complete, and the press duly began to lay down the required barrage of stories concerning the maltreatment of Germans by Poles. There was no official mobilization, merely an acceleration in the rate of call-up. Incidents began to be manufactured by the agents of the S.S. and the Gestapo. There were, of course, some genuine clashes between Germans and Poles, for excitement and uncertainty were beginning to mount in Poland, as they were in Germany.

For Germans the problem of the Corridor was by no means so remote a thing as had been the difficulties, real and alleged, of the Sudeten Germans. Even so, this new threat of war filled people with a kind of dumb fear. The mood was much what it had been in the previous year, though many still clung to the hope that Hitler would again achieve the impossible and add one more to his list of bloodless victories.

Schacht, who had now forfeited his position as president of the Reichsbank, and assumed the purely decorative office of a minister without portfolio, returned from a journey to India about this time. He sought vainly to get into touch with Halder, but the latter refused to see him. Halder knew that there was no point in reviving last year's plans for a coup.

Meanwhile Ciano had visited Ribbentrop on the latter's estate near Salzburg—the real owner of this desirable property, an Austrian legitimist, was for the time being in a concentration camp. Ciano asked his host what Germany really wanted. Was it Danzig? The Corridor? Or both? Ribbentrop looked him coldly in the eye. "We want none of these," he said. "What we want is war." Ciano was badly shaken. True, the Spanish war had ended in a victory for Franco, and Italy had occupied Albania, but Italy was not ready for war. Mussolini had not wanted war till 1942. If Hitler were willing to wait till then, he had told Ciano, the axis would have an eighty per cent chance of success. Now it had only a fifty per cent chance. Nor did Ciano find much encouragement in what he actually saw in Germany. He remarks in his diary under date August 29th: "Hitler is going to war despite an alarming shortage of armaments, and he has a disunited people behind him."

The feelings of the General Staff were very similar. In June and July, Halder had repeatedly sought quietly to warn M. Coulondre and Sir Nevile Henderson, the French and British Ambassadors. He had assured them that Hitler simply refused to believe that France and Britain would intervene on Poland's behalf and that only a firm and determined attitude on the part of their governments would deflect him from his designs on that country. He said later that he had "implored" them (*"flehentlich gebeten"*) to act before it was too late. Just as his predecessors had done, Halder feared a catastrophe in which State and people would perish together. Meanwhile, Weizsäcker, of the Foreign Office, with whom Halder was in constant touch, sought to repeat similar warnings in London.

Reports reached Rauschning in the summer of 1939 of a plan to arrange a meeting in Paris between some members of the General Staff who shared these sentiments and a French general from Daladier's *entourage*. The German generals, however, seem to have fought shy of the scheme, for even in Paris Himmler had his agents.

VII

On August 19th, Germany and Soviet Russia signed a trade agreement, and on the 22nd, when tension was at its height, the non-aggression pact with Russia was at last completed—actually, negotiations had been going on about it since the spring. On this day

Hitler ordered all commanding generals and admirals to come to Obersalzberg in mufti, and made one of his usual long-winded speeches. Quite obviously, the completion of the Russo-German agreement had given him the cue for action. Never, he said, had the situation seemed so favourable as at this moment. War must in any case come sooner or later, but England was not ready for it. "My only fear is that some *schweinehund* will now come to me with a mediation plan." A very important element in the situation was his own existence, and that of Mussolini, at this particular moment of time. Mussolini had the strongest nerves of any man in Italy, and as for himself, he was "a factor of great value" (*"ein grosser Wertfaktor"*). London and Paris had no great personalities. As to the British blockade, there was no need to be afraid of that in view of the deliveries which would come from the east. Later that day he gave a further address in which he announced that the following Saturday, the 26th, would probably be the day on which the troops would march.

Hitler's speech affected different members of his audience in different ways, and of course it was not the first speech of its kind that most of them had heard. One of the generals present actually went to sleep, while Dietrich, the Reich Press Chief, had the impression, which he communicated in a displeased tone to Halder, that most of the generals seemed depressed. Actually, a number of those present still thought it would not come to war at all. Among these was Keitel himself, who probably based his opinion on the conclusion of the agreement with Russia. Rundstedt was sceptical, while Witzleben seemed definitely to believe the crisis would take the same course as that of the previous year.

The Nuremberg documents have shed much interesting light on the week that followed. The sequence of events was roughly as follows.

On the day following the speech at Obersalzberg, on the 23rd, that is to say, Jodl, who had temporarily returned to the gunners, was recalled to Berlin to take charge of the *Wehrmachtführungsstab*. This was something of a blow for Halder, who had hopes in the event of war of pushing a man of his own into the post in the person of General von Sodenstern. However, the post went to Jodl, who on the first day of taking over noted in his diary: "Y-day declared to be 26.8. X-time 04.30 hours." This shows that Hitler had expressed a genuine intention on the previous day when he said that the attack would begin on the 26th.

On that same day, while Ribbentrop flew to Moscow to sign the new pact, Sir Nevile Henderson arrived at Obersalzberg with a personal letter from Chamberlain. In it Chamberlain declared that Britain intended to stand by the Polish guarantee, which, in point of fact, was implemented two days later by a formal treaty. On the day following, that is to say, on the 24th, Schmundt arrived in Berlin from Obersalzberg and informed Jodl that Hitler had become undecided whether England would not intervene after all—which may well have been the case, though the inference drawn from it, namely that he still might stay his hand, was gravely mistaken.

For a moment, however, there was a ray of hope, for on the next day the order went out to stop the deployment against Poland which was already in full swing. As the troops were already on the march to their assault points, it was extremely difficult to pull them back. Indeed, in some cases commanding generals could themselves have been the case, though the inference drawn from it, namely that he still might stay his hand, was gravely mistaken.

Every lover of peace now breathed a sigh of relief. Halder's immediate reaction was that the occasion should be used to persuade Hitler to draw the troops back from the frontier regions. The technical pretext could be used that it was impossible to maintain so large a concentration for long in one position. This would have provided a means of cutting right through the whole plan of attack. Canaris was immensely relieved and declared that the peace of Europe had been saved for fifty years. His view was that one simply could not order a secret mobilization in one breath, and withdraw it in the next, and then order it again. That kind of thing could only lead to one result—the complete forfeiture by Hitler of any confidence his generals had ever had in him. Even Oster, his Chief of Staff, a man who was anything but an optimist, believed that the worst was now over. As a general indication of the prevailing mood, we further have the evidence of Lieutenant-General von Buttlar-Brandenfels, who was working in the General Staff's personnel department and was later to join the Operations section of the *Wehrmachtführungsstab*. Von Buttlar-Brandenfels has told how he was overwhelmed with questions from officers who wanted to know whether the world war had now really been avoided.

However, this hopeful prospect did not last for long, and in point of fact there was very little ground for it. There is no reason to believe that Hitler seriously intended to abandon his plan, or that the postponement of the attack was actuated by any other consideration than the somewhat ill-founded hope that Britain might still withdraw from her guarantee. In any case, the Tannenberg celebrations were cancelled, as were the Party-Day celebrations which regularly took place in September.

Any hopes Hitler may have entertained of keeping Britain neutral were dashed by the signature of an Anglo-Polish treaty of alliance. Both Roosevelt and Daladier now made appeals to Hitler to preserve peace, but these only served to confirm his belief in the weakness of the Western powers. A good indication of how completely the military were shut off from what was going on at the highest level is provided by the case of a certain Birger Dahlerus, a Swedish industrialist and friend of Göring, who endeavoured to mediate at this time between London and Berlin. Dahlerus contrived to get an interview with Hitler, who seems on this occasion to have behaved like a raving maniac. When Dahlerus pointed out the dangers of a war with England, Hitler started to scream that Germany was invincible. "A short war can be won by Germany," he is stated to have cried. "If there is war, I shall build U-boats, U-boats, U-boats!" At this point the Führer appears to have begun to mutter unintelligibly, but eventually he became articulate again with the assertion that "I shall build planes, planes, planes, and I shall annihilate my enemies." Dahlerus at this stage realized that it was impossible to have any kind of sensible discussion with such a man. The historical importance of this incident resides in the fact that even Jodl was kept in complete ignorance of Dahlerus' activities and heard of them for the first time at Nuremberg.

VIII

Mussolini during the past weeks had made efforts to act ·s a mediator, as he was at this stage obviously in no condition to enter a war. Hitler, however, was determined on war and put his final demands on Poland in the form of so uncompromising an ultimatum that Poland was faced with the alternative either of fighting or submitting abjectly to Hitler's will.

Poland mobilized. The German preparations for attack were renewed, and the attack was ordered for August 30th, though at the last moment it was again postponed. On the 31st orders were again issued for an attack in the early hours of the following day, though a Polish negotiator had been asked for and the Chancellery still professed to be waiting for him. The attack was to begin at 5.45, but now, at any rate in the southern army group, the order to attack was no longer taken at its face value, and the Operations Department of the General Staff was told on the telephone that the whole thing was obviously just another phony and please when were the counter orders coming along! This time, however, Hitler meant business, although the Polish government was prepared for substantial concessions, and when, on the instructions of his government, the Polish Ambassador made yet a further call, he was brusquely asked whether he had full powers to negotiate. When he admitted that this was not yet the case, it was all over.

The German forces broke into Poland in the early hours of September 1st, with 44 divisions, including twelve armoured and motorized divisions, while the squadrons of the new German *Luftwaffe* roared through the skies, those squadrons of which Göring had said that they would fall on the enemy like an avenging angel. A relatively weak force, which was to be rapidly and continuously reinforced by reserve, second-line and *Landwehr* divisions, took over the West Wall.

At 11 o'clock, in a field grey uniform of his own devising, Hitler addressed the Reichstag. Force, he said, was now being met by force. Something of the fatefulness of this hour could be felt in his words when he said that he would return from this war as a victor or not survive it. Only one member of the Reichstag had the courage to protest against the war. This was Fritz Thyssen, one of the kings of German heavy industry, who had once financed Hitler and now felt himself betrayed by him. He looked upon the Russian pact as something that threatened the bolshevization of Germany and foresaw that the war against Poland would be bound to end in a World War which it was beyond the powers of the Reich to carry on.

Mussolini now made a last-minute attempt to save the situation by arranging a four-power conference. The conditions were that Poland should agree to an armistice, while the German troops continued in the positions they had occupied. Britain, however, was only prepared to agree on the understanding that German troops retreated to their original positions on the frontier, and put this demand in the form of an ultimatum. Berlin left Britain's communication unanswered, whereupon at 11 o'clock on September 3rd, the British Ambassador handed in a declaration of war. The French declaration of war followed at five o'clock in the afternoon. "What are we to do?" Hitler asked Ribbentrop when the English declaration of war arrived. In the ante-room Göring said to Colonel-General Schmundt, "If we lose the war, then Heaven have mercy on us!" Goebbels was deathly silent. Jodl afterwards declared that the news of the French and British declarations had struck him "like a blow from a club" (*wie ein Keulenschlag*") while Canaris declared that this was the end. Thus began the Second World War, against which the General Staff had struggled so vainly and so hard.

The reports which Ciano received at this time from Professor Attolico, the Italian Ambassador, describe something of the depressed air prevailing in the capital. This time, no cheering crowds lined the streets, as they had done in 1914, when the troops marched by. Instead, there were weeping women, while the male onlookers watched in anxious silence. Too many of them had known war at first hand.

On the evening of that same September 3rd, Hitler sent a message to Mussolini, in which he declared that he would have accepted his proposal for a conference if he had been able to obtain certain guarantees for its success, but Britain was determined to wage war in all circumstances and peace could not have lasted more than a year. The moment was particularly favourable. The Polish Army would collapse within a very short time, and it would be intolerable for the sacrifices which Germany had already made in blood to be stultified by diplomatic intrigue. He knew that this war was a battle for life and death, but he believed in his success "with the firmness of a rock".

IX

The outbreak of war presented the General Staff with a new dilemma. Prussian officers had always done their duty in war, and the officers of the General Staff were bound by their military oath to the man who had so light-heartedly conjured up a war and now presumed personally to direct its course. Now this military oath had once been given to anointed kings and had in it, therefore, the element of knightly fealty, and though the kings of Prussia had forsaken their own cause, this oath was felt to be a thing of quite peculiar solemnity. In passing judgment on the attitude of the General Staff during these, the final years of its existence, this consideration must in no wise be left out of account.

Naturally every officer among all those who had secretly opposed Hitler settled this problem of conscience in his own way. Halder, for instance, held that his moral and military duties coincided now that the war he had striven to prevent had actually broken out; but the

choice in such cases was always a difficult and often a torturing one—
most torturing of all, perhaps, for men like Beck, who understood
how strong was the oath's compulsion and yet knew that defeat was
inevitable and that ultimately those men who had felt compelled to
support Hitler would be held accountable for his misdeeds.

However, not all took the view that they were in conscience bound
to Hitler. In the course of mobilization a certain number of generals
were recalled whom their political unreliability had caused to be retired. Fritsch and Beck were under too heavy a cloud in this respect
to be called on for their services, but von Leeb was employed,
despite the fact that Hitler considered him "an incorrigible anti-
Nazi", as were also von Kleist and von Hammerstein-Equord, and
the latter for a time seems seriously to have considered the project,
charming in its simplicity, of inviting Hitler to inspect his troops and
then simply arresting him. Appropriate judicial proceedings were, of
course, to follow. It is indeed stated that just before the departure of
the British Embassy staff from Berlin, a certain von Schlabrendorff,
of the Conservative opposition (the name is not unhonoured in
Prussian history), informed one of the secretaries of the plan.

Hitler, for his part, was careful to miss no opportunity of circum-
scribing the influence of his generals. During the final occupation of
Bohemia and Moravia, he had departed somewhat from his practice
of the previous year and reverted to the traditional Prussian wartime
policy of giving the commanding general plenary powers for the
control of the district where he had his troops, though civilian commissars of the Party were attached to him. This was now changed. On
August 30th a new ministerial council for the defence of the civilian
population was set up, and at the suggestion of Göring, its president,
Hitler made arrangements which in the circumstances were entirely
without precedent. By turning the *Gauleiters* and *Reichstadthalters*
into Defence Commissars, he endeavoured to safeguard himself
against a possible coup by refractory generals and at the same time
sought to ensure the maintenance among the population as a whole
of a satisfactory *Weltanschauung*.

These measures were the precursors of other innovations, which
not only further undermined the status of the service chiefs but
tended completely to destroy the Army's traditional principle of
human relationships. Thus Hitler's "Basic Order No. 1" of January
1940 laid it down that any person charged with the carrying out of an
order should only be given such information as was absolutely necessary for its execution, and that only at the last practicable moment.

This order, born of an almost pathological distrustfulness and an obsessive craving for secrecy, went directly against the whole tradition of Moltke and Gneisenau.

X

Despite the uncertainty which had been caused by the repeated cancellation of orders, and the difficulty of the terrain over which the deployment for the great encircling movement had to be carried out, the attack on Poland proceeded according to plan. Roughly 1,300,000 German troops at this moment stood under arms. To date, the use of large closed bodies of tanks acting in co-operation with aircraft had never been tried out, nevertheless this proved to be the first of a number of triumphs for the theories of Guderian.

The Polish Army, the command of which had been personally assumed by Marshal Rydz-Smigly, had only a single tank division, and even that was incomplete. It had large forces of cavalry, one division and eleven independent brigades, but these proved themselves helpless in the face of the modernized warfare of Germany. Moreover, the weather was perfect for tanks, the ground remaining dry, and the Polish Air Force was in many cases surprised by the German bombers and destroyed on the ground on the first day of the war, while modern weapons disposed without much difficulty of the Polish cavalry, which usually charged with the sabre in close formation.

To increase its disadvantages, the Polish Army deployed its 22 divisions all along the line without concentrating special strength at any particular point. The 4th German Army attacking from Pommerania under von Kluge thus had little difficulty in establishing contact with von Küchler's 3rd Army which was based on East Prussia and was driving eastwards towards the Narev, while the 8th under Blaskowitz tied down the enemy forces in Posen. In the south, von Rundstedt and von Manstein, his Chief of Staff, were acting more or less on their own. Their orders had been to advance in a southeasterly direction, but after the first successes they swung off to the north, so that the Polish forces in Warsaw were cut off. The reckless drive of Reichenau, who commanded the 10th Army, was largely responsible for the success of this manoeuvre. The result of it was that the Polish forces were cut into two, and the Polish southern army was easily forced to surrender by the 14th Army under List.

In the second half of September the German armies began to

approach Warsaw, and it was at this stage that Hitler intervened personally in the conduct of the campaign and ordered the ruthless bombardment of that city. Brauchitsch and Halder insisted that its surrender was merely a matter of time, and that it would be more prudent to transfer their heavy artillery to the ill-equipped western front. The General Staff, however, did not know that arrangements had been made for the intervention of Russia at a particular point of time, or that Hitler in giving this order for the bombardment of Warsaw was pursuing a definite political object. He was concerned to see that the city did not fall into Russian hands. It had therefore to become German as quickly as possible. It was during this stage of the war that Fritsch fell. He had been refused the command of an army, as we have seen, but followed his regiment to the front. In all probability he sought death deliberately.

The intervention of the Russian Army, which took the General Staff completely by surprise, finally sealed Poland's fate and with it that of the old semi-feudal order of its society. There was a further unexpected development which radically changed the whole character of the war. Three divisions of the Waffen S.S. had accompanied the Army into Poland, and had for the time being been placed under the latter's commanders, though the Waffen S.S. served a purpose wholly different from that which the generals pursued. Hitler now gave it out that the governing class and intelligentsia of Poland were to be exterminated and took steps to use the appropriate instruments to that end.

The effects of his decision were soon apparent. As soon as the campaign came to an end, which it did in the latter part of September, Colonel-General Blaskowitz was made Commander in Chief in Poland with headquarters in Spala. The administration of the conquered territories was, however, turned over as quickly as possible to civilians. A demarcation line having been drawn between the Russian and German zones, the territories which had originally been German were incorporated in the Reich together with a narrow Polish fringe, while the rest of the Polish territory was turned into a "Government General" under the Austrian Seyss-Inquart, who was followed in 1940 by Frank.

It was not long before considerable friction developed between the Governor General and Blaskowitz. Blaskowitz, who was very much a man of the old school, felt compelled to take steps against the excesses of the S.S. and the German police. He objected strongly to the persecution, which now began, of the Jews and of the old

Polish governing class. Military courts were set up which in some cases condemned members of the S.S. to death for murder, arson and rape. General von Küchler also had some violent disputes with Koch, the *Gauleiter* and Defence Commissar of East Prussia, on account of the scandalous behaviour of S.S. and Party organizations in the Polish districts which had been joined to the Reich, while the deputy Commander in Chief, General Petzel, tried hard to stop the persecution of Jews in the newly-formed Warthegau and endeavoured to have the S.S. men concerned proceeded against and punished. At length, Blaskowitz made an elaborate report on the atrocities committed by the S.S. which carried the fight between the Army and S.S. into a new phase.

Ulrich von Hassell in his diaries says that this report was never sent forward, but Hitler certainly knew that it had been made and bore Blaskowitz a great deal of ill-will on account of his action, all the more so since a number of members of the *Leibstandarte Adolf Hitler* had been among those condemned by the military courts, and complained to Brauchitsch of the Army's "outmoded conception of chivalry". He also expressed his dissatisfaction with the conduct of officers who had called on Cardinal Sapieha in Cracow, and chafed at the delay in the confiscation of the property of Prince Radziwill. However, by now even the O.K.W. itself was becoming almost as concerned as the General Staff about the S.S. being turned into a separate army distinguished by its peculiar proficiency in *Weltanschauung*, since this development was producing a dualism of a most disturbing kind. This circumstance makes it all the more strange that Jodl did not feel called upon even to read Blaskowitz's report, which he regarded as uncalled for; Jodl's conduct in this matter can hardly be dismissed as wholly lacking in significance.

XI

The collapse of Poland now made the west the decisive theatre of the war. Something under a hundred divisions, all those available, in fact, except twelve used to watch the Italian frontier, were drawn up by the French along the Maginot line and in Northern France, while, as in 1914, a British Expeditionary Force had duly arrived on the scene. Apart from a local operation with limited objectives in the Saar, the French undertook nothing whatever, though according to Jodl's evidence at Nuremberg they could easily have worsted the weak German forces on this front. The German divisions mobilized at the outbreak of war numbered ninety-eight. Of these, thirty-three were gradually diverted to the west and distributed among the 1st, 5th and 7th Armies, and also among yet another set of forces under Hammerstein-Equord.

As we have seen, von Leeb was Commander in Chief on the western front. He was, as we have also seen, hostile to the régime, though oddly enough he seems to have known nothing of Hammerstein-Equord's projects for a coup. However, there can be no doubt about his attitude, to which in the main his Chief of Staff, von Sodenstern, and Prince Adalbert of Bavaria, a member of his staff, were sympathetic.

Now, as has been said, von Leeb was a leading expert in defensive strategy, but there seems little doubt that his opposite number, Gamelin, was to at least an equal degree defensively minded, so much so, in fact, that the opinion began to prevail, especially among the older General Staff officers, that France did not seriously intend to carry on the war at all. Thus, the conviction gained ground that a peaceful solution of the conflict was still well within the bounds of possibility.

Both Brauchitsch and Halder now formed the resolve to put the whole conduct of the war on a defensive basis, and this without further reference to Hitler. Brauchitsch clung desperately to Hitler's assurance that the Polish war would not lead to a world conflict. Von Stülpnagel held it inadvisable even to put any questions to Hitler on the matter. He was all for presenting him with an accomplished fact. Even Jodl and Keitel, being equally nonplussed by France's failure to relieve Poland by attacking on her own, were coming round to the view that it might be possible to localize the conflict, and indeed at first sight the situation seemed to present all the signs of a stalemate.

According to Jodl's evidence, Hitler in September 1939 was still uncertain what attitude to take. To remain permanently on the defensive seemed to him militarily inconceivable, but both *Wehrmachtführungsstab* and General Staff assured him that it was impossible to break through the Maginot line. Moreover, if a frontal attack were attempted and failed, the danger would immediately arise of an Allied flank attack directed through Holland and Belgium into the Ruhr. The nightly passage over Holland and Belgium of British aircraft on their way to Germany convinced men like Jodl that Britain would respect the neutrality of neither of these countries.

However, the speed of his victory over Poland had convinced Hitler of the excellence of the new German Army, so that he believed that he could end the war quite quickly by a similar lightning campaign in the west. A heavy-handed attempt to induce England to negotiate—it was made in the form of a public speech—bore no fruit whatever. This strengthened Hitler's determination and brought to nothing any hopes the generals may have entertained of confronting him with a defensive stalemate.

Besides the idea of a lightning campaign in the west, Hitler was turning over other plans in his mind. One was an attack on Gibraltar, to be carried out with the aid of Spain. Another was a project to gain possession of the Norwegian coast, and thus acquire new submarine bases against Britain. This last had the backing of Admiral Raeder, and its daring character appealed to Hitler's galloping imagination. It was given the name "Exercise Weser", and came more and more to take the character of a personal venture of Hitler's own, from which he largely excluded the General Staff.

The more he thought of it, the more the idea of ending the war by a brilliant *coup de main* began to appeal to Hitler's mind. He now, however, began to encounter the growing opposition of the Army's Commander in Chief, in which the latter was effectively supported by his Chief of Staff.

Halder had at first been well satisfied with the Army's performance in Poland, but as time went on doubts began to enter his mind. In many cases the infantry had lacked the offensive spirit of 1914, and it needed a ruthless sacrifice of officers' lives in order to get the rank and file to follow. The toll of regular officers had thus been unduly large. Further, the state of the Army's equipment was thoroughly unsatisfactory. Even in 1940 many of the new divisions were to be compelled to make do with Czech equipment, while serviceable numbers of the new tank models III and IV were not to be forthcoming till February. General Thoma's evidence shows that the six tank divisions committed in Poland possessed 250 tanks each, which is a good working index of the general state of things. All this taken in conjunction with the condition of morale, makes it understandable that the General Staff should have believed the German Army to be no match for the French, which in many ways it still considered the best in the world.

Meanwhile the continued failure of France to take the initiative strengthened the hopes for an early peace. Stülpnagel, still acting as *Oberquartiermeister I* in the General Staff, drew up a report in which he committed to writing his advocacy of the pure defensive, and von Leeb drew up a report in a similar sense for Brauchitsch, in which he expressed the fear that unless diplomacy were given an early opportunity to negotiate, the resulting enlargement of the war would sooner or later bring in the United States, with consequences no man could foresee.

Hitler cut any such misgivings short by issuing on October 9th his first directive for the campaign against Holland and Belgium (Directive No. 6), the code word for the campaign being "Case Yellow". In it he pointed out that a long waiting period would lead to the ending to the advantage of the Allies of Belgian and Dutch neutrality, and would strengthen the power of his enemies. He therefore proposed to defeat as strong sections of the French and British armies as possible and to acquire a large area on the Channel coast as a base for naval and air operations against Britain. Thus a new and somewhat cruder Schlieffen plan was born.

The new measure was accompanied by certain changes in command. Hammerstein-Equord had been relieved of his command (the embarrassing frequency of his invitations to Hitler to visit his troops had aroused the latter's suspicions) and out of his group of forces (the *Armee-Abteilung A*) there was now formed Army Group A. Stülpnagel was given command of this, with Manstein as his Chief of Staff and headquarters at Coblenz. Further, on October 10th, von Bock, with von Salmuth as Chief of Staff, was given command over a newly formed Army Group B, with headquarters at Bad Godesberg. This meant that with von Leeb's forces, three army groups were now concentrated on the west.

The deployment plan which the General Staff drew up and which was intended to conform as much as possible to the Schlieffen ideal, made the following provisions. Army Groups B and A, in the north and centre of the western front respectively, were, as in 1914, to advance into Northern France through Belgium, their task being to destroy the enemy forces north of the Somme and break through to the Channel coast. The task of Army Group B was, in regard to Holland, to do no more than make the frontier secure. In regard to Belgium, however, they were to push through on both sides of Liège. Should it be impossible to avoid violating Dutch neutrality in the region of the "Maestricht Appendix", this was to form the subject of friendly negotiations with the Dutch.

Army Group A was thus to form the southern wing of the enveloping movement. Meanwhile, Army Group C, consisting of the

1st and 7th Armies, was to cover the front between the Ardennes and Switzerland and hold down the troops occupying the Maginot line. All dispositions were to be complete by November 5th.

XII

All commanders of the army groups concerned now submitted reports favouring the maintenance of the defensive—a view that was shared by the Chief of the General Staff. A frontal attack by the enemy on the entire German Army seemed out of the question, and in the event of an attack through Belgium and Holland the German command would always have time for counter measures. Halder thus felt that he could take full responsibility for maintaining a waiting attitude.

Among various alternative schemes, however, which were submitted by the army groups, that of von Manstein is of peculiar interest. Manstein suggested that in the event of the enemy taking the offensive, a mass of tanks should thrust through the "Ardennes gap", the failure to fortify which had caused some disquiet to French generals prior to 1914. The direction of the thrust should be towards Sedan. Once Sedan was reached, there was excellent tank country, and the movement could then continue along the north bank of the Somme, towards Abbeville and the coast. Any forces which the enemy had thrown into Belgium would thus be cut off and compelled to fight with their front reversed. The plan was a bold one, for it left the southern flank of the advancing army exposed, but it had the advantage that, despite its offensive character, it left Germany innocent of any violation of neutrality. But precisely because its idea was novel and original, it did not find favour with the General Staff, which for a time ignored it.

On the whole, the General Staff's new Schlieffen plan took little account of the potentialities of the tank, for the employment of which the Belgian, and even more so the Dutch, terrain was not too favourable. Curiously enough, the French Commander in Chief was equally conservative in his outlook, so that his ideas moved along much the same lines as those of his enemies. He thus exactly anticipated what the German General Staff devised, and concentrated substantial motorized forces along the Belgian frontier. Thus the German General Staff might well have sustained a reverse, because their enemies were on this occasion as uninspired as themselves.

However, this second Schlieffen plan aroused grave misgivings on political grounds, not only in Brauchitsch and Halder, but in Warlimont, the head of the *Wehrmachtführungsstab*, for not even Warlimont wanted Belgium violated. Such an action might bring all the powers of the western world against Germany.

A new and serious crisis was now developing between Hitler and the Army command. Weizsäcker had detailed one of his ambassadors, von Etzdorf, to maintain liaison with the General Staff, Etzdorf being privy to the plans of the opposition in the Foreign Office. Now Halder had told Etzdorf in October, in Zossen, the General Staff's wartime headquarters, that everything must be done to prevent an offensive in the west. Eventually von Bülow-Schwante, the sometime Chief of Proctocol, now an ambassador, who was also in close touch with Beck, undertook the task of warning King Leopold of Belgium that an invasion of his country was impending. Meanwhile, Warlimont, who knew nothing of this, took a somewhat similar step on his own, though Warlimont, who acted through the military attaché in Brussels, Lieutenant-Colonel Rabe von Pappenheim, was actuated more by the fear that the presence of French troops on his border might move Leopold to abandon his neutrality.

Both Bülow-Schwante and Warlimont hoped that Leopold might use his numerous connections to bring about an offer of mediation, and in point of fact an attempt at mediation by Leopold and Queen Wilhelmina of the Netherlands was made in November. Such efforts were quite useless, however. Hitler had made up his mind.

XIII

Meanwhile the General Staff was beginning to act on its own, and since it seemed impossible to deflect Hitler from his proposed march on Paris and Brussels, gave serious thought to the only remaining expedient, which was a march on Berlin. Certain military provisions actually began to be made for this, for the Chief of the Transport Department in the General Staff, Major-General Gehrke, was in a position to control troop movements in such a way as to concentrate reliable divisions and above all to concentrate tank forces on to the capital. Halder went so far as to organize a special staff for this operation under Lieutenant-Colonel Grosscurth.

Desirable as they considered the scheme, not all General Staff officers were convinced of its practicability. Thus, Lieutenant-Colonel Röhricht, Head of the Training Department and an old colleague of Schleicher's, feared that Göring's control of the *Luftwaffe* and the A.A. presented so formidable a handicap to the enterprise that it was not worth undertaking, while Colonel-General Fromm, the Commander of the second line or *ersatz* forces, averred quite frankly that the troops would follow Hitler rather than their generals. Halder's view, however, was that a collective action by the army group commanders was quite a feasible idea and that there was no reason why a show of force should not be used to lend weight to their arguments.

Beck was given information about these plans, and was in the event of an attempted coup to take over command of the armed forces. Needless to say, Dr Goerdeler's circle was also kept informed, and there came into being a plot in which perhaps the best and most honourable men in the country were involved. Certainly the shadow government which was now formed, consisting of diplomats, high administrators and men of learning, would have compelled the respect of any country in the world.

The essence of this conspiracy was that there was to be nothing in the nature of a pronunciamento of a few conspiring generals, but that the Army was to act as a single body under its lawful leaders. Brauchitsch had knowledge of the affair and had declared that he was ready to let it take its course. Unfortunately men of very high character, such as those here concerned, are often very ill adapted to work in the twilight world in which conspirators must move, and the judgment of German generals when it came to politics was almost invariably defective. What would have happened if the plot had been pursued further, it is difficult to say, but it came to an end quite suddenly—and, one might almost say, quite needlessly.

Time was pressing, both for Hitler and for the generals. All preparations for the attack were to be ready by November 5th, the attack itself being ordered for November 12th. On that same November 5th, Brauchitsch once more sought to warn Hitler of the dangers of a precipitate offensive undertaken in what might well be unsuitable weather. Hitler's answer was an elemental outburst of rage, during which he screamed that he knew very well that the generals were planning something else than the offensive he had ordered. In actual fact, he knew nothing of the kind. The remark was simply the outcome of his fevered imagination and frustrated rage, but it frightened Brauchitsch very badly, and he naturally thought that the plot had been discovered. The result was that the whole scheme was dropped. Hitler for his part was made somewhat more anxious and suspicious than he was already by the interview. Even Keitel was told that he was conspiring with the generals at Zossen and doing nothing but encourage their resistance. Keitel for the first time asked to be relieved of his post, a request which Hitler refused, saying very characteristically that he had no right to make it.

Taking it all in all, November 1939 was a somewhat tense month. On the 7th the orders for the attack were cancelled. This process of giving and cancelling orders for the western offensive was to be repeated no less than sixteen times between November 12th and January 20th. Meanwhile, on the 9th, the Beer Hall *Putsch* was celebrated in Munich. Half an hour after Hitler had left there was a mysterious bomb explosion in the *Bürgerbräukeller*, where the festivities had taken place. The person responsible remained for some time undiscovered. Mussolini thought that the whole thing was prearranged, since the Press seemed almost suspiciously anxious to ascribe it to the British secret service. Even so, it seems most probable that it was the work of an isolated individual, for Hitler's fear of assassination rose afterwards in a most marked way and this growing conviction that he might at any time lose his life at the hands of an assassin seems to have urged him on to perfect his plans for his offensive with renewed ardour.

Two incidents that occurred about this time are worth recording. While the main conspiracy was brewing, von Leeb, who was ignorant of it, was working on a plan of his own. It was to see Hitler, with the other two army group commanders, and tell him flatly that the principal commanders of his Army refused to undertake the offensive.

The day after the Munich bomb explosion, a meeting took place at Leeb's request between the three army group commanders at Rundstedt's headquarters in Coblenz, their Chiefs of Staff being present. Leeb's initiative in this matter is significant. Von Etzdorf is said once to have remarked to von Hassell that of the three commanders, Bock was vain, Rundstedt worn out (a judgment which hardly seems confirmed by his military achievements), and that Leeb alone of the three was truly capable. However, if Leeb had the qualifications for leadership in this affair, they were not destined to be used. Bock and Rundstedt held his proposal to be mutiny. So Leeb returned to his headquarters at Frankfurt feeling that there was nothing to be done. What he did not know was that he was already under the constant surveillance of the Gestapo.

The other incident might well have had first-rate propaganda value for the military opposition, had they felt themselves in a position to use it. Himmler had published a decree the general sense of which was as follows. War was a form of bloodletting in which the best blood was often dissipated. It was therefore the duty of married women, whose husbands were in the field, not to deny themselves to members of the S.S. One of Leeb's divisional commanders, Lieutenant-General Groppe, as soon as the decree was brought to his notice, publicly refused to continue his service. He was imprisoned and condemned to death, though later released. Leeb did his utmost to protect his divisional commander, and his sharp protests ultimately brought about the withdrawal of the decree.

XIV

On November 23rd, Hitler called his service chiefs together for a secret briefing. He made a long, rambling speech, some of the points of which had already formed the subjects of secret memoranda. Its most important point was the vulnerability of the Ruhr; the more territory that was occupied to the west of it, the safer the Ruhr would be. The second point of interest is the repetition of his insistence on Germany's need for increased living space and his repeated avowal of his intention to create this for her by the sword. For the moment the situation was exceptionally favourable. Germany's rear was secured by the pact with Soviet Russia, but nobody knew how long this situation would last. The death of Stalin might present Germany with a new situation—as might that of Mussolini—and Germany could only oppose Russia when she was free in the west.

Meanwhile in Germany the dominant problem continued to be Hitler's projected offensive in the west. Halder's plan for the latter was so far the only one that was being seriously considered, though Manstein had not given up hope that his own plans of attacking through the Ardennes might still win approval. Originally conceived as a riposte to an enemy attack, it might, he felt, still be accepted as the basis of the offensive on which Hitler now seemed irrevocably determined. He saw that a frontal attack through Belgium, that being, as he rightly guessed, exactly what the enemy was anticipating, might at best lead to what Schlieffen had called "an ordinary victory" but not to the desired annihilation of the opposing force.

As has been pointed out, the Manstein plan had the double advantage of respecting Belgian neutrality and of encircling the enemy in case the latter decided to violate it, but Brauchitsch and Halder set their faces against it, hoping as they did that they could still postpone the offensive indefinitely. So when Manstein's persistence became inconvenient, they removed him from his post and set him to building up a newly organized army corps at home. But Manstein had Rundstedt behind him, and Schmundt, on a visit to the latter's headquarters, happened to see Manstein's memorandum, which he sent on to Hitler. Hitler was immediately taken by the boldness of the idea, and at a special meeting, which Schmundt arranged at the Chancellery, surprised Brauchitsch and Halder by showing a sudden interest in Manstein's scheme.

Now on January 10th, a German courier plane lost its way and landed in Belgian territory. Among the passengers, as it happened, were some General Staff officers who were carrying a copy of Halder's plan, which now fell into Belgian hands. The result was that Belgian frontier forces facing Germany were strengthened, since Leopold was determined to protect his neutrality, but the plan was not handed on to the French. Hitler raved, but as a matter of fact it would have been even more fortunate for Germany if Leopold had been less discreet, for when the Manstein plan was ultimately adopted, every effort had to be made to remedy Leopold's unfortunate omission by veiled hints through Intelligence that a new Schlieffen plan was to be carried into effect.

XV

At the beginning of February, Hitler finally abandoned the idea of carrying out his western offensive during the winter, and began increasingly to occupy himself with the Norwegian project. Nevertheless, preparations for "Case Yellow" went on, headquarters being arranged in advance for Hitler in the Black Forest, in the Eifel district and on the Ziegenberg in Hesse. Hitler, as usual, took interest in innumerable details such as the fitting of German tanks with Czech weapons, and in all the other minutiae of preparation.

On February 17th he entertained a number of generals to lunch, among them being the former military attaché in London, von Schweppenburg. Manstein was also present, and found an opportunity of talking about his plan. This time he won Hitler over, but Hitler now joined Manstein's plan on to that of a general attack on France, Belgium and Holland, thus depriving it of all its political point.

A start was immediately made on a new plan, in which a decision was to be sought on the left flank by means of a massed tank attack. Hitler's decision meant a new loss of prestige to Halder, but Warlimont was later to say that Hitler's only two real strategic achievements were his decision to strike with strong forces from East Prussia towards the Narev and his adoption of the Manstein plan.

All this time the main plan was still being shadowed by a counter plan, and the civilian opposition was still at its efforts in Switzerland and at the Vatican to bring the war to a conclusion, while Papen was working on the Dutch Ambassador in Ankara and also at long range on the King of Sweden, to undertake some step that might result in mediation. Now these hopes began to dwindle, while the General Staff began to incline increasingly to Fromm's opinion that the rank and file would stick to Hitler, all the more so since the reserve officers who were now being posted contained so many National Socialists.

Jodl's evidence at Nuremberg has a special relevance to this problem, for Jodl's point of view was that of the typical professional soldier. He declared on this occasion that an attempted coup by isolated generals would never have succeeded. He believed a revolution by the Army acting in conjunction with the workers to be a theoretical possibility, but such a revolution just wouldn't happen in the middle of a war. Here he naturally assumed in others the existence of his own point of view. In war a soldier could do nothing but perform the duty he had sworn to do. He was quite unaware of the possible existence of any conflict of conscience on such a point—perhaps he wished to be unaware of it, but Jodl's was a pretty representative opinion.

Neither Halder nor Brauchitsch, however, saw the issues quite so sharply outlined as Jodl, or were so convinced that in a war a *coup d'état* was unthinkable, but Brauchitsch was a man given to vacillation to a degree that as early as November 1939 had made some of those army commanders who were pressing for definite action uneasy. Brauchitsch indeed had been careful as far as possible to conceal his own views and in doubtful cases had hidden behind the Führer. Perhaps their dissatisfaction with Brauchitsch and Halder did less than justice to the tragic situation of these men, but the dissatisfaction was undoubtedly there. From time to time the army commanders had been tempted to suggest to Brauchitsch that he should resign and make room for a man more ready for decisive action. Many saw just such a man in Manstein. They not only believed him to have the requisite strength of character, but thought he was the one man who could succeed in making Hitler see the force of a reasoned argument founded on expert knowledge, even when its conclusions went contrary to his views.

Halder still maintained contact with the opposition. In Berlin at the Guards Cavalry Club he had a meeting with Crown Prince George of Saxony, who had become a Jesuit and was accounted one of the most brilliant minds of the Catholic resistance. In March he notes a talk with Dr Goerdeler, who again stressed the need for doing everything possible to secure a negotiated peace before the offensive was launched. Von Hassell admittedly gained the impression from Goerdeler that Halder now believed a compromise to be out of the question and thought there was nothing to be done but fight the war through until such time as defeat had given Hitler's prestige a decisive blow. He did, however, tell Goerdeler that the Army would do its duty, even if it meant going against the will of the government. Mr Sumner Welles, the U.S. Under-Secretary of State, visited Germany about this time to ascertain what chances of success were likely to attend an American effort at mediation, but Mr Welles very definitely left the generals under the impression that the Western Powers recognized Hitler as having full power to negotiate. Perhaps this was unfortunate, but if the generals enjoyed little standing in foreign eyes at the time of Mr Welles' visit, they enjoyed even less after they had launched their attack on France. Those who had maintained contact with them in England felt that they had been betrayed. After all, it had been the Army that was going to overturn Hitler, yet here was that same Army putting its heel on the West.

XVI

For the time being, however, attention began to be principally focused on "Exercise Weser", and this meant the employment of Germany's relatively weak naval forces. It also involved the overrunning of Denmark, with whom a non-aggression pact had been signed.

In the General Staff the view prevailed that such an undertaking would be impossible if it involved the commitment of large forces which had in this case to be transported by sea. Hitler, however, did not charge the General Staff with the preparation of this undertaking, but put the exclusive responsibility for it on the O.K.W. and the *Wehrmachtführungsstab*. The Commander in Chief of the Army was instructed to prepare six divisions, while a general of the Army,

Colonel-General von Falkenhorst, was put in charge of the expeditionary force. His chief qualification for the task seems to have been that he had taken part in the Finnish expedition in 1918. He was now given complete and unhampered control of an entire theatre of war. This practice, which was soon to be extended to other military undertakings, really amounted to the creation of a second General Staff. It was Hitler's answer to the General Staff's opposition. Its result was that Jodl, as head of the *Wehrmachtführungsstab*, was now recognized at the Führer Headquarters as the leading military personality of the day.

Jodl, like Halder, was a Bavarian, and there is no question that Hitler possessed in him a soldier of the highest professional attainments. Hitler's intuition could now be supplemented by a very clear sober mind, and one superbly trained in military thinking. On the human side Jodl had nothing to give, nor would Hitler have wanted any such completion of his own individuality, while Jodl himself would never have entertained the notion of stepping outside his own purely military domain.

Jodl's conception of his duty was very simple. His oath had imposed on him the sole duty of winning the war, a task which his ambition and his confidence in Hitler's genius caused him to regard as well within the bounds of possibility. This was the limit of his obligation however. Politics and questions of a general character were not his concern. He was one of the last of the experts, pure and simple, which the General Staff produced.

The way from Moltke to Jodl had been long and had led to an ever-increasing contraction of mental horizons. Thus it was that his intercourse with Hitler could produce in Jodl a conception of war that threw over not only Clausewitz but even Ludendorff, although it had some share in the latter's thought. According to this conception, war was the basic element in politics, the prime mover of all things. War was thus an end in itself. That was why none of his disputes with Hitler (and there were many of them) ever turned on fundamental values, but only on questions of military expediency.

Jodl's diary gives a good picture of Hitler's changes of mind during February and March, as he weighed the relative merits of letting "Case Yellow" and "Exercise Weser" have priority in point of time. It was only in March that Hitler decided that "Exercise Weser" was to come first. Meanwhile a great deal of improvisation had to be undertaken. Plans had never been made for a campaign in Denmark or Norway, and the necessary maps had to be got together from

Berlin bookshops—a very tricky business considering the secrecy that had to be preserved. Unfortunately both the Danish and Norwegian military attachés were quite unsuspecting, being convinced that the German Naval and Military High Commands were in no position to carry out any ventures overseas. When Admiral Canaris, in his fanatical determination to cut across every plan of Hitler's, tried to warn them of what was intended, he encountered crude incredulity. The attachés thought such warning was a feint. Sweden alone became suspicious, her apprehensions being aroused when Swedish diplomats heard of the massing of transports at Stettin. Sweden then became concerned for the safety of her iron ore deposits.

On February 5th, a special staff foregathered in Berlin to take charge of "Exercise Weser". For the moment the *Luftwaffe* was not represented, a circumstance which occasioned a burst of rage on the part of Göring. The practicability was first considered of combining the attack on Norway with an attack on Holland, so that two sally ports against England might be gained at one blow, but this idea was abandoned because the attack on Holland could not be separated from the main western offensive.

On March 13th, Jodl naïvely noted in his diary that the Führer could not yet give the order for "Exercise Weser" to begin, as he had not yet found a suitable pretext. Five days later Hitler met Mussolini on the Brenner. The Duce expressed his determination to enter the war at Germany's side, but emphasized that Italy was not in a position to carry on a long war. Hitler believed himself able to reassure Mussolini on that point, however, as his conviction that a victory in the west would end the war could not be shaken. It was on April 2nd that Hitler finally gave the order for the occupation on the 9th of Denmark and Norway.

Since the troops had to be transported almost under the guns of the British Battle Fleet, the whole of Germany's naval strength was marked down for their protection. Contrary to what might reasonably have been expected, the operation was successful, although the Navy incurred heavy losses off the Norwegian coast. On the first day, one heavy cruiser and two light cruisers were lost, also two transports and an anti-aircraft vessel. Somewhat later, a large part of the destroyers employed there were lost in an action before Narvik.

Denmark capitulated without resisting when, on the morning of the 9th, German vessels appeared in Copenhagen harbour and landed troops. The latter immediately occupied both the city and the Royal Palace. The Norwegian forces, however, resisted the aggression as best they could, despite their numerical inferiority, while the British hastily threw an expeditionary force into Norway, so that the German forces which had occupied Narvik harbour were cut off.

As Hitler's responsible Chief of Staff, Jodl now learned something of the meaning of Hitler's bad nerves and of his complete inability to control himself. Laconic entries in his diary, such as "Excitement terrible", and the single word *"Führungschaos"* (chaos in command) testify to the nature of the effect on Hitler of the continuous bad news. It was only with difficulty that Jodl persuaded his Supreme War Lord not to abandon the whole venture. It needed the intervention of Lieutenant-Colonel von Lossberg, the Army's General Staff officer in the *Wehrmachtführungsstab*, to prevent an order being sent out for the evacuation of Norway.

Hereupon Hitler went to the other extreme, and developed the idea of overrunning Sweden and sending his troops across that country to relieve those who had been cut off in Norway. Only when a Swedish admiral, who acted as the King of Sweden's representative, made it unmistakably clear that Sweden was determined to resist, did he abandon this intention.

It was not until May 4th that the situation in Norway was clarified and the British Expeditionary Force driven back to its ships. As in the case of Poland, a member of the Party was immediately sent as civil administrator to Norway. The customary clash of orders between the Party and the military now assumed proportions which aroused even Keitel's misgivings.

Meanwhile, according to Jodl's diary, Hitler had decided on April 27th that "Case Yellow" was to start between May 1st and May 7th. On the 5th Jodl notes that "the Führer has found suitable grounds for Case Yellow". Two days later he suspected that the whole plan had been betrayed. A highly remarkable telephone conversation had been tapped between the Belgian Ambassador to the Vatican and Brussels, which led to the inference that the plan had "leaked" from Germany. On the 8th, Holland mobilized, and much against his will Hitler postponed the operation to the 10th.

Jodl's anxiety in the matter of indiscretions from the German side was better founded than he knew. On May 9th, Canaris sent a last warning through Oster, his Chief of Staff, to the Dutch military attaché in Berlin. Oster was a close personal friend of the latter, and felt free to inform him that "that swine" had gone off to the western front.

XVII

The French and British forces had at this moment deployed two army groups under Generals Billotte and Prételat to the north and south of Sedan. Billotte's army group was, if necessary, to march with four armies and the six divisions of the British Expeditionary Force into Belgium in order to meet an enemy flanking thrust. On the German side, however, the centre of the attack lay in accordance with the Manstein plan with Army Group A, where under von Kleist there had been gathered together the greatest tank concentration the world had ever known. It consisted of three tank corps arranged in two blocks in echelon, with a third block containing the motorized infantry to give stiffening to the rear. A corresponding concentration of 1,000 aircraft was to support the tank thrust. The main problem of this force was not so much that of breaking through as of keeping the flow of tanks steadily moving and of keeping them supplied with fuel. It was in this connection that von Kleist's Chief of Staff, Colonel Zeitzler, first attracted notice.

On the 10th, the attack began. Hitler had chosen as his pretext the assertion that the Franco-British forces were planning to break into Holland and Belgium in order to attack the Ruhr, and so 110 German divisions were hurled against 135 of the enemy. Despite the numerical inferiority of the German forces, Jodl could note in his diary on the following day that the operation was surprisingly successful. The 6th Army, under Reichenau, forced an entry into Belgium. Parachutists and airborne troops under General Student, together with the 18th Army under von Küchler, seized Holland, which surrendered in five days. Meanwhile, von Leeb stood fast in the south awaiting developments.

The most terrible blow of all struck the Ardennes. The 9th French Army under General Corap which had been holding this part of the line had been moved off to Normandy in order to counter the thrust into Belgium. At the moment of attack the only available means of defence were four reserve divisions and the Belgian Chasseurs Ardennais. Corap's attempt to reverse the movement of his troops was unsuccessful.

Billotte's army group meanwhile had gone into Belgium together with the British, and reached the Albert Canal, but the further away they got from the main body of the French forces, the more effective was bound to be the thrust of the German tanks. These hurled themselves over the Maas on the 13th, with shrieking dive bombers preparing the way, and spread over the northern plain of France towards the coast. At the last moment they struck north in an operation which Churchill later described as a cut by a sickle.

It was not long before Hitler proved that he was wholly incapable of using the instrument that was in his hands. There was nothing about him of Moltke's calm. He alternated between fits of excessive nervousness and childish glee. On May 17th, Halder's notes carry the entry, "Führer terribly nervous", and state that he was frightened of his own success and would have preferred to hold up the whole tank drive, the southern flank of which was somewhat exposed. On the 18th, Halder witnessed Hitler in one of those rages which so often afflict hysterical types in moments of tension. Two days later, Jodl was to see a different Hitler. Now he was certain of victory and was waiting for Italy to march in over the Alps. "Führer beside himself with joy", Jodl writes on this day. "Concerning himself with peace conditions. Restoration of territory of which German people robbed for 400 years. Preliminary negotiations in Forest of Compiègne as 1918. British can have separate peace any time they like after handing over colonies."

On May 21st the German tanks reached the Channel. The British began retreating to the Channel ports while the German tanks pressed forward towards Dunkirk. It was becoming plain that four Allied armies were virtually encircled.

On the 24th, Hitler, together with Jodl and Schmundt, flew to Charleville, and it now became obvious that thanks to his mistrust of the Army and his morbid fears, he had lost all clear sense of perspective. He ordered the heads of the tank columns to halt, just as they were about to close in on the British troops embarking at Dunkirk. He gave as his reason that he wanted to avoid the danger of being over-extended, but there were certainly other ideas in his head. Göring, so Halder says, had talked him into believing that the Army must not be allowed to have so striking a success as the capture of the whole British Expeditionary Force would provide. The *Luftwaffe* could easily prevent the embarkation of the British troops by means of a running bombardment. The real truth, however, seems to be that Hitler still hoped for an understanding with Britain. He therefore refrained from inflicting upon her a military humiliation which might make such an understanding impossible.

No less than two whole days were lost in arguments between Hitler, Brauchitsch and Rundstedt before the tanks were again set

free. In that interval the British contrived to get away the great bulk
of their troops. "You can never talk to a fool," said General Thoma
to Captain Liddell Hart when in captivity. "Hitler spoilt the chance of
victory." A few days after the "Miracle of Dunkirk", von Kleist was
told by Hitler that he had had no intention of sending his tanks into
"the mud of Flanders". "The English won't show up again in this
war, anyway." Rundstedt and von Sodenstern, Manstein's successor
as Rundstedt's Chief of Staff, were favoured with another version. It
was that Hitler wanted to make an honourable peace with England.
Even Germany's colonies were not too big a price to pay for that.
Rundstedt, who had never wanted to fight England, heard these
words with relief.

XVIII

For the time being the long succession of German victories continued. The Channel ports were taken, the Belgian Army surrendered
and the German armies regrouped with perfect smoothness for the
second phase of the battle of France, which was the attack on the
Weygand line along the Somme and the Aisne. This line, named after
the new Commander in Chief who had succeeded Gamelin, protected
Paris and the Seine basin. With the destruction of Billotte's army
group, however, France had lost her best equipped troops, and even
Weygand's talents could not save the situation.

The new grand attack began on June 5th. Von Bock thrust forward
on to the Somme with three armies, Rundstedt on the Aisne with
Army Group A. On the 10th, the Seine was crossed, and the Wey-
gand line collapsed. Von Leeb now went over to the attack along the
Maginot line, while Italy entered the war and attacked along the Alps.
The troops of von Küchler entered Paris.

Streams of refugess now crammed the roads and hindered the
movement of troops. The French government fled first to Tours and
then to Bordeaux. The aged Pétain was called to save the country in its
hour of need, and formed a government together with Weygand and
other soldiers. Halfway through June, Pétain asked for an armistice,
and on the 21st the new masters of Europe accepted the surrender
of France in Compiègne, in that same railway carriage in which
Foch had accepted the surrender of the German delegation in 1918.
The German General Staff set up its headquarters at Fontainebleau.

Hitler stood triumphant at the Channel. According to Schlieffen's
doctrine, military victory should have solved the political problem.

Yet this was not to prove true. After the war, Field-Marshal von Kleist, that very enlightened man who commanded the tanks that rolled over France, remarked as follows to Captain Liddell Hart: "The German mistake was to think that a military success could solve political problems. Indeed, under the Nazis we tended to reverse Clausewitz's dictum and to regard peace as an interruption of war."

CHAPTER XIV

THE BEGINNING OF THE CAPTIVITY

I

So long as Britain possessed an air force and a fleet, there was no way of forcing a landing on her shores. Hitler believed that she was ready for peace and unofficial feelers had been put out through the Swiss Minister in London, the British Minister in Berne, the sometime High Commissioner of the League of Nations in Danzig and also through Prince von Hohenlohe. At home, actual demobilization had already begun. However, when Halder returned to Berlin on June 30th, he was told by Weizsäcker that there was no genuine basis whatever for any peace negotiations, though Weizsäcker still thought there was a peace party in England. His notes speak of letters to King George VI from Lloyd George and the Duke of Windsor in which these men had put forward pleas for peace.

On the same day that Halder had his interview with Weizsäcker, Jodl was endeavouring to clarify his own ideas on the possible ways of continuing the war. He wrote that final victory over England was now only a matter of time. It was not essential to force a landing immediately. Britain could be brought to her knees by air attack and submarine warfare. Then, at the very end, an invasion could deal the wounded enemy her death blow.

Meanwhile, the usual rivalry between the Party and the military was springing up in Paris, since the Party and the S.S. had naturally enough taken over the conquered territories. Hitler proclaimed that the Waffen S.S. was being developed as a state militarized police, whose task it would be to relieve the Army of occupation duties. In reality this represented a further stage in the building up of a special *Weltanschauung*—or "World Outlook"—possessing Army, which was soon to attain to a strength of twenty divisions and already had the pick of all equipment and personnel. That something quite unprecedented was coming into being here is proved by the fact that a French Waffen S.S. division, "Charlemagne", emerged in the latter part of the war.

During the advance into France, there was an incident between

General Hoepner, an old enemy of the régime who was commanding a tank division, and Sepp Dietrich, the commander of the *Leibstandarte Adolf Hitler*. When the latter remarked before an attack that he would complete his task and that human life mattered very little to the S.S., Hoepner, red in the face and trembling with rage, told him that that was not the language of a decent-minded officer with a sense of responsibility. Only a butcher could think like that.

In France, as everywhere else, the Army and the General Staff were on the defensive, Himmler's ambition being clearly to build a new private army of his own. There were even efforts to call a special S.S. air force into being, to the great disgust of Göring, and the S.S. most certainly organized its own counter-espionage service under *Gruppenführer* Schellenberg, the purpose of which was to absorb the corresponding service of the military.

Like Canaris, Schellenberg pursued a policy of his own, though unlike the former he was not actually working against the régime but rather seeking to modify it in such a manner as would enhance the power of his lord and master. Schellenberg represented just one more facet of this new state within a state, which now was setting up its own business organization in *S.S. Wirtschafts und Verwaltungshauptamt*, the head office that controlled slave labour and was turning the ever-growing population of the concentration camps into a source of profit. Of the full nature of this latter activity, the military knew very little.

In the east, the Russian government had hastened to gather the fruits of the non-aggression pact. The Baltic States were incorporated in the Soviet Union. Stalin voiced anew the ancient Russian aspiration in the matter of Finland and Bessarabia, the latter of which had been allotted to Rumania in 1919. Carol's comic-opera régime was coming between the millstones of the two dictatorships. Nevertheless, the attitude of the Soviet government towards the wielders of power in Berlin remained quite impeccable. The deliveries of cereals, oil and other raw materials were punctually made.

During the war in France the forces on the eastern front consisted of seven divisions, of which two had ultimately been thrown in on the west. Meanwhile, however, beside the Russian deployment of troops in the direction of Rumania there were also considerable Russian troop concentrations in Eastern Poland and Eastern Galicia. Nobody was in a position to say whether there were any aggressive intentions behind these movements, or whether they were merely security measures. The latter construction was put on them in the

German Embassy both by the Ambassador, Count von der Schulenburg, and by Lieutenant-General Köstring, the military attaché, but
already in the spring concern for the Rumanian oil fields had been
the occasion of some anxiety.

This may in part explain why, according to Halder, the General
Staff was at the beginning of July working both on the attack on
England and on plans for an offensive in the east. It was Hitler's wish
that in the event of the former operation being undertaken, the Chief
of the Operations Department, Colonel von Greiffenberg, should become *Oberquartiermeister I*. At the same time, however, the General
Staff was also drawing up plans for putting back the main Army on
to a peacetime footing, and for the creation of a special assault force
against England, the so-called "E" Army. Meanwhile, reports were
continually reaching the General Staff of Spanish and Swedish
attempts at mediation, and it is a fact that Gustav V of Sweden was
making efforts to get conversations started between London and
Berlin. Ciano notes that Ribbentrop was definitely expecting peace.

II

On July 16th, Hitler announced to the Army command that he had
definitely decided on the invasion of England, the operation being
designated as "Sea Lion". Three days later, on the 19th, Hitler made
an official offer of peace to England in a speech in the Reichstag,
using the occasion to raise a number of generals to Field-Marshal's
rank. At the head of these were the three Army commanders, Rundstedt, Bock and Leeb. Keitel was also made a Field-Marshal.
Göring was given the rank of Reichsmarshal, which was specially
invented for the occasion, while the Chief of General Staff became a
mere Colonel-General. The peace offer which was thus made from
the tribune of the Reichstag in the presence of all the galaxy of
order-bedecked generals and admirals remained unanswered. There
was therefore nothing for it but to let Operation Sea Lion
proceed.

In the original plan of campaign, thirteen divisions were to be
available for the first assault. In addition, some twenty-six divisions
were earmarked as a reserve for the operation. In this first assault
there were to be two main landings, both carried out by Army Group
A. One of these was to be effected between Margate and Hastings,
and the other between Brighton and Portsmouth. Meanwhile, airborne troops were to seize roads over the Downs. It was presumably

expected that this assault, which hoped to gain a line running roughly from Tilbury over Aldershot to Southampton, would draw the main British force, while a further force landed in the general area Weymouth-Bournemouth.

At this point, however, the German Navy, which had lost heavily in Norway, declared that there was no hope of landing anything like so large a force, as its own strength was quite insufficient to protect it. The landing would have to be made with smaller forces on a narrower front, and even then troops would have to be filtered in at a much slower rate than the Army proposed.

These suggestions, the discussion of which took an inordinate amount of time, were emphatically rejected by Halder, who declared that one might as well put the troops through a sausage machine. Ultimately Hitler settled the matter by a compromise by which landings north of Dover were abandoned, it being hoped to take Dover from the landward side and presumably also the West Kentish coast.

The compromise pleased nobody. Göring alone retained his optimism and remained confident that "his *Luftwaffe*" would knock the British out of the skies, and in point of fact Hitler now concentrated on an aerial attack by which he had some hopes, not only of destroying the British Air Force, but of so weakening the Navy that the disadvantage under which he laboured would in part be neutralized. If he was successful in this, the assault was to be made not later than September 15th.

This decision was arrived at on July 31st. In the meantime there had been other developments. Italy had started an offensive against Egypt, which from the outset proved to be ill-starred, Mussolini's old rival, Air-Marshal Balbo, who was to have conducted it, being shot down by his own anti-aircraft; but then neither Halder nor Brauchitsch expected much from Italy.

On July 30th, these two discussed the situation. Both were agreed that the invasion of England could not be postponed indefinitely, since Britain would obviously steadily build up her defences. However, they saw other possibilities of weakening England. One was an attack on Gibraltar, another was to reinforce Italy with German tanks, yet another was to use the French position in Syria for an attack on Haifa, the terminus of the oil pipe-line. They could also urge Russia to undertake actions against the Persian Gulf, the Middle East or possibly India. Both feared the possibility that Russia might ally herself with their enemy, and for this reason set great store on preserving good relations with her. They did not regard Russia's aspirations towards possession of the Dardanelles as conflicting with any German interest, and believed that in the Balkans both powers should keep out of each other's way.

There was, however, already something ominous in the very fact that the gaze of the General Staff should sweep so far afield. Total war was now obeying its own inherent law of endless self-extension. Unfortunately the powers of the German people were far less adequate to cope with that phenomenon than they had been in 1914. Economically and otherwise they were weaker, and the alliances they had contracted, as well as those which they were shortly to gain in South-Eastern Europe, were less dependable things than those of the First World War. In addition to this, the increased range of aircraft and the effort that in consequence had to be made to attain bare security by pushing forward frontiers, represented a new element of grave disadvantage. Beck had foreseen this situation, and now the hour had come, as Beck had foreseen that it would, when the war, into which Hitler had so lightheartedly led his country, would confront it with problems beyond its capacity to solve.

During these critical weeks Hitler was a picture of vacillation. The only clear resolve that can be traced to this time is that of turning the Balkans into a German sphere of influence, and of keeping them as long as possible out of the war. Meanwhile, violent air battles were beginning to take place over England, as the *Luftwaffe's* attack began to develop. British fighters were ruthlessly committed to the defence of the local skies and German losses in planes began to exceed the rate of replacement. English bombers attacked concentrations of ships in the channel ports and endeavoured to interrupt German industrial production by night attacks. Hitler, however, rapidly lost interest in his invasion plans. On September 14th he postponed the date of "Sea Lion" from the 21st to the 24th.

On the following day, the 15th, there was a violent battle over Kent. The British authorities announced that 183 German machines were shot down, though in reality German losses only amounted to 56 as against 40 British. Actually the British had thrown in their last reserves, though the German command was unaware of that, and was becoming seriously alarmed about its own losses. The task of winning command of the English sky was now regarded as impossible, and on the 17th Hitler gave out that "Sea Lion" would for the present be postponed indefinitely.

The *Luftwaffe*, hoping by this means finally to break down British resistance, now went over to night bombardment of English industrial and residential areas. The celebrated "Blitz" on London commenced. In all, 190,000 tons of bombs were dropped, and certain places, such as Coventry, one of the centres of the aircraft industry, were partly razed to the ground. Over a period of eighty-five consecutive nights, London was made the target for eighty-two attacks. The British determination to resist, however, remained unshaken, and the *Luftwaffe* lacked sufficient machines to carry out attacks on the requisite scale. Moreover, the tactics of mass attack and so-called "bomb carpets", which were to make the attacks on Germany the terrible things they were, had as yet not been developed.

III

Other plans now came into the foreground. German diplomats, German journalists and German agents of all kinds now went to Turkey, Iran and Iraq. German control officers also went to Syria, the governor of which, General Dentz, had under him a motley array of Senegalese, Foreign Legionaries, and other troops, and was himself a supporter of Pétain and of the authoritarian State. Meanwhile, Darlan, the commander of the French Navy, declared himself ready to lead it against Britain in conjunction with the Germans if a suitable treaty could be arranged.

Postponing the consideration of this attractive offer to a more convenient time, Hitler decided for the moment to pursue the less spectacular aim of integrating France into a new European order (in regard to which he proposed sounding out Pétain and Laval) and of winning Franco for an anti-British pact. This last involved certain embarrassing complications, the Caudillo having definite territorial aspirations involving Morocco and Western Algeria, which were a little difficult to reconcile with a fair deal for France. Also he was inimical to the idea of having German troops in Spain, though distressingly insistent on German aid in rearmament.

In October Hitler had the desired meeting with Pétain and Laval in Montoire, and shortly after met Franco and his Foreign Minister, Serano Suñer, on the border in Hendaye. Although Franco declared himself in principle ready and even anxious to enter the war on the side of the Axis, the Spaniards proved to be cold realists, Franco remaining completely unimpressed by Hitler's echoing harangues and showing a regrettable appetite for hard facts. The argument begun at Hendaye continued for months, and Hitler afterwards said that he would rather have several teeth pulled out than have to negotiate with Franco again. As to Suñer, he referred to him as a Jesuit whom one just couldn't talk to at all. Hitler, however, did not abandon the idea of winning Franco's help for an undertaking against Gibraltar, and new giant guns of 60 cm. calibre were constructed for this purpose.

Indeed, on November 12th, Directive No. 18 was sent out concerning operation "Felix" (Spain) and "Isabella" (Portugal). It provided for the conquest of Gibraltar by German troops and heavy artillery and, should suitable occasion arise, the occupation of Portugal, which would provide useful submarine bases, and of the Portuguese Cape Verde Islands, Madeira and the Azores. In addition, provision was made for the defence of the Canary Islands, which belonged to Spain. These plans were undeniably the product of an imagination which had lost all sense of reality.

Hitler insisted on November 12th that all preparations should be made within two months, that being the minimum time within which the General Staff could be ready. The conduct of operations was to be with Reichenau. Canaris was sent as a special envoy to Madrid. He had been employed there during the First World War as a secret agent assisting submarines, and had numerous friends both in the government and in monarchist circles. Hitler did not yet suspect that he was one of his most dangerous enemies.

Actually it was Canaris who strongly advised Franco to take no part in the war which, he was already certain, could only result in disaster for Germany. Thenceforward, Spain concentrated troops on the Pyrenees so as to be forearmed against a possible German *coup de main*. In December, Hitler finally abandoned "Felix", for he saw clearly that he could no longer count on Spanish support.

IV

After his return from Hendaye, Hitler was confronted by a new problem, which dramatically changed the whole picture. Despite the reverses which Italy's Libyan army had sustained in North Africa— or perhaps because of this very threat to its prestige—Mussolini had decided entirely on his own account to invade Greece. Apparently Hitler's habit of the *fait accompli* was proving infectious.

In this way the Balkans became a theatre of war, a development for which Hitler was not at that time ready at all. There was now the danger to be reckoned with that British troops might land in Greece. To make matters worse, Italian troops were heavily defeated, the

Greeks going over to the counter-offensive and invading Albania. Mussolini asked for help, and the subsequent appearance of German troops in the Balkans put Russo-German relations under additional strain. Jodl, though he admitted that an attack on Greece would sooner or later be inevitable, afterwards spoke most disparagingly of Mussolini's *"Extratour"*.

Actually, however, Hitler had been seriously considering an attack on Russia since the summer. First of all, the idea of procuring more *Lebensraum* for Germany belonged to the oldest and most essential part of his doctrine. That idea was now lent wings by his inherent distrust of Russia which during all this time had never died, and also by the Soviet's obvious intention of regaining not only Finland but also all the territory on its borders that had once been held by the Czars.

Further, since a quick defeat of Britain was obviously out of the question, despite the fact that Britain's western "continental sword", France, had been rendered impotent, the question now arose of a reliable source of food and raw materials sufficient to sustain a long war. All Schulenburg's reports from Moscow assured him that Stalin was honestly desirous of maintaining friendship with Germany, but Hitler always proceeded from certain fixed assumptions and rejected anything which conflicted with these. In his eyes Russia was Britain's new potential "continental sword". Jodl was told that one day the Russians would prove to be utterly cold-blooded blackmailers and they might well even attack.

At the beginning of August 1940 Hitler gave orders for Poland to be prepared as an assembly platform for an eastern campaign and for the necessary railway lines, roads, airfields and quarters to be constructed. Ten infantry divisions and two tank divisions were moved east in this month.

Halder estimated that an eastern campaign would require eighty to one hundred divisions. The combat divisions of the enemy were at one time during this period estimated at as low a figure as seventy-five, and even fifty, though the General Staff was far from being clear on this point. Neither the Foreign Armies East Department, under Colonel Kienzel, nor Seeckt's old colleague, General Köstring, the military attaché in Moscow, nor his deputy, Colonel Krebs, who had frequently visited Russia as an officer of the *Reichswehr*, could really give exhaustive information. Köstring, however, warned the authorities not to underestimate the Russian forces, an error to which the poor Russian performance in Finland had rendered people rather prone.

Initially, Major-General Marcks, Chief of Staff to the 18th Army, who, as an old collaborator of Schleicher's, had a good knowledge of Russian affairs, was ordered to draw up an eastern plan of campaign. Marcks proposed to use Rumania as the southern assembly platform, while in the north he reckoned with the participation of Finland. The objective was the destruction of the enemy forces in Western Russia, the underestimate of whose strength the General Staff began rapidly to correct. The Russians were to be prevented from retreating into the vast interior space of Russia. In this way it was hoped to gain a line in Russia sufficiently advanced to preclude air attacks on Germany from the east.

In September 1940 Lieutenant-General Paulus, Chief of Staff to the 16th (Tank) Corps, and for some time Chief of Staff to Reichenau, was made *Oberquartiermeister I* and Deputy Chief of General Staff. Halder had hoped for Colonel von Greiffenberg, a circumspect conservative type, very unlike Paulus, who was a representative of the younger generation of staff work specialists whose whole outlook was so one-sidedly military. Hitler's aim in appointing him was to put a younger man and one endowed with greater vitality at Halder's side. General Heusinger, till then G.S.O.1 of the Operations Department, was made that Department's Chief. Like Jodl and Halder, he was a Bavarian.

On the basis of Marcks' plan, Paulus ordered a war game to establish the possibilities of an eastern campaign. The conclusion therefrom was that an attacking force could reasonably hope to attain a line running from Leningrad over Smolensk to the Dnieper. After that line had been reached, new operational decisions could be made.

Before the summer was really out, the General Staff had drawn up a scheme for a new distribution of forces. One hundred and twenty divisions were earmarked for an eastern campaign, fifty for France, seven for Norway, three for Holland. One tank division was sent to Rumania in September. In November Molotov visited Berlin with the honest intention of obtaining a peaceful solution of all outstanding differences. Russia had certain specific wishes which corresponded to the bygone policies of the Czardom, and which would also give her increased security should Hitler decide that it suited his interests to attack. These may be summarized as the acquisition of Finland and of a *point d'appui* in the Dardanelles, and the consolidation of her position in South-Eastern Europe and the Balkans. Hitler sought to divert Russian ambition towards the Middle East and to sketch out a plan for partitioning the world. The two men tended to talk past each other, and Hitler, who detested being dependent on Russia for supplies, found that confirmation of his suspicion which in his heart he was only too anxious to discover.

V

On December 5th, Halder gave Hitler a seminar on the eastern campaign. He pointed out that the facts of geography made two separate deployments necessary, since the proposed front, which ran roughly north to south, was divided by the Pripyat marshes. It was with this in mind that he proposed the employment of three army groups, two of them striking into the area of Leningrad, Minsk and Smolensk, while a third was to occupy an area from Kiev downwards into the Ukraine. In Halder's view, the Russian armies could not retreat beyond the Dnieper without being forced to give battle. Hitler, it will be remembered, had stressed, and rightly stressed, the importance of preventing the Russian armies retreating too far into the interior. He was haunted by memories of Napoleon and Charles XII of Sweden.

Halder himself was in two minds about the plan. His notes show clearly that he thought it possible to eliminate Russia as a military factor by means of a quick campaign—at least, he thought this possible as far as her western armies were concerned; but he also disliked taking on new commitments before there had been a clear decision in the west. According to one story (which is probably apocryphal), he is said to have remarked that he could "trust that fool to load the Russians on our necks", but like Hitler, Halder had himself begun to doubt the sincerity of Russian intentions. The Russian troop concentrations definitely disquieted him, though these were actually heaviest in the Ukraine and somewhat weaker in the west, and seemed in his eyes to justify preventive measures. Beck, with whom he had kept in touch (though not very closely), warned him against these, though, as was so often the case, his warnings were in vain.

The plan of the eastern campaign began to take definite shape. In Halder's notes it figures at first as "Case Otto", though in Directive No. 21 of December 18th the name "Barbarossa" is used. Directive 21 deals with the need for a speedy and decisive victory over Russia, to be achieved, if need be, before the completion of operations against England. Hitler had indeed travelled far. On an earlier occasion, when Rauschning was pointing out the dangers of a coalition between

France, Russia and Britain, Hitler had remarked that such a thing could never again come to pass and that if it did all his ventures would fail. Now his exaggerated self-confidence had reached the point where he was quite ready to attack Russia on his own.

VI

Meanwhile a number of secondary problems were clamouring for the General Staff's attention, particularly in the Balkans. If the English were to attack Greece, or if the position of the Italians in Albania deteriorated, it would become necessary to penetrate over Bulgaria into Thrace and Northern Greece. This was what underlay Hitler's Directive 20 for "Operation Marita", which provided for the accumulation of a force of seven divisions in Rumania under List. Further, if the Italians sustained further reverses in Libya this would call for still more German aid. These two possibilities together with Russia and Spain meant that the General Staff had four potential fronts with which to deal, and of these all except Spain were shortly to become active.

It was unfortunate that as its responsibilities grew, the status of the General Staff should steadily decline. While Brauchitsch and Halder were wholeheartedly in agreement that the General Staff should be recognized as the brains of the service, Hitler effectively prevented it from performing any such function by forbidding criticism of any kind. If a "Führer's Order" was issued, no kind of misgiving must be allowed to find expression. Keitel was soon made to feel the heavy hand of his master, when he handed in a memo on the dangers of what Hitler called "Clearing his rear", and tried to get Ribbentrop to speak to him in a similar sense. Hitler told him brusquely that he regarded his views as wholly erroneous whereupon Keitel again offered his resignation. Hitler dressed him down and, as on a previous occasion, told him that generals had no right to expect their release because he happened to disagree with them. Keitel duly came to heel, in gratitude for which Hitler now referred to him as having the "intelligence of a cinema doorman".

Naturally, Hitler's contemptuous attitude and his continued disregard of the General Staff's advice had its own consequences. Thus the General Staff insistently demanded an increase in the Army's available reserves of manpower, but such representations might as well have been made to the wind. Army, *Luftwaffe*, Navy, Waffen S.S., O.T. and Labour services all continued to compete merrily with one another, though considering that the proposed campaign was against an eastern power with manpower in unlimited supply, the Army should obviously have received preference.

It must be admitted that optimistic estimates were now beginning to prevail even in the General Staff of the time required to secure complete victory. It was calculated that once the proposed line had been attained in Russia, only a fraction of the Army would be needed there any longer. This formed the basis of the estimate on which winter clothing was only considered necessary for a fifth of the invading force.

One of the main questions on which the success of the "lightning campaign" depended was whether the young German tank arm was strong enough for its task and was backed by a sufficiency of motorized infantry and self-propelled guns. Guderian did not think so, while General Lemelsen, who led a tank corps, was later to say that there was a grave lack of second-line tank divisions, the result being that the first-line tanks had on several occasions to be called back from more essential tasks in order to stop up gaps in the ring that had been drawn round the enemy.

According to General von Thoma's evidence, the German Army at the beginning of the campaign possessed 2,434 front-line tanks, though on paper the German tank force looked larger than it was, for the old tank division was found to be too unwieldy and was made into a smaller unit. The tank force was thus split up into no less than twenty-one divisions. Hitler waved all reports of the size of enemy tank forces aside, though it was estimated by some at 10,000 tanks. When he was told of such figures, he merely remarked that they were false, or that it was a question of outdated models. The existence of the Russian 52-ton tank, which later became the T.34, was unknown both to Hitler and the General Staff, and, as Hitler himself admitted in a letter to Mussolini, was to provide one of the embarrassing surprises of the war.

There were also profound differences between Hitler and the General Staff in the whole conception of the campaign. In Halder's eyes, the main objective was Moscow, the centre of the Russian transport system, and in the decisive conversation of February 3rd, Halder very emphatically pointed out its importance to Hitler, but Hitler cut right into all this with the remark that Moscow was of no importance and to think otherwise merely argued the possession of the outmoded General Staff point of view. Leningrad, from where he could reach out a hand to Finland, and Southern Russia, with its industrial areas, were much more vital to him. However, although in theory the main weight of the attack was now supposed to be diverted to the flanks, the original tactical scheme which put the main weight on the centre was never really dropped, for the Supreme Army Command still stuck to the idea of thrusting at Moscow.

The date for the attack was first set down for May, and in March Hitler called the Army commanders together in order to explain his Russian policy to them under the watchword "Destruction of Fighting Forces—Dissolution of State". Once this objective had been attained, he intended to create a defensive frontier in Russia which he would hold with fifty to sixty divisions. The rest of his forces would then be employed for other purposes, such as the seizure of Gibraltar, or would be demobilized so that they could be used for the arming against Britain of the *Luftwaffe* and the Navy.

At first the idea had prevailed of breaking up all territory taken from Russia into separate states. In the Baltic territories, White Russia, and the Ukraine where there were already underground movements, Halder had envisaged the creation of "Stalin-free" republics under their own governments, which would be advised by German military plenipotentiaries. These states would form a protective cordon for Germany against Russia.

At the present briefing conference, however, all such ideas went by the board. Hitler announced that there would be Reich protectorates in the areas concerned, and that these areas were to be deprived of anything in the nature of a Slav intelligentsia. The population should merely provide a labour reservoir for a future German ruling caste. Hitler demanded utter ruthlessness, the avoidance of any false chivalry, and blind obedience to his orders, whether or no they were approved. The rear areas were not to be administered by the Army but by the S.S. and the Gestapo. For "special tasks", the terrible character of which was as yet not grasped, "Special Detachments" of the S.D. were attached to the Army group commanders. Further, a special "Economic Staff East" was set up under General Stapf, sometime *Oberquartiermeister III*, for appropriating goods and materials required by the war economy.

VII

Hitler had hoped to localize the Italo-Greek conflict by drawing Rumania, Hungary, Bulgaria and Jugoslavia into his system before attacking in the east, but he was unable to prevent British troops being thrown into Greece. Partly as a result of this, a military coup took place in Jugoslavia immediately after Prince Paul had signed the three-power pact, and that country joined the camp of the Allies.

This endangered Hitler's flank, and he answered by a lightning campaign which was an extension of "Marita". Together with Hungarian troops, German troops overran Jugoslavia before she could deploy her forces, while from this new base and from Bulgaria List struck into Thrace.

Again painstaking General Staff work proved its worth, as did perfect co-operation between tanks and aircraft. On this occasion Brauchitsch and Halder flatly contravened Hitler's order to send strong forces immediately into Albania in order to help the hard-pressed Italians, since such action might well have made the success of List's operation doubtful in Northern Greece. The Italian position in the last resort depended on Germany's success in that venture. Events justified this move. British forces were expelled from Greece, and on April 27th the swastika was hoisted over the Acropolis.

Various other minor ventures formed a prelude to the Russian campaign. German airborne forces seized Crete, which was defended by Greek and British troops, but the heavy casualties incurred prevented a similar assault on Cyprus. A revolt in Irak organized with German help broke down largely because Turkey, though she signed a pact of friendship with Germany, refused to permit the passage of German troops. Shortly afterwards Free French troops of General de Gaulle moved into Syria, which made Germany's position in Iran more or less untenable, despite the fact that its ruler, Reza Khan, was friendly to the Axis.

The Italian defeat in Libya and Mussolini's appeals for help had caused Hitler to send three of his best armoured divisions to Africa. The new undertaking, which was led by General Erwin Rommel, was given the poetic name, *Sonnenblume* (Sunflower). In the General Staff the opinion prevailed that the most that could be looked for from it was to put off the day when the North African coast would be lost to the Axis. The difficulties of supply were great, and the enemy had the advantage in opportunities for moving troops to the scene of this conflict.

Rommel, however, was to cut a more spectacular figure in this undertaking than had been anticipated, so much so that English observers looked upon him as something in the nature of another Seydlitz or another Murat. He had already distinguished himself as commander of the 7th Tank Division in France, and was the author of widely read books on Infantry Tactics. He had been the Army's representative at the headquarters of the Hitler Youth and had at the beginning of the war been put in charge of the Führer's armoured train, a duty from which he secured an early release, as he found the atmosphere of intrigue intolerable. Since he had not come out of the school of the General Staff he was presumably a general very much to Hitler's taste—a fact which gives added significance to his subsequent story.

VIII

The threat that a new front might be opened in the east and that Germany might thus be faced with a two-front war, as in 1914, produced in the officer corps the first stirrings of revolt that had taken place since the first winter of the war. General Thomas worked with Goerdeler on a report for Halder on the deadly dangers of an eastern campaign, a campaign so contrary to the precepts of Seeckt, under whom Thomas had been trained. Witzleben, commanding the western front, and von Falkenhausen, who had been made Commander in Chief Belgium, were old enemies of Hitler, and Witzleben had never wholly dropped the plan for a *coup d'état*. Further, members of the "young conservative" opposition, particularly Lieutenant von Schlabrendorff, who was serving in von Bock's headquarters in Posen, sought to influence the latter to work for the cancellation of the Russian campaign.

A small resistance group came into being in the central group of armies. The persons mainly concerned were the G.S.O.1, Colonel von Tresckow, the counter-espionage officer, von Gersdorff, Bock's sometime adjutant, Colonel Schultze-Büttger, and Counts Lehndorff-Steinort and Hardenberg-Neuhardenberg, who were actually Bock's adjutants at the time. Bock himself was sceptical, but admitted that he did not know how the war could be won. Von Hassell heard von Rundstedt's adjutant, Captain von Salviati, remark that the Field-Marshal saw the truth clearly enough but that was about as far as it went. The fact is that, despite certain signs to the contrary, the chances for action were not at this moment very favourable, so that even the sceptics and those who saw clearly the disaster that lay ahead could do little more than resign themselves to it.

There can be no doubt that in the spring of 1941 Hitler's prestige in the Army had risen to its zenith. Now that the Old General Staff, and above all the "*Heulboje*" ("howling buoy", i.e. "dismal Jimmy"), as Hitler was in the habit of calling Beck, had proved themselves so have been so hopelessly at sea in their estimate of the French Army and of the impregnability of the Maginot line, they carried even less weight with Hitler than they had carried before. Prince Bismarck, the great Chancellor's grandson, who was Minister-Counsellor in Rome, did not mince his words when discussing this matter with Ciano, but told him openly that since Hitler had proved right about the Maginot line the generals did not dare to open their mouths. In any case, the best of them were now in the field and not among Hitler's *entourage*.

Hitler was thus in a position to ride roughshod over any advice he received. He rejected the General Staff plans to create new formations at home by way of a strategic reserve, and declared it unnecessary to set up a store of winter clothing, since before winter set in all operations would have been concluded. There was no influence that seemed capable of correcting his hopeless under-estimation of the task with which his armies were faced.

Admittedly those armies were good. They had so far conquered in Poland, in Norway, in France, in Belgium, in Serbia and in Greece, and these victories had everywhere begotten a new sense of strength, which contrasted most vividly with the general atmosphere of 1939. A new optimism prevailed even in the General Staff, which now made up for its earlier lack of confidence by a definite over-indulgence in that commodity. Yet Hitler's strategy, the strategy of the impossible, confronted both the Army and the General Staff with tasks which were really beyond them. The German Army, whose superiority had hitherto so largely depended on the quality of its machines, was now compelled to fight in a country where the effectiveness of those machines counted for very little and one which had inexhaustible resources of manpower.

Amongst the questions which were subjects of acute controversy were two. How far were Russian preparations advanced? And was their purpose offensive or purely defensive? Halder had information according to which the concentrations in Western Russia amounted to 200 fully-equipped divisions. He considered this a menacing sign, but believed that the German forces were sufficient to cripple their enemies—at any rate for a time. The territorial gains which could be achieved in the Baltic North-West, White Russia and the Ukraine would, in the General Staff's opinion, serve as good bargaining counters when it came to peace negotiations. Colonel Krebs, on the other hand, who was later to be the last Chief of the General Staff and who had succeeded Köstring as military attaché in Moscow when the latter fell ill, reported on his return in May that Russia would do anything to avoid a war, and that during his journey he had seen no troop concentrations in Western Russia.

Rundstedt also did not believe in any aggressive intention on Russia's part, though his G.S.O.1, General Winter, gained the definite impression during the invasion that Hitler was right and that a Russian attack had been anticipated. The forces deployed by Russia in the Carpathians seemed suspiciously large and suspiciously well-equipped with tanks. Moreover, the Russian staffs were found to possess maps of East Germany and Austria. On the whole, it seems probable that Rundstedt was right and Winter wrong, for even Jodl had to admit that Germany effected a complete tactical surprise as far as the Russians were concerned.

Whatever may be the truth of this, it seems established by the evidence of Jodl and Halder that the decision was not an easy one for Hitler to make, not that he hesitated on moral grounds but that the shadow of Napoleon fell across his path—and Hitler had a weakness for comparisons between Napoleon and himself. Halder was never certain when that decision was actually made, but inclined to the view that it was after the Balkan campaign. Hess's flight to England in June 1941 and his attempt to effect a reconciliation to be followed by an alliance with Germany against Russia, is certainly evidence that whenever the decision was made, it had by June become irrevocable. A perceptible panic in Party circles is a further indication of this. As for an alliance with Britain, this notion had certainly entered Hitler's head as well as that of Hess, for we know that the Foreign Office instructed Papen to approach the British Ambassador to Turkey in that sense on the first day of the invasion of Russia.

In order to lull the Soviet government into a false sense of security, Goebbels felt constrained to publish an article in the *Völkischer Beobachter* under the title "The Example of Crete", in which it was plainly hinted that the occupation of Crete by airborne troops was but a prototype of other operations which would be carried out elsewhere on a larger scale, the implication being that an invasion of England was imminent. The effect was further enhanced by the fact that Jodl immediately had the whole edition confiscated on professed security grounds—had not Hitler often told his generals that they should read more thrillers?—while rumours were diligently circulated in Berlin that a visit from Stalin was shortly to be expected. Meanwhile the final preparations were completed for the attack.

Just as he had made elaborate preparations for a battle head-quarters for the battle of France, and had before the projected invasion of England set up a huge shelter at Margival on the Chemin des Dames, complete with bathrooms, workrooms and bedrooms, so now he caused the "*Wolfsschanze*" to be erected in the so-called Mauerwald in East Prussia. It was a most costly affair, and was protected by mines and barbed-wire entanglements. Almost more noteworthy, however, than all these elaborate arrangements was the fact that the headquarters of the General Staff was not directly con-nected with this structure but was contained in shelters constructed half-an-hour's car-ride away. The greater part of the Army command, above all the Quartermaster-General's department, remained behind at Zossen.

IX

The German force allocated to the eastern campaign comprised 120 divisions, and in the early hours of June 22nd these began their surprise invasion of Russia. The distribution of the force was as follows. Based on East Prussia were the forces of von Leeb com-prising the 16th and 18th Armies and the 4th Tank Army under Colonel-Generals Busch, von Küchler and Hoepner respectively. Based on Warsaw were the forces of von Bock comprising the 2nd, 4th and 9th Armies and the 2nd and 3rd Tank Armies, these being under Generals von Weichs, von Kluge, Strauss, Guderian and Hoth. The southern force under von Rundstedt was based on Galicia and comprised the 6th, 11th and 17th Armies with the 1st Tank Army, the commanders being Reichenau, von Schobert, von Stülpnagel and von Kleist. All three army groups were, of course, supported by suit-able air forces.

Certain further elaborations are to be noted. Without any reference to the Army General Staff, the O.K.W. had ordered a division from Norway into Finland, and this created a new "O.K.W. theatre of war" lying outside the jurisdiction of the old General Staff. It was anticipated that Finnish forces would make contact with von Leeb before Leningrad and move against the Murman railway. Meanwhile the Rumanian Army was moving towards the Dnieper. The Secret Service had also been at work, Colonel Lahousen having established contact with Bandera and Melnyk, the Ukrainian partisan leaders. Lastly, a special formation, the "Special Purposes Regiment, Branden-burg", had been created for special missions and sabotage work. This was something wholly without precedent in the annals of the German Army.

The first result of the new enterprise was an alliance between England and Russia. Forces of both these countries entered Iran in order to secure communication between themselves through the Middle East. The occupation of Iran and the fall of Shah Reza Khan dealt a mortal blow to all the complex scheming of Germany in this region.

In Russia itself, the campaign proceeded with all the precision which careful General Staff work might have led one to expect. The northern army group advanced on Leningrad, the centre on Moscow, and the southern group on Kiev and the Ukraine. At Minsk the centre army group fought the first of those great encircling battles that were to inflict such heavy losses on the enemy, and at the beginning of July, Halder, as his notes show, believed that Russia's first effort at resistance had been shattered and that the campaign was won, though not yet ended. Even Warlimont felt that his estimate of Russia's ability to resist had been at fault. Yet despite all his successes, Hitler was still nervous and lacked all confidence in the Army and its leaders. In Halder's notes we now begin to find from time to time the sarcastic word "*Grosszustand*" in reference to what was happening at the Führer's headquarters. Literally the word means "Great circumstance", i.e. a state of general crisis and tension.

There now began to be large-scale desertions from the ranks of the enemy. Ukrainian nationalists thought their hour had come. Well known "White Guard" leaders, such as the Cossack generals Krasnow and Schkuro, offered their services as advisers to the Germans. Hitler, however, had deserters treated as prisoners of war and, what is more, forbade any Russian prisoners of war to be transported to the Reich camps. Instead he ordered them to be held in provisional camps behind the front and in Poland. Since their numbers grew enormously, it was impossible to provision them and many died of hunger. Soon the stream of refugees dried up. In due course the notorious "Commissar Order" was issued, which directed all Bolshevik commissars who were taken prisoner to be shot. Many of the principal generals were horrified. Some of them, like Leeb, Hoepner and the Tank general, Lemelsen, flatly refused to allow the order to be carried out. Brauchitsch officially informed O.K.W. that the Supreme Army Command would not issue any corresponding order. In a very marked manner, an order of his own insisted on the strict maintenance of traditional discipline and restraint (*Manneszucht*). Yet the resistance of the generals could not prevent these measures from rapidly destroying the hopes of any Russians who were hostile to the régime. The fact that the destruction of Bolshevism began soon to mean simply an effort to decimate and enslave the Slav peoples was the most fatal of all the flaws in the whole campaign.

X

Hitler's distrust of the generals caused him to interfere extensively in the conduct of operations. The policy of Gneisenau and Moltke which left the subordinate commander freedom for individual decisions within the framework of general directives, and which had become an essential part of Germany's traditional military method, was particularly in place in those great Russian spaces. Hitler, however, a victim of the illusion that he could move armies around as though they were battalions on parade, now adopted the practice of leaving commanders virtually no latitude at all. There was already a severe difference of opinion between General Staff and Supreme War Lord as to the real objectives of the campaign. Hitler, by the methods just described, introduced into it a further element of disastrous uncertainty.

By the middle of July, von Bock, having achieved overwhelming success in the centre of the front, believed the moment had come for a tank thrust to Moscow before the enemy could get his breath. At this stage, however, von Leeb was still trying to open the way to Leningrad and fighting off Russian counter attacks, while Rundstedt was still hanging back in the south. Hitler's Directive 33 of July 19th sought apparently to take this latter circumstance into account. At any rate, Bock was ordered to divert his forces north and south, Moscow not being Hitler's main objective at all. Bock was thus left with nothing but his infantry and artillery and had to rely on these since all his tanks had been ordered off to the flanking manoeuvre. On July 28th Halder noted that the Führer's orders had led to a dissipation of forces and had caused the attack on Moscow to come to a standstill.

In contrast to their recent French experience, the Germans now found that their enemy was little inclined to be affected by tank threats to his flank and rear and that despite these he made great efforts not to lose the initiative. He yielded ground, but only to return time and again to the attack, and would attack the tanks from all sides. In this way he often cut right through a German encircling movement. This was made easier for him by the fact that the Germans lacked second-line tank divisions and that owing to an insufficiency of motor transport their infantry could not be moved up fast enough. The Russians thus time and again escaped from the trap.

At length, at the end of the month, the 1st Tank Army broke through the Russian lines in the south, the Russians being defeated in a heavy battle of encirclement at Uman. Yet this too proved indecisive, and by August it was plain that despite the enemy's heavy losses in men and material, his power of resistance had by no means been broken. Halder notes that this last has been underestimated. Whereas the Germans had calculated with some 200 divisions, some 360 had already been identified. The question was now whether to break off the offensive and prepare to defend what had already been gained, or to continue to thrust forward towards certain specific objectives.

A decision had clearly to be made. The centre army group had now advanced some 900 kilometres into Russia, while the northern group was approaching Leningrad and the southern was in the Ukraine. But every step forward meant for Germany a widening of the front, though German forces at best remained constant in the different divisions while in some of them the heavy battles and marches were substantially reducing their numbers.

Meanwhile the new Colonial policy of National Socialism which dreamed of turning the Slavic East into a German India, was celebrating its first suicidal triumphs. Alfred Rosenberg was made Reichsminister for occupied territories. The fact that he was the son of a Balt and of a Latvian mother seems to have provided the chief justification for this appointment. Reichskommissars were established in the Baltic districts, White Russia and the Ukraine. An anticipatory appointment was also made of a Reichskommissar in the Caucasus, a district still in enemy hands.

Any hopes of a rational eastern policy were soon to be buried. The German *Gauleiters* and the bloody work of the special detachments of the S.S., the Police and the S.D. soon brought that about. Nay, more, the "Liquidation Detachments" of the S.D., which came under the Army groups for administrative purposes but over which the latter had no command, were the most powerful stimulus to the partisans, who now carried on the war in their enemy's rear. Russia could now appeal with renewed effectiveness to the patriotism of its people.

These "special detachments" of the S.S. and S.D. on the one hand, and the new Russian Central Staff for Partisan Warfare on the other, lent the war a new and terrible aspect. Actually, the General Staff felt themselves helpless before this latest development, as did most German commanders, for all of these were now caught between two separate manifestations of terrorism. The case of von Bock provides an excellent example of this. The so-called "Police Festival" provided the S.S. in Borisov, the headquarters of the central group of armies, with the occasion for instituting a wholesale massacre of Jews. Von Bock's outraged staff urged him to take action, but the most von Bock felt inclined to do was to make a written report to Hitler on these horrors. This was in part due to the fact that von Bock was simply afraid, but it was also due to a combination of a rather narrow conception of soldierly obedience with personal ambition, for like many of his colleagues, von Bock was anxious to prove his ability and did not wish to be removed from his post. Hence his unwillingness to disassociate himself from these detestable activities in a manner more definite than he actually displayed.

XI

The day of the lightning campaigns was over. In Russia, victory had followed upon victory, but for all that Hitler's essential objective, which was the destruction of the Russian armies west of the Dnieper, had not been obtained. The bulk of these armies stood under Marshal Timoschenko athwart the historic Smolensk-Moscow road, while Marshal Budjenny was continuing the fight in the Ukraine, and, in the north, Leningrad was being toughly defended by Voroshilov, Stalin's old comrade in arms of the civil war, who had at one time co-operated so closely with the *Reichswehr*. Further, the General Staff was receiving news of the hurried setting up of new formations east of Moscow.

For several weeks Hitler vacillated, while Brauchitsch and Halder urged him to press home the attack on Moscow so as to get possession of the Russian capital before the onset of winter and thus deal a decisive blow at the Russian government's prestige. At length, Brauchitsch committed his ideas to writing and sent them to Hitler. Hitler sent a written reply which showed the resentment he was beginning to feel for the older type of soldier, and on August 21st sent out Directive 34. The essential objective, this document stated, was not for the moment the capture of Moscow, but that of the Crimea and the Donetz basin, together with the cutting off of Russia from its Caucasian oil supplies. Brauchitsch, together with Guderian, who strongly supported him, again tried vainly to make Hitler change his mind and press home the attack on Moscow. When it became evident that they would fail in this, both seriously considered resignation. In the end, however, they stuck to their posts, feeling as they did that the troops had a right to demand this of them.

Hitler's order that forces of the centre army group and above all Guderian's 2nd Tank Army should turn south, led, between September 17th and 19th, to a gigantic new battle of encirclement in the neighbourhood of Kiev, 600,000 prisoners being taken. Kiev itself fell. On the 26th, the 11th Army broke through the barrier which was the Perekop Isthmus, and thus forced the road to the Crimea, while other forces of Rundstedt's prepared to attack the line Rostov-Kharkov. Hitler saw proof in the new battle in the Ukraine, and in the taking of Kiev, that the Russian Army's power of resistance had been finally broken, and was more convinced than ever of the inspired quality of his own generalship and of the weak and opinionated character of his General Staff. As far as he could see, there was at this moment no need of anything but to go on hammering. All objectives were now attainable.

Even before it was possible to start carrying out the operations outlined in Directive 34, Hitler had hurried along with Directive 35, which was issued on September 6th. This ordered the centre army group to begin the thrust at Moscow after all, and to do so before the winter. Both the northern and southern army groups were instructed to divert forces to this effort, the tank forces of Guderian, Hoth and Hoepner being given the task of moving in from north and south and carrying out a vast pincers movement around the capital. This operation was to begin within eight to ten days, the fact that Guderian was at the time heavily engaged in the Ukraine being disregarded. Guderian's bitterness over this profoundly unrealistic generalship grew steadily more intense.

It was not till September 30th that Guderian's tanks could start carrying out their part of the new plan by moving off in the direction Orel-Tula. The new operation, the conduct of which was in the hands of von Bock, was given the code-name "Typhoon", because it was to be in the nature of a mighty storm that blew the last of the enemy's resistance away. It began well enough. In the battle of Viasma-Briansk, Bock bagged another 600,000 Russians, which caused Hitler to boast that the Russian armies had been hurled to the ground and would never rise again. Even Halder now regained his confidence. His notes reflect his opinion that given reasonably good leadership and reasonably favourable weather, the capture of Moscow was assured. Unfortunately, neither of these conditions was fulfilled.

Around October 20th, the situation was approximately as follows. Von Kluge's 4th Army and Hoepner's 4th Tank Army lay to the east of Kaluga-Moshaisk, Hoth's 3rd Tank Army was at Twer-Staritsa, Guderian's tanks were stuck in the mud which had now begun to form and only reached Tula at the beginning of November. For all that, Hitler's star seemed at the moment at its zenith. Von Rundstedt was ordered to press forward over Rostov on the Don towards Maikop, Armavir and the oilfields of the Northern Caucasus, while von Leeb stood at the gates of Leningrad, the fall of which now seemed imminent. Voroshilov's armies had lost fearfully in blood and the last thin line of defence was held among others by companies of women, cadets and workers.

Now, however, the Hybris of Hitler stood fully revealed. Everything was to be done at once. Leeb was not only to take Leningrad but was to unite with the Finns and take the Murman railway, and so cut the connection between Moscow and Archangel. Bock was to take Moscow and at the same time send a tank corps to assist Leeb. Rundstedt was to conquer the Crimea, the Don basin and the Caucasian oilfields.

Once again Hitler believed that the war had already been won. U-boat sinkings were increasing. Russo-British staff talks were being held for the eventuality of a German pincers attack on the Middle East over Egypt on one side and the Caucasus on the other, or for that of a Turkish-German alliance. At home, Hitler ordered the disbandment of a number of reserve divisions and gave instructions for certain sections of industry to revert to peacetime production. All the while Russia was making feverish efforts to call the last man to the colours and to bring the Far Eastern Army to the threatened front in the west.

Mud now began very seriously to hinder operations. English critics were later to see in the bad condition of the Russian roads and the early arrival of bad weather a decisive factor in the war. The mud was particularly troublesome in the south, where it seriously interfered with Rundstedt's operations. Kleist could make no progress towards Rostov, while the 6th Army stood before Kharkov and the 17th before the Donetz.

XII

Meanwhile the problem of reserves was becoming acute. Halder had already noted in September that these were short by some 200,000 men. Fromm, who had a thorough knowledge of this particular difficulty, advised Hitler to make a peace offer before actually endeavouring to enter Moscow, while Rundstedt, who probably had had more experience than anybody else, was for breaking off operations and for taking up a prepared position for the winter. Bock and Brauchitsch, however, had memories of the Marne, where lack of persistence had deprived Germany of victory, and were for pushing on to Moscow. A temporary improvement of the weather in mid-November strengthened their convictions.

Hitler wavered between irrational certitude of victory and recurrent fits of pessimism, a mood which may well have been responsible for his curious action in regard to Leningrad. Quite suddenly he held Leeb's forces back. It is said that he had discovered an old memorandum of Ludendorff's in which that general dwelt on the difficulty of provisioning very large towns. Whatever the reason, Leeb suddenly received orders not to take the city but to surround it and concentrate his efforts on pushing forward in the direction of Tichwin and the Murman railway. Leeb was later to remark that one was almost tempted to think that Hitler was Stalin's ally.

On November 21st Kleist's tanks took Rostov, while the offensive against Moscow took its course. There was now panic in the city, the government and most of its officials being evacuated. There was some plundering of shops, but there was also feverish preparations for defence, with workers being formed into militia battalions and even women helping to dig trenches. The suburbs were converted into fortresses, and very slowly reinforcements began to arrive from the east.

In other parts of the front the tide now seemed to turn. In the south, Timoschenko, who had replaced Budjenny, threw back Kleist's tanks, and within a week Rostov had to be evacuated. Rundstedt now also asked for his armies to be allowed to withdraw to winter quarters on the Mius. Hitler refused, and, contrary to his usual custom, came personally to Rundstedt's headquarters at Poltava, accompanied by Brauchitsch and Halder.

When Hitler sought to put the blame for losing Rostov on Rundstedt, the old Field-Marshal coolly replied that the responsibility must lie with those who had devised the campaign. Hitler looked for a moment as though he were about to hurl himself on Rundstedt and tear the Knight's Cross from his uniform. Brauchitsch, whose health had lately been affected by the ceaseless conflict between conscience and military duty, promptly had a heart attack.

A number of commanders in the southern army group were now relieved of their posts, at the head of them Stülpnagel, who led the 17th Army, an interview between the latter and Hitler providing the occasion for another of Hitler's characteristic fits of rage. Meanwhile Rundstedt obstinately persisted in his demands for greater freedom, and when this was refused asked to be relieved of his duties. At a final meeting Hitler told him that in future he would not consider any request by generals for retirement. After all, he himself could not go to his own immediate superior, who was Almighty God, and just tell tell Him he was fed up and wanted to quit.

The fact is that Hitler's nervousness was steadily mounting as one setback followed another. On December 1st Bock told him that he believed that only slight progress toward Moscow was now possible, and that the troops were at the end of their tether. The General Staff, it must be admitted, still clung to the contrary view, and thought Moscow could and should be taken, but even O.K.W. was now beginning to suffer from a divided mind, so much so that Keitel was moved to intervene with the Führer and suggest that it might be better to withdraw to winter quarters after all.

This *démarche* had somewhat unhappy results. Hitler called him a "*Strohkopf*" (vernacular for person with a low I.Q.) whereupon, deeply insulted, Keitel walked away. Jodl found him sitting at his desk writing out his resignation with a pistol beside him. Jodl quietly took the pistol away and tried to persuade Keitel to stay on; and Keitel was weak enough to agree.

Keitel and Brauchitsch were not the only ones who were finding service under Hitler unbearable. Von Bock, too, was near breaking point, though, not unnaturally, he was, like so many, too frightened to make a stand. Once when Colonel Tresckow, one of his Staff officers, suggested that something positive should be undertaken against Hitler, Bock rushed out of the room, saying he would not listen to such talk and would defend the Führer against any that attacked him. Somewhat later he retired on grounds of health.

Bock was succeeded by von Kluge, Rundstedt's post being given to Reichenau. Reichenau soon saw that there was nothing to be done but follow the plan of his predecessor and retire to the Mius. Kluge, however, carried on with the attack on Moscow, although he already had grave doubts of its success, but Kluge's sharp understanding was offset by his ambition, nor did he ever find a way out of that conflict.

XIII

In the early days of December, Hoepner's tanks came quite close to the suburbs of Moscow, and even the infantry came just within sight of the Kremlin, while in Moscow itself signs of a complete breakdown and frantic preparations for house-to-house fighting seemed to go on side by side. It was at this moment that a heavy snow-fall set in, accompanied by intense cold, and this was too much for the German troops. There was no winter clothing, there were no fresh troops by which they could be relieved. Catastrophe was drawing near. On November 27th, Halder had noted down an utterance of Wagner, the Quartermaster-General. Wagner had said that Germany was at the end both of her human and material resources, but on that date the General Staff seems to have still been blind to the facts.

Now quite suddenly there came a change. On November 30th, Halder was writing that those in Hitler's *entourage* had no conception of what conditions were like, but were doing their thinking in a vacuum. On December 6th, Halder decided in favour of a withdrawal by the centre army groups to winter positions on the line Ostashkov-Rshev. Hitler refused to sanction this, but on that same day the counter-offensive broke out on the centre section of the front; it drove with fearful force into the German ranks, where cold and casualties had already taken a punishing toll. Two days later the German front was broken at Twer (Kalinin) and on the 10th the Russians broke through again on the front of the 2nd Army.

In more fortunate circumstances, the growing peril might have produced a searching of conscience and a sincere attempt to reform the apparatus of command in such a manner that the best military talent would be given the maximum scope. Unfortunately the rot had gone too far, and the only result of the catastrophe was a further discrediting of the very men who might have saved the situation.

At headquarters, Brauchitsch was being vehemently reproached and generally treated as though he bore the sole responsibility for the catastrophe. Actually he had told Halder two days before the start of the Russian offensive that he wanted to resign. On the 7th he had handed in his resignation on grounds of health. Meanwhile, Lieutenant-Colonel von Lossberg, the Army's representative in the

Wehrmachtführungsstab, approached Jodl and tried to win him over to the forming of a unitary General Staff for all fighting services, in other words to fuse the Army command with that of the *Wehrmacht* as a whole, the intention being presumably to put the best strategist that the Army could produce, namely Manstein, in charge, but Jodl did not like the idea. Hitler and Manstein, he said, were such different types of men that they would never work with one another.

Halder is again found complaining at this time that it was a dreadful thing how little Hitler understood of the true position of the Army and that he was only tinkering with the situation. Halder was referring here to his strict refusal of requests by all commanders for a boldly conceived manoeuvre of disengagement, though these were forthcoming with increasing frequency. Von Leeb was actually for a withdrawal as far as Poland, a proposal which embodied the traditional idea of retreating in order to regroup and renew the attack. In actual fact Hitler probably had a better understanding of what was threatening than that with which he was credited by the General Staff. He saw the danger of a complete collapse in the east well enough, but a withdrawal to a winter position (which was admittedly unprepared) was a thing he could not possibly sanction, in so far as any retreat involved a loss of prestige. He thus resisted these proposals with something like demoniac obsession and developed a determination in this from which men of such widely differing character as Jodl and Rundstedt could not entirely withhold their admiration. What he gained by this was, of course, no more than a temporary respite, and the much publicized propaganda victory over "General Winter" was paid for by the people of Germany with four years of heavy and continuous sacrifice.

The secret fear that haunted Hitler together with his inferiority complex in regard to the officer corps caused him to be absolutely ruthless whenever any commander seemed to show a will of his own, to remove old and tried generals such as Rundstedt, Stülpnagel and Hoepner, and to exact a slavish obedience such as no Prussian king had ever demanded. On December 19th von Brauchitsch's resignation was formally accepted. Hitler then summoned Halder and told him that he had decided to take over the command of the Army himself, and that Brauchitsch had not exercised that function as he had wanted it exercised. The idea of "positions in the rear" had sunk into the minds of the rank and file and had produced a decline in the offensive spirit.

Hitler also took to blaming the General Staff for not making sufficiently early provision for winter clothing. He omitted to mention that it was he himself who had insisted that the necessity for that would not arise. The Army, he insisted further, tended to work on too rigid principles. In that respect the *Luftwaffe* under Göring was a very different affair.

He then declared in these actual words: "Anybody can do that bit of operational planning. The task of a Commander in Chief is to educate the Army in a National Socialist sense. I don't know a single general in the Army who is capable of doing that in the way I want it done. That is why I have decided to assume command of the Army myself." According to the traditional code, Halder should now have followed the example of his chief and tendered his resignation. Halder, however, thought it his duty to stick it out, so that he might at least prevent the very worst mistakes from being made.

On the following day, Guderian sought to express his difficulties to Hitler in the belief that it only needed a little honest speaking of his mind to clear away any misunderstandings. He therefore declared quite openly that the principal military posts should be held by men who had had some real experience, and that a gulf was widening between the men who were conducting the war from the offices of the *Wehrmachtführungsstab* and the General Staff on the one hand, and the troops in the firing line on the other. There had, of course, always been differences between the soldiers who thought essentially in terms of infantry and artillery warfare and the creator of the new tank tactics, and quite possibly Guderian had criticized the way tanks had been used in Russia. Hitler's only reply was that he could not dissociate himself from his military *entourage* and that the latter was entirely of one mind with himself.

Ultimately Guderian, the creator of the German tank arm, the man whom the Russians feared more than they feared any other tank leader, was removed from his post like the rest for having ordered the retreat from Moscow on his own authority. For a time he was left wholly without employment and then given the post of inspector of tanks at home. In circles around Hitler the word was put about that Guderian was "a fellow without guts" (*ein schlapper Kerl*") who had lost his nerve.

It was in this winter of crisis that the atmosphere which characterized the latter years of Hitler's life became most noticeable in the shelters of the *"Wolfsschanze"*. It was an atmosphere charged with intrigue, in which schemes seemed to thrive that became ever more widely divorced from reality. Hitler now passed his days in these shelters for months on end, haunted ceaselessly by a dark malaise and by fear of the approaching end, yet still a slave to the illusion that it might be possible to win back his early good fortune and to evade his doom.

At Nuremberg, Jodl and Warlimont described something of the quality of this curious life at headquarters, with its "restricted areas", the two outer areas being for officers of the O.K.W., and the inner one for the Führer's intimates. Jodl described the general set-up as a mixture of monastery and concentration camp, and explained that officers were for the most part only tolerated guests here. It was, he said, not easy to be a tolerated guest for five and a half years.

Warlimont was particularly shocked by Hitler's abnormal and unhealthy way of life, by his long tea parties which lasted far into the night, his insufficient sleep in the early hours of the morning and his failure to get any fresh air or take any exercise whatever. Officers only met Hitler at meals and at the daily reviews of the situation. No officers were admitted to the circle of intimates except his adjutants, among whom Schmundt played an increasingly important part. Schmundt ultimately became a general.

It was here in Hitler's inner sanctum that the Chief of the Party Head Office, Martin Bormann, held sway. Here, too, were the S.A. and S.S. adjutants, among whom was the brother-in-law of Hitler's mistress, here were to be found Hitler's two medical advisers, Professor Morell and Professor Brandt. Then there were obscure personalities like his vegetarian cook, Fräulein Manzialy, and his valets, the last of whom, Heinz Linge, became a major in the Waffen S.S.

A few small administrative changes fall into this period. Two officers of the General Staff were now placed directly under Hitler, the Quartermaster-General and the recently created *General zur besonderen Verwendung* or Special Purposes General. The remainder of the General Staff still maintained its detached (and subordinate) position, and still controlled the Operations Department and such matters as training, transport, intelligence, etc. It also had under it the new "Weapons Generals" who were technical specialists in the different arms.

Further, there was now created a new liaison staff between Hitler and the Army, the so-called "Army-Staff with the O.K.W.", consisting of one general and two other officers. The conduct of this thorny office fell on Major-General Buhle, who soon contrived to raise it to one of great importance. Hitler ultimately saw in Buhle a candidate for the post of Chief of General Staff.

XIV

December 1941 represents the great turning point in the life of Hitler, as it was also the turning point of the war itself. While Hitler was trying desperately to ward off catastrophe in Russia, Japan made her attack on Pearl Harbour, an event the news of which took the General Staff completely by surprise. Indeed Hitler himself had not been informed of this intention, though Japan was already pledged as his ally in the event of complications with the United States.

Thus war began between Germany and the United States of America, of whom Ribbentrop had said that even if war broke out, they would be unable to wage it, as they would never get their armies across the Atlantic. It was an omen that shortly before Pearl Harbour, General Udet, the *Luftwaffe's* "Master General of Ordnance", should have shot himself because he refused to face the situation where the German Air Force was bankrupt of equipment.

It was perhaps another omen that about this time war, as carried on by Hitler, should have attained a stage of degradation which even Keitel could not deny. Partisan warfare spread from the areas to the rear of the eastern front into the Balkans and, above all, into Jugoslavia, where both Monarchist and Communist groups took up the fight. On December 12th, the notorious *Nacht und Nebel Erlass*, the "Dark of the Night" decree, so named presumably because S.S. arrests were usually nocturnal, was issued over Keitel's signature. This provided that any person committing an offence against the German forces could be sent to a German concentration camp without any notification of his or her relatives.

All high-ranking soldiers were agreed that Hitler's great decisive mistake was his method of inelastic defence during this winter. Hitler wanted to defend every foot of territory he had conquered. The huge Russian spaces made it impossible to defend the front by trench systems analogous to those of the First World War. Hitler therefore gave the order that wherever the enemy had broken through, troops were to "hedgehog themselves in" and thus to hold "Fortresses" in the enemy's rear which would serve as *points d'appui* when the offensive was renewed.

As against this, the General Staff favoured an elastic defence, which permitted boldly conceived retreats which in their turn could be followed by counter-offensives. Such had been Joffre's strategy in 1914 at the battle of the Marne. Such also was to be the strategy which Manstein wished to follow in Southern Russia in 1943. But Hitler feared for his prestige, and made it a reproach to the generals that they everlastingly wanted to manoeuvre.

This conflict ultimately led to the retirement of von Leeb. There is a record of an illuminating telephone conversation between Leeb and Halder concerning a certain place on which the Russians had closed in and which Hitler wanted held at all costs.

Leeb: Do you know, Halder, that one can lose an army corps this way?

Halder: Yes.

Leeb: Do you know that one can lose a whole army this way?

Halder: Yes.

Leeb: Do you know that one can lose a war this way?

Halder: Yes, but you know how it is, Herr Feldmarschall. Nothing that you and I have had to learn counts for anything to-day.

Leeb saw in Halder his last hope and he adjured him to stick at his post. When the situation grew critical near Demiansk and the Russians were closing in on a large force, he asked Hitler personally to permit the abandonment of this position. Hitler replied that he must stand where he was. Leeb left the room and went straight to Keitel to tell him he would resign. His resignation was accepted, because the reports of the Gestapo, which had long had him under continuous surveillance, left no question of his anti-Nazi sentiments. Also Leeb was a practising Catholic, and for that reason alone tended to be in disfavour. Thus there was removed the last of the three Army group commanders with whom the campaign had begun.

Towards the end of the winter Goebbels visited the Führer at his headquarters. Hitler told him he had not been feeling well lately and that he suffered from severe intermittent attacks of giddiness. Goebbels thought the long winter had left its marks on him, and the first signs of his physical decay were certainly noticeable. When shortly after this Hitler went to recuperate at Obersalzberg and snow began once more to fall in the Alps, he hastily left the place. As Goebbels noted, he could no longer bear the sight of snow.

CHAPTER XV

THE REVOLT

I

RUNDSTEDT and Kleist ascribed the breakdown of the offensive against Moscow to the early onset of winter, but Blumentritt, von Kluge's Chief of Staff, declared in an interview with Captain Liddell Hart after the war that the whole attack had been launched two months too late, August and September having been allowed to pass uselessly by. There were, however, other reasons for the failure. The strain on the armoured and motorized material had been altogether too great; repair facilities had been totally inadequate, and to this must be added a shortage of every category of supplies. The fact is that the whole eastern campaign was in reality but another manifestation of Hitler's strategy of the impossible.

Lend-Lease supplies now began to flow from America, not only to hard-pressed England but to bleeding Russia. England was thus again able to draw breath, and in the spring of 1942 the Royal Air Force began its counter-attack.

The "Blitz" on London was now answered by violent attacks on Lübeck and Cologne. Rostock was made the victim of five successive night attacks, and a great part of the town was reduced to ruins. Hitler's boast that in the event of British bombing attacks he would "erase" the enemy's towns was now turned against the people of Germany who had so blindly believed him.

In November 1941 Ribbentrop had assured Japanese diplomats that in the coming spring the German Army would occupy the Caucasus, cross the Urals and drive Stalin deep into Siberia, and even in 1942 young General Staff officers still believed the conquest of the Caucasus to be possible and were talking of trans-Caucasian enterprises into Iran and of the occupation of the oilfields of Irak. Elsewhere, however, a somewhat different mood already prevailed. In Rome, Prince Bismarck observed to an assistant of Ciano, "We are in the fifth act of the Tragedy". He was wrong. There were still a number of acts before the curtain was to be rung down.

Hitler himself seems to have believed quite seriously that if he could have had six more days of good weather, the victory would have been his, but the reign of illusion had already begun. In actual fact, the Russian winter and the Russian counter-attack had destroyed the flower of the German armies and caused the loss of a great part of its equipment.

The question of replacements was also becoming critical. That winter approximately $2\frac{1}{2}$ million men were needed to fill the gaps. Of these, a million could be provided by the normal processes of call-up, while half a million could be returned to duty from the hospitals. The remaining million had to be combed out of industry and agriculture, their places being taken by prisoners of war and foreign slave labour.

Now began the dictatorship of the labour offices. The hunt after human beings was on in a really big way. One way of finding the required manpower for the Army would have been to reduce the insanely inflated establishments of the *Luftwaffe*, the Navy and the Waffen S.S. However, neither Göring nor Himmler was prepared to reduce the private armies they might one day require for the battle behind the scenes.

America's entry into the war made the productivity of the armaments industries an even more decisive factor than it was already. Those industries were, however, affected by that condition which General Warlimont once so aptly described as "chaos of leadership within the Leader State". Once again Army, Navy and *Luftwaffe* all fiercely defended their own claims. The conflict between the Office of Economic Defence and the Administrator of the four-year plan, of course, went back to before the war.

Repeated interference by Hitler only made the confusion worse than it was already. In the autumn of 1941 he had ordered the conversion of industry to peacetime production schedules, except in the matter of aircraft. In 1942, the programme was changed again. Now the competition was between tanks, railway engines and submarines, with aircraft production relegated to second place. Since it was thought that the war would soon be over, however, the development of new inventions was shelved if their completion could not be effected within the near future—a decision that had adverse effects both on rocket development and atomic research.

Meanwhile Hitler continued his obstinate refusal to face the facts. When the General Staff sought to convince him that Russian tank production was already reaching the figure of 600-700 a month, a figure that was soon to rise to 1,200, he simply dismissed this as an impossibility. According to Thoma's statement, four new German tank divisions were established in 1942, but only ten of the twenty-five existing tank divisions actually had all the equipment which their establishment laid down.

In February 1942 Todt's mysterious death in a plane crash just after he had warned Hitler against continuing the Russian campaign, led to the appointment as Armaments Minister of 36-year-old Albert Speer, who had hitherto been Hitler's technical adviser. Despite cumulative air attacks and dwindling raw material resources, Speer devoted himself to his task with the energy of desperation and sought to bring production and distribution to all three services on to a uniform basis and also to increase productivity. In doing so he endeavoured to avoid bureaucratic procedure and was at pains to get hold of the best men he could find, irrespective of their Party orthodoxy.

Unquestionably he had some successes, and German arms production actually increased enormously. Unfortunately this welcome progress was offset by Allied bombing of communications and of synthetic petrol plants and by the loss of the Rumanian oilfields. Speer's work was thus neutralized—all of which merely proved the soundness of Beck's contention that in the days of air warfare the strategy of internal lines had been reduced to absurdity and that Germany had irrevocably lost the strategic advantages she had possessed in the era of Moltke and Schlieffen.

II

Beck once said to Schlabrendorff that this war had been lost before the first shot had been fired. Now, in retirement and torn by terrible anxiety, he watched its course from his home in Berlin Lichterfelde. He foresaw everything that was to come, the breakdown on the eastern front, the Anglo-American invasion of Italy, and the final Allied grand assault in France. He still endeavoured to keep in touch by correspondence with the commanders of the different army groups, but the fact that Beck had been so spectacularly wrong in his estimate of the French Army and his prophecy of failure for a western offensive had lowered his stock among the younger officers. Halder, however, who was haunted by much the same fears as Beck, visited him in exile, and Beck was still the secret mentor of the older generals.

Beck was also in Berlin the recognized head of that secret resistance which had originally consisted of men like Goerdeler, Hassell, Popitz and Hammerstein-Equord, and which now had established connections with sometime Social Democrats and with the trade unions. There were also a number of Socialists who were becoming secretly active in this connection, Dr Julius Leber, Carlo Mierendorff, Theodore Haubach, and in particular Leuschner, of whom previous mention has been made, the sometime Hessian Minister of the Interior.

The winter crisis of 1941/2, after the manner of such crises, caused this dormant resistance to become active again. The first concrete plan for an attempt on Hitler's life took shape in February 1942, the authors being a business man named Nicholas von Halem and Mumm von Schwarzenstein of the consular service. The carrying out of the plan, which was unfortunately all too soon betrayed, was entrusted to a former *Freikorps* leader.

Meanwhile Witzleben began to perfect a plan for a march on Berlin. The idea was that the eastern front should for the time being be held, while the help of western forces was used to reconstitute the state on a new basis which had due regard for law and human rights. Witzleben's adjutant, Count von Schwerin-Schwanenfeld, had certain connections with the small group of socialist and conservative aristocrats which centred around the elder Moltke's great grandson, Count Helmuth-James von Moltke, a lawyer in civil life, now working in counter-espionage. Together with Count Yorck von Wartenburg, Count Fritz von der Schulenburg, the son of the Crown Prince's Chief of Staff, Adam von Trott zu Solz, and a number of clergy and men of learning, Moltke was working on a programme of radical reform, which was to come into force when the final inevitable collapse eventuated. This so-called Kreisau circle, however, did not believe that they could avert catastrophe by a *coup d'état* or an attempt on Hitler's life, while Witzleben, as a great gentleman of the old school, clung to the notion that duty called not just for submission but for action.

Action, for all that, there was none. Witzleben's plan came to nothing because he himself fell seriously ill and was compelled to undergo an operation. Witzleben's place at the front was taken by von Rundstedt, who was now recalled because Hitler feared an Allied landing in the west. Colonel Zeitzler, at that time Kleist's Chief of Staff, now became the Chief of Staff to the Supreme Commander in the west.

Rundstedt looked upon any plan for a *coup d'état* in wartime as unrealistic. Although he detested National Socialism as much as Witzleben, he was not unmoved by Hitler's appeal to his patriotism.

Hitler, as a matter of fact, dismissed and then recalled Rundstedt a number of times, but this merely convinced him of his own indispensability.

III

Hitler now gave out that thanks to Germany's relentless attacks over snow and ice, Russia was already "dead". The last remnants of her strength, he declared, had been dissipated. Thus all depended on thrusting at an enemy who was already on the point of collapse. Halder and Wagner, the Quartermaster-General, expressed a very different view. So did all the *Oberquartiermeisters* on the General Staff. All were opposed to a resumption of the offensive. Halder and Wagner thought that after the catastrophe of the winter, the strength of the German forces was just sufficient to straighten out the gaps that had been made in the German front and to take up a shortened line. The German forces would then be in a favourable position to hold any Russian attacks.

Naturally Hitler saw things differently. Kleist was told that the Caucasian oil wells must be in German hands by the autumn, otherwise it would be impossible to continue the war. Kleist pointed out that such an offensive would involve an unprotected flank facing the Don, but Hitler reassured him. Italian and Hungarian troops, he said, would be used to cover that.

Field-Marshal Küchler was made Leeb's successor with the northern group of armies, von Kluge being still in charge of the centre group. Reichenau, in charge of the southern group, had a stroke in February. Von Bock was recalled to take his place, but shortly afterwards his numerous differences with Hitler and his bad health again brought about his retirement.

The proposed strategy of the summer campaign necessitated a reorganization of the forces. Two army groups, B and A, were therefore formed under Field-Marshals von Weichs and List. Army Group B, which comprised the 2nd and 6th Armies and the 4th Panzer Army, was to move forward out of the area Kursk-Kharkov towards the great curve of the Don and the bend of the Volga at Stalingrad. Army Group A comprised the 11th and 17th Armies, Kleist's 1st Panzer Army, the 3rd Rumanian Army and, at first, the Italian expeditionary corps. These were to move from the area between Kharkov and the Black Sea across the lower Don towards the Caucasus. The 11th Army, commanded after Schobert's death by Manstein, was given the special task of taking Sebastopol.

No General Staff in the world could have evaded Hitler's orders to prepare an offensive, for these were categorical and binding. Halder's final plan provided for the centre section to hold back while a surprise thrust was made into the Crimea. This induced the Russians, under Timoschenko, to make a premature diversionary attack, and provided the Germans with an opportunity to thrust successfully into their flank in the Donetz region.

Hitler, who in this matter was undoubtedly influenced by ideological considerations (which also in part had inspired his wish to seize Leningrad), had determined that Stalingrad was the main objective. His original intention, after the capture of this city, was to have his armies turn off to the north in order to eliminate the forces which had been concentrated to the east of Moscow. In the initial stages of the attack List was to establish a defensive flank along the Don. In due course, Manstein's army, having captured Sebastopol, was to move towards the Volga.

The fact that Timoschenko's attack, though ill timed, had for all that been carried out with two army groups and strong tank forces was clear proof that Russia, whatever Hitler might say, was by no means "dead". Nevertheless, these engagements which took place in the neighbourhood of Kharkov, had used up a great part of the Russian forces between the Volga and the Don. Thus, when on June 28th, 1942, Germany began the summer offensive over an area from Kursk to the Black Sea, she was able by early July to reach the Don on a broad front. The lower reaches of this river were now crossed by the 4th Panzer Army, which then swung off towards Stalingrad. The success of these operations, during which the German forces for the first time employed rocket artillery, caused Hitler again to accuse the General Staff of incompetence and lack of daring and to permit himself to be honoured as "the greatest general of all time".

It was not till it reached the territory between the Don and the Volga that Paulus' 6th Army began to encounter a certain amount of resistance. However, Hitler's conviction that he had broken Russian strength was not to be shaken. He therefore now decided to withdraw from Paulus the greater part of his armour and to throw it in towards the south. There it could help List and Kleist's panzers to press on towards Batum and Baku. This was a most disastrous *extratour* which flew flat in the face of all the obvious military facts. A particularly puzzling feature about it is the fact that Hitler should have chosen Batum as his main objective rather than Baku, which was the centre of the oilfields.

The plan of preparing at one and the same time to fight two decisive battles, one on the Volga and one on the Caucasus, the two proposed engagements being separated by enormous distances, seemed to every professional soldier to be sheer lunacy. Halder protested, saying that the whole of military history could not show any such undertaking. For Hitler, however, who was quite convinced that he could turn all the lessons of history upside down, this was not so much a deterrent as an incentive. Halder further produced evidence of the existence of powerful new Russian formations both to the east of the Volga and in the Caucasus, while Wagner declared that he could guarantee to keep one of the two ventures supplied, but not both.

Nothing was of any avail. Hitler not only transferred his headquarters to Winniza in the Ukraine, but took over direct command of the southern part of the front. List and Kleist were ordered to thrust on with their German and Rumanian divisions over the Kuban region into the Northern Caucasus, while Paulus and his 6th Army were pushed on still further toward Stalingrad and the Volga. The protection of Army Group B's ever-extending northern flank was taken over by the 3rd Rumanian, the 2nd Hungarian and the newly-formed 8th Italian Armies. None of these elements was capable of standing up to the demands of such a campaign, nor could any of them see any good reason why they should shed their blood on behalf of a German megalomaniac in the Steppes of Southern Russia. General Blumentritt paid a visit of inspection to some of the Italian and Hungarian contingents, and was particularly adversely impressed by the quality of the Italian troops. Nevertheless, the German advance went on, and Paulus' troops fought their way to the Volga at a heavy cost in men and material. List's and Kleist's German and Rumanian divisions moved forward to the northern edge of the Caucasus and occupied the first small oilfield at Maikop on August 9th.

IV

Once again Hitler seemed to have triumphed. In the late summer of 1942 German troops stood at the North Cape, in Crete, in Finland and on the Channel coast. Rommel, who had been raised to Field-Marshal's rank and quite without justification publicized as a revolutionary "People's Marshal", had pushed forward to within 80 kilometres of Alexandria. On September 1st, Paulus' troops reached the western suburbs of Stalingrad, where the Russians, under Rodinzev, put up a desperate defence. Meanwhile German mountain troops hoisted the Swastika on Mount Elbrus, the highest point in the Caucasus, and U-boat sinkings reached the unprecedented figure of 700,000 tons a month.

Rommel, who feared for his supplies, which the Italian Navy was no longer in any condition to protect, asked for his exhausted and battle-weary troops to be withdrawn in time. Hitler, however, gave orders for an attack on Cairo, while Mussolini prepared to enter that city personally at the head of his Italian troops.

In Berlin, however, General Marras, the Italian military attaché, had prophesied as early as March that the territory between Stalingrad and Astrachan on the Volga would be the grave of the German Army. A certain secretary at the Embassy, Count Lanza, was subsequently to publish highly informative memoirs under the pseudonym Leonardo Simondi. He appears at this time to have heard severe criticism of Halder in Party circles, but also—in other circles—rumours of an impending coup. He writes of Halder that with his pince-nez, his appearance suggested that of a petty employee, though actually he regarded his intelligence as being of the highest order and considered him to be the best German strategist of his day.

The rumours circulating in Berlin were simply the effect of the growing conflict between Halder and Hitler, for the truth is that some of Hitler's dispositions at this stage can only be regarded as those of a madman. On the night of August 18th, British, Canadian and American forces carried out a large-scale reconnaissance at Dieppe. Hitler promptly concluded that an invasion in the west was imminent and ordered the transport of a number of mobile *élite* units from Russia to France. Meanwhile von Manstein's army which had taken Sebastopol was sent off to the north, to take Leningrad, the same 60cm. guns being used as had been employed in the bombardment of Sebastopol. At length a great part of von Kleist's armour, aircraft and anti-aircraft guns were taken away to assist Paulus. The situation of both these commanders was precarious, and the effect of Hitler's action was simply to stop one hole by creating another. Blumentritt's impression was that the "Verdun idea" had seized on Hitler's mind. In other words, it was Hitler's intention to force Russia's armies to bleed themselves to death on this great bridgehead west of the Volga.

While the 6th Army fought its way into the interior of the town, street by street and house by house, and while the offensive of List and Kleist, now denuded of its mobile forces, was coming gradually to a standstill in the Northern Caucasus, Hitler was overwhelming the Chief of General Staff with reproaches which were as embittered as they were ridiculous, and accusing the whole General Staff of cowardice and lack of drive. Reports of the formation of new Russian armies were roundly dismissed as false—only the most simple-minded theorist could be taken in by such Bolshevik bluff; and when Halder ultimately produced proof of the size of the new enemy formations—one and a half million men north of Stalingrad, and half a million in the Southern Caucasus—he was treated to a typical Hit-lerian outburst of rage. Hitler advanced on him, foaming at the mouth and with his fists clenched, crying out that he forbade such "idiotic chatter" in his presence.

When, on September 24th, Halder still persisted in explaining what would happen when the new Russian reserve armies attacked the over-extended flank that ran out to Stalingrad, he was dismissed. According to Halder's own account, Hitler on this occasion reckoned up all the various differences he had ever had with him, giving the exact date of each, and said that this everlasting fight with the General Staff had cost him half his nervous energy and that such a price was too high. The problem which the Army had still to solve was not a matter which required technical proficiency. What was needed was the "glow of National Socialist conviction", and that was something he could never expect from officers of the old school.

When Ciano heard of Halder's dismissal, he noted in his diary on September 28th, "Bad sign", and it is true that this event marks the end of the period during which the old General Staff still conducted operations. It was also the end of the period in which German arms had enjoyed some measure of success.

Between 1939 and 1942 the aim of all planning had been the destruction of the enemy force and the regaining of the internal line which was to be pushed outwards so far that air attacks on the nerve centres of production would be rendered impossible. The basis of tactics had been the use of large numbers of tanks acting in combination with aircraft, the latter performing the functions of flying artillery. In other words, the basis of tactics had been the military exploitation of the internal combustion engine. Now began the second phase. It was marked by the contraction of the internal line which German expansion had contrived to extend and the mobilization of that same internal combustion engine by the enemy powers, a task which their superior resources enabled them to perform on a vastly greater scale.

V

Halder's successor as Chief of the General Staff was Lieutenant-General Kurt Zeitzler, at that time acting as Chief of Staff to the Commander in Chief of the West. Zeitzler, who was born in 1895, was the son of a Protestant pastor, and there was much about him that made him from Hitler's point of view a suitable candidate for his new post. He had been an infantry officer in the First World War and while in the *Reichswehr* passed through the course of "Leader's Assistant". His background, however, was certainly not that of the old Great General Staff or of the leading clique in the *Truppenamt*. In 1934 he had transferred to tanks, had later served as a Lieutenant-Colonel under Warlimont in the *Wehrmachtführungsstab* and had then become Chief of Staff to Kleist's Panzer Group in France. Finally, in the winter of 1940/41, he had carried out in civilian clothes a reconnaissance of Mount Rhodope for the future deployment of List's army group.

Halder, whose appearance so much resembled that of a teacher in a secondary school, had often had precisely that effect upon Hitler. He was a man of the quiet, learned type, suggesting something of the objectivity of the mathematician. Zeitzler, whose thickset body seemed to express an unmistakable dynamism, was essentially the man of action. Zeitzler had a thorough grasp of the problems of tank warfare; what his mind failed to recognize was the nature of the atmosphere in the Führer's headquarters and all its criss-cross of cliques and intrigue. Being an essentially practical man, he may well have believed that no more was needed than a little frankness to put Hitler, militarily speaking, on the right road. It was not long, however, before the difficulties of his position were brought home to him. This in time induced an attitude of excessive caution, which was not calculated to diminish the frequency of Hitler's temperamental explosions.

However, Hitler's distrust of the General Staff was ineradicable, and Zeitzler was only entrusted with the conduct of operations on the eastern front, which Hitler could directly control. Thus, as one of the most distinguished of the old German General Staff, Lieutenant-General Dr Hans Speidel, pointed out, the Chief of the General Staff became, for all practical purposes, the C. in C. East, but with considerably less authority than Hindenburg and Ludendorff had enjoyed in that capacity. All other theatres of war were put under the

O.K.W. and the *Wehrmachtführungsstab*, which, even in numbers, was much too weak to cope with such a task—a fact which caused all matters of supply to be left in the care of the Quartermaster-General of the Army.

The people who now really had influence on the conduct of the war were Jodl, Warlimont and Lieutenant-General von Buttlar-Brandenfels, the head of the Operations Department in the *Wehrmachtführungsstab*. Jodl for a time fell into disfavour, because he dared to try and persuade Hitler to keep Halder on. He has told us that the outburst which this attempt produced was well-nigh incredible, Hitler on that occasion swearing that he would replace him by Paulus, as soon as Stalingrad was cleaned up. For a long time Hitler behaved like an ill-mannered schoolboy, refusing even to shake hands with Jodl or to dine with the officers of his own working staff. When he finally decided to return to the common table, he had himself accompanied by S.S. officers, as though he feared that one of the other officers might draw a gun on him.

The episode of the O.K.W. theatres of war, which, however distant they might be, were all subject to Hitler's direct control, was really the beginning of the end. Warlimont saw the absurdity of the position clearly enough. The only sensible function for the *Wehrmachtführungsstab* was the co-ordination of all the different war efforts. The actual conduct of operations, as Warlimont saw it, must rest with the General Staff. For the *Wehrmachtführungsstab* to attempt to concern itself directly with distant theatres of war was wholly alien to its true purpose. Yet Warlimont's attempts to dissuade Jodl from acting as Chief of a sort of supernumerary General Staff led nowhere at all. Jodl believed too ardently in Hitler's military genius.

Zeitzler felt the need to carry out certain simplifications in the General Staff arrangements. Thus, the function of *Oberquartiermeister I* as deputy Chief of Staff was abolished. Much more drastic changes, however, were made by Hitler, who removed the personnel department lock, stock and barrel from the General Staff and put it under Schmundt, his adjutant in chief. The reintroduction of the old almighty Adjutant-General's department could now be said to be complete.

Meanwhile, Hitler continued his efforts to rob the Army of its traditional character, which had always been essentially unpolitical, so that he could turn it into a political instrument of National Socialism. It was with this general purpose in mind that he created N.S.F.O., the *Nationalsozialistische Führungsorganisation*, or National

Socialist Leadership Organization, within the officer corps, which in reality was a sort of spy ring, its members being something half-way between political commissars and political propagandists. Their task was the education of the new "Soldiers of the Revolution". Hitler often emphasized how impressed he had been by the fact that the Russian Army was permeated by the Communist ideology, and wanted the German Army to be correspondingly permeated by National Socialism. Keitel was told that he (Hitler) wanted to train General Staff officers of the Tito type.

The last stages of this process were to be represented by developments spread over the next two years. These included the transfer of the Secret Service in May 1944 to the S.S., the setting up of "People's Grenadier Divisions" and a People's Artillery Corps, which were to be the stepping stones to a future revolutionary peacetime army, and the creation of such paramilitary formations as the *Volkssturm* and *Wehrwolf*. Further, Himmler was himself made commander of the *ersatz* army and the S.S. was put in charge of "V" weapons.

In the final days of war, when everything was in dissolution, it was even decided to replace the N.S.F.O., which was under General Reinecke, the Chief of the *Wehrmachtamt*, by a new organization under Martin Bormann. This was indeed the triumph of ideology rising out of the ruins of the Army.

VI

We have already noted the fierce competition for replacements between the different arms. Actually, the ultimate arbiter in such matters was the *Wehrmachtführungsstab* and here Hitler definitely favoured the Navy, the *Luftwaffe* and the Waffen S.S. Since the *Luftwaffe's* establishment in planes had for the time being been reduced, the General Staff asked for the incorporation of its superfluous personnel into the Army. Göring, however, hastened to persuade Hitler that it would be wrong to expose men who had been so thoroughly trained in the spirit of National Socialism to the influence of reactionary generals. For this reason 22 so-called "*Luftwaffe* Field Divisions" were set up which, since they wholly lacked experience in land warfare, suffered inordinate casualties. At a later stage the *Luftwaffe's* redundant personnel was for the most part organized into paratroop formations, which ultimately reached corps and even army strength, and during the last stages of the war attained something of the status of *élite* troops.

Much damage was done in other ways to the Army by Hitler's obstinacy. The General Staff put the maximum figure for the number of divisions that could be organized at 300. Hitler, however, ordered the establishment of 450. Being able to boast of large numbers on paper was something of a propaganda asset. In order to prevent the revival of any kind of tradition, moreover, old tried units were left with their gaps unfilled, while new units were created with the manpower which would otherwise have been available for the old. The older units thus had no chance of letting others have the benefit of their battle experience.

Similar rivalries and cross purposes in high policy bedevilled the problem of using anti-Bolshevik Russians, Ukrainians and other peoples incorporated in but in the main hostile to the Soviet Union. In 1942 the different army groups in the east set up units consisting of deserters and volunteers, while, quite independently of this, the O.K.W. approved the formation of volunteer legions from the Turcoman peoples and the Caucasus. This idea of anti-Bolshevik and anti-totalitarian volunteers found considerable support in the General Staff. It was especially favoured by two officers, Major von Stauffenberg, who was the specialist for new formations in the Operations Department, and his friend Lieutenant-Colonel von Roenne, head of the section "Foreign Armies East". Neither of these men was a friend of the régime.

Thanks to Stauffenberg's initiative, a special "Weapons General" was appointed for so-called "Eastern Troops". He was General Hellmich, who had incurred Hitler's displeasure while commanding a division in the winter campaign of 1941, but had an excellent knowledge of the east. The whole thing was done without Hitler or the *Wehrmachtführungsstab* ever hearing about it. Zeitzler approved, for he saw here the beginnings of a rational eastern policy.

Shortly afterwards the O.K.W.'s propaganda department came out with a candidate of its own. This was General Vlassov, who had been made a prisoner of war and now offered to raise a "Russian Army of Liberation", composed of other captured Russians. It was all a good example of the kind of duplication and of the contradictions that were the curse of German affairs. To complicate matters further, both Stauffenberg's volunteer movement and the efforts of Vlassov (and of his friends and collaborators, Generals Shilenkov, Truchin and Malyschkin) were later nullified by the ruthless Colonial policy of the National Socialist satraps in the east. Thus, one of the greatest potential forces for the overthrow of the Bolshevik system remained unused.

After the General Staff had been eliminated so far as most theatres of war were concerned, Hitler interfered ever more actively with the detailed conduct of the war. Not everything he did was wrong, but much of what he attempted was started too late, and all too often real inspiration alternated with the most ghastly blunders. Hitler's hobby horse was the quest for new types of weapon, an urge that was bound sooner or later to clash with the whole principle of mass production. Even so, there were a number of developments which must undeniably be reckoned to his credit. The building of the new heavy "Tiger" tank, of the extra heavy "King Tiger", a somewhat lighter "Panther", all of which were to be a match for the Russian models, also the enlargement of the calibre of anti-tank weapons, the introduction of the modernized anti-tank grenade—all these were either due to Hitler's own initiative or were actively encouraged by him.

It was typical of Hitler that he should suddenly have thrown himself into the furthering of liquid fuel rockets and guided missiles, devices that had admittedly been neglected far too long, though the Army had already been studying them for a considerable time. These so-called "V" or "*Vergeltungs*" weapons, that is to say, "Retribution weapons", were to be Germany's answer to British air attacks, and a number of artillery regiments were trained under General Heinemann in the use of the new "wonder weapon". A start was made in the construction of firing ramps in France, while propaganda performed a dual function, at one and the same time cloaking the whole thing in mystery and also arousing, as it did in the matter of the Atlantic Wall, the most wildly exaggerated hopes.

The smallest details were covered by orders from headquarters, army group commanders being strictly confined to their own immediate spheres and forbidden to gather information about other parts of the front, or even to concern themselves at all with matters relating to foreign policy. Even so, as Blumentritt testifies, the quality of the order-giving was, thanks to Hitler's complete lack of mental discipline, extremely poor, though since Gneisenau's day the clarity and conciseness of military orders had been a source of pride to the Prussian Army. It must, however, be admitted that the ambiguity of these "rubber orders" often enabled commanders to exercise a certain amount of discretion, since they could often be interpreted in more ways than one.

VII

The war now began to be marked by a progressive disappearance of all restraint. On October 18th Hitler issued orders that Commandos and parachutists were in all cases to be shot, despite the fact that they were regular soldiers. On the other side, partisan warfare began to assume increasing proportions in the Balkans and particularly on the Russian front, where it was seriously endangering the supply system. It was answered by devastations, shooting of hostages and mass deportations. A number of the army group and army commanders concerned were thus brought into touch with a terror system which was in fundamental contradiction to every officer tradition but from the influence of which they could not escape. The most terrible of all the things that were done, however, such as the extermination of the Jews of Eastern Europe in the gas ovens and gas chambers of Upper Silesia and Poland, were carefully kept secret by the S.S. organizations concerned.

Zeitzler soon saw that the problem confronting him was an insoluble one. What, in the last resort, was one to do with a Supreme War Lord who insisted on regarding General Staff maps with the eye of an "artist" and asked for parts of the line to be straightened out because their appearance was displeasing to the eye? It was not long before Hitler had to recognize that even Zeitzler was no true "General of the Revolution"—all the more so when he refused the usual donation from Hitler's hand with which the Führer had been accustomed to delight his Field-Marshals, especially Keitel and Kluge.

Yet the General Staff itself cannot wholly shed its responsibility for the unfortunate situation that had developed. Despite the fact that under Halder's leadership the majority of high-ranking officers had fully recognized Hitler's military, human and moral inadequacy, the General Staff had never brought its opposition to the point of actual deeds. It still professed to adhere to the old principle of co-responsibility as Massenbach had first laid it down, and Gneisenau defined it, but shirked the difficulties of insisting on its translation into reality. Its desperate attempts to cling to the positions that it still contrived to hold merely caused it to incur odium as the executor of Hitler's orders. No wonder Beck, its would-be reformer and renovator, spoke in helplessness of a treason against its whole tradition.

Such was the inheritance that Zeitzler had taken over and such the background of the situation at the beginning of the winter of 1942, when the campaign against which the General Staff had warned Hitler but which it had nevertheless consented to plan, came to its disastrous dead end. In one of his last public speeches, Hitler had bombastically declared that the Germans were in Stalingrad and would stay there, and that no one would ever regain the territory on which the German soldier had set his foot.

For all that, it was an undeniable fact that at Stalingrad the Russians were still desperately resisting and that it was becoming a second Verdun quite as much for Germany as for Russia, a Verdun which was steadily devouring two German armies. The summer campaign had had some successes but no decisive victory. It was more true to say that Stalingrad had produced the final bankruptcy of Hitler's strategy of illusion and prestige.

On the other fronts the results were at best disappointing. Turkey refused to become Germany's ally. The offensive in the Caucasus came to a dead stop. List asked for permission to retreat, Jodl—an unusual procedure for that officer—visited him personally to size up the situation, and was compelled to admit that he was right. List was, however, removed from his command in November and replaced by von Kleist, while one of his divisional commanders, General Sponeck was dismissed the Army and sent to a military prison for retreating on his own authority. In the end, Kleist had to retire after all.

At the beginning of November, Rommel was defeated at El Alamein. A British general had for the first time been equipped with modern armoured forces and adequate aircraft. His name was Montgomery. When, on November 8th and 9th, British and American forces landed in Morocco, Rommel was caught between two fires. Italy's position in the Mediterranean grew desperate. The hasty occupation of Southern France, Corsica and Tunis by German and Italian divisions and the despatch of the 5th Panzer Army to Tunisia under Colonel-General von Arnim, could bring about no fundamental change in the situation. The only result was a further over-extension of the front and the dissipation of forces which could be more usefully employed elsewhere.

In Russia the battle for Stalingrad reached a new phase. The Russians were reinforced and, as Halder had foreseen, began the attack on the long exposed German flank that stretched towards the city. The first thrust struck at the 3rd Rumanian Army and completely overwhelmed it. The 48th Panzer Corps, composed of a German and a Rumanian armoured division, the latter equipped with old out-dated captured French material, failed to make any successful counter-attack. Hitler dismissed the commander of this force and threatened to have him shot, but that did not help the situation. Shortly afterwards the whole Don front was in ruins, and Paulus' 6th Army of 320,000 men was caught in a trap some 60 kilometres in breadth between the Volga and the Don.

Hitler's first impulse was to denude Army Group A, in the Caucasus, of the 4th Panzer Army and to use it to relieve Paulus, but Army Group A was itself far too heavily pressed for that to be possible. Both von Weichs, commanding Army Group B, and Zeitzler believed it essential to evacuate the Stalingrad position and to order Paulus to fight his way out—if necessary abandoning his heavy equipment.

While, however, the 6th Army was fighting for its life amid snow and ice, an equally embittered battle was in progress at the Führer's headquarters. The General Staff, conscious that it shared in the overall responsibility for any future development, strove to assert its traditional right to a voice in decisions. Zeitzler told Hitler to his face that it was a crime to leave the 6th Army at Stalingrad. On the night of November 23rd, he believed that he had got Hitler to the point where he was willing to order Paulus to break out, and informed Army Group B accordingly. On the morning of the 24th Weichs had resolved to issue the necessary orders on his own authority. Suddenly, however, a directive arrived from Hitler which strictly forbade anything of the kind.

The fact is that Hitler was incapable of conceiving that the 6th Army should do anything but fight where it stood. That Army had in his eyes become a bastion on which depended the collapsing fronts both on the Don and in the Caucasus. Moreover, Göring, whose aircraft had suffered heavily, and who had also lost considerable prestige, took this opportunity of thrusting himself into the foreground, and guaranteed to keep Paulus supplied by air. Göring's arguments carried more weight than those of Zeitzler; orders were sent to the 6th Army to "hedgehog itself in" and this force was somewhat pompously christened "Fortress Stalingrad" for the occasion. In this manner the battle on the home front was lost by the General Staff.

Once again that winter a number of inconvenient generals were disciplined. The commanders of the 2nd and 17th Armies, Generals von Salmuth and Ruoff, and von Wietersheim, the commander of a Panzer corps, were dismissed. Meanwhile, all efforts to supply it by air having been abandoned, the end was approaching for the 6th Army, whose supplies, fuel and munitions were severely limited.

There was only one encouraging thing about the situation. It was that Hitler was persuaded to entrust the task of reconstructing the Don front and relieving Paulus to the best strategic mind in the east, namely Manstein. The 6th Army, the remains of the 4th Panzer Army, the 3rd and 4th Rumanian Armies, and some German forces which were in process of being grouped under Colonel-General Hollidt, were all formed under Manstein into the "Army Group Don". Manstein immediately asked for the evacuation of the Caucasus, for Paulus to be given permission to retreat, and for the formation of a firm line of defence on the Donetz. Weichs was sent to command an army group in the Balkans.

Manstein's forces fought their way to within 50 kilometres of Stalingrad, but Paulus' tanks had not sufficient fuel to effect a junction. Manstein's effort failed, and as a result of the defeat of its Hungarian and Italian elements, "Army Group Don" was compelled to retire all along the line. Soon the facts of the situation were to justify a remark of Manstein's that the 6th Army was his greatest but by no means his only cause of anxiety, for the whole southern front was on the point of giving way and Manstein was soon finding himself under the necessity of supporting Kleist as the latter at last began his withdrawal from the Caucasus.

VIII

Hunger, cold and casualties were rapidly reducing Paulus' forces. There was still one way open, however, to that unfortunate soldier, namely to attempt a sortie on his own responsibility, a step which a number of his generals were pressing him to take. Now Paulus had been *Oberquartiermeister I* of the General Staff and had himself been a witness of Halder's vain struggle for authority. Yet Paulus was a typical representative of that older generation of Staff officers who purchased their military experience at the cost of any knowledge they might otherwise have of life and the world in general. He was a soldier, and his first duty, as he saw it, was obedience. He cared nothing for politics, nor could he in his isolation realize to what extent his useless continuation of the fight at Stalingrad would be the hinge on which would turn the fate both of his own organization, the General Staff, and of the people of Germany as a whole.

The impending disaster, involving as it did the pointless sacrifice of a whole army through one man's obstinate and exaggerated regard for his prestige, provided a definite spur to the military opposition. Beck came out with a plan according to which a sortie by Paulus was to be the signal for collective action by all the Field-Marshals, who were to confront Hitler and demand his resignation. Beck's plan rested on two assumptions. The first of these was that a man like Paulus could bring himself to act after the manner of Yorck at Tauroggen, the second that the Field-Marshals would all be of one mind. Both assumptions were impossible, particularly the last. Though all the officers concerned were members of the General Staff, the "unitary thinking" of that institution had long become a thing of the past. Actually neither Rommel nor Rundstedt nor Manstein would have been prepared to act in the manner desired. The last-named in particular was haunted by the picture of the battling southern front, and could only think of one thing—the danger that the flood from the east might burst the weak German dam and then submerge all of Central Europe. In such circumstances Manstein would on no account consider changing horses in midstream. Rundstedt, an old Prussian aristocrat and by no means friendly to the régime, about which his sarcasm was ready enough to vent itself, believed that the situation could still be saved if the General Staff were given freedom of action, but felt that he no longer had the strength to force Hitler to such a course.

In the General Staff itself, the most ardent advocate for the "Field-Marshals' action" was to be found in that Major von Stauffenberg to whom allusion has already been made in connection with the proposed anti-totalitarian volunteers. Stauffenberg's duties necessitated his making frequent journeys to visit the different commanders, and he used these occasions to sound them out, for Stauffenberg was profoundly convinced that it was wrong to stand by inactive while everything went down in ruin. He also believed that this was the decisive hour—perhaps the last hour—not only for the General Staff but also for the German Army.

These tentative approaches of Stauffenberg's ended in bitter disappointment. And yet it may well have been a strange remark which Manstein had occasion to make that led to a resolve which was to attain its dramatic fruition somewhat later, for Manstein told this young Staff major that that kind of thing could not be done without a definite order from above, and that somebody ought to give a proper order in the matter, an observation which was presumably meant to be ironic. It seems reasonable to suppose that Stauffenberg's later decision to usurp the authority to give orders has its roots in the impression vacillation and bankruptcy of counsel which the Field-Marshals displayed on this occasion.

Most high-ranking officers believed that matters could still be saved by a shortening of the whole eastern front, the German forces being withdrawn to a line from whence they could regain the initiative and follow a strategy of offensive defence. In this way they could in course of time wear down the enemy, despite his numbers, by repeated spoiling attacks, while at the same time husbanding their forces. If that were done, Paulus' sacrifices at Stalingrad would not have been wholly futile.

Hitler's personality, however, presented an insuperable obstacle to such a course. His imagination did not suffice to grasp the real potentialities of an elastic defence. It could only rise to the idea of obstinately maintaining what had been won. Any retirement, according to Hitler, was a defeat. Human life had never been a consideration with him, and it was the soldier's business to die where he stood.

It was Hitler's attitude that very largely caused Zeitzler, who saw no other way of saving the situation in the east, to make a despairing effort towards the complete reorganization of the whole structure of command. Zeitzler's plan involved a certain number of drastic changes. The Commander of the eastern front was to have complete independence, Keitel was to be replaced by a stronger personality, and the two *Oberkommandos* (i.e. those of the Army and the *Wehrmacht*) were to be fused into a unitary *Wehrmacht* General Staff which amongst other things would have the S.S. under its authority. It was also part of the programme that the armaments industry should be placed wholly under the control of the Quartermaster-General, who would be able to subject it to coherent planning.

What Zeitzel was aiming at, in other words, was a complete reordering of the Führer's headquarters. Under the proposed arrangements, Hitler would still have remained Supreme War Lord, but would have had the conduct of the war taken out of his hands.

Such root and branch reforms, however, were not opposed by Hitler alone, or even only by his immediate military *entourage*, but also by the commanders of the Navy, the *Luftwaffe* and the S.S. Above all, Raeder's successor, Grand Admiral Dönitz, and Himmler were violently opposed to any revival of the old great General Staff in any form whatsoever. This was, indeed, to a large extent the crucial matter on both sides, and it was the question of an adequate reform of the structure of military authority that finally decided many General Staff officers to enter the ranks of the opposition.

In the General Staff, Lieutenant-General Heusinger, Chief of the Operations Department, who already had strong moral objection to the policy of extermination pursued towards Slavs and Jews, now became a determined enemy of Hitler. The same applies to the head of the Organization Department, Major-General Stieff, and also to General Lindemann, "Weapons General" for artillery. In the Army command, Wagner, the Quartermaster-General, and Olbricht, Chief of the *Allgemeines Heeresamt*, were similarly minded.

Meanwhile events at Stalingrad were even making Ribbentrop apprehensive and caused him to plead with Hitler for a separate peace with Russia, but Hitler, though Ribbentrop had his negotiators ready in Sweden, declared that he would not consider the suggestion till the military situation had improved.

On January 22nd, an event occurred that is worthy of passing note. On that day the two main oppositional groups met in the home of Count Peter Yorck von Wartenburg in Berlin-Lichterfelde. These comprised on the one hand the men who favoured an outright *coup d'état*, namely, Dr Goerdeler, Professor Popitz, Ulrich von Hassell, and, on the other hand, the would-be architects of reform on emancipated conservative lines, Moltke, von der Schulenburg and von Trott zu Solz. Goerdeler still clung to the idea of a regency by the former Crown Prince, or possibly by his son and heir Prince Louis Ferdinand of Prussia, after Hitler had been forcibly removed, but the feeling was that the institution of monarchy had lost its meaning for the masses and the future really belonged to some kind of moderate Socialism. On the day following this meeting, however, Roosevelt and Churchill concluded their talks in Casablanca, having agreed on the formula of unconditional surrender, a formula which gave the death blow to any hopes that may have been entertained either by the "shadow government" or by the oppositional elements in the General Staff, that their enemies would negotiate with a "respectable" government. As against this, the "unconditional surrender" formula was of great help to Goebbels' propaganda, which promptly claimed that Hitler and Germany were identical with one another, and that Hitler's fate was that of the German people. When, in 1943, Anthony Eden was again told of the efforts of anti-Hitler elements to create a government charged with the conclusion of a negotiated peace, he merely replied that the world had been misled too often.

IX

On February 2nd, 90,000 men, which was all that remained of the German 6th Army, surrendered at Stalingrad. Shortly before this, when Paulus persisted in rejecting Marshal Rokossowski's numerous calls to surrender, Hitler had made him a Field-Marshal, having his eye on him as a possible future head of the *Wehrmachtführungsstab*. Thus it was that a German Field-Marshal, together with twenty-four generals and some 2,500 officers, went into captivity. It was a second Jena, and was certainly the greatest defeat in history that a German Army had ever undergone.

Hitler now took the line that the sacrifice of the 6th Army had stabilized the eastern front. Goebbels proclaimed "Total War" and appealed to the people of Germany to make their supreme effort for victory, though the chances of victory had by now long been gambled away. Amongs other things, German superiority in artillery over Russia was vanishing, and the tank arm was visibly declining. By 1944 the numerical relation between Russian and German tanks was to be five to one.

Libya was next lost, the German forces being pressed together into Tunis, where they were caught between the forces of Montgomery on the one side and Eisenhower on the other. Rommel went sick with jaundice, and was sent home. He asked to be succeeded by Guderian, though even the creator of the German tank arm could not possibly have saved the situation. Nor did Hitler accede to this request, but appointed Colonel-General von Arnim to the North African command. Warlimont flew personally to Tunis, although visits to the front by members of the *Wehrmachtführungsstab* were most unusual. The view he formed was far too optimistic and served, when its erroneous character was revealed, to add greatly to this officer's unpopularity.

The disaster of Stalingrad had a profound effect on the military opposition, which now in a marked manner changed its character. Zeitzler's battle for the reorganization of the apparatus of command now entered the acute stage, but a new oppositional stratum also began to be formed in the Army consisting, roughly speaking, of officers of the rank of major-general and of the younger Staff officers, who still carried on the General Staff tradition. From 1939 to 1942 Germany had had a shadow government in search of an army to carry out its proposed coup. Now there was a group of Army officers searching for a government—a government capable of negotiating with the enemy and of procuring a constructive peace not for Germany alone but for the whole continent. The most prominent figure in this latter movement was unquestionably Stauffenberg.

Nicholas Philip Schenk, Count von Stauffenberg, who was born in 1907, was the son of a Swabian Court Marshal. He joined the 17th Cavalry in 1926 and passed his examinations with outstanding brilliance. He was posted to the General Staff in 1938, went through the Polish campaign and a part of the campaign in France, and was posted to the Organization Department in the beginning of June 1940.

While he was still at the *Kriegsakademie*, he attracted the attention of Professor Elze, the military historian, who saw in him the man who might one day be called upon to breathe a new spirit into both General Staff and Army, and who might produce something better than the one-sided military specialization which was the weakness affecting both these institutions. The fact that on his mother's side Stauffenberg was a great-great-grandson of Gneisenau, a circumstance which, the young man felt, laid him under special obligation, would have made it peculiarly fitting for him to attain the position of Chief of General Staff, and in that capacity to re-enact the part of his great ancestor in inspiring that institution with a new idealism.

Possessed of a genuine culture both of heart and intellect, a lively interest in the world about him and an excellent understanding of all political problems, Stauffenberg stood out in a marked manner from his colleagues and contemporaries. Though he did not underestimate the value of tradition, he was nevertheless convinced that tradition alone did not suffice, but that the new age called for new methods and new ideals. Despite a strong artistic sensibility with which was connected his admiration for Stefan George and his eclectic circle, he nevertheless struck one as a natural soldier and a natural leader. He was not only a great man, however, but a charming one. His kindly manner and his readiness to hear what anyone who crossed his path had to say, made him a personality with quite unusual powers of fascination. For the first time, the evil genius which was Hitler was thus confronted in the ranks of the General Staff with a man who had something more than the essential personal decency of the older generation of General Staff officers, a man who was endowed in the noblest sense of the words with both passion and strength. Nor was Stauffenberg ignorant of the power that he possessed over men. He knew it well, and was determined to throw that asset into the scale where it was most needed.

The Stauffenbergs had always been Catholic, and their greatest son was a Christian of great moral sensibility. The enduring violation of right which was personified in Hitler, to which so many of his comrades closed their eyes, was ever before his own, and caused him to revolt against a régime which was a denial of all that was best in the spiritual inheritance both of Germany and of the West. Yet precisely because he was so very much a soldier, these convictions did not take root without a struggle. The surprising victory in the west had not failed to stir his pride, but the question of the real meaning of this victory remained unanswered. He found that victory futile unless it could make an end to the sorry story of nationalist power politics which doomed Europe to an everlasting devouring of herself, and it became increasingly plain that Hitler was not the man to end that process.

The winter crisis of 1941/2 and the disaster which ended the second summer campaign, were lived through by him at the Führer's different headquarters, and they intensified his doubts, making the certainty stronger that it was wrong to stand by inactive. At one moment fate seemed to intervene. On April 1st, 1943, Stauffenberg was severely wounded by low-flying aircraft in Tunisia. His right hand was torn off, his left one maimed, and he was blinded in the right eye. At first it seemed as though he would be completely blind. Stauffenberg himself feared this, and the experience was one of the most bitter that could befall such a man, all the more so since what he had seen in Tunisia confirmed his belief that final catastrophe both for the Reich and its Army was inevitable unless some powerful hand could seize the wheel.

Soon after Stalingrad, the first definite plan to assassinate Hitler came into being, the participants being Staff officers of the centre army group on the eastern front, members of the *Allgemeine Heeresamt* in Berlin and of the Secret Service Department. The originators of the plan were Colonel von Tresckow, G.S.O.1 of the centre army group, the Secret Service Officer of that same army group, Colonel von Gersdorff, the *aide-de-camp*, Lieutenant von Schlabrendorff, and in Berlin General Olbricht and Major-General Oster. Tresckow had made sure of a reliable force in von Boeselager's cavalry; Olbricht was contemplating using as shock troops the *Abwehr* unit which had originally been the Brandenburg "Special Purposes" Regiment, now increased to divisional strength.

The plan was to put a bomb with a time fuse into the Führer's plane when he visited the headquarters of the centre army group. The crashing of the plane on its return flight was to be the signal for the revolt. Hitler actually appeared at this headquarters in 1943, on March 13th, and the bomb, disguised as a bottle of brandy, was smuggled into the plane at its departure. However, the time fuse failed. Fortunately for the conspirators, the unexploded bomb was recovered after the plane had landed, but this misadventure for the time being put an end to this plot—but not to the plotting. There were a whole number of such schemes, which for one reason or another proved impracticable. Death was already stalking Hitler unseen— which only shows how weak was the real basis of his authority.

Hitler must, however, to some extent have been aware of the hostile attitude of the officer corps. Goebbels noted in his diary in the spring of 1943 that Hitler had remarked that none of the generals told him the truth. They were all dishonest and enemies of National Socialism. Hitler was absolutely ill when he even thought of them.

X

During the year 1943 two of the principal personalities in the shadow government were withdrawn from the scene, one of them permanently. Beck had to undergo an operation from the effects of which he never fully recovered, while Hammerstein-Equord died of cancer. As against this, however, Stauffenberg, after his recovery, was made Chief of Staff in the *Allgemeine Heeresamt* by Olbricht. While he was still in hospital in Munich, Stauffenberg had been visited by Zeitzler himself, who presented him with his wound stripe; that Zeitzler should have made this personal visit is an indication of the reputation which the young Staff officer already enjoyed. Olbricht was now deliberately giving him a post where he might have a chance to act.

On November 1st, Stauffenberg officially took over his new duties, and the military resistance movement now had a new aspect. He began working a number of his old friends of the *Kriegsakademie*, such as Colonel Merz von Quirnheim, into his department, and in the months that followed he became the man in whom the hopes of all true patriots were centred. Men began to speak of him quite seriously as the future Commander in Chief of the Army, and it went so far that careerists took pains to get in touch with him in the secret belief that he was "the coming man".

It was Stauffenberg and his immediate colleagues who now began working at a proper military deployment plan for the *coup d'état*. For this purpose they made use of Canaris, who went out of his way to inform Hitler that the critical situation on the different fronts involved the danger of disturbances among the millions of prisoners of war and foreign slave labourers within the Reich. It was therefore necessary to be ready to make use of the home or *ersatz* army, if occasion should arise, so that law and order might be restored.

Hitler was thus induced to order plans to be made for the use of the *ersatz* army in such an eventuality, the plans being given the code name "Valkyrie", and the working out of them entrusted to the *Heeresamt*. By preparing a number of secret orders in advance, Stauffenberg made ready to use this plan for his own purposes. His own chief, Olbricht, assisted him in this, and he further had close collaborators in Major Ulrich von Oertzen of the General Staff, in Lindemann, the Weapons General of the Artillery, and also in a group of friendly officers in what was for his purpose the most important militaty district, namely *"Generalkommando III"* in Berlin. At the head of these was the *Generalkommando's* Chief of Staff, Major-General von Rost, and the "3rd Defence Industry Officer", Colonel of the *Luftwaffe* Hans Gronau.

It was at this stage not yet certain whether Hitler was to be arrested or assassinated, but immediately he had been got rid of in one way or the other, the intention was to use "Valkyrie" for the setting up of a military dictatorship, which in its turn was to lead to a constitutional government based on free elections. General Lindemann, to whom more than to anybody else fell the task of approaching the commanders of the *ersatz* army, acted on the assumption that in each case either the commander himself or his Chief of Staff could be won over. They all belonged to the generation of the *Reichswehr*, and so could be looked upon as old comrades. Such men would surely not refuse their help when the Fatherland was to be saved.

Not only the actual method by which Hitler was to be removed but the whole character of the régime by which he was to be succeeded still remained subjects of dispute, for the conspirators contained men of the most varying views, Democrats, Socialists and Bavarian legitimists (such, for instance, as the Secret Service Officer of the Vienna command, Count Marogna-Redwitz). It was only the purely military side of the plan that took concrete form, this last being the work of Stauffenberg, Lindemann, von Rost and von Oertzen, with von Tresckow, of the centre army group, giving occasional advice. It was the wife of the last-named who typed out the necessary secret orders, a task in which she was assisted by a certain Margaret von Oven, sometime secretary to Fritsch and Hammerstein-Equord.

The forces available for the most decisive part of the scheme, namely the occupation of Berlin and of the principal radio transmitting stations, were first of all the "watch battalion" of the *"Grossdeutschland"* Division, itself an *élite* formation, and the different weapons schools. Some of the latter, for instance, the armourer's school, were actually in Berlin itself, while the Infantry School was in Döberitz the school for "fast troops", which had a number of scout vehicles and motor-cyclists at its disposal, was in Krampnitz, the tank school in Wünsdorf, while the artillery school was in Jüterbog. Thus troops of all arms were quite close to the capital.

Stauffenberg carefully investigated the dispositions both of the active and reserve formations of the Waffen S.S., which, with the addition of its Lettish, Bohemian-Croatian, Dutch Walloon and Scandinavian units, now totalled some 17 divisions, and included three Panzer-corps, besides an additional two such corps which were in process of formation. The majority of Waffen S.S. units were, it is true, at one or other of the fronts, but there was beside the S.S. yet another factor of uncertainty, namely the anti-aircraft personnel and the fighter planes detailed for the protection of the home front, which, together with the *Luftwaffe*'s ground staffs, came under the command of Colonel-General Stumpff. The connections which the conspirators possessed with the *Luftwaffe* were slight, as were those with the Navy. As against this, there was no reason to suppose that the various units of the *Luftwaffe* and the Navy could strike much of a blow, nor was there much doubt that once Hitler had been disposed of, the success of the first phase of the revolt would bring over the great majority of the commanders. A few isolated pro-Hitler fanatics, like Grand-Admiral Dönitz, could then very easily be rendered ineffective.

In the main, the conspiracy was confined to the staffs of the *Ersatz* army, to the Army command at Zossen and to the General Staff headquarters at Mauerwald. In Berlin itself, besides those officers in the Bendlerstrasse and in *Generalkommando III* who have already been named, especial mention should be made of the group surrounding Major-General Oster, the *Stabchef* of the Secret Service, which included Colonel Georg Hansen and Colonel von Freytagh-Loringhoven. Further, Major Hayessen of the General Staff had the special task of bringing the town commandant into line when the moment for action had come. Other members of the conspiracy within the General Staff itself were Generals Adolf Heusinger and Helmut Stieff; the chiefs of the Operations and Organization Departments; Stauffenberg's friend, Colonel von Roenne, who had taken over the

"Foreign Armies Department" in 1943, and the G.O.C. Signals, General Fellgiebel, together with his deputy, Major-General Thiele. Since these last controlled all Army communications, their co-operation was indispensable for putting "Valkyrie" into force. Last, we must not fail to mention Colonel Meichssner, the head of the Organization Department of the *Wehrmachtführungsstab*, who was also among the initiated.

In the centre army group on the eastern front, von Tresckow tried indefatigably to win over von Kluge, but von Kluge was certain neither of himself nor of his men. He listened to talks about the proposed coup, but would only agree to come in after Hitler had been eliminated. In the northern army group the conspirators had picked out Colonel von Drabich-Waechter as an intermediary between themselves and von Küchler. Von Küchler was an entirely unpolitical kind of person, but he had been a personal friend of Fritsch, and had in 1939 set his face against the terror of the S.S. in Poland. It was therefore felt that he could be counted on in an emergency.

In the southern group, Colonel Schultze-Büttger was chosen, who was Manstein's G.S.O.1. Manstein, however, though he fully recognized Hitler's failings, would hear nothing of any revolt, since he did not believe that such a scheme could be successfully carried out in the middle of a war. Guderian was approached by Goerdeler, but his attitude was negative. He had vented his displeasure against Hitler often enough, but thought it impossible for a soldier to remove his Supreme War Lord in wartime—let alone dispose of him.

The conspirators received strong backing, however, from the group of retired generals surrounding Beck, for these had always been enemies of the régime. Beck himself was chosen to take over the regency immediately after the coup, while Witzleben, who had contemplated marching on the Chancellery in 1938, was to be Commander in Chief Armed Forces. Olbricht further won over Hoepner, who had been kicked out before Moscow and who had also in 1938 placed his forces at the rebels' disposal, while a fourth ally among the retired generals was found in the person of General von Rabenau.

Von Rabenau had been an old colleague of Seeckt, and had been head of the Army archives department. At the beginning of the war he had published a biography of the *Reichswehr's* creator which, despite meticulous choice of words, gave some inkling of the profound differences that were occurring between General Staff officers and the apostles of National Socialism. Rabenau, who had himself fought for a Christian orientation in the Army, had already fallen foul of the Party leaders on that account, and could be reckoned among the defenders of the Army's Christian-conservative tradition.

A separate circle of military "resistance" also began forming in Paris, when ex-*Oberquartiermeister* Karl von Stülpnagel succeeded his relative, Otto von Stülpnagel, as Commander in Chief in France. Stülpnagel and von Falkenhausen, his neighbour in Belgium, were both impassioned enemies of Hitler, and longed for a day of reckoning with the régime. A relative of Stauffenberg's, Lieutenant-Colonel von Hofacker, who was serving on Stülpnagel's staff, built the necessary bridges with Berlin, and it was possible to enlist the aid of a number of other officers serving in the west.

The conspiracy remained a secret for three-quarters of a year, during which period the net was perfected, while those concerned waited for a suitable opportunity to act. It was soon to appear that the great majority of conspiring officers, among whom were to be found some of the greatest names of German, and above all of Prussian, history, were still profoundly conservative in outlook, and as such inwardly somewhat at variance with the methods that now lay open to them of saving their country. Conspiracy was a territory in which most generals and Staff officers felt somewhat ill at ease. Only Stauffenberg and a small number of others were to show that they were fully at home in it.

As far as the rest were concerned, the inner uncertainty of the Christian and conservative element gave the whole enterprise a peculiar character of its own and to some extent proved a brake on their determination. Von Rabenau in his biography of Seekt had written with reference to the crisis of 1923 that a Prussian general never broke his oath, and had completely failed to foresee that a few years later he was himself to be placed before the alternative of either breaking his oath or disobeying the dictates of his conscience.

Neither Stauffenberg, nor Moltke's Kreisau circle, differ though they might in many respects, were satisfied with the idea of merely rebuilding a bygone order. While the high military *frondeurs* were concerned principally with a reform of the apparatus of command, and while some of them would indeed have been quite satisfied if Hitler were merely to desist from conducting military operations, Stauffenberg was a true revolutionary with ideas and gifts of his own. As we have already seen, he had little use for Goerdeler's notion of a restoration of the monarchy. The form of the new state could only be that of a democratic republic, and the German people would have to be given the earliest possible opportunity of deciding their own fate in free elections. In such circumstances as these, the proposed Beck-Goerdeler régime could in any case be no more than transitional, and the man on whom Stauffenberg appears to have had his eye for Chancellor was Dr Julius Leber, the leader of the young Socialists, whom the President of the People's Court was ultimately to designate in a spasm of hatred as "the German Lenin". As far as the provisional government was concerned, Stauffenberg favoured the re-employment of Schacht, and did not feel disposed to raise any objection to a man like Papen conducting negotiations with the West as Foreign Minister, a proposal which was championed by Helldorf, the Chief of the Berlin Police, and by the Administrative Head of the Potsdam Government, Count von Bismarck-Schönhausen, the grandson of the first German Chancellor.

The essential future policy as far as the outside world was concerned was to open conversations with the West, all occupied territories in the west being evacuated and the troops withdrawn to the Rhine. In this way it would be possible to withdraw practically all the good divisions from the west, above all the armoured divisions, and thus make the eastern front secure. Stauffenberg looked upon it as essential to preserve the striking power of the Army, so that the new government would negotiate on a basis of equality. It was, however, quite clear to him that a *modus vivendi* with the Soviets would have to be attained—by territorial concessions if necessary. Nevertheless, negotiations with the West were the prime element in his plans, for unlike the members of the Kreisau circle, he was alive to the danger from the east.

Another way, and one even more vitiated by illusion, though it was connected with the traditional bond between the *Reichswehr* and the Red Army, was that attempted by a number of the German generals captured at Stalingrad, with General von Seydlitz-Kurzbach, lately commander of the 51st Corps, at their head. This group founded jointly with the Russians the "Free Germany" Committee, an enterprise in which they were assisted by certain German Communist emigrants and a large number of German officers and men. No doubt these people believed that in the event of a German collapse or of an internal upheaval they would be able to take control of things. Seydlitz in particular, who even before the surrender had pressed his commander to take the law into his own hands, looked upon himself as a renewer of the Tauroggen tradition. However, subsequent developments caused these officers some disappointment, for they were not all prepared to turn their principles upside down or attend the courses in Marxist doctrine which the Russians so thoughtfully arranged for them.

XI

In the late summer of 1942, when the regiments of the 6th Army reached Stalingrad and Rommel seemed on the point of taking Cairo, victory appeared to be within Hitler's grasp. With the defeat of Rommel and Paulus, however, together with the destruction of the satellite armies on the Don and the Russian counter-offensive of February 1943, there began the second phase of the war. The initiative now passed to the Allies. While still intoxicated with success, Goebbels had written in his paper *Das Reich* that Hitler's tragedy was that both as a statesman and a general he had only bad bunglers as his foils. There now appeared in the Allied camp a number of men to whom the word bungler seemed anything but applicable—Eisenhower, Montgomery, Vatutin, Koniev and Zukov.

Vatutin and Zukov are particularly interesting in this connection in so far as they developed that tactic of elastic defence which the General Staff so vainly tried to induce Hitler to adopt and which stood in glaring contrast to his own defensive methods, so costly in German blood. There is all the less excuse for Hitler in so far as Manstein succeeded in meeting the Russian counter-attack which followed Stalingrad, with an excellent demonstration of a *manoeuvre en retraite*. When the Russian armies penetrated to the crossings of the Dnieper at Dniepropetrovsk and Saporoshe, and it appeared as though the Crimea might be cut off, Manstein, by a clever wheeling movement, turned his retreat into a counter-attack on the unprotected flanks of the Russian spearheads, but the "Spirit of Saporoshe" remained incomprehensible to Hitler and indeed the words became a term of abuse with him, to be used against such generals as still believed that there was value in manoeuvring.

Both in the air and under the sea Germany began to fall badly behind. Radar and similar devices which were developed by the British, completely destroyed the effectiveness of the submarine war, while in the matter of bombing Germany was driven more and more on the defensive. As early as 1942 British Bomber Command began raids with a thousand and more machines on Essen and Cologne, and initiated the tactics of saturation bombing. The effort culminated in an attack on Hamburg on July 23rd, 1943, in which 800 air mines, 12,000 high explosive, 80,000 phosphorus and 150,000 incendiary bombs were dropped. According to official figures, 56,000 people were killed and 90,000 people rendered homeless. The German ground defences were rendered useless by a new method of jamming their radar. Only 17 machines of the first wave of 800 were shot down, equivalent to 2 per cent. Hamburg was a sort of dress rehearsal for the bombing of Berlin, and although bombing did not decisively affect German arms production it nevertheless prevented a great deal of work being carried on and had profound moral effects which communicated themselves to all the fronts.

Two additional fronts were created by the landing of British and American troops in Sicily and by the growth of the partisan movement in Jugoslavia and Northern Greece, while Hungary put out secret feelers to the West. Turkey which in the same year of 1943 had sent a military mission to the Führer's headquarters with a view to finding out the exact state of affairs in the east, turned its face finally away from Germany.

The Allied landing in Sicily was followed almost immediately by the surrender of the Italian coastal defence forces, who for the most part never fired a shot. The appearance of the enemy on the Italian peninsula was now obviously only a matter of time. At a meeting between Hitler and Mussolini in Verona, Hitler demanded that the whole of Italy up to the Po valley should be handed over to him, but the prospect of having their country turned into a battlefield strengthened the anti-Fascist opposition, now led by the former Chief of Staff, Marshal Badoglio, and the Minister of the Royal House, Count Acquarone. Mussolini called together the Grand Council of the Fascist Party, but here too the majority was against continuing the war, and on the afternoon of July 23rd Mussolini was arrested by a Colonel of the Carabinieri. Late that day, Jodl, who on his own confession had no notion what to do, told Hitler of the matter, stating that "Fascism had fallen". Hitler roared at him: "Fascism fallen! Only an officer could talk such nonsense. It only shows that generals know nothing of politics."

Despite all that Hitler could say, the first and oldest of the European dictatorships had collapsed like a house of cards. Marshal Badoglio formed a new government consisting of soldiers and of administrators who had deserted Mussolini. While it was officially given out that the war would continue, secret armistice negotiations were initiated via Madrid. It is true that the hopes which the King and the generals entertained of slipping gracefully out of the war did not fully materialize, but the whole affair nevertheless provided a sort of model for *coups d'état* carried out by the essentially conservative forces of the monarchy and the Army.

Hitler himself was very much alive to this, though he knew nothing of the actual conspiracy brewing in his own camp, and, although the architects of the latter, whom events had somewhat taken by surprise, had not yet completed their plans and so allowed this most favourable moment to slip by. Goebbels, as his diary shows, sought frantically to reassure himself and others that the Führer's genius had foreseen it all. Nevertheless those very diaries give glimpses of the confusion which events in Italy had caused at the Führer's headquarters and of the fear which prevailed there of a possible "German Badoglio". Hitler stormed against the "blue international" of the nobility and of the old princely families. Most German princes, including all Hohenzollerns, Brunswicks and Wittelsbachs, were expelled from the Army, and Goebbels clamoured for the expropriation of all the old princely houses. Himmler was made Minister of the Interior and began his tenure of office with a violent campaign against defeatists, his first victim being a *Regierungsrat* in Rostock who had declared that things would not get better till Germany had a Badoglio of her own.

XII

While these events were in progress, developments of an even more decisive character had been taking place in the east, and it was the east which was the decisive theatre of war, a fact to which Zeitzler's continued but futile struggle for a complete redistribution of forces has great relevance. Warlimont has told of a saying which at this time was going the rounds of the O.K.W. It was that the last war had been lost by the policy of the Fleet in being, and the present one would be lost by that of the "Army in being". One of the results of the extraordinary dichotomy between the General Staff and the "O.K.W. Theatres of War" was that any effort to concentrate forces at a decisive point had been rendered impossible. Instead of this, sizeable armies were standing around in all kinds of secondary theatres, because Hitler wanted to appear as strong as possible everywhere at once. In Norway were 13 actual divisions, in all 380,000 men; in Denmark were 106,500 men; in Crete 47,000, and in the Balkans 612,000.

Thus the distribution of forces alone did much to tie the General Staff's hands. As Hitler's instrument of command, the latter could only seek to make the best of his directives. When it attempted to strike out on a road of its own, as Zeitzler, Heusinger, Stieff and Wagner sometimes tried to do, the result was merely another collision with Hitler. Hitler and his *entourage* were, of course, getting daily more and more out of touch with reality, and nothing was done to put this right, nor was any attention paid to requests by the various commanders that Jodl or one of his colleagues should come and see conditions on the spot, since Hitler would have looked askance at such journeys of inspection. Thus, Jodl, too, became the typical chairborne general, who was soon caught in the toils of routine.

The principal advocates of the theory of "Defence by the milimetre", as Dönitz designated Hitler's strategy, were, as a matter of fact, Dönitz himself, on whose advice Hitler set a high value, and Himmler, though the latter had no knowledge of strategy whatever. Most military thinking by the heads of state was carried on at about that level. Thus a correct estimate of the enemy forces, a thing for which the General Staff had always held out, was invariably designated as defeatism, and it became a common habit now to speak of the "Sabotage of the generals", especially when the numbers with which the *Wehrmachtführungsstab* was reckoning turned out to be quite inaccurate, when divisions which it wanted to put into the line were found no longer to exist or when the sheer confusion of authority had produced faulty orders.

We now begin to see the rise of men like Model, Schörner and Rendulic, of whom the first two, being particularly faithful executors of Hitler's intentions, were soon made Field-Marshals. Model, who had passed through the school of the *Truppenamt*, and had made something of a name for himself by an excellent study of Gneisenau, was undoubtedly a skilful improvisor. He also quite sincerely believed in Hitler's promises that new and revolutionary weapons would turn the tide of war. Schörner, a man of lower middle class origin, had been intended for the career of a primary schoolmaster. He distinguished himself, however, in the First World War by gaining the *Pour le mérite*, and was taken over as an officer into the *Reichswehr*. He failed in his examination for the *Truppenamt*, and this, together with his lowly origin, caused him to nurse a growing resentment against the prevailingly well-born officer corps of the *Reichswehr*; he thus felt himself drawn towards Hitler, who had similar sentiments.

Rendulic was a man of a different stamp. His was an old Austrian family of soldiers, and he had been a member of the Austrian General Staff. He accounted it to his credit that while military attaché in Paris, he had been expelled from the Austrian Army for National

Socialist activities. As a soldier his nature showed a curious dualism. He took his National Socialism deadly seriously, and yet affected personally a most elegant style of life. He had a weakness for film shows at his headquarters which would be followed by genuinely entertaining conversation. On such occasions he seemed more like the representative of a dying order than a Nationalist Socialist.

Though Hitler was now being driven back from the Volga and the Don on to the Mius and the Donetz, he had not even in 1943 abandoned all hope of seizing the initiative. He nevertheless neglected to make use of the most suitable moment for such ventures, namely Manstein's *manoeuvre en retraite* in the spring of that year, by which Kharkov was recaptured, for he saw in Manstein a serious rival to himself as a general, and successful generals can always be dangerous for a dictator.

Actually, the General Staff believed that a large-scale offensive was now beyond Germany's powers, and would only have the same results as Ludendorff's "Great Battle" in 1918, namely, the dissipation of the last reserves of German strength. In a speech which he made to the *Gauleiters* in 1943, even Jodl assessed the strength of the Russian armies at 5½ millions, organized into 327 infantry and 51 Panzer divisions. Meanwhile, Russia's armament industry was in top gear and was producing tanks, guns and rocket launchers in quantities which Hitler would have deemed impossible, while America supplemented these by a steady stream of supplies.

Against these Germany could put some 200 infantry and armoured divisions, together with ten divisions from Rumania and six from Hungary, and some 160 battalions of "eastern troops" which last were being rapidly thinned by desertion. The few really battle-worthy units, such as the Turcoman contingents and General von Pannwitz's Cossacks, were never committed in the east but thrown in on the Balkan and Italian theatres.

XIII

Disregarding the insufficiency of his forces, which should have counselled the greatest possible economy in blood, Hitler decided in the summer on a large-scale attack, the so-called "Operation Citadel". The aim of this offensive was to pinch out the large Russian salient between Orel and Belgorod, and trap some 950,000 men of the two army groups "Don" and "Steppe Front" which were concentrated around Kursk; these, according to Hitler, constituted the last Russian reserves. When this had been accomplished the upper Don was to be crossed. Then either the Volga line was to be regained or Moscow threatened from the south.

Once again, a grandiose pincers movement was envisaged with the centre group under von Kluge forming the northern arm and the southern group under Manstein closing in from the south. The armoured forces available for this were 17 Panzer and 3 Panzer Grenadier divisions, which were split up among the 2nd and 3rd Panzer Armies and the S.S. armoured corps. They were furnished as to approximately sixty per cent with the new heavy "Tiger" tanks.

In all, some 500,000 men were at Hitler's disposal for his offensive. The deployment took place over a relatively restricted area because Hitler had the fixed conviction that the bulk of the enemy force was in the "Kursk Sack" and for that reason he wished to attack one of the strongest points on the whole front. The doubts of certain Chiefs of Staff of the attacking armies were disregarded, and in the case of Colonel von Schleinitz, answered with dismissal.

The offensive was launched on July 5th. After a few initial successes, it was halted by the Russian barrage, Koniev, the commander of "Army Group Steppe Front", having fully realized the nature of the German intention. Roughly forty-five per cent of the German tanks were destroyed by Russian artillery fire, while the German artillery proved itself clearly inferior to that of the enemy.

In the northern sector the battle for all practical purposes came to an end by the middle of July. In the southern sector, however, Manstein strove to press forward against "Army Group Don", and succeeded in making some deep and dangerous breaches in the Russian line, but his strength was insufficient for him to follow up his defence decisively. The battle lasted on this sector till the middle of August, and ended finally in a defeat made all the more inevitable by the fact that troops had to be withdrawn to Italy as a result of Mussolini's fall. Thus the problem posed by a multi-front war again reasserted itself.

The Russian counter-offensive in the late summer and autumn led not only to the loss of Orel and Byelgorod but also to the final loss of Kharkov and the whole Donetz basin. Von Kleist with Army Group A was still holding the Kuban bridgehead, which Dönitz had declared to be indispensable to the whole Black Sea position, and now von Kleist was compelled to retire. Hitler announced that the river line of the Dnieper was a natural line of defence, but remarkably enough forbade it to be prepared—despite Manstein's insistence that this should be done.

Army Groups A and B were now renamed "Army Groups North and South Ukraine". Manstein endeavoured to apply to the situation the arts of elastic defence, for which the wide terrain was so eminently suitable, though this merely evoked the inspired comment from Hitler that half his divisions instead of facing the enemy were perpetually on the road.

XIV

At the beginning of September, British and American forces landed in Southern Italy, and on the 8th of the month the Italian government proclaimed the signature of an armistice. The German Command was now forced in the minimum of time to occupy the whole of Italy and to disarm the numerous Italian divisions in Southern France, Croatia, Dalmatia, Albania and Greece. Rome fell into German hands, though Badoglio and the King escaped to the south. Mussolini was freed from his imprisonment and proclaimed a Fascist Socialist republic.

This last, however, had a mere shadow existence and could raise no armed forces worthy of mention. The Italian front, which was put under Marshal Kesselring, now became the scene of battles into which were hurled 20 divisions comprising some 400,000 men, while the capture by the enemy of Italian airfields served further to contract the internal line.

In Russia, in September Poltava and Smolensk had to be surrendered, and on the 29th of that month the Russians reached Kremenchug on the Dnieper, thus at last bringing the war to the Dnieper line. Five days later, on October 4th, Himmler addressed a meeting of S.S. group leaders in Posen and opened a general attack on the old officer corps. Stalin, he declared, had been well advised to have Tuchatschewski and his group of Tsarist Generals shot. With such men as those, Russia would never have endured this war for two whole years. Stalin had made an officer of the Commissar, so that the carrier of the "Weltanschauung" had also become a military leader. Hence the Russian strength.

As far as the eastern front was concerned, he could do little more than enlarge on a previous saying of his that a pig once stuck would bleed to death. A more illuminating remark was made some days later in a speech at Bad Schachen, when he issued a warning to the

"Defeatist Upper Stratum" which was seeking for a German Badoglio, adding that the war would go on till it ended in a German victory. This observation was all the more remarkable in so far as Himmler at this time already knew in a general way of the existence of a conspiracy in high military circles, but nevertheless held his hand. In a conversation he had with Popitz, the Prussian Minister of Finance, he endeavoured to find out the views of the opposition, in particular those of the Beck-Goerdeler group. It was as though he was minded at the time to end the war either against Hitler's will or possibly without him.

Nor is this entirely surprising, for even Goebbels had recognized the hopelessness of the situation. He admits in his diary that Germany lacked the strength for a two-front war, and advised Hitler either to come to an understanding with the West against the East or vice versa. Ribbentrop was similarly minded, and again put in a plea for a separate peace with Russia.

Hitler, however, whose health, as Göring saw, was failing, knew only too well that he had gambled away any international credit he ever possessed and that nobody would negotiate with him. His own hope lay in some miraculous turn of fate. Jodl made a significant speech to the *Gauleiters* on November 7th, the essence of it being that "surrender means the end of the nation, the end of Germany". Like Hitler, he could command no better counsel than that of endurance, of "sticking it out" ("*Auszustehen*"). Any "political solution" was the solution of a coward. The positive result of the eastern campaign, he said, was that the Bolshevik danger had been kept from the borders of the Reich, though whether Germany's strength would suffice to keep up the war indefinitely was a question he omitted to examine. Germany would win because otherwise the history of the world would have no meaning. All this was in reality a declaration of strategic bankruptcy made by Germany's leading military personality.

Dönitz, in speeches to the German admirals in this last hour before the catastrophe, approached the problem on different lines. In a speech in Weimar he declared that Russian territory had only been conquered to provide bases for a naval war, and for that reason the northern front, with its outlets to the Baltic, and the Crimea must be held at all costs. Like Himmler, he set his hopes on the exhaustion of Russia's offensive power, but since he was as devoid of expedients by which this end could be attained, he merely proclaimed himself as much a bankrupt as did Jodl.

Meanwhile all officers with any strategic insight continued to see the only hope of reducing the Russian pressure and carrying on a real *Guerre d'usure*, to use a favourite expression of Hitler's, in a policy of elastic defence and in a shortening of the line. In this way, and in this way alone, was there any hope of crippling Russia's offensive power. Zeitzler, Manstein, Kleist, Küchler, all expressed themselves in this sense, as did also Lieutenant-General von Tippelskirch, who was *Oberquartiermeister IV*. Heinrici and Woehler, who commanded the 4th and 8th Army respectively, held similar views. Manstein, who was still a master of the General Staff's traditional principles of generalship, exerted all his strength to hold the Dnieper line. Despite all the difficulties confronting him, he still thought it possible to cripple the Russian armies on Russian soil, but only if Hitler consented to comply with the recommendations of the General Staff and place the supreme authority in the hands of a trained soldier. He made this demand openly to Hitler, thereby appreciably raising the latter's suspicions, for Hitler recognized quite rightly that there was no man more fitted than Manstein to exercise that supreme military authority which was here in question. Indeed, despite his defective eyesight, many officers believed that Manstein was the only man who could save the eastern front.

Manstein's view was that ultimately, when Russia's offensive power had been hamstrung, the war could be ended by a restitution of territory and indeed unofficial feelers were coming from various American quarters, and particularly through Turkey, which gave grounds for supposing that the "Unconditional Surrender" formula was by no means sacramentally binding; it may also be presumed that the Russian authorities, being doubtful whether their allies really meant business with their second front, would not have been averse to negotiation.

On balance, however, it must be admitted that such hopes were at best slender. The whole character of the war made their realization unlikely. In any case it would have needed far higher diplomatic gifts than those of Hitler or Ribbentrop to bring them to fruition. Even so, however, Hitler was not averse to using certain mediation offers by Japan to encourage the more sceptical of his generals in much the same manner as he sought to bamboozle others with his tales of "Wonder Weapons".

XV

In the winter of 1943 the Russians went over to a general attack with five army groups. These were the 1st, 2nd and 3rd "Ukrainian Fronts" under Vatutin, Koniev and Malinowski, the "White Russian Front" under Rokossowski, and the "Black Sea Front" under Tolbukhin. Meanwhile the German army groups "North and South Ukraine" sought to hold the line of the Dnieper bend down to the Sea of Azov. This, however, proved to be impossible. The Crimea was cut off and Kiev was lost. During a series of violent battles in which twenty-two German divisions were destroyed, the Russians drove a wedge to Zhitomir, the railway centre on the Polish border. They were thrown back, but on December 31st a new Russian offensive led to the final capture of Zhitomir and Berdichev.

At the beginning of January 1944 the German positions on the Dnieper bend were overrun, and in February fell Nikopol, the key of the whole Dnieper front. There were still German troops on the river, however, and two army corps under Generals Lieb and Stemmermann were surrounded in the area Cherkasi-Korsun. Now for the first time von Seydlitz and the other generals of the "Free Germany" Committee sought to induce Germans to desert (though as a matter of fact their effort produced no results whatever), while Hitler again ordered the troops to stand firm, surrounded though they were. In order to avoid a second Stalingrad, the Army Command gave the order to withdraw before securing Hitler's approval. Ten divisions were destroyed, but some 35,000 men were saved.

It was during these battles that the last lot of commanders took over on the eastern front. These were coarse, drill-sergeant types like Schörner, men like Model, whose faith in Hitler could never be shaken. Then there were the tough military specialists like Colonel-General Dietl, Colonel-Generals Heinrici, Reinhardt, Harpe, Friessner and the commander of the 7th Panzer Division under Manstein, General Hasso von Manteuffel, who distinguished himself at Zhitomir.

The last representatives of the older generation now lost their posts. In the north, von Küchler was in January replaced by Model. Von Kluge was the victim of a motor accident, and was replaced by Field-Marshal Busch. In the south, where in March the Russians crossed the Dnieper and the Prut, Manstein and Kleist both resigned, Manstein making a last attempt to induce Hitler to abandon the supreme command. Hitler accepted his resignation—it was the third time he had offered it—only after a violent altercation in which he reproached Manstein with neglecting to build defences on the Dnieper in time! Kleist was succeeded by Schörner, Manstein by the now almost ubiquitous Model.

Now that Russian forces were endangering the Dniester, the necessity arose for protecting the Rumanian oilfields by constructing a strong defensive position on the Prut. Despite vigorous representations of the General Staff, the opportunity for doing this was missed. Meanwhile, the agony of the 17th Army, which had been cut off in the Crimea, continued, while the 6th Army which had been recreated in 1943 had withdrawn to the Rumanian frontier and stood there with the 8th Army of General Woehler. In the north the positions around Leningrad had been abandoned.

In December 1943 and January 1944 some 22,000 tons of bombs were dropped on Berlin. In the spring there began as a preparation for the coming invasion the strategic bombing by the British and American Air Forces of communications, synthetic petrol installations and armament works. The heavy American bombers were now able to reach targets in Poland and Eastern Germany, the tactics followed being those of daylight precision bombing.

In May the Crimea was retaken by the Russians. The "North and South Ukraine" army groups, under Model and Schörner, were pressed back into Eastern Galicia and Bessarabia. The two commanders were shortly afterwards replaced by Colonels-General Harpe and Friessner, who had both had long experience of the eastern front and of whom the former clung to the end to his belief in Hitler's genius. The northern group, commanded now by Lindemann, was forced to retreat into the Baltic border states, while Kesselring evacuated Rome and withdrew into central Italy.

XVI

On the eastern front, there still remained a balcony-like salient of about 1,000 kilometres between Kovel-Vitebsk and the areas northeast of Polotsk. The forces standing here under the command of Busch, the 2nd, 4th and 9th Armies and the 3rd Panzer Army, comprised some 42 divisions, but suffered from the disability of having their rearward communications continually endangered by strong forces of partisans. In the air they were so weak that it was almost impossible to ascertain the enemy's dispositions. And yet this salient was a positive invitation to an encircling attack by the enemy. Warnings by the General Staff, however, fell on deaf ears as far as Hitler was concerned. Others saw the peril clearly enough and the weakness of the line—there were only 27 men to the kilometre—caused some commanders to take precautions. Heinrici, for instance, had positions prepared in the rear of the 4th Army—till Hitler forbade this.

Needless to say, the inevitable thing happened here as it happened everywhere else. On June 22nd, the Russians began their offensive with 100 fresh divisions and 2,000 aircraft as against hopelessly inferior forces. It was perhaps unfortunate that at this critical juncture Krebs should have been forced to attend a course at the Ordensburg Sonthofen for the strengthening of his *Weltanschauung*, though whether his presence would have done much to change matters is questionable. In any case, the centre army group was completely destroyed, the 4th Army and 3rd Panzer Army being annihilated east of Minsk. The catastrophe was even greater than that of Stalingrad. Approximately 300,000 Germans were either killed or taken prisoner, two commanding generals being killed while defending their headquarters. All places of importance in the rearward areas were now somewhat bombastically named fortresses, but that did as little to redeem the disaster as did the passing of death sentences on commanders who allegedly failed to show sufficient vigour in their defence. Vitebsk, Bobruisk, Minsk and Wilno were now lost, and the Russian tanks moved forward irresistibly and at an astonishing speed toward the Vistula and the East Prussian border.

The northern army group was now in danger of being cut off. Hitler stormed against the commanders, and once more Model was advanced, this time replacing Busch, now a broken man. Model now made efforts to create a defensive line in Lithuania, but could only achieve a transitory success. Despite the protests of the southern army group, Panzer divisions were withdrawn from the Rumanian front, which was itself heavily threatened, and sent to stiffen the crumbling central sector. This, too, was without lasting result. Model now vainly pleaded for the evacuation of the whole Baltic region in order to free the troops of the northern army, which were now left holding another "balcony position", and throw them in at the critical point of the gigantic battle, but again Hitler refused to be instructed. Meanwhile, in a procession that took hours to pass, twelve generals and 50,000 German prisoners of war marched through the streets of Moscow.

XVII

It was now the last act of the tragedy. General Warlimont was on a later occasion to enumerate the reasons for the collapse under the following heads; first, that condition which was described in his already quoted phrase as "chaos of leadership in the Leader State" and the taking over of undivided military authority by a layman. Then the policy of inelastic defence, the decline of the *Luftwaffe*, the "standing around" of battle-worthy divisions in secondary theatres of war. How far Warlimont recognized that many of these failings were the inevitable results of a multi-front war, the record fails to disclose, not that insight on the part of Warlimont would have helped much, so long as the *Wehrmachtführungsstab* could not free itself from Hitler's strategic methods. So far from doing so, it remained Hitler's personal instrument to the end. That, no doubt, was why Warlimont's reputation among the army commanders was never more than exiguous.

After the collapse of the centre army group, Zeitzler made one last effort to persuade Hitler that a reorganization of the whole eastern front and a fundamental change in the whole method of conducting operations were indispensable. At that very moment, the Russian divisions were flooding towards Warsaw, whose lines of defenders were thin to the point of non-existence. Nevertheless, not one of Zeitzler's demands was granted. No independent commander was appointed to the eastern front, Keitel remained at his post, nor was any attempt made to appoint a properly functioning *Wehrmacht* General Staff. All hopes lay shattered that commonsense would triumph over ideology.

No less than four times this most honest man, who was becoming increasingly a victim of despair, offered Hitler his resignation, while the gulf between the Army and O.K.W. grew deeper. Now when Warlimont or Jodl at the daily conferences began his lecture on the O.K.W. theatres of war, Zeitzler together with his colleagues ostentatiously left the room. The only result of his final effort to secure some change in the whole conduct of the war was to cause Hitler's resentment at his obstinacy to vent itself in one of his outbursts of rage.

Zeitzler now seeing himself compelled to implement a strategy which he believed to be disastrous, took the desperate decision of refusing to co-operate any further. He reported himself sick, and the General Staff was thus in this critical hour deprived of its Chief. For the time being, Heusinger took over his work, though Hitler, who continued to work with the Operations Department, was actually considering General Buhle for the post.

Meanwhile the invasion had begun in the west, and naturally enough this had a profound influence on all the fronts as well as on the interior of Germany. In the ordinary course of routine, it fell to the *Wehrmachtführungsstab* to deal with this new factor. That is why the invasion was to produce a kind of laboratory demonstration of the failure of Hitler's methods, and of what must inevitably happen when a man who lacks all experience of actual conditions seeks to use modern techniques of communication to give dictatorial orders at a distance of thousands of kilometres. While on the side of the Allies desperate efforts were made to secure the maximum coherence and uniformity of command, the chaotic diffusion of authority in the west was achieving triumphs of misrule. Actually, as things were at this moment, the best General Staff in the world could hardly have achieved much since the Allies had mastery of the air, so that even a strategy carried on in the best text-book lines would have been severely handicapped. In such circumstances, the *Wehrmachtführungsstab* was completely helpless, and the task which Hitler had piled on his shoulders could be demonstrated with exceptional clarity to belong to the "strategy of the impossible".

CHAPTER XVI

GÖTTERDÄMMERUNG

I

SIXTY divisions of the most varying quality were defending 3,000 kilometres of coast between the Riviera and the North Sea. Those in the west were in part "Positional Divisions", equipped with horse transport of very limited mobility, among them being at least one division consisting entirely of men with stomach ailments. In part they were equipped with captured French, Polish and Jugoslav weapons. There were also in France considerable numbers of "*Osttruppen*", consisting of Adjerbajanese, Cossacks, Volga Tartars and Georgians, all of whom were considered too unreliable to be employed elsewhere.

The much propagandized Atlantic Wall consisted of a few strong points with protection of varying thickness and very uneven fire 'power. As a defence system its weakness resided in the fact that the chief centres of attention had been the great ports and certain obvious danger zones. Elsewhere, its strength was negligible.

As one of the O.K.W. theatres of war, the west was Hitler's personal responsibility. Rundstedt was still C. in C. West, with Blumentritt as his Chief of Staff. Eisenhower considered Rundstedt the ablest of the German generals, but Rundstedt's powers were very limited. Also, he was old and his health far from good.

Under Rundstedt, Rommel commanded Army Group B and Blaskowitz Army Group G. Army Group B, consisting of the 7th Army under Colonel-General Dollmann, the 15th Army under Colonel-General von Salmuth, and the 88th Army Corps in Holland, the whole comprising 24 Infantry and 5 *Luftwaffe* field divisions, covered the coast from Holland to the mouth of the Loire. Army Group G, with the 1st and 19th Armies and a motley combination of so-called Security Regiments, *Ostruppen* and Pétainist French, held the territory from the Loire to the Riviera. The whole of the armoured forces, consisting of two S.S. and three regular Panzer divisions north of the Loire and two S.S. and two regular Panzer divisions to the south of it, were in an emergency to have come directly under Geyr von Schweppenburg, the sometime military attaché in London. Since, however, it proved impossible to make firm plans for an operational armoured reserve, Schweppenburg's function was restricted to organizational and training questions.

Certain forces did not come under C. in C. West at all. These were the Navy Group Command under Admiral Krancke, which depended entirely on Admiralty orders, and the *Luftwaffe* formations, consisting of the 3rd Air Fleet under Field-Marshal Sperrle, and the 3rd A.A. Corps. As against the 17,000 aircraft belonging to the Allied invasion forces, the 3rd Air Fleet had only 500 machines at its disposal, these being mostly training machines. Only 90 fighters and 70 fighter bombers were actually ready for use. Hitler's promise to provide a thousand turbo jet aircraft proved to be empty words, since the production of jet aircraft was being severely handicapped by Allied bombing. Rommel had as a secondary duty that of acting as inspector of the Atlantic Wall. Since, however, this came under four different authorities, the O.T. for actual construction, the Navy for the coastal artillery, the *Luftwaffe* for air defence, the Army only being concerned with the actual manning, Rommel had virtually no power to issue any orders.

Quite apart from the activities of the Maquis, conditions in Occupied France were somewhat disturbed. A hidden triangular struggle was going on between Stülpnagel, the office of Germany's special envoy to Vichy and General Oberg of the S.S. Oberg was at pains to keep the leading generals under observation, and Stülpnagel's staff was one of the most important centres of military "resistance". In addition to this conflict behind the scenes, there was the not inconsiderable rivalry between the C. in C. West in St Germain and Rommel's headquarters at Château La Roche Guyon in Normandy. The two field-marshals did not by any means see eye to eye in the matter of defence methods. Rundstedt, as a General Staff officer of the old school, tended rather to look down on Rommel, who very definitely did not belong to it. He was later to speak of him to Major Liddell Hart as a man suited for minor operations. Rundstedt's view was that the defence of the coastline, which Rommel considered vital, was of secondary importance. Regarding, as he did, the Atlantic Wall as an illusion, he wanted to treat it merely as a first line of defence. His plan was to rely on a strategic reserve in the interior of France consisting of his best infantry and the great mass of his armour, and he believed that these should be used to counter the enemy in a war of movement. It was in the nature of things for Guderian, as Germany's leading tank expert, to share this view.

Rommel, on the other hand, thought the coastline a matter of prime importance, and his staff criticized Rundstedt's failure to appreciate the merits of static defence. Rommel also had doubts whether the enemy's superiority in the air would not make it well nigh impossible for large bodies of armour to manoeuvre at all. He believed that the fate of the invasion would be decided within twenty-four hours of its being attempted, and that the war could be looked upon as lost once a bridgehead had been established, and so held it to be essential that all the armour should be concentrated near the coast.

Hitler very largely shared Rommel's views, though he arrived at his conclusions on somewhat different grounds. He went so far as to forbid the preparation of any plans which presupposed the success of the landing, though, needless to say, in this particular instance his orders were not obeyed. He also reserved to himself the sole right to commit the armoured forces, which he proposed to do from his headquarters in East Prussia.

The upshot of the Rundstedt-Rommel controversy was a compromise. The infantry forces holding the coast were strengthened, as was also the artillery, while the armour was held back. Actually both commanders were agreed that the best thing for Hitler to do was to end a war which no longer held the remotest prospect of a successful issue. They were sufficiently of one mind in this for them to ask him to come to France so that they could lay this view before him, but their request proved abortive. Montgomery expressed the view in his memoirs that the belated dribbling through of the armour and the failure on Germany's part to make an immediate strategic counter-thrust contributed in a marked degree to the success of the landing.

II

Although the General Staff might look upon Rommel as an outsider, the fact remains that thanks to National Socialist propaganda he was since the days of his African victories the most popular of all German commanders. This made it all the more remarkable that a centre of the military conspiracy should have been formed in his own *entourage*. Yet so it was, for the Chief of Staff of Army Group B was Lieutenant-General Dr Hans Speidel. Speidel had passed through the *Truppenamt*, and later gone to the *Luftwaffe*, from which he had been expelled for resisting Hitler's orders. He had been duly degraded but then taken over again by the General Staff.

Now, before Speidel, who was accounted one of the severest critics of the régime, had come on the scene, Rommel had been strongly influenced by an old friend and fellow Württemberger, Dr Strölin, Lord Mayor of Stuttgart, who was in close touch with Goerdeler. Moreover, after paying a visit to the Führer's headquarters, Rommel had found abundant confirmation of his doubts whether Hitler could bring the war to any end that was not a disaster. He had also had talks with Zeitzler, who communicated his views on the subject of a change in the structure of command. Rommel seems at this stage to have established contact with both Beck and Goerdeler, and in May 1944 had a conversation with Stülpnagel. There is reason to believe that both officers on this occasion agreed that the western armies should be used to make an end of the Hitler régime. Rommel was further informed by Wagner, the Quartermaster-General, of the Stauffenberg plan, though nothing was said of the proposed assassination of Hitler. Only an arrest was discussed. Stauffenberg himself declared his intention of visiting Rommel, but failed to do so.

It looks as though Rommel may now have formed a plan of his own. If so, the essence of it was that a radio appeal should be sent out to the people of Germany. This was to be the signal for the various resistance groups in the General Staff and the *ersatz* army to arrest Hitler and to transfer the government to the Beck-Goerdeler group. Rommel was relying on the possibility of holding a line from Memel along the Vistula and the Carpathians in the east, while armistice negotiations were opened in the west. Whether the western powers would have considered such a suggestion for a separate armistice must remain in doubt.

III

Since Stauffenberg never carried out his intention of visiting Rommel, the latter's plan, whatever it was, was never fully co-ordinated with that of Goerdeler and the General Staff. Moreover, the invasion took place before it could be fully perfected. From the early part of 1944 it was known to the German command that the enemy was withdrawing his best divisions from Italy to England. This circumstance, together with the concentration of large quantities of shipping in the southern ports of England, the intensified bombing of bridges and communications, and the increase of French underground activities made it obvious that a landing would not long be delayed. Both Rommel and Rundstedt, being entirely ignorant of the enemy's preparation of an artificial harbour, thought the capture of a port would be essential to him.

Blumentritt was later, while in captivity, to comment on the complete failure of the German Intelligence services. In point of fact, the imprisonment of Oster and one of his colleagues in 1943 had dealt this department a heavy blow. Nor were matters improved when the desertion to the British of one of Canaris' agents in Turkey made the latter's position impossible. Canaris was given a minor job in the O.K.W.'s Economic Warfare Department, while intelligence was taken over in its entirety by Heydrich's successor, S.S. *Obergruppenführer* Ernst Kaltenbrunner. Intelligence was thenceforward wholly concerned with the special interests of the S.S. There can be little doubt that Himmler was at this time contemplating making an end to the war on his own account—in opposition to Hitler.

Rundstedt thought that the landing would take place between the mouth of the Somme and the Pas de Calais, while the Navy believed that it would be attempted near Havre and looked upon a Normandy landing as impossible. Rommel came near to the truth with his forecast that the landing would be made between the Calvados coast and the mouth of the Seine, though he, too, believed that the Allies' fortunes depended on their ability to seize a large port. Hitler was certain that the landing would take place in the Pas de Calais, but also wanted stronger security for Normandy.

Rommel's staff complained of inadequate information of what was going on in enemy territory, though it received reports from C. in C. West, from the General Staff's Foreign Armies Department and from the *Wehrmachtführungsstab*. Further, O.K.W. did not elect to keep Army Group B adequately informed of the new weapons in preparation. In the case of Rundstedt, at any rate, this led to very exaggerated hopes being entertained of the effectiveness of such devices.

IV

The invasion began between 1.30 and 2 a.m. on June 6th, with the dropping of paratroops and airborne troops, after which thousands of planes began the bombing of the German batteries and fortifications. At daybreak some 130,000 men, with 20,000 tanks and other vehicles, effected a landing under a curtain of fire from naval vessels. The German command was taken completely by surprise, and it was not till 5 a.m. that the first counter-measures could be taken.

Since Hitler, who in these days was in Obersalzburg, was in the habit of sleeping late, the news did not reach him till the midday conference. Even Jodl had not dared to apprise him earlier. Thus the orders to commit the armoured reserve together with the Panzer training division and the 12th Panzer division were only sent out in the early afternoon, though they were coupled with the strict injunction to "clean up" the landing by the evening of that same day.

Zeitzler declared that this was impossible, and he proved quite right. On the evening of June 6th, two bridgeheads had taken shape. One lying between the Orne and the country north of Ryes was 25 kilometres broad and 10 deep, the other, which had a breadth of 15 kilometres and a depth of 4, was in the south-eastern corner of the Cotentin Peninsula.

Of the armoured divisions in France, only three could be brought into action. All roads were being attacked by low-flying aircraft, while the French Partisans perpetrated a large number of acts of sabotage against bridges, railway stations, etc. The entire staff of the Commander of Armoured Forces was eliminated by an air attack.

Hitler insisted on believing that a further landing would be made in the Pas de Calais. For this reason the majority of the troops concentrated in this area were kept where they were. As a result, the Allies, despite bad weather, were able to get through the first stage of the invasion without serious opposition.

Between June 7th and June 12th, a union was effected between the two Allied bridgeheads, and the Allies held a line some 90 kilometres long. The Cotentin Peninsula, with the harbour of Cherbourg, was sealed off. Rundstedt and Rommel increased their pressure on Hitler to come and examine the position for himself, a position of which they took a highly pessimistic view. Both men knew that it was now impossible to throw the Allies into the sea. On June 17th, Hitler at last complied with this request and received the two Field-Marshals with their Chiefs of Staff in the shelters of Margival, the so-called "Command Post W.II" which had been constructed for the invasion of England. Speidel has described Hitler's appearance on this occasion. He was pale, showed signs of lack of sleep, played nervously with his pencils and he loaded his commanders with reproaches. He wore spectacles now when reading, though pictures which showed him wearing these were not allowed to be published. Nobody must be allowed to think that the Führer had any weakness at all.

Rommel spoke with scathing frankness of the enemy's overwhelming superiority and the senselessness of Hitler's habit of trying to hold fortified positions in the enemy's rear. He had no qualms in describing the O.K.W.'s strategy as a "strategy of the green table", pursued wholly without knowledge of actual conditions. He also foretold that the enemy would succeed in breaking out towards Paris and the south unless a new method of countering his intentions was adopted. Between 22 and 25 motorized and armoured divisions had already been landed and two to three fresh divisions were being landed daily. There was now no chance of a landing in the Pas de Calais. He therefore asked for freedom to manoeuvre and for permission to withdraw behind the Orne. Hitler had to stand by and listen while Rommel accused him of demanding the confidence of other people but of withholding his own from his generals. He then asked Hitler straight out how he imagined the war would end, to which Hitler replied: "Don't bother yourself about the course of the war. Attend to your invasion front."

Both Field-Marshals pressed for the employment against the Allied landing places of the "V" weapon, which had begun to be used against England on the 13th. However, the officer in charge, General Heinemann, said that this was impossible, since the missiles were too inaccurate and might fall anywhere within 18 kilometres of their target. The fact is that when Hitler decided on their employment, these weapons were far from having been perfected. Hitler further forbade their use against the British ports of embarkation. He was determined to concentrate on London, believing, as he did, that this would make Britain more willing to come to terms. To the end he seems to have had the most erroneous notions about the "V" weapon's effectiveness.

Rundstedt tried to explain to Hitler that a much greater degree of regrouping was essential if the west front were to be maintained. He asked for the evacuation of Southern France up to the Loire so that Army Group G could be incorporated into a new strategic force of nine to ten infantry and three to four armoured divisions. With these he could carry on a war of manoeuvre on an extended scale. Hitler's reaction was merely to say, "You must remain where you are." Some time after this interview, Keitel telephoned Rundstedt from East Prussia and asked despairingly, "What are we to do?" Rundstedt replied, "End the war, what else can you do?"

Rommel's reproach that the O.K.W. was pursuing a strategy of the green table moved Hitler to announce his intention of visiting the troops on the following day but in the evening a faulty flying bomb fell near Hitler's shelter, whereupon he returned that same night to his own headquarters.

On June 19th there began another phase of the struggle which led to the final capture of Cherbourg and to the creation of an Allied bridgehead on the Odon river. Larger German tank formations were now hurled into the battle. Despite the collapse of the eastern front, two S.S. armoured divisions arrived from Hungary, and the attempts to press in on the Allied landing zone increased in intensity. Three armoured divisions were virtually destroyed in this fierce battle, and five more thrown into it and heavily mauled. In this way the forces which Rundstedt wanted to use as an operational reserve were destroyed. The end of this phase came when, on July 1st, the enemy broke out into the plains of Northern and Central France, which gave excellent opportunities to the American armour.

After the meeting in Margival, Rommel expressed his mind more or less openly to Dollmann and Salmuth, his two army commanders, neither of whom was enthusiastic for the régime. Indeed, Dollmann had once remarked, whilst an artillery commander in the *Reichswehr*, that a National Socialist had no business in a German officers' mess.

V

On June 29th, the day on which Dollmann, already inwardly a broken man, died of a heart attack at his battle headquarters, Rundstedt and Rommel were again ordered into Hitler's presence in Obersalzberg. Hitler treated them to a monologue about final victory and the great change which the "Wonder Weapons" would bring about, but proved himself completely impervious to any objection which his generals raised.

On his return to France, Rundstedt found that he had again been dismissed in disgrace. His successor was von Kluge, who had now recovered from his accident and had been the Führer's guest at Obersalzberg, where in long interviews he had been prepared for his task. Rommel knew that Kluge was privy to all plans for a coup, and was all the more surprised when this same man now demanded unconditional compliance with all Hitler's directives and criticized the extreme pessimism of the West. Kluge was one of those men who always take their opinions from the man they happen to have spoken to last. Tresckow had contrived to convince him of the necessity for a coup while Kluge was in the east. Now Hitler had made him equally convinced that the success of the invasion was wholly due to the faults of Rundstedt and Rommel, and had expressed his complete confidence in Kluge's ability to put matters right. Rommel was profoundly shocked to hear Kluge speak in the "Berchtesgaden style". However, as soon as the new Commander in Chief had spoken to the army commanders, to S.S. *Obergruppenführer* Hausser, who was Dollmann's successor, and to General Eberbach of the 5th Panzer Army, he veered round completely and apologized to Rommel. He now saw that the position was hopeless. When an enquiry reached him from Beck whether the western front should not be opened to the Allies, he remarked sadly that this was no longer necessary, the front would in any case collapse within a few days.

Rommel now resolved on one final step. He sent Kluge a report which was to be forwarded by the latter to Hitler. In this he called upon Hitler to face the consequences of the collapse of the western front and bring the war to an end. When sending it, he told his staff that if Hitler refused to act, he would act himself. What he did not know was that Stauffenberg's group had planned an attempt on Hitler's life for the 16th.

On July 17th, Rommel was in the neighbourhood of Caen, the critical point of the battle. When returning to his headquarters, his car was attacked by enemy aircraft on the Livaroth-Vimoutiers road, near Ferme Montgomery, reputed to have belonged to one of his great opponent's ancestors. His driver was killed, he himself severely wounded and actually believed dead. In order to prevent an S.S. general taking it over, as Hitler desired, von Kluge himself took over Army Group B.

VI

Thus ended the last attempt to end the war by using the western army to produce a change of government. There can be no doubt that the support of a man as popular as Rommel would have been a great source of strength to the movement on July 20th, though psychologically, of course, there was always the danger that the eastern armies, which had developed their own distinctive types and outlook, might have regarded such a venture as a "stab in the back". The removal of Rommel from the scene, however, did not make the crisis less acute. Hitler himself had admitted to Warlimont in January 1944 that if the invasion succeeded, or if Rumania was lost, the war could no longer be won. Now the success of the invasion was a fact, and the Russians were at Rumania's gates. This meant that the resistance movement was placed before the alternative of acting forthwith or abandoning its plans. An additional spur was provided by the circumstance that the effects of Canaris' elimination would grow more serious as time went by—and there was always Himmler, who might strike at any moment. Helmuth-James von Moltke had already been arrested, and Himmler had told Canaris that he knew very well that a revolt was being planned in high military circles and had named Beck and Goerdeler, saying that all this would lead to nothing as he would put a stop to the thing in time.

The final plan of action was essentially the work of the innermost circle around Stauffenberg, Beck and Lindemann, and its provisions were as follows. Hitler and Himmler were to be got rid of by a time-bomb concealed in a brief case. Stauffenberg himself volunteered to place this bomb. Stauffenberg was to be accompanied by a second conspirator, who would carry a duplicate bomb. At the critical moment, Fellgiebel, the general in charge of communications, was to cut off the Führer's headquarters from the outside world, while in Berlin the commander of the *ersatz* army put "operation Valkyrie" into effect. The Watch Battalion and the weapons schools were to occupy the capital and hold the surrounding radio stations. Helldorf, the Police President of Berlin, was ready to put the police at the conspirators' disposal. At the last moment the town commandant of Berlin, Lieutenant-General Paul von Hase, was also initiated.

Once power had passed to the "Deputy Commanders", which means the men whom Lindemann had chosen and who were in his confidence in the staffs of the different commands, the following measures were to be carried into effect. All *Reichsstatthalters* and *Gauleiters*, Ministers, S.S. leaders and similar Nazi instruments were to be arrested. All communication-centres, gas, electricity and water works were to be occupied, and all concentration camps broken up, after political prisoners had been separated from actual criminals. Finally, the security service and Gestapo were to be abolished, while the Waffen S.S. was to come directly under the Army.

A new government would then be established in Berlin under the Army's protection with Beck as provisional Regent, Goerdeler as Chancellor, and either von Hassell or the sometime ambassador in Moscow, von der Schulenburg, as Foreign Minister. The last-named had always had good personal relations with Stalin. The Propaganda

Ministry was to become an Information Office under Lindemann, and Witzleben was to take over command of the armed forces.

The Crown Prince and his son, Prince Louis Ferdinand, were apprised in a general way of what was afoot, and Prince Louis was prepared ultimately to take the regency into his own hands. The conspirators were, however, determined that the actual form of the constitution was to be decided by the German people in free elections. The military dictatorship and the provisional government were conceived as purely transitional affairs.

There remained the question of establishing contacts with the governments of enemy powers. Here the prospects were not wholly discouraging. In the autumn of 1943 some kind of contact seems to have been established with Churchill through the Swedish banker, Wallenberg. In addition to this, another member of the civilian resistance movement, Count Kanitz-Podangen, sometime Reich Food Minister, was endeavouring to establish contact with the Western Allies through the former League of Nations Commissioner of Danzig, Carl Burckhardt, in Switzerland. No connection was, however, established with the "Free Germany" Committee in Russia, and it was an open question what the attitude of Soviet Russia would be towards a government that consisted so largely of members of the old German governing class. In point of fact this latter consideration also applied to America, which was almost equally tied down by certain ideological preconceptions. As far as purely military measures were concerned, Stauffenberg wished to withdraw all troops in the west to the Rhine and to transfer all battleworthy divisions, and particularly all tank units, to the eastern front.

Certain special measures were planned for Berlin. The Watch Battalion was to shut off the area in which the government offices were situated, while special squads of reliable officers and men were to be held in readiness under a colonel in the *Zeughaus* to carry out the necessary arrests. The Propaganda Ministry was to be occupied by three companies under Colonel Gronau. The planning was thus reasonably complete, though the continual shifts of headquarters resulting from the air raids prevented it from being faultless.

VII

In the last resort everything depended on the success of the attempt on Hitler's life, though the attempt was only to be made if a blow could be struck at Hitler and Himmler simultaneously.

Stauffenberg did not form his resolution without a severe inner struggle and until it had become apparent to him beyond any shadow of doubt that tyrannicide was the only course to be adopted. He did not feel that he was the man to play the part of Brutus, and yet something must be done or everything would go down in ruin and shame. He felt that this expiatory deed was owing not only to his own order and to his comrades on the General Staff, but to the German people. The tragic dilemma in which these heirs of German idealism were caught was this. The very deed which purchased freedom would lay a guilt of blood on the initiator of the revolt which would make his future rôle as a soldier and a statesman extremely difficult. Yet this dilemma could not be resolved, and its existence can only increase our admiration for the courage of this man who sought under such terrible auspices to save his country from disaster.

Thanks to the co-operation of his fellow conspirators in the Supreme Army Command, Stauffenberg was, on July 1st, appointed to the post of Chief of Staff of the *ersatz* army, and thus obtained a decisive key position for the venture in hand. It was something of a setback that one of the principal members of the conspiracy, Major-General von Rost, who commanded the 3rd military district, was transferred in May to the Italian front, where he was killed shortly afterwards. His successor in Germany was Major-General Herfurth, whom it was considered unwise to initiate. This badly upset the plan for carrying out "Operation Valkyrie" in the manner that Lindemann had suggested. Nevertheless, Stauffenberg told his commander, Colonel-General Fromm, that he looked upon the war as lost—nor did Fromm endeavour to contradict him.

The network of conspiracy now stretched very far. It went from the Supreme Army Command through the General Staff and the *Allgemeines Heeresamt*, where General Olbricht's new Chief of Staff, Colonel von Quirnheim, and the head of the Infantry section, Colonel Wolfgang Müller, were now also won over, to the staffs of the military governors of France, Belgium and Jugoslavia, and to Army Group B in the invasion zone.

It is true that the conspirators' connections with the West were by no means of a uniform character. Also the network of those who were in the know had necessarily to be loosely knit; the danger of possible indiscretions made that inevitable. Reliance had ultimately to be placed on the effect of the news of Hitler's death, and Stauffenberg depended on that to bring all the generals in.

Even so, however, there was a considerable network of sympathetic civilian functionaries in existence in the Prussian provinces and the South German *länder*; to this belonged sometime high officials like the ex-*Oberpräsident* of Westphalia Freiherr von Lüninck, and certain political figures of the past, such as Gessler and Noske. There were also a number of great landowners in the affair. Count Lehndorff-Steinort in East Prussia and Count Hardenberg-Neuhardenberg in Mark Brandenburg are typical examples.

Hitler still did not know how near he was to death, for the issue of a warrant for Goerdeler's arrest and the arrest of most of the Young Socialist leaders who surrounded Dr Leber (they were alleged to be in touch with the Communist underground) only served to give additional strength to Stauffenberg's resolve, while the worsening situation in the west acted as an added spur. On July 16th, Stauffenberg made the first attempt to place the brief case containing the bomb in the conference room at Obersalzberg. A deputy with a second bomb accompanied him. A "stand by" order was sent to the weapons schools, the fact that the tanks and "recce" cars in Wündsdorf and Krampnitz were held in battle readiness arousing considerable and unwelcome comment. On this occasion, however, Hitler was not present at the conference, and Stauffenberg returned with his purpose unaccomplished. On July 18th, the plan was again put into operation, this time at the *Wolfsschanze*, but Hitler prematurely left the room.

Nervousness increased among the conspirators. Goerdeler was on the run from the Gestapo and time was pressing. Unfortunately, when it was decided that Stauffenberg should make a third attempt it proved impossible to warn all the centres of the conspiracy in time. The risk had now to be taken that members of the General Staff who were actually in the conspiracy and whom it might be impossible to warn in time without arousing suspicion might be blown up along with Hitler. Even the manufacture of pretexts which would enable Stauffenberg to come into Hitler's presence was a very troublesome business.

On July 20th an appointment had been made for Stauffenberg to go to the Führer's headquarters in Rastenburg to explain certain proposed new formations in the *ersatz* army, and Stauffenberg decided to use this opportunity to make his third attempt. The question of Himmler's presence was treated as no longer material. Also, the second bomb carrier was not present, as the General Staff officer who had been detailed for this task had been recalled by his division. In estimating the actual effect of the bomb, it had been assumed that the conference would take place, as was customary, in an underground shelter. Somewhat surprisingly, however, owing to the heat, it was held in a wooden hut above ground. Here only the end walls were of concrete. Further, because of the heat, the windows were open. Mussolini was expected in Rastenburg that afternoon, together with the Italian Commander in Chief, Graziani, and there were present at the conference: Keitel, Jodl, Warlimont, Buhle, Schmundt, General Scherff, who was the specialist for questions of military history in the O.K.W., the Army Command and the General Staff being represented by Heusinger, the Chief of the Operations Department, and his G.S.O. 1, Colonel Brandt. There were also present the *Luftwaffe's* Chief of Staff, Colonel Korten, Hitler's naval adjutant, Admiral von Puttkamer, and a number of other high-ranking officers.

VIII

Stauffenberg entered the conference room. Hitler, suspecting nothing, offered him his hand. Stauffenberg now quietly placed the briefcase with its deadly contents close to Hitler, against one of the supports of the table. Then he left the room under pretence of having to make a telephone call to Berlin, and, together with his orderly officer, Lieutenant von Haeften, watched further developments from a respectful distance. At 12.28 there was a fearful explosion. Pieces of wood were hurled in all directions, while a cloud of smoke and dust covered the hut. The two officers also thought they saw a human body hurled into the air.

There were confused cries. Stauffenberg believed that Hitler must certainly have been killed. All exits were now automatically blocked off, but the officers with some difficulty reached the plane which was to take them to Berlin, where Stauffenberg was to send out the order for "Operation Valkyrie".

Utter confusion prevailed in the Führer's headquarters. Keitel rushed out of the building, blackened with smoke, and kept on shouting, "Where is the Führer?" It was thought at first that the deed had been the work of one of the O.T. workers who were continually engaged in adding to the buildings. The casualties were as follows. Berger, the stenographer, was killed outright. Schmundt was mortally wounded, as were Colonel Brandt and Colonel Korten, of the *Luftwaffe*. General Buhle was seriously injured. Jodl and Heusinger, himself one of the conspirators, sustained minor injuries. Warlimont suffered from severe concussion, though he did not notice its effect at the time. Hitler himself suffered a few small burns on his right hand

and arm, had his ear drums broken and suffered somewhat from shock. The circumstance that just before the explosion he had got up to look at a map on the wall had saved his life. After Professor Morell had examined him and given him a stimulant, he received Mussolini at the railway station the same afternoon. He was perfectly collected though deathly pale. Hitler showed his guest the wreckage of the hut, and remarked that his escape was a proof that he stood under the direct protection of Providence, which had spared him to complete his great work.

It was only gradually that the real meaning of what had happened was realized. A telephonist caused suspicion to fall on "a one-eyed Staff officer" who had left the headquarters with suspicious haste immediately before the explosion. Yet this same suspect Staff officer did not know that he had failed to kill Hitler, and that the essential condition for his projected stroke had thus failed to materialize. The result of this, among other things, was, of course, that the conspirators in the Führer's headquarters did not drop the mask. Meanwhile Fellgiebel had failed to sever communications, so that Hitler was left for some time in the belief that the attempt at assassination was the act of an isolated individual.

Stauffenberg finally managed to reach Berlin at about half past three. From the airport in Rangsdorf he had already notified Olbricht that everything had gone off well. Olbricht's offices were in the Bendlerstrasse at the corner of the Tirpitz-Ufer, as were those of the commander of the *ersatz* army, and there were now present Beck, Witzleben, Hoepner and a number of civilian conspirators, particularly Yorck von Wartenburg, who was to become state secretary to the Foreign Office, Konsistorialrat Gerstenmaier and Gisevius who had illegally returned from Switzerland. Goerdeler could not be reached and did not put in an appearance.

Olbricht in good faith reported the death of Hitler to Fromm. Now Fromm was the typical professional officer of the old *Reichswehr*, who maintained a very reserved attitude towards National Socialism but had a great respect for Hitler's almost magical influence on the masses of the German people. Being that kind of man, he wanted first to get confirmation from Keitel that Hitler was really dead. When he called up the *Wolfsschanze*, he heard from Keitel's own lips that Hitler was alive and only slightly injured. He then told Olbricht that the orders for "Valkyrie" could not go out.

IX

Meanwhile other men had already acted. Colonel von Quirnheim had sent out in Fromm's name the orders that were to come into force in the event of an internal disturbance. Helldorf, of the police, and von Hase, the town commandant, reported to the Bendlerstrasse and asked for instructions. Hase was given orders to arrest Goebbels, who was in Berlin, though this duty was originally to be given to Gronau, a substitution which was to prove unfortunate. Hase was a pleasant man and of high moral sensibility, but wholly unsuitable for the work of a *coup d'état*. He acted strictly according to regulations and alerted the Watch Battalion so that the Wilhelmstrasse could be cordoned off.

Now the commander of the Watch Battalion was Major Remer, who had shortly before this been decorated by Hitler with the oak leaves of the Knight's Cross of the Order of the Iron Cross. Remer was incredulous when he was given the news of Hitler's death, and at this point the National Socialist *Führungsoffizier* of the battalion, Lieutenant Hagen, who in civilian life was one of the heads of Department in the Propaganda Ministry, intervened and offered to get Goebbels to confirm personally the truth or falsity of the report. Meanwhile, the Watch Battalion could cordon off the Wilhelmstrasse pending further clarification.

Von Quirnheim's emergency orders had yet further consequences. The tank schools in Krampnitz and Wünsdorf set about getting their vehicles ready in order to move on Berlin, but there was a bad hitch in the case of the Infantry school at Döberitz. The commandant, General Hitzfeld, who had been initiated into the conspiracy, was absent at a funeral, so that all that resulted from the orders were long arguments between the officers concerned. This was particularly disquieting in so far as it had been planned that the Infantry school should occupy the radio stations and also Concentration Camps I and II at Oranienburg.

By this time Stauffenberg had appeared at the Bendlerstrasse and repeated to Fromm that there could be no doubt of Hitler's death since he himself had carried out the assassination and observed the effects of the bomb, adding that if Keitel said anything different, he was not speaking the truth. Olbricht, who was present at the interview, declared that von Quirnheim had already sent out the orders for "Operation Valkyrie". Fromm summoned von Quirnheim and told him he was under arrest, while Stauffenberg was informed that there was nothing for him to do but to shoot himself as quickly as possible, since his attempted assassination had failed. Hitler was alive, and so long as the sinister master of the masses was still among the living, Fromm thought that a coup had no prospect of success. Olbricht made a last attempt to persuade Fromm not to cripple a movement the aim of which was to save the country, whereupon Fromm threatened to put Olbricht under arrest as well. A short tussle ensued in which Fromm was overpowered by the conspirators and locked in his office, the command of the *ersatz* army being assumed by Hoepner.

At this stage, Beck and Witzleben were themselves beginning to grow doubtful about the question of Hitler's death. Beck was nevertheless determined to go through with the plan. When Hoepner somewhat anxiously objected that this involved an actual trial of strength, Beck replied with conviction that they owed the German people a readiness to take that risk. Everything now depended on the length of time needed for the armoured contingents and the other troops of the weapon schools to reach Berlin and on the success or failure to isolate the government offices and the radio stations. Beck insisted that it was essential for him to get to the microphone before Hitler. Beck also established communication with the different army groups, and sought in particular to get von Kluge to take sympathetic action in the west.

Kluge, however, evaded the request and telephoned to Keitel, Warlimont and Stieff. He thus learned that Hitler was still alive. Witzleben, who had waited for years for this hour and had grown old and grey in waiting, now began to doubt whether it was possible to occupy the capital in the short time still remaining. Further, Beck's health was in a precarious state. There were times when the dreadful nature of the moment seemed to overwhelm him, and on more than one occasion he lost his voice when speaking on the telephone. Some of the younger officers who observed him on these occasions began to doubt whether Beck was the man who, as they had been told, could save Germany.

Stauffenberg, however, leaped into the breach. In the late hours of that close afternoon, his personality unfolded in all its passion and grandeur. He went from telephone to telephone in his effort to try and carry the deputy commanders in the provinces along with him, adjuring one, encouraging another, issuing peremptory orders to a third, always displaying what seemed to be a sixth sense in the choice of the manner and tone most suited to the person concerned. Beck remarked that everything depended on the time the tanks would take to arrive, and that a good general should be able to wait. Olbricht as usual kept his poise. When Beck asked him whether the sentries were reliable and would shoot if the Gestapo suddenly appeared, Olbricht replied drily that he did not know. Beck rejoined, "Olbricht, Olbricht, if it had been for Fritsch the men would have been ready enough to take their chance of a bullet."

Minutes became hours. No previous warning having been given, it would take an hour and a half to get the hundred or so tanks of the tank school at Wünsdorf loaded up and ready for the road. They could thus only reach the centre of Berlin in the early hours of the evening. The same applied to the armoured "recce" cars at Krampnitz. Late that afternoon, the radio gave out officially that an attempt had been made to assassinate the Führer, but that he had remained unharmed and would address the nation that evening. With that the whole plan slipped out of its authors' hands.

X

Meanwhile in Berlin an incident had occurred the effects of which proved decisive. The Watch Battalion went over to Hitler. Lieutenant Hagen had gone to see Goebbels, and Goebbels had little difficulty in persuading him that the news of Hitler's death was false and that the orders for the Army to take over supreme power against the S.S. were without validity. Goebbels had immediately recognized that a full-blown *coup d'état* was in progress, for the Wilhelmplatz was already shut off by the troops. He told Hagen to bring his commanding officer along. Goebbels then asked Major Remer if he would care to reassure himself that the Führer was alive, and had a call put through to the latter's headquarters. Remer then heard that well-known voice which had once sent the people of Germany into transports of delight.

Hitler by now had realized the seriousness of the danger which threatened him, and like a man in a fever gave Remer on the spot the command of all troops in and around Berlin, and Remer obeyed, feeling that the greatest hour of his life was at hand. The *coup d'état* which had begun with telephoned orders was thus ended by a telephone conversation.

By evening the situation had become hopeless for the conspirators in the Bendlerstrasse in so far as they had been unable to occupy a radio station. They still had no reliable force at their disposal, though an S.S. *Gruppenführer* who had innocently arrived with two high

S.S. officers to arrest them, was, at Stauffenberg's suggestion, himself arrested. The question, however, was what would happen when units of the S.S. appeared in force. At this stage, Colonel Müller, the head of the Infantry section in the *Allgemeines Heeresamt*, decided to order the Infantry School and the Infantry Training Battalion to Berlin on his own account, and drove to Döberitz about 7.30. He harangued the troops, and then, as his intervention seemed to have been successful, drove back to Berlin. On his return journey he found the streets empty, the chains which had surrounded the government offices withdrawn. Major Remer had made a job of it. The magic words "Führer's orders" had had their effect. When, at 10 o'clock, he saw the men of the Armourers' School moving into the Bendler-strasse Colonel Müller thought that this was on the orders of the conspirators. In reality, it was on those of Major Remer, the dictator of that hour.

In the Ministry, meanwhile, there had been something like a counter-revolution; such officers as were faithful to Hitler or had made up their minds to refrain from action till they knew of his death, armed themselves with machine guns, pistols and hand grenades, took over the telephone exchange, released Fromm, and went from room to room calling out that people had been misled, and putting the threatening question, "For or against Hitler?" Stauffenberg was wounded by shots and arrested. Fromm declared to Olbricht, Hoepner and Beck that he would now deal with them as he had himself been dealt with that afternoon, and duly arrested them. Beck refused to hand over his pistol, since he was determined not to survive that day. Fromm thereupon compelled him to shoot himself before the eyes of those present in the room. When, shaken as he was by the events of that hour, he missed with the first shot and with the second merely inflicted a wound in his head which was not fatal, Fromm ordered an officer to despatch the sometime Chief of General Staff as though he were a wounded animal. The officer passed the order on to an N.C.O. who fired the fatal shot.

Hastily now Fromm set up a court martial, which condemned Stauffenberg, Olbricht, Quirnheim and Haeften to death by shooting. Fromm was moved at this moment not only by the fear that the propriety of his own conduct might be questioned but also by the old tradition of the *Reichswehr* as an *imperium in imperio*. He was anxious that possible witnesses for the prosecution should be got rid of before the S.S. could intervene. Thus at one o'clock the four victims were shot by the light of an armoured car in the gutter of one of the quadrangles of the War Ministry, troops of the army-fireworkers acting as their executioners. Stauffenberg cried out "Long live Free Germany!" but the soldiers did their duty in sullen silence. They understood nothing of the meaning of these words. Later S.S. men threw the bodies, including that of Beck, on to a lorry. Their present whereabouts is unknown.

XI

In Paris events at first took an entirely different course. They provided a perfect object lesson of what might have happened if action ·in the different military districts had been more energetic. Immediately Stauffenberg telephoned to von Hofacker, who was a relative of his, that Hitler was dead, Stülpnagel set about arresting the Gestapo and the S.D., and the town commandant of Paris, Lieutenant-General von Boineburgk-Lengsfeld, was instructed to have this operation carried out that evening by the Security Regiment I Gross-Paris, which was equipped with armoured "recce" wagons. At 18 hours the regiment was alerted, and at 21.30 hours the action began, with the regimental commander, Colonel von Kraewel, leading his men, pistol in hand. Not a shot was fired by Hitler's myrmidons. The head of the S.S., General Oberg, and the leader of the Security Services, an S.S. *Standartenführer*, (who was found in a night club), made no resistance to arrest.

Now, no warning had reached von Kluge that the assassination was to have been attempted on that day, and when he returned that evening to B Group headquarters at La Roche Guyon from a visit to the front, he found matters in some confusion. Blumentritt, his Chief of Staff, had already been informed by one of the conspirators, namely the *"Oberquartiermeister* West", Colonel Finckh, that Hitler was dead. He had also been informed some time previously by Speidel that some kind of action against Hitler was intended. He contrived, however, to get into touch by telephone with Major-General Stieff at headquarters, who, knowing that the plot had failed and being anxious not to give himself away, asked where they got the story about Hitler's death, adding "The Führer is perfectly well and in excellent spirits." Blumentritt's impression was that some kind of an attempt had been made and that it had failed. Kluge then said that if the thing had succeeded he would immediately have stopped the V.1's on England and tried to start talks with the Allies.

That evening Kluge asked Stülpnagel and Sperrle of the *Luftwaffe* to join him to discuss the situation, while a new crisis developed near Caen. At about 7.30 Stülpnagel arrived, together with Lieutenant-Colonel Hofacker, at the headquarters of Army Group B, Sperrle coming somewhat later. Stülpnagel disclosed what Stauffenberg's plans had been. Kluge then remarked, "Well, gentlemen, the attempt has failed. It's all over."

Stülpnagel: "Herr Feldmarschall, I thought you were acquainted with the plans. Something must be done."

Kluge: "Nothing more can be done. The Führer is still alive."

According to Blumentritt's account, Sperrle showed no signs of wanting to be drawn into this fruitless discussion, and eventually Stülpnagel, who was obviously badly scared, had an interview with Kluge alone and told him that before leaving Paris he had taken the "first precautionary measures" and had arrested the Gestapo and the Security Services. Kluge's reaction was immediate. He told Stülpnagel that he had acted without orders and must take personal responsibility for anything he had done. Blumentritt called up Colonel von Linstow, Stülpnagel's Chief of Staff, who informed him that Stülpnagel's orders were in process of being executed and that nothing could stop them. Kluge thereupon declared that it would be best for Stülpnagel to put on civilian clothes and disappear, but Stülpnagel was not the man for such a course.

Meanwhile the position was becoming more critical. Admiral Krancke, who had grown suspicious as the result of a long telephone conversation with Witzleben, threatened to use his 5,000 naval ratings to free the S.S. in Paris. Sepp Dietrich, commanding the 1st S.S. Panzer Corps, who had been alarmed by rumours, threatened likewise to march on Paris with this force. When eventually Hitler himself spoke over the radio and made "a clique of megalomaniac and criminal officers" responsible for the attempt on his life, Boineburgk-Lengsfeld and Kraewel, who were carrying out the operation against the S.S. in Paris, threw in their hands. At length, Stülpnagel himself returned to Paris and ordered the release of such S.S. as were being held.

The night of July 20th brought changes of the most decisive kind to the Army. Late in the evening the commander of the Reich Air Fleet was entrusted with the highest military power over all troops within the Reich. An order was sent out that orders must only be obeyed if given by officers personally known to the troops concerned. Further, General Buhle having been seriously injured by the bomb explosion, Colonel-General Guderian was entrusted with the conduct of the office of Chief of General Staff. This decision was due to pure chance. Guderian, who had had no knowledge of the plans for a coup, and who had not been in Berlin on July 20th, but had that morning been inspecting an armoured unit in Hohensalza, had returned in the afternoon to the estate which had been presented to him in the Warthegau, and there had heard of the attempted assassination at about 7 o'clock. It so happened that at this particular moment he was, as far as Hitler and his advisers were concerned, the only high-ranking officer who was available in the neighbourhood who knew something of the eastern problems, and who had most palpably not been associated with the bomb explosion.

On July 21st, Heinrich Himmler, once a Bavarian ensign, then a poultry farmer and a bank clerk, now *Reichsführer S.S.*, took over command of the *ersatz* army, and Keitel sent Stülpnagel word that he had backed the wrong horse and would have to pay. At von Kluge's headquarters there appeared, by direction of Goebbels and Keitel, the highest *Führungsoffizier* in the west, with representatives of the *Wehrmacht* propaganda section, who asked for a congratulatory telegram to be sent to Hitler and for a radio address to be delivered which would put an end to all rumours of independent action. Kluge, already a broken man, contrived to evade at least the latter of these demands.

When Guderian, on the afternoon of that same day, went to take over the General Staff at Mauerwald, he found utter confusion. Zeitzler had been dismissed from the Army and deprived of his right to wear a uniform, and some of the most important officers had been wounded at the time of the bomb explosion. Others had necessarily to expect their arrest. As part of the plot, most of the telephone connections had been transferred to Zossen. Guderian found the Chief of Staff's office empty and in the entire hut he finally discovered only a solitary corporal who was supposed to be acting as telephone operator but who was actually asleep.

Now Guderian had been a soldier all his life. He came from the German East, where he had been born in 1888, the son of a Prussian officer and the grandson of a landowner. Before his eyes there stood in this hour the picture of the pitifully thin line holding the East Prussian border, and his mind was haunted by the terrible danger of a Russian breakthrough. He had never believed that much could be changed by a plot against the government, and it seemed to him that precisely such conduct as that of Stauffenberg might make it possible for the Russians to pour over the country right up to the Rhine, while the Allies were still engaged in heavy battles in the west. The atmosphere of the Führer's headquarters was fundamentally alien to him, as alien as the idealism which had moved men like Stauffenberg. He believed that nothing but persistence and fearlessness was needed to correct Hitler's strategic errors. He also felt that his being relieved of his post in the winter of 1941 had been a severe setback, and that he could now show what he was made of.

He felt a fearful bitterness against the men who were seeking to defend the traditions of the General Staff, and one of the first orders that he sent out branded that institution with the guilt of having helped prepare the plot. His order of July 29th directed to all General Staff officers laid it down that every officer must become a "National Socialist *Führungsoffizier*". Anyone having objections to this was to apply for transfer. It was an order for which the champions of the military opposition never forgave him. It produced a division in the ranks of the General Staff which could never be bridged. Guderian, who simply viewed the matter as a soldier, was trying to apply purely external means to preserve a purely external discipline.

In the Führer's headquarters, Hitler was raging against the General Staff and the old officer corps. With foam on his lips he cried out that he would hang his enemies as though they were so many carcasses of beef. A special commission of the Gestapo comprising 400 officials went to work to examine the background of the plot. Arrests and suicides among high-ranking officers multiplied, as the extent of the conspiracy was disclosed. Two days after Guderian had assumed office, Heusinger, Chief of the Operations Department, was arrested, his fate being shared by Stieff. In Zossen, Wagner committed suicide when he was about to be taken.

Stülpnagel was removed from his post and summoned to Berlin to explain his conduct. On the journey there he endeavoured to take his life, but merely blinded himself and was taken to hospital unconscious. When scarcely recovered, he was condemned to death by garroting. Witzleben was arrested on his estate by a general. A court of honour was instituted by the *Wehrmacht*, Keitel, Rundstedt and Guderian being members, and expelled from the service all officers who had taken part in the conspiracy, so that these became subject to proceedings in the civil courts—in this case, a "People's court". Among the first who went to the gallows as a result of this were Witzleben, Hoepner, Hase, Stieff and Yorck von Wartenburg.

All old enemies or suspected enemies were now arrested, including

Schacht, Falkenhausen, Thomas and Halder, the last-named having entered into correspondence with ex-Chancellor Wirth, who was living in Switzerland. Also Halder's wife and his daughter-in-law, Frau von Hobe, whose husband, a lieutenant-colonel in the General Staff, had taken part in the conspiracy, were sent to concentration camps.

The court martial which Fromm had hastily improvised on July 20th helped him not at all. His equivocal attitude during the crisis was considered to justify his arrest and in due course he was beheaded. Herfurth was hanged, as were also Fellgiebel, Finckh, von Roenne and others too numerous to mention. Speidel was arrested in September, and when it transpired that Rommel, who was just recovering from his wounds, was mixed up in the conspiracy. Rommel was handed poison by two generals from the O.K.W. and told that he must take it or face his trial before a People's court. Rommel took the poison, and was given a state funeral. The official announcement was that he died from his wounds. Goerdeler was also hanged—after being arrested by two Army paymasters in East Prussia.

Hitler's fury gradually spent itself. The execution of Witzleben and the other culprits in the Bendlerstrasse had been by the garrotte, a method by which the agonies of the condemned were prolonged. These executions were filmed and Hitler saw this film in his private cinema. His first intention was that the film should be shown to the troops, but this idea outraged even the National Socialists in the officer corps, and it was dropped. Men like Warlimont considered these exhibitions of sadism so disgusting that they found it difficult, as self-respecting officers, to continue serving such a man. Warlimont made the concussion he had suffered as a result of the bomb explosion a pretext for resigning on grounds of health.

XII

When, after the failure of the plot, Himmler assumed command of the *ersatz* army, the story of the General Staff as an autonomous entity may be said to come to an end. Its task had also ended, for there was little now to be done, beyond liquidating a lost war. Guderian held that his main duty was to hold the eastern front.

Guderian, who had started his military career as a Jäger officer, had passed through the school of the General Staff and had served in the *Truppenamt*, but he did not really belong to the charmed circle of General Staff officers. Beck, after the manner of his kind, had treated his revolutionary theories with extreme reserve, and this now led to some misunderstanding. Many General Staff officers bore Guderian a grudge for carrying on quietly with his duties while their comrades were sitting in the cellars of the Gestapo in the Prinz Albrecht Strasse or had ended their lives on the gallows. Such men, though quite wrongly, believed that old rivalries were being pursued.

Guderian's attempt to make Hitler see reason failed, as it was bound to fail, and when he too followed his predecessors in trying to bring about a recasting of the apparatus of command and pressed for the constitution of a *Wehrmacht* General Staff with Manstein at the head of it, he had no more success than the rest. Needless to say, there were a number of changes both in the General Staff and in the Army as a whole. General Alfred Toppe was made Quartermaster-General, while General of Tanks Walter Wenck became *Chef des Führungsstabs*, an office which replaced that of *Oberquartiermeister I*. Colonel von Bonin became head of the Operations Department, Lieutenant-Colonel von dem Knesebeck became its G.S.O.1, and General Gehlen took over "Foreign Armies East". The appointments of Wenck and von Bonin put tank men into the key positions of the General Staff, unfortunately at a time when German superiority in this arm had become a thing of the past, but it was a belated triumph of the tank school of thought. Undoubtedly Wenck was a competent General Staff officer, but strategic talent was now of little use.

In the O.K.W., General Winter became Warlimont's successor as deputy Chief of the *Wehrmachtführungsstab*, while one of Hitler's all-out admirers, General Burgdorf, took the place of Schmundt (who had died of his injuries) as Adjutant in Chief of the *Wehrmacht* and head of the *Heeres-Personalamt*.

These changes in the General Staff were carried out under the shadow of the terror—a circumstance which Guderian had certainly not bargained for, such considerations being wholly alien to his clear soldierly mind. From a purely military point of view, there were still other shadows that darkened the scene. The end was drawing near. Despite rising armaments production, by means of which 130 infantry and 40 armoured divisions had been equipped in the spring of 1944, despite the fact that feverish work was being done on new weapons— the new V.2 rockets, a new anti-aircraft aerial torpedo rocket, a turbo-jet plane and a new type of submarine, Speer, the Armaments Minister, recognized that the war was lost when the strategic bombing of the Allies had destroyed Germany's synthetic fuel installations. According to Speer, Germany was at the end of her strength in the late autumn of 1944, and he did not fail to explain this to Hitler in a series of memoranda. Hitler deliberately misled him by talking of Japanese attempts at mediation between Germany and Russia, precisely as he fooled Jodl and Keitel by his talk about new weapons.

In the west there began that breakdown of the front which Rommel had prophesied long before. On July 24th, Hitler at last decided to throw into the battle the German units which were stationed in the Pas de Calais. They came too late and suffered heavily from the low flying aircraft which commanded all the roads. On the 25th, one day after Hitler's decision, the Allies broke out of their landing zone, American armoured forces breaking through at Avranches, the hinge of the German front. Kluge, remembering Joffre's manoeuvre *en retraite* at the Battle of the Marne, advocated a boldly conceived retirement to the Seine, from where he could launch a counter-attack, and asked Jodl to arrange to let him see Hitler.

Hitler, however, wanted to hear nothing of such plans and gave a categorical order for a counter-attack on the spot with all available armoured forces. General Eberbach, of the 5th Panzer Army, was to be in charge of the operation. Sepp Dietrich himself protested to von Kluge against the order, but von Kluge could only remark resignedly that it was "Führer's orders".

The attack failed completely owing to inadequate air cover, the German tank concentrations providing perfect targets for the enemy planes. Eventually, the 5th Panzer Army and the 7th Army began to be encircled in the Morton-Falaise pocket, and a French Stalingrad came into being. The American generals further distressed their enemies, who had hitherto made a somewhat supercilious estimate of their capacity, by a thoroughly inconsiderate display of talent, though it needed a week's hard fighting before the signs of disintegration among the German formations became too palpable to be denied.

On August 12th, von Kluge went to the Falaise area for a conference with his army and corps commanders and his mobile radio transmitter became a casualty, so that for a considerable time it was impossible to reach him. Hitler immediately suspected that he had gone over to the Allies and gave strict orders against any withdrawals out of the trap, but actual impressions from the battle area had already decided Kluge to take the law into his own hands. On the 16th of the month, however, Model suddenly arrived with a handwritten letter from Hitler authorizing him to take over the command both of the

western armies as a whole and of Army Group B. Two days later
Kluge started his journey home full of dark forebodings that his guilty
knowledge of the plot had been discovered. Between Verdun and
Metz he took poison, and so ended his life. He left a letter for Hitler
in which he adjured him either to commit the new weapons or end
the war.

On August 20th the last attempt of the 5th Panzer Army to break
out ended in failure, and the battle of Morton-Falaise drew to an end.
German losses were 1,500 tanks, 3,500 guns, 240,000 killed or
wounded and 210,000 prisoners. Since June 6th, 53 German divisions
had been destroyed, 22 corps and divisional commanders were either
killed, wounded or prisoners of war.

Meanwhile the 7th American Army had landed at Marseilles and
Toulon on August 15th and had begun to push its way up the Rhone
Valley. Von Kluge had left the forces of Army Group G in southern
France and had refused to unite them with his main body. These,
however, were now forced to beat a costly retreat through the Burgundian Gates, while the Allied forces, having been completely
successful at Morton-Falaise, streamed towards Paris and towards
the rocket sites on the coast.

Paris fell in due course, and thereafter Brussels and Antwerp, and
now that the front at last began to crumble, it disclosed the extent of
the moral breakdown which had taken place in the armies of occupation. Scenes were witnessed which nobody would ever have deemed
possible in the German Army. Naval troops marched northward
without weapons, selling their spare uniforms to the French as they
went. They told people that the war was over and that they were
going home. Lorries loaded with officers, their mistresses and large
quantities of champagne and brandy contrived to get back as far as
the Rhineland, and it was necessary to set up special courts martial to
deal with such cases. However, Field-Marshal Model took charge
with an iron hand, and managed to effect a substantial regrouping of
units in Southern Belgium and Holland. In September Rundstedt
was reappointed C. in C. West, given a highly experienced Chief of
Staff in the person of Cavalry-General Siegfried Westphal and allotted
the task of re-forming the front, which was temporarily stabilized
on a line running from the Lower Rhine, along the Meuse, through
Southern Holland, Brabant and Lorraine, then along the western
edge of the Saar territory to the Burgundian gates. Montgomery believed that it was now possible to thrust on to Berlin, and if he had
done so the heart of Central Europe would have fallen into the hands

of the Western Allies, not those of the Russians. Eisenhower, however, who had no distrust of the latter, feared such an extension of his communications, and his decision gave the German command a breathing space. How quickly it took advantage of this is shown by the failure of the British attempt to seize a bridgehead over the Lower Rhine at Arnhem by means of a large-scale airborne operation.

Behind this front Himmler now began to stamp new formations out of the ground. The so-called *Volks* or "People's" Grenadier Divisions and *Volks* Artillery Corps were created, which were also intended to be models for a sort of National Socialist peacetime army, and mass production began of such Bazooka-type anti-tank weapons as the *Panzerfaust* and *Panzerschreck*. Meanwhile Guderian was using every means to strengthen the eastern front. He planned to withdraw the 30 divisions of the Courland army, now commanded by Field-Marshal Schörner, and to use the new *Volks* Grenadier divisions and the *Volks* Artillery for the defence of Poland. He planned a strong defensive system in the east which could be held by *Landwehr* units created for the purpose, by so-called fortress battalions of physically low-grade troops armed with 2,000 captured heavy guns. Hitler rejected these plans one after another, for his gaze was fixed on the west. He ordered the Courland army to stay where it was, while the fortification of the east was placed into the hands of the Party and into those of the eastern *Gauleiters* and Reich Defence Commissars. Bormann created a special "Inspectorate of Fortresses" for the occasion. The *Volks* Grenadier divisions were distributed among all the fronts, while Himmler appropriated the idea of a *Landsturm*, for use in the less exposed positions in the east, and converted it into the nonsensical *Volkssturm*, to which all men were to be called once the enemy had set foot on German soil.

Thus the inevitable catastrophe in the east drew nearer. It is true that heavy battles in Poland and the East Prussian frontier, battles which were fought both with the Russians and with the Polish underground which now rose in Warsaw, enabled Germany to hold for a time the line of her frontier, and a distribution of forces was effected which was roughly as follows. The line from the northern corner of East Prussia to the Narev was held by the centre army group under Colonel-General Reinhardt, comprising the 2nd and 4th Armies (the latter commanded by Hossbach, the sometime *Wehrmachtadjutant*) and the 3rd Panzer Army. Between Modlin and Kasshau was Army Group A under Colonel-General Josef Harpe, comprising the 17th and 4th Armies and the 4th and 1st Panzer Armies. The numerical relation of German and Russian divisions was one of one to nine, that of tanks one to six and that of guns between one to ten and one to fifteen. Most German armoured divisions were at a third of their original strength, being reduced to about 70 to 80 battle-worthy tanks apiece. Only the S.S. Panzer units were at full strength.

The weakest point on the whole German line was the Southern Rumanian front, commanded by General Friessner, from whom Hitler had in June taken nearly all his tanks in order to throw them in on the central sector. In August Antonescu had paid a last visit to Hitler and had expressed his surprise that so many high-ranking generals had taken part in the plot of the previous month. He himself, he assured the Führer, could rely absolutely on his generals. Actually, of course, King Michael was already planning to get Rumania on to the Allied side in the hope of winning Allied support against Russia's threat to the monarchy. In this most of his generals were supporting him.

Friessner's warnings to Hitler fell on deaf ears, and his request to withdraw his forces behind the Prut was refused. When, therefore, on August 20th Russia attacked on the Dniester, the inevitable result ensued. Dimitrescu's Rumanian army group dissolved. The 6th German Army, which had been re-formed since the catastrophe of 1943, experienced something like a second Stalingrad, and was surrounded. What remained of the 8th Army retreated to the Eastern Carpathians and Transylvania. On August 23rd, King Michael carried out his plans, and Rumania went over to the enemy.

Friessner was unable to hold the Transylvanian passes, and the Russians under Malinowski and Tolbuchin broke into the Hungarian plain. Soon the whole of the Balkans had to be evacuated, while in Hungary, Admiral Horthy tried to open simultaneous negotiations with the Americans, the Russians and Tito. Horthy was deposed and taken under German arrest, and a puppet government set up of Szalassi's Fascist Arrow Cross organization. By mid-September, however, the Russians stood in the Banat, and the fight for the Danube crossings began.

XIII

Guderian's boldly conceived plan of defence for the east remained a torso. Its whole basis, which was the preparation of a defensive line

in the rear, could only be realized by means of a bluff, Guderian sending out the necessary orders in Hitler's name but without any actual
authorization. Hitler, however, sent to the West Wall the fortress
battalions and the captured guns which Guderian had wanted to use
in the east. Thus the earthworks and trenches which the *Gauleiters* of
East Prussia, Pommerania and Silesia had constructed by the most
ruthless use of all the available labour forces, and for the construction
of which they had not hesitated to use the labour of women, lacked
any forces by which they could be held, and were worthless from the
start.

Guderian was quite clear in his mind that his plan of defence could
not change the ultimate issue of the war; he knew that all he could
achieve was a change in the relative potential of his eastern and
western enemies. He fought for his plan with all the toughness and
obstinacy of which he was capable, sacrificing even his health in this
cause, but the plan perished in the atmosphere of the Führer's headquarters. Guderian, like Zeitzler, had failed to appreciate the complete impossibility of getting such a man as Hitler to work with him
in a reasonable and objective spirit.

Unlike the General Staff, for which the decisive theatre of operations was the east, and which feared the threat of Bolshevism much
more than it feared a victory by the Western democracies, Hitler, as
before, saw his principal enemy in Britain, and now returned to the
idea of eliminating her. Then, he thought, he would get a free hand
in the east—a shocking piece of unrealism. His last resources were
now concentrated on renewing the Ardennes offensive of 1940. Those
Panzer divisions which were grouped together in the 6th S.S. Panzer
Army under Sepp Dietrich were all equipped with new material. The
fronts in Poland and Hungary were ruthlessly weakened. The purpose which Hitler had in mind was to break through the historic
Ardennes gap and to cut off the British from the Channel Ports, and
so force a second "Dunkirk" upon them. Montgomery himself was
later to describe the plan as bold. The point of attack, he said, was
skilfully chosen, since the Ardennes were only held by four American
divisions. Nevertheless, Hitler had here engaged on an undertaking
which went far beyond any realistic estimate of his resources.

Old Field-Marshal Rundstedt, now once again C. in C. West, was
the last representative of that long line of field marshals who had led
the German armies to victory in Poland, France, Jugoslavia and
Russia, and the most Rundstedt would concede was that an offensive
might be feasible which had the limited objective of cutting off the

enemy forces around Aix-la-Chapelle. However, as always, he ulti-mately gave in, confined himself to private sarcasm and lent his name, the name of a military specialist of great experience, to a scheme which went wholly beyond Germany's strength. For all that he no longer could be accounted among the favourites on whom Hitler banked for success. That rôle now belonged to men like Model, com-manding Army Group B, the commanders of the two Panzer armies, General Hasso von Manteuffel and Sepp Dietrich.

Besides these, there was yet another personality, namely *S.S. Sturmbannführer* Skorzeny, the man who had rescued Mussolini and was now entrusted with the task of using special squads in American uniform to create confusion behind the enemy's front. Skorzeny was an apostle of Tito's brand of partisan warfare which always made a strong appeal to Hitler, and so a man after Hitler's own heart. It had been a long way—and a shameful one—from Moltke to Skorzeny.

Hitler believed that he had at last found truly "revolutionary generals" in Sepp Dietrich and Manteuffel, although the latter bore one of the best names of the old Prussian nobility. Manteuffel had begun his career as commander of Rommel's old ghost division, the 7th Panzer, fighting under Manstein in the desperate battles round Zhitomir. Actually his judgment of Hitler was that of most other soldiers. He believed Hitler to have a certain magnetism in his personality and conceded that he occasionally had flashes of insight, but he denied he had any real strategical or tactical talent or even any schooling in that direction. This meant that he lacked the means of carrying his occasional inspirations into effect.

In November 1944 Hitler transferred his headquarters from the *Wolfsschanze* to the Ziegenberg near Nauheim in Hessen, the fortified complex of shelters prepared for "Case Yellow". The Chief of the General Staff went to the Maibach camp in Zossen. Hitler travelled not by plane but by rail, and for the first time saw the ruins of Berlin. Till now he had carefully avoided visiting a single one of the bombed cities. This involuntary experience elicited the remark that he had not imagined "that".

The new plan laid down that Manteuffel's armour were to thrust forward to Brussels while Dietrich's S.S. divisions were to move on Antwerp. On the third or fourth day of the attack, the 15th Army under Blumentritt was also to follow through towards Antwerp. Model, Manteuffel and, particularly, Rundstedt, were highly scepti-cal. Later they were to tell Captain Liddell Hart how impossible it was to persuade Hitler to abandon an idea once he had made up his mind on it. None of them seems to have considered the alternative of refusing obedience. In war, soldiers obeyed. The supply both of munitions and fuel was, however, quite insufficient for the undertaking. Manteuffel asked for five units of petrol to be in reserve, and Jodl promised this, but it was only possible to provide one and a half units. Further, exaggerated measures of secrecy prevented subordinate commanders from being adequately acquainted with their tasks.

The surprise of the enemy, however, was complete. Neither Eisenhower nor Montgomery had credited the Germans with the strength for a counter-attack. The offensive began without previous artillery preparation in the early hours of December 16th. It was launched on a front of 100 kilometres between Monschau and Echternach, and it was soon evident that it was not going to go according to plan—this despite the fact that Allied aircraft were grounded by fog.

While ridiculous reports were being circulated among the troops of the 15th Army (which was to form the second wave) that Namur had been taken by airborne troops, the 6th S.S. Panzer Army had been held at Stavelot. Monschau could not be taken, and Manteuffel's 47th Panzer Corps encountered stiff resistance from two American airborne divisions at Bastogne. The woolly schemes of Skorzeny and his terror groups proved completely impracticable. Manteuffel sought to besiege Bastogne with *Volks* Grenadier divisions and to by-pass it with the 2nd Panzer and Panzer-Lehr divisions, hoping to reach the Meuse at Dinant, and on the 24th his spearheads actually reached that city. Now, however, clear frosty weather set in, and the Allied air force was able to intervene and covered all his communications with a hail of bombs. He had no air support from his own side, while an attack on the Allied airfields proved ineffective. Meanwhile, the 30th British Army Corps and the 3rd American Army, under the brilliant General Patton, had begun its counter-offensive.

On this same 24th, Manteuffel asked for reinforcements, fuel and air cover. He proposed to Hitler that he should make a roundabout advance on Liège with the help of the 6th S.S. Panzer Army and the O.K.W. reserve in order thus to establish a bridgehead over the Meuse. Hitler vacillated till the 26th. Manteuffel afterwards found hard words to say about "a corporal's war". He now went to the other extreme and proposed as a final solution a general retreat to the starting line and to the Rhine.

XIV

While on December 24th Manteuffel was thus asking for help, a request from Guderian reached the Ziegenberg. Since the Ardennes offensive had failed, Guderian asked for all available divisions to be sent to the east. The centre army group which was defending the front between Memel and Warsaw had only 12 weak divisions available to spread over a distance of 800 kilometres, though all news of what was going on in the enemy's camp showed that a large-scale winter offensive was being prepared. Meanwhile, 400,000 men were standing idle under Falkenhorst in Norway, while 300,000 first-class troops were defending the now isolated Courland Bastion under Schörner. Grand Admiral Dönitz was insisting that the latter position should be held so as to secure the Baltic as a training ground for his submarines, while Hitler hoped to make it the basis for a flank attack. Guderian now pressingly demanded that Courland should be abandoned so that the troops concerned could be released to strengthen the rest of the front.

Hitler, however, decided to renew the Ardennes offensive, and to relieve the eastern front by an offensive in Hungary. He hoped in this way to regain the Rumanian oilfields and to be able then to wheel round and strike into the Russian southern flank. The immediate objective, however, was the relief of Budapest. Three of the best armoured divisions were transferred from Poland to Hungary for this purpose. Despite these preparations, Hitler showed his real mind by remarking, the observation being confirmed by Jodl, that Germany could still afford to lose territory in the east, but not in the west.

In order to preserve the appearance of unity, Guderian, about the turn of the year, made certain public utterances which were incomprehensibly optimistic. Nevertheless, he was all this time sticking with desperate determination to his demands on Hitler, though such persistence proved quite useless. The only result was one of Hitler's hysterical outbursts of rage. Keitel afterwards reproached him, saying that it was obvious the Führer was in bad health, and indeed the latter had at this time become a mere shadow of his former self. When he appeared at the map table his face was ashen, his hands trembled and his back was bent like that of an old man.

Again the inevitable happened. The Ardennes offensive petered out, and its consequences were far worse than those of the "Great Battle" of 1918. It merely succeeded in taking the last ounce of strength from the western front before the general Anglo-American assault had even begun. The Hungarian offensive failed, nor could it prevent the fall of Budapest. In Vienna, members of the Austrian resistance group "O5" in the deputy commander's office sought to establish contact with the Russians. The persons concerned were Major Sokol, the G.S.O.2, and Lieutenant Huth. They gathered troops for an attempt at Austria's liberation. In Vienna several artillery detachments were at their disposal, as was the *Ersatz-batallion* of the *"Hoch-und Deutschmeister"* regiment and several other units. As will be told later, however, this effort was destined to fail.

Meanwhile, Zukov, commanding the 1st "White Russian front", was gathering together some 300 fresh divisions for the final battle. At the same time the 2nd and 3rd White Russian fronts under Marshals Czerniakowski and Rokossowski were concentrating on the East Prussian border and before Warsaw at the entry gate of the road to Berlin. In Galicia, round Cracow, the entry gate to Silesia and Saxony, stood the 1st Ukrainian front under Koniev, while the 2nd and 3rd Ukrainian fronts threatened Austria from Budapest and Pressburg.

When the offensive was opened on the night of January 11th with an assault from the Baranov bridgehead, the 4th Panzer Army was completely destroyed and the Russians broke right through Army Group A. A few days after the initial assault, the latter's staff only escaped with difficulty from the Russian tanks. Harpe was removed from command of this army group and replaced by Schörner, the army group itself being shortly thereafter rechristened Army Group Silesia. Meanwhile some forty Russian mobile and armoured divisions continued their preparations for a blow on Silesia.

On the 13th of the month, Zukov attacked East Prussia. Here too the enemy broke through the 2nd Army and the 3rd Panzers, while the 9th Army, desperately defending Warsaw, was split in two. Guderian again strove furiously to win his freedom of action. In vain! The head of the Operations Department, von Bonin, and his G.S.O.1, Lieutenant-Colonel von dem Knesebeck, were arrested for prematurely announcing Warsaw's fall. Guderian himself, who tried to protect his subordinates, had to submit with such grace as he could muster to an examination by Kaltenbrunner, Himmler's security chief. Hitler, by now almost blind with hatred, remarked on this occasion that he was not concerned with any individual officer, he wanted to strike at the General Staff.

Even Hitler, however, could not completely dispense with trained General Staff officers, and Bonin's successor was Wenck's old G.S.O.1, Major-General von Trotha. He did not last for long, but was chased away two months later. Hitler still believed that such changes of personnel could alter the fundamental situation.

The Russians succeeded in breaking into East Prussia and the Warthegau, where no measures had been taken for an orderly evacuation of the inhabitants. A few islands remained in the red flood, Posen, Thorn, Graudenz took on the character of fortresses and continued to defend themselves. The Party officers for the most part lost their heads and fled. It was obvious that the Russians intended to press forward over Elbing and so to cut East Prussia off from the west. Hossbach finding himself thus threatened on the flank, decided, with the army group commander's permission, to retire to the Vistula and there to effect a junction with the defeated 2nd Army. The effect of this would be to allow the population of East Prussia to escape westwards. While he was endeavouring to carry this decision into effect, Hitler removed both Hossbach and the army group commander, Reinhardt, from their posts, and Rendulic, whose curious character has already been described, took over command of the centre army group.

Hitler now moved to his elaborate shelter in the half-ruined Reich Chancellery in Berlin, and the reign of terror commenced anew. In addition to many civilian victims, a colonel of the General Staff, Count von Rittberg, was shot for saying the war was lost. Meanwhile Himmler, as commander of the *ersatz* army, was conjuring more new formations into being—Naval Rifle divisions, divisions from the Labour Service composed of half-grown boys, Naval Storm units, Police combat groups and Police Regiments. Military schools, weapon schools, schools for N.C.O.'s, specialist units such as the Ski-Jäger division, the "*Führerbegleit* division" or Führer Personal Attendance division, commanded by General (formerly Major) Remer, the "Jahn" division, the Reichsmarschall's division and the Brandenburg division, represented the final offerings of Germany's manhood. All these efforts, however, did not stop the advance of the Russian tanks, which poured irresistibly over the snow covered plains towards Pommerania, Neumark, Silesia and the Upper Silesian industrial region. They broke into the last-named during the 23rd and 24th of the month, though the 17th Army and 1st Panzer Army strove desperately to hold this, the second largest industrial region of Germany.

XV

Murder, arson, rape and devastation marked the trail of the Russian armies, excited as the latter had been by an unimaginable propaganda of hate. Huge columns of refugees were moving westward. Often they were overtaken by Russian tanks, in which case they were massacred or crushed beneath the treads. Ships carrying thousands of refugees were sunk by Russian submarines. All the horrors perpetrated in Russia by the S.S., all the deeds of shame committed in this "degenerate war" of *Weltanschauungen* which Hitler had so impiously proclaimed, were now revenged a hundred and a thousand fold, the innocent population of the German East being the victims. The culture which had taken centuries to build was buried within a matter of days.

Under cover of the Russian Army, yet another process was initiated: the agrarian revolution of Prussia, the end of the East Elbian landlords, which had been so long deferred, and with it the end of that military aristocracy which had formed the backbone of the Prussian Army. Many old Prussian families who had already made heavy sacrifices of blood in the war, had also been the victims of the persecution following the plot of July 20th. Now such people had either to flee or suffer all the horrors which, as Russia and Poland had already shown, were incidental to the revolutionary spirit. Where they either could not escape, or elected not to do so, they were deported, or failing that, tortured, shot or hanged. Many preferred not to survive the end of their world, and took their own lives. A few died defending their lands and houses, displaying to the end that obstinate pride which had always marked them as an order, and forcing as many of their enemies as they could to share their death.

It was the end of many an ancient house. The von Arnims lost no less than ninety-eight estates and farms; thirty of this family's sons had fallen in the course of the war, one had died in a concentration camp, two were shot by the Russians, three were transported, and eight died by their own hand. In the case of the von der Schulenburgs, which family had produced three field-marshals and thirty-five generals, the record is as follows: Two of its leading members took part in the plot and were executed. Fourteen others fell in the war. Seven committed suicide when the Russians broke in. This family is fortunate in still having property in Western Germany. In the east it lost twenty-three estates. One can prolong such a list indefinitely.

A great part of the daily conferences in Hitler's shelter were now devoted to two subjects, the reduction of manpower and industrial potential through the progressive loss of territory, and the question which of the generals was a sticker. Meanwhile towards the end of the month Zukov penetrated deep into Brandenburg, so that the threat to the capital became serious. Schörner, sparing neither himself nor anybody else, sought to collect the remnants of Army Group A and establish a frontier in the Lausitz and in the Tatra. Both Koniev and Zukov by now were under the necessity of building up their communications and thus gave the Germans a temporary respite.

Guderian was anxious to use this lull to build up a counter-offensive, which if it could not indefinitely stop the enemy, might at least delay his progress. He suggested to Hitler that all available forces between the Vistula and the Oder should now be gathered together into a single army group under Weichs, whose staff, thanks to the destruction of Army Group F in the Balkans, was now without employment. Weichs was further to be given the Courland Army, and from the west the 6th S.S. Panzer Army. He would thus have a force of thirty to forty divisions and some 1,500 tanks, and could strike from Pommerania into Zukov's over-extended northern flank. At the same time other forces were to strike from around Crossen and so effect a pincers movement which might at least throw the enemy back over the Vistula. Possibly even Silesia might be regained. This Pommeranian offensive was the last plan of any military importance which the General Staff drew up.

Everything depended on maintaining the element of surprise. Speed was essential. Hitler's and Jodl's first objection was to the employment of Weichs, for the latter was a Catholic. Hitler declared that such a task could only be accomplished by a man who was permeated by the National Socialist faith, and eventually, after heated arguments, forced Guderian to agree to the appointment of Himmler as Commander in Chief. He also modified Guderian's plan in accordance with certain conceptions of his own. These involved the greater part of the Courland Army remaining where it was, since it was to be used for a flank offensive at a later stage. Only a small part of it was transferred to Pommerania. The 6th S.S. Panzer Army, on the other hand, was sent, not to Pommerania, but to Hungary, from where Hitler was planning yet another offensive against the Southern Russian flank with a vague hope of regaining the Rumanian oilfields. All of this shows that the Supreme War Lord had completely lost all sense of perspective.

Himmler as a military commander proved quite impossible. He was entirely without military knowledge and unwilling to choose any military advisers. His Chief of Staff was an S.S. *Brigadeführer*, his G.S.O.1 being the only officer whom the General Staff of the Army was permitted to supply. Also he displayed a marked disinclination to go near the front. There were now more violent arguments between Hitler and Guderian, who tried hard to get his deputy in the General Staff, General Wenck, appointed as Himmler's Chief of Staff, and a great deal of the precious time that was still available was wasted with these disputes, which lasted from February 9th to 13th. Then suddenly Hitler changed his mind, agreed to Wenck's appointment and ordered the offensive to begin on the 15th. After the decision was made, Hitler remarked, "The Chief of the General Staff has won a battle to-day," but it was the last battle Guderian was to win.

The operation was ill starred from the start. Just after his return from the Führer's headquarters, Wenck was involved in a motor accident and sustained severe concussion, and in Himmler's incompetent hands the attack was a complete failure. Zukov now struck north with strong forces and on March 17th, after a ten-day battle, there fell the old fortress of Kolberg, where Gneisenau had first won fame. Large Russian forces now appeared before Stettin.

Himmler went down with influenza and withdrew to the sanatorium of Hohenlychen. He was by now positively anxious to lay down his command, and Guderian, who visited him, persuaded him to hand over the command of the Oder front to Colonel-General Heinrici, who at that particular moment was in command of the 1st Panzer Army in Northern Hungary. The Oder front, at that time defended by the 3rd Panzer Army under Manteuffel, and the 9th Army under General Busse, became the nation's last hope.

XVI

Everything now was in progressive dissolution, and the most astonishing plans began to be conceived. S.S. *Gruppenführer* Schellenberg, head of the S.S. Secret Service, developed a scheme for making Himmler Chancellor and interning Hitler at Obersalzberg. In this way Himmler, it was thought, could become free to negotiate with the Western powers and enter into an alliance with them against Russia. This, incidentally, was a hope which many General Staff officers entertained, though it was based on nothing more substantial than the Western powers' disputes with Russia on the subject of

Greece, in which country the British had forestalled a Communist attempt to seize power. The Yalta conference, however, made it clear that whatever differences there might be about Greece, there was perfect unanimity on the subject of Germany.

The more Guderian recognized that Hitler intended to identify the fate of the German people with his own, the more he sought to counter the worst consequences of his megalomania. He asked Ribbentrop to try and open negotiations with the West, and when this suggestion was turned down put the frank question to him what he thought would happen when in some four weeks' time the Russians reached Berlin. Ribbentrop informed his lord and master of this conversation, and Hitler declared that it was high treason for the Chief of Staff to pass such information to the Foreign Minister.

Guderian's days were now numbered. His successor was General Hans Krebs, a man who still had an unqualified belief in Hitler's genius. Hitler stated that in Krebs he had at last found the ideal Chief of Staff, the man who was really prepared to give his own ideas sympathetic consideration. Halder had always wanted to know better, Zeitzler had had no brains, and Guderian had been a fathead. Since Wenck had left it, the post of the Chief of the *Führungsstab*, i.e. that of the old *Oberquartiermeister I*, had remained vacant. It was now abolished. Only the Operations Department, of which Colonel Dettleffsen was in charge, now remained. The tasks of the General Staff were now ever more rapidly intermingling with those of the *Wehrmachtführungsstab*. It was for the latter, however, a Pyrrhic victory.

The decline of the Army's strength was not without its effects on the General Staff. Merely in point of numbers such catastrophes as Stalingrad, Tunis, Morton-Falaise and Rumania, which had devoured whole army groups, had also inflicted heavy losses in trained Staff personnel. The number of qualified Staff officers had proved itself too small at the time of the rearmament, a fact which had been painfully evident at the outbreak of war. July 20th had brought further irreplaceable losses, and now nearly the whole of the old Army Command had been either retired, killed, wounded or executed; failing that, they had gone to concentration camps or committed suicide. The pressure of circumstance had long since made nonsense of picking an *élite* from among the officer corps and subjecting it to a long and careful training. As in the First World War, the training courses for young General Staff officers had to be drastically shortened. The "Sedan Courses" now appeared in an even more thoroughly abridged edition than in 1918. At last the Staff posts, particularly in the *Volks* Grenadier divisions, could hardly be filled at all. The case of the final scratch divisions with the resounding names "Clausewitz", "Jahn", "Reichsmarschall" and the rest, was even worse. It was indeed not rare to find divisions which could only boast of a single Staff officer. Quite young officers from the front were now passing through the General Staff training courses and immediately obtaining high and responsible posts. That need not necessarily have been a fault. It merely meant that since the training was quite insufficient, everything depended on personality, and the selection of these young men was bound in the nature of things to be imperfect. At best, many such young men continued to act with the dash, one might even say the *naïveté*, of a front-line officer, and made little effort to cultivate the cool objectivity of a General Staff officer of the old school. Many let themselves drown in the details of routine and lost their perspective over their problems as a whole. The true General Staff officer, whose heart belonged to the troops while his head belonged to his science, the man who could take responsibility and dared to have a mind of his own, became ever harder to find. As against this, the mere executors of orders, who desired nothing more than to remain what they were, multiplied exceedingly.

The National Socialist Party was still to win a final barren victory over Prussian conservatism. On March 15th, the *N.S. Führungsorganisation* was dissolved, its reconstitution being entrusted to the Chief of the Party head office, Martin Bormann. Hitler's order that in a critical situation, when there was a failure of leadership on the part of the responsible leader, the soldier who held himself capable of solving the problem in question should be chosen as commander spelt the end of the whole German tradition of leadership, the end of everything for which the General Staff had stood. It spelt the liquidation of that Prussian principle of obedience, from which Hitler had himself drawn such marked benefits. Just as in the east the traditional leading stratum had now been wiped out or driven into the wilderness, so now within the Army its rule was coming to an end.

Meanwhile in the west the last great offensive had begun. In February "Operation Grenade" pressed in the defensive positions on the left bank of the Rhine, and the enemy thrust forward to the river. Rundstedt was again retired and replaced by Kesselring, who was transferred from Italy. Thus the oldest and one of the last field-marshals disappeared from the scene. Among field-marshals only Keitel and Busch remained, and among the younger ones, Model and

Schörner. Of the other field-marshals, von Bock had been killed on the road with his wife and daughter by enemy aircraft, Witzleben and Rommel had lost their lives following the events of July 20th, Kluge had committed suicide, Paulus was a prisoner, while Brauchitsch, Leeb, Manstein, Kleist, List, Küchler and Weichs lived on in retirement and with a cloud over their names. For the rest, of the thirty-six colonels-general who held that rank at the outbreak of war or had been subsequently raised to it, seven had fallen, three had been executed after July 20th, two had been expelled from the Army, twenty-one had been dismissed in disgrace. In all, out of about 800 General Staff officers, approximately 150 had found death upon the home front of this war of *Weltanschauungen*.

Germany's death agony began in March. On the 7th of that month, the Americans most surprisingly succeeded in seizing a bridgehead at Remagen. The officers charged with the duty of blowing up the bridge and protecting this sector of the front were shot by Hitler's orders. Some 60 divisions, including paratroops, *Volks* Grenadiers, *Volkssturm*, A.A. units and one Panzer corps of two divisions still held the line of the Rhine. On the 23rd, however, Montgomery's airborne forces effected a crossing at Wesel, and Montgomery now thrust forward towards the line Hamburg-Magdeburg. Meanwhile American forces on a wide front broke through into central and southern Germany. Army Group B was surrounded in the Ruhr and disintegrated. When Field-Marshal Model saw that Hitler had deceived him and that no wonder weapons would be forthcoming, he shot himself after vainly requesting his *aide-de-camp* to do him this last service.

XVII

Hitler now gave orders for a scorched earth policy, for the destruction of all industrial plant and communications. In West Germany alone, some 10,000 bridges were destroyed in response to this piece of lunacy. Speer, the armament minister, endeavoured in co-operation with Lieutenant-Colonel von Poser, his liaison officer on the General Staff, to sabotage these measures as best he could, and even made plans to kill Hitler by introducing poison gas into his shelter, but at the last moment these plans were abandoned. On much the same level as this scorched earth policy and inspired by similar motives was Hitler's expressed intention to have ten thousand Allied airmen prisoners of war shot in reprisal for the raid on Dresden, which cost sixty thousand lives. Goebbels at this time advocated the use of the two new poison gases, Tabun and Sarin, which German industry had developed, but Allied air superiority made even Hitler think this too dangerous.

In the Army Group South-West in Southern Italy, commanded by Colonel-General von Vietinghoff, a new military conspiracy came into being. With the full approval of the highest local S.S. functionary, S.S. *Obergruppenführer* Wolf, contact was established with the Allied command and an armistice ultimately negotiated. Meanwhile Himmler, who was feverishly endeavouring to build up an underground movement, the so-called "Werewolf", to make the Allied advance more difficult, was also busying himself with peace plans of his own. With the help of Count Folke Bernadotte, the President of the Swedish Red Cross and a nephew of the King of Sweden, who had come to negotiate the release of Norwegian inmates of concentration camps, he suggested to the Western powers a separate peace excluding Russia. He was, however, fated to learn that the Allies were as little prepared to negotiate with him as they were with Hitler, and that this way out was closed.

In the east, the Oder front under Colonel General Heinrici (with Colonel Kinzler as his Chief of Staff) formed the last barrier, a fact which Heinrici stressed in vain. In the presence of Göring, Keitel, Jodl, Dönitz and Krebs, the new Chief of Staff, Hitler took away from the Oder group a great part of its tanks to transfer them to the Lausitz. Göring promised 100,000 men from the *Luftwaffe's* ground forces, while Dönitz offered naval units amounting to 12,000 men, and Himmler 25,000 of the S.S. Hitler, however, believed that the enemy's plainly discernible concentration of forces between Küstrin and Frankfurt am der Oder was a ruse and declared that the Russian objective was Dresden and Prague and not Berlin. Despite all his representations, Heinrici never got back his tanks.

At the beginning of April, some two million Russian troops were ready to attack between the Baltic and Bohemia, and Russian contingents were approaching Vienna, where on April 5th the S.S. discovered Major Sokol's conspiracy. Major Sokol, who had now become G.S.O.1 to General Brünau, the Commandant of Vienna, was arrested, together with the whole Operations Department of that Command. He himself was hanged on the Floridsdorf bridge together with two fellow conspirators, while the remaining twelve General Staff officers were shot in a courtyard of what had once been the old Royal Imperial War Ministry. His plot thus had failed but he had succeeded in introducing a considerable element of confusion among the S.S. who were charged with the defence of Vienna, which was occupied by Tolbuchin's troops on the 13th.

One day before this, the drum fire of the new offensive began on the Oder. Opposite the 9th Army alone, which now had only some 200 tanks, there stood two Russian Panzer armies and four fast corps with 2,000 tanks. Up to the 18th, Heinrici's army group put up a desperate resistance, then the Russians broke through on both sides of Küstrin. On that same day, Koniev attacked on the Neisse and tore open Schörner's flank. Koniev thrust forward, then wheeled north and marched on Berlin. The Russians could now concentrate 5,000 tanks and an equal number of planes and 2,000 guns in readiness for the battle for the capital. On the 21st, the General Staff were compelled to evacuate Zossen, and on the next day Russian spearheads reached the Autobahn to the south of Berlin.

XVIII

In Berlin, Goebbels sought to whip up the population for a battle of desperation, but the slogan "Berlin stays German, Vienna will be German again" was drowned in the thunder of cannon. Hitler told Keitel and Jodl that he would conduct the defence of the city himself, and that when the end came he would shoot himself so as not to fall into Russian hands. Jodl's last plan was to turn the whole western front about face and bring its troops into battle with the Russians and thus to show the Western powers that Germany's real battle was against Bolshevism.

For a moment the sudden death of President Roosevelt on April 12th had aroused the most fantastic hopes, but the notion that it had ended the co-operation between Russia and the West was soon exploded, and Russian and American shook hands with each other at Torgau on the Elbe.

Dönitz and most of the Reich ministers went from Berlin to Schleswig-Holstein—first to Eutin and then to Flensburg—while the O.K.W. under Keitel and Jodl, together with the *Wehrmachtführungsstab*, retired to Fürstenberg in Mecklenburg, where it found security in the woods. Jodl still held to the idea of turning the western front around, but only wanted to do this in the north and not on the whole front. Meanwhile General Winter undertook to form a new *Führungsstab B* to organize the various units in Southern Germany.

Göring went to Southern Germany from whence he addressed a

letter to Hitler asking officially whether as his deputy he was now to take over plenary power and open negotiations with the West. Hitler promptly ordered the S.S. to intern him at Berchtesgaden. When Himmler's efforts towards a similar end became known to him, he cast out Himmler too and clamoured to have him shot. In fact, the heads of this great Party, who were also the heads of the State, began to act very much after the manner of gangsters who are expecting arrest.

On the Oder front, the 3rd Panzer Army had put up a desperate resistance, aided by Hitler Youth formations, Police regiments and similar bodies, but could not hold the Oder crossing at Stettin. It was ultimately driven back into Mecklenburg. A part of the 9th Army was driven back into the suburbs of Berlin, the rest being surrounded in the neighbourhood of Lübben and Fürstenwalde. The Chief of Staff of the Army group in question, Colonel Kinzler, had agreed with Speer that his troops would be withdrawn in such a manner that Berlin would not become a battlefield, but circumstances made it impossible for him to honour his undertaking. Hitler's decision to remain in Berlin meant fighting to the last round. Heinrici was relieved of his post, General von Tippelskirch being put in command of the troops in Mecklenburg. Since, however, he could no longer be reached, Student, the creator of Germany's paratroops, who according to Göring had always been a "sticker", took over his command. But nothing now was any use. Surrender was the only course open, the struggle had become senseless.

Hitler, however, ordered the Reich to be divided into a Northern and a Southern Command, Dönitz being made C. in C. North and Kesselring C. in C. South. Thus Hitler, giving full rein to his suspicion against the old order of generals, had put Germany's last remaining armies under an Admiral and an Air Marshal.

There could now no longer be any ordered planning. The General Staff's Operations Department was ignorant even of the location of most units. Jodl set his last hopes on a counter-offensive for the relief of Berlin. In the Elbe area, Wenck managed to set up a new army command which was supposed to comprise 12 divisions. Actually it had only three, composed largely of the labour service, N.C.O.s' schools and similar scratch units. Keitel drove to see Wenck and discussed the attack which both he and Jodl were hoping to co-ordinate with the turn about of the western front. Hitler saw in Wenck his last saviour, for a plan to reconstitute the 11th Panzer Army under S.S. *Gruppenführer* Steiner, using S.S. and *Luftwaffe* personnel for this purpose, had come to nothing.

XIX

General Wenck's offensive was to begin on April 25th. Street fighting was already in progress in Berlin. *Volksturm* units, companies of Hitler Youth armed with the *"Panzerfäust"*, a few *Wehrmacht* units and the crews of the great A.A. towers were the last defenders of the capital. Terror still reigned. Men were still being hanged and shot in the street because of their unwillingness to die for a Führer who at that moment was discussing with his friends the most appropriate method of suicide.

One "battle commandant" after another in that doomed city was relieved of his duties for "cowardice and incompetence". General von Hauenschild, Major-General Kunze, Lieutenant-General Reimann, Major-General Kaether, a young N.S. *Führungsoffizier* who was suddenly made a general because of "the glow of his National Socialist convictions"—all experienced the transient nature of power. At last command was assumed by General of Artillery Weidling, despite the fact that Hitler had once wanted to have him shot for cowardice.

On the 27th, the heads of Wenck's columns had contrived to fight their way to Ferch, some twelve kilometres from Potsdam, but a Russian thrust in the flank ended their progress. Hitler thereupon got into telephonic communication with General von Natzmer, Chief of Staff to Schörner's army group, who was near Königgrätz, and sought to move him to relieve Berlin. However, the project was quite impossible and was not attempted.

On the 28th, the day on which Mussolini was shot by Italian partisans while attempting to escape to Switzerland, Hitler and his mistress, Eva Braun, were married by Bormann, whereupon both bride and groom took their lives.

In his will, Hitler expelled both Göring and Himmler from the Party, and named Dönitz as his successor. British and American troops now continued to drive forward towards Mecklenburg and Holstein, while Russian tanks thrust on towards the Kiel Canal. American troops advanced from Bavaria into Bohemia. The Czechs revolted. All serious opposition was over.

The last Chief of General Staff, General Krebs, disappeared in Berlin. Together with General Burgdorf, he had planned to take his life when the Russians appeared. Probably, however, he was taken prisoner. As to the O.K.W., its last task was so to direct the movement of troops that the smallest possible number would fall into Russian hands.

One after another the German armies capitulated. First to surrender were the defenders of Berlin. On the same day, May 2nd, Army Group South-West followed their example, though they had been in negotiation with the enemy for some time. On May 5th, all remaining German forces in Northern and Southern Germany, Austria, Holland, Denmark and Norway laid down their arms. The Courland pocket and Schörner's army group were the only exceptions. On May 7th, Admiral Dönitz formally entered into negotiations and on the 8th formalities were complete. Jodl signed the instrument with the Western powers and Keitel with the Russians. The war ended with this purely military act.

Thus was concluded the second multi-front war which the German Reich had waged in the twentieth century, and with its conclusion the German General Staff ceased to exist. A military organization had been twice confronted with tasks the carrying out of which was beyond the strength of the people to which that organization belonged. On the first of these occasions the memory of the wars of unification which it had waged successfully in the preceding century may have led its members to believe that a task wholly beyond its powers could be accomplished, but its shrewdest minds had clearly seen before the Second World War that such a war was but another attempt to bring the impossible within the bounds of possibility.

This being so, the accusation made against the General Staff before the international court in Nuremberg that it was one of the organizations that had played a leading part in unleashing the Second World War was found impossible to sustain.

INDEX